A Short History
of Opera

ONE-VOLUME EDITION

A Short History of Opera

by DONALD JAY GROUT

PROFESSOR OF MUSIC, CORNELL UNIVERSITY

ONE-VOLUME EDITION

COLUMBIA UNIVERSITY PRESS · NEW YORK

A. M. D. G.

A.M.D.G.

Preface

VOLUMES ALMOST BEYOND COUNTING have been written about opera, but no systematic historical survey since the publication of Hermann Kretzschmar's *Geschichte der Oper* in 1919. This work, though valuable for the early periods of opera history, ends to all intents and purposes with Wagner; moreover, it has never been translated. Most books in English which profess to deal historically with opera are either mere collections of plot synopses strung on a thin thread of continuity, or else obvious bids for popular success without serious pretensions to accuracy or thoroughness. There are a few excellent books which treat of opera in a non-historical manner, among which may be especially mentioned Edward J. Dent's *Opera* (New York, Penguin Books, 1940). But the bulk of serious writing about opera at the present time is in the form of specialized studies of limited scope and is read for the most part only by specialists.

Recognizing this fact, it would seem that there might be room for a book which has for its purpose to offer a comprehensive report on the present state of our knowledge about the history of opera. In compressing such a long and diversified history into the compass of a single book it is obvious that many things must be omitted. The reader will not find here, for example, many synopses of opera plots or much gossip about the personal affairs of composers and singers; no attempt has been made to furnish complete statistical information about the output of composers or complete records of performances; biographies have been treated summarily; and digressions on the relation of opera to contemporary production in literature and the other arts, to politics, economics, and the *Zeitgeist* generally have been regretfully held to a minimum. On the other hand, a conscientious effort has been made to present the essential points in the history of opera clearly, fairly, in proper proportion, and with constant reference to the music. Musical examples have been provided, especially for the earlier periods from which scores are not readily available, and some technical analysis of important representative works or passages is included. The bibliographical material has been made full enough, it is hoped, to provide the student with adequate information for beginning research on almost any desired special topic. An elementary acquaintance on the reader's part with the history of music is assumed, though this is perhaps not essential; knowledge of music theory will be found necessary for understanding some of the technical analyses.

Generous help has been given by many friends in the course of preparation of this work. The author wishes especially to express his thanks to the Trustees of the Wesley Weyman Fund, Harvard University, for a grant of one thousand dollars for aid in research. Professor Otto Kinkeldey kindly read the manuscript and made many suggestions which are gratefully acknowledged. Advice on various special topics has been most cheerfully given by Mr. Gilbert Chase, Professor Archibald T. Davison, Mr. Richard S. Hill, Professor Scott Goldthwaite, Dr. Henry L. Clarke, Dr. Walter Rubsamen, Professor Chase Baromeo, and many others. To Mr. Lawrence Apgar, Mr. Leonard Burkat, and their helpers, thanks are due for skilled and devoted labor on bibliographical problems, and to Mr. John Scabia for preparation of the musical examples. Lastly to my wife, who typed most of the manuscript and who has been both a patient sufferer and an encouraging companion throughout the entire labor, a special debt of gratitude must always stand.

Acknowledgment is made to the following publishers for permission to use copyrighted material in the musical examples: Edwin Arnold & Co., London (Ex. 76); E. de Boccard, Paris (Ex. 72); Choudens, Editeur, Paris (Ex. 95); Durand & Cie., Paris (Exs. 53, 110, 111, 112); Heugel & Cie., Paris (Exs. 124 and 126); Novello & Co., Ltd., London (Exs. 57, 58, 59, 93, 101, 102); G. Schirmer, Inc., New York (Ex. 103); and Joseph Williams, Ltd., London (Exs. 54, 55, 56).

It is perhaps not out of order to warn the reader against the delusion that the history of any kind of music can be learned simply by reading a book. The principal use of any book about music is to serve as an introduction to the music itself, which must always be the central object of study. If beyond this essential point it is possible to suggest some of the implications of the music, some of its relation to the culture of which it is a part and some of its significance for our own time, so much the better. The landscape of history is not alone the solid earth of fact; above must spread the rolling cloudbanks of imagination.

DONALD JAY GROUT

Skaneateles Lake, New York
September 1, 1947

Contents

*That day the sky was cloudless; the
wind blew softly where we sat. Above
us stretched in its hugeness the vault
and compass of the World; around us
crowded in green newness the myriad
tribes of Spring. Here chimed around
us every music that can soothe the ear;
was spread before us every color that
can delight the eye. Yet we were sad.
For it is so with all men: a little while
(some by the fireside talking of
homely matters with their friends,
others by wild ecstasies of mystic
thought swept far beyond the boundaries of carnal life) they may be easy
and forget their doom. But soon their
fancy strays; they grow dull and list-
less, for they are fallen to thinking that
all these things which so mightily
pleased them will in the space of a
nod be old things of yesterday.*

WANG HSI-CHI (A.D. 353)

A Short History
of Opera

AfMf	*Archiv für Musikforschung*
AfMw	*Archiv für Musikwissenschaft*
AMZ	*Allgemeine musikalische Zeitung*
art.	article
B&H	Breitkopf & Härtel
C.E.	Collected Edition (*Gesamtausgabe*)
C.F.	*Chefs d'œuvre de l'opéra français*
DdT	*Denkmäler deutscher Tonkunst*
DTB	*Denkmäler der Tonkunst in Bayern*
DTOe	*Denkmäler der Tonkunst in Oesterreich*
ed.	edition, editor, edited by
HAM	*Historical Anthology of Music*, Vol. II (Davison and Apel)
JMP	*Jahrbuch der Musikbibliothek Peters*
K	Köchel, *Chronologisch-thematisches Verzeichnis sämtlicher Tonwerke Wolfgang Amade Mozarts*, 3d ed., rev. Einstein
MA	*Musical Antiquary*
MfMg	*Monatshefte für Musikgeschichte*
M&L	*Music & Letters*
MM	*Mercure musical*
MMus	*Modern Music*
MQ	*Musical Quarterly*
MTNA	*Proceedings of the Music Teachers National Association*
mus.	music (by)
OHM	*Oxford History of Music*
perf.	performed, performance
PIMG	Publikationen der internationalen Musikgesellschaft
PMA	*Proceedings of the Musical Association* (London)
RassM	*La rasssegna musicale*
RdM	*Revue de musicologie*
RHCM	*Revue d'histoire et de critique musicales* (with No. 10 of Vol. II, 1902, became SIM *Revue musicale*)
RM	*Revue musicale* (Paris, 1920–)
RMI	*Rivista musicale italiana*
SB	Schering, *Geschichte der Musik in Beispielen*
SIM	*Société internationale de musique*
SIMG	*Sammelbände der internationalen Musikgesellschaft*
SzMw	*Studien zur Musikwissenschaft* (Beihefte der DTOe)
VfMw	*Vierteljahrsschrift für Musikwissenschaft*
ZfMw	*Zeitschrift für Musikwissenschaft*
ZIMG	*Zeitschrift der internationalen Musikgesellschaft*

I

Introduction

THE CUSTOM OF USING MUSIC IN CON-
nection with dramatic presentations is
universal. It is found throughout the
history of European culture and among primitive and civilized
peoples alike. This is perhaps because the desire to add music to
drama is really part of the dramatic instinct itself. The motives may
be either religious or secular: drama with music may have as its
end either edification or entertainment. Of religious dramatic music
we know today such forms as the cantata, the oratorio, and the
Passion; the two last (aside from their subject matter) differ from
opera essentially only in that they include some narrative portions
and that they do not require scenery, costumes, or stage action. Even
this difference is little more than a historical accident; it arises from
the traditional antipathy between church and theatre which has
existed especially since the period of the Renaissance. The dramatic
impulse is retained in these types of sacred music but purified of
those external trappings most closely associated with its secular
manifestations. The opera itself is, with rare exceptions, a secular
form. Its aim is like that of all the secular arts: the enrichment and
embellishment of civilized life.

The first work now known as an "opera" was performed in 1597.
The word itself, however, was not used in its present sense before
1639.[1] It means literally a "work" (compare "opus") and is a shortened form of the Italian *opera in musica,* that is, a "work of music."

It is a remarkable fact that not only had both music and the
theatre existed for hundreds of years before an opera was written,

---

[1] Cavalli's *Le nozze di Teti e Peleo* ("The Wedding of Thetis and Peleus"), performed
at Venice in that year, was called an *opera scenica.* A list of designations used for operas
in the seventeenth and eighteenth centuries is given in Haas, "Geschichtliche Opernbe-
zeichnungen," in *Festschrift . . . Kretzschmar,* pp. 43–45. See also Dent, "The Nomenclature of Opera," M&L XXV (1944) 132–40, 213–26. The most common terms were
favola (lit. "fable"), *tragedia* ("tragedy"), or *dramma.* These general terms nearly always had characterizing words or phrases attached, e.g., *favola in musica, favola pastorale,
tragédie lyrique,* etc. The word "opera" in our sense came into general use earliest in
England (from 1656); it was not common in France or Germany until the eighteenth
century and has only recently been accepted in Italy.

but also that both music and drama have since flourished during periods and in countries in which opera has shown no comparable vitality. Such is the condition, for example, in the United States at the present time. In eighteenth-century Italy, on the other hand, the production of operas far exceeded, in both quantity and quality, that of other musical or dramatic forms. It seems necessary, therefore, to consider what special inherent features of opera may account for such anomalies.

The first is undoubtedly its luxuriousness. Opera is an expensive affair because it is so difficult to stage and perform. It involves the co-operation of a large number of experts, from the librettist and composer through the conductor, the singers, the orchestra, the stage designers, managers, technicians, and so on. All these people must be persuaded or compelled to work together harmoniously, and they must be paid. A large theatre, with all kinds of special equipment, has to be maintained. Since there have seldom been enough persons in any community who are both able and willing to pay the high admission prices necessary to make opera self-supporting, some form of patronage is necessary. The patron may be a wealthy noble maintaining an opera company for the amusement of himself and his friends; or it may be a private association of individuals who attempt with greater or less success to sell opera to the public by exploiting it both as an art work and as a prestige symbol; or again, the state may be the patron, supporting opera by means of subsidies from the public funds. In any case the result is the same: opera is conditioned poetically, musically, scenically, and to the last detail by the ideals and desires of those upon whom it depends, and this to a degree and in a manner not true of any other musical form. The opera is the visible and audible projection of the power, wealth, and taste of the society which supports it. For this reason, the study of its history may be of value for the light it sheds on the history of culture in general.

Another inherent feature of opera is its artificiality. Opera is always laden with certain conventions, which people agree to accept while at the same time acknowledging them to be unnatural or even ridiculous. Take for example the practice of singing instead of talking. Nothing could be more unnatural, if imitation of actual life were the purpose of opera. Yet it is now accepted as a matter of course, as the basic unreality in a whole structure of unrealities. Not only are there such timeless conventions in opera, but every age has a set of them peculiar to itself, which the second or third generation following begins to find old-fashioned and the next generation finds insupportable. And so all the music and poetry which were tied to these conventions suffer their fate and are forgotten. Nothing in music dates more quickly than an opera. Handel's oratorios are still widely performed, but, except for an occasional historical revival, do we ever hear a Handel opera? Shakespeare's plays are still produced at a profit, but what modern opera house has ventured to stage commercially Monteverdi's *Orfeo,* which was written during Shakespeare's lifetime? It is not that the music of these operas is inferior, but that it is bound up with a hundred details which interfere with our understanding it—operatic conventions which, passing out of knowledge, carry the music with them to oblivion.

All of this points to the necessity for approaching the study of an opera, particularly one of a past period, with especial care. An opera score must be studied with imagination as well as attention. It will not do merely to read the music as if it were a symphony or a series of songs accompanied by an orchestra. One must at the same time imagine the work as it appears in performance, with the stage action, the costumes, and the scenery; and one must be aware of the operatic conventions by which the librettist and composer were governed, so as not to judge them according to the conventions of a different period, committing the absurdity (for example) of condemning an opera of Lully or Handel merely because it is not like the operas of Verdi or Wagner, or some other familiar composer.

The luxuriousness and artificiality of opera have always provoked reactions. Just as every age has its own kind of opera, so every age has its own humbler counterparts of the form, designed to appeal to persons of less wealth or less cultivation. These stepchildren of opera have been known by many different names: *opera buffa, opéra comique,* ballad opera, "intermezzo," comic opera, vaudeville, operetta, musical comedy, and so on. Whatever the name, all have certain common features: they are less expensive than the opera, their social standing is lower, their tone is more familiar, and many of them caricature or parody the serious opera. They are the poor man's opera, even (as the title of one of the most famous of them

has it) the *Beggar's Opera*. So far as artistic merit goes they may be
equal or even superior to the more pretentious form and must certainly be considered along with it in any historical treatment.

What is an opera? One common definition, "a drama, either tragic
or comic, sung throughout, with appropriate scenery and acting, to
the accompaniment of an orchestra," [2] requires a correction and
certain amplifications. The correction is simply that many operas
are not "sung throughout." Comic operas, except Italian ones, almost always use spoken dialogue. The French opéra comique of the
nineteenth century, much of which is not "comic opera" but romantic musical drama, has spoken dialogue (for example, Bizet's
Carmen). Mozart's *Magic Flute*, Beethoven's *Fidelio*, and Weber's
Freischütz are other operas in which singing and speaking alternate.
It is clear that the criterion of continuous music does not apply
universally, although it is true that most serious operas, and some
comic ones, are sung in their entirety.

The basic point in the definition is that opera is "a drama." This
serves to distinguish it from such kindred forms as the ballet. But
what kind of drama? Is there any essential difference between a good
opera libretto and a good play? Evidently so; if there were not, con-
ceivably any of Shakespeare's tragedies could be set to music exactly
as it stands—a feat which has probably never been attempted. The
difference is one of emphasis. A play centers about characters and a
plot; it may contain episodes which could be omitted without dam-
aging its unity or continuity, but if this is the case, it is, strictly
speaking, a defect in the structure. An opera libretto, on the other
hand, may almost be said to center about the episodes; at least, it
admits and even requires many portions which contribute little or
nothing to characterization or to development of the action, such as
dances, choruses, instrumental or vocal ensembles, and spectacular
stage effects. Even the solo songs (arias) are often, from the dramatic
point of view, mere lyrical interruptions of the plot. All these things,
which (on a comparable scale at least) would be out of place in a
spoken drama, are the very life blood of opera. Composers may
accept them frankly as episodes or may try to make them contribute
in a greater or less degree to the depiction of character or the development of the dramatic idea; but they are so much a part of opera

2 *Grove's Dictionary of Music and Musicians* (4th ed.), art. "Opera."

that it is difficult to find an example which does not include them to some extent, even among the so-called "realistic" operas of the late nineteenth and twentieth centuries.

On the other hand, plot and characterization in an opera libretto are likely to be sketched in broad outline rather than in detail. The action is usually simpler than in a play, with fewer events and less complex interconnections among them. Subtle characterization is exceptional. Most important of all, the entire dramatic tempo is slower, so as to allow time for the necessary episodic scenes and especially for the deployment and development of the musical ideas.

There is another kind of difference between a play and a libretto, one which has to do with the poetic idiom employed, the choice of words and images. It is a commonplace that not all poetry is suitable for music; it would be nothing short of impertinence, for example, to add music to such lines as Shakespeare's

> Cloud-capp'd towers, the gorgeous palaces,
> The solemn temples, the great globe itself,
> Yea, all which it inherit, shall dissolve
> And, like this insubstantial pageant faded,
> Leave not a rack behind.

But consider the following:

> When I am laid in earth, may my wrongs create
> No trouble in thy breast. Remember me, but ah!
> Forget my fate.

Judged as ordinary poetry this passage, from Nahum Tate's *Dido and Aeneas,* could hardly merit high praise. Yet it is excellent poetry for music. It suggests in simple terms the image of a woman desolated by an emotion which the words by themselves cannot completely convey, an emotion so overpowering that only with the aid of music can it be given full expression. Moreover, the passage has a maximum of the appropriate dark vowel sounds and liquid consonants, with few sibilants. The important words (laid, earth, wrongs, trouble, remember, fate) are not only well adapted for singing but also are full of emotional suggestion. The very imperfections, the incompleteness, almost formlessness, of the passage considered purely as poetry are its greatest merit as a text for music, since they leave so much for the composer to add.

Making due allowance for the special requirements of the form, an opera libretto will usually reflect the prevailing ideas of its time with regard to drama. Similarly, opera music will be, in general, very much like other music of the same period. It must be remembered that in an opera, music is only one of several factors. It is necessarily always a kind of program music, in that it must (even if only to a slight degree) adapt itself to the dramatic and scenic requirements instead of developing in accordance with purely musical principles. As a rule it is somewhat simpler, more popular in style than contemporary larger forms of nondramatic music, more tuneful, more obvious in its rhythms, less contrapuntal in texture—though there are some exceptions to this, notably the music dramas of Wagner. On the other hand, an opera score is apt to be more varied and original in instrumental color, partly because an opera is so long that more variety is needed, and partly in consequence of the composer's constant search after new dramatic effects by means of instrumentation. Thus the trombones had been used in opera two hundred years before they were admitted to symphonic combinations; the devices of string tremolo and pizzicato were first used in dramatic music; Wagner introduced a whole new group of instruments, the so-called "Wagner tubas," in his *Ring*.

Neither the poetry nor the music of an opera is to be judged as if it existed by itself. The music is good not if it happens to make a successful concert piece but primarily if it is appropriate and adequate to the particular situation in the opera where it occurs, and if it contributes something which the other elements cannot supply. If it sounds well in concert form, so much the better, but this is not essential. Similarly, the poetry is good not because it reads well by itself, but primarily if, while embodying a sound dramatic idea, it furnishes opportunity for effective musical and scenic treatment. Both poetry and music are to be understood only in combination with each other and with the other elements of the work. In beginning the study of an unfamiliar opera it is always best to start with the libretto, which is where the composer himself usually starts.

In an opera, as elsewhere, music may serve four different purposes in relation to the words. Music may be used (1) for *declamation,* as a vehicle for reciting the words—whence the name "recitative" for this kind of music; (2) for *decoration:* the music may set out to charm on its own account, using the text only as a kind of spring-board from which to launch itself; (3) for *depiction:* the music may attempt to illustrate certain picturesque details of the text, imitating natural sounds (such as bird songs) or suggesting by conventional running passages the action conveyed by such words as "run," "fly," and the like; (4) for *expression,* to give utterance to the emotional implications of the text or situation. This last is, of course, its most important function. Sometimes these various musical activities are kept comparatively separate, as is the case in Italian opera gener-ally; or they may be all going on at once, as in the last scene of Wagner's *Walküre.*

Throughout the history of opera, in all its many varieties, two fundamental types may be distinguished: those in which the music is the main issue, and those in which there is more or less parity between the music and the other factors. The former kind is some-times called "singer's opera," a term to which some undeserved opprobrium is attached. Examples of this type are the operas of Rossini, Bellini, Verdi, and indeed of most Italian composers; Mo-zart's *Magic Flute* also is a singer's opera, in which a complicated, inconsistent, and fantastic libretto is redeemed by some of the most beautiful music ever written. On the other hand such operas as those of Lully, Rameau, and Gluck, not to mention the music dramas of Wagner, depend for their effect on a balance of interest among many different factors of which music is only one, albeit the most important.

Theoretically it would seem that there should be a third kind of opera, one in which the music was definitely subordinated to the other features. As a matter of fact, the very earliest operas were of this kind; but it was found that their appeal was limited, and that it was necessary to admit a fuller participation of music in order to establish the form on a sound basis. Consequently an opera is not only a drama but also a type of musical composition, and this holds even for those works which include some spoken dialogue. The exact point at which such a work ceases to be an opera and becomes a play with musical interludes is sometimes difficult to determine; no rule can be given except to say that if the omission of the music makes it impossible to perform the work at all, or alters its fundamental character, then it must be regarded as an opera.

Throughout its career opera has been both praised and censured in the strongest terms. It was lauded by its creators as "the delight of princes," "the noblest spectacle ever devised by man." [3] On the contrary, Saint-Evremond, a French critic of the late seventeenth century, defined an opera as "a bizarre affair made up of poetry and music, in which the poet and the musician, each equally obstructed by the other, give themselves no end of trouble to produce a wretched work." [4] Opera has been criticized on moral as well as on aesthetic grounds; the respectable Mr. Haweis in 1872 regarded it "musically, philosophically, and ethically, as an almost unmixed evil." [5] Despite both enemies and friends, however, it has continued to flourish, and there is no reason to expect that it will not, in some shape or other, be with us for a long time to come. Like all other forms of art, it contains many things today which cannot be understood without a knowledge of its history. It is hoped that this book will not only serve as an introduction to the opera of the past but may thereby contribute as well to understanding the opera of the present.

[3] Marco da Gagliano, preface to *Dafne*. In Solerti, *Origini del melodramma*, p. 82.
[4] Saint-Evremond, *Œuvres* (ed. 1740) III, 249.
[5] Haweis, *Music and Morals*, p. 423.

Part I

Music and Drama
to the end of
the Sixteenth Century

2

The Lyric Theatre
of the Greeks

IT IS INDISPENSABLE FOR A STUDENT OF the history of opera to know something of the history, literature, and mythology of the ancient world, if only because so many opera subjects have been drawn from these sources. The myth of Orpheus and Eurydice has been used for over thirty operas, the story of Iphigenia (first dramatized by Euripides toward the end of the fifth century B.C.) for at least fifty, and the myth of Hercules for probably twice as many. Over half of the ninety-four operas of J. A. Hasse (1699–1783) are on classical themes. Berlioz's masterpiece, *Les Troyens,* is an outstanding nineteenth-century example. More recently there have been such works as Richard Strauss's *Elektra* (1909), Fauré's *Pénélope* (1913), Wellesz's *Alkestis* (1924), Křenek's *Leben des Orest* (1930), Milhaud's *Médée* (1939), and Malipiero's *Ecuba* (1941), though on the whole the preference for classical subjects is now much less pronounced than in the eighteenth century.

Greek drama, however, is of particular interest to us for the reason that it was the model on which the creators of modern opera at the end of the sixteenth century based their own works; it was the supposed music of Greek tragedy which they sought to revive in their "monodic style." Unfortunately, they did not know (nor do we) just how this music sounded. The only surviving specimen of Greek dramatic music is a very short mutilated fragment of unison melody from a chorus of Euripides' *Orestes* (408 B.C.),[1] and even this was not known to the early Florentine opera composers.

That music did play an important part in Greek tragedy we may learn from Aristotle's definition in the *Poetics,* written about a cen-

[1] A reproduction of the papyrus fragment (which itself is at least four centuries later than the time of Euripides) and transcription of the melody may be found in Sachs, *Musik der Antike,* pp. 17–18; see also Mountford, "Greek Music in the Papyri and Inscriptions," in *New Chapters in the History of Greek Literature,* pp. 168–69; Reinach, *La Musique grècque,* pp. 175–76.

tury later than the works of Sophocles and Euripides, which still served as models:

"Tragedy, then, is an imitation of some *action* that is *important, entire,* and of a proper *magnitude*—by language, embellished and rendered *pleasurable,* but by different *means* in the different parts. . . .

"By *pleasurable language,* I mean language that has the embellishments of rhythm, melody, and metre. And I add, by *different means in different parts,* because in some parts metre alone is employed, in others, melody." [2]

The last sentence of this passage would seem to indicate that the tragedies were not sung in their entirety, as has sometimes been stated. It is believed, however, that some kind of musical declamation was employed for at least part of the dialogue, and the fact that the plays were given in large open-air theatres makes this probable on acoustical grounds, if for no other reason. Such declamation may have been a kind of sustained, semimusical speech, perhaps like the *Sprechstimme* of Schönberg's *Pierrot Lunaire* or Berg's *Wozzek,* but moving within a more limited range of pitch. It is also probable that regular melodic settings were used in certain places.

Whatever may have been the manner of performing the dialogue, there can be no doubt that the choruses were really sung, and not merely musically declaimed. When Greek drama developed out of the earlier Bacchus-worship ceremonies, it took over from them the choral songs (dithyrambs) and solemn figured choral dances which have such an important place in the tragedies. The role of the chorus in these works is that of the "articulate spectator," voicing the audience's response to the events portrayed in the action, remonstrating, warning, or sympathizing with the heroes. Formally, the choruses are generally so placed as to divide the action into parts, corresponding to the division of a modern play into acts or scenes, resulting in an alternation of drama with the comparatively static or reflective choral portions. It is significant that this same formal arrangement is characteristic of opera in the seventeenth and eighteenth centuries, with its clear distinction between the dramatic action (recitative or spoken dialogue) and the lyrical or decorative scenes (arias, choruses, ballets) to which the action gives rise. The typical use of the chorus in Greek

[2] Aristotle, *Poetics* (tr. Twining) p. 75.

drama is best seen in the tragedies of Sophocles (495–406 B.C.) and Euripides (484–407 B.C.), the choruses of the latter's *Iphigenia in Tauris* being particularly beautiful examples. In Aeschylus (525–456 B.C.) the choruses are more numerous, and sometimes serve to narrate preceding events (*Agamemnon*) or take a direct part in the action (*Eumenides*).

All the actors in Greek tragedy were men, and the chorus was no exception. Although in later ages it numbered no more than twelve or fifteen singers, in Periclean times it was undoubtedly larger; [3] the chorus of Furies in Aeschylus' *Eumenides* numbered fifty, whose singing and dancing were said to have such a terrifying effect that children in the audience were thrown into convulsions from fright. The leader of the chorus (*choregos, choryphaios*) was chosen from among the wealthiest and most prominent citizens of the community. The position was regarded as a distinction, but since the leader had to train and equip the chorus at his own expense he sometimes found himself ruined by the honor, which the satirists listed among the possible calamities of life, like lawsuits and taxes.

The choral songs were unison melodies (like all Greek music), one note to a syllable, with accompaniment of instruments of the kithara or aulos type.[4] Theorists prescribed certain modes as appropriate for certain kinds of scene, the Dorian being generally favored for majestic verses and the Mixolydian for lamentations in dialogue between the chorus and a soloist. Such dialogues are quite frequent; there are also dialogues between the choregos and one of the actors, and occasionally (as in the *Alcestis* of Euripides) various members of the chorus have short solo parts. The choruses occasionally have a refrain, a passage recurring several times in "ritornello" fashion (Aeschylus, *Eumenides*).

No composers are mentioned, but poets are sometimes stated to have composed the music for their own plays. This does not mean so much as it would in the present day, for it is probable that the

---

[3] Cf. Hamilton, "The Greek Chorus," *Theatre Arts Monthly* XVII (1933) 459.
[4] The kithara was an instrument like the lyre, the strings being plucked either with the fingers or with a plectrum. The aulos was a double-reed wind instrument, the tone of which probably resembled that of the oboe but with a more piercing character. These instruments may have played short introductions and interludes to the choral songs. The "accompaniments" consisted in either doubling the voices at the unison or embellishing the vocal melody in a manner similar to "coloration," a practice known to the Greeks as "heterophony."

declamatory solo portions of the drama were for the most part improvised, only slight general indications of the rise and fall of the voice being given by the poet; the choruses may possibly have employed certain standard melodies (*nomoi*), though on occasion new melodies might be composed.

The Greek comedy assigned to music a much less important role than did the tragedy, although Aristophanes (*ca.* 448–385 B.C.) has choruses of Clouds, Wasps, Birds, and Frogs. In keeping with the general satirical spirit of the comedies, the chorus was dressed in fantastic costumes and indulged in imitation of animal and bird sounds. There was probably very little if any solo singing in the comedies.

By the second century B.C. the chorus had disappeared from Greek drama altogether. Aristotle in the fourth century already speaks of its decline and complains that the poets of that day introduce choral songs which "have no more connection with their subject, than with that of any other Tragedy: and hence, they are now become detached pieces, inserted at pleasure."[5] Solo singing still remained a feature of the Roman drama, as we learn from a passage in Lucian's dialogue "On the Dance," written about A.D. 165, describing an actor in tragedy "bawling out, bending forward and backward, sometimes actually singing his lines, and (what is surely the height of unseemliness) melodising his calamities. . . . To be sure, as long as he is an Andromache or a Hecuba, his singing can be tolerated; but when he enters as Hercules in person and warbles a ditty . . . a man in his right mind may properly term the thing a solecism."[6]

There are still many unanswered questions about the way in which Greek drama was performed, but we may be certain that, although it was not precisely like modern opera, neither was it entirely in spoken dialogue like a modern play. The function of music was that of an embellishment, though a very important one.[7] It was this conception which Gluck expressed as his theory of the relation of music to drama, namely, that its purpose should be to "animate the figures without altering their contours."

5 Aristotle, *Poetics*, p. 103.
6 Lucian (tr. Harmon) V, 240.
7 Cf. Aristotle: "Music . . . of all the pleasurable accompaniments and embellishments of tragedy, the most delightful." (*Poetics*, p. 78.)

3

Medieval
Dramatic Music [1]

THE HISTORY OF THE THEATRE DURING the Middle Ages is obscure. Ancient drama seems to have disappeared, although it is possible that traces of Roman comedy may have been retained in the popular farces and other pieces performed by strolling bands of players and (later) by the jongleurs. So far as our actual knowledge goes, however, the significant theatre of the Middle Ages is religious. It develops within the liturgy and emerges only partially from the church in the fifteenth century. Two stages of this religious theatre are to be distinguished: the liturgical drama (eleventh to thirteenth centuries) and the mysteries (fourteenth to sixteenth centuries). We shall give first a brief summary of their course and then a somewhat more detailed description of the features of each.

The origin of the religious theatre appears to have been the practice of performing certain portions of the service dramatically, that is, the officiating priests actually representing the characters rather than merely narrating the events. This technique was first applied to the story of the Resurrection, and soon after to that of the Nativity. Around the original kernel there was a steady growth by accretion: in the Resurrection dramas the episode of the three Marys at the tomb of Christ (Matthew 18:1–7) was preceded by the scene of the buying of the ointment and followed by scenes representing the appearance of the risen Christ to the women and later to the apostles; the story was extended backward to include the crucifixion, the trial, and eventually all the events of Passion Week. Similarly in the Nativity dramas the scene of the shepherds worshiping at the manger was expanded by taking in the Annunciation, the flight into Egypt, the Massacre of the Innocents, and so on. Before this process of

[1] The two leading works in English on this period are Chambers, *The Medieval Stage*, and Young, *The Drama of the Medieval Church* (on liturgical dramas only). See also Mantzius, *A History of Theatrical Art* II.

accretion was completed, the drama had been removed from its primitive position as part of the church service and reserved as a special feature of feast days, often coming as the climax of a procession and being performed on the church porch or steps, still however with priests and clerks as the actors, though the people might take part as a chorus. Next, the vernacular began to replace Latin; stage properties and costumes grew more elaborate; and with the constantly increasing size of the spectacle, the charge of the performances was finally given over to guilds of professional actors, and the arena of the action changed from the church to the market place. This transformation of the liturgical drama from an ecclesiastical to a municipal function was completed by about the middle of the fourteenth century and led into the mysteries, the typical late medieval form of sacred drama. But alongside the latter, the tradition of the older, simpler form survived; its manifestations are to be found in such works as the "school dramas" (plays on sacred subjects performed in schools and colleges), the oratorio, and certain aspects of opera in the seventeenth century, especially in Rome and northern Germany.

THE LITURGICAL DRAMA.—Like Greek tragedy, the liturgical drama grew out of religious ceremonies. The origin of the Resurrection dramas is found in a trope [2] of the tenth century which was prefixed to the Introit for Easter:

> INT. Quem quaeritis in Sepulcro, o cristicolae?
> RESP. Jesum-Nazarenum crucifixum, o celicolae.

As these phrases were sung, music was retained in the scenes which grew up around them. In the earliest liturgical dramas, everything was sung; the further these plays grew away from the church, the more speaking and the less music they included, thus approaching in form the later mysteries. The music of the liturgical dramas

---

[2] Tropes are passages not forming part of the official liturgy, but added or inserted. They flourished from the ninth to the twelfth centuries, and their invention has been attributed by legend to Tuotilo, a monk of St. Gall in Switzerland, though modern research has shown that they originated earlier in France (see *The Winchester Troper*, ed. W. H. Frere, p. xii). It has been suggested that, since the trope never formed a part of the liturgy, the name "liturgical drama" applied to plays developed from tropes is inappropriate; however, since this term is well established there seems little point in attempting to replace it by the more accurate designation "ecclesiastical drama." Cf. Reese, *Music in the Middle Ages*, pp. 185–86, 193–97.

is of two kinds: (1) Nonmetrical plainsong of a simple though not purely syllabic type. For texts taken from the liturgy or the tropes the existing melodies were usually retained. For the added portions new melodies were selected or composed. Many of those chosen were from the antiphonary, and it has been shown [3] that there was an evident tendency to select melodies of which the original liturgical texts have some relation to the words to which the melody is sung in the drama: for example, the words in the drama "Ne timeas, Maria" are sung to the tune of the antiphon "Beati qui ambulant in lege tua, Domine." (2) Songs of a more or less distinctly metrical character, either hymn melodies or perhaps tunes of popular origin. These are less common, but they tend to occur more frequently in the later dramas. Their rhythm is not evident from the original notation [4] but is apparent from the metrical form and presence of a rhyme scheme in the texts. The latter are usually strophic, with two to fifteen or more stanzas, and may be either in Latin or in the vernacular. It is possible that some of these songs were sung by the congregation.

There are songs for both soloists and chorus. In the earlier dramas they may have been accompanied by the organ; there are occasional mentions of other instruments, but it is not clear to what extent these were intended to be actually used in performances.[5] So far as the manuscripts show, all the music was sung as single-line melody. The term "conductus," which sometimes occurs, refers not to a musical form [6] but to the procession from one part of the stage to another, marking the division of the drama into scenes.

Over two hundred liturgical dramas have been unearthed; twenty-two are published in Coussemaker's *Drames liturgiques du moyen âge*. The subjects of these cover a wide range: the Resurrection, the Nativity, miracles of saints, the prophets (for example *Daniel*), a melodrama with a kidnaping (*Le Fils de Guédron*), and a comedy (*Le Juif volé*). Adolphe Didron has pointed out how the liturgical drama must have represented for the medieval church a visible em-

[3] See Liuzzi, "L'espressione musicale nel dramma liturgico," *Studi medievali, nuova serie* II (1929) 74–109.
[4] The manuscripts are in the square "choral" notation, except for some of the earliest ones, which have the older neumes.
[5] See Coussemaker, *Drames liturgiques*, pp. 50, 59, 60.
[6] Cf. Ellinwood, "The *Conductus*," MQ XXVII (1941) 167.

bodiment of the sacred stories commemorated in the statues and stained glass windows of the cathedrals, as though the figures in these monuments "descended from their niches and panes . . . to play their drama in the nave and choir of the vast edifice." [7] There is about them certainly an air of profound and simple piety, a naïve blending of sacred and profane without the least sense of incongruity, which is one of the most engaging features of medieval art.

As an example of the liturgical drama we may take *The Three Marys,* which is found in a manuscript of the late thirteenth or early fourteenth century.[8] This is one of the Resurrection dramas which grew up around the Easter trope. To this original scene, five others have been added: (1) The lament of the three Marys. (2) The scene of the merchants who sell oil and spices; after this comes the scene at the tomb which contains the trope. (3) A long dialogue between Mary Magdalene and the angels. (4) The scene of recognition between Mary and the risen Christ; and finally (5) the arrival of the apostles, who join the Marys about the tomb. Thus the action increases in interest and animation to the end, and the work is followed by the customary "Te Deum laudamus."

Following is part of the dialogue between Mary Magdalene and the angels at the tomb:

Ex. I.

The angels then announce the Resurrection, and there follows a song in French, of a simple *rondeau* type (a a b a), with four equal phrases, and obviously intended to be performed in a regular metrical pattern:

7 Coussemaker, *Drames,* p. ix.
8 Published in Coussemaker, *Drames,* No. 18, pp. 256–79. For other forms of this liturgical drama, see *The Winchester Troper,* Plates 26a (cf. p. 17) and 26b. See also Young, *Drama of the Medieval Church,* chaps. VII–XV. There are summaries of other liturgical dramas from Coussemaker in Dent, "Social Aspects of Music in the Middle Ages," in OHM, 2d ed., Introductory Volume, pp. 195–99.

The examples here given are transcribed from Coussemaker's version, which is in modern plainsong notation; consequently, the suggestions as to rhythm and metre are the responsibility of the present author, as are also the accidentals placed above the staff.

Ex.2.
Angels:
Dou-ce da - me, qui si plou-rés, di-tes nous ou vo - lés a - ler.

Je crois mout bien, se Diex nous gart, de'vrais a - mour, le cuer vous art.
(Rhyme-scheme: a a bb)

Mary replies in a song beginning with the same melody, but breaking off into a variant with expressive melismata on the words "dolante" ("sorrow") and "plante" ("lament"):

Ex.3.
Mary:
Las-se do-lan - te, que fer-ai de mon Seig-neur que per - du ai?

Je cuit de duel me tu - er-ai. Do-lan - te!

ta mors au cuer grant duel me plan - te!

(*) This variant does not occur in every stanza.

The closing scene reverts to Latin. Notice the effective dramatic entrance of the chorus on higher notes at "et ille alius discipulus":

Ex.4.
Apostles: Chorus:
Cor-re-bant du - o si - mul. Et il-le a-li-us di - sci - pu-lus pre-cu-
cur-rit ci-ci-us* Pe - tro, et ve-nit ad mo-nu-men-tum. Al-le - lu-ia!

*"Cicius"(sic in Coussemaker) for "citius."

Toward the end of the scene occurs the closing part of the Easter sequence "Victimae paschali laudes," other portions of which had been
used in preceding scenes: [9]

Ex.5.

1.(Chorus)

Cre-den-dum est ma-gis so-li Ma-ri-e ve-ra-ci quamJu-de-o-rum tur-be fal-la-ci.

2.(Three Marys)

Sci-mus Chris-tum sur-rex-is-se ex mor-tu-is ve-re. Tu no-bis vic-tor rex mi-se-re-re!

THE MYSTERIES.—The mysteries,[10] which flourished during the
fifteenth and sixteenth centuries, differed considerably from the
earlier liturgical dramas. Although the church still collaborated and
the bishop's permission was necessary for a performance, the sponsor
was the community as a whole and the actors were recruited from
professional guilds, such as the Confrérie de la Passion in France
and the Compagnia del Gonfalone in Italy. National differentiations
are evident, and the vernacular is used consistently. The Italian
works of this class were known as *sacre rappresentazioni*,[11] and are
generally regarded as forerunners of the oratorio, though their influence is apparent in some seventeenth-century Italian operas as
well. The subjects of the mysteries are sacred but of much greater
scope than those of the liturgical dramas; thus there was the *Mystery
of the Old Testament,* which ran for twenty-five days consecutively,[12]
and the *Mystery of the Acts of the Apostles* performed at Bourges
in 1536, which lasted forty days. The performance was usually on
a large outdoor stage, using the principle of "simultaneous décor,"
that is, with all the scenes disposed in various places about the
stage and each being used as required. Paradise was always placed
at a higher level, and it was here that the singers and players were
stationed, whence the hauntingly beautiful recurrent phrase in the
stage directions, "Adoncques se doit resonner une melodye en Para-

[9] This sequence is found in many of the Easter plays (Young, *Drama of the Medieval
Church,* chap. XII). For a more detailed musical analysis of other liturgical dramas see
Albrecht, *Four Latin Plays of St. Nicholas.*

[10] This word is probably derived from the Latin *ministerium* ("service").

[11] For the other Italian names for these pieces, and a general account of them in Italy,
see D'Ancona, *Origini del teatro italiano* I, 370 ff.

[12] Modern edition by Rothschild, 6 vols.

dis" ("Now shall a melody be sung in Paradise"). The middle level was for Earth, and there might be a still lower stage to represent Hell. The walls of Jerusalem, Herod's palace, Noah's Ark, the hill of Golgotha, the Garden of Eden, limbo, purgatory, and scores of other scenes were represented. All the miracles had to be shown visibly: descents and ascents of angels, Lucifer on a fire-breathing dragon, Aaron's rod blossoming, the souls of Herod and Judas carried off by devils, water changed to wine, eclipses, earthquakes, the Deluge, even tortures and beheadings took place on the stage.[13] The juxtaposition of sacred scenes and crude displays no longer gives the impression of naïve piety, as in the liturgical dramas, but rather of almost blasphemous incongruity; the large number of characters, the grotesque, disorderly crowding of episodes, all make of the mysteries a typically Gothic spectacle, reminiscent of the sprawling confusion of incidents and personages in the medieval epics and romances. There were also comic insertions, improvised antics or farces, often of an indecent nature. Finally the mysteries went so far as to permit mockery of the church and priests, and the introduction of pagan deities on the stage. The awakened conscience of the church, together with the revival of classic ideals of the drama, eventually led to the condemnation of the mysteries on both moral and aesthetic grounds. By the end of the sixteenth century they were virtually extinct, but some remnants of the medieval love of profusion and grotesquerie survived in the operas and ballets of the seventeenth century.

Music in the mysteries was of relatively much less importance than in the liturgical dramas. In most cases its function was purely incidental, and since none of it has come down to us we learn of its existence only by occasional references in the stage directions and from other indirect sources. Hymns and other parts of the liturgy were sung, as in the *Mystery of the Resurrection* (fifteenth century) where at the moment when Christ descends into Hell all the spirits sing "Veni creator spiritus." [14] Most of these selections were probably simple plainsong, but there were occasionally pieces in polyphonic style. In the *Mystery of the Passion* (Angiers, 1486), the voice

---

13 Similar scenes are to be found in the pre-Shakespearean drama in England, in early Spanish and Italian tragedy, and in many of the sixteenth-century Italian *novelle*.
14 Jubinal, *Mystères inédits du quinzième siècle* II, 339.

of God is represented by three singers, soprano, tenor, and bass [15] —this being doubtless intended to symbolize the Trinity. Sometimes the angels in Paradise sing three-part motets, as in the *Mystery of the Incarnation* (Rouen, 1474), the author of which (or a later commentator) makes many references to, and quotations from, a treatise *De arte musica* which he ascribes to Jean de Muris.[16] In addition to music of this kind the mysteries included popular airs, in the singing of which the audience joined. In Germany, where the Nativity plays were especially cultivated, one such song was the well-known "In dulci jubilo." [17]

There was also a considerable amount of instrumental music in the mysteries. Before the performance there would be a procession (*monstre*) through the town, with music by pipe and tabor. Entrances of important personages were announced by a *silete*, similar to the "flourish of trumpets" in Shakespeare. Instrumental music accompanied the procession of the actors to a different scene on the stage. Angels played concerts of harps—or rather pretended to play them while musicians concealed behind the scenes furnished the music. Instruments were also played for dancing: in the *Mystery of the Passion* Herod's daughter dances a *moresca* to the accompaniment of a tambourine; in Italy we learn of morescas, galliards, pavanes, and many other dances in these spectacles, which frequently concluded with a general dance. For the monstre of the *Mystery of the Acts of the Apostles* there was an orchestra of flutes, harps, lutes, rebecs, and viols. Trumpets, *bucinae,* bagpipes, cornemuses, drums, and organs are also mentioned; in the *Mystery of the Passion* the march of Jesus to the Temple is accompanied by "a soft thunder of one of the large organ pipes," and in the *Mystery of the Resurrection* the descent of the Holy Ghost is similarly signalized.[18]

---

[15] "Et est à noter que la loquence de Dieu le père se doit pronuncer entendiblement et bien atraict en trois voix cest assavoir ung hault dessus, une hault contre et une basse contre bien accordées et en cest armonie se doit dire toute la clause qui s'ensuit . . ." (quoted in Cohen, *Histoire de la mise en scène*, p. 140).

[16] No work of this title by Jean de Muris is known. The references are probably to the *Speculum musicae* (ca. 1350), the former attribution of which to De Muris is probably erroneous.

[17] Moser, *Geschichte der deutschen Musik,* 5th ed., I, 320; Hoffmann von Fallersleben, *In dulci jubilo . . . ein Beitrag zur Geschichte der deutschen Poesie.*

[18] Cohen, *Histoire,* pp. 136, 159.

There was at least one mystery in which music, instead of being merely incidental, was used throughout. This was the *Festa d'Elche,* a Spanish mystery performed in the sixteenth century, which had instrumental pieces, unaccompanied plainsong solos, and a number of three- and four-part choruses by the Spanish composers Ribera, Pérez, and Lluis Vich.[19] This instance of continuous music in the mysteries is probably not unique. Some of the Italian sacre rappresentazioni and similar pieces of the fifteenth century seem to have been sung throughout.[20]

The medieval liturgical dramas and mysteries, although they did not lead directly into the opera, are more than merely isolated precursors of the form. The Italian sacre rappresentazioni were the models from which the first pastoral dramas with music were derived. We shall have occasion later to see how the traditions and practices of such works manifest themselves in some of the operas of the seventeenth century. But their music was completely unsuited to modern dramatic expression. The immediate predecessors of the opera must be sought in the secular theatre of the late Middle Ages and the Renaissance.

SECULAR DRAMATIC MUSIC.—Aside from the dramas of antiquity, the earliest known secular play with music is Adam de la Hâle's *Li Gieus de Robin et de Marion,* performed probably at the court of the king of Naples in 1283 or 1284.[21] Although this work is sometimes called "the first opéra comique," it actually has no historical connection with the latter form, and indeed differs in no way from other *pastourelles* of its period, except that Adam chose to omit the customary narrative portions and make it simply a little pastoral comedy, in which the spoken dialogue is interspersed with a score of short songs or refrains, a number of dances, and some instrumental music. It is doubtful whether Adam himself wrote either the words or the music of the songs. All are single-voice melodies notated without accompaniment. Their naïve, folk-song-like character, and the fact that several phrases of their texts occur also in

19 Ambros, *Geschichte der Musik,* 3d ed., IV, 274; Pedrell, "La Festa d'Elche," SIMG II (1900–1901) 203–52; Trend, "The Mystery of Elche," M&L I (1920) 145–57.
20 Rolland, "L'Opéra avant l'opéra," in his *Musiciens d'autrefois,* p. 24.
21 *Œuvres complètes du trouvère Adam de la Halle,* ed. Coussemaker (1872); other modern editions by E. Langlois (1896) and G. Cohen (1935). See also H. Guy, *Essai sur la vie et les oeuvres littéraires du trouvère Adan de la Hale* (1896).

other pastourelles,[22] point to the probability that some at least were simply popular chansons of the time, fitted into the situations of the play.

Ex.6.

In any event, *Li Gieus de Robin et de Marion*, although a charming work, is of little importance for the history of opera, since it is an isolated instance of the introduction of music into a secular dramatic piece in this early period.[23]

---

[22] Cf. Bartsch, *Romances et pastourelles françaises, passim*.
[23] The other *jeux* of this period are not, strictly speaking, dramatic in form. Adam's own *Li Jus Adan ou de la Feuillie* contains but a single line of music.

4

The Immediate Forerunners
of Opera

WITH THE COMING OF THE RENAISSANCE, interest in all forms of non-churchly music increased. Throughout the fifteenth and sixteenth centuries music was a feature of courtly entertainments, banquets, tourneys, festivals, triumphal entrances, and similar brilliant occasions.[1] This music cannot properly be called "dramatic," since it did not serve to carry on the action of a drama; nevertheless, its connection with the history of opera is important, for these courtly displays of the Renaissance established the practice of bringing together many different artistic resources—singing, playing, dancing, scenery, costumes, stage effects—in a single spectacle calculated to appeal equally to the eye, the ear, and the imagination. Scenes of this kind, nondramatic displays with accompaniment of music, came into opera very early in the seventeenth century and have remained characteristic of opera ever since. In the sixteenth century the most important of the many types of entertainment in which music served were the ballet and the *intermedio*.

THE BALLET.—The ancestor of the ballet was the *mascarade* (Italian *mascherata*, English masque). Originally a popular spectacle associated with carnival time, the Italian mascherata had developed into a favorite court amusement which was imitated by the French and English in the sixteenth century. The French mascarades frequently formed part of the ceremonies of welcome to a distinguished personage, as on the occasion of a visit of Charles IX to Bar-le-Duc in 1564, when actors representing the four elements, the four planets, and various allegorical and mythological personages, including the god Jupiter, united in a fulsome ceremony of homage

---

[1] See Nolhac and Solerti, *Il viaggio in Italia di Enrico III, re di Francia* [1574], for some notable instances. Comparatively little of this music has been preserved. The best treatment of all this preoperatic music is in Ambros, *Geschichte der Musik*, 3d ed., IV (revised by H. Leichtentritt), 161–346.

to the king. Mascarades of this sort later became the models for the French opera prologues. By the sixteenth century, as these mascarades show, aristocratic poetry had taken over the whole panoply of ancient pagan deities, demigods, nymphs, satyrs, and heroes, together with scores of figures from the pages of medieval epics and romances; all these were freely introduced on the stage, usually more lavishly than logically. In those mascarades where the purpose was the entertainment of an entire company rather than the complimenting of an illustrious guest, dancing was the chief attraction, and it was from mascarades of this sort that the characteristic French form of the ballet was derived. The English masque, somewhat similar to the mascarade, developed later in the sixteenth century, and its heyday was the time of James I and Charles I (1603–1649). The French word *ballet* comes from the Italian *balletto,* the diminutive of *ballo,* an Italian dance much in favor at the French court in the later sixteenth century. The most famous ballet of the period was *Circe, ou le Ballet comique de la reine,* performed at the Petit-Bourbon palace in Paris, October 15, 1581, on the occasion of the marriage of Mademoiselle de Vaudemont, the queen's sister, to the Duc de Joyeuse. A complete account of this incredibly lavish production (it cost nearly a half million dollars) was published with the score in the following year.[2] The principal author and director, Balthasar de Beaujoyeulx, explains in his introduction that the word "comique" refers to the fact that here for the first time an attempt was made to unify all the elements of the ballet by means of a coherent plot (*comédie*), a very simple dramatic framework which gave occasion for the introduction of many different stage settings and dances. Slight as it was, this introduction of a dramatic action into the ballet might have led at once to the creation of French opera if only the musicians had undertaken to solve the problem of setting dramatic dialogue, thereby making continuous music possible. But neither their interest nor that of their audiences lay in this direction. The dramatic ballet survived for a few decades in France, but by 1620 all pretence of a unified plot was abandoned, and the ballet reverted to a mere diversified spectacle for the amusement of the court. The music of the *Ballet comique de la reine* was by Lambert de Beaulieu and Jacques Salmon. It consists of six

2 Modern edition (piano-vocal score) in C.F.

choruses, two dialogues with choral refrains, two solos, and two sets of instrumental dances. The choruses are comparatively dull. The bass solos, as was customary in the period, merely follow the bass of the harmony. Some of the soprano airs are highly ornamented— a style of writing frequently found in solo madrigals and also used by Monteverdi for one aria in his *Orfeo*. The most interesting pieces are the dances, with their formal, stately, geometrical rhythms. One of them, "Le Son de la clochette," is still played today (Example 7).

BALLET COMIQUE DE LA REINE (1582) p.31

Ex.7.

Both the ballet and the masque exercised a strong influence on the formation of the respective French and English national operas, as we shall see later.

THE INTERMEDIO.—It will be observed that in such pieces as the mascarades and ballets the function of music is essentially that of adjunct to a visual spectacle. There is another class of sixteenth-century works in which the role of music was to offer diversion in connection with a regular spoken play. As is well known, one of the features of the Renaissance was the revival of secular drama. The movement began in Italy toward the end of the fifteenth century with performances of Latin plays, in the original or in translation, under courtly auspices, at various centers, of which Ferrara, Rome, Florence, Mantua, and Venice were particularly prominent. Many new plays were written, in Latin or Italian, imitated from classical models. Practically all these plays made use of music to a greater or less extent, though in a subordinate, decorative fashion. There were occasional solos or duets, choruses (these especially in tragedies based on Greek originals), madrigals, and instrumental pieces. The general tendency was to separate the musical numbers from the play itself by placing them in the prologue and at the ends of the acts, so that each appeared as an "intermezzo" or "intermedio," that is, something "intermediate" in the action of the play. Their subjects were, as a rule, connected in some allegorical way with the subject of the drama: "that which is enacted by the Gods in the fable of the Intermedii, is likewise enacted—as it were, under constraint of a higher power—by the mortals in the comedy." [3] On especially festive occasions, such as princely marriages, the intermedi might be very elaborate. Those performed at Florence in 1539 at the marriage of Cosimo I and Eleonora of Toledo, with music by Francesco Corteccia, included three solo songs and four madrigals for four to eight voices with varied instrumental accompaniment.[4] The intermedi by Corteccia and A. Striggio for D'Ambra's *La cofanaria* (Florence, 1565), had solos, madrigals, and other ensemble pieces, with accompaniments by large and varied orchestral groups.[5] Striggio's intermedio *L'amico fido* (Florence, 1569) was presented with a pomp of staging and music which foreshadows many seventeenth-century operas.[6] Other composers of intermedi include Alfonso della Viola (Cinthio's *Orbecche,* Ferrara, 1541, and several others), Antonio dal Cornetto (Cinthio's *Eglè,* Ferrara, 1545), Claudio Merulo (Dolce's *Marianna,* Venice, 1565, *Troiana,* 1566, and others), and Andrea Gabrieli (Giustiniani's *Edipo,* Vicenza, 1585). Perhaps the most famous intermedi of the sixteenth century were those for Bargagli's comedy *La pellegrina,* performed at Florence in May of 1589 as part of the festivities attending the wedding of the Grand Duke

3 Il Lasca, foreword to the intermedi *Psyche ed Amore,* reprinted in Sonneck, "[The] Intermedi *Psyche and Amor,*" in his *Miscellaneous Studies,* pp. 269–86; also MA III (1911) 40–53.
4 SB 99. See also Schering, "Zur Geschichte des begleiteten Sologesangs," ZIMG XIII (1911–12) 190–96; idem, *Aufführungspraxis alter Musik,* p. 67. The instrumentation mentioned is found in a later edition of the comedy: *Il commodo, comedia d'Antonio Landi con i suoi intermedi* [etc.] (1566) p. 95.
5 Sonneck, "[The] Intermedi *Psyche and Amor,*" pp. 276–86.
6 See description by Balduccini in Ambros, *Geschichte* IV, 245–51.

Ferdinand de' Medici and Christine of Lorraine.[7] The six intermedi
were planned by Count Giovanni Bardi; some of the texts were by
Ottavio Rinuccini, and the music was by several different composers, including Luca Marenzio, Emilio de' Cavalieri, and Cristofano Malvezzi. Forty-one of the most celebrated musicians of the
time took part in the performance. There were five- and six-part
madrigals, double and triple choruses, and a final madrigal calling
for seven different vocal ensembles in a total of thirty parts, each
part sung by two voices. These songs were accompanied by various
groups of instruments, which also played a number of "sinfonie."
The orchestra included organs, lutes, lyres, harps, viols, trombones,
cornetts,[8] and other instruments, used in different combinations for
each number. The style of orchestration is like that in Monteverdi's
Orfeo.[9] Three of the six solos are in ordinary madrigal style with the
lower voices played on instruments. The others exemplify the florid
solo style of the sixteenth century, the voice ornamenting a melodic
line which is given simultaneously in unornamented form in the
accompaniment. Example 8, for soprano with accompaniment of
a *chitarrone* (bass lute), is by Cavalieri.

With intermedi on such a scale as this, we can well imagine that
the audience must have had little attention to give to the play itself, and such was no doubt often the case with such performances
in Italy in the sixteenth century. "For the majority of the audience
the dances and pageants formed the chief attraction. It is therefore
no marvel if the drama, considered as a branch of high poetic art,
was suffocated by the growth of its mere accessories." [10]

It must not be imagined that the coming of opera at once put an
end to the intermedi and similar spectacles. On the contrary, they
remained popular at Italian courts well into the seventeenth cen-

[7] See Solerti, *Musica, ballo e drammatica alla côrte Medicea*, pp. 12–22; idem, *Albori
del melodramma* II, 15–42; *Atti dell' accademia del R. Istituto musicale di Firenze, Anno
XXXIII* (1895) pp. 103 ff. The two principal source documents differ in some details
as to the composers, and the general music histories are full of confusion on the subject.
[8] The cornett (It. *cornetto*, Ger. *Zinke*) is not to be confused with the modern cornet.
See Karstädt, "Zur Geschichte des Zinken," AfMf II (1937) 385–432.
[9] Unlike most of the sixteenth-century intermedi, the music of these was published
(Venice, 1591). The only complete set of part books is (or was, according to Eitner) in
the Vienna National Library. There are reprints of selected numbers in Schneider, *Die
Anfänge des Basso Continuo*, pp. 116–57; see also Haas, *Musik des Barocks*, pp. 20–22;
Goldschmidt, *Studien* I, 374–80; Kinkeldey, *Orgel und Klavier*, pp. 306–12.
[10] Symonds, *The Renaissance in Italy: Italian Literature* II, 143.

tury; the opera eventually took over many features of the earlier form, but without supplanting it. The intermedio is important as a forerunner of opera for two reasons: first, because it kept alive in the minds of Italian poets and musicians the idea of close collaboration between drama and music; and second, because in these works, just as in the French dramatic ballet, the external form of the future opera is already outlined—a drama with interludes of music and dancing. As soon as the drama itself could be set to music and sung instead of recited, opera would be achieved.

INTERMEDIO VI

Ex.8.

Cavalieri

VOICE

Go - di tur-ba — mor - tal fe - - - li - - œe lie - ta go - - - - - di di tan - - - - - to do - no E col can - to e col suo - - - - -

CHITARRONE

- - - - noi fa - ti - co - sì tuoi tra - va - gli ac - que - ta

ac - - - - - - - - - - - - - - - - que - ta.

(Original, as transcribed in Schneider:)

It is clearly evident that the theatre music of the sixteenth century, far from being a mere tentative and imperfect experiment, was a well-developed, essential feature of the entire Renaissance movement. The academies of Italy and France quite naturally interested themselves in music as one aspect of their interest in the revival of ancient art and letters. The texts of the ballets and intermedi imply a degree of familiarity with Greek mythology on the part of their audiences which is hardly conceivable at the present day; while mingled with this, as a heritage from the Middle Ages, is a pervasive, subtle use of allegory and personification. Yet these works were not intended only for the erudite. They were a common part of the luxurious, pleasure-loving court life of cultivated persons. Princes and nobles, poets, painters, and musicians, amateur and professional alike, all participated in their composition and performed in them side by side. The music itself, as has been said, was not dramatic; all the action and passion of the drama were in spoken dialogue, leaving for music only the adornment of the spectacular, reflective, or lyrical scenes. But in these, the important musical forms of the sixteenth century found their place: instrumental dances, airs, madrigals, choruses, chansons, canzonets—everything that music had to offer, with one tremendous exception: the learned contrapuntal art of the Netherlanders. By the last decade of the sixteenth century the world was on the verge of opera. It remained only to transform the relation between drama and music from a mere association into an organic union. For this end, two things were necessary: a kind of drama which should be suitable for continuous music, and a kind of music capable of dramatic expression. The former was found in the pastorale, and the latter in the monodic recitative of the Florentine composers Galilei, Peri, and Caccini.

THE PASTORALE.—Toward the middle of the sixteenth century the pastorale began to displace all other types of dramatic poetry in Italy. So complete did its dominance become that Angelo Ingegneri, the foremost writer on the theatre in the latter part of the century, remarked that "if it were not for the pastorales, it might almost be said that the theatre was extinct." [11] A dramatic pastorale is a poem, lyric in substance but dramatic in form, intended for either reading or stage presentation, with shepherds, shepherdesses, and sylvan deities for the chief characters, and with a background of fields, forests, or other idyllic and pleasant natural scenes. The dramatic action is restricted to mild love adventures and a few incidents rising out of the circumstances of pastoral life and usually ends happily. The attraction of the pastorale consisted, therefore, not in the plot but in the scenes and moods, the sensuous charm of the language, and the delicately voluptuous imagery, at which the Italian Renaissance poets excelled. The sources of the pastoral ideal lay partly in literary studies (Theocritus, Vergil), but it was redeemed from affectation by the sincere and profound Italian feeling for the beauties of "nature humanized by industry." "The vision of a Golden Age idealized

[11] Ingegneri, *Della poesia rappresentativa*, p. 8.

man's actual enjoyment of the country, and hallowed, as with inexplicable pathos, the details of ordinary rustic life. Weary with courts and worldly pleasures, in moments of revolt against the passions and ambitions that wasted their best energies, the poets of that century, who were nearly always also men of state and public office, sighed for the good old times, when honor was an unknown name, and truth was spoken, and love sincere, and steel lay hidden in the earth, and ships sailed not the sea, and old age led the way to death unterrified by coming doom. As time advanced, their ideal took form and substance. There rose into existence, for the rhymsters to wander in, and for the readers of romance to dream about, a region called Arcadia, where all that was imagined of the Golden Age was found in combination with refined society and manners proper to the civil state." [12]

The earliest pastoral drama was Poliziano's *Orfeo,* performed sometime between 1472 and 1483 at Mantua, with music consisting of at least three solo songs and one chorus, interspersed with the spoken dialogue.[13] The pastoral poem was firmly established by Sannazaro's *Arcadia* (1504), but the real beginning of the pastoral drama is usually dated from the performance of Agostino Beccari's *Sacrificio d'Abramo* at Ferrara in 1554. The music of this work, by Alfonso della Viola, has been reprinted by Solerti.[14] In the third scene of Act III occurs a strophic monologue for bass, with a choral refrain. The solo part is a kind of psalmodic recitative on the bass notes of the harmonies, which were undoubtedly filled in (improvised?) by a lute or similar instrument (Example 9).

The finest examples of the pastorale, and indeed two of the most beautiful poems in all sixteenth-century Italian literature, are Torquato Tasso's *Aminta* (Ferrara, 1583) and Battista Guarini's *Pastor fido* (written at Ferrara between 1581 and 1590).[15] The pastorales

---

[12] Symonds, *Renaissance* II, 196–97 (paraphrased from Tasso's *Aminta,* closing chorus of Act I).

[13] Poliziano, *Le stanze, l'Orfeo e le rime,* pp. 369–507; see also Symonds, *Renaissance* I, 409–15, and Henderson, *Some Forerunners of the Italian Opera,* chaps. 4–9. Modern edition of *Orfeo,* for voice and piano, by A. Casella (Milan, 1934).

[14] See his "Precedenti del melodramma," RMI X (1903) 207, 466; and his *Albori del melodramma* I, 12–13. Cf. also Schering, "Zur Geschichte des begleiteten Sologesangs," ZIMG XIII (1911–12) 193–94.

[15] See Solerti, *Vita di Torquato Tasso;* and, on the unique significance of Ferrara and the ducal family of the Este in the history of Italian sixteenth-century music, the same author's *Ferrara e la corte Estense.* See also Neri, "Gli intermezzi del Pastor fido," *Giornale storico della letteratura italiana* XI (1888) 405–15.

lent themselves naturally to musical treatment not only because of their preponderantly lyric content, their brevity, and their use of choruses, songs, and dances, but also because of the very language, "flowery and sweet . . . so that one may even admit that it has melody in its every part, since there are shown deities, nymphs, and

IL SACRIFICIO

Ex.9.   Alfonso della Viola

Tu c'hai le cor-na ri-guar-dan-ti il cie-lo   Fis-se ne l'am-pia fron te, e spaci-o-sa

O Pan Li - ce - o,   O Pan Li - ce - o!

shepherds from that most remote age when music was natural and speech like poetry." [16] In *Aminta* the words are hovering on the edge of song at every moment; every phrase is filled with that unheard music which Tasso himself called "the sweetness and, so to speak, the soul of poetry." [17] Tasso, like all the Italian artists and poets of his time, was an amateur of music and particularly admired Gesualdo, who made settings of a number of his madrigals. He was a friend of Cavalieri, who composed the incidental music for a performance of *Aminta* at Florence in 1590.[18] Rinuccini, the librettist of the first operas, was a disciple of Tasso, and his poems *Dafne* and *Euridice,* as well as Striggio's *Orfeo* (composed by Monteverdi in 1607) and many of the other early operas, are simply pastorales on the model of Tasso's and Guarini's works. "Great tragedy and great comedy were denied to the Italians. But they produced a novel species in the pastoral drama, which testified to their artistic originality, and led by natural transitions to the opera. Poetry was on the point of expiring; but music was rising to take her place. And the imaginative

---

[16] Doni, "Trattato della musica scenica," Cap. 6 (quoted from Solerti, *Origini del melodramma,* p. 203).

[17] "La dolcezza, e quasi l'anima della poesia." *Dialoghi* III, 111.

[18] The music of two other pastorales by this composer—*Il satiro* and *La disperazione di Fileno* (Florence, 1590)—has not been preserved. According to Doni ("Trattato della musica scenica," Cap. 9), it was not in recitative style.

medium prepared by the lyrical scenes of the Arcadian play, afforded just that generality and aloofness from actual conditions of life, which were needed by the new art in its first dramatic essays. . . . *Aminta* and the *Pastor fido* . . . complete and close the Renaissance, bequeathing in a new species of art its form and pressure to succeeding generations." [19]

THE MADRIGAL COMEDY.—In any study of sixteenth-century Italian music as a whole, attention is usually concentrated on two fields: the sacred polyphonic music stemming from the Netherlands tradition and brought to its culmination by Palestrina, and the polyphonic madrigal, represented at its height by Marenzio, Gesualdo, and Monteverdi. With the great body of sixteenth-century church music the history of opera has simply nothing to do. With the madrigal, however, the case is different. The experiments of the latter part of the century include a number of works [20] now known as madrigal comedies, which represent attempts to adapt the madrigal to dramatic requirements. The most famous of these was Orazio Vecchi's *Amfiparnaso,* published in 1597.[21] Whether the *Amfiparnaso* was actually staged or merely sung as a madrigal cycle has long been an unsettled question, but the latter method of performance is more probable.[22] Vecchi's pupil, Adriano Banchieri, in the preface to his madrigal comedy *La saviezza giovanile* (1598), gives directions which indicate that in this work the singers and players were placed behind the scenes, while the actors on the stage mimed their parts. (It is not clear whether there was also spoken dialogue by the actors.) [23] The *Amfiparnaso* and similar works show clearly in their plots, character types (Pantalone, Pedrolino, Isabella, and the like), and use of dialect their derivation from the *commedia dell' arte.* In the *Amfiparnaso* there are eleven dialogues and three monologues, the same kind of musical setting being used for all, namely five-part (one four-part) madrigal ensembles or choruses. In the monologues, all five voices sing; in the dialogues, the differentiation of persons is commonly

19 Symonds, *Renaissance* II, 241, 245.
20 Solerti in his "Primi saggi del melodramma giocoso," RMI XII, XIII, reprints a famous predecessor of these works: Striggio's *Cicalamento delle donne* (1567).
21 Republished in Eitner, *Publikationen* XXVI, and Torchi, *L'arte musicale in Italia* IV, 148–280; new ed. in full score by C. Perinello (Milan, 1938); see also SB 164.
22 Dent, "Notes on the *Amfiparnaso*," SIMG XII (1910–11) 330–47; idem, "The *Amfiparnaso*," *Monthly Musical Record* XXXVI (1906) 50–52, 74–75; Hol, "Horatio Vecchi et l'évolution créatrice," in *Gedenkboek . . . Scheurleer,* pp. 159–67.
23 Rolland, *Les Origines du théâtre lyrique moderne; histoire de l'opéra en Europe,* p. 43.

suggested by contrasting the three highest with the three lowest voices (the *quinto* or middle part thus being in both groups), though at times all five are used even here. The music of the comic characters is mostly in the simple note-against-note style of the Italian "villanella," with a fine sense of the animation of comic dialogue:

On the other hand, some of the five-voice pieces are beautiful examples of the sixteenth-century serious Italian madrigal style, such as the "soliloquy" of Lucio in Act II, scene 1 (Example 11).

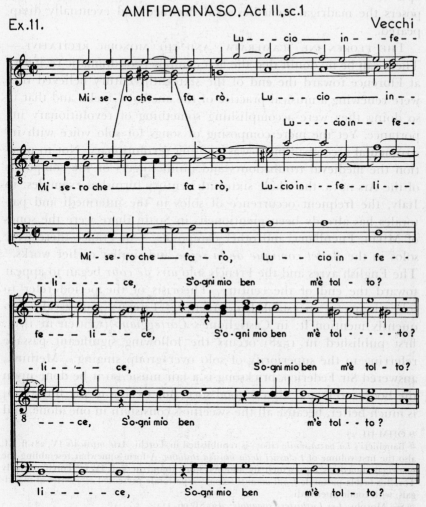

The madrigal comedies were an early attempt to combine farce comedy with music, to exploit the lively, popular commedia dell' arte as against the languid, aristocratic pastorales. But they were not essentially dramatic music. So far as their contribution to opera is concerned, their chief usefulness was to prove that madrigals were not suitable for dramatic purposes. It has even been surmised [24] that Vecchi intended the *Amfiparnaso* (the title has been freely translated "The Lower Slopes of Parnassus") as a satire on the early attempts at operatic music. In the hands of Banchieri [25] and other later composers the madrigal comedies soon declined and eventually disappeared.

THE FLORENTINE "CAMERATA" AND THE MONODIC RECITATIVE.— There can be no doubt that the first composers of dramatic recitative at Florence toward the end of the sixteenth century believed they were renewing a musical practice of the ancient Greeks, and that in so doing they were accomplishing something of revolutionary importance. Yet the mere composing of songs for solo voice with instrumental accompaniment was nothing revolutionary. Not to mention the medieval troubadours and minnesingers or the composers of the Ars nova, the whole sixteenth century furnishes examples: in Italy, the frequent occurrence of solos in the intermedi and pastorales has already been mentioned; in Spain there were the songs of Milan, Fuenllana, and other composers; [26] in France there were solos in the *Ballet comique de la reine* and similar earlier works. [27] The English ayres and the French solo *airs de cour* began to appear toward the end of the century. Theorists of the period refer to solo singing as an established practice. [28] Literary sources also frequently mention it; in Castiglione's *Corteggiano* (written in 1514, first published in 1528) occurs the following significant passage referring to the superiority of solo over group singing: "Methink, answered Sir Federico, pricksong is a fair music, so it be done upon the book surely and after a good sort. But to sing to the lute [viol] is much better, because all the sweetness consisteth in one alone, and

---

[24] OHM III, 27.

[25] Banchieri's *La pazza senile* (1607) is republished in Torchi, *Arte musicale* IV, 281 ff. Cf. also the first volume of *I classici della musica italiana*. A form somewhat resembling the madrigal comedy is represented by another work found in Vol. IV of Torchi, namely Torelli's favola pastorale *I fidi amanti* (1600)—a pastorale presented as a series of madrigals, with comic intermedi.

[26] See Morphy, *Les Luthistes espagnols;* also SB 96, 114.

[27] Prunières, "Ronsard et les fêtes de cour," RM V, No. 7 (May, 1924) 27–44; Comte, "Ronsard et les musiciens du XVIe siècle," *Revue d'histoire littéraire de la France* VII (1900) 341–81; Tiersot, "Ronsard et la musique de son temps," SIMG IV (1902–03) 70–142; see also "Hortus musarum de Pierre Phalèse, deuxième partie," in *Chansons au luth et airs de cour français du XVIe siècle.*

[28] Glareanus, *Dodecachordon* (1547) Lib. II, Cap. 39; Vicentino, *L'antica musica ridotta alla moderna prattica* (1555), Lib. IV; Zarlino, *Istituzioni harmoniche,* Lib. II, Cap. 8, 9.

a man is much more heedful and understandeth better the feat manner and the air or vein of it, when the ears are not busied in hearing
any more than one voice; and, beside, every little error is soon perceived; which happeneth not in singing with company, for one bear-
eth out another. But singing to the lute [viol] with the ditty, methink,
is more pleasant than the rest, for it addeth to the words such a grace
and strength that it is a great wonder." [29]

Even in Italian polyphonic music of the sixteenth century there
was a constantly increasing tendency to give the highest voice the
character of a solo and to reduce the others to the function of accompaniment.[30] This is evident not only in such native forms as the
frottola, the later villanella, and the *canti carnascialeschi* but also in
the madrigal, which, owing to its more contrapuntal texture, might
not be expected to show such traits. Italian madrigals (and the same
is true of other polyphonic vocal works of this period) were certainly
not invariably performed by an *a cappella* group; instruments, if
available, might double some or all the parts, or even replace the
four lowest voices altogether, leaving the highest one to be sung by a
soloist accompanied by (perhaps) a quartet of viols,[31] or accompanying himself on a lute or viola da braccio with a simplified "intabula-
tion" of the supporting parts. "Solo" madrigals for one, two, or three
voices with accompaniment of a keyboard instrument were composed
in the last part of the sixteenth century by Luzzasco Luzzaschi in

[29] Hoby's translation. "Bella musica, rispose Messer Federico, parmi il cantar bene a libro
sicuramente, e con bella maniera; ma ancor molto più il cantare alla viola; perchè tutta
la dolcezza consiste quasi in un solo; e con molto maggior'attenzio si nota, ed intende
il bel modo, e l'aria, non essendo occupate le orecchie in più che in una sol voce; e meglio
ancor vi si discerne ogni piccolo errore; il che non accade cantando in compagnia, perchè
l'uno ajuta l'altro: ma sopra tutto parmi gratissimo il cantare alla viola per recitare;
il che tanto di venustà, ed efficacia aggiunge alle parole, che è gran meraviglia" (Castiglione, *Il cortegiano,* Lib. 2). Cf. Bukofzer, "The *Book of the Courtier* on Music,"
MTNA XXXVIII (1944) 230–35.
"Cantare alla viola" refers to singing a solo and accompanying oneself on the viol—
presumably the "arm viol" (viola da braccio), though the tenor viola da gamba or the
large lyre were also suitable for chord playing (cf. Schneider, "Zur Geschichte des begleiteten Sologesangs," in *Festschrift . . . Kretzschmar,* pp. 138–40). The phrase "per
recitare" is not elucidated; it may refer to a freely rhythmed, recitative style of song,
possibly (as Schering points out, "Zur Geschichte des begleiteten Sologesangs," p. 196) like
the solos in the intermedi of 1539 and *Il sacrifizio* of 1554.
[30] See Einstein, "Die mehrstimmige weltliche Musik von 1450–1600," in Adler, *Handbuch der Musikgeschichte,* pp. 358–73; Einstein, "Firenze prima della monodia," RassM
VII (1934) 253.
[31] Cf. Schering's edition of Marenzio's "Solo e pensoso," SB 165; Greulich, *Beiträge zur
Geschichte des Streichinstrumentenspiels im 16. Jahrhundert.*

Ferrara.[32] The large amount of embellishment in the voice part of these madrigals exemplifies, to a virtuoso degree, the kind of ornamentation which singers were expected to provide in solos; such ornaments were usually improvised [33] and were a regular feature of late sixteenth-century vocal music. The melodic style of Luzzaschi is not like the Florentine monody but rather more regularly metrical and more tuneful in character.

The rise of solo singing was paralleled by a growing emphasis on the harmonic (as against the contrapuntal) aspect of music, a tendency evident even in church compositions with the frequent occurrence of syllabic, note-against-note passages, or even by entire compositions in this style, such as Palestrina's *Stabat Mater,* where the expressive effect of chordal progressions is clearly exploited. The rise of *basso continuo* in the last quarter of the century [34] was, of course, a sign of the final establishment of this harmonic conception of music.

The growth of solo song and of harmonic feeling in Italy has the character of a reaction against the contrapuntal style of music which had been implanted in that country by the Netherlands composers in the early part of the century. It is a manifestation of certain deep-rooted Italian traits which have remained constant throughout the musical history of that nation: hatred of complexity and obscurity, a profound feeling for melody as constituting the essence of music, and (this partly as a result of the whole mental attitude of the Renaissance) a preference for the individual artist as against the communal group represented by the church choir or the madrigal vocal ensemble.

Now it is a fact provable by many examples in the history of music that the establishment of a new practice, particularly if it be in conflict with an older practice, sooner or later inevitably calls forth a theory by which the new practice is sought to be justified. In the present case the development of the theory, as well as its practical

---

[32] SB 166; see also Kinkeldey, "Luzzasco Luzzaschi's Solo-Madrigale," SIMG IX (1907–08) 538–65.
[33] Haas, *Aufführungspraxis,* pp 117–21; Ferand, *Die Improvisation in der Musik,* chap. 6; Chrysander, "Ludovico Zacconi," VfMw VII (1891) 337–96, IX (1893) 249–310, X (1894) 531–67; Kuhn, *Die Verzierungskunst in der Gesangs-Musik.*
[34] The *term* "basso continuo" was first used by Viadana in his *Cento concerti ecclesiastici* (1602), but the practice of accompanying a polyphonic vocal piece on chord or keyboard instruments was much earlier. See Kinkeldey, *Orgel und Klavier in der Musik des 16. Jahrhunderts;* and Schneider, *Die Anfänge des Basso Continuo.*

application, was the work of a small group of composers, poets, scholars, and cultivated amateurs of art in Florence, known in music history as "the Camerata." [35] The leading spirit of the Florentine Camerata at the beginning was Count Giovanni Bardi di Vernio, a wealthy amateur and patron of artists, at whose house the group held its meetings, beginning sometime before 1580. It was a kind of academy, or rather a *ridotto*, of which so many were established in Italy at the time of the Renaissance. One of its earliest members was Vincenzo Galilei, father of the famous astronomer, whose *Dialogo della musica antica e della moderna* ("Dialogue of Ancient and Modern Music"), published in 1581,[36] was the first "declaration of war against counterpoint" and the basis of all the later theory and practice of the Camerata.[37] After 1592, when Bardi was called to Rome, the patron of the group was another nobleman and amateur composer, Jacopo Corsi. His principal associates were the poet Ottavio Rinuccini and the composers Emilio de' Cavalieri, Jacopo Peri, and Giulio Caccini. Rinuccini was the author of the librettos of *Dafne* (composed by Peri in 1594 and by Marco da Gagliano in 1608), *Euridice* (composed by both Peri and Caccini in 1600), and *Arianna* (composed by Monteverdi in 1608). Cavalieri composed and produced at Rome in 1600 the *Rappresentazione di anima e di corpo* ("The Spectacle of the Soul and the Body"), a work commonly (and erroneously) known as the "first oratorio." Peri was a singer, organist, and director of the ducal chapel. Caccini was a famous virtuoso singer and teacher; two of his daughters were also well-known singers, and one of them, Francesca, was a composer as well.

In the writings of Galilei and other members of the Camerata the theory of the "new music" was fully developed.[38] And since the music is, to some extent, the result of the theory, it will be well to outline the latter before proceeding to a study of the music itself. Like all Renaissance philosophers, the Camerata appealed for authority to the ancient Greeks. But the actual Greek music was unknown

---

[35] Martin, "La 'Camerata' du Comte Bardi," RdM XIII (1932) 63–74, 152–61, 227–34; XIV (1933) 92–100, 141–51; Brownlow, "The Bardi Coterie," PMA XXII (1896) 111–27.
[36] Facsimile reprint, Rome, R. Accademia d'Italia, 1934.
[37] For a study of the life and works of Galilei and an edition of some of his music, see F. Fano, ed., *La camerata fiorentina: Vincenzo Galilei (Istituzioni e monumenti dell' arte musicale italiana* IV).
[38] For a list of these writings see Ambros, *Geschichte* IV, 292, note 1. The most important documents are reprinted in Solerti, *Origini del melodramma*.

to them; Galilei had published three examples in his *Dialogo* but had not been able to transcribe them.[39] Consequently, it was necessary to deduce the character of the music from such writings of the ancients on the subject as were available. Long study and discussion of these writings led to the formulation of a basic principle, namely that the secret of Greek music lay in the perfect union of words and melody, a union to be achieved by making the former dominate and control the latter. "Plato and other philosophers . . . declare that music is none other than words and rhythm, and sound last of all, and not the reverse." [40] From this basic principle three corollaries followed. First, *the text must be clearly understood:* therefore the performance must be by a solo voice with the simplest possible accompaniment, preferably a lute or similar instrument played by the singer himself. There must be no contrapuntal writing, for this distracts the mind and produces confusion owing to different words being heard at the same time with different rhythms in different parts, leading to distortion of pronunciation (in Caccini's phrase, "laceramento della poesia"), and in general appealing not to the intelligence at all but only to the sense of hearing. (This wholesale condemnation of counterpoint was due rather to the exigencies of the theory than to ignorance or lack of appreciation and need not be taken altogether seriously.) The second corollary was that *the words must be sung with correct and natural declamation,* as they would be spoken, avoiding on the one hand the regular dancelike metres of popular songs such as the villanelle, and on the other the text repetitions and subservience to contrapuntal necessities found in madrigal and motet writing. "The idea came to me," says Caccini, "to introduce a kind of music whereby people could as it were speak in tones [*in armonia favellare*], using therein . . . a certain noble negligence of melody [*sprezzatura di canto*], now and then running over some passing-tones [*?false*], but holding firmly to the chord in the bass." [41] Peri is even more explicit: "I believed that the ancient Greeks and Romans (who, according to the opinion of many, sang their tragedies throughout) used a kind of music more advanced than ordinary

39 Two Hymns to the Muse, a Hymn to Nemesis (by Mesomedes of Crete, *ca.* A.D. 130), and a Hymn to the Sun (also probably by Mesomedes). See Sachs, *Musik der Antike,* pp. 13, 16, 18.
40 Caccini, preface to *Le nuove musiche.* In Solerti, *Origini,* p. 56.
41 Caccini, *Le nuove musiche.* In Solerti, *Origini,* p. 57.

speech, but less than the melody of singing, thus taking a middle position between the two." [42] The third and final corollary had to do with the relation between music and words. *The melody must not depict mere graphic details in the text but must interpret the feeling of the whole passage,* by imitating and intensifying the intonations and accents proper to the voice of a person who is speaking the words under the influence of the emotion which gives rise to them.[43] This pronouncement was, of course, directed against certain aspects of text treatment in the sixteenth-century madrigals and motets.

It was in these aesthetic principles and their practical consequences, not in the mere employment of the solo voice, that the revolutionary character of the Florentine reform consisted. They formed the necessary foundation for true dramatic music and thus made possible the creation of opera. There were tentative experiments in the new style by Galilei as early as 1582, when he composed a setting of Ugolino's monologue from Dante's *Inferno* (Canto XXIII, verses 4–75), which he sang to the accompaniment of four viols; neither this music nor his setting of part of the Lamentations of Jeremiah from about the same date, has been preserved. It seems that the new ideas must have made their way very slowly at first, for no trace of them is to be found in the music of the famous intermedi of 1589, most of which was written by members of the Camerata. In 1595 a little pastorale by Cavalieri, *Il giuoco della cieca*,[44] was performed at Florence, a work which probably made use of the new style of singing. Early in 1597 [45] the first opera, *Dafne*—Rinuccini's text set to music by Peri, with some parts by Corsi—was played before a small audience in Corsi's palace and repeated annually with changes and additions for two or three years following. In view of the great historical interest of this score it is singularly unfortunate that none of the music has survived, with the exception of two frag-

[42] Preface to *Euridice*. In Solerti, *Origini*, pp. 45–46.
[43] Galilei, *Dialogo*, pp. 88–89.
[44] Text arranged by Laura Guidiccioni from Act III, sc. 2, of Guarini's *Pastor fido*. Cf. Solerti, "Laura Guidiccioni," RMI IX (1902) 797–829.
[45] Probably not 1594, as is sometimes stated. The exact date is uncertain. See Sonneck, "*Dafne*, the First Opera," SIMG XV (1913–14) 102–10 (also Library of Congress, *Catalogue of Opera Librettos*, pp. 340–45). Tirabassi has argued that the "first opera" was not *Dafne* but Belli's *Orfeo dolente*, but the evidence he adduces is not convincing; see MQ XXV (1939) 26–33.

ments by Corsi,[46] neither of which serves to give much idea of the monodic style.

The earliest remaining examples of Florentine monody are undoubtedly some of the songs in Caccini's *Nuove musiche*,[47] which, although not published until 1601, were composed at least ten years previously. The collection consists of arias (strophic) and madrigals (through-composed) for solo voice with accompaniment of a lute or other stringed instrument. The music is in the *stile recitativo* ("reciting style") which, unlike the *stile rappresentativo* ("theatre style") of the operas,[48] permits a more symmetrical organization of phrases and a certain amount of text repetition and vocal embellishment—in other words, a free *arioso* type of melody.[49] The arias have simpler and more regular rhythms than the madrigals. A typical melodic line of the latter is illustrated in Example 12.

LE NUOVE MUSICHE

Ex.12.   Caccini

Fi - gli,   mi - rando il cie _ _ _ lo   Di - cea do-glio - sa, e in -

tan-to Em - pia di cal - de   per - le un bian _ _ _ co ve _ _ _ lo

One other early monodic work must be mentioned before going on to a discussion of the first operas. Cavalieri's *Rappresentazione*

46 In Schneider, *Die Anfänge des Basso Continuo*, p. 109.

47 *Le nuove musiche di Giulio Caccini detto Romano*. In Firenze, appresso J. Marescotti. MDCI (MDCII). Facsimile reprint, Roma, 1930. See also Francesco Mantica, *Prime fioriture del melodramma italiana* II. Selections in *I classici della musica italiana* IV. Other examples in Riemann, *Musikgeschichte* II, Pt. 2; and Haas, *Musik des Barocks*.

48 This distinction between "reciting" and "theatre" styles was first made explicit about 1635 by Doni in his "Trattato della musica scenica," Cap. 11. (See his *Lyra barberina* II, 28–30.)

49 Riemann, *Musikgeschichte* II, Pt. 2, 1–30. See also the aria "Arde il mio petto" and the madrigal "Amarilli mia bella" in SB 172, 173.

di anima e di corpo,[50] performed before the Congregazione dell' Oratorio at Rome in 1600, is the first known attempt to apply the principles of Florentine monody in a sacred composition. The text, with its moralizing purpose and its allegorical figures (Soul, Body, Pleasure, Intellect, and the like), shows its connection with the sacred dramas and morality plays of the sixteenth century. The extensive use of the chorus (twenty-four places in all, with many instances of choral refrains) is in marked contrast with the earliest opera scores, as is also the frequent appearance of solo songs of a distinctly tuneful and popular character. Dances and instrumental interludes also occur. The prologue is spoken; the alternation of speaking and singing, as in the medieval mysteries, remained during the first half of the seventeenth century a characteristic feature of the sacred dramas which flourished at Rome and Florence.[51]

The "new music" immediately found imitators all over Italy and soon spread to other countries. The older contrapuntal art of the sixteenth century did not, of course, immediately disappear; but the first half of the seventeenth century witnessed a gradual modification of the language of music due to the interaction of the new monodic idea with the older contrapuntal principles, and the efforts of composers to find a means of reconciling the two. For a long time they existed side by side. Christoph Bernhard in his *Tractatus compositionis* (written about 1648) distinguished between the *stylus gravis* or *antiquus* (marked by slow notes, little use of dissonance, "music mistress of poetry"), and *stylus luxurians* or *modernus* (some fast notes, unusual skips, more dissonance, more ornamentation, more tuneful melody); the latter in turn he subdivided into *communis* (poetry and music of equal importance) and *theatralis,* in which poetry was the "absolute mistress" of music.[52] The integration of monody with the traditional practices of music, and the earliest adaptation of the resultant new style to opera, took place chiefly in three centers: Florence, Rome, and Venice.

---

[50] Facsimile reprint in Mantica, *Prime fioriture del melodramma italiana;* selections in *I classici* X; SB 169; see also OHM III, 37–40. The text was written by Padre Agostino Manni, a disciple of San Filippo Neri; see Alaleona, "Su Emilio de' Cavalieri," *La nuova musica,* Nos. 113–14 (1905) 35–38, 47–50.

[51] For a theoretical justification of this practice see Doni, "Trattato," Cap. 4–6, and the two "Lezioni" following Cap. 49 of the same work.

[52] *Die Kompositionslehre Heinrich Schützens in der Fassung seines Schülers Christoph Bernhard,* ed. Müller-Blattau (1926).

Part 2

Renaissance and
Baroque Opera

5

The Florentine Operas

THE EARLIEST OPERA OF WHICH THE MU-
sic has survived is *Euridice*. The poem
is by Rinuccini; there are two com-
plete musical settings, one by Peri and one by Caccini, both composed
in 1600 for the wedding of Henry IV of France and Marie de' Medici.
Peri's version (with some numbers by Caccini) was performed October 6, 1600, at the Pitti Palace in Florence and published in 1601.[1]
Caccini's setting was published in the same year, but not performed
in its entirety until 1602.[2] The poem is a pastorale on the myth of
Orpheus and Eurydice—a favorite subject for operas, owing not only
to the fact that the hero is himself (according to legend) a singer, but
also to the combination of a simple action with a variety of emotional
situations (love, death, suspense, rescue from danger) and possibilities
for striking scenic effects. In the classic version of the myth, it will
be remembered, the condition of the rescue of Eurydice from Hades
is that Orpheus shall not look back or speak to his wife until they
arrive at the upper world; but in his anxiety he looks back and
Eurydice is returned to death irredeemably. Opera audiences have
always found this tragic outcome unbearable, and the poets have
invented all sorts of expedients to avoid it. Rinuccini's solution is
simplicity itself: no condition at all is attached to the rescue, and
Eurydice is happily restored to life. The divisions of Rinuccini's
poem are as follows: [3]

Prologue: "Tragedy" announces the subject and makes flattering allusions to the noble auditors (35–36, *1–2*).

[1] The dedication is dated February 6, 1600 (old style), i.e., 1601 (new style).
[2] Peri's *Euridice* has been published in a facsimile of the first edition by the R. Accademia
d'Italia (Rome, 1934); it is found also in Torchi, *Arte musicale* VI (not always accurate,
and with overelaborate realizations of the figured bass); selections in *I classici* XXIV;
SB 171, HAM 182.
  Caccini's *Euridice* (incomplete) in Eitner, *Publikationen* X. See also Solerti, *Musica,
ballo e drammatica;* Ehrichs, *Caccini;* and *Commemorazione della riforma melodrammatica (Atti dell' accademia del R. Istituto musicale di Firenze, Anno XXXIII,* 1895).
[3] The page numbers in ordinary print refer to Eitner's edition of Caccini's score, those
in italics to Torchi's edition of Peri.

Scene 1.[4] Shepherds and nymphs celebrating the wedding day of Orpheus and Eurydice: choruses, alternating with soli (36–40, 3–7).

Scene 2. Eurydice and chorus (40–47, 7–17). At her invitation, all leave to form a general dance of rejoicing. Ritornello chorus "Al canto, al ballo."

Scene 3. Orpheus (solo) expresses his happiness and prays to the goddess Venus (47–49, 17–21).

Scene 4. Arcetro and Tirsi join Orpheus, bringing good wishes (49–53, 21–30). In both versions Tirsi sings a little metrical song; in Peri, there is a ritornello for three flutes.

Scene 5 (53–66, 30–52). The messenger Daphne announces Eurydice's death.[5] Orpheus and his friends break out in lamentations: long scene, ending with ritornello chorus "Sigh, heavenly breezes! Weep, O forests, O fields!"

Scene 6. Arcetro and chorus (66–76, 52–67). Arcetro as messenger relates how Orpheus in his grief wished to kill himself and how Venus came down from Heaven to console him. The chorus goes to the temple to sacrifice.

Scene 7 (change of scene). Venus encourages Orpheus to demand Eurydice from Pluto in Hades (68–70).

Scene 8. Orpheus, Pluto, Proserpine, other infernal deities. Orpheus by his prayers obtains the release of Eurydice (71–100).

Scene 9 (101–117). Stage as at the beginning. Dawn. Shepherds and nymphs are bewailing Orpheus and Eurydice. A messenger announces their happy return.

Scene 10 (117–134). They enter amid general rejoicings; choruses and dances.

The two versions of Peri and Caccini are very similar. Peri is perhaps somewhat more forceful in tragic expression, whereas Caccini is more tuneful, excels in elegiac moods, and gives more occasion for virtuoso singing. Neither score has an overture, and there is almost no independent instrumental music. At the first performance of Peri's work (as we learn from his preface) there were at least four accompanying instruments, placed behind the scenes: a *gravicembalo* (harpsichord), *chitarrone* (bass lute), *lira grande* (large lyre, a bowed chord-instrument with as many as twenty-four strings), and *liuto grosso* (literally "large lute," that is, probably a theorbo). Doubtless these continuo instruments alternated or were used in various combinations, making possible a considerable variety of tonal color.

4 The division into scenes is not indicated in the score or libretto. Apparently only two stage "sets" were used: the woodland scene (at the beginning and end) and the scene in Hades. (Cf. Solerti, *Albori* II, 113.)

5 The messenger, a common figure in Italian sixteenth-century drama, is a device used to avoid representing unpleasant events on the stage.

What notes did they play? The score gives only the bass, with a few figures,[6] below the melody of the solo part; the exact realization of the bass is a problem about which editors have differed, and it is essential to keep this fact in mind when dealing with modern editions of early operas. In the case of Peri and Caccini, the probability is that the harmonies were simple (that is, not many non-harmonic tones or chromatics); certainly the basses do not suggest many contrapuntal possibilities in the texture of the inner parts. The bass has no importance as a line, as may be recognized not only by its stationary, harmonic character but also by the absence of any sustaining bass instrument in the orchestra.

At the first performance of Peri's opera the part of Orpheus was sung by the composer himself, while that of Eurydice was sung by Vittoria Archilei, one of the most celebrated women singers of the time.

The action in both *Euridice* operas is carried on by solo voices in the new Florentine theatre style (stile rappresentativo), consisting of a melodic line not so formal as an aria or even an arioso, yet on the other hand not at all like the recitative of eighteenth- and nineteenth-century Italian opera, which is characterized by many repeated notes and an extremely rapid delivery. The operatic monody of Peri and Caccini is different from all these. Its basis is an absolutely faithful adherence to the natural rhythms, accents, and inflections of the text,[7] following it in these respects even to the extent of placing a full cadence regularly at the end of every verse—an insistent and annoying mannerism. It presents no organized independent melodic structure, and when considered apart from the words appears almost meaningless. It is there solely to provide a background of sustained sound, to add the ultimate fulfillment of musical delivery to a poetic language already itself more than half music (Example 13).

[6] On the figuring of the basses and their realization in the early monodists, see Arnold, *The Art of Accompaniment from a Thorough Bass*, Pt. I, secs. 5–8. Cf. also Wellesz, *Die Aussetzung des Basso Continuo in der italienischen Oper;* Torchi, "L'accompagnamento degli istrumenti nei melodrammi italiani della prima metà del seicento," RMI I (1894) 7–38, II (1895) 666–71; Goldschmidt, "Die Instrumentalbegleitung der italienischen Musikdramen," MfMg XXVII (1895), 52–62.

[7] A theory of the relationship between the emotions of the text and the technical melodic and harmonic procedures of the music is given by Peri in his preface to *Euridice* (Solerti, *Origini,* pp. 46–47).

EURIDICE

Ex.13.   Caccini

Spar-gea il bel vol - to e le do-ra-te chio-me un su-

dor via più fred-do as-sai che ghiac-cio;in-di s'u-dio il tuo no-me tra le lab-bra so-

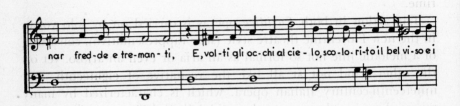

nar fred-de e tre-man-ti, E,vol-ti gli oc-chi al cie-lo,sco-lo-ri-to il bel vi-so ei

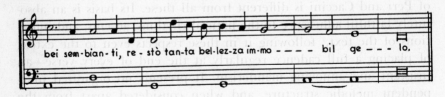

bei sem-bian-ti, re-stò tan-ta bel-lez-za im-mo - - - - bil ge - - - lo.

On occasion, effective use is made of the contrast between static
and quickly moving harmonies, with expressive suspensions. Note
in Example 14 the dramatic change from G minor to E major on
the word "ohimè," and the subtly delayed closing cadence.

In contrast with the free-rhythmed portions, there are a few songs
in regular metre, either solos or solos alternating with chorus. These
songs are in the nature of lyrical interludes in the action; they are
placed usually at the ends of scenes, where the effect of dropping
into a metrical pattern is similar to the effect produced by a pair of
rhymed verses at the end of a scene in Shakespeare, contrasting with
the preceding blank verse. One such air is the well-known "Gioite al

EURIDICE   Peri

Ex.14

Las - sa, che di spa-ven-to e di pie - ta - - de

Ge-la-mi il cor nel se-no Mi-se-ra - bil bel-ta - te

Co-m'in un pun-to ohi - mè ve-ni-sti me - no

canto mio" with two strophes, sung by Orpheus in the closing scene
(Example 15).

In addition to the solo parts, there are a number of choruses in
Euridice. Some of these are monophonic, the entire chorus or sec-

EURIDICE   Peri

Ex.15

Gio - i-te al can-to mio sel-ve fron-do - se Gio-i-te a-ma-ti
col-li e d'ogn' in-tor - no. Ec-co rim-bom-bi dal-le val-li a-sco-se.

tions of it singing the melody in unison; such places may be either
in the usual free monodic style or in regular metre, exactly like the
solos. As in Greek drama, a scene will sometimes take the form of
a dialogue between the chorus and an actor (for example, scene 6).
There are also polyphonic choruses, occurring commonly at the ends
of scenes, where the chorus frequently has a refrain alternating with
soli or small solo groups. In such places both chorus and solo parts
may show the typical sixteenth-century florid coloratura lines (Example 16).

EURIDICE

Ex.16.   Caccini

Non   ve - de un si - mil   par d'a-man - ti'l —

so - le.

The choral writing is not so highly developed as that of the best
Italian madrigals, and there is little counterpoint. The simple, note-
against-note style is particularly evident in those choruses which are
intended to accompany dancing, as in the closing scene of the opera
or at the end of scene 2 (Example 17).

Another early opera in the Florentine style is Marco da Gagliano's
Dafne, first performed at Mantua in 1608 and in Florence two years
later.[8] The libretto of this work is adapted from Rinuccini's poem
of 1594;[9] the action is divided into two parts: Apollo slays the

[8] Reprinted in Eitner, *Publikationen* X, 77–117 (incomplete). Gagliano (*ca.* 1575–1642)
was director of music at the church of San Lorenzo in Florence. In addition to *Dafne*,
he composed *La Flora* in collaboration with Peri (Florence, 1628), as well as two other
operas, the music of which has been lost. Selections from *La Flora* are reprinted in
Goldschmidt, *Studien* I, 180–84. Cf. Vogel, "Marco da Gagliano," VfMw V (1889) 396–
442, 509–68.

[9] For the changes and additions, see Solerti, *Albori* II, 77 ff.

Python with his arrows but is himself in turn wounded by the
arrows of Love; he vainly pursues the nymph Daphne, who is changed
into a laurel tree just as he is about to seize her. The latter episode
does not take place on the stage, but is narrated by a messenger. The

prologue is sung by Ovid, from whose *Metamorphoses* the legend is
taken. The music is essentially like that of the Florentine monodists,
to whose doctrines Gagliano professes adherence, but the monody
is more animated in the melodic line and supported by more logical
basses and richer harmonies. The free monody occasionally alternates

with aria-like sections, and it is possible to see in certain places the outline of the future "recitative and aria" grouping.[10] Some of the arias have instrumental ritornellos, and there is an instrumental dance (ballo) at the end as in Peri's *Euridice*. There is no overture, but Gagliano in his preface states that a "sinfonia of the various instruments which accompany the choruses and play the ritornellos" should be played before the prologue [11]—a direction which suggests that similar introductory pieces may have been performed before the earlier operas of Peri and Caccini. There are many choral songs, combined with strophic solos, duets, and instrumental interludes. The elaborate "echo song" [12] is an example of a musical and poetic fancy which long remained popular in opera. The whole score, in sum, shows more abundant and varied musical resources, while not departing fundamentally from the Florentine ideal (Example 18).

DAFNE

Ex.18.   Gagliano

SOLO
Se la sù tra gl'au-rei chio-stri potè un cor — tro-var mer-cè,

CONTINUO

o-di il pian-to e pre-ghi no-stri o del ciel — Mo-nar-cha e Re.

Chorus
O-di il pian — to e pre-ghi no-stri, o del ciel Mo-nar-cha e Re.

10 See for example pp. 110–12 in Eitner's edition.   11 Solerti, *Origini*, p. 83.
12 Eitner ed., pp. 84–89.

The weaknesses of the early Florentine operas, which came to be recognized as soon as the novelty of the new stile rappresentativo wore off, were the lack of individual characterization, the limited range of emotional expression, and above all the monotony of the solo style, resulting from the constantly recurring cadential formulae and the absence of any principles of musical organization. The foremost opera theorist of the early seventeenth century, G. B. Doni, still argued for this reason that the ideal dramatic work was one in which music alternated with spoken dialogue and strongly advocated the use of choruses and arias to vary the monotony of the recitative.[13] The Florentine opera in the beginning was the outgrowth of a limited musical theory applied to an artificial, stylized poetic form. There were no first-rate musicians among the founders but only noble amateurs, poets, and singers, all actuated by an enthusiastic misconception of antiquity. They have often been compared to Columbus, who set out to find the East Indies and accidentally discovered a new continent: so the Florentines, seeking to revive Greek drama, opened the way to modern opera. Like all pioneers, they were soon outdistanced; it was left to others to exploit and develop the new form. The annals of the Medicean court for the first thirty-seven years of the century show many performances of ballets, comedies with intermedi, tourneys, rappresentazioni, and other musical spectacles but less than a half-dozen operas.[14]

[13] "Trattato," Cap. IV–VI.
[14] Solerti, *Musica, ballo e drammatica.* Among the poets represented in these Florentine spectacles was Chiabrera, one of the last of the great Renaissance literary figures.

6

Monteverdi's
Early Operas

O F THE TWENTY-ONE DRAMATIC OR SEMI-
dramatic works composed by Monteverdi, only six (including three operas)
have been preserved in their entirety.[1] *Orfeo*, his first opera, was
performed at Mantua in 1607. The poem, by Alessandro Striggio,[2]
is on the same subject as Rinuccini's *Euridice* but with different
divisions and a different ending:

Prologue: Sung by "Music" (a significant contrast to Rinuccini's prologue, sung by "Tragedy").
Act I: Rejoicings by Orpheus and Eurydice; choruses of nymphs and
shepherds. Orpheus' solo "Rosa del ciel" (SB 176).
Act II: Further rejoicings: strophic songs with instrumental ritornellos.
The messenger announces Eurydice's death ("Ahi, caso acerbo"); Orpheus
mourns ("Tu se' morta") and resolves to seek his beloved in the realms of
the dead; choruses of lamentation.
Act III: "Hope" encourages Orpheus; his song ("Possente spirto")
lulls Charon to slumber, and Orpheus crosses the Styx; chorus of infernal
spirits.
Act IV: Hades. Orpheus wins Eurydice from Pluto, but on the return
journey he looks back, whereupon she is delivered over to death ("O
dolcissimi lumi"); chorus of spirits.
Act V: Lament of Orpheus (echo song "Voi vi doleste, o monti"); Apollo
in pity transports Orpheus to heaven; closing chorus and ballet (a
moresca).[3]

[1] For a complete list of Monteverdi's works (including modern editions) and a selected
bibliography, see the *Supplementary Volume* of *Grove's Dictionary* (1940) pp. 442–43 and
add: special number of RassM (October, 1929). There is a recent biography by Domenico
de' Paoli (1945). Reference will be made here to Malipiero's edition of the complete
works (C.E.), of which fifteen volumes have so far been published.
[2] Not to be confused with his father, composer of intermedi and madrigals, who bore
the same name.
[3] This ending in Monteverdi's score differs from that of Striggio's poem, which is based
on the original myth. Cf. Solerti, *Albori* III, 270 ff.

The music of *Orfeo* [4] was greeted by contemporaries as a new example of the Florentine style, and indeed the general plan of the opera—a pastorale, with monodic declamation—justifies this view. Nevertheless, there are important differences, stemming from the fundamental fact that Monteverdi was a musician of genius, soundly trained in technique, and primarily concerned with musical and dramatic effects rather than antiquarian theories. He combined the madrigal style of the late sixteenth century with the orchestral and scenic apparatus of the old intermedi and a new conception of the possibilities of monodic singing.[5] Externally, *Orfeo* represents the first attempt to apply the full resources of the art of music to opera, unhampered by artificially imposed limitations, while at the same time it shows a breadth of conception, a power and variety of expression, far removed from the somewhat bloodless, unimpassioned, intellectual art of the Florentines.

The imposing list of orchestral instruments at the front of the score gives an idea of the extent and importance of the instrumental music of *Orfeo*. The similarity of this orchestra to those of the earlier intermedi may be seen by a glance at the table on p. 62.[6] The great number and variety of "fundament" (chord-playing) instruments is characteristic of the sixteenth century. Of course, not all the instruments were used at once, and undoubtedly many of the players doubled, so that there were not so many performers as there were different instruments. All the players united for certain numbers (for example, the opening toccata, some of the sinfonie, accompaniments of some of the choruses), but at many places Monteverdi indicated in the score precisely what instruments were to be used, his choice obviously being dictated not only by the desire to secure variety of color but to help characterize the dramatic situation as well. A detailed study of the score in this respect is extremely interest-

[4] First printed in Venice, 1609; 2d ed., 1615. Facsimile reprint of 1609 edition by A. Sandberger (Augsburg, 1927); in C.E. XI; seven other modern editions (see *Sup. Vol., Grove's Dictionary* [1940], pp. 442–43); recording, "Musiche italiane antiche," Edizione del Magazzin Musicale, CBX 1462–85.

[5] Tessier, "Les Deux Styles de Monteverdi," RM III, No. 8 (June, 1922) 223–54.

[6] It must be remarked that the exact nature of all these instruments and of the various combinations is not yet definitely established. Cf. Sachs, *Handbuch der Musikinstrumentenkunde*, p. 195; Goldschmidt, *Studien* I, 132–38; Westrup, "Monteverdi and the Orchestra," M&L XXI (1940) 230–45.

	MONTEVERDI'S "Orfeo," 1607	INTERMEDI of 1589	"Ballet comique," 1581	"Psyche ed Amore," 1565
Fundament instruments	2 clavicembalos 1 double harp (one more needed in performance?) 2 chitarrones (one more called for in score) 2 bass cithers (not listed, but called for in score) 3 bass gambas 2 organs with wood (flute) pipes 1 organ with reed pipes	1 small cembalo 2 harps 6 lutes 2 chitarrones 2 guitars 1 psaltery 1 cither 1 mandola 1 viola bastarda 2 lyres 1 organ with wood pipes 1 *organo di pivette* (?)	lutes lyres harps organ with wood pipes	4 clavicembalos 4 lutes 1 lyre 1 bass lyre 1 small rebec
Stringed instruments	2 small violins *alla francese* 10 viole da braccio (i.e., a string ensemble, possibly 4 violins, 4 violas, 2 violoncellos) 2 contrabass viols	1 small violin (*sopranino di viola*) 1 *violino* 3 tenor viols 2 bass viols 1 contrabass viol (and perhaps additional viols)	violons (generic name for all bowed instruments)	1 soprano viol 4 "bowed viols" 4 bass viols 1 contrabass viol
Wind instruments	4 trombones (one more called for in score) 2 cornetts 1 *flautino alla Vigesima seconda* (i.e., a high recorder; one more (?) called for in score) 1 high trumpet (*clarino;* possibly referring to use of high range of ordinary trumpet) 3 soft trumpets (*trombe sordine*)	4 trombones 2 cornetts 1 traverse flute 1 (or more) tenor oboes bassoons	trombones cornetts flutes oboes	4 trombones 1 large cornett 2 soft-toned cornetts 2 recorders 4 traverse flutes 2 tenor flutes 1 tenor oboe 5 (!) serpents
Percussion instruments	None	None	None	2 drums

ing. The following outline of the instrumentation of Act III will give an idea of the method:

1. Dialogue, Orpheus and Hope: continuo instrument(s) not specified.
2. Charon challenges Orpheus: continuo (organ with reed pipes).
3. Sinfonia in five parts: instruments not specified.
4. Orpheus begins his appeal ("Possente spirto"); four strophes, all with continuo (organ with wood pipes, chitarrone), each with a different set of concertizing instruments as follows:
    a. Two violins
    b. Two cornetts
    c. Two harps
    d. Two violins and a violoncello (*basso da brazzo*)
5. Orpheus: continuo, three arm viols, one contrabass viol ("very softly").
6. Dialogue, Orpheus and Charon: continuo instrument(s) not specified.
7. Charon sleeps. Sinfonia (No. 3 above) repeated "very softly": wood organ, arm viols, contrabass viol.
8. Orpheus crosses the Styx in a boat; his song is accompanied only by the wood organ.
9. Sinfonia in seven parts: instruments not specified (full orchestra).
10. Chorus of spirits: reed organ, wood organ, two bass gambas, five trombones, one contrabass viol.
11. Sinfonia (No. 9) repeated (full orchestra).

There are altogether twenty-six instrumental pieces in *Orfeo*. The overture, called "toccata" (compare English "tucket"), is probably a dressed-up version of the customary opening fanfare; it consists of a brilliant flourish on the chord of C major, played three times by the full orchestra. The prologue opens with a ritornello [7] for strings, which recurs in shortened form after each stanza, and in its original form at the end of the prologue, forming an introduction to Act I. The same ritornello is heard near the end of Act II, and again as an introduction to Act V. There are other instrumental pieces which

---

[7] On the difference between ritornello and sinfonia, both of which designations occur in *Orfeo*, see Heuss, *Die Instrumental-Stücke des Orfeo*, Appendix 3, and cf. Wellesz, "Cavalli," SzMw I (1913) 45–48. The essential difference is that a ritornello is a recurring interlude between parts of a song, whereas a sinfonia is an independent instrumental piece, usually having as its aim the musical depiction of a scene on the stage. The composers are not consistent in their use of the terms—a common observation for the early seventeenth-century period.

recur in similar fashion, thus serving as a means of formal unity in the midst of the more rhapsodic vocal monody. The style is distinctively instrumental. The sinfonie are like the orchestral music of

ORFEO, Act I

Ex.19.   Monteverdi

Giovanni Gabrieli: serious, solidly chordal, with occasional short points of imitation, a very full texture, and much crossing of parts. The ritornellos are more lightly scored, sequential in structure, and more contrapuntal in texture, as in Example 19 (for strings) from Act I, with its canonic imitation and rather modernistic dissonances.[8]

The aria "Possente spirto" in Act III is a remarkable example of the florid vocal style of the sixteenth century. There are five strophes, each consisting of a different set of embellishments (written out in full by Monteverdi) of the given melody, and each accompanied by different instruments. The practice of having instruments concertize —that is, compete—with the voice was one destined to become very important in the style of late seventeenth- and eighteenth-century vocal music. The deployment of such elaborate vocal and instrumental effects at this place in the opera is not merely for purposes of display but is calculated to suggest the supreme effort of Orpheus to overcome the powers of Hades by all the strength of his divine art; at the same time, the wild, fantastic figures of the music seem to depict the supernatural character of the scene.

Quite different types of songs are found in the first part of Act II. The act begins with a little air by Orpheus in periodic phrasing and three-part form—a miniature *da capo aria*. This whole scene is a kind of lyric interlude, containing no dramatic action; and appropriate to the joyous pastoral atmosphere are the duet of the shepherds ("In questo prato adorno"), with its ritornellos for two high recorders played behind the scenes, and Orpheus' strophic solo "Vi ricorda, o boschi ombrosi," with its effect of alternating 6/8 and 3/4 metres (Example 20).

ORFEO, Act II

Ex.20.   Monteverdi

Vi ri - cor-da o bos-chi om - bro - si   Vi ri - cor-da o bos-chi om-

bro - si   de' miei   lungh'   as - pri   tor - men - ti

---

8 Heuss points out (p. 18) that the austere contrapuntal style of this ritornello is employed deliberately to suggest a churchly atmosphere; it occurs in the scene where Orpheus and Eurydice are supposed to be in the temple (off stage) sacrificing to the gods.

Songs of this kind, which show the traits of popular style, establish the background for the abrupt contrast at the entrance of the messenger with the news of Eurydice's death. Nowhere is Monteverdi's superiority to the early Florentine composers more manifest than in the startling change of mood which he achieves at this place and in the dialogue immediately following, with the alternating E major and G minor harmonies at Orpheus' exclamations (Example 21).

The ending of the messenger's account (Example 22) may be compared with the corresponding passage in Caccini's *Euridice* (Example 13), as showing Monteverdi's grasp of the dramatic possibilities of the monodic style.[9]

[9] As a warning of the way in which editors can make practically two different pieces out of the same given bass and melody, the reader is invited to compare Leichtentritt's realization of Examples 21 and 22 (Ambros, *Geschichte der Musik* [3d ed.] IV, 564, 567) with that of Malipiero (C.E. XI, 59, 61). An equally instructive comparison may be made between two versions of Orpheus' "Tu se' morta" by Riemann (*Musikgeschichte* II, Pt. 2, 200 ff.) and Malipiero (C.E. XI, 62–64).

The choruses of *Orfeo* are more numerous and important than in the early Florentine operas. Some are intended to accompany dancing, such as the chorus "Lasciate i monti" in Act I; others are in madrigal style, such as the ritornello chorus "Ahi, caso acerbo" at the end of the second act. The choruses of spirits at the end of the third and fourth acts exploit the somber color of the lower voices in a thick texture, supported by the trombones—instruments traditionally associated in opera with the depiction of "infernal" scenes.

ORFEO, Act II

Ex.22.

Monteverdi

e te chia-man-do Orfe-o, Or-fe-o. Do-po un gra-ve so-

spi-ro spi-rò fra ques-te brac-cia ed io ri-ma-

si pie-na il cor di pie-ta-de e di spa-ven-to.

Perhaps the most remarkable feature of *Orfeo* is Monteverdi's sense of form, of a logically articulated, planned musical structure. This is apparent not only in the use of such devices as the strophic songs and instrumental ritornellos but even in the monodic portions, such as the entire recitative of the messenger in Act II from which Example 22 is quoted. Such places in Peri and Caccini were mere formless vocal rhapsodies; here they are clearly organized into musical units in which the freedom of declamation is admirably balanced by the careful plan of the passage as a whole. On a larger scale, the architectural symmetry of the third act is especially noteworthy.

Monteverdi's second opera, *Arianna*, was written (perhaps in collaboration with Peri) and performed at Mantua in 1608. Only the famous "lament" has been preserved.[10] This song was probably the most celebrated monodic composition of the early seventeenth century and was declared by Gagliano to be a living modern example of the power of ancient (that is, Greek) music, since it "visibly moved the entire audience to tears." [11] Monteverdi later arranged it as a five-part madrigal [12] and used the music again for a sacred text.[13]

In 1613 Monteverdi received an appointment as choirmaster of St. Mark's at Venice, in which city he remained for the rest of his life. His last two operas will therefore be considered later, in connection with the Venetian school. One of his other works, the dramatic cantata *Il combattimento di Tancredi e di Clorinda* (performed at Venice in 1624), may be briefly mentioned here because of its significance in the development of a new type of musical expression and because of its use of two new devices of instrumental technique. In the preface to his *Madrigali guerrieri ed amorosi* ("Madrigals of War and Love," the collection in which the *Combattimento* was first published in 1638) [14] Monteverdi explains that music hitherto has not developed a technique for the expression of anger or excitement, and that he has supplied this need by the invention of the *stile concitato* ("agitated style"), based on the metre of the pyrrhic foot (two short syllables).[15] This is a typical Renaissance theory to justify the use of rapidly reiterated sixteenth notes on one tone—in modern parlance, a tremolo of the strings. Monteverdi claims credit for the discovery of this device, as well as for the pizzicato, which he likewise uses in this work to depict the clashing of weapons in combat. The orchestra of the *Combattimento* consists of only strings and continuo, an instance of the trend during the early seventeenth century toward reducing the number and variety of the older instrumental groups and centering the interest on the strings.

[10] C.E. XI; SB 177 (incomplete). See Epstein, "Dichtung und Musik in Monteverdis *Lamento d'Ariana*," ZfMw X (1927–28) 216–22.
[11] Gagliano, *Dafne,* preface; in Solerti, *Origini,* p. 82.
[12] Sixth book of Madrigals (1614); in C.E. VI.
[13] "Pianto della Madonna," in *Selva morale e spirituale* (1641), C.E. XV, 757–62.
[14] C.E. VIII; HAM 189.
[15] Kreidler, *Heinrich Schütz und der Stilo concitato von Claudio Monteverdi.*

7

Opera at Rome[1]

THE MONODIC STYLE WAS INTRODUCED AT Rome in 1600 with Cavalieri's *Rappresentazione di anima e di corpo* and soon found adherents, notably Agostino Agazzari, whose *Eumelio*, a pastorale with moralizing aim, was given in 1606. The first secular opera to be performed at Rome was F. Vitali's *Aretusa* (1620),[2] a pastorale which shows no advance over the earlier works of Peri and Caccini.[3] Signs of departure from the Florentine ideal may be found in Domenico Mazzocchi's *Catena d'Adone* ("The Chain of Adonis," 1626).[4] The libretto, based on an episode in Marini's epic *Adone*, tells the story of the rescue of Adonis by Venus from the wiles of the enchantress Falsirene.[5] The various mythological personages are no longer the statuesque and serious figures of early Florentine opera but conduct themselves like characters in a bedroom farce; the complicated intrigue is bolstered by all kinds of magic tricks and particularly by the use of disguises—credulity in this respect knowing no bounds in opera from this early day to the present—sudden transformations of scene, conjurations, descents of gods, and by the familiar pastoral background and the sympathetic chorus. The typical baroque opera plot, with its multitude of characters, fantastic scenes, and incongruous episodes, is already foreshadowed in this work. Musically, *La catena d'Adone* is important

[1] The fundamental book in this field is Goldschmidt's *Studien zur Geschichte der italienischen Oper im 17. Jahrhundert* I (1901), which contains numerous musical examples. Cf. Rolland's review in SIM *Revue musicale* II (1902) 20–29. Additional information may be found in Ademollo's *I teatri di Roma nel secolo decimosettimo.*

[2] Filippo Vitali (birth and death dates unknown) came to Rome from Florence, where he had been director of music at the Cathedral. In addition to *Aretusa* (his only opera) he published many volumes of madrigals and songs, as well as some church music.

[3] S. Landi's *Morte d'Orfeo* was written in 1619, but there is no record of its performance. The score is remarkable for an eight-part chorus of shepherds at the end of Act I and a comic bass solo in Act V. See Goldschmidt, *Studien* I, 192–201.

[4] Domenico Mazzocchi (b. *ca.* 1600) published songs and madrigals which show his adherence to the traditional Roman choral style. *La Catena d'Adone* is his only opera. Cf. Finney, "Comus," *Studies in Philology* XXXVII (1940) 482–500.

[5] The female magician has always been a favorite character in opera, appearing under many names, e.g., Circe, Medea, Armida, Dido, Venus, Isolde.

for the number and size of its choruses and for its embryonic line
of demarcation between recitatives and arias, the former becoming
less significant musically, with many repeated notes and frequently
recurring cadential formulae, while the latter, without showing the
traits of popular melody or dance rhythms, begin to be organized
into clear-cut sections and to have a distinct melodic contour. Adonis'
aria "Dunque piagge ridenti" in the second scene of Act II has a
"walking bass" which with its stereotyped phrases and periodic cadences strongly suggests the *passacaglia* style (Example 23).[6]

LA CATENA D'ADONE

Ex.23.   D.Mazzocchi

The leading patrons of opera at Rome were the powerful family
of the Barberini, princes of the church. Their palace had a theatre
with a capacity of over three thousand, which was opened in 1632 [7]
with one of the most important operas of the Roman school: Stefano
Landi's *Sant' Alessio*,[8] with libretto by Rospigliosi. *Sant' Alessio* was
the first opera to be written about the inner life of a human character: it is based on the legend of St. Alexis (fifth century), but the
persons and scenes (some of them comic) are obviously drawn from
the contemporary life of seventeenth-century Rome. The music shows
a further development of the distinctive features of the recitative,
already noted in *La catena d'Adone* (Example 24).

The aria of Alessio from the same scene shows a clear conception
of form and tonality in the modern sense, together with an appreciation of the structural value of the sequence and of the dramatic
possibilities of text repetition. The first section of thirteen measures
(Example 25), cadencing on the relative minor, is balanced by a

6 Cf. Fischer, "Instrumentalmusik von 1600–1750," in Adler, *Handbuch,* p. 570.
7 Rolland, "La Première Représentation du *Sant Alessio* . . . à Rome," RHCM II
(1902) 29–36, 74–75. See also Pastor, *History of the Popes* XXIX, 408–544.
8 Stefano Landi (*ca.* 1590–*ca.* 1655), contralto singer in the Papal Chapel, was distinguished for sacred music, cantatas, and canzonas as well as his two operas.

SANT'ALESSIO, Act II, sc.5

Ex.24 *(Recitative) Angel:*   S.Landi

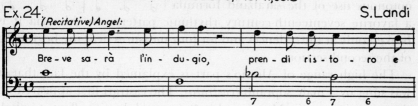

Bre-ve sa-rà l'in-du-gio, pren-di ris-to-ro e

spe-me, E giun-to al-l'o-re e-stre-me Non pa-ven-tar di mor-te; il

var-co om-bro-so, che, a chi pe-ne sof-fri, mi-ro e ri-po-so.

sixteen-measure second part which cadences on the tonic. After a short instrumental ritornello the aria is repeated (with different

SANT'ALESSIO, Act II, sc.5

Ex.25.   S.Landi

ARIA. Alessio:

O mor-te gra-di-ta, Ti bra-mo, ti as-pet-to, Dal duol o al di-let-to, Tuo

cal-le m'in-vi-ta; O mor-te, o mor-te, o mor-te gra-di-ta. Dal

text), and the ritornello is played again. Notice the somewhat mo-
notonous use of the saraband formula (𝅘𝅥 𝅘𝅥. 𝅘𝅥 | 𝅘𝅥 𝅘𝅥. 𝅘𝅥),
a favorite seventeenth-century rhythmic pattern. In this aria it is
broken only at the cadences and for four measures near the beginning
of the second section.

The high range of Alessio's part is explained by the fact that it
was sung by a male soprano (*castrato*). The castrati first appeared on
the operatic stage in Monteverdi's *Orfeo,* and despite efforts to abol-
ish the custom it became increasingly prevalent, especially in Italy,
throughout the seventeenth century.[9]

Among the ensemble numbers of *Sant' Alessio* are a comic duet [10]
and a very expressive trio.[11] There are choruses at the end of each
act and in other places; the finale is a particularly impressive ensemble in which a smaller group, accompanied only by the continuo,
alternates or joins with the full chorus and orchestra.[12] In the latter,
the old-fashioned viols are replaced throughout by violins (in three
parts) and violoncellos. Harps, lutes, and theorbos go for the most
part with the strings, but the harpsichords have a separate staff in
many of the instrumental numbers. It will be noted that the outlines
of the modern orchestra are here distinct; only the number and
variety of fundament instruments remind us of the earlier practice,
and these will remain in the orchestra (though in ever decreasing
numbers) until the time of Haydn and Mozart. The wind and percussion instruments (flutes, oboes, trumpets, trombones, tympani,
and so on) become from now on ever less conspicuous; in the opera
they are used only for special effects, or in full subordination to the
string group.

SANT'ALESSIO

Ex.26.   S.Landi

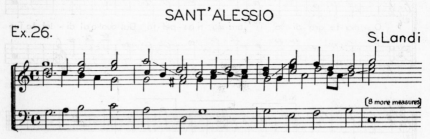

[8 more measures]

9 Maugars, "Response faite à un curieux," MfMg X (1878) 18.
10 Goldschmidt, *Studien* I, 210–12; HAM 209.
11 *Ibid.,* pp. 233–36.
12 *Ibid.,* pp. 238 ff.

The overture to *Sant' Alessio* is another departure from earlier operatic practice. It consists of a solid chordal introduction, evidently in slow tempo (Example 26), followed by a *canzona* beginning in this way (Example 27):

SANT'ALESSIO

Ex.27.   S.Landi

The canzona continues for sixty measures in a somewhat aimless fashion and in contrapuntal style to the end, with the exception of one more homophonic section consisting of alternating forte and piano phrases and one interlude in the rhythm of a saraband, in strict note-against-note writing. Toward the end, the subject of the canzona appears a fifth below its original pitch, in the first violins doubled by the basses in the lower octave (!); the piece is then brought to a close with a stretto-like passage in eighth notes and a final broad cadence in G major.[13] The formal resemblance of this canzona overture to the later *sonata da chiesa* is obvious; and it has further historical importance as being the model for the type of "French overture" perfected about thirty years later by Lully.[14] The prelude to the second act of *Sant' Alessio* is likewise a canzona in three movements but without a slow introduction, thus giving it a resemblance (though a purely superficial one) to the later "Italian overture" arrangement (fast-slow-fast).

Conditions at Rome on the whole did not favor the growth of serious opera on secular themes. The influence of the church tended

[13] The entire overture may be found in Goldschmidt, *Studien* I, 202–207, in Riemann, *Musikgeschichte* II, Pt. 2, 255–61, and in HAM 208. The overture to Francesca Caccini's ballet *La liberazione di Ruggiero* ("The Liberation of Roger," 1624) begins with a theme in canzona rhythm but does not have the fugal entrances. An overture similar to that of *Sant' Alessio* is Michelangelo Rossi's "sinfonia" to *Erminia sul Giordano* (1637), reprinted in H. Botstiber, *Geschichte der Overtüre*, Beilage 2.

[14] The relation between the canzona and the sonata da chiesa has been studied in an unpublished Radcliffe doctoral dissertation by Eunice Crocker, "The Instrumental Ensemble Canzona" (1943).

rather to the cultivation of the oratorio or similar quasi-dramatic forms, or at most permitted operas of a pious, allegorical, or moralizing nature, such as *Sant' Alessio* or Marco Marazzoli's *Il trionfo della pietà ossia la Vita humana* ("The Triumph of Piety or the Life of Man," 1656, libretto by Rospigliosi).[15] Secular productions were represented chiefly by the harmless, diverting genre of the pastorale. Michelangelo Rossi's *Erminia sul Giordano* ("Erminia at the Jordan," 1637, librettist unknown)[16] is based on the sixth and seventh cantos of Tasso's *Gerusalemme liberata,* with some elements from the same author's *Aminta.* It consists of an imperfectly connected series of scenes featuring elaborate stage settings and machines. The music including a hunting chorus with echo effects and a chorus of soldiers on a trumpet-like motif to the words "All' armi," shows on the whole no significant advances in style.

La Galatea (1639), with words and music by the famous castrato, Loreto Vittori,[17] is almost the last Italian pastorale of this period. Musically it is a superior work, and Romain Rolland calls it "the finest lyric drama of the first half of the seventeenth century."[18] The arias show progress in the direction of formal organization based on a clear system of tonal relationships; the recitatives include occasional expressive dissonances but on the whole tend toward the *secco* style. Some of the finest music of this opera is found in its ensembles (Example 28).

The last important Roman composer of serious opera was Luigi Rossi,[19] who was also famous for his cantatas. Only two operas by Rossi are known: *Il palazzo incantato* ("The Enchanted Palace,"

[15] Marco Marazzoli (d. 1662) was a singer in the Papal Chapel; he composed oratorios and at least four operas, one of which was performed at Venice in 1642. For others see Ademollo, *Teatri di Roma, passim.* It is not always easy to make a clear distinction between opera and oratorio in Rome at this period. Cf. Alaleona, *Studi su la storia dell' oratorio,* pp. 213 ff.; Schering, *Geschichte des Oratoriums,* pp. 93–95.

[16] Michelangelo Rossi (birth and death dates unknown), a pupil of Frescobaldi, was active at Rome from 1620 to 1660 as singer and composer. Some of his keyboard works are reprinted in Torchi, *Arte musicale* III. *Erminia* is his only known opera.

[17] Loreto Vittori (1604–1670) came from Florence to Rome, where he was a soprano in the Papal Chapel. He composed a number of sacred operas, songs, and dialogues. See Rau, *Loreto Vittori.*

[18] Rolland, "L'Opéra au XVIIe siècle en Italie," in Lavignac, *Encyclopédie,* Pt. I, Vol. II, p. 711.

[19] Luigi Rossi (1598–1653) was a singer as well as a composer of operas, an oratorio, and over one hundred cantatas.

Ex.28

Vittori

(Example 28 continued)

Rome, 1642) [20] and *Orfeo,* performed at Paris in 1657 under the title
Le Mariage d'Orphée et Euridice. The Paris performance was the
consequence of political changes at Rome resulting in the election
of Pope Innocent X in 1644, which forced the Barberini family to
emigrate. At the invitation of Cardinal Mazarin many of their
musicians, including Rossi, came with them to Paris to give the
French public its first taste of Italian opera.[21] The poem of *Orfeo,* by

[20] See Prunières, "Les Représentations du *Palazzo d'Atlante* à Rome," SIMG XIV (1912–13) 218.
[21] Rolland, "Le Premier Opéra joué à Paris: 'L'Orfeo' de Luigi Rossi," in his *Musiciens d'autrefois,* pp. 55–105. Pastor, *History of the Popes* XXX, 48–72.

Francesco Buti, reads like a caricature of the Orpheus myth; the whole plot is a marvel of confusion, a hodgepodge of serious and comic episodes intermingled with ballets and spectacular scenic effects. The only way a composer can deal with such a libretto is to ignore the drama (or lack of it) and concentrate on the musical op-

ORFEO

Ex.30.   L.Rossi

portunities offered by each scene. The score of *Orfeo* is as variegated as its poem: there are recitatives, da capo arias, arias with *ostinato* bass, two-part arias, *buffo* (comic) arias, and many ensembles of different kinds. These numbers are distinguished by that grace and perfection of style, that refinement of sensuous effect, for which their composer (along with Carissimi and Cesti) was so admired in the seventeenth century. The lamentation on the death of Eurydice is a fine example of writing for four sopranos, with masterly use of dissonance (Example 29).[22]

Equally expressive, and in similar vein, is Eurydice's aria "Mio ben," in which the melismatic figures of the solo voice stream out above an ostinato descending bass figure (Example 30).

With all its beauty of detail, however, Rossi's *Orfeo* as a whole is no more a dramatic entity than Berlioz's *Damnation de Faust;* it is a succession of lyrical and scenic moments in which the beauty of music and *décor* successfully conceals the lack of any serious dramatic purpose. As such, it illustrates the extent to which opera in the course of forty years had moved away from the Florentine ideal in the direction of the formal exterior of the later baroque.

THE FIRST COMIC OPERAS.—There were no comic scenes in the earliest operas. Italian popular comedy at this period was represented by the commedia dell' arte, which found its musical counterpart in the madrigal comedies of Vecchi and Banchieri. There are some comic episodes of the sort common to Italian pastorales, in Landi's *Morte d'Orfeo* and Cornachioli's *Diana schernita* ("Diana Ridiculed," 1629),[23] and more realistic comic characters are to be found in *Sant' Alessio*. But the creation of comic opera as a separate form, the foundation of the long Italian opera buffa tradition which was to culminate in Mozart and Rossini, was the work of Giulio Rospigliosi, friend of the Barberini family, distinguished man of letters, papal secretary, and eventually cardinal (from 1657) and Pope (Clement IX, 1667–1669).[24] Rospigliosi's operas include *Sant' Alessio, Il palazzo incantato, La vita humana,* and several others, in addition to the two comedies *Chi soffre, speri* ("Who Suffers May Hope") and *Dal male il bene* ("Good from Evil"). *Chi soffre, speri,* with music by Vergilio Mazzocchi[25] and Marco Marazzoli, was performed at the Barberini

22 For another ensemble from *Orfeo,* see SB 199.

23 Giacinto Cornacchioli (Cornachioli) D'Ascoli was a priest who later (*ca.* 1635) held a position at the court of Munich (Rudhardt, *Geschichte der Oper am Hofe zu München,* p. 28).

24 See biographical sketch in Ademollo, *Teatri di Roma,* chap. VIII; Salza, "Drammi inediti di Giulio Rospigliosi," RMI XIV (1907) 473–508; Pastor, *History of the Popes* XXXI, 314–37.

25 Vergilio Mazzocchi (d. 1646), brother of Domenico, was director of music at St. Peters.

palace in Rome in 1639.[26] It has a romantic plot, with comic scenes featuring character types of the commedia dell' arte (Zanni, Coviello) and other figures from the common walks of Italian life, in the manner established by Michelangelo Buonarroti with his comedies *La Tancia* (1612) and *La Fiera* (1618), and already used by Rospigliosi in his own opera *Sant' Alessio.* The dialogue of *Chi soffre, speri* is conveyed in a kind of recitative which differs essentially from the quasi-melodic monody of the Florentines; it is, in short, the style which later came to be called *recitativo secco:* a quick-moving, narrow-ranged, sharply accented, irregularly punctuated, semimusical speech, with many repeated notes sustained only by occasional chords—a style for which the Italian language alone is perfectly adapted and which has always been a familiar feature of Italian opera. Although tendencies toward this type of recitative were manifest in earlier Roman works, the necessity of finding a musical setting for realistic comic dialogue led to its fuller development here:

CHI SOFFRE, SPERI

Ex 31.   Mazzocchi and Marazzoli

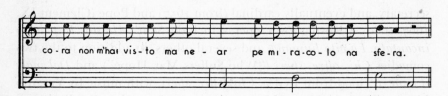

Apart from the recitative and one lively ensemble scene depicting the bustle and noise of a fair with the cries of the merchants, the music of *Chi soffre, speri* offers no points of interest. In the quality of both libretto and songs it is surpassed by *Dal male il bene,* with music by Marco Marazzoli (Act II) and Antonio Maria Abbatini (Acts I and

[26] This work is probably the same as *Il falcone,* which is sometimes listed separately. See plot synopsis in Goldschmidt, *Studien* I, 90–94.

III),[27] performed in 1654 after the return of the Barberini to Rome, to which event the title obviously alludes. Rospigliosi, who had served as papal legate in Madrid from 1646 to 1653, showed in the construction of this work some influence of the Spanish playwright Calderón de la Barca; it is a romantic comedy in which, after complications and misunderstandings, two pairs of lovers are happily united. The servant characters are evidently drawn from life, and one of them, Tobacco, is very similar to Leporello in *Don Giovanni*. The music is notable for the skill of the recitatives and for another feature which later became characteristic of the opera buffa, namely the ensembles, especially the trio at the end of Act I and the sextet which forms the finale of the opera.[28] There is also a bass "arietta" for Tobacco, which shows a well-developed tonal and formal scheme, together with a good sense of comic style.[29]

Another excellent comic opera is Andrea Moniglia's *La Tancia, overo il podestà di Colognole* ("Tancia, or the Mayor of Colognole"), with music by Jacopo Melani,[30] performed in 1657 at Florence.[31] Among the ensembles of this work is a parody of the famous incantation scene from Cavalli's *Giasone*, which had been first performed at Venice eight years before.[32] *La Tancia* contains many more arias in proportion to the recitative than did the earlier comic works, and it is possible to observe clearly some of the standardized forms into which the aria, in both serious and comic opera, was settling down during the latter half of the seventeenth century. These forms divide themselves, with few exceptions, into three groups:

1) *Strophic songs,* in which the solo part may be either literally repeated for each stanza or more or less varied. The style in many of these

[27] Abbatini (1597 or 1598–1670) was director of music at a number of churches in Rome and distinguished himself as a composer of sacred music. His other dramatic compositions include an opera *Ione* (Rome, 1666) and a religious drama *La comica del cielo* (Rome, 1668, text by Rospigliosi). See biography by Coradini.

[28] Goldschmidt, *Studien* I, 330, 341.

[29] *Ibid.,* p. 335. Another arietta from this opera will be found in SB 204.

[30] Jacopo Melani (b. 1623), director of music at the Cathedral of Pistoia, composed at least four comic operas between 1657 and 1673.

[31] Goldschmidt, *Studien* I, 107 ff.; Ademollo, *I primi fasti del teatro della Pergola*, pp. 8–12. The libretto of *La Tancia* bears only a slight resemblance to Buonarroti's comedy of the same name.

[32] Goldschmidt, *Studien* I, 371. The original scene from Cavalli is in SB 201. A *rispetto* from *La Tancia* (dance song with instrumental interludes) is reprinted in *Atti dell' Accademia del R. Istituto musicale di Firenze, Anno XXXIII* (1895), Supplement No. 3.

is comparatively light and simple, frequently showing traces of popular song-types or dance metres. Others are more serious in mood. There is usually an orchestral ritornello or a short section of recitative between the stanzas. (Example: Tancia's "S'io miro il volto," Act I. scene 9, Goldschmidt, *Studien* I, 357.)

2) *Through-composed arias.* These show a wide variety of types, both serious and comic, but all have a broader formal pattern and are less regular in melodic and rhythmic structure than the strophic songs. They consist of a number of sections, each ending with a full cadence in the tonic or a related key, and separated by orchestral ritornellos. (Examples: Isabella's "Son le piume acuti strali," Act I, scene 1, Goldschmidt, *Studien* I, 349; Leandro's "Sovra il banco di speranza," Act I, scene 8, Goldschmidt, *Studien* I, 355.) The basic form of these arias is two-part, without marked contrast of thematic material. Sometimes, however, the second section may be more contrasting, followed by a repetition of the first, resulting in a three-part form. (Example: Lisa's "Se d'amore un cor legato," Act I, scene 1, Goldschmidt I, 352.)

Arias of this second group represent the main channel of development of operatic style in the later seventeenth century. In the course of time the formal scheme is expanded, the orchestra enters into the accompaniment proper as well as at the ritornellos, concertizing instruments appear, a fully developed da capo form gradually replaces the simple two-part structure, and eventually a number of stereotypes develop—arias of definite categories, each distinguished by certain stylistic procedures and appearing in the opera in a more or less rigidly fixed order of succession. This final degree of stylization, however, is not achieved until the early part of the eighteenth century.

3) *Arias over an ostinato bass.* Most arias of this group are serious in mood and belong to a recognized type known as the *Lamento*. (Example: Isabella's "Lungi la vostra sfera," Act I, scene 20, Goldschmidt I, 360.) They are most often in triple metre, with slow tempo, and the usual bass figure is the passacaglia theme consisting of a diatonic or chromatic stepwise descent of a fourth from the tonic to the dominant, or some variant of this.[33]

Apart from the three works which we have mentioned and a few others, little is known about the history of comic opera as a separate genre in the seventeenth century.[34] There was a school of comic and satirical opera at Venice after 1650.[35] Comic scenes persisted in serious opera until after the end of the century, and the incongruous

[33] A familiar example of this kind of aria is the lament of Dido "When I am laid in earth," from Purcell's *Dido and Aeneas.*

[34] D'Arienzo, "Origini dell'opera comica," RMI II (1895) 597–628.

[35] Wolf, *Die Venezianische Oper in der zweiten Hälfte des 17. Jahrhunderts,* pp. 107–41.

mingling of the two moods is one of the typical features of baroque opera.

The native school of Roman opera composers virtually came to an end after the middle of the century. During its comparatively short period of activity—spanning hardly more than a generation—this school had contributed certain features to opera which were of historical importance. The prominence of the chorus in their works was in part a heritage from the Florentines and in part a reflection of the traditional Roman interest in choral music dating from the days of Palestrina and earlier; but the chorus did not maintain its place in Italian opera, which after 1640 concentrated its attention on solo songs. More significant, therefore, were the first steps made by the Roman composers toward establishing the main outlines of the structure of opera as a whole, founded on the separation of recitative from aria and the working out of musical forms for the latter, with distinct tonal relationships. Along with this formal progress went the discovery of new types of expression: the comic opera began its career, with its typical secco recitative and ensemble numbers, while for serious opera the possibility of successful musical treatment of other subject matter than the conventional pastorale was demonstrated by Rospigliosi and Landi. Finally, the modern orchestra, centering around violin instruments and continuo, was established, and an important type of overture (the canzona overture) originated. The Roman opera was the link between the Florentine and the Venetian schools, preparing the way for the developments of the second half of the century.

8

Opera at Venice[1]

ALTHOUGH THE BEGINNING OF OPERA IS commonly reckoned from the Florentine performances of 1600, it would be almost more appropriate to date it from the opening of the first public opera house in Venice in 1637. Florentine and Roman opera was a court entertainment and for this reason kept always a certain reserve, a refinement, almost preciosity of both form and content. Venetian opera, on the contrary, very early became a public spectacle and one of tremendous popularity. Between 1637 and the end of the century, 388 operas were produced in seventeen theatres in Venice itself and probably at least as many more by Venetian composers in other cities.[2] Nine new opera houses were opened during this period; after 1650 never fewer than four were in operation at once, and for the last two decades of the century this city of 125,000 people supported six opera troupes continuously, the usual seasons filling from twelve to thirty weeks of the year. Citizens were admitted on payment of about fifty cents, and wealthy families rented loges by the season. Within a short time the whole typical modern organization of opera, based on a combination of broad popular support and strong prestige appeal to the upper social classes, was in evidence at Venice. Opera had stepped out of the salon with its little circle of connoisseurs, onto the public stage with its mass audiences.

The transformation which took place in the character of both

1 Bibliography: *Mercure galant* (Paris, 1672–1674, 1677–1714); Solerti, "I rappresentazioni musicali di Venezia dal 1571 al 1605," RMI IX (1902) 503–58 (intermedi, pastorales, etc., at the ducal court; no music preserved); Wiel, *I codici musicali contariniani;* Groppo, *Catalogo;* [Salvioli], *I teatri musicali di Venezia nel secolo XVII;* Kretzschmar, "Die venetianische Oper," VfMw VIII (1892) 1–76; idem, "Beiträge zur Geschichte der venetianischen Oper," JMP XIV (1907) 71–81; Wellesz, "Cavalli und der Stil der venetianischen Oper," SzMw I (1913) 1–103; Prunières, *Cavalli et l'opéra vénétien au XVIIe siècle;* Rolland, "L'Opéra populaire à Venise; Francesco Cavalli," MM II, No. 1 (1906) 61–70, 151–60; Prunières, "I libretti dell'opera veneziana nel secolo XVII," RassM III (1930) 441–48.

2 Less than one-sixth of this number are preserved, and these exclusively in manuscript. The librettos were always printed, the musical scores never. If an opera was played in a different theatre the score was adapted to local tastes and conditions or composed entirely anew.

libretto and music is attributable in part to these new circumstances; yet signs of the change had already become apparent in Rome, and the whole movement was part and parcel of the changing literary and musical tastes of the time. The genuine Renaissance interest in antiquity being exhausted, only the shell of classical subject matter remained, and even this was frequently abandoned in favor of episodes from medieval romances, especially as embodied in the epics of Ariosto and Tasso. Moreover, the facts of history or legend were overlaid with so-called *accidenti verissimi* [3] to the point of being no longer recognizable. Perseus, Hercules, Medea, Alcestis, Scipio, Leonidas, Tancred and Clorinda, Rinaldo and Armida were, in these operas, not so much human (or superhuman) persons as mere personified passions, moving through the drama with the stiff, unreal air of abstract figures (despite the vehemence with which their emotions were expressed), preoccupied with little more than their eternal political or amorous intrigues and caricatured in comic episodes which might fill half the opera. Mistaken identity—a device rendered somewhat less implausible by the presence of castrati in male roles— was a dramatic stock in trade. The Aristotelean unities gave way before a bewildering succession of scenes, sometimes as many as fifteen or twenty in a single act, full of strong feeling and suspense, abounding in sharp contrast and effects of all kinds. Lavish scenic backgrounds added to the spectacle. Pastoral idylls, dreams, incantations, descents of gods, shipwrecks, sieges, and battles filled the stage. In particular the machines, ingenious mechanical contrivances for the production of sudden miraculous changes and supernatural appearances, attained a degree of development never since surpassed.[4] Heritage of the medieval mysteries, beloved adjunct of the Renaissance intermedi, the machines formed an indispensable part of the brilliant opera of the early Venetians, though their magnificence declined before the end of the century.[5]

One of the first effects of these conditions was the virtual disap-

[3] Literally, "truest accidents," i.e., incidents invented and added by the librettist.
[4] Grout, "The 'Machine' Operas," *Bulletin of the Fogg Museum of Art, Harvard University*, IX (1941) 100–103.
[5] Sabbattini, *Pratica di fabricar scene, e machine ne'teatri*; Haas, *Musik des Barocks, passim; idem, Aufführungspraxis*, pp. 163 ff.; see also Burnacini's stage designs in the edition of Cesti's *Pomo d'oro* (DTOe III², IV²); *Denkmäler des Theaters*, Pt. II; Kinsky, *History of Music in Pictures*; Zucker, *Theaterdekoration des Barock*.

pearance of the chorus. This was primarily a matter of aesthetic propriety, for the stately, antique choral group of the Florentine pastorales had no place in the lusty melodrama of Venetian opera. Moreover, the public cared little for choral singing on the stage, preferring to hear soloists. Bontempi, in the preface to his opera *Il Paride* (1662), stated bluntly that the chorus belonged only in the oratorio,[6] and the managers soon found that the money it cost to maintain such a large body of singers could be more advantageously spent for other purposes.[7] Only in festival operas, for which extraordinary sums were available, did the chorus remain. Its place was taken by ensemble solo voices, particularly in the prologues and epilogues, where divinities and allegorical figures of all kinds came forward to sing greetings to distinguished spectators or make general moral observations and topical allusions to events of the day. The decline of the chorus was accompanied by the rise of a typical operatic phenomenon, the virtuoso soloist, for whose sake numerous songs having no connection with the drama were interpolated in the score.

Along with these external changes, the music of Venetian opera in the course of the seventeenth century developed some fundamentally new features of style. The works of the Florentines and early Romans were essentially chamber operas: relatively short, with a limited range of musical effects, sophisticated in feeling and declamation, calculated to appeal to invited guests of aristocratic tastes and education. The Venetian operas, on the other hand, were destined for performance in large public theatres before a mixed audience who had paid admission. Broad effects by simple means, direct and vivid musical characterization, continual sharp contrasts of mood were required. Tuneful melodies, unmistakable major-minor harmonies, a solid but uncomplicated texture, strong rhythms in easily grasped patterns, above all a clear formal structure founded on the sequential repetition of basic motifs—these became the elements of a new operatic style.

MONTEVERDI.—A glance at the scores of the two Venetian operas of Monteverdi which have been preserved, *Il ritorno d'Ulisse in patria* ("The Return of Ulysses to His Country," 1641) and *L'incoro-*

6 Kretzschmar, "Die venetianische Oper," p. 22.
7 Cavalli's earliest operas (to 1642) have choruses, and he also used the chorus in *Doriclea* (1645) and in *Ercole amante* (1662, Paris); but these are exceptions to the general rule.

nazione di Poppea ("The Coronation of Poppea," 1642),[8] shows
what striking changes had taken place in the generation since his
Orfeo. The recitative in *Il ritorno d'Ulisse* [9] is no longer a mere
rhapsodic declamation of the text, with dramatic high points underlined by startling shifts of harmony; it is constantly organized into
patterns, with sequences and canonic imitation between the solo
voice and the bass. Sections of free "parlando" on a single note alternate with melodic phrases at the cadences. The recitative frequently gives way to short arias, mostly in triple metre and strophic
form. There are several arias on a ground bass. The parts of the gods
and goddesses are filled with elaborate coloraturas. Ensembles, particularly duets, are abundant. Conventional word painting is evident.[10] Serious, comic, and spectacular scenes follow one another
closely. Every possible occasion for emotional effect is exploited.
From beginning to end one senses the effort to be immediately
understood, along with an almost nervous dread of monotony, of
that *tedio del recitativo* which had been so severely criticized in the
early Florentine operas. There is little instrumental music: a few
sinfonie which recur in the same fashion as the ritornellos in *Orfeo*,
and one *sinfonia da guerra* to depict the combat between Ulysses and
the suitors at the end of Act II. The high points of the opera are
undoubtedly the monologue of Penelope in the first scene of Act I
(reminiscent of the famous lament of Arianna) and the opening solo
of Ulysses in the seventh scene of this act. At the beginning of Act III
there is a comic lament, a clever parody of this favorite type of scene.
Some of the little strophic songs in popular style, such as Minerva's
"Cara, cara e lieta" (Act I, scene 8), are very attractive.

On the whole, however, *Il ritorno d'Ulisse* is not to be compared
with Monteverdi's next (and last) opera, *L'incoronazione di Poppea*,[11]
a masterpiece of the composer's old age paralleled only by the last
two operas of Verdi. The libretto of this work, by Francesco Buse-
nello, deals with the love of the Roman emperor Nero for Poppea,

8 Two others—*Adone* (1639) and *Le nozze d'Enea con Lavinia* (1641)—have been lost.
9 C.E. XII; DTOe XXIX. Cf. also DTOe Beihefte IX, 3–42.
10 Long-held notes over a moving bass for words like "costanza" (Act I, sc. 8); melismatic
runs on "lieto" (Act I, sc. 9); long coloratura phrases on "aria" (Act II, sc. 3), etc.
11 C.E. XIII; Goldschmidt, *Studien* II; see also Kretzschmar's analysis in VfMw X (1894)
483 ff. On the interpretation of the time values in Malipiero's edition of the score, see
Redlich, "Notationsprobleme," *Acta Musicologica* X (1938) 129–32.

the wife of Nero's general Ottone; Nero banishes Ottone and divorces
his own wife Ottavia in order to make Poppea his empress. This
eminently tragic subject is handled by the poet with consistency,
good taste, and real dramatic insight. Monteverdi altered many details of the libretto in the course of composition, for the sake of more
effective musical treatment. The music is not spectacular; there are
no display scenes and few ensembles (except duets). The composer's
greatness lies in his power of interpreting human character and passions—a power which ranks him among the foremost musical dramatists of all times. Take for example the dialogue between Nero and
Seneca,[12] where the grave admonitions of the philosopher contrast
with the petulant outbursts of the wilful young emperor (Example
32).

POPPEA.Act I,sc.9

Ex.32.   Monteverdi

The delineation of comic characters is delightful. The song of the
page boy Valletto has a naïveté comparable to Mozart's Cherubino
(Example 33).

12 Act I, sc. 9.

Not less remarkable is the power of pathetic expression, as in the noble resignation of Ottone's "E pur io torno" (Act I, scene 1)[13] or the profound grief of Ottavia's lament "Disprezzata regina" (Act II, scene 5). The love scenes can only be compared to Wagner's *Tristan* or Verdi's *Othello*. The frankly sensuous passion of Nero

POPPEA, Act II, sc.5

Ex.33.

Monteverdi

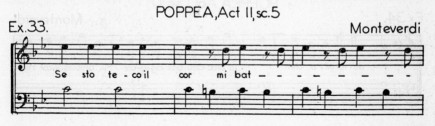

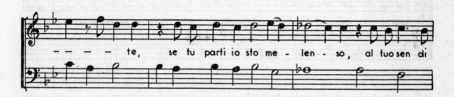

and Poppea is matched by a voluptuous, incandescent music, as in the closing duet (a da capo form over a passacaglia bass),[14] or in the third and tenth scenes of the first act, which are in a free mixture of recitative and arioso (Example 34).

No operatic score of the seventeenth century is more worthy of careful study, or even of revival in performance,[15] than *Poppea*. In it Monteverdi applied the full resources of a mature technique to a dramatically valid subject, creating in a great variety of musical forms and effects a unified, moving whole. The perfect balance be-

[13] The recurrence of the theme of this song in sc. 12 and again in Act II, sc. 11, is an early instance of the leitmotif technique.

[14] SB 178.

[15] Both *Poppea* and *Orfeo* have been performed successfully in modern times.

tween drama and music here achieved was soon to be upset by a trend
toward musical elaboration at the expense of dramatic truth and
consistency. Yet the influence of the work was far-reaching. Just as
Orfeo marked the climax of the old-style pastorale, so *Poppea* marked

POPPEA, Act I, sc.10

Ex.34.

Monteverdi

the definitive step (already foreshadowed ten years earlier in Landi's
Sant' Alessio) in the establishment of modern opera, centering about
the personalities and emotions of human characters instead of the
pallid figures of an ideal world.

CAVALLI.[16]—The leading figure in the first period of the history

[16] Goldschmidt, "Cavalli als dramatischer Komponist," MfMg XXV (1893) 45-48, 53-58,
61-111 (many musical examples); Wiel, "Cavalli," MA IV (1912-13) 1-19; album of
twenty arias, ed. Zanon (Wien-Trieste, Verlag Schmiedel, 1909).

of Venetian opera was Monteverdi's pupil Pier Francesco Caletti-Bruni, who (following a common practice of the time) took the name of his patron, Cavalli. About forty of his operas appeared at different Venetian theatres between 1639 and 1669. Cavalli's fame during his lifetime is attested by the fact that many of his works were performed also in other cities, including Paris.[17] His best-known opera was *Giasone* (1649, poem by Cicognini),[18] based on the legend of Jason, Medea, and the Golden Fleece. Since this work so well illustrates many of the salient features of the Venetian style in this period, we shall consider its music in some detail.

The overture ("Sinfonia avanti il Prologo") is in two sections: a slow, majestic introduction of eight measures in duple rhythm, followed by a quicker movement [19] in triple time, the theme of which is derived from the introduction (Example 35).[20]

GIASONE, overture

Ex. 35.   Cavalli

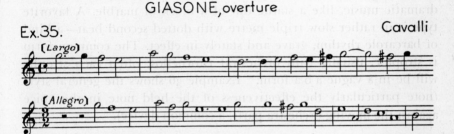

The presence of a second (fast) movement in the overture was something of an innovation at this time. The overtures of most early Venetian operas consisted only of a slow, pompous sinfonia of a few measures' length, a mere general "call to attention," an intimation of the ceremonious nature of the work to follow. The addition of a quicker movement was partly in the interests of variety and partly to connect the overture more closely with the particular opera which it preceded; many of these Venetian overtures introduced themes

17 *Serse*, 1660 (first performed at Venice in 1654); *Ercole amante*, 1662. See HAM 206.
18 Prologue and Act I in Eitner, *Publikationen* XII.
19 There are no tempo indications in the score; the contrasting tempi are inferred from the nature of the music itself.
20 This thematic similarity with change of metre is like the pavane-galliard combination of the dance suites. It was used by Marenzio in one of the sinfonie of the Florentine intermedi of 1589 and by Monteverdi in the opening sinfonia of *L'incoronazione* as well as by Cavalli and Cesti in their overtures. See Haas, *Musik des Barocks*, p. 143; Heuss, *Die Instrumental-Stücke des Orfeo und die venezianischen Opern-Sinfonien*, pp. 94–96.

which were later used in the prologue or body of the opera itself.[21]
It is noteworthy that in early instances the second movement was
not fugal, and that the overture as a whole was not nearly so complex in style as the canzona overture of Landi's *Sant' Alessio*.[22] Only
after 1660 did the fugal second movement come into the Venetian
overtures, and then doubtless under the influence of the French
overture type as established by Lully.[23] Apart from the overtures, and
a few descriptive sinfonie,[24] the Venetian operas contain comparatively little instrumental music.

The score of *Giasone* shows a number of well-developed arias,
serious in character and set forth in balanced periods. The origin
of this kind of aria is undoubtedly to be sought in the expressive
arioso phrases so often found in the midst of the recitative. It is thus
a style indigenous to opera, not a mere transfer of popular song-types
to the stage;[25] its forms are carved out of the very substance of
dramatic music, like a statue out of a block of marble. A favorite
type is in rather slow triple metre with dotted second beat—a kind
of barcarole rhythm, grave and stately in effect. The common form
is strophic, usually with orchestral ritornellos; often each strophe
will be in a vague a b a form.[26] Example 36 shows the general style
(note particularly the effectiveness of the held note in the voice
against the moving orchestra parts, a common device).

[21] See for example the overture to Cesti's *Pomo d'oro* (SB 202), the second theme of which
recurs in a chorus of the prologue.
[22] Cf. the overture to Zamponi's *Ulisse* (performed at Brussels in 1650) as given by Haas
in ZfMw III (1921) 390–91. This difference between the Roman and the Venetian overture types is usually attributed to the fact that in the former city the composer was
writing for an audience accustomed to hearing canzonas, whereas in Venice the audience
was not "educated up" to that kind of music. It may be pointed out in addition that
Landi was a master of the canzona form and therefore wrote it naturally when an instrumental piece was required, whereas Cavalli and most of the other Venetians composed little instrumental music and would hardly turn to the canzona, a difficult form,
under such circumstances.
[23] Cf. the second movement of the overture to Cesti's *La Dori* as given in OHM III, 172
(this overture is probably of a later date than the first performance of the opera in 1661);
the overture of Legrenzi's *Totila* (1677) is of the French type (Heuss, *Venezianische
Opern-Sinfonien*, p. 85.) See also overtures by M. A. Ziani (1674) and Franceschini
(1677), *ibid.*, pp. 118, 120; and Pallavicino's *Messalina* (1680) in Wolff, *Die venezianische
Oper in der zweiten Hälfte des 17. Jahrhunderts*, Anhang No. 67.
[24] See example in OHM III, 131.
[25] Wellesz, "Cavalli," p. 13.
[26] There are no instances of full-fledged da capo arias in this period, though this
form is sometimes suggested by the practice of repeating the orchestral introduction at
the end of a song.

Cavalli's comic style is marked by robustness, even crudity. Quite unlike the badinage of Monteverdi's page boy and waiting maid is the scene in *Giasone* [27] between Orestes and his servant Demo, who

GIASONE, Act I, sc. 2A

Ex. 36.

Cavalli

[Violins]

Voice — De - li - zie con - ten - te, che l'al - me be - a - te

Continuo

fer - ma - - - - - - -

te, fer - ma - - - te sù

que - sto mio co - re, deh! più, deh! più non stil - la - - - - - - - - te le

gio - ie d'a - mo - re - - - de - li - zie mie ca - re, fer - ma - te - vi qui

[27] Act I, scene 7a; Eitner, *Publikationen* XII, pp. 41–46.

is a stutterer—a typical farce figure, one of many such characters which were always welcomed on the Venetian stage.

Certain other features of Cavalli's style must be especially noted. His characteristic method of establishing a mood was by means of the persistent reiteration of one striking figure, as in the famous conjuration scene from *Giasone* (Example 37), where the motif (♩ ♩ ♩ | ♩) is repeated twenty-one times with hardly a break, using (except at the cadences), only the chords of E minor and C major (Example 37). Another token of Cavalli in this example is the melodic

GIASONE, Act I, sc. 15A

Ex. 37   Cavalli

line moving by leap, frequently outlining the triad. Notice also the subtle phrase structure: if this example were barred regularly in 3/2,[28] the grouping would be $6 + 5 + 5 + 5$ measures, the five-measure phrases being obtained by an overlapping of one measure at the beginning and end of each phrase of the solo; in this way the dotted portion of the vocal phrase is transferred from the first to the second

28 Cf. Schering's edition, SB 201.

half of the accompaniment motif. Thus Cavalli avoids a mere mechanical repetition of the prevailing rhythmic figure, which is itself momentarily interrupted at the cadence.

Despite the presence of well-marked arias and distinct sections of recitative, the formal separation of the styles is by no means complete in the operas of Cavalli. Most of the scenes are a mixture, or rather a free alternation of the two, as in Monteverdi, except that the arias in Cavalli form a somewhat larger proportion of the whole than is the case with the older composer. The method is not fixed; the form arises in each case out of the dramatic requirements. A typical example is the scene from *Ormindo* (1644) reprinted in Schering's *Geschichte der Musik in Beispielen* [29] which consists of (a) a dialogue in recitative, C minor, eighteen measures; (b) an eight-measure solo recitative, ending in G minor; (c) a lament on a ground bass, in E flat major, fifty-six measures; and (d) a closing solo recitative in G minor, thirteen measures. The constant use of "scene complexes" of this sort (that is, scenes made up of different musical elements freely assembled) shows that the Venetian opera in Cavalli's time had not yet altogether sacrificed dramatic values to the demands of abstract, symmetrical musical form. Cavalli was not critical of his texts, and his manuscripts show signs of haste and carelessness; he was not an artist of Monteverdi's caliber, but his music has virility and a kind of elemental directness in dramatic expression comparable to Mussorgsky— qualities which justify his position in history as the first great popular composer of opera.

CESTI.—The outstanding composer of the second generation of the Venetian school was Marc Antonio Cesti.[30] He is said to have written over one hundred operas, of which, however, only eleven have come down to us, all from the period 1649–1669. The most famous were *Orontea* (Venice, 1649), *La Dori* (Florence, 1661), and *Il pomo d'oro*

---

[29] SB 200; the measure numbers are given according to this edition.

[30] Cesti is ranked with the Venetian school by virtue of his musical style and his librettists rather than for biographical reasons. He was born at Arezzo, probably traveled in France, worked in Innsbruck, Rome, and Vienna, and died in Florence. He never held an official position in Venice, and only three of his known operas were first performed there. See Coradini, "P. Antonio Cesti," RMI XXX (1923) 371–88; Wellesz, "Zwei Studien," SIMG XV (1913) 124–54; Sandberger, "Beziehungen der Königin Christine . . . zur italienischen Oper," *Bulletin de la Société union musicologique* V (1925) 121–73. There is a modern edition of *Il pomo d'oro* in DTOe III² and IV² (the music of Acts III and V has not been preserved); selections from *La Dori* and other operas in Eitner, *Publikationen* XII, 86–206; selections from *Il pomo d'oro* in HAM 221.

("The Golden Apple," Vienna, 1667). Compared to Cavalli, Cesti's music is more facile, less vigorous, more feminine; he excels in the setting of idyllic, tender scenes; his melodies are clearly defined and graceful; his harmony is more conventional than Cavalli's—that is to say, it sounds less bold and experimental, more like the style of the eighteenth century; his rhythmic patterns are more regular, sometimes almost stereotyped. In his operas the already growing fissure between recitative and aria is noticeably widened: the center of musical interest shifts from the former, reserving the chief attention of composer and audience for the lyrical songs. The latter, by way of compensation, achieve larger proportions and clearer outlines, blossoming forth in an unprecedented variety of forms and types, offering frequent opportunities for vocal display. Thus the whole outline of the future singer's opera begins to come into focus in the works of Cesti.

This step, involving as it did a complete reorientation of operatic ideals, was of capital importance for the future. The doctrines of the Camerata had emphasized poetic values at the expense of music. Monteverdi, by means of organizing the recitative, deepening its content, and introducing arioso or aria forms at critical points in the action, had made the music an equal partner with the text, thus restoring the balance. But now by the middle of the century, as composers were becoming more familiar with the new musical idiom, their interest in problems of form began to outweigh their concern for dramatic propriety. It must be said in their defence that the poor quality of the librettos which the poets supplied in some measure justified this attitude. The trend was hastened, moreover, by another influence, namely the cantata, a genre in which both Cesti and his teacher, Carissimi, excelled. The cantata, although semidramatic in form and employing recitatives and arias like the opera,[31] was not theatre music. Designed for performance before a small audience, a vehicle for fine singing rather than for genuine dramatic expression, its virtues were those appropriate to the chamber: symmetrical forms, correctly balanced phrases, pleasing melodies, unadventurous harmonies; logic, clarity, elegance, and moderation. It was a musical style founded on these ideals, a style for which the widespread popu-

[31] "Eine Cantata siehet aus, wie ein Stück aus einer Opera," Hunold, *Die allerneueste Art, zur reinen und galanten Poesie zu gelangen* (1707) p. 285.

larity of the cantata had already prepared both composers and audiences, which Cesti introduced into the opera.[32] With him may be said to begin the reign of the composer over the dramatist, and of the virtuoso singer over both, which was to characterize Italian opera for the next hundred years.

Cesti's most famous work, *Il pomo d'oro*, was written for the wedding of the Emperor Leopold I of Austria with the Infanta Margherita of Spain, and performed at Vienna early in 1667 with a magnificence of staging appropriate to an imperial court desirous of not being outdone by the royal festivals of Louis XIV at Versailles.[33] The five acts included sixty-six scenes, in the course of which twenty-four different stage sets were required, some of them involving exceedingly elaborate machines. There were several ballets in each act and a grand triple ballet at the end.[34] The story of *Il pomo d'oro* was based on the myth of Paris and the golden apple; in the epilogue (*licenza*) the god Jupiter presents this prize of beauty to the new empress, as being more worthy than all the goddesses whose contention for it had brought about the Trojan War. In addition to the chorus there were forty-eight roles, though not necessarily this number of singers, since doubling was customary. All the gods of Olympus, as well as a host of heroes and other legendary personages, were represented in the cast. All the parts were sung by men, with the quaint consequence that some of the male characters in the opera have higher voices than the female ones—a situation not uncommon in Italian seventeenth-century opera even when there were women singers, for the composers favored the woman's alto voice and commonly reserved the soprano roles for castrati.[35] The orchestra con-

---

[32] Rolland, "L'Opéra au XVIIe siècle en Italie," in Lavignac, *Encyclopédie*, Pt. I, Vol. II, p. 722. Dent, "Italian Chamber Cantatas," MA II (1911) 142–53, 185–99.

[33] See Wellesz, "Ein Bühnenfestspiel aus dem 17. Jahrhundert," *Die Musik* LII (1914) 191–217. *Il pomo d'oro* was one of nine new operas performed at Vienna in 1667 (including Draghi's *Monarchia latina trionfante*) and was said to have run continuously for a year, three performances a week—a doubtful claim.

[34] Ballets were not a common feature of Italian opera but were frequently introduced into court spectacles, in imitation of the French taste. The music was often written by a different composer. For some of the ballets in the Vienna court operas, see DTOe XXVIII², and cf. Nettl, "An English Musician at the Court of Charles VI," MQ XXVIII (1942) 318–28.

[35] In Monteverdi's *Incoronazione*, Ottavia and Poppea are altos while Nero and Ottone are sopranos. A similar situation is found in Cavalli's *Didone* and other operas. In Cesti's *La Dori* the leading male role (Oronte) is for an alto castrato. See further on this subject Haböck, *Die Kastraten und ihre Gesangskunst*, chap. V, pt. 1.

sisted of six violins, twelve viols (alto, tenor, and bass), two flutes
(for pastoral scenes), trumpets in two parts (used chiefly in sinfonie
and choruses), a *gravicembalo* (harpsichord), which was occasionally
replaced by a *graviorgano* (a theatre organ, that is, probably a *positiv*
or one-manual organ with wood pipes), and other continuo instruments (lutes, theorbo). There was also a special group of instruments
for infernal scenes,[36] consisting of two cornetts, three trombones, a
bassoon, and a *regale.*

The prologue and each act are opened by stately instrumental
"sonatas," and there are also many short sinfonie and ritornellos in
the course of the opera. Choruses, found chiefly in the prologue,
epilogue, and ballet scenes, are of comparatively little musical interest. The recitatives are for the most part mere perfunctory settings
of dialogue, with the usual continuo accompaniment; there are,
however, a few very beautiful accompanied recitatives (continuo
and strings), notably that of Aurindo in Act I, which show what Cesti
could do in the expressive style when he had occasion.[37]

The favorite ensemble medium of all the Venetian composers was
the duet. In Monteverdi and (to a lesser degree) in Cavalli, the duet,
when not merely a recitative dialogue, showed, by its imitative
style, the derivation from the older madrigal. In Cesti, the contrapuntal feature is less favored, often being only suggested in the opening phrase and then giving way to melismatic passages in double
thirds or sixths. The opening measures of "Se perfido Amore" from
La Dori (Example 38) are typical of this graceful, amiable style.
Note particularly the cadence: the device of taking the final unaccented syllable on the penultimate (unaccented) note and slurring
or tying it over to the closing note is a characteristic of this period
(compare Examples 34, 36). This duet is in da capo form, with a
different text on the repetition of the first section.

Cesti's arias are not usually of large dimensions, but they show a
remarkable variety of types and much care in planning the order
in which these occur. There are serene, long-breathed, noble Handelian melodies;[38] playful airs with graceful and piquant rhythms such

---

[36] E.g., opening of Act I; Act II, sc. 6.
[37] DTOe III², 97, 100 ff. Also in Lavignac, *Encyclopédie*, Pt. I, Vol. II, pp. 729–31. The
recitatives in Cesti's *La Dori* are on the whole more flexible and expressive, more closely
related to the earlier Venetian style of Cavalli, than those of *Il pomo d'oro*.
[38] Aria from *L'Argia* in SB 203; air of Oenone in *Pomo d'oro*, Act I, sc. 6 (DTOe III², 83).

as Arsete's "Non scherzi con amore" from *La Dori*,[39] a complete da
capo form with the ritornello repeated between the first and second
parts and again at the end; martial airs with strong rhythms and

LA DORI, Act I, sc.9A

Ex.38   Cesti

much bravura passage work; [40] and buffo arias, lively, moving by
wide intervals, exploiting the virtuoso powers and comic possibilities
of the bass voice (Example 39).

IL POMO D'ORO, Act I, sc.11

Ex.39.   Cesti

The traditional strophic air is well represented in Cesti's operas;
the characteristic form of each strophe in these airs is two part, frequently with the second part repeated (a b b). Arias on a ground bass
are also used, and there is a considerable number of complete da
capo arias. Yet the forms are not stereotyped; subtleties of detail
abound. One feature of Cesti's melody, found typically in slow-mov-
ing airs of an elegiac character, is the melodic interval of the di-

[39] Act I, sc. 2a, Eitner, *Publikationen* XII, pp. 116–18.
[40] Adrasto's "Hor voi donzele" in *Il pomo d'oro*, Act II, sc. 13 (DTOe IV[2], 215–17).

minished third at cadences—or, harmonically expressed, the Neapolitan sixth followed by the dominant (Example 40).

One other trait of this formal, stately, mid-baroque Venetian style
is the rhythmic formula almost always found at the cadences of pieces
in triple metre: while the rhythmic unit keeps the same value, the
last two measures before the final chord are grouped as 3 x 2 instead
of 2 x 3 beats—equal to a change of metre from ⅝, ⅚, or ⁶⁄₂ to
¾, ³⁄₂, or ³⁄₁. It is a rhythmic alteration common in the courantes
of the seventeenth century.[41] Example 41 is from a chorus in the prologue of Cesti's *Pomo d'oro*.

LATER SEVENTEENTH-CENTURY ITALIAN OPERA.[42]—The principal
Venetian composers after Cesti were Antonio Sartorio (*L'Adelaide*,
1672),[43] Giovanni Legrenzi (*Eteocle e Polinice*, 1675; *Totila*, 1677),[44]

[41] This is usually expressed in the original score by "blackening" the notes affected, a
survival of the fifteenth- and sixteenth-century "hemiolia" notation (Wolf, *Handbuch
der Notationskunde* I, 398 ff.; Apel, *The Notation of Polyphonic Music*, p. 127).

[42] Wolff, *Die venezianische Oper in der zweiten Hälfte des 17. Jahrhunderts* (many musical examples).

[43] Sartorio (*ca.* 1620–1681), after a period of service as music director at the court of
Hanover, took a similar post at St. Mark's, Venice, in 1676. Thirteen of his operas are
listed in the Venetian repertoire between 1661 and 1679. Aria from *L'Adelaide* in SB 223.

[44] See OHM III, 177–81; aria (on a ground bass) in SB 231.

P. A. Ziani,[45] and Carlo Pallavicino.[46] Toward the end of the century the leading composer was C. F. Pollarolo.[47] Later Venetian opera composers included Antonio Lotti,[48] while M. A. Ziani, Albinoni, Vivaldi, and Antonio Pollarolo [49] continued the school in the eighteenth century. The general trend of the Venetian libretto after Cesti and Sartorio was toward comedy and parody, and this is reflected in the style of the music. Although the works of Legrenzi still preserve some of the serious qualities of the earlier period, the tendency was all toward simplicity and popular appeal: folklike melodies, dance rhythms, and conventional patterns prevailed; the musical interest of the recitative weakened, while the aria increased in importance; gradually the da capo form became the universal rule.[50] At the same time, the orchestra was assuming a more important position as an accompanying medium, relegating the simple continuo accompaniments to the background.

The songs of the earliest operas had been accompanied only by the continuo instruments, improvising in a more or less elaborate texture over a figured bass. Orchestral ritornellos, first used on an extensive scale by Monteverdi in *Orfeo,* were eventually brought into close relation with the

[45] Pietro Andrea Ziani (*ca.* 1630–1711) became second organist of St. Mark's in 1669. He composed a total of twenty-seven operas for Venice, Bologna, and Vienna.

[46] Pallavicino or Pallavicini (1630–1688), after an early period of composition at Venice, was active chiefly at Dresden, where he held various official posts at court. Of his twenty operas, the best known is *La Gerusalemme liberata* (Dresden, 1687). The overture to his *Diocletiano* (Venice, 1675) is printed in SB 224.

[47] Carlo Francesco Pollarolo (1653–1722) was a pupil of Legrenzi. He had seventy-three operas performed at Venice between 1684 and 1722.

[48] Like Pollarolo, Lotti was a pupil of Legrenzi; he was at Dresden from 1717 to 1719. Aria in SB 270. See Spitz, *Antonio Lotti in Seiner Bedeutung als Opernkomponist; idem,* "Die Opern *Ottone* von Händel und *Teofane* von A. Lotti," in . . . *Sandberger Festschrift,* pp. 265–71.

[49] Marc Antonio Ziani (*ca.* 1653–1715) was a nephew of P. A. Ziani. Forty-five of his operas and serenades were performed at Venice from 1676 to 1700; during the remainder of his life he was at Vienna.

Tommaso Albinoni (1674–1745) wrote fifty-one operas, mostly for Venice.

Antonio Vivaldi (*ca.* 1675–1741), known chiefly for his instrumental music, was the composer of forty-six operas. There are twelve ms. volumes of operas attributed to him in the R. Biblioteca Nazionale at Turin, which have not yet been fully studied. See *Vivaldi; note e documenti* (articles by Mortari and Rolandi); biography by Rinaldi. A complete edition of Vivaldi's works has been undertaken by the Istituto di alta cultura, Milan.

Antonio Pollarolo (1680–1746), son of Carlo Pollarolo, had thirteen operas performed at Venice between 1700 and 1729.

[50] Illustrations of the late seventeenth-century Venetian style will be found in the music of Pallavicino's *Gerusalemme liberata,* in the following chapter.

vocal part by the simple device of using the same thematic material in both.[51] A further step was taken when the orchestral instruments, instead of being confined to the pauses between sections or stanzas of the aria, played with the voice, either as a continuous supporting accompaniment [52] or constantly alternating with the vocal phrases in echoes or imitations.[53] During the latter part of the seventeenth century the simple continuo accompaniment of arias diminished in favor. In Cavalli's *Giasone* (1649) only nine out of twenty-seven arias had been accompanied by the orchestra; in Cesti's *La Dori* (1661) only five out of thirty-two; in Stradella's *Floridoro* (*ca.* 1680?) the proportion is sixteen to thirty-seven; in Steffani's *Servio Tullio* (1686) twenty-three to fifty-two; in Pallavicino's *Gerusalemme* (1687) eleven to fifty-one. The number varied according to circumstances; the Vienna opera had a large orchestra, and we consequently find many orchestral accompaniments in Draghi. The later Venetians, especially Pollarolo, introduced the orchestra more frequently, while Handel in his *Agrippina* (Venice, 1709) has thirty-one of the forty arias accompanied by the orchestra, and Scarlatti in *Telemaco* (Rome, 1718) dispenses with the continuo-accompanied arias altogether.[54] Mattheson in 1744 laments the passing of the continuo arias, which he says have long since gone out of fashion.[55]

The opera at Venice was often described by travelers in the seventeenth century, and it may be of interest to read some of their accounts. John Evelyn wrote in 1645: "This night, having . . . taken our places, we went to the Opera, where comedies and other plays are represented in recitative music, by the most excellent musicians, vocal and instrumental, with variety of scenes painted and contrived with no less art of perspective, and machines for flying in the air, and other wonderful motions; taken together, it is one of the most magnificent and expensive diversions the wit of man can invent. The history was, Hercules in Lydia; [56] the scenes changed thirteen times." [57]

In 1680 the French traveler Limojon de St. Didier reported as follows: "At Venice they Act in several Opera's at a time: The Theaters are Large and Stately, the Decorations Noble, and the Altera-

[51] Landi's *Sant' Alessio* (Goldschmidt, *Studien* I, 211); Rossi's *Orfeo* (Goldschmidt, *Studien* I, 301); Monteverdi's *Ritorno* (finale of Act III) and *Incoronazione* (see Wellesz, "Cavalli," p. 32).
[52] See for example Oronte's aria "Renditimi il mio bene," in Act I of Cesti's *La Dori*, in Eitner, *Publikationen* XII, 129 ff.
[53] See above, Ex. 36.   [54] Haas, *Musik des Barocks*, p. 202.
[55] *Die neueste Untersuchungen der Singspiele*, p. 162.
[56] *Ercole in Lidia*, music by G. Rovetta.   [57] *Diary* I, 202.

tions of them good: But they are very badly Illuminated: The Machines are sometimes passable and as often ridiculous. . . . These Opera's are long, yet they would divert the Four Hours which they last, if they were composed by better Poets, that were a little more conversant with the Rules of the Theater. . . . The Ballets or Dancings between the Acts are generally so pittiful, that they would be much better omitted; for one would imagine these Dancers wore Lead in their Shoes, yet the Assembly bestow their Applauses on them, which is meerly for want of having seen better.

"The Charms of their Voices do make amends for all imperfections: These Men without Beards [that is, the castrati] have delicate Voices ["des voix argentines"] besides which they are admirably suitable to the greatness of the Theater. They commonly have the best Women Singers of all *Italy*. . . . Their Airs are languishing and touching; the whole composition is mingl'd with agreeable Songs [chansonettes] that raise the Attention; the Symphony [orchestra] is mean[,] inspiring rather Melancholy than Gaiety: It is compos'd of Lutes, Theorbos and Harpsichords, yet they keep time to the Voices with the greatest exactness imaginable. . . .

"They that compose the Musick of the Opera, endeavor to conclude the Scenes of the Principal Actors with Airs that Charm and Elevate, that so they may acquire the Applause of the Audience, which succeeds so well to their intentions, that one hears nothing but a Thousand *Benissimo's* together; yet nothing is so remarkable as the pleasant Benedictions and the Ridiculous Wishes of the *Gondoliers* in the Pit to the Women-Singers . . . for those impudent Fellows ["canailles"] say whatever they please, as being assured to make the Assembly rather Laugh than Angry." [58]

Ten years later Maximilien Misson, obviously no enthusiastic devotee, had this to say about the Venetian opera: "The Habits are poor, there are no Dances, and commonly no fine Machines, nor any fine Illuminations; only some Candles here and there, which deserve not to be mentioned . . . they have most excellent Ayres . . . but I cannot forbear telling you, that I find a certain Confusion and Unpleasantness in several Parts of their Singing in those Opera's: They dwell many times longer on one Quavering, than in singing Four whole Lines; and oftentimes they run so fast, that 'tis hard to

[58] *La Ville et la république de Venise,* English translation, 1699, Pt. III, pp. 61–63.

tell whether they Sing or Speak, or whether they do neither of the
Two and both together. . . . The Symphony is much smaller than
at *Paris;* but perhaps, it is never the worse for that. There is also one
Thing which charms them, which I believe would not please you;
I mean those unhappy Men who basely suffer themselves to be

TRESPOLO, Act II, sc.9

Ex.42.
                                             Stradella

maimed, that they may have the finer Voices. The silly Figure! which, in my Opinion, such a mutilated Fellow makes, who sometimes acts the Bully, and sometimes the Passionate Lover, with his Effeminate Voice, and wither'd Chin[,] is such a thing to be endured? . . . There are at present Seven several Opera's at *Venice,* which Strangers, as we are, are in a manner oblig'd to frequent, knowing not, some times, how to spend an Evening any where else." [59]

Venice by no means had a monopoly of Italian opera in the second half of the seventeenth century. Public opera theatres were opened at Florence, Rome, Genoa, Bologna, and Modena soon after 1650 and at many other cities within the next few decades.[60] There was no longer, however, any question of several distinct local schools, such as were associated with the early days of Florentine, Roman, or Venetian opera. The style founded by Cesti and developed by his followers became a national, or rather an international, type. One of its representatives was Alessandro Stradella,[61] whose four operas and over two hundred cantatas and other semidramatic works show a facility and sensuous grace of melodic invention which justify his position in history as one of the forerunners of Scarlatti and the Neapolitan school of the eighteenth century (Example 42).

[59] *A New Voyage to Italy* I, 269–70.
[60] For a list of the local histories dealing with these theatres see Bustico, *Bibliografia delle storie e cronistorie dei teatri italiani.*
[61] Hess, *Zur Geschichte des musikalischen Dramas im Seicento; die Opern Alessandro Stradellas.* So little is known about Stradella's life that it is impossible to assign him pre-eminently to any one city. He was born at Naples about 1645 and, in consequence of a love affair with the mistress of a Venetian nobleman, was assassinated in 1682 (Bourdelot, *Histoire de la musique, et de ses effets,* pp. 59–66); see Richard, "Stradella et les Contarini," *Le Ménestrel* XXXII (1864–65), XXXIII (1865–66), *passim.* His life has been made the subject of an opera by Flotow (1844). Manuscripts of his operas are found at Modena (Catelani, *Delle opere di Alessandro Stradella;* Roncaglia, *Le composizioni di Alessandro Stradella*). Aria from *Il Corispero* (ca. 1665) in HAM 241.

9

Italian Opera in Germany

THE SOUTH GERMAN COURTS WERE NOT slow to import Italian opera. Performances are recorded in Salzburg as early as 1618; Vienna and Prague soon followed (1626, 1627). Cesti's works were performed at Innsbruck from 1655 to 1665, and there was Italian opera at Regensburg and Munich from 1653. The chief center, as might be expected, was Vienna.[1] Monteverdi, Cavalli, and Cesti were heard here at the middle of the century; subsequent composers included Antonio Bertali, G. F. Sances, P. A. Ziani, the Emperor Leopold I (reigned 1658–1705), and (the most prolific of all) Antonio Draghi, who from 1663 to 1699 contributed some one hundred and seventy dramatic pieces of various kinds to the Viennese repertoire.[2] Draghi, his librettist Nicolo Minato, and the court architect Ludovico Burnacini were the leaders of opera at Vienna during the last three decades of the century. Draghi was a court composer of skill and facility, if not of distinction. The airs of his early works are usually short and in strophic form, typically with the first part returning after a middle section in the dominant (or relative major), either with or without thematic contrast. In his later works, this is evolved into a full da capo form, with much text repetition and extremely difficult bravura passages. His recitatives are of the parlando variety, generally barren of musical interest, though occasionally a few measures of arioso are introduced, as in the older Vene-

---

[1] Bibliography: Köchel, *Die kaiserliche Hofmusikkapelle in Wien von 1543 bis 1867;* Nettl, "Zur Geschichte der kaiserlichen Hofkapelle von 1636–1680," SzMw XVI, XVII, XVIII, XIX; *idem,* "Exzerpte aus der Raudnitzer Textbüchersammlung," SzMw VII (1920) 143–44; Weilen, *Zur Wiener Theatergeschichte; idem, Geschichte des Wiener Theaterwesens;* Haas, *Die Wiener Oper;* Adler, "Die Kaiser . . . als Tonsetzer," VfMw VIII (1892) 252–74; Wellesz, "Die Opern und Oratorien in Wien," SzMw VI (1919) 5–138.

[2] Bertali (1605–1669 was at Vienna from 1637, where he produced eight operas.

Sances (*ca.* 1600–1679) came to Vienna in 1637 as a tenor singer; in 1669 he succeeded Bertali as court chapelmaster. He composed four operas, including one in collaboration with Leopold I: *Apollo deluso* ("Apollo Deluded"), 1669, text by Draghi.

Draghi (1635–1700) came to Vienna about 1660. See Neuhaus, "Antonio Draghi," SzMw I (1913) 104–92, which includes a complete catalogue of works and nineteen pages of musical examples.

tian style.[3] His overtures, like those of Cesti, resemble the French form, frequently with dance movements added at the end.

A style similar to Draghi's is found in the later works of Pallavicino, director of the first permanent opera theatre at Dresden (from 1686). About twenty of Pallavicino's operas had been performed at Venice before he composed his *Gerusalemme liberata* for Dresden in 1687.[4] The libretto of this work combines three episodes from Tasso with a number of newly invented incidents in considerable confusion, but with opportunity for several of the favorite spectacular scenes. The comic episodes are much less conspicuous than in most Venetian operas; each of the three acts ends with a ballet. Despite readiness of melodic invention and surety of style, the music gives a total impression of monotony. With the exception of two duets, everything is for solo voice. The sixty-six arias are for the most part very short and preponderantly in da capo form; the orchestral ritornello, played either at the beginning or end, is based on a motif from the aria itself. Certain mannerisms obtrude: phrases are constantly repeated in echo style,[5] whether or not the text justifies such a procedure (Example 43). The device of sequence is ever present;

GERUSALEMME LIBERATA, Act II, sc.12.
Ex.43.   Pallavicino

Vit-to - - - - - - ria, vit-to - - - - - - ria, vit-to - - - - -
- - - - - - ri-a, vit-to - - - - - - - - - ri-a

there are many passages of brilliant coloratura, especially in the larger arias accompanied by the full orchestra. On the other hand, many of the smaller arias are in simple, popular style including examples of the barcarole and siciliano types. The formal balance is

[3] See example, SB 226.
[4] This opera was performed at Venice in the same year. It was revived at Hamburg in 1695 under the title *Armida*. Modern edition DdT LV, with introduction by H. Abert on the style of Pallavicino's earlier works.
[5] Cf. Kretzschmar, "Einige Bemerkungen über den Vortrag alter Musik," JMP VII (1900) 63 ff.

always clear, the middle section of the da capo arias being shorter than the first part and usually offering contrast of key, material, phrase structure, and general design (Example 44).

There are three accompanied recitatives and two ostinato bass arias. One of the latter (Act I, scene 1), in genuine passacaglia style, is nevertheless in a b a form, the third and last variation being a literal repetition of the first—a striking instance of the imposition of the da capo idea on an older form, recalling the combination of chaconne and sonata-allegro in the finale of Brahms's Fourth Symphony.

One feature of the instrumental music in Pallavicino is the frequent repetition of phrases. Sometimes this is merely the echo effect common in the songs, but the repetition may involve also a contrast of instrumentation. The second movement of the overture, for example, consists only of five two-measure phrases, each of which is first played by the continuo instruments alone and then immediately repeated by the full orchestra. Similar places are found in many of the ritornellos: usually (as in the overture) a mere antiphony of short phrases between different instrumental groups, but occasionally a more freely developed concerto-like structure in miniature.[6] Essentially, of course, this procedure amounts to no more than taking over into the instrumental field a practice already established in the orchestrally accompanied arias, with their interplay of solo voice and orchestra. Yet it is worth noting that the appearance of the concerto principle in the instrumental music of opera at this time coincides with the earliest independent compositions for string orchestra in concerto style.[7]

One of the leading Italian composers in Germany was Agostino Steffani (1654–1728), most of whose eighteen operas were written between 1681 and 1696. Steffani was at Munich in the years 1668–1671 and 1674–1688, after which he went to Hanover. His teachers were the Munich chapelmasters J. K. Kerll and Ercole Bernabei. Steffani was the intermediary between the Italian opera of the late seventeenth century and the German operas of Keiser and Handel, so that

---

[6] DdT LV, 55, 113, 152, 177. See also the overture to *L'amazoni corsara* (1688) in Heuss, *Venetianischen Opern-Sinfonien*, p. 121.

[7] The trumpet concerto, a favorite of a slightly earlier period, is represented in the overture to Pallavicino's *Diocletiano* (Venice, 1675) and in a sinfonia from the first act of M. A. Sartorio's *Adelaide* (Venice, 1672). See SB 223, 224, and cf. Schering, *Geschichte des Instrumentalkonzerts*, pp. 27 ff.

GERUSALEMME LIBERATA, Act II, sc.3

Ex.44.   Pallavicino

Don-na rea, di me tu ri-di, ma di te mi ri-de-rò,

ma di te mi ri-de-rò ———— mi ri-de-rò, mi ri-de-rò.

(Fine)

Por-ge-rò pre-cial to-nan-te, che non de-stra

ful-mi-nan ———————————— te

arda un dì chi m'ol-trag-giò — — — chi m'ol-trag-giò.

D.C.

* *These six measures are repeated.*

even apart from his own achievements as a composer his historical position is an important one.[8]

The librettos of Steffani's operas differ from those of Pallavicino and other contemporary composers of the Venetian school only in their use of subjects from German history and a diminished emphasis on mythological and spectacular elements; in form, there is the usual regular alternation of recitative and aria, relieved only by an occasional accompanied recitative or duet. But the contrapuntal texture of the music marks a profound break with the prevailing tendencies in Italy, which were toward the homophonic style of the Neapolitans. Steffani's basses in the continuo arias are independently moving contrapuntal lines. In the orchestrally accompanied arias the voice is treated as one instrument among several, yet without ever sacrificing its position as "chief among equals" or taking on any nonvocal traits. Concertizing instruments (solo flutes, oboes, violins, bassoon, or trumpet) weave strands of melody about the vocal part, while the full orchestra joins in at the cadences. The characteristic arias are lyrical rather than dramatic, noble and serious in expression—long-breathed, leisurely melodies, effortlessly flowing (Example 45).

Attention must be called in Example 45 to the way in which the voice makes a false start, beginning the first phrase of the aria only to abandon it during a short instrumental interlude, after which the phrase is begun again and continued normally. This peculiarity (to which Riemann gave the name *Devise*) first came prominently into operatic music with Legrenzi: twenty-six of the arias in his *Eteocle e Polinice* (Venice, 1675) begin in this way. Instances may be found also in Cesti and earlier; it was very commonly used by Pallavicino and P. A. Ziani and by the end of the century had become an almost unconscious mannerism of style, constantly present in the arias of Steffani, Handel, Fux, and other composers.

The fundamental simplicity of Steffani's songs does not exclude melismatic passages, many of which have no particular justification

---

8 Bibliography: Chrysander, *Händel* I, 309–73; Fischer, *Musik in Hannover;* Untersteiner, "Agostino Steffani," RMI XIV (1907) 509–34; De Rensis, "Un musicista diplomatico," *Musica d'oggi* III (1921) 129–32; Werner, "Steffanis Operntheater in Hannover," AfMf III (1938) 65–79; A. Einstein, "Agostino Steffani," *Kirchenmusikalisches Jahrbuch* XXIII (1910) 1–36. Reprints: *Alarico* (Munich, 1687) DTB XXI; selections from other operas, DTB XXIII; duets in DTB X; aria from *Henrico Leone* (1689) in HAM 244.

ALCIBIADE, Act I, sc. 3

Ex. 45.

Steffani

(*Example 45 Continued*)

in the text but seem to well forth as the natural completion of the musical idea (Example 46).

The bravura aria is less characteristic of Steffani, though it was a favorite of Cesti, P. A. Ziani, Sartorio,[9] and other Venetians. Written for texts of stirring or martial character,[10] these airs abounded in virtuoso passage work; trumpet-like figures in the melody or the addition of an actual trumpet obbligato rendered the effect even more brilliant (Example 47).

Steffani's arias are nearly all in da capo form. In keeping with the contrapuntal character of his music, there is an unusually high proportion of arias on a ground bass, which sometimes itself determines the form but more often is simply incorporated in the da capo pattern. In many instances the ostinato principle is modified, leaving a bass consisting of a steady movement in quarter or eighth notes (walking bass), or of a characteristic rhythmic motif constantly repeated.[11] In view of Steffani's fame as a composer of vocal chamber duets it is surprising that few duets are found in his operas, and these for the most part short and not highly developed. In the accompanied recitatives, with their flexible structure and free mingling of declamatory and arioso phrases, the old Monteverdi-Cavalli ideal of purely dramatic song is recalled. It was customary in the Venetian opera to accompany scenes of a supernatural character (especially the appearance of specters, the *ombra* scenes) with the full string orchestra; and a curious echo of this tradition is heard in the string

[9] SB 223.

[10] Cf. Bücken, *Der heroische Stil in der Oper, passim.*

[11] Cf. Riemann, "*Basso ostinato* und *Basso quasi ostinato*," in *Festschrift Liliencron,* pp. 193–202.

accompaniment to the recitatives of Christ in Bach's *Passion According to St. Matthew.*

Steffani's overtures are obviously modeled on those of Lully, with whose music he had become acquainted on a visit to Paris in 1678–

TASSILONE, Act IV, sc.8

Ex.47.   Steffani

1679. Steffani is credited with being the first to introduce trio sections in the fast movement of the overture—short interludes for solo instruments, contrasting with the *tutti* quite in the manner of the *concerto grosso.*[12]

12 Lully had earlier used trio sections of this sort, but not in the overture.

Steffani is one of the culminating points of operatic style at the end of the seventeenth century. A spontaneous genius on the order of Mozart or Schubert rather than a dramatist like Cavalli or Handel, his works represent in pristine perfection the musical opera toward which the whole epoch had been more or less consciously striving. In his music at last is achieved the reconciliation of the monodic principle with the contrapuntal tradition. Steffani's operas, like the (contemporary) trio sonatas of Corelli, exemplify that balanced classical style of the late baroque which led the way in the next generation to the monumental achievements of Bach and Handel. The aristocratic, dignified, musically serious opera of Steffani found successors in the early eighteenth century only in the works of a few exceptional northern composers, notably Keiser and Handel. In Italy it was a stranger; there the demand for simplicity and melody, always immanent in the Italian temperament as well as in the nature of opera itself as a large public spectacle, led ineluctably to the *galanteries* of the Neapolitan school.

An echo of the older style is heard in J. J. Fux's festival opera *Costanza e fortezza* ("Constancy and Fortitude"),[13] performed at Prague in 1723 to celebrate at the same time the coronation of the Emperor Charles VI and the birthday of the Empress. The occasion called for an exceptional work, like Cesti's *Pomo d'oro,* filled with elaborate scenic effects, choruses, and machines. Both libretto and music are stiff, ceremonious, and old-fashioned. The texture is contrapuntal, as befits the author of the most celebrated textbook of that science in the eighteenth century,[14] with steady rhythms and frequent suspensions in the manner of Corelli. The whole opera is interesting as an example of the kind of music which in this period was more characteristic of the church than of the theatre.

[13] Full score in DTOe XVII, edited with an introduction by E. Wellesz; also in Smith College Archives, No. 2, edited by Gertrude P. Smith (piano-vocal score, with omissions and alterations, "adapted for modern performance"); aria in SB 272. Johann Joseph Fux (1660–1741), a learned theorist and organist, became court chapelmaster at Vienna in 1713. In addition to eighteen operas and ten oratorios, he wrote a large quantity of church music. See Köchel, *Johann Josef Fux.*

[14] *Gradus ad Parnassum,* 1725.

10

Opera in France to 1760[1]

I TALY WAS THE NATIVE SOIL OF OPERA.
Transplanted to other lands it either
flourished as an exotic or else took on
new characteristics essential to survival in a new environment.
The first French opera was performed in 1671. This late date is
surprising if we reflect that throughout the first part of the seventeenth century (that is, during the reigns of Henri IV, Louis XIII,
and the minority of Louis XIV, who assumed power on the death of
Mazarin in 1661) there were close political and cultural relations between Italy and the French court. But opera was not congenial to
the Gallic mind, with its rationalistic bias and its quick awareness
of absurdities; furthermore, the French for many years held that
their language was not suited to recitative, which is the foundation
of musical drama. They preferred their drama unadulterated and
regarded music in the theatre as only an auxiliary to dancing and
spectacle. Having their tragedy and their ballet, each the best of its
kind in the world, they were of no mind to risk spoiling both by
trying to combine them in the form of opera. Yet once launched, the
French opera was the only national school in Europe able to maintain itself unbroken through the eighteenth century in the face of
Italian competition. The reason for this was that Lully,[2] who established the fundamental pattern, was clever enough to take up into
his operas every musical and dramatic form which had already proved
itself in France. These forms were the French classical tragedy (ex-

[1] General works: Blaze, *De L'Opéra en France;* Chouquet, *Histoire de la musique dramatique en France;* Lajarte, *Bibliothèque musicale du théâtre de l'opéra;* Campardon,
L'Académie royale de musique au XVIIIe siècle; Borland, "French Opera before 1750,"
PMA XXXIII (1907) 133–57; Vallas, *Un Siècle de musique et de théâtre à Lyon.* See also
works cited below.

[2] Jean-Baptiste Lully, a Florentine by birth, came to Paris at the age of fourteen. Trained
as a dancer and violinist, his commercial talents and skill as a courtier contributed
materially to a successful career under the protection of Louis XIV. See biographies by
La Laurencie and Prunières, in which references to sources and other bibliographical
material will be found; see also RM, *Numéro Special* (January, 1925); Rolland, "Notes
sur Lully," in his *Musiciens d'autrefois,* pp. 107–202; Lavignac, *Encyclopédie,* Pt. I,
vol. III, pp. 1343–1425.

emplified in its perfection by the works of Corneille and Racine),
the pastorale, the Italian opera, and the French ballet.[3]

Lully's librettist, Philippe Quinault,[4] had begun his career as a
playwright. In general form and in dramatic framework his operas
are similar to contemporary French tragedies. The subject matter,
however, is restricted to mythology or legend, including three works
(*Roland, Amadis, Armide*) derived from medieval romantic sources;
there were no historical subjects, as in Venetian opera. The pastorale
genre, which had remained popular in France long after its decline
in Italy, and which Lully had used with success in some of his early
works, came into his operas especially in the prologues, though in
Isis and *Roland* there are long pastoral scenes in the body of the
opera as well.

Italian opera was known in France [5] from about a dozen works
performed by visiting troupes between 1645 and 1662, including L.
Rossi's *Orfeo*, and Cavalli's *Serse* (1660) and *Ercole amante* ("Hercules in Love," 1662). The last-named work showed evidence of
Cavalli's efforts to adapt his music to French tastes both in the style
of the melodies and recitatives and in the inclusion of many ballet
scenes, the music of which was furnished by Lully and other French
composers. Italian opera, however, was not a success in France. Undoubtedly audiences were impressed by the fact that an entire drama
could be set to music; they enjoyed the ballets; but their real enthusiasm was for the machines invented by Giacomo Torelli,[6] the
like of which had not been seen on such a scale in France since the
sixteenth century. The influence of Italian opera was therefore indirect; it stimulated the French to emulate the Italians by trying to
create an opera of their own, and it probably led them to favor a
large proportion of machine scenes.

The determining factor in the background of French opera, however, was the ballet, which had flourished in France steadily since the
famous *Ballet comique de la reine* of 1581.[7] The accession of the

[3] Schletterer, *Vorgeschichte . . . der französischen Oper;* Grout, "Some Forerunners of
the Lully Opera," M&L XXII (1941) 1–25.

[4] Gros, *Philippe Quinault.*

[5] Prunières, *L'Opéra italien en France.*

[6] On Torelli, see works by Bragaglia and Torrefranca listed in bibliography; see also
Nicoll, *The Development of the Theatre,* pp. 215–28.

[7] Prunières, *Le Ballet de cour en France avant Benserade et Lully;* Lacroix, *Ballets et
mascarades de cour;* Ménestrier, *Des Ballets anciens et modernes.*

young Louis XIV stimulated a revival of the ballet under Benserade [8] and Lully, as well as a series of "comedy ballets" which Lully wrote in collaboration with Molière during the 1660's. In these works Lully perfected all the elements of his mature style; indeed, some of the later ballets and comedy ballets had such elaborate musical and scenic interludes as to be little short of full operas, lacking only a continuous dramatic action developed musically, that is, in recitative.

The official existence of French opera dates from the founding of the Académie Royale de Musique in 1669, under the direction of Pierre Perrin and Robert Cambert. They staged two operas, or rather pastorales, with music by Cambert,[9] before going bankrupt three years later. Lully, who had hitherto loudly maintained that opera in French was impossible, changed his opinion when his favor with the king enabled him to seize control of the Academy and establish a monopoly of operatic performances in France.[10] From 1673 until his death he produced an opera nearly every year.[11] These works, all perfectly consistent in form and style, established a type of French national opera destined to endure for a hundred years, essentially unchanged by Rameau and hardly dethroned by Gluck himself.

The nature of opera as conceived by Lully is expressed in his designation of the form as a *tragédie en musique,* that is, a tragedy first and foremost, which is then set to music. Interest in the poem of an opera, and insistence that it should be of respectable dramatic quality, was one of the basic differences between the French and Italian viewpoints in the seventeenth and eighteenth centuries and indeed (though perhaps to a lesser degree) since. Contemporary French

---

[8] Silin, *Benserade and His Ballets de Cour.*

[9] *Pomone,* 1671, text by Perrin; *Les Peines et les plaisirs d'amour,* 1672, text by Gilbert. Both in CF; scene from *Pomone* in SB 222; overture in HAM 223. Cambert (*ca.* 1628–1677) was a pupil of Chambonnières and held an official court post from 1665. In 1672 he emigrated to London, where (according to legend) he was assassinated.

[10] See La Laurencie, *Les Créateurs de l'opéra français;* Nuitter and Thoinan, *Origines de l'opéra français;* the account by Pougin (*Les Vrais Créateurs de l'opéra français*) makes Lully out more of a scoundrel than he really was in this matter, according to Prunières.

[11] The following is a complete list of Lully's operas (librettos are by Quinault unless otherwise indicated): *Cadmus et Hermione,* 1673; *Alceste,* 1674; *Thésée,* 1675; *Atys,* 1676; *Isis,* 1677; *Psyché,* 1678 (Fontenelle); *Bellérophon,* 1679 (T. Corneille); *Proserpine,* 1680; *Persée,* 1682; *Phaëton,* 1683; *Amadis de Gaule,* 1684; *Roland,* 1685; *Armide et Renaud,* 1686; *Acis et Galatée,* 1686 (Campistron); *Achille et Polyxène,* 1687 (Campistron; Act I by Lully, score completed after his death by Colasse). All except *Amadis, Roland, Acis,* and *Achille* are in CF (piano-vocal scores); *Armide* is in Eitner, *Publikationen* XIV (full score); those marked * have appeared in Prunières' edition of Lully (full scores); selections from *Alceste* in HAM 224, 225.

criticism was directed fully as much to Quinault's texts as to Lully's music. The operas, divided into five acts, always had a prologue devoted to the glorification of Louis XIV, with allusions to important recent events of his reign. The action, unrolling with majestic indifference to realism, presented a series of personages discoursing lengthily on *l'amour* or *la gloire* in the intervals of all kinds of improbable adventures. There were no comic figures, except in *Cadmus* and *Alceste;* everything was stately, formal, and detached from ordinary life—the kingly opera par excellence, designed not for a general public as in Venice, not even for an aristocracy as in Rome and Florence, but for a single individual who was conceived to embody the perfection of national artistic taste and whose approbation alone was sufficient to guarantee success: what Louis approved, few either dared or cared to condemn.

The music was in keeping with this ideal. Its fundamental character may be described by the word "conventional": aspiring not to be new or different but to create the accepted effects supremely well. There were no startling intervals, chords, or modulations; everything was kept within moderate bounds, avoiding violence or passion. At its best, therefore, early French opera was impressive, noble, rich, and dignified; at its worst, barren, stereotyped, pale, and thin. Considered solely as music, it is likely to be less appealing to modern ears than contemporary Italian scores; but considered as opera, and in its proper setting, the French school stands comparison with the Italian very well.

One of Lully's achievements was the creation of a musical recitative suited to the French language. His model for the recitative is said to have been the declamation employed in tragedies at the Comédie Française.[12] Almost strictly syllabic, it often falls into monotony of rhythmic and melodic patterns; yet where the feeling of the text permits, the recitative may display extraordinary variety and naturalness, necessitating for its notation continual changes of time signature.[13] The relatively more complex notation of French recitative has sometimes led to an exaggerated view of the contrast between it and the Italian recitative. To a considerable degree this is a matter of notation rather than of actual sound, although naturally the differ-

12 Le Cerf de la Viéville, *Comparaison* III, 188.
13 See for example the scene from *Armide* (Act II, sc. 5) in SB 234.

ence in accent and tempo of the two languages determines the characteristics of the recitative in each case. Modern singers need to be cautioned against taking Lully's recitative too slowly and songfully, forgetting the composer's dictum "mon récitatif n'est fait que pour parler." [14]

Occasionally, at points where the emotion expressed by the words is more lofty or concentrated, the usual recitative will give way to a melodic phrase, which may recur several times in rondo fashion—a procedure analogous to that of Monteverdi or Cavalli, welding recitative and arioso into a unified and expressive whole. A very beautiful example of this is the lament in *Persée,* in which the recurring vocal phrase is first announced in the orchestral introduction (Example 48).[15]

A word is necessary on the interpretation of the time signatures in Lully and Rameau. The signs 2 (=2/2) and ₵ are two-beat measures, in which ordinarily the beat is *half as fast* as in C (a four-beat measure). Thus where the signatures alternate in the same piece, in changing from 2 or ₵ to C, two quarter notes in the latter have the same value as one half note in the former. The same holds true if the change is from 2 or ₵ to 3 (=3/4), or from 3/2 to 3 or C. In other words, the duration of a quarter note is approximately the same whether the measure is divided into two beats or four; the different signatures are indications of different metres rather than different tempos. However, the signatures do serve in some degree as tempo indications, especially in instrumental pieces.[16]

The vocal airs in Lully's operas differ considerably from the Italian arias. Relatively less numerous and important, they are for the most

[14] Le Cerf de la Viéville, *Comparaison* III, 188.
[15] For the entire selection, see SB 232.
[16] See Georg Muffat's *Florilegium,* Pt. II, Introduction, sections reprinted in Vol. I of Prunières' edition of Lully's ballets, with notes by A. Tessier.

part shorter, narrower in range, and more irregular in form and phrasing. They do not use coloratura, except for conventional short passages on such picture words as *lancer, briller,* and the like, though the vocal line is ornamented by a multitude of *agréments* (short trills, grace notes, passing tones, and so on). These are seldom indicated in the score, unless by a little *t* or cross above the note affected, which signifies only that some kind of agrément is expected without specifying what one. Their correct choice and placing were largely a matter of custom and taste, both for singers and instrumentalists.[17] Thus for the French singer there was required less technical vocal cultivation than for the Italian but a clearer enunciation and a more intelligent grasp of the text. A favorite type of air in Lully, derived in part from the French popular chanson and in part from instrumental dance music, is illustrated in Example 49; the minuet rhythm is fre-

PHAËTON. Act I, sc. 7

Ex. 49.   Lully

Que Pro-tée a - vec nous par - ta - ge   La dou - ceur de nos

chants nou - veaux: C'est de   tous les Pa - steurs, le Pa - steur le plus

sa - ge,   Pais - sez heu - reux trou - peaux Du Dieu des Eaux

[17] See Aldrich, "The Principal Agréments of the Seventeenth and Eighteenth Centuries" (Harvard Dissertation, 1942); Goldschmidt, *Die Lehre von der vokalen Ornamentik.*

quent in these airs, as is also the rondo-like recurrence of the opening
phrase in the middle and again at the end of the song.

A more serious type of air goes back to the French air de cour,
cultivated in the early and middle seventeenth century by such composers as Antoine Boesset and Michel Lambert.[18] The well-known
"Bois épais" from *Amadis* (Example 50), and the equally famous
"Plus j'observe ces lieux" from *Armide* (Example 51), both occurring in pastoral scenes, show this style at its best.

AMADIS, Act II, sc. 4

Lully's operas are filled with long scenes having nothing to do
with furthering the action but existing solely to furnish pleasure
to eye and ear—pastoral episodes, sacrifices, combats, descents of
gods, infernal scenes, funeral and triumphal processions. These
pompous displays are the heritage of the seventeenth-century ballet,
and the generic French term *divertissement* well describes their place
in the scheme of the opera. They give occasion for most of the chor-

18 Gérold, *L'Art du chant en France au XVIIe siècle.*

Ex. 51.   Lully

lieux,   et   plus   je les ad - mi - re.   Ce fleu-ve cou-le len-te-

ment,   et s'é - loigne à   re - gret d'un   sé - jour si   char- mant.

uses, instrumental numbers, and dances which are so prominent in
Lully. The choruses are generally homophonic and massive; those
sung to accompany dancing are characterized by strongly marked
rhythms. Scenes with choruses are particularly numerous in *Bellérophon*.

The orchestra in Lully consists chiefly of the strings (in five parts),
which play the ritornellos, double the chorus parts, and occasionally
accompany solos. Flutes or oboes are used especially in pastoral
scenes, either in combination with the strings or playing short episodes in trio style with continuo. Bassoons may be added to the
ensemble, and the martial scenes employ trumpets and drums. The
orchestra of the Paris opera, carefully selected and strictly drilled by
Lully himself, achieved a quality of performance which made it celebrated throughout Europe.

Instrumental ritornellos are usually placed at the opening of acts
or scenes, and descriptive symphonies (for example, the "Songes

agréables" in *Atys,* Act III, scene 4) are common. For the ballets there are dances and airs. The most frequent dances are the minuet and chaconne;[19] an instrumental air in French ballet or opera of this period is a piece played to accompany any dance or other movement on the stage which does not fall into one of the standard dance categories (such as the minuet).

The French overture, descended from the older canzona, the sonata da chiesa, and the early Venetian overture, and first definitively established by Lully,[20] is a large two-part (not three-part) form. The introductory section, in duple metre, is slow, sonorous, and majestic, marked always by dotted rhythms and usually by suspensions; it cadences on the dominant and is repeated. The second section, the theme of which may be derived from the introduction, is lively and in either triple or duple metre; it begins with imitative entries in the manner of a canzona, but once the voices have come in all pretence of systematic imitation is abandoned, though a pseudocontrapuntal texture is maintained throughout, with much sequential treatment (Example 52). This part (which is also usually repeated) may conclude with a broad *allargando* somewhat in the style of the opening section, though not necessarily having any thematic resemblance thereto. The French overture form was one of the most influential musical patterns of the late baroque period, being taken over into the instrumental suite.[21] Later opera composers (for example, Handel), borrowing in turn from the suite, often introduced one or more dance movements at the end of a French overture.

The dignified, formal splendor of Lully's works, veritable embodiments of the glory of the age of Louis XIV, offered a model to be imitated by lesser European courts. The high quality of the librettos, the careful composition of the recitative, the prominence of instrumental music, and the importance of chorus and ballet (all contrasting with the prevailing tendencies in Italy) helped to characterize a distinctive national type of opera which eventually made its influence felt on composers of other countries.

In France itself, Lully established the opera as an institution of the state—a source at once of weakness and of strength: of weak-

19 Chaconne from *Roland,* SB 233.
20 In the ballet *Alcidiane,* 1658. Cf. Prunières, "Notes sur les origines de l'ouverture française," SIMG XII (1910–1911) 565–85.
21 Cf. W. Fischer, "Instrumentalmusik von 1600–1750," in Adler, *Handbuch,* p. 553.

ness, because it tended to perpetuate forms which, whatever meaning they may have had during the great days of the Sun King, became mere empty show when that triumphal age was past; [22] yet of strength,

PHAËTON, overture

Ex.52.   Lully

for without such a foundation French opera might never have survived the series of second-rate composers and the general relaxation of taste which set in toward the end of the century. [23] Between the

22 Quantz (*Versuch*, 1752, XVIII. Hauptstück, sec. 65) reproached the French with the opposite fault of the Italians; whereas the latter are "too changeable," the French are "too obstinate and too slavish" in clinging to outworn musical styles.

23 The principal composers of operas and ballets between Lully and Rameau were: Pas-

death of Lully (1687) and the first opera of Rameau (1733) the gradual
change from the severe formality of Louis XIV to the galanterie of
the days of the Regency (1715–1723) and Louis XV was reflected in
the introduction of more lightness, gaiety, and charm on the French
operatic stage. The symbol of this was the creation of a new form
known as "opéra ballet," first exemplified in Campra's *Europe galante*
of 1697. The *opéra ballet* differed from the older court ballet in that
it was exclusively a public spectacle with professional dancers and
was set to music throughout. It was decidedly ballet rather than
opera, for it had no unified dramatic action, though each of its three
acts (*entrées*) might have a little plot, the chief purpose of which was
to furnish occasions for dancing and beautiful stage effects. Fantastic, pastoral, whimsical, or exotic scenes were featured and treated
with the profusion and originality of imagination which had characterized French ballet from the beginning. Even the opera itself,
the tragédie lyrique, was invaded by irrelevant ballet and display
scenes to an extent never imagined by Lully.

Another sign of change in this period was the infiltration of Italian
characteristics—a tendency stoutly opposed by conservative critics,
who remained loyal to the pure tradition of French opera as represented by Lully. The conflict between French and Italian styles flared
up many times in the course of the eighteenth century and led to a
tremendous amount of polemical writing.[24] The Italian taste was
represented by the use of Italian background in scenes of operas and
ballets (for example, Campra's *Festes vénitiennes,* 1710), by the insertion of Italian arias and cantatas, or of French "ariettes" in Italian
style,[25] by the occasional use of the da capo form, and more particularly by certain harmonic innovations foreign to the idiom of
Lully but common in the music of Scarlatti and other Italian composers, such as freer modulations, a more liberal use of appoggiaturas,

---

cal Colasse (*Thétis et Pélée,* 1689; *Les Saisons,* 1695), Marin Marais (*Alcyone,* 1706), Marc-
Antoine Charpentier (*Médée,* 1693), André Campra (*L'Europe galante,* 1697; *Tancrède,*
1702; *Les Festes vénitiennes,* 1710), and André Cardinal Destouches (*Issé,* 1697; *Omphale,*
1701; *Les Eléments,* 1725). All the works mentioned except those of Marais and Charpentier are in CF.
24 The two chief polemical essays of the early part of the century were Raguenet's
Parallèle des Italiens et des Français (1702) and Le Cerf de la Viéville's *Comparaison de
la musique italienne et de la musique françoise* (1705–1706).
25 The term "ariette" for a French aria in Italian style in early eighteenth-century
French opera is not to be confused with the use of the same term after 1752 in the
opéra comique to signify an originally composed air or song as against a borrowed tune.

seventh chords (especially the diminished seventh), chromatic alterations, and more florid or expressive vocal writing.[26]

Developments of this sort paved the way for the style of Rameau [27]
who, having begun his career as an organist and theorist (his epoch-
making *Traité de l'harmonie* was published in 1722), made his debut
in serious opera at the age of fifty-one with *Hippolyte et Aricie* (1733).
He was immediately hailed by the progressives as the savior of
French opera, and condemned by the conservatives as a hopeless
pedant, a *distillateur d'accords baroques,* whose capitulation to Italian
style was tantamount to musical treason. The reasons for this criticism are not to be sought in the outward aspects of his operas, which
conform essentially to the Lully model, but rather in the music itself,
which represents the late thorough-bass style in France as Bach represented it in Germany and Handel in England. Tonalities are absolutely clear, often being emphasized by Rameau's predilection for
outlining triads in the melody; large-scale forms are common, supported by definite modulatory schemes with systematic use of secondary sevenths (a particularly fine example is the great chaconne
in the finale of *Castor et Pollux*).[28] The whole style is more contrapuntal than Lully's, though not so much so as that of Bach. Short
airs intermingled with the recitative recall the practice of Lully; other
arias, longer and more fully developed, perhaps with da capo form
and some coloratura (this being the case particularly in the Italian-
inspired ariettes),[29] are formally set apart. Some of the larger arias
foreshadow the profound, serious moods of Gluck (Example 53).

The contrast between Lully and Rameau is particularly evident

[26] Examples in the music of Campra and especially Destouches. See La Laurencie in
Lavignac, *Encyclopédie,* Pt. I, Vol. III, pp. 1374, 1382–84.

[27] References to the extensive literature on Rameau will be found in La Laurencie's
"La Musique française de Lulli à Gluck" (Lavignac, *Encyclopédie,* Pt. I, Vol. III, p.
1388) and in the biography by La Laurencie (1926). See also P.-M. Masson's exhaustive
work *L'Opéra de Rameau.* Attention should be called to the introductions in the
monumental edition of Rameau's works in full score published by Durand at Paris, in
18 volumes (1895–1913, uncompleted). Following are the principal operatic works (roman
numerals refer to the volume number in the C.E.): *Hippolyte et Aricie,* 1733, VI, CF;
Les Indes galantes (opéra-ballet), 1735, VII, CF; *Castor et Pollux,* 1737, VIII, CF; *Les
Festes d'Hébé ou les talents lyriques* (opéra ballet), 1739, IX, CF; *Dardanus,* 1739, X,
CF; *Platée* (comédie lyrique) 1745, XII, CF; *Zaïs* (pastorale héroïque), 1748, XVI;
Zoroastre, 1749, CF. A number of piano-vocal scores, based on the C.E., have been pub-
lished by Durand. See also SB 297 and HAM 276.

[28] Full score, pp. 337–55. This number is not found in the CF score, which is based on
a later (revised) version of the opera.

[29] See examples in the closing scenes of *Hippolyte et Aricie* and *Castor et Pollux*.

DARDANUS, Act IV, sc.1

Ex. 53.   Rameau

Lieux fu - nes — tes où tout res - pi - re La honte et la dou-

in the choruses, which are more numerous and varied in the latter
and often extremely brilliant, recalling the style of Handel (for example, "Brillant soleil" in *Les Indes galantes,* Act II, scene 5). In
his use of the chorus for dramatic purposes (as in the impressive
opening of Act I of *Castor et Pollux*) Rameau showed the way for
developments which were to culminate in the later operas of Gluck.

Above all, Rameau is distinguished for the instrumental music
in his operas. The Paris opera orchestra in 1756 numbered forty-
seven players, comprising two flutes, four oboes, five bassoons, one
trumpet, and percussion, in addition to the strings and continuo instruments;[30] extra players were hired when needed for musettes,
horns, and clarinets (from 1749). The three main types of instrumental pieces in Rameau are the overtures, the descriptive symphonies, and the dances.

The overtures of the earlier operas are in the conventional form,
but in certain cases Rameau, unlike Lully, connects the overture
with the particular opera for which it is written. Thus the opening
theme of the overture to *Castor et Pollux,* in G minor, reappears
in the finale in A major for the scene of the apotheosis of the two
heroes.[31] *Zoroastre* has a program overture aiming to summarize the
main outlines of the plot of the opera.[32] In his later works Rameau
experimented with different overture forms: that of *Zoroastre* is in
three movements (fast-slow-fast), approaching not only in general
outline but also in many details—the texture of the music, the na-

[30] Masson, *L'Opéra de Rameau,* p. 513.   [31] C. E. VIII, 322.   [32] See introduction, CF.

ture of the themes, the form of the last two movements, the rhythms, methods of motivic development, use of devices like parallel thirds, unison passages, and echoes—the style of the early classical symphony.

The descriptive symphonies are short instrumental pieces intended to depict in music certain scenes or happenings on the stage. They are typical of an age whose music aesthetic was based on the ideal of imitation of nature, thus leading to a whole conventional language of musical images [33] for conveying landscapes, sunrises, babbling brooks, thunderstorms, earthquakes, or other natural phenomena. Rameau never wrote a piece of nature music more perfectly expressive of pastoral tranquillity than the slumber scene in Lully's *Armide,* but he excelled in more violent episodes, of which the earthquake in the second entrée of *Les Indes galantes* is a good example.[34] There are in his operas also many short symphonies for filling in awkward pauses in the action (such as descents of celestial beings) or suggesting off-stage battles.

Most numerous of all are the dances, which comprise all types from the simple minuet to the elaborate chaconne, with an astounding variety, freshness, and fertility of rhythmic invention. These are a noble flowering of the oldest instrumental tradition in France, a line descending from the sixteenth-century ballet through Chambonnières, Lully, François Couperin, and many other distinguished composers. In Rameau perhaps more than in any other of his countrymen the music has the strange power of vividly suggesting the movements of the dancers; it is in truth "gesture made audible."

The common dance types in duple metre are: gavotte, *bourrée, rigaudon,* tambourin, *contredanse;* in triple metre: saraband, *chaconne,* minuet, *passepied;* in compound metre; *loure, forlane, gigue;* others, variable in metre and form: musette, march, *entrée,* air (the last usually qualified by a descriptive term, as *air majestueux* or *grave, air pour les Fleurs, pour les Ombres,* and so on). The principal forms are: two part, rondo, chaconne. Many of these dances are sung by solo, ensemble, or chorus as well as played

[33] Du Bos, *Critical Reflections,* Pt. I, sec. xlv.
[34] One of the earliest "storm symphonies" is found in Matthew Locke's music for *The Tempest* (1670?; see OHM III, 289). There was a *tempête* in Colasse's *Thétis et Pélée* (1689), and a more famous one in Marais's *Alcyone* (1706); a favorite form of musical depiction throughout the eighteenth century, the orchestral storm has left its traces in Beethoven's Pastoral Symphony and many lesser instrumental works, not to mention the numberless instances in opera.

by the orchestra. Examples are too numerous and varied to warrant mention of any in particular. Only a study of the scores can give an idea of Rameau's inexhaustible richness in this field.

Rameau is not to be regarded as a mere way station between Lully and Gluck; any conception of him as no more than a composer of graceful dance trifles is completely false. On the contrary, he is one of the very few really first-rank composers whose work happens to fall largely in the realm of opera. If he is less consistently a dramatist than Lully, the fault is that of the age in which he worked; as a musician, he is by far Lully's superior. His relatively limited success in France is to be attributed to the poor quality of his librettos (for which his own indifference was partly responsible) and to the fact that in his day the old French opera itself, encumbered by so many conventions of a bygone era, was on its way toward decline, and Rameau's music went down to obscurity with it. Today it stands as a classic example of great music forgotten because it cannot be detached from a dead operatic style—for Rameau's opera cannot be revived as a living art without reviving the age of Louis XV. Yet by means of the requisite knowledge and imagination, one can in some measure learn to hear and see it as it lived in Paris under the *ancien régime* and thereby alone arrive at a just estimate of its greatness.

Opera in England[1]

AS IN FRANCE OPERA GREW OUT OF THE ballet, so in England it was rooted in the masque. English opera, like the French, developed late in the seventeenth century into a distinct national type retaining many traces of the parent form. Unlike the French, however, English national opera succumbed to Italian taste soon after 1700. The untimely death of its master, Henry Purcell, is symbolic of its own fate—"a spring never followed by summer."

The English masque was an entertainment something like the French ballet, allegorical in character, with the main interest in lavish costumes and spectacle, but including spoken dialogue, songs, and instrumental music.[2] The principal author of masques in the early seventeenth-century period was Ben Jonson, and one of his colleagues was Inigo Jones, who designed costumes and scenery. None of the great Elizabethan composers wrote masque music, but the form became a proving ground for experiments in solo singing soon after the beginning of the seventeenth century. It may be recalled that this was also the age of the solo ayre; John Dowland, whose first collection appeared in 1597, was followed by many other composers (Jones, 1600; Rosseter, 1601; Coprario, 1606; Ford, 1607; Ferrabosco, 1609; Campion, 1610). Alfonso Ferrabosco and Thomas Campion [3] were among the earliest composers of masques, but the first recitative in England was probably written by Nicolas Lanier in his music (now lost) for Ben Jonson's *Lovers Made Men* in 1617.[4] This and similar

---

[1] Dent, *Foundations of English Opera;* Parry, *The Music of the Seventeenth Century* (OHM III); Forsyth, *Music and Nationalism.*

[2] Reyher, *Les Masques anglais;* Herford, "Jonson," in *Dictionary of National Biography* (1917) X, 1069–79; Mark, "The Jonsonian Masque," M&L III (1922) 358–71; Noyes, *Ben Jonson on the English Stage;* Lawrence, "Notes on a Collection of Masque Music," M&L III (1922) 49–58; H. A. Evans, *English Masques;* W. M. Evans, *Ben Jonson and Elizabethan Music;* Prendergast, "The Masque of the Seventeenth Century," PMA XXIII (1897) 113–31; Finney, "*Comus,* Dramma per musica," *Studies in Philology* XXXVII (1940) 483–500.

[3] The surviving music of Campion's *Masque in Honor of the Marriage of Lord Hayes* (1607) is published in the Old English Edition, Vol. I, ed. G. E. P. Arkwright.

[4] An example of Lanier's recitative from a later masque, *Luminalia* (1637), is found in OHM III, 200.

efforts to adapt the new Italian stile recitativo to English words were
of no immediate importance for English music, which in the course
of the seventeenth century developed its own style in the airs and
songs, preferring to leave most of the rest of the masque (that is, those
portions which in an Italian opera would have made up the recitative)
in spoken dialogue. The songs, being simply inserted pieces and not
evolving laboriously out of the recitative as did the Italian arias, retained a simple and even popular flavor which gave a distinctive
national stamp to the English masque music and, by inheritance, to
the later English opera.[5]

The masque flourished especially during the reigns of James I
(1603–1625) and Charles I (1625–1649). Under the Commonwealth
(1649–1660), opposition to the stage prevented large public performances of masques, though some were still given privately, for example, Shirley's *Cupid and Death* (1653 or 1659), with music by Matthew
Locke.[6] Masques were also performed in schools during this period.
The professional theatre flourished briefly under the management
of William D'Avenant, who in 1656 presented a five-act work entirely in music, *The Siege of Rhodes.* The music (which has not been
preserved) included recitatives and arias; it was written by a number of different composers, among whom were Henry Lawes and
Matthew Locke. Apparently in order to avoid trouble with the Puritan authorities, the acts were called "entries" and the whole spectacle
was known not as an opera (which word, in any case, was still new
in England at the time) but "A Representation by the art of Pros-
pective in Scenes and the Story sung in Recitative Musick." In spite
of this subterfuge, however, *The Siege of Rhodes* was actually the
"first English opera." Though successful, it was not followed up, for
the Restoration soon brought influences to bear which gave a different direction to English dramatic music.

The Puritans had not aimed to suppress secular music, but they
did oppose the theatre,[7] and this resulted in an attempt to evade
their prohibition by disguising a theatrical spectacle as a musical concert. English opera, therefore, as represented by *The Siege of Rhodes,*

---

5 Parry in OHM III, 196–97. The song "Back, shepherd, back" in Henry Lawes's setting
of Milton's *Comus* (perf. 1634) is typical of this style (music in OHM III, 203).
6 Examples in Dent, *Foundations of English Opera,* pp. 89–96, and OHM III, 213–18.
7 Scholes, *The Puritans and Music,* chap. XIII *et passim;* Bannard, "Music of the
Commonwealth," M&L III (1922) 394–401.

was born four years before the return of Charles II in 1660. Paradoxically, the result of that event was to put a stop to opera by removing the prohibition against stage plays. English audiences preferred spoken drama, and once this was permitted they no longer had any interest in maintaining a form which to them represented only a makeshift, called forth by special circumstances. Theatre music, to be sure, was composed after the Restoration, but not in the form of opera; it was confined for the most part to masques and incidental music for plays, and the style in both these fields was affected by foreign influences.

The English tendency to underrate their own music in comparison with that of continental composers has been a bane of their musical history ever since Elizabethan times. That a true English style in dramatic music survived as long as it did—that is, until the end of the seventeenth century—was due partly to the strength of the old tradition, partly to the Commonwealth (which had decidedly not welcomed continental artists), and partly to the genius of a very small number of English composers who were either conservative enough or of sufficiently original genius to resist foreign domination. In the sixteenth and early seventeenth centuries the predominant foreign influence had been Italian; a number of Italian musicians appeared in the first years of the Restoration: there were Italian operas at the court in 1660; G. B. Draghi arrived in 1667; [8] Nicola Matteis about 1672 introduced the works of the Italian school of violin composers in England; [9] a celebrated castrato, Giovanni Francesco Grossi (known as "Siface"), tarried briefly in London in 1687 and probably introduced there some of the music of Scarlatti.[10] But Charles II, who had learned to admire French music at the court of Versailles during his exile, and who soon after his restoration organized a band of twenty-four violins (that is, a string orchestra) in emulation of the *vingt-quatre violons* of Louis XIV, showed himself disposed to encourage French composers rather than Italian. Thus in 1666 a Frenchman, one Louis Grabu, was appointed Master of the King's Music, the highest official musical post in England. Grabu was undoubtedly a better courtier than composer, if we may judge by his chief work, a setting of Dryden's *Albion and Albanius* (1685)

[8] Pepys, *Diary*, Feb. 12, 1667.   [9] Cf. Evelyn, *Diary*, Nov. 19, 1674.
[10] *Ibid.*, Jan. 30 and April 19, 1687; Dent, *Alessandro Scarlatti*, p. 37.

in three acts, along the lines of a French opera prologue. The music, a feeble imitation of Lully, dealt the death blow to this "monument of stupidity" [11] as far as public success was concerned. King Charles tried to lure Lully from Paris but failing in the attempt was obliged to be content with Cambert, who found himself out of employment in Paris when Lully took over the Académie de Musique in 1672. Cambert was in London from 1673 until his death in 1677, and two of his operas were performed there in 1674.[12] In addition to these and other importations, Charles sent a number of young English musicians, among them Pelham Humfrey, to acquire a French polish under Lully at Paris.[13]

In spite of foreign influences, however, the vitality of English music was preserved in the latter part of the seventeenth century by three composers: Matthew Locke, John Blow, and Henry Purcell.

Locke, the eldest of the three, had received his training during the Commonwealth and was at the height of his powers during the early years of the Restoration. He composed music for revivals of Shakespeare's *Tempest* in 1670 and *Macbeth* in 1673.[14] These and similar Shakespearean performances were decked out with machines and added songs, ballets, and instrumental pieces; the language was altered, the order of scenes changed, prologues and even new episodes and characters were added to make an operatic entertainment of a sort frequently burlesqued in the popular theatres. Nevertheless, this tradition of plays with incidental music is important, since it was for such productions that Purcell later wrote some of his best dramatic compositions. Another work for which Locke furnished some of the music was *Psyche* (1673),[15] an adaptation by Shadwell of the "tragi-comedy-ballet" of the same name by Molière, Quinault, and

11 Dent, *Foundations of English Opera*, p. 165; examples of the music, *ibid.*, pp. 166–70.

12 *Ariane ou le mariage de Bacchus* (probably with revisions by Grabu) and *Pomone*. See Tessier, "Robert Cambert à Londres," RM IX (December, 1927) 101–22; Flood, "Cambert et Grabu à Londres," RM IX (August, 1928) 351–61.

13 Pepys, *Diary*, Nov. 15, 1667.

14 Selections (respectively) in OHM III, 289–90, and Dent, *Foundations of English Opera*, pp. 131–35. The dates given are somewhat uncertain, and there is also some doubt as to whether the *Macbeth* music is by Locke. It has been ascribed to Purcell and other composers. Matthew Locke, or Lock (*ca.* 1632–77), although he excelled in theatre music, was also composer of many anthems, songs, and instrumental pieces, as well as author of *Melothesia, or Certain General Rules for playing upon a Continued Bass*, the first work of this kind published in England (1673). See article in Pulver's *Biographical Dictionary of Old English Music*.

15 Excerpts in OHM III, 291–93, and Dent, *Foundations of English Opera*, pp. 117–19.

Corneille with music by Lully (1671). *Psyche* (which Locke subtitled "The English Opera") is of interest as showing the strong French influence in English theatre music at this time and for the skillful setting of English recitative, but on the whole the music lacks distinction and is generally regarded as inferior to Locke's earlier dramatic pieces or his instrumental works.

John Blow's [16] only dramatic composition is *Venus and Adonis*, performed probably in 1685.[17] Although subtitled "A masque for the entertainment of the king," *Venus and Adonis* is actually a little pastoral opera, with the simplest possible plot and continuous music. The first act, after a long dialogue between Venus and Adonis, ends with a chorus of huntsmen and a dance. The entire second act is an interlude: first a scene in which Cupid instructs all the little Cupids (in the form of a spelling lesson) in the art of causing the wrong people to fall in love with each other; then a half-serious conversation between Venus and Cupid, ending with a dance of Cupid and the three Graces. The farewell of Venus and Adonis, and the latter's death, are set to beautiful and expressive strains in the third act; Venus bids Cupid bear Adonis to heaven, and the chorus calls on Echo and the Nymphs to mourn his death.

In its musical style and proportions, *Venus and Adonis* (like Purcell's *Dido and Aeneas*) shows the influence of the Italian cantata rather than the opera; certain details, however, suggest that Blow was well acquainted with the works of Cambert and with at least the instrumental portions of those of Lully.[18] The overture is on the French pattern, though with a rather more contrapuntal style and an individual harmonic idiom. The prologue, like many of Lully's, introduces allegorical figures discoursing on love in general terms, and ends with an "entry," that is, a ballet. Little coloratura phrases on descriptive words in the recitatives and songs are reminiscent of the French practice, as is also the common device of echoing the final phrase of a chorus or solo. An important part is given to ballets and choruses, and there is a relatively large amount of instrumental mu-

[16] Clarke, "Dr. John Blow" (Harvard Dissertation), 1947.
[17] The Old English Edition, Vol. 25 (piano-vocal score); Paris, Oiseau-lyre, 1939 (full score and reduction, original text); aria in HAM 243. The author of the words is unknown. There have been some recent revivals of this work (London, 1920; Oxford, 1937 and 1938; Cambridge, Mass., 1941).
[18] Clarke, "Cambert, Lully, and Blow" (unpublished article).

sic, including particularly a "ground" (that is, a passacaglia) in the
finale of Act II and a lovely "sarabrand" in the same scene, beginning
with a descending chromatic bass (Example 54).

VENUS AND ADONIS, Act II

Ex.54.   Blow

Typically English are the forthright melodies, such as the duet
"O let him not from hence remove" in Act I (Example 55). Above all
there is in Blow's music (despite certain crudities of detail) a quality

VENUS AND ADONIS, prologue

Ex.55.   Blow

Oh let him not from hence re-move Till ev'ry bo-som's full of love,

Oh let him not from hence re-move Till ev' — ry bo-som's full of love.

of seriousness, of sincerity, which lifts it out of the realm of mere
courtly show and gives to his characters a living human likeness beside which the conventional figures of French opera seem like puppets. The lamenting cry of Venus on hearing of Adonis' death (Example 56), the nobly elegiac final chorus, exemplify this quality which
has marked so much of English music, whether in the national folk
songs, the motets of Tallis, or the madrigals of Wilbye, and which
at the end of the seventeenth century is incarnated in Blow and his
great pupil, Henry Purcell.

Purcell's music,[19] like that of so many late baroque composers,
represents a fusion of different national style qualities. His early
training under Captain Henry Cooke, master of the boys of the
Royal Chapel, made him familiar with the English musical tradition; from Pelham Humfrey he undoubtedly learned something of
the French manner of composition, and from Blow the Italian, but
these elements were always dominated by a genius essentially in-

[19] Complete edition in process of publication by the Purcell Society (26 volumes have so
far appeared). The best general biography of Purcell is that by J. A. Westrup (1937).
Attention should be called to the articles by H. C. Colles in *Grove's Dictionary* (which
include bibliographies); the relevant sections in the histories of Hawkins (IV, 495–539)
Burney, and Parry (OHM III); Rolland's study of English opera in the Lavignac *En-
cyclopédie*, Pt. I, Vol. III, pp. 1881–94; the last three chapters of Dent's *Foundations of
English Opera;* and Barclay Squire's bibliographical study, "Purcell's Dramatic Music,"
SIMG V (1903–4) 490–564.

dividual and imbued with national feeling. The dramatic work of Purcell includes only one opera in the strict sense—that is, sung throughout—namely *Dido and Aeneas*.[20] Composed for performance at a girls' school in 1689 or 1690, it is on the scale of a chamber opera rather than a full stage work, though exquisite in detail and very effective in performance. The rest of Purcell's theatre music consists of overtures, interludes, masques, songs, dances, choruses, and other incidental music for plays; [21] but in some cases the amount and importance of the music is so great that the works may be considered as operas; indeed the word "opera" was constantly used in England at the time for such productions.[22]

When we examine Purcell's music, we are impressed first of all by the fresh, engaging quality of his melodies, so like in feeling to English folk songs. The air "Pursue thy conquest, love" from Act I of *Dido and Aeneas,* with its horn-call figures and constant lively echoing between melody and bass, suggests the sounds and bustle of the chase. In *King Arthur* the martial "Come if you dare" shows an English adaptation of the popular trumpet aria of Italian opera, with two of these instruments concertizing in the introduction and interlude, and the characteristic rhythmic motif ♩ ♩ common in French music and so appropriate to the declamation of English words (Example 57).

KING ARTHUR, Act I

Ex.57.   Purcell

"Come if you dare," our trum-pets sound.

The duet "Fear no danger" from *Dido and Aeneas* (Act I) is similar in rhythm and in its note-against-note style to the duets of Lully. No less characteristic, though in a different mood, is an aria such as "Charon the peaceful shade invites" from *Dioclesian* (Example 58),

---

[20] C.E. III; vocal score, ed. by E. J. Dent, Oxford Univ. Press, 1925; recitative and aria in HAM 255. The date of this work was formerly thought to be 1680 or 1682.
[21] *Dioclesian*, 1690 (C.E. IX); *King Arthur,* 1691 (C.E. XXVI); *The Fairy Queen,* 1692 (C.E. XII); *The Indian Queen,* 1695; *The Tempest,* 1695 (both in C.E. XIX); *Bonduca,* 1695 (C.E. XVI); and the masque in *Timon of Athens,* 1694 (C.E. II).
[22] Cf. Locke's preface to *Psyche,* 1675.

Ex.58.

Purcell

with the two concertizing flutes, the three- and six-measure phrases, the delicate cross relations, and the word painting on "hastes." There are also many fine comic airs and duets, particularly in the lesser theatre pieces.[23] Da capo arias are not frequent in Purcell, but he uses most effectively the older form of the passacaglia or ground, the best example of which is Dido's "When I am laid in earth" from the last act of *Dido and Aeneas,* one of the profoundest and most affecting expressions of tragic grief in all opera. Another air of this kind is the "plaint" ("O let me weep") from Act V of *The Fairy Queen.*

Purcell's recitative is found at its best in *Dido and Aeneas,* the only one of his operas which gives opportunity for genuine dramatic dialogue. The treatment, as Dent points out,[24] has nothing in common with the Italian recitativo secco; rather, the style is that of free arioso, admitting expressive florid passages, and always maintaining a clear rhythmic, formal, and harmonic organization, yet without sacrificing correctness of declamation or expressive power. The dialogue in the parting scene between Dido and Aeneas (Act III) and the beautiful arioso phrase which introduces Dido's last aria show what can be done by way of dramatic musical setting of the English language, that despised tongue which has been so often condemned as "unsuitable for opera." In Purcell's other works there are isolated examples of recitative phrases, including one from *The Indian Queen* which Dr. Burney called "the best piece of recitative in our language" (Example 59).[25]

The overtures to Purcell's operas are in the same general form as the French overtures of Lully; one of the finest examples is found in *Dioclesian.* Other instrumental music includes "act tunes" (that is, interludes or introductions), and there are some interesting examples of the canzona and other forms.[26] There are dance pieces of all kinds, including the hornpipe, *paspe* (French *passepied*), canaries, and special descriptive dances as in Lully; a favorite type (also common in French opera) is the chaconne or ground, which is often placed for climax toward the end of a scene, and in which dancing

---

23 Examples: "Dear pretty youth" (*The Tempest*), "Celia has a thousand charms" (*The Rival Sisters*), "I'll sail upon the dogstar" (*A Fool's Preferment*), "Celimene pray tell me" (*Oroonoko*), and the song of the drunken poet "Fi-fi-fi-fill up the bowl" (*The Fairy Queen,* Act I).

24 *Foundations of English Opera,* pp. 188–92.   25 *History* (2d ed.) II, 392.

26 *Indian Queen,* Acts II (C.E., p. 25) and III (p. 61); *Fairy Queen,* Act IV (p. 103); *King Arthur,* Act V (p. 142).

is combined with solo and choral singing as well as with instrumental accompaniment.[27] Descriptive symphonies occur, such as the introduction to the song "Ye blustering brethren" in *King Arthur*[28] or

THE INDIAN QUEEN. Act III

Ex.59.   Purcell

Bass solo   Ye twice ten hun-dred dei-ti-es,   to
B.c

whom,   to whom we dai-ly   sa-cri-fice,   Ye

pow'rs,   ye pow'rs   that   dwell   with fates   be-

low   and see what men   are doo-m'd to

do, Where e-le-ments in dis _____ cord dwell,
4   3

the famous "Cold" symphony and chorus "See, see, we assemble" from the same opera[29]—a scene perhaps suggested by the chorus of *trembleurs* in Lully's *Isis*.

The choruses in Purcell's operas contain some of his best music. Such numbers as "Sing Io's" from *Dioclesian*,[30] with stately vigorous rhythms, brilliant voice groupings, orchestral interludes, and passages of harmony contrasting with contrapuntal sections, deserve to be described as Handelian, so strongly do they foreshow the broad, sonorous choral movements in the oratorios of the later composer. Other choruses in Purcell are more like those of Lully, in strict chordal style with piquant rhythms;[31] still others clearly show the influences

[27] Examples in *King Arthur*, Act III, pp. 121–34; *Dioclesian*, Act III, pp. 57–59 (in canon form).
[28] Act V, p. 136.   [29] Act III, pp. 84, 92.   [30] Act II, p. 13.
[31] E.g., " 'Tis love that hath warmed us" from *King Arthur*, Act III, p. 101.

of the English madrigal tradition.[32] Finally, there are the choruses of lamentation, such as "With drooping wings," from *Dido and Aeneas,* which (like many other features of this opera) has a worthy predecessor in the closing number of Blow's *Venus and Adonis.* Except for *Dido and Aeneas,* where the chorus has a part in the action, Purcell's choral numbers usually occur in scenes devoted to spectacle or entertainment, corresponding to the ceremonies, ballets, and the like in French opera. There are scenes of this kind in *Bonduca* (Act III), *King Arthur* (Acts I and III), and *The Indian Queen* (Act V). The masques, of which examples may be found particularly in *Timon of Athens* and *The Fairy Queen,* also contain many choruses and dances; for parallels to these masques, with their fantastic settings and characters, we must look not only in the French opera but also in the contemporary popular plays of the Italian Theatre at Paris, which contain many scenes of a similar nature.[33]

On the whole, it is difficult to accept unreservedly Romain Rolland's estimate [34] of Purcell's genius as "frail" or "incomplete." It is difficult to believe that the composer of the closing scenes of *Dido and Aeneas* could not have created a true national opera in England if he had not been frustrated by the lack of an adequate librettist and by his apparently inescapable servitude to an undeveloped public taste.[35] As it was, however, Purcell's death in 1695 put an end to all hope for the future of English musical drama. London was even then full of Italian musicians; audiences became fascinated with Italian opera, and English composers did no more than follow the trend. The success of M. A. Bononcini's *Camilla, regina de' Volsci* in 1706 marked the capitulation, and the fashion was completely established by the time of Handel's arrival and the performance of his *Rinaldo* in 1711.

There was at least one Englishman who viewed this state of operatic affairs with regret. Joseph Addison in the *Spectator* frequently alluded to the absurdities of Italian opera in England and in one issue [36] wrote a long essay in criticism of Italian recitative, with acute observations on the relation of language to national style in music and an exhortation to English composers to emulate Lully by invent-

---

[32] "In these delightful pleasant groves," from *The Libertine* (C.E. XX, 51).

[33] Gherardi, *Théâtre italien.*   [34] In Lavignac, *Encyclopédie,* Pt. I, Vol. III, p. 1894.

[35] Cf. the preface to *The Fairy Queen.*   [36] No. 29, Tuesday, April 3, 1711.

ing a recitative proper to their own language: "I would allow the
Italian Opera to lend our *English* Musick as much as may grace and
soften it, but never entirely to annihilate and destroy it." That this
was a vain hope, Addison had virtually admitted in an earlier letter
which so well sums up the situation of opera in England at the beginning of the eighteenth century that it deserves to be quoted at
length:

"It is my Design in this Paper to deliver down to Posterity a faithful Account of the Italian Opera, and of the gradual Progress which
it has made upon the English Stage: For there is no Question but
our great Grand-children will be very curious to know the Reason
why their Forefathers used to sit together like an Audience of Foreigners in their own Country, and to hear whole Plays acted before
them in a Tongue which they did not understand.

"*Arsinoe* [37] was the first Opera that gave us a Taste of Italian
Musick. The great Success which this Opera met with, produced
some Attempts of forming Pieces upon Italian Plans, that should give
a more natural and reasonable Entertainment than what can be met
with in the elaborate Trifles of that Nation. This alarm'd the Poetast-
ers and Fiddlers of the Town, who were used to deal in a more
ordinary Kind of Ware; and therefore laid down as an established
Rule, which is receiv'd as such to this very day, *That nothing is capable of being well set to Musick, that is not Nonsense.*

"This Maxim was no sooner receiv'd, but we immediately fell to
translating the Italian Operas; and as there was no great Danger of
hurting the Sense of those extraordinary Pieces, our Authors would
often make Words of their own, that were entirely foreign to the
Meaning of the Passages which they pretended to translate. [Here
Addison gives some instances of inept translations, and continues:]
By this Means the soft Notes that were adapted to Pity in the Italian,
fell upon the Word Rage in the English; and the angry Sounds that
were turn'd to Rage in the Original, were made to express Pity in
the Translation. It oftentimes happen'd likewise, that the finest Notes
in the Air fell upon the most insignificant Words in the Sentence.
I have known the word *And* pursu'd through the whole Gamut, have

[37] *Arsinoe* was performed in 1706; the text was a translation from the Italian, the music
by Thomas Clayton. See Burney, *History* (2d ed.) II, 655; Fassini, "Gli albori del melodramma italiano a Londra," *Giornale storico della letteratura italiana* LX (1912) 340–
76; Nicoll, "Italian Opera in England," *Anglia* XLVI (1922) 257–81.

been entertain'd with many a melodious *The,* and have heard the most beautiful Graces Quavers and Divisions bestow'd upon *Then, For,* and *From;* to the eternal Honour of our English Particles.

"The next Step to our Refinement, was the introducing of Italian Actors into our Opera; who sung their Parts in their own Language, at the same Time that our Countrymen perform'd theirs in our native Tongue. The King or Hero of the Play generally spoke in Italian, and his Slaves answer'd him in English: The Lover frequently made his Court, and gain'd the Heart of his Princess in a Language which she did not understand. One would have thought it very difficult to have carry'd on Dialogues after this Manner, without an Interpreter between the Persons that convers'd together; but this was the State of the English Stage for about three Years.

"At length the Audience grew tir'd of understanding Half the Opera, and therefore to ease themselves intirely of the Fatigue of Thinking, have so order'd it at Present that the whole Opera is per-form'd in an unknown Tongue. We no longer understand the Lan-guage of our own Stage. . . .

"It does not want any great Measure of Sense to see the Ridicule of this monstrous Practice; but what makes it the more astonishing, it is not the Taste of the Rabble, but of Persons of the greatest Po-liteness, which has establish'd it. . . .

"At present, our Notions of Musick are so very uncertain, that we do not know what it is we like, only, in general, we are transported with anything that is not English: so if it be of a foreign Growth, let it be Italian, French, or High-Dutch, it is the same thing. In short, our English Musick is quite rooted out, and nothing yet planted in its stead." [38]

[38] The *Spectator,* No. 18, Wednesday, March 21, 1711.

12

Early German Opera

THE EARLY HISTORY OF OPERA IN GER-many is not one of a comparatively unified development, as in France or England, or even of a comparatively consistent musical style evolution, as in Italy. The numerous political subdivisions of Germany in the seventeenth century, with many different cultural traditions, the conflicting elements in both the dramatic and the musical background, and the extremely strong infusion of foreign styles (chiefly Italian, but some French) to different degrees in different parts of the country—all combine to produce a complicated task for the historian. Abstractly speaking, a purely "German" opera is one written for performance by German artists for German audiences, with an original libretto in the German language and on a German (or at least, not a typically foreign) subject, composed by a German, and with music in a German (or at least, not predominantly foreign) style. In actuality, there are few, if any, operas of the early period which correspond to this admittedly narrow abstract definition. In actuality, we find foreign conductors and singers performing before German courts whose tastes are often formed on Italian and French models, librettos in Italian or German translations or paraphrases of Italian or French texts, Italian composers, German composers aping the Italian manner, and all possible permutations and combinations of these factors. Add to these conditions the fact that many composers were active in different places; that frequently the same opera poem appeared under different names, or different poems under the same name; that composers habitually used music from their own earlier works or inserted music from other sources in their scores; and add finally that the scores themselves, a study of which alone could resolve many of the problems, are in the great majority of cases utterly lost or survive only in fragments—and it will be readily seen that a complete history of German opera in the seventeenth and early eighteenth centuries is, if not quite impossible, at least far beyond the scope of the present work. It has seemed best, there-

fore, in this chapter to begin with a brief survey of the political and
social conditions under which German opera was composed and of
the dramatic and musical factors which entered into it, to indicate
some of the principal developments at important centers, and then
to concentrate our study on the most distinctive of the many local
schools, that of Hamburg.[1]

Germany in the seventeenth century was not a nation but a loose
confederation of some 1700 more or less independent states; most
of these were petty "knights' dominions," but there were also fifty-
one free imperial cities (of which the chief were Hamburg, Bremen,
Frankfort am Main, Nuremberg, Augsburg, Ulm, and Strassburg),
sixty-three ecclesiastical holdings, and nearly two hundred secular
principalities and counties, a few of which were of considerable size
and importance. The semblance of unity arising from an ill-defined
allegiance to the Holy Roman Empire was disrupted by the Thirty
Years' War (1618–1648), a calamity which left the country eco-
nomically prostrated and bereft of almost all pride in its national
heritage. Like a body weakened by illness, German culture was invaded by foreign elements. The language became filled with French
and Spanish words; French became the common tongue of polite
society;[2] the little local courts, narrow, paternalistic, and extrava-
gant, aspired to imitate the glories of Versailles. Italian opera thus
made its appearance as a courtly show, particularly in southern Germany, where we have already traced some of its manifestations at
Vienna, Dresden, and Munich. Other centers of Italian opera were

1 The conditions of early German opera are reflected in the fact that the great majority of
the studies in this field are in the form of local or regional histories, embodying chronicles
and statistics. References to this extensive literature will be found in the three chief
general surveys of the period: Kretzschmar, "Das erste Jahrhundert der deutschen
Oper," in his Geschichte der Oper, pp. 133–57, also SIMG III (1901–02) 270–93; Moser,
"Die frühdeutsche Oper," in his Geschichte der deutschen Musik II, Bk. II, chap. 3;
and Schiedermair's Deutsche Oper, Pt. I. See also Haas, "Die Oper in Deutschland bis
1750," in Adler's Handbuch; Schletterer, Das deutsche Singspiel; G. F. Schmidt, "Zur
Geschichte, Dramaturgie und Statistik," ZfMw V (1922–23) 582–97, 642–65; VI (1923–24)
129–57, 496–530; Schreiber, Dichtung und Musik der deutschen Opernarien. A bibliography of regional and local histories of German music will be found in Moser's Musik
Lexikon, pp. 988–89. Biographies of many composers are to be found in Mattheson's
Ehrenpforte (1740).
2 A proverb at the Brunswick court in the latter part of the seventeenth century ran:
"Wer nicht französisch kann, Der kommt bei Hof nicht an" (Hartmann, Sechs Bücher
braunschweigischer Theatergeschichte, p. 85). See also Braunschweigischer Magazin IX
(1903) 116–17.

Hanover (Steffani's operas from 1689 to 1696), Düsseldorf, and Bonn.[3]
Yet many courts tried at first to encourage German talent. The early
Italian operas at Vienna occasionally had German songs inserted.
The "first German opera" [4] was performed at Torgau in 1627 at the
marriage of Princess Luise of Saxony and Landgraf Georg von
Hessen-Darmstadt. This work was the old *Dafne* of Rinuccini, trans-
lated and adapted by the leading German poet of the time, Martin
Opitz, and set to music by no less a composer than Heinrich Schütz.[5]
Before the opening of the Italian opera in 1686, Dresden had a few
works in German; one of these, *Apollo und Daphne* (1671) by G. A.
Bontempi and M. G. Peranda, is preserved in manuscript—one of
the three complete German opera scores prior to Keiser's *Adonis*
(1697) still known to exist.[6]

At Brunswick the court opera employed native poets, subjects,
and composers (Erlebach, Philipp Krieger, Bronner, Kusser, Keiser),
but with the opening of a public theatre in 1690 the demand for foreign goods became so strong that French and Italian works had to
be added to the repertoire. A temporary revival of native opera in
the early eighteenth century was led by Georg Caspar Schürmann,
one of the most significant of the German composers, whose dignified, serious musical style has much in common with Keiser, Handel,
and Bach.[7] At Leipzig, where operas were played during the Fair

---

[3] Four numbers from Johann Christoph Pez's Italian opera *Trajano* (Bonn, 1696, 1699)
are found in DTB XXVII/XXVIII, pp. 75–90.

[4] The German equivalent of the term "opera" was *Singspiel*, a literal translation of
the Italian *dramma per musica*. Cf. Hunold: "Eine *Opera* oder ein Sing-Spiel ist gewiss
das galanteste Stück der Poesie, so man heut zutage æstimieren pfleget" (*Die allerneueste
Art* [1707], p. 394). Ayrer's comedies on popular song-tunes at Nuremberg (from 1598)
bear the designation *singets Spil;* the first operas at Hamburg were called *Sing-Spiele*.
The term was applied in the seventeenth and early eighteenth centuries both to works
sung in their entirety and to those having some spoken dialogue. In the second half
of the eighteenth century its meaning was restricted to pieces of the latter type. (It may
be added that, in the absence of scores, it is not always possible to ascertain in the case
of some seventeenth-century German operas whether the recitatives were sung or
spoken.) The word "opera" does not often occur in German scores before 1720. (See
Schmidt, *Die frühdeutsche Oper und die musikdramatische Kunst Georg Caspar Schürmann's* II, 45–54.)

[5] The score has not survived. Schütz also wrote music for one or two ballets; a *Ballet
von der Zusammenkunft und Wirkung der sieben Planeten* (Dresden, 1678), formerly
attributed to him, has recently been ascribed, on the basis of internal evidence, to his
pupil, Christoph Bernhard (Bittrich, *Ein deutsches Opernballett des siebzehnten Jahrhunderts*).

[6] One aria reprinted in Hugo Riemann's *Musikgeschichte in Beispielen*, No. 197.

[7] Schürmann (*ca.* 1672–1751) composed about forty operas for Wolfenbüttel, of which

seasons from 1693 to 1720, the texts were mostly translations of
Venetian librettos; poets and composers, players and singers were
largely recruited from the students of St. Thomas's, and so successfully that Kuhnau in 1709 complained that church music suffered
from the competition.[8] The general enthusiasm for opera at Leipzig
was such that even J. S. Bach did not altogether escape its influence.[9]
Another center of German opera was Weissenfels (ca. 1680–1732);
here the leading composer was Johann Philipp Krieger, whose opera
songs were in the simple German "lied" tradition.[10] The subject
matter of the Weissenfels operas, however, was not distinctively German; the repertoire shows a strong preponderance of mythological
dramas and ballets. A similarly ambiguous picture is presented at
many of the lesser courts—German elements struggling against an
increasing tide of Italian opera, which by the fourth decade of the
eighteenth century had definitely won the lead everywhere.

The characteristic German forerunner of opera was the school
drama, a play in Latin or German, usually of a moral or religious
nature, didactic in aim, performed by the students of a school or
seminary.[11] Many of these dramas in the sixteenth century included
instrumental dances, solo odes, and choral pieces.[12] In the early seventeenth century the musical portions became even more extensive.
Although the Thirty Years' War put an end to the most flourishing

---

eleven have been preserved. His *Ludwig der Fromme* (1726) was published (incomplete)
as Vol. 17 of the Eitner *Publikationenen;* an aria from the same opera in SB 293; an
aria from *Heinrich der Vogler* in MfMg XVII (1885) Beilage, pp. 148–60; three volumes
of arias ed. by G. F. Schmidt. See also Schmidt's masterly study *Die frühdeutsche Oper
und die musikdramatische Kunst Georg Caspar Schürmann's.*

8 Spitta, *Johann Sebastian Bach* (4th ed.) II, 854.

9 The most obviously dramatic work of Bach is *Phoebus und Pan* (composed for the Leipzig *Collegium Musicum* in 1731), which one contemporary called a "Gesprächspiel"
(Spitta, *Bach* II, 740). Several of the secular cantatas, so called, actually bear the designation "Drama" or "Drama per Musica," and others (e.g., the "Coffee Cantata") are semidramatic—not to mention the Passions and oratorios, in which the influence of dramatic
forms is clearly evident.

10 Krieger (1649–1725) was noted for his church and chamber music as well as operas
(see church music in DdT 53/54 and DTB VI, 1; instrumental music in DTB XVIII,
Appendix.) A selection of arias from the operas is found in MfMg XXIX (1897) Beilagen,
pp. 37–65; one aria in *Neue Musik-Zeitung* XLIX (1928) Musikbeilage Nr. 6 (Heft 10),
pp. 3–4; two arias in SB 236; twenty-four in *Lieder und Arien*, ed. H. J. Moser. See also
Wagner, "Beiträge zur Lebensgeschichte J. P. Kriegers," ZfMw VIII (1925–26) 146–60.

11 The Jesuits were particularly active in this field. See Flemming, *Geschichte des Jesuitentheaters.*

12 Liliencron, "Die Chorgesänge des lateinischen-deutschen Schuldramas," VfMw VI
(1890) 309–87; Schünemann, *Geschichte der deutschen Schulmusik*, pp. 67 ff., 137.

era of the school drama, its influence may be seen in the earliest
German opera whose music has survived: *Seelewig,* a "spiritual pastorale" by Philipp Harsdörffer, set to music by Sigmund Theophil
Staden, and published at Nuremberg in 1644 in a family periodical.[13]
As with the first Hamburg opera, nearly thirty-five years later, the
subject matter of this work is religious. The form is allegorical.
"Seelewig" is the soul; the villain of the piece is one Trügewalt, who
attempts to ensnare Seelewig with the help of other characters representing Art, the Senses, and so on, while Wisdom and Conscience
act as her defenders. The final triumph of virtue is celebrated by
an invisible chorus of angels. This highly moral drama is placed in a
fashionable pastoral setting: the sylvan scenes are described in poetry
filled with moral symbolism; Seelewig's companions are nymphs and
shepherds, while Trügewalt is figured as a satyr. Sinnigunda's "nightingale song" (Act III, scene 3) displays remarkable coloratura passages
and other instances of word painting, together with a deliberate quotation of the chorale melody "Wann mein Stündlein vorhanden ist"
(on the words "Und gleich eim Totenlied"). Two examples of the
echo song testify to the popularity of this device, so frequent in
early Italian operas. The prologue is sung by Music, the epilogue by
Painting. Each of the three acts is introduced by a symphony, and
there are a few other short instrumental pieces, together with the
composer's direction that more may be added if necessary in order
to avoid pauses during the changing of the scenery. The orchestra
consists of a theorbo, "lutes," three violins,[14] three "flutes" (that is,
recorders), one or more traverse flutes, three shawms (instruments of
the oboe family), three bassoons, and a horn; [15] each class of instru-

---

[13] *Frauenzimmer Gesprechspiele* IV, 31–165, 489–622. Reprinted by Eitner, MfMg XIII
(1881) 65–150. Cf. also Narciss, *Studien zu den Frauenzimmergesprächspielen,* pp. 93–
96; Tittmann, *Kleine Schriften zur deutschen Literatur und Kulturgeschichte,* Theil I;
Schmitz, "Zur musikgeschichtlichen Bedeutung der Harsdörfferschen 'Frauenzimmergesprächspiele,' " in *Festschrift Liliencron,* pp. 254–77. According to Moser (*Geschichte der
deutschen Musik* II, 169), no performance of this work can be traced; it is evident from
the text that it was intended only for private use. Puttmann (*Die Musik* III [1903–
1904] 345) mentions a performance at Augsburg in 1698 (*sic*) by a troupe of professional
comedians; no authority is given for this statement, and we have been unable to find
any record of such a performance. Staden (1607–1655), son of a Nuremberg organist and
composer, was himself organist at St. Lorenz's from 1635 to his death.
[14] *Geigen;* the last symphony (p. 616 of the original edition) is notated for "3. Violen";
two in the treble G clef, one in the alto C clef, going below the violin range.
[15] *Grobes Horn,* literally a "rough" or "rude horn"; either a crude instrument of this
type or possibly a horn or trumpet played in the second octave above the fundamental

ments is associated with particular characters—violins and flutes with
the nymphs, flutes (and shawms?) with the shepherds, and the horn
with Trügewalt. In the solo songs (which comprise most of the
music) there is evidence of some effort to write in the recitative
style, but Staden has not acquired the knack; consequently, most of
the songs are short melodies, and nearly all are in strophic form (two
to seven stanzas). This form, especially when there are many stanzas,
is far from ideal for dramatic purposes, even with a number of performers alternating in dialogue fashion. It may be that Staden had
in mind the music of some of the ballad plays performed by English
troupes in Germany in the early part of the seventeenth century, or
by their German imitators at Nuremberg, in which the same melody
might be used throughout an entire play for twenty, thirty, fifty, or
even more stanzas.[16] The strophic lied, so highly cultivated in Germany in the early and middle seventeenth century,[17] naturally found
its place in opera, into which it was indeed completely absorbed for
a time. Staden's songs in *Seelewig* are not at all of the folk type but
rather in the style of the more serious solo melodies of Heinrich Albert. Perhaps the best is Seelewig's outburst of thanksgiving in the
closing scene (Example 60).

Seelewig was not the only effort of Harsdörffer [18] along operatic
lines. If there he showed himself a follower of the Italian pastorale,
in *Die Tugendsterne* ("The Stars of Virtue") [19] he sought to turn to
moral purposes another favorite genre, the ballet with machines;
still another play, *Von der Welt Eitelkeit* ("Of Worldly Vanity"),[20]
consists of four allegorical scenes, each representing a worldly Vanity, with an epilogue sung by Death. No doubt such works are ex-

---

(cf. Speer, *Grund-richtiger . . . Unterricht*, p. 94). The direction on p. 517 of the original
edition of the score ("Trom od' grob Horn") indicates that a trumpet might substitute.
The term *grobes Horn* is still current in Styria to describe a primitive instrument made
from the horn of a cow.

16 J. Ayrer's first "singets Spil," *Von dreyen bösen Weibern* (probably performed at Nuremberg *ca.* 1598), consists of forty-seven stanzas to the tune of "The English Roland."
See Bolte, *Die Singspiele der englischen Komödianten*, pp. 12, 167–69, *et passim*.

17 The two leading composers were Heinrich Albert (eight books from 1638 to 1650;
modern edition, DdT XII, XIII; see also SB 193) and Adam Krieger (1657; DdT XIX;
see also SB 209).

18 For a fuller treatment of the moral and biblical opera in Germany, see Schmidt, *Die
frühdeutsche Oper* II, 66–85.

19 Text in *Frauenzimmer Gesprechspiele* V, 280–310. No music is preserved.

20 *Ibid.* III, 170–242. A nearly complete reprint, with the music, by Eugen Schmitz in
Festschrift Liliencron, pp. 264–75.

ceptional, as being designed primarily for reading rather than actual performance; but they show what kind of stage spectacles presumably interested the good citizens of Nuremberg at this period. A later Nuremberg composer, Johann Löhner (1645–1705), is represented for us by some surviving arias but no complete scores.[21]

SEELEWIG, Act III, sc. 6

Ex. 60.

Staden

With the increase of Italian opera everywhere in the South, the native school found a home not in one of the courts but in the free imperial North German city of Hamburg. Here for sixty years (1678–1738) flourished with varying fortunes a public opera house, the first in Europe outside Venice, where German composers were able for a time to combine contributions from Italian and French sources with their own genius to make an original, truly national form.[22]

21 Music from Löhner's *Triumphierende Treue* (1679) and *Theseus* (1688) is reprinted in Sandberger, "Zur Geschichte der Oper in Nürnberg," AfMw I (1918) 84–107.
22 Bibliography: Lindner, *Die erste stehende deutsche Oper*; Chrysander, articles on the Hamburg opera (1678–1706) in *Allgemeine musikalische Zeitung* XII (1877)–XV (1880), *passim*; Kleefeld, "Das Orchester der Hamburger Oper," SIMG I (1899–1900) 219–89; Moller, *Cimbria literata*.

The earliest Hamburg operas show the influence of the school drama. The first one presented the story of Adam and Eve, under the title *Der erschaffene, gefallene und aufgerichtete Mensch* ("The Creation, Fall, and Redemption of Man"), with music by Schütz's pupil Johann Theile,[23] and a number of similar titles appeared in the first few years. Such material was not only traditional but was also useful in retaining the good will of the Lutheran church authorities and providing a defense of the opera against frequent attacks on the ground of its worldly and immoral character.[24] Despite sporadic opposition, secular operas soon gained the ascendancy; composers and poets began to introduce subjects from the Italian and French stages—chiefly translations or adaptations from Venetian librettists (especially Minato), but also occasionally from Corneille (*Andromeda und Perseus*, 1679), from Quinault (*Alceste*, 1680), and from Italian comedies; a few foreign operas were performed in French or Italian (Lully's *Acis et Galatée*, 1689; Colasse's *Achille et Polyxène*, 1692; Cesti's *Schiava fortunata* [in M. A. Ziani's revision?], 1693; Pallavicino's *Gerusalemme*, 1693; and others). Many of Steffani's works were presented in German translation, and a number of German composers chiefly associated with other cities or courts were represented in the Hamburg repertoire, notably J. S. Kusser (Brunswick), Johann Philipp Krieger (Weissenfels), and G. C. Schürmann (Wolfenbüttel). So far as their literary quality is concerned, the Hamburg librettos were on the average neither worse nor better than those of contemporary Italian opera, on which they were modeled. As in Venice, the machines played a conspicuous role. The leading poets were Christian Heinrich Postel (1658–1705), Friedrich Christian Bressand (*ca.* 1670–1699; also active at Brunswick), Lucas von Bostel (1649–1716), and Barthold Feind (1678–1721), the last of whom in the eighteenth century took the lead in cultivating caricature and parody.

The chief composers of the period were Nikolaus Adam Strungk,[25] the Nuremberger Johann Wolfgang Franck, and Johann Philipp

---

23 Zelle, *Johann Theile und Nikolaus Adam Strungk.*
24 An account of the quarrels on this issue at Hamburg is given by Flemming in his introduction to *Die Oper,* pp. 12–18. The entire introduction is a brilliant study of the German opera primarily from the literary standpoint.
25 Strungk (1640–1700) was active at Hamburg from 1679 to 1682, with about nine operas. Over twenty other operas of his were performed at Leipzig. See Berend, *Nicolaus Adam Strungk.*

Förtsch.[26] Of the fourteen Hamburg operas of Franck [27] (1679–1686), one is available in a modern edition: *Die drey Töchter Cecrops* ("The Three Daughters of Cecrops"), probably composed for Ansbach in 1679 and produced at Hamburg the next year in a shorter version.[28] The text of this work (by the Countess Maria Aurora von Königsmarck) is one of the comparatively few German opera poems not translated or adapted from a foreign libretto; the story is taken from Ovid (*Metamorphoses,* Book II), but its form clearly shows traces of Venetian models. Franck's music is serious in tone, as might be expected from a composer distinguished for sacred songs.[29] His arias, both with continuo alone or with orchestral accompaniment, show a fine feeling for the long-phrased, expressive melodic line (Example 61). Most of the songs are in two-part form. There is little use of the strophic structure so characteristic of Staden; on the other hand, the favorite Italian da capo hardly appears at all, and there are few coloratura passages, though Italian influence is evident in the suavity of the melodies as well as in occasional effective use of chromatic alterations. As in the Venetian operas, there are comic episodes, one of which includes a stammering song for this stock figure of the baroque opera stage (Act IV, scene 5). Folklike, cheerful strains are heard in Sylvander's "Wenn man seinen Zweck erhält" ("When one has achieved his goal") in Act V (Example 62). There are a few short duets, occurring for the most part at the end of recitative dialogue scenes. Chorus and ensemble sections are found in the prologue; in a few places in the opera itself, the chorus is used dramatically.[30] The overture (*Intrade*) is like those of the contemporary Venetian school —a slow, serious introduction, followed by a 3/4 allegro in almost

26 Förtsch (1652–1732) was also a singer and poet. He composed about a dozen operas at Hamburg from 1681 to 1690, in addition to some church music and two theoretical works. No opera scores have been preserved. One aria is reprinted in Zelle, *Johann Philipp Förtsch,* pp. 9–10.
27 Zelle, *Johann Wolfgang Franck;* Barclay Squire, "J. W. Franck in England," MA III (1911–12) 181–90; Sachs, "Die Ansbacher Hofkapelle," SIMG XI (1909–10) 105–37; Klages, *Johann Wolfgang Franck.*
28 *Das Erbe deutscher Musik, Landschaftsdenkmale, Bayern,* Bd. 2 (DTB XXXVIII), edited by Gustav Friedrich Schmidt. See also Schmidt's monograph on this opera in AfMf IV (1939) 257–316. Nine arias from Franck's *Cara Mustapha* (Hamburg, 1686) are reprinted in Zelle, *Johann Wolfgang Franck,* pp. 17–24.
29 Cf. his settings of Elmenhorst's songs in DdT XLV.
30 German opera composers on the whole used a chorus less than the French but more than the Italians; they "borrow what suits them in this matter from one nation and another" (Mattheson, *Der vollkommene Capellmeister,* p. 216).

DIE DREY TÖCHTER CECROPS, Act IV, sc. 1

Ex. 61.   Franck

Da-rum so wünsch ich bald von mir zu schei - den

durch den von Un - ge-lück ———— und Pein er -

sü — — sten Tod,   da - rum so wünsch ich bald

von mir zu schei - den   durch den von Un — ge-lück —

— und Pein er-sü — — — sten Tod.

completely homophonic style, ending with a short allargando in the
manner of the introduction. The only other orchestral pieces are the
short ritornellos, which derive their motifs from the (usually) preceding aria. Franck's recitative is more melodic, slower in tempo, and
altogether of more musical significance than the recitativo secco of

DIE DREY TÖCHTER CECROPS, Act V, sc. 4

Ex. 62.   Franck

Wenn man sei - nen Zweck er - hält, muss man sich um nich - tes
küm - mern, und da - durch sein Glück ver - schlim - mern, das doch, eh' man's meynt ver-
fällt, ———————————— das doch, eh' man's meynt, ver - fällt.

contemporary Italian opera; its style rather resembles the recitative
of German seventeenth-century church composers, half declamation
and half arioso, measured and dignified in tone, composed with great
care for both the rhythm and the expressive content of the text. Altogether, this opera shows a full-textured, stiff-rhythmed baroque
music, unmistakably Italian in inspiration but tinged with the
serious, heavy formality of Lutheran Germany.

A lighter and at the same time more cosmopolitan style was represented at Hamburg by Johann Sigismund Kusser's *Erindo* (1693).[31]

31 Kusser, or Cousser (1660–1727), had spent eight years in Paris, where he enjoyed the
friendship of Lully and acquired a taste for the French style of music. He was chapelmaster at Wolfenbüttel from 1682, director of the Hamburg opera 1694–95, worked at

The poem was a pastorale by Bressand, and the score included eight duets and ten choruses in addition to the arias and the customary ballets. There are three distinct musical idioms. One is represented by a number of short airs in dance metres, similar to contemporary French chansons, and with French names: passepied, gavotte, bourée, minuet, *branle de village,* and so on. A second type of song is the simple German lied, of which there are several beautiful examples (Example 63). More numerous and important, however, are the arias in Italian style, in da capo form, with many different combinations of concertizing instruments, in which the influence of Steffani is strikingly apparent. Kusser's work, both as composer and as impresario, was decisive in transforming Hamburg from a local school into the most important operatic center of Germany, preparing the way for Keiser and the early dramatic works of Handel.

Reinhard Keiser was the most talented of the Hamburg composers. He is reputed to have written over one hundred and twenty operas, of which, however, only twenty-five have been preserved.[32] Writing with a sureness of style and fertility of invention which remind one of Mozart, Keiser completed the process begun by Franck and Kusser, taking over a full measure of contemporary Italian and French operatic achievements but uniting them in a highly individual way with fundamental German qualities. A worldly, adventurous, impulsive, energetic personality, a musician who commanded the deepest respect of other musicians, his historical importance lay not only in his own work but also in his direct influence on Handel, whose early Hamburg success stung the older composer at one time to open

---

Stuttgart from 1698 to 1704, and in the latter part of his life was in the service of the viceroy of Ireland. His compositions include eleven operas (four for Hamburg) in addition to several orchestral suites. He was lauded by Mattheson as a model conductor (*Der vollkommene Capellmeister,* pp. 480–81). See Scholz, *Johann Sigismund Kusser.* Arias, duets, and choruses from *Erindo* are reprinted in *Das Erbe deutscher Musik, Landschaftsdenkmale, Schleswig-Holstein,* Bd. 3, edited by H. Osthoff. One aria also in SB 250.

32 There are modern reprints of: selections from *Pomona,* 1793 (Lindner, *Die erste stehende deutsche Oper* II); *Octavia,* 1705 (Händelgesellschaft edition, Supplement, Vol. 6); *Croesus,* 1710/1730 (DdT XXXVII–XXXVIII, with introduction by M. Schneider); *L'inganno fedele,* 1714 (DdT XXXVII–XXXVIII, incomplete); *Der lächerliche Printz Jodelet,* 1726 (Eitner, *Publikationen* XVIII); see also SB 268, 269 and HAM 267. Bibliography: Leichtentritt, *Reinhard Keiser in seinen Opern;* Voigt, "Reinhard Keiser," VfMw VI (1890) 151–203.

ERINDO, Act I, sc. 5

Ex. 63.   Kusser

Schö - ne Wie - sen, ed - le Fel - der,
Und ihr an - ge'- neh-men Wäl - der,

die ich je - tzund las - sen soll,
zum Be - schluss ge - habt euch wohl!

Kann ich euch gleich fort nicht se - hen durch der

Ster - nen stren-gen Neid, soll in mei - nem Her - zen

ste - hen doch eur Denk - mal je - der - zeit. - zeit.

rivalry.[33] Keiser in the course of his works traversed the road from the heavy-textured music of the late baroque to the light, thin, and playful *style galant* of the eighteenth century. His career was thus an epitome of an age of transition. It was also, unfortunately, an epitome of the declining fortunes of the Hamburg opera. The librettos of his later works (*Prinz Jodelet* may serve as an example) show an increasing tendency toward the burlesque, the trivial, the vulgar, and the indecent; unskillful poets, pandering to the lowest tastes of an ignorant public, led the way to extinction of German opera, while Keiser lacked either the will or the greatness of soul to fight against the current. Yet at its best, the music of Keiser will stand comparison with the greatest of his contemporaries—Purcell, Steffani, Scarlatti, even Handel. The influence of Lully and the French school may be traced in his choruses, ballets, and instrumental pieces. He made no fundamental changes in opera, but his work is remarkable for three features: the flexibility of form in the arias, the skill and elaborateness of the orchestral accompaniments, and the mastery of effect in lyrical and tragic scenes. The da capo does not predominate in Keiser's arias, as it did in those of his Italian contemporaries; when used, it is often modified in subtle ways which suggest the freedom of the earlier Venetian period.[34] In addition, there are many shorter types—arioso melodies, German lieder— occurring at places where the dramatic situation requires something other than the da capo pattern. On the whole, Keiser's melodic lines, although certainly not unvocal, do not show that instinctive adaptation to the qualities and limitations of the voice which is the gift of nearly all Italian composers: there are more wide intervals, angular phrases, and instrumental idioms. The characteristic mood is more energetic and aggressive than in Steffani. No composer of opera demands a higher degree of virtuosity in bravura-type arias; this is especially true in those arias with Italian texts which are often found in the midst of otherwise German operas—a peculiar practice beginning with *Claudius* in 1703 and increasing in the later works,[35] and for which parallels may be found in both France and England at

[33] Chrysander, *Händel* I, 129–34. For a list of some of Handel's thematic "borrowings" from Keiser, see the preface to the Händelgesellschaft edition of *Octavia*.
[34] See for example the aria "Hoffe noch" in *Croesus,* Act I, sc. 2.
[35] The audiences were usually provided with a libretto giving German translations of these arias.

the same period. There are some arias with simple continuo accompaniment, and on the other hand a very few in which the continuo
instruments are omitted from the orchestra. A special effect is created
in the arias *all' unisono*, where the violins or violas in unison (sometimes with an oboe added), or all the strings in octaves, concertize
with the voice, while the continuo fills in the harmonies.[36] Sometimes
the vocal line will be doubled at the unison by a solo instrument

OCTAVIA, Act II, sc.6

Ex.64.   Keiser

[36] The *unisono* was fashionable in Venetian opera around 1700; it is found also in Handel
and Scarlatti.

or by all the strings. Repeated chords or broken-chord figures are frequent in the orchestral accompaniments. The orchestral parts are particularly noteworthy in the many arias with obbligato solo instruments, which appear sometimes in novel combinations (for example, four bassoons or three oboes), producing great richness and variety of texture. Instruments are used effectively for descriptive touches, as in Octavia's aria "Wallet nicht zu laut" (Example 64).

Keiser's recitative is somewhat short breathed, cadencing frequently; it is no mere colorless declamation of text, however, but freely introduces expressive phrases and arioso passages, thus harking back to the older Venetian practice. Such phrases are sometimes used in recurring fashion to give point to the dramatic situation, for example, *Octavia,* Act I, scene 4 (Example 65). Note the descent from

OCTAVIA, Act I, sc. 4

Ex.65.   Keiser

the third at the cadence, which is characteristic). The vitality of Keiser's treatment of the text is well summed up by Mattheson: "I believe assuredly that in the time he flourished there was no composer who . . . had set words to music so richly, naturally, flowingly, attractively, or (above all) so distinctly, understandably, and eloquently." [37]

Keiser's chief opera is *Der hochmütige, gestürtzte und wieder erhabene Croesus* ("Croesus Haughty, Overthrown, and Again Raised Up"), on one of the most popular librettos of the Venetian poet Minato, translated and arranged by von Bostel.[38] The plot in its outlines is an amusing hodgepodge of impossible melodramatic situations, but it has the operatic virtue of providing many opportu-

[37] *Ehrenpforte,* p. 129.
[38] See Beare, *The German Popular Play "Atis" and the Venetian Opera.*

nities for strong expression of moods (*Affekten*) as well as for pastoral scenes in the second act. There are two versions of this work, one from 1711 and the other a revision by Keiser for a revival in 1730. The two versions show some interesting differences in detail, aside from the generally higher quality of music in the latter. For example, the ballets were omitted in 1730. In the original version, the overture was on the French pattern; in 1730, an overture of the Italian type was substituted: a fanfare-like opening movement in simple texture, with musical material and formal treatment like the first movement of an early symphony; a short adagio consisting of broken-chord figures over a sequential series of seventh chords; and a "third" movement which is nothing but a da capo repetition of the first.

Examples of Keiser's lyrical and tragic power are plentiful in *Croesus:* the spontaneous charm of Elmira's "Sobald dich nur mein Auge sah," with the clever cadence at which Atis (a mute personage in this scene) responds to her question by a gesture on the chord of resolution, is unequaled (Example 66); the pastoral solo and duet

"Mein Kätchen ist ein Mädchen" (Act II, scene 3) is in the purest German lied style; Croesus' aria "Götter, übt Barmherzigkeit," over a recurring bass motif, is filled with noble pathos (Example 67). Altogether, there is ample justification in the music for Mattheson's punning laudatory reference to the composer as "ein Kaiser des Gesangs" ("an emperor of song"). [39]

The Hamburg composers after Keiser need not detain us long. Johann Mattheson [40] is more important as a theorist and historian

---

[39] *Ehrenpforte*, p. 133.
[40] Autobiography in his *Ehrenpforte*, pp. 187–217; Meinardus, "Mattheson und seine Verdienste um die deutsche Tonkunst," in Waldersee, *Vorträge* I, No. 8, pp. 215–72; H. Schmidt, *Johann Mattheson*; Haberl, "Johann Mattheson," *Caecilien Kalender* 1885, pp. 53–60; Cannon, *Johann Mattheson*.

than as a composer. Christoph Graupner is noted more for his church works and instrumental pieces than for his operas.[41] G. C. Schürmann, Handel, and K. H. Graun all appear in the Hamburg list, but their work chiefly centered elsewhere. The change in musical style announced by Keiser's *Prinz Jodelet* and other later works was

CROESUS, Act III, sc. 12

Ex. 67.   Keiser

completed by Georg Philipp Telemann,[42] whose fabulous productivity included some forty operas for the Hamburg stage. But Telemann, so far as can be judged from the little of his music which is accessible, belongs fully to the "gallant style" of the eighteenth century. His *Pimpinone*, first performed at Hamburg in 1725,[43] is in every detail a perfect model of the Italian opera buffa, strikingly similar, both in subject and style, to the much more famous *Serva padrona* of Pergolesi, which it antedates by eight years.

The closing of the Hamburg opera in 1738 marked the end of German opera for nearly half a century; although scattered native companies held on for a few years in other cities, the creative impulse which had called them into being was long since spent. As in England, so in Germany, the earliest national opera finally fell before the all-conquering power of the eighteenth-century Italian schools.

[41] See Noack, "Die Opern von Christoph Graupner in Darmstadt," in *Bericht über den I. Musikwissenschaftlichen Kongress,* pp. 252–59.

[42] Autobiography in Mattheson's *Ehrenpforte,* pp. 354–69; Ottzen, *Telemann als Opernkomponist;* Rolland, "L'Autobiographe d'un illustre oublié," in his *Voyage musical au pays du passé,* pp. 105–52; Valentin, *Georg Philipp Telemann;* Schering, *Musikgeschichte Leipzigs* II, 437–71.

[43] Reprint in *Das Erbe deutscher Musik, Reichsdenkmale* VI. Cf. Werner, "Zum Neudruck von . . . *Pimpinone,*" AfMf I (1936) 361–65; see also SB 266.

Part 3

The Eighteenth Century

13

The Operas of Handel[1]

H ANDEL'S OPERAS DO NOT LOOM LARGE IN
the estimation of most of his present-
day admirers. Passage of time and
changes in operatic style have thrust them into ill-deserved oblivion;
modern revivals,[2] while revealing a multitude of beauties, at the
same time have raised many problems with regard to the proper
"adjustment" of these works for twentieth-century audiences. They
conform to the conventions of their time, and the music, much of
which was composed under extremely unfavorable conditions, is not
always at the highest level of inspiration. Nevertheless, the best of
Handel in this field is not only superior to anything his contemporaries were writing but also forms historically a culminating point
which makes the works of Steffani and Keiser seem almost like preliminary stages. Like Bach at Leipzig, Handel in London worked
in comparative isolation from the so-called "advanced" currents of
the day—an isolation due not to ignorance but to independence:
and though his later operas make some concessions to the fashionable
Neapolitan style, he never capitulated to it entirely and indeed
abandoned opera for oratorio when it became evident that his own
way of writing could not hold the favor of the London opera-going
public against the combined competition of the new ballad operas

1 Handel's forty known operas are printed in full score in the Händelgesellschaft edition
of the complete works (the music of two early Hamburg works—*Nero* and *Florindo
und Daphne*—is lost). In addition, the following are available in piano-vocal scores
published in Germany between 1922 and 1927: *Amadigi, Ezio, Giulio Cesare, Ottone,
Poro, Rodelinda, Serse, Tamerlano;* also *Ptolomäus (Tolomeo),* 1939. There are modern
collections of opera arias published by the Oxford University Press and by Boosey &
Co. For a list of the writings about Handel, see Coopersmith, "Thematic Index," Appendix H; and K. Taut's "Verzeichnis" (*Händel-Jahrbuch* VI, 1933). The following books
are the most important: Chrysander, *Händel,* the basic work; biographies and studies by
Leichtentritt (containing plot synopses of all the operas), Abert, Rolland, Dent, Rockstro.
Flower, and Mainwaring (the first biography); Burney, *History* (2d ed.) II, 672–835 *et
passim;* Hawkins, *History* (1776) Vol. V, Book III, chaps. 6–7; Mattheson, *Ehrenpforte,*
pp. 93–101.
2 Ten of the operas were staged in Germany during the 1920's, and there have been
other recent revivals in England and America. See articles by R. Steglich in ZfMw and
Zeitschrift für Musik, 1920–1927, *passim; idem,* "Die neue Händel-Opern-Bewegung,"
Händel-Jahrbuch I (1928) 71–158.

on the one hand and the modern Italian music of Porpora, Hasse, and Galuppi on the other.

Handel's first opera, *Almira*, was successfully performed at Hamburg in 1705. The poem, a typical Hamburg libretto with comic scenes and ballets, is a mixture of German and Italian, and the music shows many traces of Keiser's influence. A visit to Italy from 1707 to 1709 resulted in the Italian operas *Rodrigo* (Florence, 1707) and *Agrippina* (Venice, 1709), and also a number of other stage works and Italian cantatas. In 1710 Handel succeeded Steffani as chapelmaster of the court of Hanover. The maturity of style evident in *Agrippina*, where Handel showed himself fully capable of assimilating the art of the Italian masters Legrenzi and Scarlatti, came to even fuller realization in *Rinaldo* (1711), the work by which he was first introduced to London, and one of the most popular of all his operas.[3] The London visit was so successful that Handel obtained permission from his master, the elector of Hanover, to return in 1712; and this time, whether by intention or negligence, he overstayed his leave. With the sudden death of Queen Anne in 1714 the elector ascended the English throne as George I, and the famous "reconciliation" between king and composer took place shortly afterwards.[4] Between 1712 and 1741, Handel produced thirty-six operas in London, of which the most notable were *Radamisto* (1720), *Ottone* (1723), *Giulio Cesare*, *Tamerlano* (1724), and *Rodelinde* (1725). The later works (for example, *Orlando*, 1733; *Serse*, 1738, his only comic opera) show a tendency toward a more facile kind of music, influenced to some extent by the newer Italian style with which Handel had refreshed his acquaintance on a trip to Italy in 1728–29. During much of the time in London, Handel was not only composer and conductor but manager and impresario as well, with all the troubles incident to such a position. The Royal Academy of Music, which had been opened in 1720, was for a time highly successful but finally had to close its doors in 1728. A new company, founded under Handel's direction the following year, soon fell into difficulties; reorganized

---

[3] *Rinaldo* was revised in 1731; both versions are in the C.E. Vol. 58. On the original London performances see the *Spectator*, No. 5 (Tuesday, March 6, 1711) and No. 14 (Friday, March 16, 1711). Cf. Babcock, "Francis Coleman's 'Register of Operas,'" M&L XXIV (1943) 155–58.

[4] The story of the reconciliation and the composition of the "Water Music" (which has been doubted by some authorities) is told by Mainwaring in his *Memoirs* (1760) pp. 89–92.

in 1733, it was opposed by a rival group (the "Opera of the Nobility"), and both undertakings ended in complete bankruptcy four years later. A breakdown in health forced Handel to retire from active work for some months, and his last operas were produced in London between 1738 and 1741 by the Swiss impresario Heidegger. A blow to the prosperity of Italian opera in London was the fabulous success of the *Beggar's Opera* (1728), and its numerous offspring, with their satirical tendencies, evidencing a reaction in England against the "foreign growth" of which Addison had complained twenty years earlier. Wearied by the material difficulties and discouraged by the waning fortunes of opera, Handel had already begun in the 1730's to turn his attention to oratorio; *Saul* and *Israel in Egypt* were performed in 1739, and in the following years came the other masterpieces by which the composer is best known today.

Handel's operas will not be understood if they are regarded merely as examples of an outworn operatic formula, composed because such was the fashionable thing to do or the best way to make money, and unworthy of remembrance except for a few isolated arias to be sung in modern recital programs. Such views have been advanced by persons who should know better; unqualified acceptance of them can be founded only on ignorance of the nature of this type of opera, on insufficient knowledge of the scores, or on a shameful misunderstanding of Handel's character. The Italian opera of this period, as Leichtentritt has pointed out,[5] is based on the presentation of moods not mixed and modified as in "real" life, but each pure, so that a character at any given moment of expression is for the time being simply the incarnation of a certain state of mind and feeling; thus the complete picture of the character is to be obtained by the synthesis of all these expressive moments rather than (as in modern drama) by the analysis of a complex of moods expressed in a single aria or scene. For such an aesthetic, the questions of consistency and plausibility in the plot are relatively secondary: it is of little importance what a situation is or how it comes about, provided only that it gives occasion for expression of a mood. On the other hand, music, being free to devote itself to its peculiar function of unmixed emotional expression, expands freely into forms which are conditioned fundamentally by its own nature, unrestricted by any requirements

5 *Händel*, pp. 592 ff.; *Music, History, and Ideas*, pp. 150–51.

of so-called "naturalness" on the stage. Once this fundamental idea is grasped—and its difficulty is due only to the fact that it happens to be different from modern dramatic principles—then it is easy to perceive that the form of a Handel opera, with its continual succession of recitative and aria, its ubiquitous da capos, and all the other apparently artificial features, is in reality a musical structure of perfect artistic validity, whose restrictions, far from being arbitrary, exist only to assure freedom in essential matters.[6]

Handel was not a revolutionist in opera; he accepted the forms he found but filled them with his own inimitable genius. The subject matter is conventional, drawn from history (*Tolomeo*), mythology (*Admeto*), or romantic legend (*Orlando*). The chief librettists were Nicola Haym (*Radamisto, Giulio Cesare, Ottone, Tamerlano,* and others) and Paolo Rolli (*Floridante, Scipione, Deidamia,* and others); Handel set only three of Metastasio's texts: *Siroe, Poro* (from *Alessandro nell' Indie*), and *Ezio.*

The overtures are for the most part of the French type, frequently with added movements after the allegro.[7] The sinfonie, marches, and the like, which are used to introduce an act or scene or to accompany some stage business, are neither numerous nor distinctive, and the same may be said of the choruses as a general rule—the dramatic use of the chorus [8] (as in the pastorale *Acis and Galatea*) being quite exceptional. Ballets are few and of little importance.[9] The favorite ensemble form is the duet, in which Handel learned much from the example of Steffani.

The recitatives are remarkable for correct declamation and for the richness and variety of their harmonic patterns, taking full advantage of modulatory possibilities and of the expressive quality of chords such as the Neapolitan sixth and the diminished seventh to underline the dramatic situation. In the comparatively rare accompanied recitatives (see Example 69) and even occasionally in the

---

6 Cf. Abert, "Händel," in *Gesammelte Schriften,* pp. 232–63.

7 One of the best overtures is that to *Agrippina;* in *Ottone* the allegro is followed by a gavotte, and then closes with a fast movement in concerto grosso style with solo passages for two oboes.

8 It is hardly necessary to mention the supreme importance of the chorus in the oratorios of Handel, where his indebtedness to Purcell is most manifest both in technique and in dramatic treatment, as Dent has pointed out (*Foundations of English Opera,* p. 231).

9 Roth, "Händels Ballettmusiken," *Neue Musik-Zeitung* XLIX (1928) 245–52.

recitativo secco, the dramatic element is more prominent.[10] At times the recitative encloses distinct arioso passages or is combined with an aria in a free manner which relieves the prevailing regular alternation between the two styles [11] and recalls the scene-complex technique of Cavalli and other seventeenth-century composers.

With few exceptions, Handel's opera arias follow the da capo pattern, but within this framework there is inexhaustible variety.[12] The principle of musical development is the unified working out of one or two basic motives, by voice and instruments jointly, in a continuous flow, within which the various periods are organized by a clear key scheme and a systematic use of sequences. In many of the longer arias, a fairly distinct binary form may be perceived in the principal section. The middle section most often uses the same or similar thematic material, though it is usually shorter than the first section and somewhat contrasting in mood, accompaniment, and tonality. Even where at first glance the middle part of a da capo aria appears to be in complete contrast with the first, often subtle thematic relationships may be discovered. In sum, the whole formal treatment of the aria in Handel may be regarded as a climax of perfection in a style of which Steffani and Keiser were the forerunners. For details, one can only refer the student to the scores themselves, a careful study of which will be found to be both fascinating and rewarding.

The orchestra in Handel's operas is important chiefly (aside from the overtures) for its part in the accompaniment of the solo voice. Here it functions, as in Steffani and Keiser, as an equal partner with the singer. The basic instrumental group is formed by the strings and continuo, to which various instruments are frequently joined for obbligato parts (for example, solo violin, flutes, oboes, bassoons). The principle of opposition between *ripieno* and *concertino* is retained; accompaniments during the singing are entrusted to the smaller group, while the full orchestra joins in at cadences and for the ritornellos. Horns, trumpets, and trombones are used only with the chorus or for special effects. Many of the shorter arias are accompanied only by the continuo and one or two solo instruments, or by

10 E.g., *Agrippina,* Act II, sc. 4.
11 E.g., in *Poro,* Act I, sc. 9; *Serse,* Act I, sc. 2; and (on a greater scale) *Tamerlano,* Act III, sc. 10.
12 Flögel, "Studien zur Arientechnik in den Opern Händels," *Händel-Jahrbuch* II (1929) 50–156.

continuo and unisono violins. A few have accompaniment by continuo alone. In general, the cembalo parts are very sparsely indicated in the originals, since Handel usually played this instrument himself and needed notes only as a reminder. There are even occasionally some blank measures, marked only "cembalo" in the score, at which places we are to understand that the composer improvised.[13]

Handel's use of tonality is a subject which has received considerable attention in recent years. Of the importance of the tonal scheme as a formal element within the aria there can be no doubt. Leichtentritt [14] has also emphasized the composer's tendency to associate certain keys with certain moods, as F major with calm, pastoral, or idyllic sentiments, G major for arias of a cheerful character, F-sharp minor for the expression of suffering, and so on. Similar concepts were fairly widespread in the eighteenth century.[15] But an interesting problem is raised by what often looks like evidence of a tonal plan extending over not merely a single aria or scene but entire acts and even entire operas. The first act of *Amadigi* has a symmetrical tonal structure which it is difficult to believe could be accidental.[16] Many of the operas show a preference for one tonality which is established in the overture or at the beginning of the first act, returns briefly perhaps somewhere in the second, and is strongly confirmed in the finale.[17] A similar procedure is found in Keiser's *Croesus*, where the overture and first chorus are in D major, and each of the three acts ends in the same key. Purcell's *Dioclesian* seems to be in C major; his *Dido and Aeneas* is not unified in this way, though there is an evident tonal plan for each act.[18] But these observations, whatever significance they may have, are far from establishing any kind of general rule. Indeed, it seems hardly probable that we should find consistent,

13 See C.E. LVIII, 78, 117–19.
14 See "Handel's Harmonic Art," MQ XXI (1935) 208–23.
15 Cf. Borrel, "Un Paradox musicale au XVIIIe siècle," in *Mélanges de musicologie*, pp. 217–21.
16 Leichtentritt, *Händel*, p. 643; idem, *Music, History, and Ideas*, p. 145; Steglich, "Händels Opern," in Adler, *Handbuch* II, 663–67.
17 Examples: *Almira* (B-flat), *Scipione* (G), *Alessandro* (D), *Alcina* (B-flat, with instrumental pieces and chorus in G at the end, corresponding to similar forms in the same key in the second scene of Act I), *Atalanta* (D), *Silla* (G, with closing chorus in D), *Floridante* (A minor and major, closing chorus in D), *Flavio* (B-flat), *Ottone* (B-flat), *Tolomeo* (F), *Ricardo* (D), *Siroe* (F), *Ezio* (F), *Arianna* (D minor and major), *Ariodante* (G minor and major).
18 Act I: C-F; Act II: D-A; Act III: B-flat–G minor. Cf. Dent, *Foundations of English Opera*, pp. 180–83.

conscious, tonal architecture throughout many operas of this period, where the choice of key for a given number was so often dictated by external considerations, such as the limitations of wind instruments, the presence of a certain singer, the transference of whole numbers from earlier compositions, or the mood suggested by the text. Nevertheless, the question remains open; a comprehensive study of the large-scale works of the late seventeenth and early eighteenth centuries (operas, oratorios, Passions) from this point of view might lead to more definite conclusions.[19]

One trait which Handel shares with all composers of his epoch is the constant use of tone painting and musical symbolism. This ranges all the way from naïve, playful imitation of natural sounds [20] through the brilliant trumpet arias [21] to such awe-inspiring effects as Claudio's "Cade il mondo" ("Let the world fall") in *Agrippina* (Act II, scene 4) with its downward plunge through two octaves to the low bass D (Example 68). Such places show the play of fancy, now whimsical,

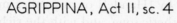

AGRIPPINA, Act II, sc. 4

Ex.68.   Handel

Ca-de il mon - do,

now earnest, on the surface of baroque musical forms, but they are no mere externals. All these picturesque or conventional figures are part of the music itself, inseparable from the structure they adorn— so much so that though, as in the London performance of *Rinaldo*, live birds may be released to flutter about the stage while flutes twitter in the orchestra, and the unreflecting person may hear only that the music is imitating the birds, yet the musician feels that this is not so, but rather that it is the birds who are imitating the music. Handel's art, like that of Bach, has the power of glorifying the apparently

19 Cf. Schmidt, *Die frühdeutsche Oper* II, 315–17; Lorenz, after an exhaustive examination of A. Scarlatti's operas, could find no evidence of a consistently applied tonal plan, though in certain works (especially among the earlier works) there are traces of it (*Scarlatti's Jugendoper*, p. 177 *et passim*). Gerber (*Der Operntypus Johann Adolf Hasses*, pp. 39–42) finds no evidence whatever in Hasse.
20 E.g., *Rinaldo*, Act I, sc. 6, "Augelletti, che cantate."
21 E.g., *Radamisto*, Act I, sc. 3, "Stragi, morti."

trivial by showing it to be a manifestation of the eternal; as the rhythm of walking feet becomes in Bach's chorale prelude the rhythm of the soul's march to Heaven, so in Handel the song of the birds is a magic window opening on a glimpse of pastoral Eden.

This universal quality is, of course, most apparent in those arias which are pure expression of moods, with few or no picturesque external details. The number and variety of these arias is so great, and the power of capturing the most subtle nuances of feeling so astounding, that one is tempted to believe there is no emotion of which humanity is capable that has not found musical expression somewhere in Handel's operas. Referring the reader once more to the only adequate source of information, the scores themselves, let us call attention to a half-dozen examples: (1) the famous "Ombra mai fù" (*Serse,* Act I, scene 1), known universally (in transcriptions, alas) as the "Largo from Xerxes"; (2) the nobly mournful "Lascio ch'io pianga" (*Rinaldo,* Act II, scene 4); (3) the deeply moving "Cara sposa" (*Rinaldo,* Act I, scene 7), "one of the best airs in that style that was ever composed by [Handel] or any other master; and by many degrees the most pathetic song, and with the richest accompaniment, which had been then heard in England"; [22] (4) a whole class of arias of the siciliano type, adopted by Handel from the example of Scarlatti and other Italian composers, elegant in contour, elegiac in feeling, moving in langorous 12/8 metre (example: "Con saggio tuo consiglio," from *Agrippina,* Act I, scene 1); (5) the idyllic arias, musical pastorales, and landscapes of tranquil charm, filled with sunlight (example: "Se in un fiorito ameno prato" from *Giulio Cesare,* Act II, scene 2); (6) the light, playful, "Un cenno leggiadretto" (*Serse,* Act I, scene 15), representative of a less numerous class of arias appropriate to the comic style; in a similar category may be mentioned also the bass songs of Polyphemus in *Acis and Galatea.*

A fine example of the energetic, passionate, brilliantly displayful aria is Radamisto's "Perfido" (*Radamisto,* revised version, Act I, scene 6), with its recurring rhythmic figure (♪ ♫) curiously prophetic of the motif of the Scherzo in Beethoven's Ninth Symphony. Coloratura passages such as we find in this aria are frequent in Handel; often they were composed to show off a particular singer, and Handel's mastery of his craft is evident in the brilliant virtuosity of this vocal

22 Burney, *History* II, 674.

writing. Yet he seldom employed such passages solely for display; they spring naturally from the tension of the music or from some obvious image in the text and are strictly organized within the musical structure. Occasionally a melismatic passage occurs which recalls the softer style of Steffani.[23]

Surely one of the most beautiful of Handel's arias is Cleopatra's "Se pietà di me non senti" (*Giulio Cesare,* Act II, scene 8), which is preceded by an accompanied recitative (notable for its wide range of modulations) and introduced by an orchestral ritornello, from which the characteristic "drooping" motif of the obbligato violin is derived (Example 69 pages 176–77).

It must be emphasized that in every case the realization not only of mood but also of personality comes from the music. Caesar in Haym's libretto is a stage hero in the manner of the early eighteenth century; only through Handel's music does his character receive those qualities which make him a truly dramatic figure. Caesar and Cleopatra, Radamisto and Zenobia, Bajazet (in *Tamerlano*), and others of Handel's dramatic creations are universal, ideal types of humanity, moving and thinking on a vast scale, the analogue in opera of the great tragic personages of Corneille. This quality is more than the reflection of a certain musical style or a consummate technique; it is the direct emanation of Handel's own spirit, expressed in music with an immediacy that has no parallel outside Beethoven. It is the incarnation of a great soul. If his characters suffer, the music gives full, eloquent expression to their sorrows—but it never whines; there is not a note in it of self-pity. We are moved by the spectacle of suffering, but our compassion is mingled with admiration at suffering so nobly endured, with pride that we ourselves belong to a species capable of such heroism.

[23] See Example 69, end; also the beautiful closing cadence of the first part of "Forte e lieto" (*Tamerlano,* Act I, sc. 1).

GIULIO CESARE, Act II, sc. 8

Ex.69.   Handel

(*Example 69 continued*)

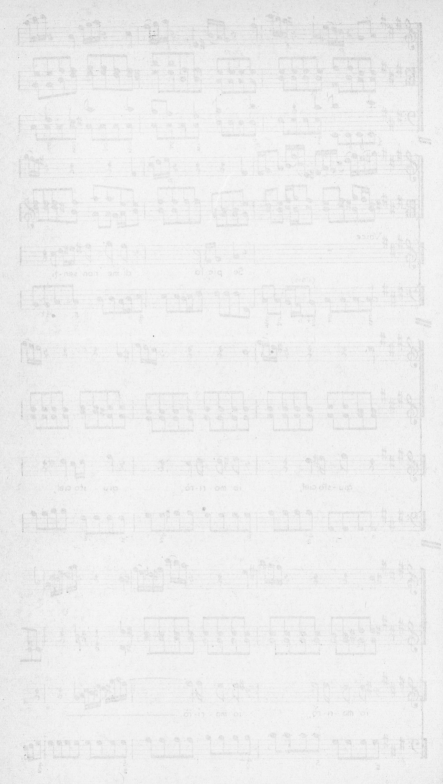

14

Neapolitan Opera

TYPE AND PERFORMANCE

WE HAVE SEEN HOW, FROM ITS EARLIEST beginnings at Florence and Rome, Italian opera in the course of the seventeenth century passed out of the experimental stage. Radiating from Venice with its public opera houses, it established itself on a firm basis of public interest and support which made it by the end of the century the most widespread and most popular of all musical forms. We have also seen how, in the course of this development, three important national schools of opera rose outside Italy. One of these, the French, maintained its existence and individuality; the English school died with Purcell, while the German gradually lost its identity by absorption into the Italian style. At the beginning of the eighteenth century, therefore, it is possible practically to perceive one single operatic type which dominated all western Europe except France—a type which, despite variations in different countries and composers, showed certain fundamental common features everywhere. From the standpoint of the libretto, we identify this type as the opera of moods or *Affects*.[1] Its intention was to present a series of discrete expressive moments, each devoted exclusively to a particular mood; in order to call forth the necessary variety and intensity of moods, situations were contrived with little attention to unity or consistency of plot, and with corresponding indifference to realism either in subject matter or in details of dramatic development. The form in which this intention was realized was one which we may call the "aria opera"; musically speaking, that is to say, it consisted of a series of arias separated by passages of recitative. Throughout the latter half of the seventeenth century the tendency had been more and more to differentiate these two styles and, in general, to concentrate the musical interest more and more on the aria. Ensembles,

[1] Kretzschmar, "Allgemeines und Besonderes zur Affektenlehre," JMP XVIII (1911) 63–77; XIX (1912) 65–78.

ballets, and instrumental pieces were of only incidental importance.

Now within this general type of opera two distinct directions were perceptible in the late seventeenth century. These have been designated by German historians as respectively the "aristocratic" and the "democratic" type of opera. The distinction involves many criteria, but with respect to musical style it is simply this: the aristocratic opera was polyphonic, the democratic was homophonic. The former admitted the orchestra as an equal partner with the voice, aiming at a contrapuntal kind of bass and often interweaving the vocal line with one or more strands of instrumental melody; the latter tended to relegate the orchestra to a position of simple accompaniment, with a bass whose function was entirely harmonic, concentrating all musical attention on the singer. Mattheson remarks on the contrast in this respect between his own time and the seventeenth century; [2] in the earlier period "hardly anyone gave a thought to melody, but everything was centered simply on harmony." Quantz laments that, though most Italian composers of the present day (that is, 1752) are talented, they start writing operas before they have learned the rules of musical composition; that they do not take time to ground themselves properly, and that they work too fast.[3] To these criticisms, with their implications of frivolousness and lack of counterpoint in Italy, may be opposed, as representing the Italian viewpoint, Galuppi's classic definition of good music: "Vaghezza, chiarezza, e buona modulazione," which Dr. Burney translates "beauty, clearness, and good modulation," [4] though there are really no words in English capable of conveying the exact sense of the original.

The polyphonic opera was represented by Legrenzi, Steffani, and Keiser; the homophonic tendencies became decisive in the works of the later Venetians, notably Pollarolo and Albinoni. The division took place, as might be expected, between northern and southern composers, the north emphasizing counterpoint and complexity, the south melody and simplicity. Perhaps the clearest way to illustrate the distinction is to consider the contrasting types of operatic overture which are associated with each of the two schools. The older, aristocratic type was the French *ouverture,* first outlined by the early Venetians, given definitive form by Lully, and adopted in its essen-

---

[2] *Ehrenpforte.* p. 93.   [3] *Versuch,* XVIII. Hauptstück, par. 63.
[4] *The Present State of Music in France and Italy,* p. 177.

tial features by Steffani, Keiser, and Handel; the newer, democratic type was the Italian *sinfonia*, first established by Scarlatti about 1700, and gradually ousting the French overture everywhere as the eighteenth century went on. The difference between these two kinds of overture is usually stated in terms of the order of movements—the French beginning (and often also ending) in slow tempo, whereas the Italian began fast, had a slow movement in the middle, and an allegro or presto at the end. This distinction, however, is superficial; the essential difference between the two was a matter of musical texture. The French overture was polyphonic: it derived from the past; it was one of the highest manifestations of instrumental form in the late thorough-bass period. The Italian overture was homophonic: it looked to the future; it represented those principles of structure, thematic material, and methods of motivic development which were to lead eventually to the style of the classical symphony.[5]

Both the polyphonic and the homophonic opera existed in the early part of the eighteenth century, but the former was obviously on the decline, at least so far as popularity was concerned. The general change in the language of music which characterized the middle of the century, and which led through the rococo or gallant style to the later classical idiom, was evident in opera as everywhere else. The growing taste for simplicity, ease, lightness of texture, tuneful melody, and facile ornamentation brought to the fore a certain type of opera, Italian in origin but international in practice, generally known as "Neapolitan." The term is traditional but somewhat misleading. Its origin is due to the fact that most of the composers (including Alessandro Scarlatti) who were first associated with this kind of opera lived and worked at Naples. The Neapolitan school in the eighteenth century held the same sort of dominant position in the world of opera that the Venetian school had held in the seventeenth century. The word "Neapolitan" has been applied indiscriminately by many writers to operas as far apart in style as those of Handel on the one hand and Pergolesi on the other, thus obscuring really important differences.[6] It would seem better to restrict it specifically to that

[5] On the early history of the Italian overture cf. Heuss, *Die venetianischen Opern-Sinfonien*, pp. 88–92. Wellesz's designation of Cavalli's overture to *Ercole* (*Cavalli*, pp. 53–54) as an early example of the Italian type seems to rest on questionable assumptions.
[6] Cf. Abert, "Wort und Ton in der Musik des 18. Jahrhunderts," in his *Gesammelte Schriften*, pp. 173–231.

style of opera (developed largely at Naples) which was the logical outcome of the democratic, homophonic tendency observable in Italy in the late seventeenth century, and which gradually replaced the conservative, polyphonic, aristocratic opera inherited from an earlier period. This limitation of meaning will explain why we have dealt with Handel and Fux in the section devoted to baroque opera rather than in the present chapter; although their operas have many features in common with the Neapolitans, fundamentally they belong to the earlier, aristocratic type. Needless to say, the distinction (like all classifications in the arts) is not absolute. The works of Scarlatti, for example, have many characteristics of the older style; but since he is, after all, a Neapolitan composer, and since his work is commonly regarded as being the starting point for the eighteenth-century Neapolitan schools, he finds his place appropriately in connection with them.

One other division within the general field of Neapolitan opera must be clarified, namely that between the serious and the comic opera. The latter is, at least in the beginning, a quite distinct form and will be treated later. At present we are concerned exclusively with the Neapolitan *opera seria*, the characteristic type of the age, cultivated in all countries by imported Italian composers and singers as well as by natives imitating the Italian style, maintaining itself throughout the eighteenth century, and continuing its influence far into the nineteenth. We shall attempt first to give a general idea of this operatic type and, if possible, to dispose of certain misconceptions which prevail regarding it; afterwards, we shall study the music of particular composers. The latter undertaking, however, is hampered by the fact that so few scores are available. Almost none of this music was printed; hundreds of manuscripts have been lost, and hundreds of others exist only in rare copies; only an infinitesimal fraction of it is accessible in modern editions.

In view of the chorus of criticism which modern writers have directed against the Neapolitan opera, it is interesting to note that its practical foundation was a reform of the seventeenth-century libretto. The two poets chiefly associated with this reform were Apostolo Zeno (1668–1750)[7] and Pietro Metastasio (1698–1782).

---

[7] Zeno was born and died in Venice but passed most of his life at Vienna, where he was for a time court poet (1718–1729) and historian. He wrote sixty-six librettos for operas

Zeno, under the influence of the French dramatists, favored historical subject matter and sought to purge the opera of erratically motivated plots, reliance on supernatural interventions, machines, irrelevant comic episodes, and the bombastic declamation which had reigned in the seventeenth century.[8] This movement was brought to fulfillment by Metastasio,[9] the guiding genius of eighteenth-century opera and a literary figure of such influence that his compatriots seriously compared him with Homer and Dante. The modern reader is apt to find Metastasio's plays mannered and artificial, elegant rather than powerful; his characters seem more like eighteenth-century courtiers than ancient Romans; sentimental love pervades all the action, and the stock figure of the magnanimous tyrant is often in evidence. Yet in spite of all this, if one is willing to allow for the dramatic conventions of the time, some of his works may still be read with pleasure. His achievement consisted in the creation of a consistent dramatic structure conforming to the rationalistic ideals of the period, but which incorporated lyrical elements suited for musical setting in such a way as to form an organic whole. As an example of the Metastasian libretto at its best, let us take *Attilio regolo* (1740). Attilio, having been taken captive by the Carthaginians, is offered his freedom if he will use his influence with the Roman Senate to obtain certain advantages for Carthage. Under parole to return if unsuccessful, he is permitted to go to Rome; but once there, he urges the Senate to stand firm, scorning to purchase his own life by betraying the interests of his country. Resisting the entreaties of his friends and family, of the Senate (who are willing to make national sacrifices

and oratorios. See Negri, *Vita di Apostolo Zeno;* Fehr, *Apostolo Zeno;* Wotquenne, *Alphabetisches Verzeichnis der Stücke in Versen aus den dramatischen Werken von Zeno, Metastasio und Goldoni.*

[8] Metastasio, letter to Fabroni, December 7, 1767; in Burney, *Memoirs* III, 19. See also Wellesz, Introduction to Fux's *Costanza e fortezza,* DTOe XXXVII, xiii.

[9] Metastasio's real name was Trapassi. On Zeno's recommendation he became court poet at Vienna in 1730 and lived in that city for the rest of his life. He wrote twenty-seven drammi per musica, besides many other dramatic and semidramatic pieces. There were over a thousand settings of his operas in the eighteenth century, certain ones having been composed as many as seventy times. There are numerous editions of his works. See Burney, *Memoirs of the Life and Writings of the Abate Metastasio;* De Calzabigi, *Dissertazione;* Mattei, *Memorie;* Stendhal, *Vies de Haydn, de Mozart et de Métastase;* Callegari, "Il melodramma e Pietro Metastasio," RMI XXVI (1919) 518–44: XXVII (1920) 31–59, 458–76; Rolland, "Métastase, précurseur de Gluck," in his *Voyage musical,* pp. 153–70, and also in MM VIII, No. 4 (1912) 1–10; Della Corte, "Appunti sull' estetica musicale di Pietro Metastasio," RMI XXVIII (1921) 94–119; Gerber, *Der Operntypus Hasses,* chap. I.

to save him), and of the entire populace, he voluntarily boards the ship which will take him back to captivity and death.[10]

Now we may well ask where, in such a drama, there is any place for lyricism. The answer is to be found in the peculiar construction of the scenes. A typical scene consists of two distinct parts: first, dramatic action (in recitative); and second, expression of sentiments by the chief actor (in an aria).[11] In the first part of the scene, the actor is a character in the drama, carrying on dialogue with other actors; in the second part, he is a person expressing his emotions or conveying some general sentiments or reflections appropriate to the current situation—not to his fellows on the stage but to the audience. While this goes on, the progress of the drama usually comes to a complete stop. Consequently, the play is made up of regularly alternating periods of movement and repose, the former representing the rights of the drama (recitative) and the latter the rights of the music (aria); the former occupying the larger part of the scene in the libretto, but the latter far exceeding it in the score, by reason of the extended musical structure of the aria being built on (usually) only two stanzas of four lines each. There results from this scheme an endlessly repeated pattern of tension and release, each recitative building up an emotional situation which finds outlet in the following aria.[12] This is the classical compromise operatic form, in which drama and music each yield certain rights and thereby find a means of living together compatibly. It permits free development of both elements within conventional limits. So long as these limits were tolerable (as they were to the early and middle eighteenth century), the form was found satisfactory; it lost favor only when other ideals of drama began to prevail. Moreover, the apparent stiffness of the scheme was mitigated in Metastasio's operas by the skill and naturalness of the transition from recitative to aria, by the musical quality of the language in the recitative, and by the interesting variety of verse forms in the aria.

One paramount fact emerges from this view of eighteenth-century operatic form, namely the central position of the aria as a musical

---

10 The tragic ending was an innovation in opera with Metastasio. It is found also in his *Didone* and the original version of *Catone in Utica,* but in none of his other works.

11 The placing of the aria at the end of the scene in Zeno and Metastasio was different from the seventeenth-century Italian practice, and German operas even in the eighteenth century retained the older custom of ending a scene with recitative.

12 "The recitative loads the gun, the aria fires it" (Flemming, *Die Oper,* p. 58). A somewhat similar pattern is seen in the verse and chorus of a modern popular song.

unit. Musically speaking, that is to say, an opera is a succession of arias; other elements—recitatives, ensembles, instrumental numbers —are nothing but background. From this fact stem certain consequences which, in their totality, explain all the essential features of the Neapolitan opera: (1) the variety and degree of stylization of aria types, (2) a corresponding looseness of structure in the opera as a whole, and (3) the importance of the singer not only as an interpreter but also as a creative partner of the composer.

ARIA TYPES.—Eighteenth-century writers on opera classify arias into certain well-defined types, having distinct characteristics. Thus the Englishman John Brown mentions five traditional varieties:

"*Aria cantabile,*—by pre-eminence so called, as if it alone were Song: And, indeed, it is the only kind of song which gives the singer an opportunity of displaying at once, and in the highest degree, all his powers. . . . The proper subjects for this Air are sentiments of tenderness.

"*Aria di portamento* . . . chiefly composed of long notes, such as the singer can dwell on, and have, thereby, an opportunity of more effectually displaying the beauties, and calling forth the powers of his voice. . . . The subjects proper to this Air are sentiments of dignity.

"*Aria di mezzo carattere* . . . a species of Air, which, though expressive neither of the dignity of this last, nor of the pathos of the former, is, however, serious and pleasing.

"*Aria parlante,*—speaking Air, is that which . . . admits neither of long notes in the composition, nor of many ornaments in the execution. The rapidity of motion of this Air is proportioned to the violence of the passion which is expressed by it. This species of Air goes sometimes by the name of *aria di nota e parola,* and likewise of *aria agitata.* . . .

"*Aria di bravura, aria di agilita,*—is that which is composed *chiefly,* indeed, too often, *merely* to indulge the singer in the display of certain powers in the execution, particularly extraordinary agility or compass of voice." [13]

A less scientific but more vivid tabulation is given by the Frenchman Charles de Brosses, writing from Rome about 1740:

"The Italians . . . have airs of great agitation, full of music and

[13] *Letters on the Italian Opera* (2d ed.) pp. 36–39.

harmony, for brilliant voices; others are of a pleasant sound and charming outlines, for delicate and supple voices; still others are passionate, tender, affecting, truly following the natural expression of emotions, strong or full of feeling for stage effect and for bringing out the best points of the actor. The 'agitato' airs are those presenting pictures of storms, tempests, torrents, thunder-claps, a lion pursued by hunters, a war-horse hearing the sound of the trumpet, the terror of a silent night, etc.—all images quite appropriate to music, but out of place in tragedy. [This is the so-called "comparison aria," the stock-in-trade of eighteenth-century opera.] This kind of air devoted to large effects is almost always accompanied by wind instruments—oboes, trumpets, and horns—which make an excellent effect, especially in airs having to do with storms at sea. . . .

"Airs of the second kind are madrigals, pretty little songs with ingenious and delicate ideas or comparisons drawn from pleasant objects, such as zephyrs, birds, murmuring waves, country life, etc. . . .

"As to airs of the third kind, which express only feeling, Metastasio takes great care to place them at the most lively and interesting point of his drama, and to connect them closely with the subject. The musician then does not seek for embellishments or passage-work, but tries simply to portray the feeling, whatever it may be, with all his power. . . . I should also place in this class the airs of spectres and visions, to which the music lends a surprising power." [14]

It goes without saying that these and similar classifications cannot always be applied in all their details to the actual music; but their very existence is of interest as showing the high degree of organization—of stylization—which the aria reached in this period. There were other conventions as well, notably the one which decreed that practically every aria must be in the da capo form. Even the order and distribution of the different types were prescribed: every performer was to have at least one aria in each act, but no one might have two arias in succession; no aria could be followed immediately by another of the same type, even though performed by a different singer; the subordinate singers must have fewer and less important arias than the stars; and so on.[15] At first glance, the whole system

---

[14] *Lettres familières sur l'Italie* (1931) II, 348–51. (Author's translation.)

[15] Hogarth, *Memoirs of the Opera* II, chap. 3; Goldoni, *Mémoires,* chap. 28. Cf. also the letter of the Abate Giuseppe Riva to Muratori in 1725, on the requirements for a London libretto, quoted in Streatfeild, "Handel, Rolli," MQ III (1917) 433.

seems artificial to the point of absurdity; later in the century, in fact, it was attacked on this very ground. Yet, granted the postulates of early eighteenth-century opera aesthetic, it was quite logical, and justification could be found for every rule. (Moreover, the composers did not hesitate to break the rules if it suited their purposes to do so.) It was one of the secrets of Metastasio's success that he could construct a drama which met these rigid requirements without being too obviously constrained by them.

THE "PASTICCIO."—A second consequence of overconcentration on the aria was a certain looseness of structure in the opera as a whole. With few exceptions, the composer's responsibility for formal unity was limited to each single number.[16] Apart from the libretto, there was nothing to bind these into a larger musical unit except the general requirements as to variety and the custom of placing the two most important arias at the end of each of the first two acts. To use a familiar comparison, the arias were not like figures in a painting, each fulfilling a certain role in the composition and each in some measure conditioned by the others; rather they were like a row of statues in a hall, symmetrically arranged but lacking any closer bond of aesthetic union. The conception corresponded to the baroque ideal of dynamics, where the various degrees of loudness or softness were distinct, without transitions of crescendo or diminuendo; or to forms such as the sonata and concerto, in which each movement was a complete, thematically independent unit. The arias were like Leibniz's monads, each closed off from the others, and all held together only by the "pre-established harmony" of the libretto. Thus their order could be changed, new numbers added, or others taken away, without doing real violence to the musical plan of the opera as a whole—though, needless to say, the drama might suffer. Composers therefore freely substituted new arias for old in revivals of their works, or for performances with a different cast. A composer at Rome, for example, who had orders to revise a Venetian opera to suit the taste of the Roman singers and public, would have no compunction about replacing some of the original composer's arias with some of his own, perhaps taken from an earlier work where they had been sung to different words. Indeed, it was exceptional for an opera to be given in exactly the same form in two different cities.

[16] Exception to this statement must probably be made in the case of Handel and perhaps a few other composers.

This patching of new materials on old operatic garments, if carried far enough, resulted in a kind of work known as a *pasticcio*—literally, a "pie," but perhaps translatable more expressively for modern readers as a "hash." There were two distinct kinds of pasticcio. One is well illustrated by the opera *Muzio Scevola* (London, 1721), the first act of which was composed by Mattei, the second by G. B. Bononcini, and the third by Handel.[17] But the typical pasticcio was the result of a more haphazard process; it was an opera which had migrated from city to city, undergoing patchwork and alteration at every stage, until it might one day arrive at London (its usual final home) with a libretto in which Metastasio shared honors with "Zeno, Goldoni, Stampiglia, Rossi, and other librettists," while "Gluck, Ciampi, Galuppi, Cocchi, Jommelli, Latilla, Handel and several more might be pasted together" in the same musical score.[18]

THE SINGERS.—A third effect—which operated at the same time as a cause—of the importance of the aria was the glorification of the singer. The virtuoso singer was to the eighteenth century what the virtuoso pianist was to the nineteenth, or the virtuoso conductor to the twentieth. The operatic songbirds of the Neapolitan age have been so often and so unsparingly condemned that it seems worth while to try to correct this judgment by quoting a passage from Vernon Lee's *Studies of the Eighteenth Century in Italy,* a book naïve in many of its musical opinions and perhaps too uncritical in its enthusiasm for everything Italian, but which nevertheless states the case for the singer with sympathy and insight:

"The singer was a much more important personage in the musical system of the eighteenth century than he is now-a-days. He was not merely one of the wheels of the mechanism, he was its main pivot. For in a nation so practically, spontaneously musical as the Italian, the desire to sing preceded the existence of what could be sung: performers were not called into existence because men wished to hear such and such a composition, but the composition was produced because men wished to sing. The singers were therefore not trained with a view to executing any peculiar sort of music, but the music was composed to suit the powers of the singers. Thus, ever since the

---

17 This kind of pasticcio is comparable to the French ballets of the seventeenth century, which were commonly the work of several different composers.
18 Cf. Sonneck, "Ciampi's *Bertoldo*," SIMG XII (1911) 525–64.

beginning of the seventeenth century, when music first left the church and the palace for the theatre, composition and vocal performance had developed simultaneously, narrowly linked together; composers always learning first of all to sing, and singers always finishing their studies with that of composition; Scarlatti and Porpora teaching great singers, Stradella and Pistocchi forming great composers; the two branches . . . acting and reacting on each other so as to become perfectly homogeneous and equal. . . .

"The singer, therefore, was neither a fiddle for other men to play upon, nor a musical box wound up by mechanism. He was an individual voice, an individual mind, developed to the utmost; a perfectly balanced organization; and to him was confided the work of embodying the composer's ideas, of moulding matter to suit the thought, of adapting the thought to suit the matter, of giving real existence to the form which existed only as an abstraction in the composer's mind. The full responsibility of this work rested on him; the fullest liberty of action was therefore given him to execute it. Music, according to the notions of the eighteenth century, was no more the mere written score than a plan on white paper would have seemed architecture to the Greeks. Music was to be the result of the combination of the abstract written note with the concrete voice, of the ideal thought of the composer with the individuality of the performer. The composer was to give only the general, the abstract; while all that depended upon individual differences, and material peculiarities, was given up to the singer. The composer gave the unchangeable, the big notes, constituting the essential, immutable form, expressing the stable, unvarying character; the singer added the small notes, which filled up and perfected that part of the form which depended on the physical material, which expressed the minutely subtle, ever-changing mood. In short, while the composer represented the typical, the singer represented the individual." [19]

We read much about abuses on the part of eighteenth-century opera singers, but we are seldom told why these abuses were tolerated, being tacitly allowed to infer that audiences and composers were either blind to the evil or too supine to resent it. This was not the case. The abuses were recognized, but they were endured because they seemed to be inseparable from the system out of which they

[19] Pages 117–18.

grew and because, on the whole, people liked the system. The principle of absolute dominance of the aria in the form entailed the absolute dominance of the singer in performance; and in their submission to this principle audiences, composers, and poets alike allowed excesses on the part of the singers which would not have been endured in another age. Only rarely was even an autocrat like Handel (who had the incidental advantage of combining the offices of composer and manager in one person) able to control them, and then only by an extraordinary combination of tact, patience, humor, personal force, and even threats of physical violence.[20] But usually the singers reigned supreme. Metastasio might insist all he pleased that poetry should be the "dictator" in opera, and complain of the mutilation of his dramas by "those ignorant and vain vocal heroes and heroines, who having substituted the imitation of flageolets and nightingales to human affections, render the Italian stage a national disgrace" [21]—but he was powerless to alter a situation which his own works had contributed so much to bring about.

A lively, though unquestionably exaggerated, picture of the singers may be drawn from the critical and satirical writings of the seventeenth and early eighteenth centuries.[22] The most famous satire was Marcello's *Teatro alla moda* ("The Fashionable Theatre"), which first appeared in 1720.[23] Marcello's work is in the form of ironically worded counsels to everyone connected with opera, from the poets down to the stagehands and singing teachers, and gives a living detailed picture of the operatic practices of the time. Thus, he says, the composer "will hurry or slow down the pace of an aria, according to the caprice of the singers, and will conceal the displeasure which their insolence causes him by the reflection that his reputation, his

---

20 Cf. Flower, *Handel,* p. 144.   21 Burney, *Memoirs* II, 325; III, 43.

22 Salvator Rosa, *La musica;* Adimari, *Satira quarta;* Muratori, *Della perfetta poesia,* Lib. III, Cap. V (refutation of Muratori is undertaken by Mattheson in his *Neueste Untersuchung der Singspiele*); memoirs of Casanova, Da Ponte, Goldoni, and others; Jommelli's comic opera *La critica,* 1766 (Abert, *Jommelli,* p. 426); and similar works (cf. Abert, *Mozart* I, 415, note). See also "Die Oper und ihre Literatur bis 1752," in Goldschmidt, *Musikästhetik des 18. Jahrhunderts,* pp. 272–87; Cametti, "Critiche e satire," RMI IX (1902) 1–35; Frati, "Satire," RMI XXII (1915) 560–66; Monnier, *Venise au XVIIIe siècle,* pp. 48 ff.

23 Modern editions in Italian (E. Fondi, 1913; A. D'Angeli, 1927), French (E. David, 1890), and German (A. Einstein, 1917). Marcello's *intreccio* (lit. "intrigue") *Arianna,* a mythological and allegorical opera in two acts (1727), is published as Vol. IV of Chilesotti's *Biblioteca di rarità musicali* (1886). This work was performed (for the first time?) at Venice in 1913.

solvency, and all his interest are in their hands.[24] . . . . The director
will see that all the best songs go to the *prima donna,* and if it becomes necessary to shorten the opera he will never allow her arias
to be cut, but rather other entire scenes." [25] If a singer "has a scene
with another actor, whom he is supposed to address when singing
an air, he will take care to pay no attention to him, but will bow to
the spectators in the loges, smile at the orchestra and the other players, in order that the audience may clearly understand that he is the
Signor Alipi Forconi, Musico, and not the Prince Zoroaster, whom
he is representing." [26]

"All the while the ritornello of his air is being played the singer
should walk about the stage, take snuff, complain to his friends [27]
that he is in bad voice, that he has a cold, etc., and while singing his
aria he shall take care to remember that at the cadence he may
pause as long as he pleases, and make runs, decorations, and ornaments according to his fancy; during which time the leader of the
orchestra shall leave his place at the harpsichord, take a pinch of
snuff, and wait until it shall please the singer to finish. The latter
shall take breath several times before finally coming to a close on a
trill, which he will be sure to sing as rapidly as possible from the
beginning, without preparing it by placing his voice properly, and
all the time using the highest notes of which he is capable." [28]

The cadenzas and ornaments to which Marcello here alludes were
carefully prepared beforehand: "If [a singer] have a role in a new
opera, she will at the first possible moment take all her arias (which
in order to save time she has had copied without the bass part) to
her Maestro *Crica* so that he may write in the passages, the variations,
the beautiful ornaments, etc.—and Maestro Crica, without knowing
the first thing about the intentions of the composer either with regard
to the tempo of the arias, or the bass, or the instrumentation, will
write below them in the empty spaces of the bass staff everything he can
think of, and in very great quantity, so that the *Virtuosa* may be able
to sing her song in a different way at every performance . . . and if
her variations have nothing in common with the bass, with the violins which are to play in unison with her, or with the concertizing

---

[24] *Il teatro alla moda,* pp. 19–20.   [25] *Ibid.,* p. 23.   [26] *Ibid.,* p. 26.
[27] This is an allusion to the eighteenth-century custom of seating spectators on the stage.
[28] Marcello, *Il teatro,* pp. 26–27.

instruments, even if they are not in the same key, that will be of no consequence, since it is understood that the modern opera director is both deaf and dumb." [29]

The more serious critics viewed with alarm the overemphasis on vocal virtuosity, as attracting attention at the expense of both drama and music. Thus Metastasio writes, "The singers of the present times wholly forget, that their business is to imitate the speech of man, with numbers and harmony: on the contrary, they believe themselves more perfect, in proportion as their performance is remote from human nature. . . . When they have played their Symphony with the throat, they believe they have fulfilled all the duties of their art. Hence the audience keep their hearts in the most perfect tranquillity, and expect the performers merely to tickle their ears"—to which Dr. Burney adds, "If, forty years ago, Metastasio speaks with so much indignation of the abuse of execution, which has been increasing ever since, what would he say now?" [30]

There can be no doubt that the technique of singing reached a level in the eighteenth century which has never since been equaled. In the nature of things, it is difficult to find out much about the details of this art in specific cases, for the singers' greatest displays of skill were improvised, and consequently no record remains in the scores. In general, however, it may be said that there were two related practices, one having to do with ornamentation of the given melodic line (coloratura), and the other with the insertion of improvised passages at the cadences (cadenzas).

Ornamentation of the melodic line by solo singers was a custom inherited from the Renaissance and carried on through the whole baroque period.[31] Kept within reasonable bounds by the serious dramatic ideals of the early Venetian opera composers and by the contrapuntal texture of the scores, it rose to greater prominence in the latter part of the seventeenth century in Italy, when the aria came into its commanding position and the accompaniment suffered a corresponding lapse into a mere harmonic support for the soloist. The climax was reached in the eighteenth century, the age of the great Italian singing schools. Particularly on the da capo repetition

---

[29] *Ibid.*, pp. 39, 41.   [30] Burney, *Memoirs* II, 135–36.

[31] For a general survey of this subject see Haas, *Aufführungspraxis;* see also Aldrich, "The Principal Agréments," which gives full references to the sources; and Goldschmidt, *Die Lehre von der vokalen Ornamentik.*

of the first part of an aria the singer was expected to show his full powers: "Among the Things worthy of Consideration, the first to be taken Notice of, is the Manner in which all *Airs* divided into three Parts are to be sung. In the first they require nothing but the simplest Ornaments, of a good Taste and few, that the Composition may remain simple, plain, and pure; in the second they expect, that to this Purity some artful Graces be added, by which the Judicious may hear, that the Ability of the Singer is greater; and, in repeating the *Air,* he that does not vary it for the better, is no great Master." [32]

In the rapid bravura arias, opportunity for improvised ornamentation was less than in those arias in slower tempo. The well-known "Largo" from Handel's *Serse* would probably have been ornamented by the singer as shown in Example 70.[33]

The practice of improvising cadenzas likewise originated in the sixteenth-century solo song, and was revived in the eighteenth-century opera. Examples are found in Scarlatti. The natural place for a cadenza was on the 6–4 chord of an important cadence, just as we find it commonly in the concertos of the classical period.[34] Inserted in arias, where they served par excellence for the display of the singers' powers, the cadenzas were often extended to ridiculous lengths.[35] Tosi criticizes them in these words: "Every *Air* has (at least) three *Cadences,* that are all three final. Generally speaking, the Study of the Singers of the present Times consists in terminating the *Cadence* of the first Part with an overflowing of *Passages* and *Divisions* at Pleasure, and the *Orchestre* waits; in that of the second the Dose is encreased, and the *Orchestre* grows tired; but on the last Cadence, the Throat is set a going, like a Weather-cock in a Whirlwind, and the *Orchestre* yawns." [36] Examples of cadences sung by Farinelli in Giacomelli's *Merope* (Venice, 1734) have been preserved in a manuscript dedi-

[32] Tosi, *Observations on the Florid Song,* pp. 93–94.

[33] For examples of elaborate bravura arias, see R. Broschi's "Son qual nave" from *Artaxerxes* (London, 1735) in Burney, *History* II, 833–37, and Pergolesi's [?] "Tremende oscure atroci" from *Meraspe* (perf. London, 1742) in OHM IV, 221–32. For the realization of the ornamented melodic line in Example 70 I am indebted to Dr. Putnam Aldrich.

[34] Cf. Tovey, "The Classical Concerto," in *Essays in Musical Analysis* III, 3–27.

[35] Ange Goudar quotes a burlesque "request" presented to the manager of the Paris opera "par les eunuques italiennes" which includes the statement "Une cadenza, pour être dans les regles, doit durer sept minutes & trente-six seconds, le tout sans prendre respiration; car il faut que toute cette tirade soit d'une seule haleine, l'acteur en dût crever sur la scene" (*Le Brigandage de la musique italienne,* 1777, p. 127).

[36] Tosi, *Florid Song,* pp. 128–29.

cated to the Empress Maria Theresa and now in the Vienna library;
one of them well illustrates the remarks of Tosi quoted above (Example 71).

Ex.70.

SERSE, Act I, sc.1

Handel

All this outburst of virtuosity was closely bound up with the peculiar seventeenth- and eighteenth-century Italian institution of the castrato.[37] There are many references to the presence of eunuchs among the singers of Italian and German chapels of the sixteenth century; they are found at Florence in 1534, in the Papal Chapel at

Cadenza in Giacomelli's MEROPE

Ex. 71.   Farinelli

[37] Haböck, *Die Kastraten und ihre Gesangskunst;* Raguenet, *Paralele des Italiens et des François;* Villeneuve, *Lettre sur le méchanisme de l'opéra italien* (1756); Lalande, *Voyage d'un françois en Italie* VI, chap. XVI. Rogers, "The Male Soprano," MQ V (1919) 413–25.

Rome by 1562. By the end of the seventeenth century they were a usual feature in Italian churches, despite periodic pronouncements by the Popes against the custom. They came into opera first in Monteverdi's *Orfeo;* the Roman and Venetian operas made use of them to the almost total exclusion of women singers. Castrato singers flourished especially during the period 1650–1750. Both male and female roles in the operas were entrusted to them. Their popularity began to decline in the latter part of the eighteenth century, and the last Italian opera castrato died in 1861.[38] Their extraordinary vogue was due in part to the remarkable shortage of women singers after the first few years of the seventeenth century, coupled with the fact that for a long time (especially at Rome) women were forbidden to appear on the public stage; [39] even where women did take part in opera, as at Paris (there were no castrati in the French opera), they were generally regarded as morally outside the pale of respectable society. But the castrati held their ground even in the eighteenth century, a period when there was no dearth of first-rate women singers (such as Faustina Bordoni, wife of the composer Hasse), by reason of sheer superiority in their art. Educated from early childhood in the famous "conservatories" of the Italian cities, their long and thorough training gave them a solid grounding in musicianship in addition to developing a really miraculous vocal technique. Their voices (known as *voci bianchi,* literally "white voices") were more powerful and flexible, if less sweet and expressive, than those of women, and the quality often remained unimpaired after as many as forty years of singing. So great were the rewards of a successful career that even the slightest sign of a promising voice was often sufficient to induce hopeful parents to offer a boy for emasculation, with the inevitable result that (according to Dr. Burney) in every great town of Italy could be found numbers of these pathetic creatures "without any voice at all, or at least without one sufficient to compensate for such a loss." [40]

Of all the Italian castrati, the most renowned was Carlo Broschi (1703–1782), known as Farinelli, who had a legendary career in Eu-

38 Parolari, "Giambattista Velluti," RMI XXXIX (1932) 263–98. Cf. also Hogarth, *Memoirs* II, 306–13.
39 Cf. Lalande, *Voyage en Italie* V, 179.
40 *The Present State of Music in France and Italy,* p. 303. See also Lalande, *Voyage* VI, chap. 16 *passim.*

rope. Brilliantly successful as a singer in every country, the friend of princes and emperors, for twenty-four years the confidant of two successive Spanish kings and virtually prime minister of Spain, the hero of popular tales, and the subject of an opera, he was a figure in the public imagination of the eighteenth century comparable only to Liszt or Paganini in the nineteenth.[41]

COMPOSERS AND AUDIENCES.—The amount of music written by eighteenth-century opera composers testifies to the popularity of this entertainment.[42] A tabulation of forty leading composers of the period shows nearly two thousand works, or an average of about fifty operas apiece. The sum total of the production of all composers would, of course, be much greater. One reason for this was that audiences insisted on new music each season, though they welcomed the old familiar librettos year after year.[43] Then, too, the writing out of the score was not the time-consuming process that it is in modern times, since so much was left to be improvised. The score was really little more than a memorandum of the composer's intentions, to be filled in by the performers. A composer commonly completed a score in a month or six weeks, and received for it a sum amounting to $100 or $150, plus the price of the first copy of the arias—in manuscript usually, though favorite airs of popular operas were often published in London. Once the first copy was sold, the composer's income from his work ended, for there was no copyright protection for him.

Contemporary audiences, far from regarding the opera as a serious dramatic spectacle, looked upon it merely as an amusement. De Brosses reports that the performances in Rome began at eight or nine in the evening and lasted to midnight. Everyone of any consequence had a box, which was a social gathering place for friends. "The pleasure these people take in music and the theatre is more evidenced by their presence than by the attention they bestow on the performance." After the first few times, no one listened at all, except to a few favorite songs. The boxes were comfortably furnished and lighted so that their occupants could indulge in cards and other games.

---

[41] For an account of Farinelli, see Burney, *Present State of Music in France and Italy*, pp. 202–17. See also Monaldi, *Cantanti evirati celebri;* Haböck, *Die Gesangskunst der Kastraten.*

[42] Cf. Monnier, *Venise au XVIIIe siècle*, chap. VI; Grosley, *New Observations on Italy, passim;* Villeneuve, *Lettre sur le méchanisme de l'opéra italien.*

[43] Lalande, *Voyage* VI, 352.

"Chess is marvellously well adapted to filling in the monotony of
the recitatives, and the arias are equally good for interrupting a too
assiduous concentration on chess." [44] Dr. Burney mentions the faro
tables at the Milan opera; [45] at Venice, where the pit was usually
filled with gondoliers and workmen, "there is a constant noise of people laughing, drinking, and joking, while sellers of baked goods and
fruit cry their wares aloud from box to box"; [46] at Florence it was
the custom to serve hot suppers in the boxes during the performance.[47]

Some understanding of the circumstances under which these operas
were performed will explain why we of today often fail to see what
there was in the music to arouse such enthusiasm on the part of the
audiences. We must realize that those things which were the very
life of the performance were just the things which could never be
written in the score—the marvellous, constantly varied embellishments by the singers, the glamour of famous names, the intoxication
of the lights and scenery, above all the gay, careless society of the
eighteenth century, the game of chess during the recitatives, and
the gabble of conversation, hushed only for the favorite aria and the
following rapturous applause.

OTHER ELEMENTS OF NEAPOLITAN OPERA.—Although the arias were
the chief musical feature, there were a few other elements. The
chorus was limited to occasional interjections, or at most to short
recurring phrases which could be memorized without difficulty.
Hardly more important practically was the overture, since the composer knew there would be too much noise in the house for it to be
heard. The orchestra [48] in accompaniments, however, was carefully
managed, so as to support the singer without obscuring him. The first
violins frequently played in unison with the voice—or rather, they
played the simple written version of the melody which the singer
was ornamenting. Ensembles were few; in the early part of the century there was usually no more than a perfunctory closing number for
all the singers, but later this feature took on more importance, largely

44 De Brosses, *Lettres . . . sur l'Italie* II, 336 *et passim*. But see also Lalande, *Voyage* V,
chap. X.
45 *Present State of Music in France and Italy*, pp. 81–82.
46 Maier, *Beschreibung von Venedig* II, 284.
47 Doran, *'Mann' and Manners at the Court of Florence.*
48 See diagram of the Dresden Opera orchestra under Hasse in Rousseau, *Dictionnaire de
musique*, art. "Orchestre."

under the influence of the comic opera ensembles. Duets were more common, though even here the writing was more often in dialogue than in strictly ensemble form.

There were two distinct types of recitative, both inherited from the seventeenth century. The recitativo secco (literally, "dry recitative") was so called because it was accompanied only by the continuo instruments.[49] Its function was simply to carry on the action in dialogue; as a rule it received very little serious attention either from the audience or from the composer, though on occasion (particularly in Scarlatti) it might still show some traces of the earlier seventeenth-century care for dramatic emphasis, harmonic variety, and even some formal organization. In sharp contrast to this type was the *recitativo accompagnato* or *stromentato* ("accompanied recitative"), so called because it was accompanied either by the strings or the full orchestra in addition to the continuo. These recitatives were reserved for the two or three most dramatic points in the opera, for monologues expressing strong emotion at the climaxes of the action. The voice, declaiming in flexible, varied, and expressive phrases, alternated with orchestral outbursts of chords, tremolando figures, or rhythmic motifs. Sudden changes of mood, abrupt modulations, were featured. The essential function of the orchestra, indeed, was not so much to accompany the singer as to express, during the pauses of his song, the emotions which words were insufficient to convey—to suggest, in combination with the attitudes and gestures of the actor, those further depths of feeling which only music and movement, transcending the too definite ideas and images of a text, could adequately render.[50] The close union between words and music, together with the natural freedom of form, gave these places great dramatic power, and all contemporaries speak of them with enthusiasm. They were almost the only relief from the monotony of the recitativo secco on the one hand and the strict formality of the aria on the other, and it is significant that the accompanied recitative was especially cultivated by the later Neapolitan composers Hasse, Graun, and Terradellas, above all by Jommelli, Gluck, and Traetta, who were striving to break down the rigidity of the old operatic framework.

[49] On the performance of the accompaniment in the eighteenth century, see Schneider, "Die Begleitung des Secco-Rezitativs um 1750," *Gluck-Jahrbuch* III (1917) 88–107.
[50] Cf. Rousseau, "Récitatif obligé," in his *Dictionnaire de musique.*

THE COMPOSERS

"Music is the special triumph of the Neapolitans. It seems as if in that country the membranes of the ear-drum are more taut, more harmonious, more sonorous than elsewhere in Europe. The whole nation sings; gesture, tone of voice, rhythm of syllables, the very conversation—all breathe music and harmony. Thus Naples is the principal source of Italian music, of great composers and excellent operas; it is there that Corelli, Vinci, Rinaldo [di Capua], Jommelli, Durante (learned in harmony above all the rest), Leo, Pergolesi, Galuppi, Perez, Terradeglias, and so many other famous composers have brought forth their masterpieces."[51]

The high esteem in which the Neapolitan school was held, as shown by these words of Lalande, rested on a long tradition of achievement. Naples, the largest city in Italy in the seventeenth century and the seat of a royal court, was quick to take an interest in opera.[52] Although regular seasons did not begin before 1668, there are notices of isolated performances as early as 1654. The first Neapolitan composer of importance was Francesco Provenzale,[53] whose music shows a fine quality of expressiveness and a subtle use of chromatic harmony comparable to the best Italian style of the late seventeenth century (Example 72; see also HAM 222).

The real founder of Neapolitan opera, and the composer who is

IL SCHIAVO DI SUA MOGLIE, Act I, sc.8

Ex. 72.   Provenzale

(Strings and continuo)

[51] Lalande, *Voyage* VI, 345.

[52] Florimo, *La scuola musicale di Napoli* (the basic work, a thoroughgoing study of the Neapolitan conservatories, teachers, composers, and singers to the middle of the nineteenth century); B. Croce, *I teatri di Napoli*; Roberti, "La musica in Italia nel secolo XVIII," RMI VII (1900) 698–729; VIII (1901) 519–59; Grosley, *New Observations on Italy* (1769); Schletterer, "Die Opernhäuser Neapels," MfMg XIV (1882) 175–81, 183–89; XV (1883) 12–19.

[53] *Ca.* 1630–1704. Little is known about Provenzale's life. Some of the music from his eight operas is reprinted in the Supplement of Rolland's *Histoire de l'opéra en Europe*. See Goldschmidt, "Francesco Provenzale als Dramatiker," SIMG VII (1905–1906) 608–34.

generally regarded as the fountainhead of eighteenth-century Italian music, is Alessandro Scarlatti.[54] The historical importance of Scarlatti lies in the fact that his works embody the transition from the seventeenth-century style, as founded and developed by the Venetian composers, to that of the Neapolitans. His eminent position and the lack of sufficient knowledge about his contemporaries have sometimes led to his being made the scapegoat for the alleged shortcomings of the whole Neapolitan school. As a matter of fact, Scarlatti began much in the style of Legrenzi and Stradella; their influence is apparent in his first operas performed at Rome previous to 1684. The small forms, the free mixture of recitative and aria passages, and the use of the ground-bass are all characteristics of the Venetian opera of this period. It was during his first stay at Naples (1684–1702) that Scarlatti began to develop more individual characteristics. The pres-

[54] Scarlatti (1659–1725) claimed to have composed 115 works for the stage. Of these, 36 are known to exist complete today in full score; 16 others are preserved in part, and 19 more are known only through librettos (Lorenz, *Alessandro Scarlatti's Jugendoper* I, 6–38). *La Rosaura* (1690) is published (incomplete) as Vol. XIV of Eitner's *Publikationen*. There are 135 arias and many more short excerpts from the early operas in Lorenz, *Jugendoper* II; see also SB 258, 259, HAM 259. Dent, "The Operas of Alessandro Scarlatti," SIMG IV (1902–1903) 143–56; *idem, Alessandro Scarlatti;* Lorenz, *Alessandro Scarlatti's Jugendoper;* van den Borren, *Alessandro Scarlatti et l'esthétique de l'opéra napolitain;* Prota-Giurleo, *Alessandro Scarlatti.* According to Lorenz, a full bibliography of works relating to Scarlatti is given in Strüver, "Die cantata da camera Alessandro Scarlattis."

ence of comic characters (as in the Venetian librettos) led to his custom of ending each of the first two acts of a serious opera with a comic
duet in lively style, clearly the ancestor of the later opera buffa finale.
By 1700 Scarlatti had definitely established the new Italian overture
with its quick opening movement, short slow interlude, and closing
movement in two-part form with marked dance rhythms.[55] During
this period also there is evident a growing differentiation between
Scarlatti's cantata and opera styles. *La Rosaura* (1690) has many details which suggest the cantata. Most of the arias are of small dimensions, and the harmonies are often intricate and subtle. The recitatives, carefully composed, are far from mere stereotypes, and there
are many scenes in which recitative, arioso, and aria passages are
freely intermingled. The music shows to perfection that quality of
pleasure in sensuous effect which is such a strong characteristic of
the Italian composers. The moods range from tender melancholy
to charming playfulness, occasionally touching vehement grief on
the one hand or outright broad comedy on the other. The whole
is suffused with an aristocratic elegance, avoidance of excess, and
perfect understanding of the powers of the solo voice for dramatic
expression. The variety of the music makes it impossible to give a
single typical illustration, but Climene's arias "Non far mi più
languir" (Act II, scene 6) and "Son si dolce le catene" (Act I, scene 2)
are good examples of the simple, lighthearted Italian melody so
often found in Scarlatti, as well as of his constant habit of repeating
nearly every phrase, as though to make sure that the audience should
not lose anything of its beauty. A masterpiece of dramatic characterization is the first scene of Act II in which Rosaura laments the
betrayal of her love, while her servant Lesbo attempts to divert her
by singing a little ballad about "La bella Margarita" (Example 73).

LA ROSAURA, Act II, sc.1

Ex.73.   Scarlatti

---

[55] See for example the overture to *Eraclea* (1700), reprinted in Haas, *Musik des Barocks*,
pp. 207–208.

But Rosaura's emotions are too strong; she breaks out in reproaches against her false lover (Example 74), which are interrupted at the moment of greatest excitement by a sudden return to the thought

LA ROSAURA, Act II, sc. 1

Ex. 74.
concitato   Scarlatti

of her overwhelming grief. The entrance of the strings at this point is of striking effect (Example 75).

In contrast to *La Rosaura*, *La Statira* (performed at Rome in the same year) is "a very fine example of the grand manner"; [56] some of the arias are on a broad scale, impressive in their rhythms, showy and effective in a masterful way, with copious use of coloratura passages after an opening phrase in long notes with wide harmonic

56 Dent, *Scarlatti*, p. 63.

intervals.[57] This eminently theatrical style is further exemplified in
Eraclea (1700), *La principessa fedele* (Naples, 1710), and *Tigrane*
(Naples, 1715), the last-named work being also remarkable for its
comic scenes. In contrast to this distinctly popularizing tendency is
Mitridate Eupatore, composed for Venice in 1707. This work, with

LA ROSAURA, Act II, sc.1

Ex. 75.   Scarlatti

its dignified, serious, deeply expressive music, shows Scarlatti as a
worthy companion to the great Venetian composers of the baroque
period. The recitative "O Mitridate mio" from Act IV is a remarkable example of passionate declamation, supported by skillful chromatic harmonies with sudden, though always appropriate, modula-

[57] See for example the opening measures of the aria "Resista chi può," OHM III, 385–86.

tions (Example 76). The aria in B minor which follows ("Cara tomba") is marked by many suspensions between the voice and concertizing solo violin; in its mood of mingled pathos and resignation it is similar to many of the lyrical effusions of Steffani and equally beautiful.[58]

MITRIDATE EUPATORE, Act IV

Ex. 76.   Scarlatti

O va - na spe - me! o rot - ta fe - de! o bre - ve, lu-sin-ghie-ra, fu - nes-ta, em-pia al-le-grez-za! Da chi più cer-co ai - u - to, o più con - for - to? o in cie - lo o in ma-re o in ter-ra, o ne - gli ab-bis-si? Ahi! ahi! Mi-tri-da-te è mor-to!

The popular or folk element in Scarlatti is represented by the realistic dialogue in the comic scenes of his serious works, as well

58 Both recitative and aria are reprinted (incomplete) in Dent, *Scarlatti*, pp. 109–12.

as his one comic opera, *Il trionfo dell'onore* (1718). In addition, there are many tunes which in their strongly characteristic rhythms and melodic turns are clearly of popular derivation. Perhaps the most common of these are the rather insinuating, languid, minor melodies in 12/8 metre to which the name "siciliano" [59] is generally applied, though it is notable that Scarlatti himself restricts this term to those airs in which the flatted supertonic is a prominent feature. This note and its harmonization by means of the Neapolitan sixth are not confined to the siciliano-type airs but form a conspicuous mannerism of Scarlatti's style.[60]

The later operas show an increasing emphasis on vocal ensembles (especially in *Griselda*, 1721) and a growth in the size and importance of the orchestra. In *Tigrane* the horns are introduced for the first time. The orchestra of *Telemaco* (1718) is large, and in this work there is not a single aria with simple continuo accompaniment. The beginning of the overture to *Griselda* shows evidence not only of a clearly homophonic style in orchestral writing but also of the typical later classical division between strings and winds according to function—the strings having arpeggios and tremolandos while oboes and trumpets reinforce with chords on the strong beats.[61] An even more significant development in the later works is the accompanied recitative, which evinces a growing recognition of the essential feature of this style, namely antiphonal dialogue effect between voice and orchestra, in free declamatory rhythms and irregularly recurring motifs. An interesting example of the influence of the accompanied recitative on the aria itself is found in Act II of *Griselda*, where the aria "Figlio! Tiranno," although accompanied throughout in steady rhythm of eighths or sixteenths, is nevertheless so broken and interjectional, with its phrases alternately echoed by the strings or interrupted by rushing scale passages, as to give almost the impression of being a recitative—an effective, original, and highly dramatic treatment.[62]

On the whole, and judging as well as we are able from the ex-

---

[59] This type of melody is not new in Scarlatti. One is found in Monteverdi's *Orfeo*, and there are many in P. A. Ziani's *Galatea* (1660). Their predecessors may be found in the slower, 3/2 metre, barcarole arias typical of Steffani and Pallavicino (cf. DdT LV, Introduction, p. ix).

[60] Dent, *Scarlatti*, pp. 146–47.   [61] Music in Dent, *Scarlatti*, p. 171.

[62] See music in Dent, *Scarlatti*, pp. 165–67.

tremely small amount of Scarlatti's opera music (especially of his later period) which is accessible, it may be said that if he did not actually initiate the movement toward the eighteenth-century Neapolitan style, at least he was himself carried along by the same powerful currents which brought other composers even further on that road. Professor Dent points out how Scarlatti's writing gradually evolved from the serious, contrapuntal idiom of the seventeenth century toward the homophonic, sharply accentuated, obviously melodic style of the preclassical period. Like his contemporaries, he came to use the da capo pattern almost exclusively in his arias. Yet there is much evidence to show that he deplored the extremes toward which music, especially in Italy, was then tending. That evidence is found not only in the scores themselves but also in the attitude of Scarlatti's noble patrons (who were forever urging him to write down to the level of his audience) and in the significant fact that for the last four years of his life, during which he resided at Naples, he wrote no operas, but only cantatas and church music. His fate, like Bach's, was to be outmoded before his death, "a great man . . . forgotten by his own generation." [63] His influence, except on Handel and Hasse, was only partial and indirect. His own happy combination of strength and sweetness, of passion and humor, was not to be heard again in music until the time of Mozart.

Of all the Neapolitan composers of Scarlatti's time and the generation following, whose music delighted the ears of early eighteenth-century audiences, and about whose relative merits eighteenth-century writers debated so earnestly, scarcely one today is more than a name in the history books. Leonardo Vinci [64] is remembered as having advanced the style of accompanied recitative and for having expanded the form of the da capo aria (which in Scarlatti is always a comparatively short piece) by introducing a contrasting theme within the principal section. His style was vigorous and energetic,

[63] Dent, *Scarlatti*, p. 193. A striking illustration of the contrast between Scarlatti's later style and the fashionable "new" manner may be seen in the respective settings (1721, 1723) of Zeno's *Griselda* by Scarlatti and Pietro Torri (*ca.* 1665–1737), an Italian resident at Munich. See Junker, "Zwei 'Griselda'-Opern" in *Festschrift . . . Sandberger,* pp. 51–64. (Additional opera music by Torri in DTB XIX–XX.)

[64] Vinci (1690–1730) was an official of the Royal Chapel at Naples. He is said to have written forty operas, of which over half survive in manuscript. He was distinguished in the field of comic as well as serious opera. Cf. Silva, *Illustri musici calabresi;* Dent, "Notes on Leonardo Vinci," MA IV (1912–13) 193–201.

concentrating dramatic expression in melodic phrases of striking rhythms. The avoidance of contrapuntal texture and the tendency toward an easy, popular melodic style evident in Vinci are less strong in the music of Francesco Feo (*ca.* 1685–*ca.* 1745) and Leonardo Leo,[65] both of whom were distinguished in church music as well as opera. Leo's important contributions to the stage were his comic works, which were immensely popular. One other Neapolitan of this period deserves mention here, not as a composer of operas but as a distinguished church musician and teacher of many of the most famous opera composers of the eighteenth century: Francesco Durante (1684–1755), whose pupils included Vinci, Pergolesi, Terradellas, Jommelli, Traëtta, Piccini, Sacchini, and Paisiello. The more serious, learned art of the eighteenth-century Roman school, represented in Naples by such masters as Leo and Durante, served in some measure to counteract the extreme tendencies of some of the Neapolitan opera composers and preserved a tradition which became increasingly important as the century went on.

The archrepresentative of the florid, virtuoso singer's opera among the early Neapolitans was Niccolo Porpora,[66] a man of no particular distinction as a dramatic composer (though he wrote over fifty operas) but perhaps the greatest singing teacher who ever lived, the master of Farinelli, Caffarelli, Mingotti, and many another famous eighteenth-century singer, who wrote arias so full of vocal pyrotechnics that Dr. Burney was once moved to remark, "I never saw Music in which shakes were so lavished; Porpora seems to have composed the air *Contrasto assai* [from his opera *Temistocle*], in a shivering fit." [67]

The most famous of the early Neapolitan composers after Scarlatti was Pergolesi, now remembered chiefly as the composer of the *Stabat Mater* and the comic intermezzo *La serva padrona* [68] but distinguished in opera particularly for his setting of Metastasio's *Olim-*

65 Leo (1694–1744) studied at Naples under Provenzale and Nicola Fago. He became first organist of the Royal Chapel on the death of Scarlatti in 1725. See article by Dent in *Grove's Dictionary* and titles listed under Cav. G. Leo in bibliography. An aria is printed in the musical supplement of Marx, *Gluck und die Oper*, No. 3.
66 Porpora (1686–1767) had a motley career, being active at various times in Vienna, Dresden (where for a time he was a serious rival of Hasse), and London (in opposition to Handel), as well as his native Naples. In addition to operas he wrote church music, cantatas, and a large amount of instrumental chamber music. See Villarose, *Memorie dei compositori;* Di Giacomo, *Il conservatorio dei poveri; idem, Il conservatorio di Sant' Onofrio;* Fassini, *Il melodramma italiano a Londra.*
67 *History* II, 842.   68 See below, pp. 248 ff.

piade (Rome, 1735), one of the favorite librettos of the eighteenth century. Pergolesi may be called the Bellini of the Neapolitan school; his serious music is characterized by "tenderness of sentiment. a noble, attractive, enthusiastic feeling, an innocent, touching, childlike quality." [69] His serious dramatic works, despite their merit (or, perhaps, because of it), procured him no popular success among his compatriots.

Outside the city of Naples itself, the Neapolitan style made its way rapidly during the early part of the eighteenth century. Venetian opera composers of this period [70] include Francesco Gasparini (1668–1727), Antonio Vivaldi, Giovanni Porta (*ca.* 1690–1755),[71] and Giovanni Battista Pescetti (*ca.* 1704–1766), none of whose dramatic music is available for study. A number of well-known composers were associated at various times with the Austrian imperial court, including the brothers Giovanni Battista Bononcini (Handel's London rival) [72] and Marc Antonio Bononcini; [73] the latter's *Trionfo di Camilla* ("The Triumph of Camilla"), first performed at Naples in 1696 and at Vienna in the following year, was one of the most popular scores of the early eighteenth century, being heard in various Italian cities as late as 1719 and holding the stage in London four seasons (1706–1709) for a total of sixty-four performances in English.[74] Still another Italian composer who made his way to London was Attilio Ariosti,[75] who was associated with Handel and Bononcini

69 Kretzschmar, *Geschichte der Oper*, p. 172.
70 Wiel, *I teatri musicali di Venezia nel settecento*.
71 Westermann, "Giovanni Porta als Opernkomponist" (Munich dissertation, unpublished).
72 G. B. Bononcini (1672–*ca.* 1750) was court composer at Vienna from 1700 to 1711, divided his time between Vienna and Italy during the next decade, and was in London from about 1720 to 1732; he apparently then lived for some time in France, returned for a while to Vienna, and passed the closing years of his life at Venice. Besides operas (of which over thirty are preserved) he wrote many instrumental pieces, church works, and cantatas.
73 M. A. Bononcini (1675–1726), whose biography is obscure, wrote at least twenty operas between 1690 and 1723, which were performed in Naples, Vienna, and London and which won the admiration of Padre Martini. See Valdrighi, *I Bononcini da Modena*.
74 Burney, *History* II, 663.
75 Ariosti (1666–*ca.* 1740) was a Servite monk who, under dispensation, gave up his religious profession to devote himself to music. His wandering career, so characteristic of the time, brought him to many different European cities. He was conductor and composer at Berlin from 1697 to 1703. He wrote about twenty operas, also cantatas, oratorios, and some "lessons" for the viola d'amore, on which instrument he was a performer. See Ebert, *Attilio Ariosti in Berlin;* Frati, "Attilio Ottavio Ariosti," RMI XXXIII (1926) 551–57.

in the Royal Academy of Music (1720–1728); Burney reprints an aria from his *Vespasiano* (London, 1724) "as an exhibition of all the furbelows, flounces, and other vocal fopperies of the times." [76]

At Vienna, the principal operatic successors of Fux were Antonio Caldara [77] and Francesco Conti,[78] in whose music the change from baroque to Neapolitan traits is manifest, though the Vienna opera always retained somewhat of the formal, contrapuntal style, the magnificence of staging, and the participation of chorus and ballet which we have already seen so conspicuously in Fux's *Costanza e fortezza*.[79]

One of the most popular composers of the Neapolitan school in the first half of the eighteenth century was not an Italian by birth, but a German, Johann Adolph Hasse of Dresden.[80] A tenor singer, a pupil in composition of Porpora and Scarlatti, Hasse's style was so thoroughly Italianized that he became the leading representative of the characteristically Neapolitan type of opera. He was called by Italians "il caro Sassone" ("the beloved Saxon") and acclaimed by public and critics alike in all countries as the greatest living composer of vocal music.[81] He was the favorite musician of Metastasio and set all of that poet's librettos, many of them two or even three and four times. There is undoubtedly much in his music to justify criticism that he was merely another composer gifted with facility and understanding of the voice but without real dramatic insight and completely uninterested in the instrumental parts of his operas; nevertheless, such

[76] *History* II, 726.

[77] Caldara (1670–1736), a Venetian by birth and a pupil of Legrenzi, became vice-chapelmaster at Vienna under Fux in 1716. He wrote eighty-seven operas (none of which has been published) but is said to be superior in his church and instrumental music and shorter lyrical songs. See Gmeyner, "Die Opern M. A. Caldaras."

[78] Conti (1681–1732), born at Florence, was a celebrated performer on the theorbo. He became court theorbist at Vienna in 1701 and court composer in 1713. He wrote sixteen operas, besides other dramatic works, of which *Don Chisciotte* (1719) was the most successful. See a minuet from his *Griselda* (1725) in SB 274.

[79] See Lady Mary Wortley Montagu, *Letters* (3d ed.) I, 239, Sept. 14 (O.S.), 1716.

[80] Hasse (1699–1783) is of considerable significance as a symphonic and church composer and was one of the most important creators of the early classical style. His activity as a dramatic composer extended from 1721 to 1771. Not one of his eighty or more operas is available in a modern edition (*Alcide al Bivio* was published in piano score in 1763). Short examples of his music may be found in some of the music histories (Bücken, *Rokoko und Klassik*, pp. 108–109; Adler, *Handbuch* II, 724). See also Gerber, *Der Operntypus Johann Adolf Hasses*; Mennicke, *Hasse und die Gebrüder Graun als Symphoniker*; idem, "Johann Adolph Hasse," SIMG V (1903–1904) 230–44, 469–75; Zeller, *Das Rezitativo accompagnato in den Opern Johann Adolf Hasses*; Burney, *The Present State of Music in Germany* I, *passim*.

[81] Burney, *Present State of Music in Germany* I, 234.

criticism must be tempered by remembrance of the operatic ideals of his time and of the peculiar qualities of the Metastasian librettos, which required only that a score should be filled with agreeable and singable music. This requirement Hasse completely understood and fulfilled, untroubled by any revolutionary impulses. His arias are models of that musical feeling which dissolves and transmutes everything into beautiful, elegant, and sensitive melody—superficial perhaps, but with a surface of such perfection that it seems almost captious to demand more (Example 77). Yet even within this style, Hasse

DIDONE ABBANDONATA, Act II, sc.10

Ex.77.   Hasse

is not without certain traits here and there which foreshadow a change in operatic ideals. His arias, though still in the prevailing da capo form, are well constructed, with a feeling for real development rather than mere repetition of the themes. In the later works, even the da capo form itself becomes more plastic. His respect for the integrity of the drama is in marked contrast to the carelessness of the earlier Neapolitans in this regard; he is no slave to the conventional pattern of regular alternation of arias and secco recitatives but will on occasion freely intermingle passages in different styles as the situation demands. His handling of the orchestra is above the general level of opera composers of his time. Moreover, and particularly in the numerous accompanied recitatives for which he was so celebrated, he sometimes shows a depth and power of expression which may be attributable to his Germanic origin (as German historians are fond of pointing out), but which in any case are not qualities for which Neapolitan composers of the early eighteenth century, except Scarlatti, were distinguished.

The typical da capo aria as found at its highest point of development in Hasse has the following scheme:

A (first four-line stanza): ritornello I; first section, cadencing on the dominant or relative major; ritornello II; second section, in the nature of a development of the material of the first, with extended coloratura passages, modulating back to the tonic and sometimes with a return of the theme of the first section; cadenza; ritornello III.

B (second four-line stanza): In one section, shorter than A, in a related key, and with material either (1) continuing and developing that of A, or (2) contrasting with A; ending with cadenza, then ritornello IV (usually = ritornello I).

A da capo (usually without ritornello I), with additional improvised coloraturas and a longer cadenza.

The above scheme is frequently shortened in later composers (for example, Di Majo) by omitting a portion of part A in the da capo; or by setting both stanzas in a one-movement ABA′ form.

Another Italianized German, contemporary with Hasse, was Karl Heinrich Graun,[82] the official composer of Frederick the Great of

---

[82] Graun (1704–1759) is remembered today chiefly as the composer of the popular oratorio *Der Tod Jesu* ("The Death of Jesus"). He began his career in opera as a tenor at Brunswick, where he became acquainted with the operas of Lotti and other Venetians. He took part in the performance of Fux's *Costanza e fortezza* at Prague in 1723. In 1740 he became chapelmaster to Frederick the Great and was entrusted with the direction of the new opera house at Berlin, for which city he composed most of his thirty-six operas,

Prussia. This monarch, who supervised with the closest interest all musical productions at his court, was enamoured of Hasse's operas, and as a natural consequence Graun's music for the Berlin opera was similar in style to that of his famous compatriot. The libretto of Graun's *Montezuma*, written by King Frederick himself in French prose and translated into Italian verse by the court poet, is remarkable as being one of the comparatively rare modern subjects in eighteenth-century opera—the conquest of Mexico by Cortez.[83] On the strength of this background the ballets even make some attempt at local color, though with rather feeble results. The chief historical importance of *Montezuma* is the preponderance (in the ratio of about two to one) of the "cavatina" over the traditional da capo aria.

The word "cavatina" comes from the Italian *cavare*, "to draw out, to excavate"; hence one meaning of *cavata* is that of something buried or concealed. Thus in vocal compositions of the fifteenth and sixteenth centuries there were *soggetti cavati*, for example, themes (in the tenor) which "concealed" a name, each vowel of which was represented by a note (a by *fa*, e by *re*, i by *mi*, and so on). Walther's *Lexikon* (1732) defines cavata as a short arioso passage, occurring usually at the end of a recitative, in which the mood or meaning of the recitative is concentrated or drawn forth. Cavatina (the diminutive of cavata) is used in the eighteenth century as opposed to aria in the sense of a vocal number which "gathers together" an aria (that is, a da capo aria) in shorter and simpler form. In the nineteenth-century opera, it signifies merely a short song of a lyric nature, usually forming part of a larger *scena*.

The cavatinas in *Montezuma* are in two-part form without repeats and with the following key scheme: Tonic→Dominant ‖ Dominant→ (modulations)→Tonic, the ending of the second part repeating that of the first more or less exactly but in the tonic key. Thus the scheme is that already exemplified in the principal section of many of the large-scale da capo arias in the works of Vinci, Schürmann, and Hasse, corresponding to the typical contemporary instrumental sonata first-movement form (K. P. E. Bach). It may be regarded as a truncated da capo aria: an elaborate first section, but without the traditional

---

to Italian texts (a few earlier works for Brunswick are in German). *Montezuma* (1755) has been published as Vol. XV of the DdT; selection in HAM 282. See A. Mayer-Reinach, "Carl Heinrich Graun als Opernkomponist," SIMG I (1899–1900) 446–529; *idem*, "Zur Herausgabe des Montezuma," MfMg XXXVII (1905) 20–31.

[83] Cf. Spontini's *Cortez*, 1809; there were some half-dozen other Cortez operas in the second half of the eighteenth century.

middle (contrasting) section or the traditional recapitulation of
Part A. The decline of the da capo had already begun in Germany
by the 1730's; many of the German scores of that period bear the
direction *senza da capo* at the end of the arias.[84] Predecessors of the
two-part form of the cavatina may be found as early as Landi's *Sant'
Alessio,* Vittori's *Galatea,* or L. Rossi's *Orfeo* in the songs of two
stanzas, the second of which is written to a different melody from the
first; but the genuine cavatina differs from this or any other simple
two-part song form in its less symmetrical structure, its more elaborate vocal style, its continuity of rhythm, and its constant text repetition.

It is uncertain whether the large proportion of cavatinas in *Montezuma* is due to the librettist or the composer. Graun had used the
form in earlier works, but Frederick claims the credit in this instance: "As for the cavatinas, I have seen some by Hasse which are
infinitely more beautiful than the arias [that is, da capo arias]. . . .
There is no need of repetition, except when the singers know how to
make variations [note that "except"!]; but it seems to me, in any
case, that it is an abuse to repeat the same thing four times. Your
actors . . . were never obliged to do such a stupid thing." [85] This
statement is interesting not only as the comment of an intelligent
contemporary on one of the conventions of eighteenth-century opera
but also as a distinct presentiment of the theories of Gluck on the
same subject.

Graun's music is in typical mid-eighteenth-century style. The overture [86] is of the Italian type, in three movements, with homophonic
texture, short themes, a simple harmonic vocabulary, many repetitions and sequential patterns, broken-chord figures, and the so-called
"Lombardic rhythm" or "Scotch snap" (♪♩.), a device very common
in the music of this period.[87] The arias are well written and effective,
though occasionally, as in Keiser, there are figures which suggest the
instrumental rather than the vocal idiom. The secco recitatives show
some harmonic variety and are enlivened by the use of deceptive

---

84 See G. F. Schmidt, *Die frühdeutsche Oper* II, 397 ff.

85 In a letter to his sister May 4, 1754, quoted in DdT XV, Introduction, p. ix.

86 On the overtures to Graun's other operas see Mennicke, *Hasse und die Gebrüder
Graun,* chaps. III and IV.

87 Quantz (*Versuch,* ed. Schering, p. 241) says this rhythm was introduced "about the
year 1722." Burney (*History* II, 847) complains of its abuse in operas sung at London
in 1748.

cadences. (Musical improvement of the secco recitative is a noticeable feature in the work of many composers by the middle of the
century.) The accompanied recitatives are excellent examples of this
style (Example 78).

Among the Italianized German composers after Hasse and Graun
we may mention Johann Gottlieb Naumann [88] of Dresden, one of

MONTEZUMA, Act III, sc. 1

Ex. 78.   Graun

Sen-za pe-na ab-ban-do-no u-na gran-dez-za, che fra-gil trop-po e
(Strings and continuo)
va-na ò co-no-sciu-ta, e sen-za in-su-per-bir-ne ò pos-se-
du-ta.   Sem-pre a la-sciar quei be-ni

---

[88] Naumann (1741–1806) was trained in Italy and brought out the first of his twenty-
four operas at Bologna in 1763; he also composed church and chamber music, and
many songs. See Meissner, *Bruchstücke;* Engländer, *Naumann als Opernkomponist.*

the most brilliant musical figures of his time and a typical representative of the *Empfindsamkeit* of the late eighteenth century. Curiously enough, the best-remembered opera of Naumann is his *Cora*, composed to a Swedish libretto for Stockholm about 1780 and subsequently performed in Germany in German translation.

THE LATER EIGHTEENTH CENTURY

There is on the part of certain writers a tendency to regard everything in eighteenth-century opera before Gluck as being somewhat in the nature of a necessary but regrettable episode, declining about the middle of the century to a hopelessly low state of affairs, which Gluck, practically singlehanded, redeemed through his so-called "reforms"—the very word carrying with it an aura of moral uplift, implying simply that something bad was replaced by something better. This point of view—a relic of the evolutionary philosophy of history —has had the vicious consequence of leading to the neglect of early and middle eighteenth-century Italian opera composers, a failure to appreciate their real merits and the qualities of their music in relation to its period and the circumstances for which it was composed. The situation has been aggravated by the fact that Italian scholars, who of all people should be most concerned to set this matter in its true light, have so far not made much of the music of their own composers available in modern editions.[89] The German musicologists, as is only natural, have concerned themselves chiefly with either composers of German birth (Fux, Hasse, Graun) or composers who were active in Germany (Jommelli), and even here they have been more attentive to those qualities of the music which appeal to Germans (for example, more serious quality of expressiveness, richer texture, greater importance of the orchestra) than to the fundamentally vocal and melodic traits characteristic of Italy. The result is that the importance of Gluck—great as it unquestionably is—has been exaggerated by an inadequate idea both of the real nature of the situation against which he was striving and of the contributions of other composers who to some extent anticipated many of his doctrines.[90]

The reform of opera was no new thing with Gluck. Opera is always being reformed; that is to say, it is always changing, and one is presumably entitled to call any marked change which he regards as being in the right direction, a reform. A more objective viewpoint is neatly stated by Martin Cooper: "Opera is constructed of three elements—the musical, the literary, and the spectacular; and at different times each of these three elements has in fact gained an undue supremacy over the other two. For this reason the history of opera is the history of a series of reformations and counter-reformations, no two countries and no two epochs agreeing on the role that each element should ideally play in the constitution of the whole. Neither

[89] The outstanding example of neglect is, of course, Alessandro Scarlatti: for the only comprehensive book about his life and music we are indebted to an Englishman (Dent), and for the only modern edition of an opera to a German (Eitner).

[90] Goldschmidt, "Die Reform der italienischen Oper des 18. Jahrhunderts," *III. Kongress der I.M.G.*, pp. 196–207.

evolutionary nor unified, it is the history of perpetually recurring schools of thought, one never victorious over the other, though occasionally gaining the majority of popular opinion." [91]

Granting, then, that in much of the Italian opera of the early eighteenth century the elements of melody and display of singers' virtuosity had usurped too large a place in the scheme, it was natural that a reaction should take place calculated to restore the balance. Then, too, by the middle of the century there was a general turning away from the frivolities characteristic of the age of the Regency, and with this went a desire to make music to some degree more serious and expressive. The new Empfindsamkeit, which was at first nothing more than an infusion of a tender and pretty sentimentality into the fabric of rococo music, prepared the way for the classical style of Haydn and Mozart. A deepening of the texture, an increased attention to harmonic variety and to the inner voices in the composition, were natural concomitants of this change. The growth of interest in symphonic music, and the gradual solution of the larger problems of form within the new instrumental style, helped call attention to the possibilities of the orchestra in opera, which the early Neapolitans had generally neglected. The older operatic formula, by which every drama was forced into a pattern of alternating recitatives and arias, began to give way to a more flexible arrangement, in the interest of greater truth and naturalness of dramatic presentation. French opera, with its emphasis on ballet, chorus, and spectacle, began to exert some influence on composers in other countries. Finally, the comic opera, constantly increasing in popularity, acted as a goad through parody and satire and at the same time provided a living example of the effects to be gained through simplicity of style and new types of subject matter, forcing the creators of serious opera to take stock and adapt themselves to a new generation of audiences.

Not all the influences came from the side of music. The rise of the sentimental novel (Richardson) and above all the cult of naturalness popularized by Rousseau wrought such changes in literary thought and expression that the opera libretto, and consequently opera music, could not possibly remain aloof. But as these changes

[91] *Gluck* (New York, Oxford University Press, 1935), p. 4. Quoted by permission of the publisher.

are to be more clearly observed in the field of comic opera (through which in large measure their effects were transmitted to the serious opera), we shall defer a more detailed consideration of them until later.

We have already intimated that Gluck was not the only reformer in the eighteenth century. As a matter of fact, there was hardly a single composer of serious opera after 1740 who was not touched by the general movement of reaction against the older Neapolitan opera type. As in all such changes, there were conservatives, moderates, and radicals. Among the conservatives we may certainly class Hasse and Graun, the extent of whose innovations has already been noted. A slightly younger and more progressive group includes Davide Perez,[92] one of the little-known masters of this period, whose scores are remarkable for their wealth of feeling as well as for the importance and skill of their instrumental music. "Had all the Neapolitan composers been of his stamp, there would have been no need of a Gluck." [93] Another Spanish composer active in Italy, Domingo Terradellas,[94] was remarkable for his depiction of violent emotions and for the originality and daring quality of his modulations. Two Italians of this period, Gaetano Latilla and Rinaldo di Capua,[95] both of whom enjoyed considerable reputation in their day, have left so

[92] Davide Perez (1711–1778) was born at Naples of Spanish parents. After a career at Naples, Palermo, and other cities, he went to Lisbon in 1752, where he was director of the Royal Theatre from its foundation in 1755 until 1780. He composed about thirty operas, of which the most notable was *Solimano* (Lisbon, 1757). None of his music is available in modern editions.

[93] Kretzschmar, *Geschichte der Oper*, p. 189.

[94] Domingo Terradellas, whose name is often Italianized as Domenico Terradeglias (1713–1751), was born at Barcelona, and studied for a short time under Durante at Naples. His fourteen operas were produced in Italy and London; the chief work is *Artaserse* (Venice, 1744). A splendid example of an accompanied recitative and aria from his *Merope* (Florence, 1743) is found in SB 298; see also HAM 298. Carreras y Bulbena, *Domenech Terradellas* (contains musical examples); Volkmann, "Domenico Terradellas," ZIMG XIII (1911–12) 306–309; Mitjana, "Les Espagnols italianisants" in Lavignac, *Encyclopédie*, Pt. I, Vol. IV, pp. 2195–2209.

[95] Gaetano Latilla (1713–1789), a pupil of Gizzi at Naples, wrote thirty-six operas, of which only seven are extant (none in modern editions). The two chief works are *Orazio* (Rome, 1738) and *Antigono* (Naples, 1775). See Bellucci La Salandra, *Saggio cronologico delle opere teatrali di Gaetano Latilla*.

Rinaldo di Capua (*ca.* 1720–*ca.* 1778), about whose life very little is known, produced about thirty operas and comic intermezzi, chiefly at Rome; only fragments of these works survive, with the exception of one intermezzo, *La zingara* ("The Gypsy Girl"), performed at Paris in 1753. See Spitta, "Rinaldo di Capua," VfMw III (1887) 92–121; Dent, "Rinaldo di Capua" in *Grove's Dictionary*.

little music that it is difficult justly to judge their merits or estimate their historical position.

Three other representatives of the Neapolitan school may be mentioned here, though belonging to a later generation than the composers listed above. Francesco di Majo [96] ranks with Perez and Terradellas as one who brought into the regular tradition of Italian opera certain individual qualities, particularly in the expression of sorrowful emotions and in the fineness and elegance of his style, of which the aria "Se mai più saro geloso" from *Alessandro* (Naples, 1767) is an example.[97] Johann Christian Bach, the youngest surviving son of J. S. Bach, who moved to Milan shortly after his father's death, turned Catholic, and became as completely Italianized in his music as Graun or Hasse, was one of the most popular of the later composers in the Neapolitan style.[98] His music, sweet and expressive without being deeply emotional, clear in form, expert in detail, most characteristic in lyrical moods and cantabile melodies, was much admired by the young Mozart.[99] Dr. Burney states that in his arias "the richness of the accompaniments perhaps deserve [*sic*] more praise than the originality of the melodies; which, however, are always natural, elegant, and in the best taste of Italy at the time he came over. The Neapolitan school, where he studied, is manifest in his cantilenas, and the science of his father and brother in his harmony." [100] One of the last composers in the Neapolitan style was Giuseppe Sarti,[101] whose scores show, along with many traditional fea-

96 Gian Francesco di Majo (*ca.* 1740–1771) was a pupil of Padre Martini. His nineteen operas were performed in various Italian cities from 1758 to 1771. Two arias are reprinted in Marx, *Gluck und die Oper*, Musical Supplement Nos. 5 and 6.

97 Printed in Bücken, *Rokoko und Klassik*, p. 115.

98 Johann Christian Bach (1735–1782) is known as the "Milan" or the "London" Bach. His importance in the development of the classical instrumental style, and his profound influence on Mozart, have long been recognized. A pupil of Padre Martini, he worked principally at Milan from 1754 and in London from 1762 until his death; operas of his were also performed at Mannheim (1772, 1776) and Paris (Quinault's *Amadis des Gaules*, 1779). None of these opera scores exists in modern editions. The principal book is Terry's *Johann Christian Bach*, with a thematic catalogue (important review, with corrections, ZfMw XVI [1934] 182–88). See also Schwarz, "Johann Christian Bach," SIMG II (1900–1901) 401–54; Abert, "J. C. Bach's italienische Opern," ZfMw I (1918–19) 313–28.

99 Abert, *Mozart* I, 58, 242–49; cf. Köchel, *Verzeichnis* (3d ed.) No. 293e.

100 *History* II, 866.

101 Sarti (1729–1802), a pupil of Padre Martini and the teacher of Cherubini, had a long and successful career, of which the years 1755–1775 were spent chiefly at Copenhagen and 1784–1801 at St. Petersburg. His best works were the opera seria *Giulio Sabino* (Venice, 1781) and the opera buffa *Fra i due litiganti il terzo gode* (Milan, 1782). No opera is available in modern editions. See Scudo, *Le Chevalier Sarti*, and the sequel "Frédérique," *Revue des deux mondes* (1863–1864); Rivalta, *G. Sarti*.

tures, some influence of newer ideas, especially in their powerful accompanied recitatives and in the effectiveness of the orchestral accompaniments. His graceful melodies and the profusion of his ideas often suggest the style of Mozart. Both Bach and Sarti, however, represent the more conservative tendencies of the later eighteenth-century opera seria, distrusting the changes introduced by German-influenced composers and attempting to preserve the spirit of Metastasio and Hasse with emphasis on melodic expression and sensuous appeal of the music rather than dramatic force or profundity.

We turn now to two Italians whose innovations in opera went beyond anything attempted by the composers so far considered, and who may be regarded not only as the forerunners but in some respects as the colleagues of Gluck in the work of reform: Nicola Jommelli and Tommaso Traëtta.[102] Jommelli's early works were quite in the old Neapolitan style, but the example of Hasse, and especially the teachings of Padre Martini, filled him with doubts and set him experimenting, so that signs of change appeared in his music about 1745. Perhaps unfortunately, in 1749 Jommelli became acquainted with Metastasio at Vienna and remained under his spell ever thereafter, with the result that he was never moved to make a fundamental break with the older type of opera libretto. The climax of Jommelli's life was his period of service (1753–1769) as chapelmaster to the Duke of Württemburg at Stuttgart—a German court, but one in which French taste was an important factor. His last operas, written after his return to Naples in 1769, were received coldly by his countrymen, who found his new style "too German." So strong was the admixture

---

[102] Nicola Jommelli (1714–1774) studied at Naples under Durante, Feo, and Leo, later under Padre Martini at Bologna. Over fifty of his operas and other dramatic works, both serious and comic, have been preserved, in addition to a quantity of church music. *Fetonte* (Stuttgart, 1768) is published as Vols. 32–33 of DdT. The standard study is Abert's *Niccolo Jommelli als Opernkomponist*. See also the same author's "Zur Geschichte der Oper in Württemburg," *Kongress-Bericht* (1909), pp. 186–93; also Alfieri, *Notizie biografiche di Niccolò Jommelli* (1845).

Traëtta (1727–1779) was also a pupil of Durante. He wrote forty-two operas, his work centering chiefly at Parma (1758–1765) and St. Petersburg (1768–1774), where he succeeded Galuppi as court composer to Catherine II. Selections from his operas are published in DTB XIV[1] and XVII. The principal works are *Ifigenia in Tauride* (1758), *Sofonisba* (1762), and *Antigona* (1772). Bibliography: Nuovo, *Tommaso Traetta;* Damerini, "Un precursore italiano di Gluck: Tommaso Traetta," *Il pianoforte* (July, 1927); idem, "Tommaso Traetta," *Bolletino bibliografico musicale* II (July, 1927) 1–13; Raeli, "Tommaso Traetta," *Rivista nazionale di musica* (March, 1927); idem, "The Bi-Centenary of Tommaso Traetta," *The Chesterian* VIII (1926–27) 217–23.

of Northern elements in his music that he has been called "the Italian Gluck." [103] Traëtta likewise, by both temperament and circumstances, was led to even greater departure from the accepted Italian models of his time.

What are the qualities in the operas of Jommelli and Traëtta that have caused their composers to be numbered among the re-formers in the eighteenth century?

The first is their international character. The earlier Italian composers, though they traveled a great deal, always took with them the Neapolitan tradition and preserved it untouched by foreign musical influences, even of those countries in which they worked. At this time there was only one school of opera in Europe outside Italy, namely that of France, which had been preserved by virtue of almost complete isolation from Italian music in the first half of the century. By 1750, the French opera had begun, though slightly, to make itself felt by composers in those courts and cities which in other respects also were touched by French culture—meaning, in effect, the German courts and a few in northern Italy. French influence was still strong on German life throughout the eighteenth century to the time of Lessing, Herder, and Goethe, as witness in literature the doctrines of Gottsched (1700–1766) and in manners Frederick the Great of Prussia (1712–1786), the great friend of Voltaire, who habitually spoke and wrote French and despised German as "the language of boors." It happened that both Jommelli and Traëtta came into this French orbit, the former at Stuttgart and the latter at Parma. The very subjects of some of Traëtta's operas are significant, for example, I tantaridi (1760), a translation of Rameau's Castor et Pollux; Le Feste d'Imeneo (1760), a festa teatrale or opéra ballet similar to Rameau's Fêtes d'Hébé of 1739; and Ippolito ed Arice (1759), the same subject as Rameau's Hyppolite et Aricie. Traëtta's principal librettists, Coltellini (ca. 1740–1775) and Frugoni (1692–1768), were well acquainted with Rameau's works. Coltellini was a pupil of Calzabigi; in 1765 he was engaged to prepare the libretto of Telemacco for Gluck, and in 1772 Calzabigi designated him as his successor at the Vienna court. The importance of the ballets in both Jommelli's and Traëtta's operas is another sign of French influence. At Stuttgart the ballet master was Jean-Georges Noverre (1727–1810), author of a famous

103 Abert, Jommelli, p. 106.

treatise (*Lettres sur la danse et les ballets,* 1760) and later ballet master at the Paris Opéra, who advocated a return to Greek ideals of the dance, with naturalness of movements, simplicity of costume, and emphasis on the dramatic content of the ballet rather than on abstract figures or virtuosity of the dancers.[104] Another evidence of French taste in Traëtta and Jommelli is the greater prominence of the spectacular element in their operas, as in Traëtta's *Sofonisba* (1762), with temple scenes, battle scenes, the submarine palace of Thetis, the transformations of Proteus—all reminiscent of Lully and Rameau. Equally French are the pictorial details in the music, touches of that imitation of nature so dear to eighteenth-century aestheticians: storms, battles, pastoral idyls, even the rhythm of a horse's galloping imitated in the second violins throughout an aria,[105] or the direction *urlo francese* (literally, "French howl"), a cry rather than a musical note, literally imitating the sound of the voice under stress of emotion.[106]

The specifically German influence on Jommelli and Traëtta is seen first in their treatment of the orchestra, in a greater complexity of texture and increased attention to instrumentation in the modern sense. The orchestra was the great medium through which German music in the eighteenth century began its conquering career in Europe; the Mannheim orchestra was famous by 1745, while those of Dresden under Hasse and Stuttgart under Jommelli (there were forty-seven players for his *Fetonte* in 1768) were hardly less celebrated. Likewise due to German influence is the greater richness and variety of the harmonies in both Jommelli and Traëtta, as compared with their Italian contemporaries.

Another aspect of the operas of Jommelli and Traëtta is the way in which they consistently aim at a closer co-ordination of music and drama. One sign of this is the sharply decreased proportion of secco recitative, a style which by its very nature excludes any thorough participation of music in the action. To a greater extent than ever before, secco recitatives are replaced by the accompanied variety. In the second act of Jommelli's *Demofoonte* (1764) only two of the eleven scenes are secco, all the rest being accompanied by full orchestra; this is an extreme instance, but it illustrates the whole tendency of

[104] See Abert, "J. G. Noverre" in *Gesammelte Schriften,* pp. 264–86.
[105] "Quel destriere" in Jommelli's *Olympiade.*   [106] Traëtta's *Sofonisba,* DTB XVII, 90.

the century which culminates in the later works of Gluck, where the
secco recitative is abolished altogether. Among the accompanied
recitatives in these operas are some splendid examples of dramatic
power, such as the tenth scene of Act III of Traëtta's *Sofonisba*.[107] The
treatment of the aria also undergoes a change: many are so contrived
as to further the action rather than interrupt it as in the older
Neapolitan opera; the melodic style is more expressive and covers a
wider range of emotions. A distinctly Mozartean quality is apparent
in some of the cantabile arias, such as "Non piangete" from Traëtta's
Antigona (1772) (Example 79). A sense of climax and proportion, a

ANTIGONA, Act III, sc. 2

Ex. 79.   Traëtta

Non pian - ge - te   i   ca — — — — si   mie-i,

Non v'af - fan - ni   il mio   tor - men - to,

non   v'af - - fan - - ni   il   mio —— tor - men-to.

sure grasp of the problems of musical form and its adaptation to the
dramatic situation, are everywhere evident.[108] The tendency is constantly toward greater fluidity, toward breaking down the old hard-
and-fast boundaries between recitative and aria. We often find long
scene complexes in which accompanied recitative, arioso, aria, ensemble, and chorus all participate freely. Even the conventional da
capo pattern of the arias is artfully concealed: more prominence is
given to the middle (contrasting) section, especially in Traëtta; in
repetition, the principal section is shortened or otherwise altered;
changes of mood, of metre, and of tempo are incorporated; declamatory (recitative) sections occur in the midst of an aria; or an accompanied recitative and the following aria will use the same thematic

[107] DTB XVII, 165–73.   [108] See for example Jommelli's *Fetonte*, Act II, scs. 8–9.

material—all changes from the old order, some of which had, however, been anticipated by earlier composers.

The changing conception of the overture is another eighteenth-century tendency which finds reflection in the works of Jommelli and Traëtta. The Neapolitan overture was merely an introductory symphonic piece, having no particular relation to the opera which followed; the overture of one opera could be, and frequently was, used for another without anyone being the wiser. One of the points of Gluck's reform manifesto of 1769 is a statement of the new ideal of an overture which should be specifically connected with the drama following; though neither Jommelli nor Traëtta consistently aimed at this ideal, their operas do show certain interesting features. Thus in Traëtta's *Sofonisba* the theme of the slow movement of the overture recurs in a quintet in the last scene of the opera—a device similar to that employed by Rameau in *Castor et Pollux* twenty-five years earlier—and the finale leads without pause directly into the first scene of Act I.[109] Both here and in Jommelli's *Fetonte* the overture evidently suggests the general course of the drama—as in Rameau's *Zoroastre* of 1749. In *Fetonte,* the very short first movement of the overture leads at once into the first scene of the opera (an andante solo with chorus) which replaces the usual second movement; [110] then follows the "third" movement, a musical depiction of an earthquake (as in many French operas), after which, with the second scene of Act I, the opera proper begins. The overture to Di Majo's *Ifigenia in Tauride* (1767) is a similar compromise between the old Neapolitan concert overture and the later nineteenth-century program type, which was first exemplified in Gluck's *Iphigénie en Aulide* (1772) and brought to full realization in Beethoven's *Fidelio* (1806).

The French example, and the departure from the Italian norm, are most clearly evidenced in Jommelli and Traëtta by the return of the chorus to an important place in their operas. Choruses are numerous and often of large dimensions; they do not merely appear in the spectacle scenes but also form part of the action. Perhaps the most notable instance is the fourth scene of Act II of Traëtta's *Ifigenie*

109 The immediate connecting of the overture with the opening scene was common in Hasse (Mennicke, *Hasse und die Gebrüder Graun,* p. 147). For a survey of eighteenth-century theory and practice of the relation between overture and opera, see Mennicke, chap. VI.

110 Mozart used a similar device in his serenata *Ascanio in Alba,* 1771.

in Tauride, in which the pleadings of Orestes are interrupted by outbursts of the Chorus of Furies. Although the librettos are not the
same, an interesting comparison may be made between this and the
parallel scene in Gluck's *Iphigénie en Tauride* (Act II), written
twenty years later. In spite of their impressive scale and appearance,
the choruses in Traëtta never attain the real solemnity and impact
of the great choral scenes of Rameau, Gluck, or Mozart (*Idomeneo*).
The eighteenth-century Italians apparently lacked feeling for the real
dramatic possibilities of the chorus, and their choral writing (not
alone in opera!) all too frequently succumbed to facile tunefulness
and to triviality of harmonies and rhythms.

In sum, while the operas of Jommelli and Traëtta show important
advances over many of the weaknesses and limitations of the old Neapolitan school, they do not mark a fundamental break with it. In
Jommelli particularly, and in Traëtta to a lesser degree, the old type
of libretto still prevails. The old duality of poem and music is weakened but not overcome. In spite of all changes in detail, the works
remain singers' operas, with the old virtuoso display, improvised embellishments, and cadenzas. Furthermore, and by comparison with
Gluck, the style of the music itself is still essentially rococo: it is, for
the most part, primarily elegant and polished rather than simple and
passionate; attention is directed to a brilliant surface rather than to
depth; melody is still the chief issue, not harmony; the rhythms are
restless, nervous, almost as though the composer felt the audience
would go to sleep if not constantly titillated by new and unexpected
turns. The whole is, from the standpoint of a genuine classicism, over-
ornamented; it is full of merely decorative short notes, trills, graces,
snaps, runs, and appoggiaturas—a frilly, lace-valentine texture, related to that of Gluck as a courtier's dress to a simple peasant costume.

In all consideration of composers like Perez, Di Majo, Traëtta,
and Jommelli as predecessors of Gluck it is essential to remember
that their kind of opera was not absorbed or superseded by Gluck's,
but continued to live side by side with the latter's reform works.
When the old opera seria finally declined, it was in favor of the opera
buffa, which had become the dominant Italian type by the end of
the eighteenth century. To this type belong the best operas of Piccinni, Paisiello, Cimarosa, and above all Mozart, whose own *Figaro*
and *Don Giovanni* show the new Italian opera buffa in its perfection.

15

The Operas of Gluck [1]

CHRISTOPH WILLIBALD GLUCK WAS BORN in 1714, the son of a Bohemian forester. After acquiring some knowledge of music in the elementary schools, he went to Prague, where he remained four years (1732–1736). In 1736 he removed to Vienna as a chamber musician in the employ of Prince Ferdinand Philipp Lobkowitz; he was soon sent by another noble patron to study with Sammartini at Milan. No details of his very early musical education are certainly known; he must have become acquainted with the current Italian opera (as represented by Hasse) in Prague, while at Vienna he would have heard the older style of Caldara. At Vienna likewise he met Metastasio, whose poetry appealed to him as to every other opera composer; Gluck's first three operas were on Metastasian librettos. His studies with Sammartini opened to him the new world of modern symphonic music. His first ten operas were successfully performed at Milan and other Italian cities in the years 1741–1745. They are distinguished from those of contemporary Italian composers only by a certain melodic freedom and individual energy of expression but they show no traces of the revolutionary principles for

[1] Of Gluck's approximately one hundred dramatic works, about half have been preserved either wholly or in part. Modern full-score editions sponsored by Mlle. Pelletan and edited by Saint-Saëns, Tiersot, and others were published at Paris as follows: *Orphée et Euridice* (1898?), *Alceste* (1874), *Iphigénie en Aulide* (1873), *Armide* (1889), *Iphigénie en Tauride* (1874), and *Echo et Narcisse* (n.d.). The following full-score editions have appeared in Germany: *Le Nozze d'Ercole e d'Ebe* (DTB XIV²), *L'innocenza giustificata* (DTOe XLIV), *Orfeo*, the original Italian version (DTOe II. Folge, Nr. 1), and the ballet *Don Juan* (DTOe XXX²). Eulenburg has published a full score of *Iphigénie en Tauride*, ed. H. Abert (1927). There are many piano-vocal scores of the principal later operas, as well as of the following opéras comiques: *Le Cadi dupé*, *L'Ivrogne corrigé* (Paris, 1925), *L'Arbre enchanté* (1911), and *La Rencontre imprévue* (Breitkopf & Härtel; also Paris, R. Legouix, 1923). Two arias are found in HAM 292, 293.

The extensive literature on Gluck cannot be fully listed here. The leading biographies are those of Schmid (1854), Marx (1863), and Arend (1921). There is a thematic catalogue of Gluck's works by Wotquenne (supplement by Liebeskind, additions and corrections by Arend). Important material is found in the publications of the Gluck-Gesellschaft (4 vols., 1913–1918). See Wortsmann, *Die deutsche Gluck-Literatur* (1914) for bibliography. The best book in English is that of Alfred Einstein (translated by Eric Blom), which may be supplemented by the useful works of Ernest Newman and Martin Cooper.

which he later became famous.[2] In the season of 1745–1746 Gluck visited London. He traveled by way of Paris, where he may have had occasion to hear some of the music of Rameau (the latter's *ballet héroïque Les Fêtes de Polymnie* was performed for the first time October 12, 1745); if so, there is no evidence that it produced any remarkable immediate impression. At London he presented two operas with no particular success and drew upon himself the oft-quoted remark of Handel to the effect that "he [Gluck] knows no more of counterpoint than Waltz, my cook." Nevertheless, Gluck made friends with the older composer and was undoubtedly much impressed by his music,[3] though the influence exerted itself only considerably later and then indirectly, in the form of an ideal of grandeur which Gluck embodied in his own particular way in the reform operas. The two years following the visit to London were spent in touring Germany as conductor with a traveling opera company. *Le nozze d'Ercole e d'Ebe* ("The Marriage of Hercules and Hebe"), a serenata [4] performed at a wedding in Pillnitz (near Dresden) in 1747, shows Gluck as an accomplished composer in a rather pretty, trifling Italian style. In this work, as indeed in all his operas, Gluck followed the eighteenth-century custom of borrowing numbers from his own previous works or even from those of other composers; several arias are from earlier Gluck operas, and the first movement of the overture is taken from a symphony of Sammartini, with only slight alterations. The aria "Cosi come si accese," from the epilogue, is typical of the graceful, tuneful, Pergolesi-like melody in which this work abounds (Example 80).

In 1750 Gluck was married at Vienna. The substantial dowry which his wife brought him undoubtedly encouraged a certain independence which Gluck began to manifest about this time. Concrete evidence of the new attitude is found in the scores of *Ezio* (Prague, 1750) and *La clemenza di Tito* ("The Mercy of Titus," Naples, 1752),

2 Only one of these earliest operas is preserved entire: *Ipermestra* (Venice 1744). For a technical study of all the operas before *Orfeo*, with musical examples, see Kurth, "Die Jugendopern Glucks," SzMw I (1913) 193–277. Cf. also Abert, "Glucks italienische Opern," *Gluck-Jahrbuch* II (1915) 1–25, and the same author's introduction to *Le nozze d'Ercole e d'Ebe*, DTB XXVI.
3 Cf. Kelly, *Reminiscences* I, 255.
4 A serenata is the eighteenth-century name for a small opera or dramatic cantata, often of a pastoral nature and employing few characters, composed for a special occasion (such as a birthday or wedding) in a patron's household.

which in carefulness of orchestral writing, nobility of melody, and seriousness of expression surpass not only the earlier operas but also most of the Italian works of the next ten years. The characteristic vigor which had always been remarked in Gluck's music, and the growing individuality of his methods, may have been what caused

LE NOZZE D'ERCOLE

Ex.80.   Gluck

Co - sì co - me si ac - ce - se la vo-stra fiam-ma bel - la nel - la na-ti - va stel -la, nel - la na-ti - va stel - la, co - sì ris - plen - de - rà, ri - splen-de - rà.

Metastasio about this time to describe him as a composer of "surprising fire, but . . . mad." [5] It was the cry of the conservative, instinctively recognizing the presence of a force inimical to the old settled state of affairs. Yet it was to be ten years before Gluck composed *Orfeo;* and during this time he still produced some works in the old manner, as well as one sparkling buffo opera, *Le cinesi* ("The Chinese Ladies," 1754), for the imperial court. The success of this work was instrumental in securing for him the position of official court composer of theatre and chamber music under the superintendency of Count Durazzo, whose influence and encouragement played a large part in determining the new artistic ideals which were then developing in Gluck's mind. Their first collaborative work, the one-act *Innocenza giustificata* (1755), although apparently conforming to the Metastasian type of libretto, is in actuality a significant forerunner of the monumental simplicity of *Orfeo*, with the musical resources (including a chorus) largely subordinated to the dramatic aims. This work was revised by Gluck in 1768 under the title *The Vestal;* it is the same subject as that of Spontini's opera (1807).

[5] Letter to Farinelli, Nov. 16, 1751; in Burney, *Metastasio* I, 402.

Another important influence on Gluck in the years immediately preceding the composition of *Orfeo* was his contact with the French *opéra comique*.[6] This distinctive national form of comic opera had grown up at Paris, at first using only popular melodies to which poets fitted their words but coming toward the middle of the century to make use of more and more original music and at the same time improving in poetic quality and musical interest. The Viennese court being curious to hear these pieces, Durazzo arranged for some to be sent from Paris. Gluck was charged with the duty of conducting the performances, which entailed arranging the music and composing new numbers where it was thought the original melodies might not be suited to the Viennese taste. These performances of opéras comiques at Vienna began in 1755, and it is noteworthy that the proportion of new music steadily increased, until in the last of them, *La Rencontre imprévue* ("The Unexpected Meeting," 1764), not one of the original French airs was retained, the entire text having been newly composed by Gluck. Thus, as it were by accident, the composer in his forties went to school to the French opéra comique, learning a syllabic style of text setting, a melodic restraint, a freedom of phrase structure, and a close adaptation of music to poetry which contrasted with the typical Italian arias in an extreme degree. How thoroughly he assimilated the French musical idiom may be gathered not only from the scores but also from the testimony of the French poet and manager Favart, who speaks with highest praise of Gluck's settings of his librettos: "They leave nothing to be desired in the expression, the taste, the harmony, even in the French prosody." [7]

A final stage of preparation for *Orfeo* was the composition of Angiolini's ballet *Don Juan* in 1761,[8] a work which seems as though designed to illustrate the new principles outlined by Noverre in his book on the dance, published only a year previously. As in the opéras comiques Gluck had learned to subordinate music to text, so here he adapted his art to the service of pantomime. There is in this music something of Rameau's wonderful power of depicting gesture in sound; and, as in the older opera, the score is divided into many short numbers, each complete in itself. But the music is more than

6 Haas, *Gluck und Durazzo;* Holzer, "Die komischen Opern Glucks," SzMw XIII (1926) 3–37.
7 Letter to Durazzo, Nov. 19, 1763; in Favart, *Memoires et correspondances* II, 169.
8 Haas, "Die Wiener Ballet-Pantomime im 18. Jahrhundert," SzMw X (1923) 3–36.

mere accompaniment to patterns of motion; it enters into the action and becomes a partner of the drama figured forth by the dancers. Part of the closing scene between Don Juan and the Statue will serve to show this quality and also to suggest how Mozart must have remembered, perhaps unconsciously, the music of Gluck when composing his own *Don Giovanni* (Example 81). Indeed, comparison between the two works is almost inevitable, though it is not in super-

DON JUAN, No. 30

Ex.81.   Gluck

ficial thematic resemblances but rather in the whole spirit of the music that Mozart's indebtedness to the older composer is evident.

With the composition of *Don Juan* Gluck stood at the parting of the ways; having begun with the conventional Italian operatic formulas and having reached the point of instilling into this framework a new breath of dramatic life, he might have continued along the lines of Jommelli and Traëtta, toward the type of opera which Mozart eventually brought to unsurpassable heights. That Gluck's genius now took a different turn was not owing to any inner compulsion of Gluck the musician but rather to a quite unexpected development of Gluck the dramatist—a development for which at this moment external forces were largely responsible. These forces were immanent in the whole intellectual and artistic atmosphere of the later eighteenth century.[9] Fundamental was the profound yearning for free, simple, unaffected expression of human feelings. The baroque had been an age of order, authority, and formality, to which the early eighteenth century had reacted with the critical and skeptical philosophy of rationalism, summed up in the works of Voltaire. Into the vacuum created by this essentially negative criticism there rushed the earlier manifestations of mannered sentimentality and capricious, superficial ornamentation, extending through all the details of life, and mirrored in music of the gallant style. But mere caprice was not enough. To the gallant ideal succeeded that of naturalness, whose great prophet was Jean-Jacques Rousseau with his *Nouvelle Héloïse* (1760) and *Emile* (1762), the fountains of the romantic movement in literature. Yet naturalness, however valid as an ideal, was too vague to furnish by itself a sure foundation for art; not only an ideal but a form as well was needed, and the form, the regulating, ordering principle without which great artistic creation is impossible, was sought now, as it had been at the time of the Renaissance, in the models of the classical age of ancient Greece. In 1764 a German archaeologist, Johann Joachim Winckelmann, published his *Geschichte der Kunst des Alterthums* ("History of Ancient Art"), embodying the fruits of nearly twenty years of study and meditation; from this publication may be said to date the epoch known par excellence in the history of European art as the classical period.

9 Cf. Abert, "Gluck, Mozart und der Rationalismus," in his *Gesammelte Schriften*, pp. 311–45.

Winckelmann's work was not only a history but a philosophy of art, which served in some degree to counteract the dangers of unrestrained individualism implicit in the doctrines of Rousseau. Beauty, according to this philosophy, can be attained only when individual, characteristic details are subordinated to the general plan of the whole, thus creating an ideal, suprapersonal work marked by harmonious proportions and a certain repose in the total effect—in Winckelmann's phrase, "noble simplicity and calm greatness." [10]

It may be doubted whether Gluck ever read either Rousseau's or Winckelmann's books, though he probably had met Winckelmann at Rome in 1756. In any case, the question is not important, for the ideas which both men expressed were so much in the air at this time that no thinking person could possibly have escaped them. With regard to the classic models, of course, the same difficulty was present as in the Renaissance, namely the lack of actual specimens of ancient music. But theorists in the eighteenth century did not trouble to speculate, as the Florentine Camerata had done, on the nature of Greek music; rather, they attacked the problem of opera at its root, advocating fundamental changes in the libretto and in the relations between composer, poet, and performing artists. The most influential writer in this field was the Italian Francesco Algarotti, a highly esteemed philosopher, a friend of Voltaire and Frederick the Great, and artistic adviser to the court of Parma where Traëtta was stationed. His *Saggio sopra l'opera in musica* ("Treatise on the Opera"), first issued in 1755, became the most popular manifesto of operatic reform, influencing even in details both the practice and the theory of Gluck.[11] The resemblance between Algarotti's book and Gluck's preface to *Alceste* (1769) leaves no room for doubt on this point.

The fundamental impulse, the suggestion of a model, and the detailed aesthetic theory were thus present. And at this moment appeared the poet, Raniero Calzabigi (1714–1795),[12] from whose collaboration with Gluck *Orfeo* and *Alceste* resulted. Calzabigi was

---

10 Winckelmann, "Gedanken über die Nachahmung der griechischen Werke," ¶79. He may have obtained the phrase from Gottsched: "Man sollte in der Opernmusik mehr auf eine edle Einfalt sehen, als auf die unförmlichen Ausschweifungen der Italiener" (*Kritische Dichtkunst* III, 1734; quoted by E. Reichel in "Gottsched und Johann Adolf Scheibe," SIMG II [1900–1901] 665).
11 A summary of Algarotti's teachings, with copious quotations, will be found in Newman, *Gluck and the Opera*, Pt. II, chap. II.
12 See Michel, "Ranieri Calzabigi," *Gluck-Jahrbuch* IV (1918) 99–171.

the real standard-bearer of the revolt against Metastasio,[13] in spite of the fact that he had earlier brought out at Paris an edition of the latter's works which in the preface he characterized as "perfect trage- dies." He had led an adventurous life in Italy, Paris, and elsewhere; he was known as a literary amateur and aesthetician and was an admirer of Shakespeare. Gluck handsomely acknowledged his in- debtedness to Calzabigi: "If my music has had some success, I think it my duty to recognize that I am beholden for it to him. . . . How- ever much talent a composer may have, he will never produce any but mediocre music, if the poet does not awaken in him that en- thusiasm without which the productions of all the arts are but feeble and drooping." [14] Calzabigi even went so far as to claim, and without contradiction from Gluck, that it was he who had taught the composer exactly how to write his recitatives and had persuaded him to banish both coloratura passages and the secco accompaniment of recitative from his operas.[15]

Orfeo ed Euridice, the first joint work of Calzabigi and Gluck, was performed at Vienna October 5, 1762.[16] Thus the new reform began with the same subject as that of the first Florentine operas of 1600. Aside from two incongruous features—the irrelevant overture and the artificial happy ending (both due to the festive occasion for which the opera was written, where too much tragedy would have been out of place)—the work is a profound contrast to the contem- porary Italian operas. The contrast begins with the libretto, in which the action is simplified to the verge of austerity; it is, in fact, a series of tableaux rather than a connected story. Eurydice has died before the action begins, and the curtain rises to show Orpheus and the chorus lamenting about her bier; this was a favorite type of scene in French opera, the *tombeau,* a fine example of which may be found at the opening of Act I of Rameau's *Castor et Pollux.* The choral lament is intensified by Orpheus' moving cries of "Euridice!" There follows a short recitative and a ballo, that is, a solemn dance, after which the chorus is resumed. At its conclusion Orpheus sings his aria "Chiamo il mio ben così" ("Thus I call my beloved"), in F major, three strophes separated by short recitatives, a simple, sincere expres-

---

[13] Cf. Einstein, "Calzabigi's 'Erwiderung' von 1790," *Gluck-Jahrbuch* II (1915) 56–102; III (1917) 25–50.
[14] Einstein, *Gluck,* pp. 67–68.   [15] Letter in *Mercure de France,* August, 1784, p. 135.
[16] See Tiersot, "Etude sur Orphée," *Le Ménestrel* LXII (1896) *passim.*

sion of grief, made more poignant through echo repetitions of the closing phrases by a second orchestra behind the scenes. A final outburst of sorrow is interrupted by the appearance of the God of Love, who in pity directs Orpheus to seek his departed wife in the realms of the dead. The second act opens with the highly dramatic scene of the Furies guarding the gates of the underworld, whose fierce denials Orpheus overcomes by the magic power of his singing. The gradual diminution of intensity leads naturally into the next scene of the Elysian Fields, where a mood of bright, serene happiness is sustained throughout with remarkable consistency. This scene is introduced by the famous "Ballet of the Happy Spirits" and the lovely aria "Che puro ciel" ("What pure sky"), with its delicately pictorial accompaniment. Eurydice appears, conducted by a train of Blessed Spirits. Everything moves with a still, unearthly, dreamlike motion. With the third act, the mood is abruptly broken; we suddenly find ourselves watching a human interest drama. The first part of this act is less interesting musically, though it brings the catastrophe of the action. Orpheus, no longer able to withstand the pleadings of Eurydice, looks back; and her death is followed by that ideal, classic outpouring of grief "Che faro senza Euridice?" ("What shall I do without Eurydice? Whither shall I go without my beloved?"), which in its profoundly simple feeling is matched in opera only by the closing solo of Purcell's *Dido and Aeneas*. Here the action properly concludes; but since the occasion required a happy ending, the God of Love once more appears and restores Eurydice to life. General rejoicings, with ballets and chorus, furnish the closing scene, which thus, with the overture, frames this antique tragedy for presentation to a European court of the eighteenth century.

In no other work did Gluck realize so consciously and so fully the effect of classic, statuesque repose as in *Orfeo*. The music, like the libretto, is denuded of all unnecessary ornament; nothing in it calls attention to itself. The forms are symmetrical and clearly perceived but freely intermingled and always appropriate to the moods and situations; the extremes of dull secco recitative on the one hand and of coloratura aria on the other are abolished; always the simplest means are used, and yet these produce an effect apparently out of all proportion to their simplicity. It can hardly be said that the music is in any degree suppressed in favor of poetry, even in the recitatives, which are certainly more musical and expressive than those of Lully or Rameau.[17] Rather, the music is purified; it is as though Gluck, by voluntarily abandoning the outward charms of Italian operatic melody, stimulated the sources of inward beauty. *Orfeo* was performed at Paris in 1774 with a French libretto, some added ballets, and a change of the role of Orpheus from contralto to tenor, which also involved some changes in the key scheme. The full score was printed at Paris in 1764—the first Italian opera (except Handel's) to be thus published since 1639. Its popularity may be inferred both from this fact and from the number of parodies which appeared in the latter half of the eighteenth century.[18]

The five years after *Orfeo* were filled with the composition of two other Italian operas and a number of lesser works. On December 16, 1767, occurred the performance of the second opera in which Gluck and Calzabigi collaborated, *Alceste*. Here is another Greek subject, first dramatized by Euripides. Like *Orfeo,* the opera exists in both the original form and a revision made for Paris in 1777. The differences between the two versions are more extensive than in *Orfeo,* and, as in the earlier work, it is hardly possible to decide dogmatically which is superior. Both have certain faults of dramatic construction, chiefly the artificial ending. King Admetus lies at the point of death; an oracle decrees his life may be spared if another will die in his stead. His wife, Alcestis, offers herself as the victim but is rescued and restored to Admetus—in Calzabigi's poem by Apollo, and in the Paris version by Hercules. The latter is according to the Greek original, but in both librettos the interference has the character of a mere arbitrary act of magnanimity on the part of a conventional eighteenth-century *deus ex machina* instead of being motivated, as in Euripides, by a feeling of gratitude for hospitality. But (as Einstein points out) [19] the strength of this motive, however it may have been appreciated by the Athenians, could not have been made clear to a modern audience, for whom the spectacle of Alcestis' sacrificial devotion was bound to overshadow all other interests. Thus the opera centers around the heroine, in comparison with whom the other figures count for little.

17 See Meyer, "Die Behandlung des Rezitativs in Glucks italienischen Reformopern," *Gluck-Jahrbuch* IV (1918) 1–90.
18 See Cucuel, "Les Opéras de Gluck dans les parodies du XVIIIe Siècle," RM III, No. 5 (1922) 201–21 and No. 6 (1922) 51–68.
19 *Gluck,* p. 107.

Gluck had called *Orfeo* a "dramma per musica," the usual designation of an opera. But *Alceste* he called a "tragedia messa in
musica," a "tragedy set to music," like the scores of Lully. The entire
action is on a grander scale than in *Orfeo*. It is organized, in a manner
similar to Traëtta, into monumental scene-complexes with large
choruses, which are the most promient features of the score. The
first act is the most unified and satisfactory, from the truly tragic
overture which leads directly into the opening outburst of the chorus,
the announcement by the herald of Admetus' impending death, the
choruses of mourning, proceeding in an unbroken crescendo of interest through the pronouncement of the oracle, and climaxing with
Alcestis' heroic resolve and her famous aria "Divinités du Styx."
The second act (in the Paris version) opens with the needed contrast,
the dances and choruses of rejoicing over Admetus' recovery; the
dramatic entrance of Alcestis, and the revelation to the king of the
identity of his rescuer, lead to some remarkable recitative dialogue,
ending with Alcestis' cavatina "Ah! malgré moi," the agitated second
part of which is broken by a short choral interlude. The third act is
dramatically an anticlimax, the action remaining for a long while
just where it was at the end of Act II; but the music is notable for
the choruses, the strangely calm and yet moving aria of Alcestis, "Ah,
divinités implacables," and a fine passionate aria of Admetus, "Alceste, au nom des Dieux." [20] After a banal final chorus, the opera
closes with the customary suite of ballets.

When the score of *Alceste* was published at Vienna in 1769 it con-
tained a dedicatory preface which is the clearest and fullest statement
of Gluck's and Calzabigi's new ideals for opera. This preface has been
reproduced so many times, and is so easily accessible in translation,
that it does not seem necessary to quote it again here. Like many
history-making documents, it embodied no ideas that had not been
stated before; it was a defense of a *fait accompli* rather than a program
for the future. It voiced the usual arguments against the caprice and
vanity of singers and against the domination of musical stereotypes
over the requirements of the text; it set forth the purpose of the
overture in much the same way that Algarotti had done; most significantly, it enunciated Gluck's musical aesthetic in a famous sim-

[20] The aria of Hercules "C'est en vain que l'enfer" was probably arranged (by Gossec)
from an aria in Gluck's *Ezio*.

ile: "I have striven to restrict music to its true office of serving poetry
by means of expression and by following the situations of the story,
without interrupting the action or stifling it with a useless superfluity
of ornaments; and I believed that it should do this in the same way
as telling colors affect a correct and well-ordered drawing; by a well-
assorted contrast of light and shade, which serves to animate the
figures without altering their contours." [21] Such self-abasement
would have been inconceivable to an Italian composer of the old
school, for whom the story existed only as a pretext for the music.
In the preface to *Paride et Elena* (1770), Gluck (or Calzabigi) was
even more explicit: "He who is concerned with truthfulness must
model himself to his subject, and the noblest beauties of harmony
and melody become serious faults if they are misplaced." [22] Such a
theory strongly suggests the later doctrines of Wagner, and it has
sometimes been cited as evidence of the latter's ignorance of operatic
history, or of his egoistic jealousy, that he failed to recognize the
fundamental kinship of Gluck's ideas with his own when he proclaimed that "the famous revolution of Gluck . . . really consisted
only in the revolt of the composer against the arbitrariness of the
singer." [23] But Wagner was right inasmuch as he was judging by results, not by professed intentions; for Gluck did not fully carry out
the implications of his own theories. How far the comparative simplicity of his music was the result of his aesthetic beliefs, and how
far the beliefs were *ex post facto* attempts to justify his practice, is
not easy to say. He was not a great technician; and though he probably did know more about counterpoint than Handel's cook, he certainly was not a match for either Hasse or Jommelli in facility of
invention or power of sustained thematic development in long arias.
Moreover, the art of singing was already on the decline; there were
no more artists of the caliber of Farinelli, even if Gluck could or
would have written for them. By way of compensation, orchestral
technique was steadily improving. One cannot therefore totally exclude the possibility that Gluck's ideas of the subordination of music,
of formal freedom, plainness of diction, and importance of orchestration were, if not actually inspired, at least supported by very
practical considerations. At any rate, they had a certain measure of

21 As translated in Einstein, *Gluck*, pp. 98–99.   22 Quoted in Cooper, *Gluck*, p. 143.
23 "Oper und Drama, Erster Theil," in *Gesammelte Schriften* III, 237.

success. When Dr. Burney visited Vienna in 1772 he reported the operatic situation in these words:

"Party runs as high among poets, musicians, and their adherents, at Vienna as elsewhere. Metastasio, and Hasse, may be said, to be at the head of one of the principal sects; and Calzabigi and Gluck of another. The first, regarding all innovations as quackery, adhere to the ancient form of the musical drama, in which the poet and musician claim equal attention from an audience; the bard in the recitatives and narrative parts; and the composer in the airs, duos, and choruses. The second party depend more on theatrial effects, propriety of character, simplicity of diction, and of musical execution, than on, what *they* style, flowery descriptions, superfluous similes, sententious and cold morality, on one side, with tiresome symphonies, and long divisions, on the other [24] . . . the chevalier Gluck is simplifying music . . . he tries all he can to keep his music chaste and sober, his three operas of *Orfeo, Alceste,* and *Paride* are proof of this, as they contain few difficulties of execution, though many of expression.[25] . . . I cannot quit Hasse and Gluck, without saying that it is very necessary to use discrimination in comparing them together. Hasse may be regarded as the Raphael, and . . . Gluck the Michael Angelo of living composers. If the affected French expression of *le grand simple* can ever mean anything, it must be when applied to the productions of such a composer as Hasse, who succeeds better perhaps in expressing, with clearness and propriety, whatever is graceful, elegant, and tender, than what is boisterous and violent; whereas Gluck's genius seems more calculated for exciting terror in painting difficult situations, occasioned by complicated misery, and the tempestuous fury of unbridled passions." [26]

Reading between the lines it is easy to see that Dr. Burney's sympathies are temperamentally with Hasse rather than Gluck; and this lends added weight to his testimony as to the enthusiasm with which both *Orfeo* and *Alceste* were received at Vienna. By comparison *Paride ed Elena,* the next production of Gluck and Calzabigi, was a failure, and whether for this reason or another, they collaborated no more. Gluck remained dissatisfied. His new style met with no understanding and but little attention outside the Vienna circle.

[24] Paraphrased from the preface to *Alceste.*
[25] *The Present State of Music in Germany* II, 232–33, 237.   [26] *Ibid.* II, 349–50.

Durazzo meanwhile had gone as ambassador to Venice in 1764, and Calzabigi left in 1771. Gluck's native tenacity rebelled at the prospect of only an incomplete triumph. Moreover, he had suffered financial reverses and doubtless felt the need to recoup his fortunes. Only one city in Europe offered the possibilities he sought, and his inclination to try his luck in Paris was strengthened by the fact that the new dauphine of France, Marie Antoinette, who had formerly been his singing pupil at the imperial court, was still interested in his career. Fortunately also, the situation in Paris was favorable for him. The old French opera, incurably conservative, had declined steadily in prestige since the middle of the century and was under constant critical attack from the partisans of Italian music, led by Jean-Jacques Rousseau. Although Gluck himself was probably not well known in Paris, the works of the German symphonists had been favorably received there for many years. In 1772 Gluck began the composition of *Iphigénie en Aulide,* a libretto adapted from Racine's tragedy by Du Roullet, a member of the French embassy staff at Vienna. By a combination of skillful diplomacy and the powerful intercession of Marie Antoinette the score was accepted; Gluck directed the carefully rehearsed first performance at Paris on April 19, 1774, and the work had an immediate success.

The chief thing which distinguishes *Iphigénie en Aulide* from *Orfeo* and *Alceste* is the greater rapidity and decisiveness of the action; it is a drama of events rather than a series of comparatively static pictures. As a consequence, the rhythm is more animated, the declamation more pointed, and the musical units shorter, more continuous, more completely intermingled, less self-sufficient than in the earlier works. When Dr. Burney visited Gluck at Vienna, the composer sang for him almost the whole of *Iphigénie,* which he had (according to his custom) already composed in his mind, though not yet set down on paper; and it was doubtless this work which led Burney to remark that "It seldom happens that a single air of his operas can be taken out of its niche, and sung singly, with much effect; the whole is a chain, of which a detached single link is but of small importance." [27] This observation is particularly true of the great scene at the end of Act II, where Agamemnon, wavering between his supposed duty to his country and his love for his daughter,

27 *The Present State of Music in Germany,* II, 262.

in a magnificent monologue finally resolves to save Iphigenia's life. Gluck's moving power as a dramatist in this scene is surpassed only by some of the pages of his own later *Iphigénie en Tauride*. Another beautiful place is the farewell of Iphigenia in the third act ("Adieu! conservez dans votre âme"), surely, as Newman says, "one of the most perfect emotional utterances of the eighteenth century." [28] The overture to *Iphigénie en Aulide,* Gluck's finest instrumental composition, still holds a place on symphonic programs.

The triumph of *Iphigénie en Aulide* was followed by Paris performances of the revised versions of *Orfeo* (1774) and *Alceste* (1776), as well as by unsuccessful revivals of two of Gluck's French *opéras comiques*. Meanwhile the inevitable happened. A group of literati, headed by Marmontel, determined to furnish Paris the spectacle of a musical combat between the new lion and a representative of the pure Italian school. Their chosen champion was Nicola Piccinni,[29] who lent himself to the project in all innocence and came out of it a distressed and chastened man.[30] The excitement in Paris over the "Quarrel of the Gluckists and Piccinnists" (as over that of the Buffonists twenty-five years earlier) was a manifestation of a side of the Gallic temperament which usually leaves the Anglo-Saxon cold. Benjamin Franklin, then commissioner of the United States of America in Paris, was moved to satire in the manner of Swift: "We had been shown numberless skeletons of a kind of little fly, called an ephemera, whose successive generations, we were told, were bred and expired within the day. I happened to see a living company of them on a leaf, who appeared to be engaged in conversation. You know I understand all the inferior animal tongues. . . . I listened through curiosity to the discourse of these little creatures; but as they, in their national vivacity, spoke three or four together, I could make but little of their conversation. I found, however, by some broken ex-

---

[28] *Gluck and the Opera*, p. 128.

[29] Piccinni (1728–1808) was educated at Naples under Leo and Durante. He began his career as a rival of Logroscino in comic opera at Naples, but it was the success of his *Cecchina zitella, o La buona figliola* at Rome in 1760 which made his European reputation. Numerous other serious and comic works followed. His career in France practically ended before the Revolution, though toward the end of his life he became an "inspector" at the Paris Conservatory. The operas *Roland* and *Didon* are in CF (piano-vocal scores); selection from *Le Faux Lord* (1783) in HAM 300. See Cametti, "Saggio cronologico," RMI VIII (1901) 75–100; Abert, "Piccinni als Buffokomponist," in his *Gesammelte Schriften*, pp. 346–64; biographies and studies by Ginguené, Della Corte, La Rotella, Napoli.

[30] For the details of this affair see Desnoiresterres, *Gluck et Piccinni*.

pressions that I heard now and then, they were disputing warmly on
the merit of two foreign musicians, one a *cousin*, the other a
moscheto; in which dispute they spent their time, seemingly as regardless of the shortness of life as if they had been sure of living a
month. Happy people! thought I, you live certainly under a wise,
just, and mild government, since you have no public grievances to
complain of, nor any subject of contention but the perfections and
imperfections of foreign music." [31] Franklin's badinage is less wither-
ing than the straight-faced observation of Symonds: "At times when
politics have been dull, theology dormant, and science undemon-
strative, even music has been found sufficient to excite a nation." [32]

The pleasant idea was conceived of having both Gluck and Piccinni compose the same libretto, Quinault's *Roland*. When he found
that Piccinni was already working on it, Gluck refused and produced
instead a setting of Quinault's *Armide*, which was performed in
September, 1777, four months before Piccinni was ready with his
Roland. The latter had a better reception than its composer had
hoped, though his reputation in French opera was not made secure
until the later success of *Atys* (1780) and *Didon* (1783). Meanwhile,
Gluck's *Armide* was received with enthusiasm by his friends and
disparagement by his enemies. The score is indeed very uneven,
partly because of the old-fashioned five-act libretto which included
many scenes not capable of stimulating the composer to his best
efforts. Comparisons with Lully were to be expected, and verdicts
were freely rendered in favor of one or the other according to the
prepossessions of the critic in each case. The most remarkable feature
of the music is its idyllic, sensuous charm, giving a foretaste of the
romantic style. This may be heard particularly in the air "Plus
j'observe ces lieux" (Act II, scene 3) and in the scene of parting
between Armide and Renaud (Act V, scene 1), a surprisingly passionate love duet for the eighteenth century. The chaconne in the
following scene is one of Gluck's noblest instrumental creations, a
worthy companion to the chaconne in Rameau's *Castor et Pollux*.

The last important work of Gluck, and certainly his masterpiece,
was *Iphigénie en Tauride*, first performed at Paris May 18, 1779.

31 "The Ephemera," a "bagatelle" written in 1778; in *Writings*, ed. Smyth (New York,
Macmillan, 1907) VII, 207. Quoted by permission of the publisher.
32 *The Revival of Learning* (N.Y., 1883) p. 244.

The libretto, written by Guillard on the model of Euripides, is the best poem Gluck ever set, and the entire work, a real drama in music, probably comes as close as possible to the ideal of a modern revival of the spirit of Greek tragedy. It is an extraordinary and happy mixture of ancient and modern motifs—the sense of an inexorable Fate which drives human beings on to catastrophe is combined with vivid, contrasting characterization and masterly depiction of emotion: the noble pathos of Iphigenia, the sullen, superstitious cruelty of Thoas, the fearful remorse of Orestes, the friendship between him and Pylades, and the mysterious brother-sister love between Orestes and Iphigenia. All these were things calculated to call forth Gluck's highest powers. These are displayed in the accompanied recitative near the beginning of the first act "Cette nuit j'ai revu le palais de mon père," where Iphigenia relates her dream which obscurely prefigures the course of the entire tragedy and serves in a manner as a substitute for the prologue of Euripides. It is not difficult to see in the music of these pages the source and model for nineteenth-century composers of similar scenes—Cherubini, Weber, Berlioz, even Wagner and Richard Strauss. Equally powerful is the gloomy air of Thoas, "De noirs pressentiments," with its heavy dotted rhythm and rising arpeggio figures in the bass reaching up "like tentacles of the underworld." [33] The choruses intensify by contrast the outlines of these individual characters. Unlike *Alceste* and the earlier *Iphigénie,* the chorus here takes no direct part in the action, except for a moment at the climax of the last act; the priestesses of Diana (sopranos and altos) furnish an immobile, neutral-colored background for Iphigenia; the chorus of Scythians (tenors and basses) is little else than spectacle, closely connected with a series of ballets whose descent from the exotic scenes of the traditional French ballet is obvious despite the conventional "Turkish" instruments of the late eighteenth century; the chorus of the Eumenides in Act II is merely the personification of Orestes' conscience, haunting him in a symbolic and terrible dream.

Iphigénie en Tauride has no formal overture, but rather an introduction depicting first "the calm," then a "storm"—no mere tour de force of nature painting (as often in earlier French opera) but

[33] Marx, *Gluck* II, 273. This rising broken-chord figure in the bass is characteristic of Gluck for the suggestion of the supernatural.

a prelude leading naturally into the first scene, which opens with the cry of Iphigenia and the chorus "Grands dieux! soyez-nous secourables!" Of the many fine details of the orchestral accompaniment in the course of the opera, one in particular may be mentioned: Orestes, left alone after his friend Pylades has been arrested by the temple guards, falls in a half stupor; in pitiable self-delusion he tries to encourage the feeling of peace which descends upon him momentarily, singing "Le calme rentre dans mon cœur." But the accompaniment, with a subdued, agitated sixteenth-note reiteration of one tone, and with a *sforzando* accent at the first beat of every measure, betrays the troubled state of his mind, from which he cannot banish the pangs of remorse for his past crime. It is perhaps the first occurrence in opera of this psychological device of using the orchestra to reveal the inward truth of a situation, in distinction from, even in contradiction to, the words of the text—a practice which Wagner was later to develop into a complete system.

One feature of this opera is the way in which Gluck returns to long-breathed, purely musical, even lyrical forms in the arias. It is as though the extreme of revolt against the dominance of music over poetry had passed, and the two were coming together again on equal terms. It is an example of the final stage of artistic revolutions, which usually end by taking over much of that which at first they had rejected. We are accustomed to regard Monteverdi, Gluck, and Wagner as the three revolutionary figures in the history of opera; but we tend too much to emphasize what each rejected of the past and to lose sight of the fact that the end result in every case was an enrichment of the musical substance of opera by the incorporation of many earlier musical achievements, though in a new guise or with new significance. Gluck, as we have already mentioned, often used numbers from his earlier operas when composing a new score; borrowings of this sort are especially frequent in his reform operas, and we are thus confronted with the realization that the works in which he is supposed to have renounced the ways of Italian opera are, to a considerable degree, made up of music from his own Italian operas of earlier date. The opening of the overture and of the aria "Diane impitoyable" in *Iphigénie en Aulide* comes from an aria of *Telemacco,* which work likewise supplied the overture to *Armide* and the opening chorus of *Alceste;* "Che puro ciel" of *Orfeo* is a final version of an aria used in three previous works; in *Iphigénie en Tauride* the chorus of the Eumenides is taken from *Semiramide* (1748), Iphigenia's aria "O malheureuse Iphigénie" from *La clemenza di Tito,* and other portions from *Telemacco*. The reversion to musical opera, however, is more than a matter of a few borrowed numbers. The whole score of *Iphigénie en Tauride,* particularly the arias, shows a tendency toward gathering the music into longer, more continuous, and more highly developed units. Even the old da capo reappears in Orestes' "Dieux qui me poursuivez," a fine instance of the dramatically appropriate use of this form. Thus we may see here a triumphant reconciliation of the two elements, words and music, the conflict of which had so much occupied the thoughts of Gluck and his contemporaries.

Gluck's last opera, *Echo et Narcisse* (1779), was not a success at Paris in spite of some beautiful individual numbers, and he took the disappointment badly. He returned at once to Vienna, where he died in 1787.

It is difficult to define Gluck's true significance for the history of opera. His essential achievement was the restoration of a more even balance between music and poetry, between what we may call the audible surface of opera and its dramatic content. His task was to elevate the drama to a more important place and to reduce the musical excrescences of the preceding period. Paradoxically, he accomplished this by simplifying the drama and enriching the music, by replacing the complexities of Metastasian intrigue with the statuesque figures of Greek legend, the roulades and ornaments of Hasse with his own harmonically conceived, orchestrally supported, oratorically declaimed melody, for which he obtained many suggestions from French opera. He combined the simplicity of the opéra comique, the grandeur of the tragédie lyrique, the vocal charm of Italian opera seria, and the symphonic achievements of the Italian and German schools in an international, or rather supernational, opera, which answered at once the contemporary demand for naturalness, its interest in classical forms, and its passion for art with the moral aim of offering great models of virtue and heroism for contemplation. His success was due not only to his powers as a musician but also to his intellectual grasp of the moving ideas of his age, his gift for taking practical advantage of the means at hand, his willingness to compromise when necessary, and a certain peasant-like obstinacy in the pursuit of his fundamental aims.

Nothing could be more misleading on the subject of Gluck than his own oft-quoted statement to the effect that when composing an opera he endeavored above all things to forget that he was a musician. Such a remark has all the characteristics of an epigram for the benefit of the French literary critics whom it was his interest to conciliate. Even if he himself by any chance believed there was an atom of meaning in it, there is no reason for us to take it seriously. On the contrary, he never forgot he was a musician; but he also never forgot that it was a drama he was composing, and, so far as the later works are concerned, he composed it so carefully, his settings were so uniquely right, that he marks the beginning of the end of that era which regarded any libretto as any composer's property and saw nothing extraordinary in seventy different settings of the same poem, all, if not perhaps equally good, at least equally suitable to the words. Gluck's operas survive not because of their poems, or of anyone's theories, but because of Gluck's music; and his music survives while that of many cleverer composers is forgotten because it is in itself the drama, not a mere fashionable dress to cover a text.

The influence of Gluck on later composers was comparatively small. He founded no school and had few disciples. We may trace his style of serious opera on heroic subjects treated in the grand manner through his one-time rival Piccinni, his pupil Salieri, through Cherubini, Méhul, and Spontini, to the greatest of his spiritual descendants, Berlioz.[34] But the line of descent is through similarity of dramatic aims and ideals rather than actual musical idiom. Outside France, Gluck made little permanent impression; Italy practically ignored him, and Germany remained under the Italian spell until a national opera began to develop with the approach of romanticism. Gluck was, like Handel, the end of an epoch rather than the beginning. He sums up the classical age of serious opera, as Handel does that of the late baroque. The qualities of sincerity, uprightness, and honest dealing with the art of music are common to both men.

[34] The nineteenth-century school of grand opera—Rossini's *Tell*, Meyerbeer, Halévy, Wagner's *Rienzi*—belongs in a different class.

16

Eighteenth-Century Comic Opera

IN THE SEVENTEENTH-CENTURY OPERA, comic episodes of all kinds were regularly mingled with serious scenes. One of the reforms of Zeno and Metastasio was the abolition of the comic as being irrelevant to the plot and incongruous with the tragic style. In the first part of the eighteenth century, therefore, we find a complete separation of the two types, which flourished for a long time side by side but with hardly any mutual influence. The comic opera grew up independently in each country, developing a number of quite diverse national forms, such as the Italian opera buffa, the French opéra comique, and the English ballad opera; after the middle of the century arose the German Singspiel and the Spanish *tonadilla*. Certain features were common to all these works in the early stages of their history: all showed signs of their humble origin in the choice of light or farcical subjects and the preference for scenes, personages, and dialogue taken from familiar popular comedies or from the everyday life of the common people (if fantasy was present, it was treated comically); all were performed by comparatively unskilled singers, often by inferior actors with whom music was, to say the least, only an avocation; [1] all (except the Italian opera buffa) used spoken dialogue; all occasionally parodied the serious opera; and all cultivated a simple, easily grasped musical style in which national popular idioms played a decisive part. Finally, in the course of the eighteenth century, all underwent a radical change in character from low-class farce to middle-class comedy of various sorts, acquiring in the process so many new features, both in the libretto and in the music, that by the end of the century the original distinction of serious and comic opera no longer had much meaning. Comic opera in its beginning was a "low-brow" entertainment, regarded by opera-

[1] The castrato, that symbol of opera seria, found no place in comic opera, but male roles were sometimes sung by women.

goers as something about on the level of a circus midway show; within a little over fifty years, it became of equal respectability and importance with serious opera; in less than fifty years more, it dominated the stage, having supplanted or absorbed the old opera seria almost completely. Mozart is the representative of comic opera at the end of the eighteenth century as Scarlatti was of opera seria at the beginning of that period.

OPERA BUFFA.[2]—The typical transformation of comic opera in the eighteenth century may be clearly traced in Italy. The early works of this period show the derivation from the commedia dell' arte (the national improvised comedy) in their distinct character-types, dialects, stereotyped incidents and situations, and a constant robustness of action and dialogue, seasoned with crude horseplay and supported by appropriate music. The characteristic form, first developed at Naples, was the intermezzo, which (as the name implies) was a short farce designed to be played between the acts or scenes of longer operas or plays. The commedia in musica, on the other hand, was a full-length opera on a comic libretto; it is historically descended from the pastoral comedies of the seventeenth century.[3] The custom grew up of making the two intermezzi which were required for a three-act opera form a continuous plot, so that performances in effect consisted of two operas, one serious and one comic, in alternation. Understandably, foreigners sometimes complained of the resultant confusion.[4] Sometimes the intermezzo was performed at the end of the opera as an afterpiece, thus becoming to all intents and purposes an independent work, retaining a vestige of its origin in its division into two acts instead of the three customary in full-length operas. Of the hundreds of comic pieces produced by famous as well as obscure composers in the first half of the eighteenth century, Pergolesi's intermezzo La serva padrona ("The Maid Mistress," 1733) has deservedly maintained its popularity to our own time.[5] It is characteristic of such

2 D'Arienzo, "Le origini dell' opera comica," RMI II (1895) 597–628, IV (1897) 421–59, VI (1899) 473–95, VII (1900) 1–33; Della Corte, L'opera comica italiana nel 1700; Scherillo, Storia letteraria dell' opera buffa napolitana; Abert, Mozart I, 400–58; Roncaglia, Il melodioso settecento italiano.   3 See Dent, Scarlatti, p. 127.
4 Cf. Wright, Some Observations Made in Travelling Through France, Italy, &c, p. 85.
5 Pergolesi (1710–1736), who studied under Durante and Feo at Naples, produced many church works and serious operas as well as intermezzi. There are modern editions of La serva padrona, Livietta e Tracollo (1734), and Il maestro di musica ("The Music Master," 1734?). A C.E. (piano-vocal scores) is being published by Bärenreiter, ed. F. Caffarelli. There are modern "performing editions," in English, published by The Music

works in its economy of musical resources—only two singers (soprano and bass) and a third mute character, with orchestra of strings and continuo. The musical style is likewise typical: prevailingly major, rapid in movement, having much repetition of short motifs, a disjunct melodic line, comic effects produced by sudden offbeat accents, wide skips, and an infectious gaiety and vigor of utterance, offering much to the tone and gesture of the actor (Example 82). Beside the

LA SERVA PADRONA, Act I

Ex.82.   Pergolesi

e sì   e no,   e no   e sì, e qua e là, e su e giù, e si e
no, e no e sì e sì e   no; or que-sto ba - - - sti, ba - -
- sti, ba-sti;   fi - nir si   può, fi - nir si può, fi - nir si può.

more common allegro arias there is found in the intermezzi a slower, cantabile style, sometimes in minor, which often features chromatic melodies and harmonies for mock-pathetic effects. Folk-songish canzonettas and bass-buffo patter songs frequently appear. Throughout the scores, one is impressed by the absolute fidelity of music to text; the singing seems to be simply a highly flexible, sensitive, melodic declamation of the words, preserving and heightening every detail which might contribute to the comic effect. At the same time, there is never a suggestion that the words impede in any way the spontaneous flow of the music; text repetition is a constant feature but somehow never gives the impression of artificiality. One consequence of this perfect union of text and music is the extraordinary variety of forms in the arias of the intermezzi, in marked contrast to the stock da capo pattern of the contemporary opera seria. The recitativo secco, which is so well adapted to rapid speech, takes an important place in the intermezzi, and the recitativo accompagnato is tellingly used for comic or parodistic purposes, as in Act I of Pergolesi's *Livietta e*

Press, New York, of *The Music Master, The Jealous Husband, The Brother in Love,* and *Olympiade.* See also HAM 286, 287. The principal biography of Pergolesi is by Radiciotti.

Tracollo, where there is a delightful burlesque of the grandiloquent style of serious opera.[6]

Characteristic of the intermezzi was the use of the bass voice, which had been practically abolished from opera seria. The presence of basses along with the higher voices made possible one of the most distinctive features of Italian comic opera, namely the ensembles, particularly those at the end of each act.[7] The opera seria, with its emphasis on solo singing, had not developed the ensemble forms, with the exception of the duet. Occasionally there would be a trio or quartet, but these were either unimportant, short, chorus-like pieces, or else merely arias in which the various phrases or sections were taken by each voice in turn.[8] The problem undertaken in the opera buffa was to create an ensemble finale which was not simply a closing set piece, but in which the action of the play was still continued. Nicola Logroscino[9] was the first to attempt a solution to this problem, but his finales, though influential on later composers, suffered from the lack of any organized musical scheme, being simply through-composed in accordance with the action. In the comic operas of Galuppi[10] the Logroscino finale was supplanted by the "chain finale," where the action is broken up into short units, each being composed as a separate piece.

Galuppi's association with Carlo Goldoni[11] at Venice, which be-

6 Tracollo's "Misero! A chi mi volgerò" (*I classici* XXIII, Quad. 90–91, pp. 17–19). See also Uberto's "Ah! quanto mi sa male" in Act II of *La serva padrona* (*I classici* XXIII. Quad. 89–90, pp. 41–45).

7 Fuchs, "Die Entwicklung des Finales in der italienischen Opera Buffa vor Mozart"; Dent, "Ensembles and Finales in 18th Century Italian Opera," SIMG XI (1909–10) 543–69; XII (1910–11) 112–38.

8 Cf. Dent, *Scarlatti,* p. 165–66.

9 Logroscino (1698–*ca.* 1765) produced comic operas at Naples from 1738. He was known as "Il dio dell' opera buffa" ("The God of Comic Opera"). Little of his music has been preserved, and no works are available in modern editions. See Kretzschmar, "Zwei Opern Nicolo Logroscinos," JMP XV (1908) 47–68 (also in *Gesammelte Aufsätze* II, 374–400), and biography by Prota-Giurleo.

10 Baldassare Galuppi (1706–1785), known as "Il Buranello" from the name of his island birthplace near Venice, was a pupil of Lotti. His 112 operas (mostly comic) were produced chiefly at Venice, though he spent the years 1765–1768 as chapelmaster at the Court of St. Petersburg (Catherine II), where Bortnianski was one of his pupils. Selections from *Il filosofo di campagna* (1754) in *I classici* XIII (Quad. 54–58). See Wotquenne, "Baldassare Galuppi . . . ; étude bibliographique," RMI VI (1899) 561–79; Piovano, "Baldassare Galuppi; note bio-bibliografiche," RMI XIII (1906) 676–726, XIV (1907) 333–65, XV (1908) 233–74; Bollert, *Die Buffoopern Baldassare Galuppis.*

11 Goldoni (1707–1793) was active at Venice until 1761, after which he lived in Paris. He was the leading figure in the reform of Italian drama in the eighteenth century. His comedies, rejecting the stock character types and plots as well as the improvised dialogue

gan about 1749, was a turning point in the history of the opera buffa. From this time on, the early Neapolitan farce underwent a process of reform, becoming more dignified, more orderly in structure, and more refined in action and language. New kinds of comic opera librettos began to appear—works which must be called dramas rather than farces, and which were often sentimental or even pathetic in character. These newer tendencies did not, of course, replace the old comic elements altogether but rather existed side by side or intermingled with them, so that the comic opera libretto in the second half of the eighteenth century was distinctly varied and, on the whole, much more interesting than that of the opera seria. One of the most successful examples was Goldoni's *Buona figliuola* ("The Good Girl"), composed by Nicola Piccinni in 1760 for Rome, where it enjoyed a two-year run and soon became known all over Europe. The story was taken from Richardson's *Pamela; or, Virtue Rewarded* (1740). The score is remarkable for the long, complex, and carefully planned finales of each act. Piccinni was probably the first composer to try to unify these sections by means of a recurring musical theme ("rondo finale"), thus making a step toward the highly organized symphonic finale which was to be perfected by Mozart. In other ways also, for example, in the assigning of independent motifs to the orchestra and in the relatively greater continuity and self-sufficiency of the instrumental parts, Piccinni advanced the style of opera buffa.

As the century went on, the music of comic opera grew more ambitious, broadening its range of expression in accordance with the broadening subject matter of the librettos. Three composers of this period were Pasquale Anfossi (whose musical talent was akin to Piccinni's),[12] Pietro Guglielmi,[13] and Giovanni Paisiello, whose

---

of the old commedia dell' arte, are models of natural characterization and spontaneous action; the old farcical material is replaced by humorous, tender, even sentimental plots. He wrote many opera librettos. His *Mémoires* are important for the history of the theatre and opera in the eighteenth century. See biography by Chatfield-Taylor; Della Torre, *Saggio di una bibliografia;* Spinelli, *Bibliografia goldoniana.*

[12] Anfossi (1727–1797), a pupil of Piccinni, wrote seventy-six operas, of which the most successful was *L'incognita perseguitata* ("The Persecuted Incognita," Rome, 1773). He directed the Italian opera in London 1781–1783. During the last years of his life he was chapelmaster at the Lateran in Rome, where he composed some church music.

[13] Guglielmi (1728–1804) studied under Durante at Naples. He is said to have composed nearly two hundred dramatic works, mostly of the comic genre, besides a number of oratorios, Masses, etc. He worked at Dresden and Brunswick, and was in London from 1772 to 1777. See Piovano, "Elenco cronologico," RMI XII (1905) 407–46; Bustico, *Pier Aless. Guglielmi.*

Barbiere di Siviglia (1782),[14] remained such a favorite in Italy that even in 1816 Rossini had to overcome popular prejudice against the presumption of any other composer attempting to set the same libretto. Paisiello's *Socrate immaginario* ("The Man Who Thought He Was Socrates," Naples, 1775) is an example of parody, a frequent resource of comic opera librettists. The objects in this case are the classicist movement in general and Gluck's *Orfeo* in particular—the scene between Orpheus and the Furies being burlesqued in broad, though clever, fashion. In *La molinara* ("The Maid of the Mill," Naples, 1788) Paisiello displays many of those expressive qualities and turns of phrase which we are accustomed to associate with Mozart, while his *Nina* (Naples, 1789) is one of the best examples of sentimental comedy in this whole period (Example 83). Paisiello was, in short, a many-sided genius, a master of musical characterization, perhaps the greatest figure in eighteenth-century opera buffa next to Mozart himself, and one who exercised a strong influence on the musical style of the latter. Paisiello's gifts are especially apparent in the orchestral writing, which is more varied and more important dramatically than in any earlier buffo composer. In his ensemble finales, Paisiello rivaled the achievements of Piccinni both in scope and in the skill with which musical forms were adapted to the action of the text. He also was one of the first composers to introduce ensemble finales in serious opera.

An immediate forerunner of Mozart at Vienna was Florian Leopold Gassmann,[15] whose two most celebrated comic operas were

14 Paisiello (1740–1816), another pupil of Durante, wrote a large quantity of church and instrumental music in addition to more than one hundred operas. His *Barbiere di Siviglia* was produced at St. Petersburg, where he resided from 1776 to 1784. *Il re Teodoro* ("King Theodore") was performed in the latter year at Vienna. Otherwise, the principal scene of his activity was Naples. Seven of his operas were printed during his lifetime. The following are available in modern editions: *Die schöne Müllerin* [*La molinara*] (Leipzig, Senff, [1890]); *Nina*, selections (piano-vocal) in *I classici* XX; *Socrate immaginario*, piano-vocal score, ed. Assoc. dei musicologi italiani (1931); *Il barbiere di Siviglia* (Ricordi, full score 1868; piano-vocal score, ca. 1880 and 1903). The literature on Paisiello is too extensive to be listed here. See particularly Abert, "Paisiellos Buffokunst," in his *Gesammelte Schriften*, pp. 365–96 (also in AfMw I); biographies and studies by Della Corte, Pupino, Speziale, and Faustini-Fasini; Cortese, "Un' autobiografia inedita di Giovanni Paisiello," RassM III (1930) 123–35.
15 Gassmann (1729–1774), by birth a Bohemian, studied two years with Padre Martini at Bologna, and was active as conductor at Vienna from 1764. He wrote seven serious and fourteen comic operas; *La contessina*, first performed in 1770 and later translated into German by J. A. Hiller, has been published in a two-act arrangement as Vol. XXI of the DTOe. See Donath, "Gassmann als Opernkomponist," SzMw II (1914) 34–211.

L'amore artigiano ("Love among the Laborers," 1767) and *La contessina* ("The Countess," 1770), both on librettos by Goldoni. Gassmann's ensemble finales are remarkable for the way in which the orchestra carries on the music in continuous fashion, giving unity and direction to the entire scene. The orchestral part is important

NINA

Ex 83.   Paisiello

also in the arias, sometimes even having greater melodic interest than the voice. Gassmann's melodic style shows the transition from the characteristic Italian vocal line to the plainer, less mannered, more lyrical and expressive melody of Mozart.[16]

The pure Italian comic opera at the end of the century is best represented by Domenico Cimarosa,[17] whose *Matrimonio segreto*

[16] See for example the aria "Curiosità mi sporno" from *La notte critica* (1768) in Donath, "Gassmann," SzMw II (1914) Ex. 4, pp. 182–99.

[17] Cimarosa (1749–1801) was educated at Naples, where his earliest works were performed. A typically fecund Italian composer, he produced about eighty operas, serious and comic, as well as many church works and a quantity of instrumental music. He enjoyed a European reputation and was at the Court of St. Petersburg from 1789 to

("The Secret Marriage," Vienna, 1792), one of the most popular
works of its time, fairly rivals Mozart in tunefulness and spontaneity,
though lacking Mozart's profundity and musical constructive power.
But profundity was far from being an Italian ideal in this field; the
qualities of wit, liveliness, and melodic flow, a never ending vein of
loquacity and good humor, constituted the charm of Cimarosa as of
all his Italian confreres. He continued the tradition of Paisiello and
the other eighteenth-century buffo composers in that inimitable musical style which led in the nineteenth century to Rossini, Donizetti,
and (ultimately) Verdi's *Falstaff.*

OPÉRA COMIQUE.[18]—The founders of the French comic opera were
Molière and Lully, whose comedy ballets, pieces in which spoken
dialogue alternated with songs and dances, were presented before
Louis XIV during the 1660's.[19] When Lully assumed control of the
Academy of Music in 1672 his monopoly cut off all but the barest
musical resources from other Paris theatres, and the death of Molière
in the following year put an end to the first stage of the comedy
ballet. At this juncture an Italian Theatre, which had been established on a permanent basis at Paris in 1661, began to intermingle
French scenes, including music, with its improvised Italian comedies.
In the course of the next two decades, the French language gradually
replaced Italian: eventually the "Italian" troupe gave nothing but
comedies and farces (of a rather low sort) in French, which still
retained many traces of their commedia dell' arte predecessors, and
which were embellished by fanciful displays with ballets and songs.[20]
The Italians were expelled from Paris in 1697, and their repertoire
was taken over, in a still cruder form, by various small popular theatres which played a few weeks in each year at the two large fairs of

---

1792. The most recent biographies of Cimarosa are by Vitale (1929) and Tibaldi (1939); see
also Magni-Dufflocq, "Domenico Cimarosa, note biografiche," *Bolletino bibliografico-
musicale* V (1930) 5–15.

[18] Cucuel, *Les Créateurs de l'opéra-comique; idem,* "Sources et documents," *Année musicale* III (1913) 247–82; Genest, *L'Opéra-comique;* Campardon, *Les Comédiens du roi
de la troupe italienne; idem, Les Spectacles des foires;* La Laurencie, "L'Opéra-comique,"
in Lavignac, *Encyclopédie,* Pt. I, Vol. III, pp. 1457 ff.; Grout, "Origins of the Opéra-
comique."

[19] Tiersot, *La Musique dans la comédie de Molière;* Böttger, *Die "Comédie-ballet" von
Molière-Lully;* music in Prunières ed. of Lully.

[20] Parfaict, *Histoire de l'ancien théâtre italien;* Du Gerard, *Tables;* Gherardi, *Théâtre
italien;* Grout, "The Music of the Italian Theatre at Paris, 1682–1697," in *Papers of the
American Musicological Society . . . 1941,* pp. 158–70; *idem,* "Seventeenth Century Parodies of French Opera," MQ XXVII (1941) 211–19, 514–26.

Paris. Practical exigencies forced these groups to simplify their music to an extreme degree. They used for the most part little popular tunes ("vaudevilles"—Example 84) to which the authors adapted new words—a process known technically as "parody." Little by little the fortunes of the Fair Theatres improved, until in 1715 they were brought under one management and formally established as the Théâtre de l'Opéra-comique. For a long time they continued giving popular comedies in which the vaudevilles were the principal source of music [21] and burlesque of the serious opera a frequent device.[22] As a competitor, they had the so-called "New Italian Thea-

Vaudeville Airs from
THÉÂTRE DE LA FOIRE, vol. I

Ex.84.

tre," which had been re-established in Paris after the death of Louis XIV in 1715.[23] Among the literary talents attracted to the latter theatre was Charles-Simon Favart, who during the 1740's raised the vaudeville comedy to its highest level and at the same time en-

[21] Carmody, *Le Repertoire de l'opéra-comique en vaudevilles;* Parfaict, *Mémoires;* Lesage, *Théâtre de la foire;* Barberet, *Lesage et le théâtre de la foire;* Calmus, *Zwei Opernburlesken.*
[22] Cf. Cucuel, "La Critique musicale," *Année musicale* II (1912) 127–203; Grannis, *Dramatic Parody in Eighteenth Century France.*
[23] *Le Nouveau Théâtre italien; Les Parodies du nouveau théâtre italien* (with *Supplément*); Geulette, *Notes et souvenirs;* Desboulmiers, *Histoire anecdotique;* Origny, *Annales du théâtre-italien;* Cucuel, "Notes sur la comédie italienne de 1717 à 1789," SIMG XV (1913–14) 154–66.

couraged the introduction of new music—airs parodied from operas and even some originally composed songs—in place of the old-fashioned vaudevilles.[24] From 1752–1754 the performance at Paris of a dozen Italian buffo operas (including Pergolesi's *Serva padrona*) by a visiting troupe gave rise to a famous quarrel, the "War of the Bouffons," [25] in the course of which the relative merits of French and Italian music were argued *ad nauseam*. One of the peculiar features of this quarrel was that no one seemed to realize that all the comparisons were being made between French *serious* opera and Italian *comic* opera, and therefore the real point at issue was missed. However, the results of the Italians' visit were important, for they led a new generation of French composers to create a national comic opera with original music, in which the native popular idiom of the vaudeville was overlaid and enriched by a more refined, varied, and expressive style.

A forerunner of this new opéra comique was Jean-Jacques Rousseau's *Devin du village* ("The Village Soothsayer"),[26] which was performed at the Academy of Music in 1752 and remained in the repertoire for sixty years. This charming little work is Italian in form— that is, it has continuous music, with recitatives—but French in style and feeling. The melodies show kinship with both the vaudeville and the popular romances of the day, while the harmonizations are amusingly naïve. Rousseau's attempt to found a French comic opera had no immediate results; he himself, with typical inconsistency, declared in the following year that "the French have no music and

[24] Favart, *Théâtre; idem, Mémoires et correspondances;* Monnet, *Mémoires;* Font, *Favart;* Iacuzzi, *The European Vogue of Favart.*

[25] Richebourg's *Contribution à l'histoire de la "Querelle des Bouffons"* contains a bibliography of the principal documents in this affair. See especially Grimm, "Lettre sur Omphale"; *idem, Le Petit Prophète de Boemischbroda; idem, Correspondance littéraire;* Kretzschmar, "Die *Correspondance littéraire*" in *Gesammelte Aufsätze* II 210–25, also in JMP X (1903) 77–92; Rousseau, *Lettre sur la musique française;* Diderot, *Le Neveu de Rameau;* La Laurencie, "La Grande Saison italienne de 1752," *Mercure Musical* VIII, No. 6 (1912) 18–33; Nos. 7–8, pp. 13–22; Hirschberg, *Die Enzyklopädisten und die französische Oper.*

[26] Rousseau (1712–1778) was an accomplished amateur whose lifelong interest in music is evident both from his writings (see especially his *Dictionnaire de musique,* 1768, based on articles contributed to the *Encyclopédie*) and from his compositions, which include an opera (*Les Muses galantes,* 1745) and a collection of romances entitled *Les Consolations des misères de ma vie* (1781). See Tiersot, *Jean-Jacques Rousseau;* Masson, "Les Idées de Rousseau sur la musique," SIM *Revue Musicale* VIII, No. 6 (1912) 1–17; Nos. 7–8, pp. 23–32; Pougin, *Jean-Jacques Rousseau musicien;* Arnheim, "*Le Devin du village,*" SIMG IV (1902–1903) 686–727. Music from *Le Devin* in HAM 291.

never can have any—or if they ever do, so much the worse for them." [27]
Yet after a few years of experimentation, the new French comic opera
came to full growth in the works of Duni, Philidor, and Monsigny,
while Gluck independently was producing a series of similar pieces
at Vienna.[28]

The new opéra comique differed in many ways from both the
earlier vaudeville comedies and the Italian opera buffa. The form
was known as a *comédie mêlée d'ariettes*, a "comedy [in spoken dia-
logue] mingled with songs." (The term "ariette" was used as the
diminutive of the Italian "aria" to distinguish a newly composed
song from the traditional vaudeville melodies.) The subject matter
was varied: oriental fantasy (Gluck's *Rencontre imprévue*, Grétry's
Zemire et Azor), realism (Philidor's *Tom Jones*, based on Fielding's
novel), intrigue comedy on the Italian model (Monsigny's *On ne
s'avise jamais de tout*), sentimental drama (Monsigny's *Déserteur*),
or medieval tales (Grétry's *Richard Coeur-de-Lion*). An important
group of opéras comiques were those with scenes and characters representing an idealized peasantry, with a naïve heroine (a character
type inherited from Favart) and a manly young hero who, oppressed
by a wicked noble, are finally saved either by virtue of their own
innocence and honesty or by the intervention of a more powerful
noble or the king himself. Such pieces abounded in the advanced
ideas of the day, and their criticism of the current social order reflected, although in a perfectly harmless fashion, the doctrines of
Rousseau and the other encyclopedists and reformers. The music,
seldom profound, was always tuneful and charming (see Example 85).
Ensembles, especially duets, were common, though the French never
developed the dramatic ensemble finale to the extent the Italians

[27] End of his *Lettre sur la musique française*.
[28] Egidio Romualdo Duni (1709–1775), a pupil of Durante at Naples, came to Paris
in 1755. He wrote about twenty opéras comiques, of which *L'Isle des fous* (1760) and *La
Fée Urgèle* (1765) are the best.

François André Danican-Philidor (1726–1795), the last of a distinguished family of
musicians, was known equally as composer and chess player. He wrote some twenty
comic operas, of which the most successful were *Le Maréchal ferrant* (1761) and *Tom
Jones* (1764); also a few serious operas (including *Ernelinde, princesse de Norvège*, 1767)
and some church music. See Bonnet, *Philidor et l'évolution de la musique française*.

Pierre-Alexandre Monsigny (1729–1817), though not a thoroughly trained musician,
succeeded as a composer of comic operas on the strength of his melodic gifts, which lay
in the direction of tender and sentimental expression. His use of orchestral color is
often imaginative. His best work was *Le Déserteur* (1769). See Pougin, *Monsigny et son
temps*. Cf. also Arnoldson, *Sedaine et les musiciens de son temps*.

did. Short descriptive orchestral background pieces were frequent—a heritage from Lully and Rameau. Every opéra comique ended with a "vaudeville final," a strophic song with refrain, the tune either a popular vaudeville or in imitation of that style. The form of the vaudeville final established itself not only in the later French opéra comique but in other countries as well (see for example the finales of Gluck's *Orfeo,* Mozart's *Entführung,* Rossini's *Barbiere di Siviglia*).

LE DESERTEUR, Act I, sc.1

Ex.85.　　　　　　　　　　　　　　　　　　　Monsigny,

Peut - on af - fli - ger c'e qu'on ai - me? Pour-quoi cher -
cher à le fâ - cher? Peut -
on af - fli - ger c'e qu'on ai - me? C'est bien en vou -
loir à soi mê - - - - me, c'est bien en vou -
loir à soi mê - - - - me.

The leading composer of the eighteenth-century opéra comique was Grétry,[29] whose music happily combines the melodic grace of Italy with the delicate imagination, simplicity, lyricism, and rhythmic finesse of the French. His masterpiece, *Richard Coeur-de-Lion* (1784), is a landmark of early romantic opera, based on the legend of the rescue of King Richard from prison by his faithful minstrel Blondel.

[29] The best work of Grétry (1742–1813) falls between his *Tableau parlant* (1769) and *Richard Coeur-de-Lion* (1784). A collected edition (45 volumes so far) is being published under the auspices of the Belgian government; air from *Richard* in HAM 306. See Grétry's *Mémoires* and *Réflexions d'un solitaire;* there are numerous biographies and monographs, of which those of Bobillier and De Curzon may be especially noted (see bibliography in Lavignac, *Encyclopédie,* Pt. I, Vol. III, p. 1481; also *Grove's Dictionary,* 4th ed., and *Supplementary Volume*).

The rescue plot was a favorite in operas of the late eighteenth and early nineteenth centuries, blending the emotions of suspense, personal loyalty, and triumph of virtue over evil in an effective dramatic pattern, familiar to us still through Beethoven's *Fidelio*. By way of added romantic color, Grétry introduced in *Richard* an imitation of a simple troubadour song, which pervades the work almost like a leitmotif. The ballad "Que le sultan Saladin" (Act I), introduced simply as a song external to the action, is the type of many such interpolations in later opera. Blondel's air "O Richard, O mon roi" ("O Richard, O my king," Act I), by its elevated, sincere, and ardent expression, lifts this opéra comique into the realm of serious romantic drama, setting an ideal to which many later composers paid homage (Example 86).

The opéra comique continued to flourish during the revolution and early years of the nineteenth century,[30] though it had no composers comparable to Grétry either in ability or popularity until the success of Boieldieu's *Jean de Paris* in 1812. Like the Italian opera buffa, the French opéra comique in the course of the eighteenth century had undergone the transformation from low popular comedy to varied, semiserious human drama, from the music of popular folk song to the efforts of able composers. It was destined for greater triumphs in the nineteenth century and for such further changes of style and subject matter as to leave the designation "comique" merely a memento of its origin and a conventional indication of one vestige of its early days, the use of spoken dialogue.

BALLAD OPERA.[31]—When Addison in 1711 complained that "our English Musick is quite rooted out," he uttered no more than the melancholy truth, so far as the theatre was concerned. Yet the enthusiasm for Italian opera which prevailed during the first quarter of the eighteenth century eventually provoked a reaction. The English, unable to compete with foreign opera seria on its own ground, took revenge by creating the ballad opera, which at the same time ridiculed Italian music and originated a national comic type as distinctive and popular for the British as opera buffa was for the Italians or opéra comique for the French. The best-known of these works,

[30] Pougin, *L'Opéra-comique pendant la révolution.*
[31] Tufts, "Ballad Operas," MA IV (1912–1913) 61–86; Squire, "An Index of Tunes in the Ballad-Operas," MA II (1910–1911) 1–17; Gagey, *Ballad Opera.*

Ex.86.   Grétry

Ò Ri - chard, ò mon Roi! L'u-ni - vers t'a-ban-

don - ne, Sur la ter-re il n'est donc que moi Qui s'in-té-resse à

ta per-son - ne, Moi seul dans l'u-ni-vers, Vou-drais bri-ser tes

fers, Et tout le re-ste t'a-ban-don - - ne.

and one which has survived to our own time, was *The Beggar's Opera,*
written by John Gay with music arranged by Pepusch and first performed at London in 1728.[32] The characters are pickpockets, bawds,
jailbirds, and similar gentry (in keeping with Swift's suggested title
"The Newgate Pastoral"), the language is low and racy, and the play
is full of satirical thrusts both at the absurdities of Italian opera and
at the reigning Whig politicians of the day. The songs, which alternate
with spoken dialogue, are for the most part familiar ballad tunes
(Example 87), though there are some borrowings from other sources

THE BEGGAR'S OPERA, air XVI
Over the Hills and Far Away
Ex.87.

(for example, the march from Handel's *Rinaldo*). The motifs of
political and musical satire are particularly congenial to the English in comic opera, as witness Gilbert and Sullivan; neither in the
eighteenth nor the nineteenth century were the Londoners inclined
to take opera seria with complete seriousness.

The success of the *Beggar's Opera* struck a blow at the fortunes of
Handel and marked the beginning of the decline of Italian opera

[32] John Christopher Pepusch (1667–1752), by birth a German, came to London from
Berlin in 1700 and was one of the founders of the Academy of Ancient Music (1710). A
learned and conservative musician, he was long director of Lincoln's Inn Theatre, for
which he composed several masques and arranged three ballad operas. He also composed
some sonatas, cantatas, and motets. See Burney, *History* (2d ed.) II, 985–90; Hughes, "John
Christopher Pepusch," MQ XXXI (1945) 54–70. There is a modern edition of the *Beggar's Opera* in Calmus. *Zwei Opernburlesken aus der Rokokozeit;* piano-vocal score, rev.
by F. Austin (Boosey & Hawkes); selections in HAM 264. See also studies of Gay and the
Beggar's Opera by Benjamin, Kidson, Schultz, and Berger.

in England. There was a spate of ballad operas during the next ten years, and they continued to be produced throughout the century. The form underwent an evolution similar to that of the vaudeville comedy in France: people tiring of the same old tunes, composers turned to other sources or began to introduce their own songs into the scores, though keeping in general to the ballad style. Indeed, the typical English comic opera of the later eighteenth century is such a hodgepodge of popular tunes, songs from favorite operas, and original music that the elements are hard to disentangle, though the genuine folk ballads of the early days gradually disappeared. The influence of the opera buffa and opéra comique is increasingly apparent after the middle of the century, not only in the outright appropriation of both librettos and music but also in the whole trend from broad comedy and burlesque toward a semiserious, sentimental type of plot with simple half-Italian, half-English music—a singularly innocent, naïve kind of entertainment which was tremendously popular in its day and is still not without a certain appeal.[33]

One of the composers of comic opera was Dr. Thomas Arne,[34] whose *Thomas and Sally* (1760?) has been recently revived; his *Love in a Village* (1762) is a typical pasticcio of the period. Dr. Arne, incidentally, is known as the composer of the only successful English serious opera of the eighteenth century, *Artaxerxes* (1762; the text translated and adapted by the composer from Metastasio), which is a good imitation of contemporary Italian style but otherwise undistinguished. The chief later composers were Charles Dibdin, William Shield, and Stephen Storace.[35] Of these, the most gifted (though not

---

33 The basic study of English opera in the second half of the eighteenth century is Winesanker, "The Record of English Musical Drama, 1750–1800." See also Kelly, *Reminiscences* II, 36, 66, *et passim.*

34 Thomas Augustine Arne (1710–1778), "the most eminent English composer of his generation" (Grove), first made a reputation with his music for an adaptation of Milton's *Comus* in 1738. His masque *Alfred* (1740) contains the celebrated "Rule, Brittania." Aside from nearly fifty theatre works, Arne composed two oratorios, many songs, catches, glees, etc., and some instrumental pieces. Oxford gave him the degree of Mus. Doc. in 1759.

35 Dibdin (1745–1814) led a varied life in London as singer, actor, manager, author, and composer. He published a five-volume *History of the Stage* (1795), besides memoirs and several novels; he wrote the texts as well as the music to most of his comic operas, of which he produced nearly one hundred from 1764 to 1811. A series of "table entertainments" (from 1790) included many of his most popular songs. His most successful comic operas were *Lionel and Clarissa* (1768), *The Padlock* (1768), *The Waterman* (1774), and *The Quaker* (1775). See Sear, "Charles Dibdin," M&L XXVI (1945) 61–65.

Shield (1748–1829) wrote forty comic operas, besides many songs, and two books of

the most popular) was Shield, whose *Rosina* (1783) is a good example
of English comic opera in this period. His librettos, like those of
Storace (*The Haunted Tower*, 1789; *The Pirates*, 1792; *The Chero-
kee*, 1794), show an expansion of subject matter to include popular
supernatural and adventurous tales in the early romantic taste. Storace's music betrays to some extent the influence of Mozart, especially
in the use of the concerted finale (as in Act I of *The Pirates*). The
comic opera was continued in the early nineteenth century by Sir
Henry Rowley Bishop (1786–1855), of whose 120 dramatic compositions or arrangements nothing is known to present-day audiences but
a setting of Shakespeare's "Lo, here the gentle lark" and the melody
of "Home, sweet home," from the comic opera *Clari, the Maid of
Milan* (1823).

English comic opera, unlike that of either Italy or France, remained a local development, without influence on the course of serious opera anywhere. In the American colonies it flourished for a
time, but with no important historical consequences. In a century
which, to speak mildly, was not the Golden Age of British music, the
ballad opera appeared as a vigorous but solitary gesture of revolt
against foreign musical domination; but it lacked the principle of
growth within itself, nor did external conditions favor the rise on
its basis of an independent serious national opera. The harmless
trifles of Dibdin, Shield, and Storace are less the flowers of English
genius than the somewhat childish pastimes of a people whose real
energies were wholly occupied with the growth of industry and the
expansion of empire.

THE SINGSPIEL.[36]—The collapse of German opera in the first half
of the eighteenth century discouraged any systematic attempt at
native musical drama for many years. Even the regular theatre,
though spurred on by the reforms of Gottsched, did not succeed in
shaking off its baroque crudities and its later subservience to French

---

violin trios and duets.

Storace (1763–1796) had the advantage of a thorough early musical training. After
studying at Naples, he produced two Italian comic operas at Vienna (1785–1786), where
he associated with Mozart. (His sister, Ann Storace, was the original Susanna in Mozart's
Figaro.) He wrote eighteen English comic operas, also some songs and instrumental
music. See Kelly's *Reminiscences*, which give many interesting details on the state of the
English stage at the end of the eighteenth century.

[36] Schletterer, *Das deutsche Singspiel*; Eitner, "Die deutsche komische Oper," MfMg
XXIV (1892) 37–92; Lüthge, *Die deutsche Spieloper*.

tragedy until after the middle of the century. As for opera, with a few insignificant exceptions, nothing corresponding to the Italian opera seria or the French tragédie lyrique ever appeared. Yet the seeds of a new growth were present, and the soil in which they were to flourish was the same that had nurtured comic opera in Italy, France, and England—namely the theatre of the common people. Bands of strolling players discovered that they could attract larger audiences by mingling music with their plays, and so the new German Singspiel arose, somewhat like the French opéra comique, as a spoken comedy with interspersed lyrical songs. The latter, since they were to be performed by actors not skilled in music, had to be of the simplest possible kind. A model was at hand in the new German lied, which, from the publication of Sperontes' collection *Die Singende Muse an der Pleisse* (1736–1745), entered upon a revival destined to continue uninterruptedly through the century and eventually lead up to the works of Schubert.[37]

Although there were earlier isolated instances of popular comic music in cantatas, school dramas, and intermezzi,[38] the first definite impulse to the new Singspiel came from England. In 1743 a ballad opera by Coffey, *The Devil to Pay; or, the Wives Metamorphos'd* (*Der Teufel ist los; oder, Die verwandelten Weiber*), was performed at Berlin, in German translation but probably with the original English tunes; in a new arrangement by Christian Felix Weisse, and with new music by J. C. Standfuss,[39] it was given again at Leipzig in 1752 with great success. Another Singspiel by the same two men, likewise based on one of Coffey's ballad operas, *The Merry Cobbler* (*Der lustige Schuster*), was presented at Lübeck in 1759. The music of Standfuss is very fresh and jolly, with the true breath of German folk song. His successor, and the most important early composer of the Singspiel, was Johann Adam Hiller,[40] who with Weisse produced a

---

[37] Friedländer, *Das deutsche Lied im 18. Jahrhundert;* Kretzschmar, *Geschichte des neuen deutschen Liedes.* Modern edition of Sperontes in DdT xxxv–xxxvi; facsimile ed. B&H, 1909.

[38] Cf. Moser, *Geschichte der deutschen Musik* II, 371; Schering, "Zwei Singspiele des Sperontes," ZfMw VII (1924–25) 214–20.

[39] Nothing is known about the life of Standfuss beyond the fact that he was a violinist attached to a theatre troupe in Leipzig. Examples of his and Hiller's music are found in SB 309 and in the most important study in this field, Calmus' *Die ersten deutschen Singspiele von Standfuss und Hiller.* On Weisse (1726–1804), see biography by Minor.

[40] Hiller (1728–1804) was the first conductor of the Leipzig *Gewandhaus* concerts, editor of an important musical periodical (*Wöchentliche Nachrichten*) from 1766–1770, author

series of Singspiels at Leipzig beginning with a new version of *Der Teufel ist los* in 1766 and climaxing with *Die Jagd* ("The Hunt") in 1770, the most popular German opera before Weber's *Freischütz*. Although Hiller's early works show some Italian influence, the music of *Die Jagd* is characteristically German; the score is filled with melodies of the purest folk-song type, contrasting (as in all his Singspiels) with the intentionally more elaborate and Italianate arias which Hiller considered appropriate for kings and other highly placed characters. Some of the songs, without departing from the prevailing simple style, have a sweep of line which almost reminds one of Beethoven (Example 88). There are nine ensembles, including three with chorus, and an orchestral storm in addition to the usual three-movement overture.

DIE JAGD, Act II

Ex.88.   Hiller

O dass mich noch sein Her - - ze lieb - te so
wie mein Herz, so wie mein Herz ihn liebt!

The success of Hiller's Singspiels was not due alone to the music. Weisse's librettos, adapted nearly every one from contemporary French opéras comiques,[41] reflected the same preoccupation with scenes and characters from common life, the same touches of romantic fancy, the same exaltation of sentiment and glorification of the peasantry, the same inevitable triumph of simple virtue over

of a series of biographies of German musicians and of singing and violin instruction books, as well as composer of a dozen Singspiels. songs, choruses, and other works. His autobiography has recently been reprinted (Leipzig, 1915). See also Peiser, *Johann Adam Hiller*. There is a modern edition of *Die Jagd* (ed. Kleinmichel), and copies of the numerous eighteenth-century editions of all the Singspiels (mostly in piano-vocal reduction) are not rare; see also HAM 299.

41 The derivation of the principal librettos is as follows: *Lisuart und Dariolette* (1766) from Favart's *Fée Urgèle, ou Ce qui plaît aux dames*, mus. Duni, 1765; *Lottchen am Hofe* (1767) from Favart's *Ninette à la cour*, mus. pasticcio, 1755; *Die Liebe auf dem Lande* (1768) from Mme. Favart's *Annette et Lubin*, mus. mostly vaudevilles, 1762, and Anseaume's *Clochette*, mus. Duni, 1766; *Die Jagd* (1770) from Sedaine's *Roi et le fermier*, mus. Monsigny, 1762; *Der Dorfbarbier* (1771) from Sedaine's *Blaise le savetier*, mus. Philidor, 1759.

the wickedness of the nobles, and the same motif of devotion to the king as protector and father of the innocent—in short, all those ideas which made such a deep appeal to the feelings of the people in this prerevolutionary period, and which made the comic opera of both nations a genuine popular manifestation. The folk basis is even more pronounced in Germany than in France; many of Hiller's melodies became national folk songs.[42] French opéras comiques, or translations and imitations, with the original music or in new settings by German composers, appeared by scores after 1770.[43] The growth of the Singspiel went hand in hand with the ever increasing popularity of the lied; authors and composers, professional and amateur alike, all over the country, joined in a universal outpouring of song; for sheer quantity, it was one of the most productive periods in the history of German music.

Two distinct branches of the Singspiel developed. In the North, where the influence of Weisse and Hiller predominated, the literary framework remained that of the idyllic, sentimental, lyrical comedy on the model of the French opéra comique, with music of a simple melodic type closely allied to folk song. The adherence to a national musical language and the increase of romantic elements in the libretto [44] led naturally in the nineteenth century to the romantic German opera of Weber.

Of the many North German composers after Hiller we may mention particularly Georg Benda,[45] who was noted not only for his Singspiels but also for his "melodramas." A melodrama is a stage piece without singing, but with action and speaking by one or two performers accompanied by or alternating with the orchestra (there may also be choral interludes). Rousseau had already written a melodrama Pygmalion (performed 1770, with music by Coignet),[46] but

42 Burney, The Present State of Music in Germany I, 84; Hoffman von Fallersleben, Unsere volkstümliche Lieder, Nos. 48, 265, 304, 947.

43 Theater-Kalendar (Reichard), passim.

44 E.g., Kunzen's Holger Danske (Copenhagen, 1789) from Wieland's Oberon; cf. Schmidt, Geschichte der Märchenoper.

45 Benda (1722–1795) was court chapelmaster at Gotha from 1748 to 1788, where he produced fourteen Singspiels and melodramas. Ariadne has been published in a modern edition (A. Einstein, Munich, 1920). See studies by Hodermann and Brückner. See also Istel, Die Entstehung des deutschen Melodrams; musical examples in Martens, Das Melodram (fuller bibliography of this subject in Moser's Lexikon).

46 On the debated question of Rousseau's music for his Pygmalion see Istel, Studien zur Geschichte des Melodrams. I. Jean Jacques Rousseau als Komponist seiner lyrischen Szene "Pygmalion," and (contra) Hirschberg, Die Enzyklopädisten, pp. 88–90; cf. also Mason, "The Melodrama in France."

Benda's *Ariadne auf Naxos* (1775) was the first important German work in this form and had many successors.[47] The chief historical importance of the melodrama lay in the effective use made of the style by later composers for special scenes in opera: the grave-digging scene in *Fidelio* and the Wolf's Glen scene in *Der Freischütz* are familiar examples.

The principal other North German composers (most of whom were equally distinguished in the field of the lied) are: Anton Schweizer (*Die Dorfgala,* 1772), Johann André (*Das tartarische Gesetz,* 1789), Christian Gottlob Neefe (*Die Apotheke,* 1771), and Johann Friedrich Reichardt (1752–1814), the composer of Goethe's Singspiels and originator of the *Liederspiel,* a comedy with familiar popular songs analogous to the French vaudeville or the English ballad opera. There was a Danish branch of the Singspiel, of which the leading composers were Johann Abraham Peter Schulz (1747–1800) and Friedrich Ludwig Aemilius Kunzen (1761–1817). Two other composers prepared the way for Danish national opera in the nineteenth century: Christoph Ernst Friedrich Weyse (1774–1842) and Friedrich Kuhlau (1786–1832).[48]

In South Germany the Singspiel took on a different character, owing in part to the strong influence of Italian opera buffa. The Viennese found the quiet, lyrical melodies of the North "too Lutheran" and demanded more liveliness and display. The librettos tended to be gay and farcical, with not a hint of any social significance; the supernatural, which in the North was an accepted means of romantic expression, here became usually an object of spectacle or of ridicule. A national opera theatre, founded at Vienna by Emperor Josef II, was opened with a performance of Ignaz Umlauf's *Bergknappen* ("The Miners") in 1778,[49] and Mozart's *Entführung* was performed there four years later. The leading Viennese Singspiel com-

---

[47] Schletterer, *Das deutsche Singspiel,* p. 225.
[48] Krogh, *Zur Geschichte des dänischen Singspiels;* Behrend, "Weyse und Kuhlau," *Die Musik* III, No. 22 (1904) 272–86; Thrane, *Danske Komponister.*
[49] Ignaz Umlauf (1746–1796) was conductor of the German Opera at Vienna from 1778 and deputy chapelmaster at court from 1789. His *Bergknappen* is in the DTOe XVIII 1, ed. with important introduction by R. Haas. On the Vienna Singspiel in general see also Haas, "Die Musik in der deutschen Stegreifkomödie," SzMw XII (1925) 1–64; *idem,* "Wiener deutsche Parodieopern um 1730," ZfMw VIII (1925–26) 201–25; Helfert, "Zur Geschichte des Wiener Singspiels," ZfMw V (1922–23) 194–209. For examples of the music see (in addition to works of separate composers) *Deutsche Komödienarien 1754–1758* (DTOe XXXIII) and *Wiener Komödienlieder aus 3 Jahrhunderten,* ed. Glossy and Haas (Vienna, 1924).

poser, however, was Dittersdorf,[50] whose music shows traces of the
Italian comic style in its vivacious rhythms, bravura passages, effective chromatic touches, short-phrased interjectional melodic lines,
long ensembles which continue the action, and lively comic details
of all sorts. Yet Dittersdorf is no mere imitator of the Italians, as
Hasse was. Many of his melodies are unmistakably Viennese (Example 89). His facility, energy, and humor, together with his melodic
gift, his imaginative use of the orchestra, and his grasp of formal
structure, make it easy to understand the success of his works at
Vienna and show him as a composer of comic opera not unworthy to
be named along with Mozart.

Later Viennese Singspiel composers include Johann Schenk,[51]
whose *Dorfbarbier* ("The Village Barber," 1796) looks forward to
the comic style of Lortzing, and Wenzel Müller,[52] in whose works
there is apparent an increasing popularization of both libretto and
musical idiom, in a manner destined to lead to the nineteenth-century
Viennese operetta. The latter is, indeed, the natural successor of the
lighthearted, melodious Singspiel of the eighteenth century.

No treatment of the Viennese opera would be complete without
reference to Haydn's works in this form.[53] Haydn wrote one German
Singspiel, the music of which has been lost, and five marionette
operas, of which only *Philemon und Baucis* survives. His Italian operas (thirteen comic and two serious) were for the most part composed
between 1762 and 1784 for the private theatre of Count Esterhazy

50 Karl Ditters von Dittersdorf (1739–1799) composed a large quantity of instrumental
music—symphonies, concertos, quartets, etc. (selections in DTOe XLIII 2)—in addition
to fifteen Italian and twenty-nine German comic operas. His chief Singspiels are *Doktor
und Apotheker* (1786), *Betrug durch Aberglauben* (1786), *Die Liebe im Narrenhaus*
(1787), *Hieronymus Knicker* (1787), and *Das rote Käppchen* (1788). See his *Autobiography; Krebs, Dittersdorfiana* (with thematic catalogue); Holl, *Dittersdorfs Opern;*
Riedinger, "Dittersdorf als Opernkomponist," SzMw II (1914) 212–349; *Doktor und
Apotheker* and *Hieronymus Knicker* are published in Senff's *Opernbibliothek;* selection
from the former in HAM 305.
51 Schenk (1753–1836) was a singer and composer of church and instrumental music as
well as many Singspiels. *Der Dorfbarbier* is in DTOe XXIV; autobiography in SzMw
XI (1924) 75–85.
52 Müller (1767–1835) is the composer of 225 musical works for the stage (complete list
in Riemann, *Opernhandbuch,* pp. 816–20). See studies by Krone and Raab. Müller's
Schwestern von Prag (1794) is published in a modern edition.
53 On Haydn's operas, see the biographies of Pohl and Geiringer, and cf. Larsen, *Die
Haydn-Überlieferungen;* also Wendschuh, *Ueber Jos. Haydns Opern;* Wirth, "Haydn
als Dramatiker"; Geiringer, "Haydn as an opera composer," PMA LXVI (1939–40) 23–
30; Láng, "Haydn and the Opera," MQ XVIII (1932) 274–81. The following have been
published: *Orfeo ed Euridice, Lo speziale, Orlando Paladino, L'incontro improviso,
L'isola disabitata,* and *Il mondo della luna.*

DAS ROTE KÄPPCHEN, Act II, finale

Ex.89.   Dittersdorf

1. Herr Schultz auf ein Wort warum bleibt er zu
2. Ich dan - ke fürs Es - sen, ich dan - ke fürs

Haus, und will nicht er - schei - nen beim heu - ti - gen Schmaus? Da
Trin-ken, wenn Män - ner be - trunk-en vom Stuhl her-ab sinken.

Orch.

mögt' es wohl ü - bel den Wei - bern er - geh'n,

mögt' es ü - bel den Wei - bern schon geh'n, doch

bleibt man zu Hau - se, da kann nichts ge - scheh'n

but were also publicly performed in German translations. They show no outstanding talent for dramatic effect and little departure from the current Italian fashion either in subject matter or treatment, though they are pleasant enough and marked, of course, by a sure sense of form and symphonic continuity. In fact, their musical attractiveness is sufficiently divorced from details of the text and from the stage conventions of their time to make them excellent material for modern revivals.

EARLY SPANISH OPERA: THE "ZARZUELA" AND THE "TONADILLA." [54]— From its beginnings in the fifteenth century the Spanish secular theatre, like the Italian, called on music to adorn and supplement the spoken dialogue of its dramas. Most of the plays of Juan del Encina (1469?–*ca.* 1529) end with a *villancico,* a little song for four voices somewhat similar to the Italian frottola, which was both sung and danced.[55] The plays of Gil Vicente (d. 1557) and Diego Sánchez de Badajoz (1479–*ca.* 1550) also commonly used music, not only at the beginning and end but sometimes intermingled with the action. In the sixteenth century also flourished the *ensalada* (literally "salad," that is, "hodgepodge"), a humorous type of piece reflecting popular scenes and character types, and having many features in common with the Italian madrigal comedy.

During the Golden Age of Spanish drama, the seventeenth century, there arose the characteristic national "zarzuela." [56] The name comes from the "Palace of the Zarzuela" near Madrid, where these pieces were first performed. The zarzuela of this period, of which Calderón's *El laurel de Apolo* (1658) is a typical example, was in two

[54] Soriano Fuertes, *Historia de la música española;* Chavarri, *Historia de la música;* Mitjana, "La Musique en Espagne" (with many musical examples) in Lavignac, *Encyclopédie de la musique,* Pt. I, Vol. IV, pp. 2003–17 (madrigals), 2027–35 (sixteenth-century theatre), 2052–71 (seventeenth-century zarzuela), 2108–14 (late seventeenth century), 2123–28 (Italian opera in Spain), 2150–80 (eighteenth-century theatre), 2195–2209 (Spanish composers of Italian opera), 2227–57 (tonadilla); *idem, Histoire du développement du théâtre dramatique et musical en Espagne;* Pedrell, *Teatro lírico español* (many musical examples); Reiff, "Die Anfänge der Oper in Spanien," *Spanien, Zeitschrift für Auslandskunde* Jahrgang I, Heft 3 (1919); Subirá, *La música en la casa de Alba; idem,* "Le Style dans la musique théâtrale espagnole," *Acta Musicologica* IV (1932) 67–75; Chase, *The Music of Spain.*
[55] Examples of music in Barbieri, *Cancionero musical de los siglos XV y XVI.* Cf. Subirá, *La participación musical en el antiguo teatro español;* Livermore, "The Spanish Dramatists and Their Use of Music," *M&L* XXV (1944) 140–49; Beau, "Die Musik im Werk des Gil Vicente," *Volkstum und Kultur der Romanen,* IX (1936) 177–201.
[56] Cotarelo, *Historia de la zarzuela.*

acts, often on pastoral or mythological subjects, and with emphasis on elaborate scenic effects; it was in spoken dialogue but included much music (choruses, dialogues, and solos). In form and general plan it corresponded most closely to the contemporary comedy ballet of Molière and Lully,[57] but its vitality and significance were greater. All the great Spanish playwrights of the seventeenth century interested themselves in the zarzuela and similar forms, such as the *comedia harmónica* (comedy with music), the *egloga* (pastorale), or the *auto sacramentale* (a religious play). Most of the musical scores of these plays seem to have been lost, and if we may judge from the published examples of those which survive, it is a loss greatly to be regretted. The zarzuela attained the height of its development toward the end of the seventeenth century. Its historical career is strikingly parallel to that of the national English and German operas of the same period, for in the course of the eighteenth century it was abandoned owing to the popularity of Italian opera, which first came to Spain in 1703.[58]

Among the zarzuelas of the seventeenth century there were a few which were sung throughout. The earliest was Lope de Vega's pastorale *La selva sin amor* ("The Forest without Love," 1629) the music of which is not known.[59] In 1662 was performed a *fiesta cantada*, *Celos aun del aire matan,* by Calderón, with music by Juan Hidalgo; the music of the first of the three acts has recently been discovered and published.[60] It consists for the most part of simple solo songs in dancelike triple metre, with frequently recurring themes connected by recitatives; there are also a few short choruses. Other similar works, often designated as *zarzuelas a la italiana,* appeared in the eighteenth century; but they were few in number, too much under the influence of Italian style, or too insignificant dramatically to establish a genuine Spanish opera in this period.

The different musical numbers in the zarzuelas and plays of the seventeenth and early eighteenth centuries appeared in various forms,

---

57 The comedy ballets show traces of Spanish influence in their occasional Spanish scenes (*Mariage forcé, Ballet des Muses, Bourgeois Gentilhomme*).
58 Cotarelo, *Orígenes y establecimento de la ópera en España;* Carmena, *Crónica de la ópera italiana en Madrid;* Virella, *La ópera en Barcelona.*
59 There is some doubt also as to whether *La selva sin amor* was really sung throughout. Cf. Chase, "Origins of the Lyric Theater in Spain," MQ XXV (1939) 300.
60 Barcelona, 1933, ed. J. Subirá. The title means literally "Jealousy, even from the air, kills." See Ursprung, "*Celos* usw.," in *Festschrift Arnold Schering*, pp. 223–40.

some of which developed considerable importance of their own.[61] Among these was the *entremés* (intermezzo), which was usually performed as an interlude between the acts of a play. Frequently the entremés ended with a song, called a *tonadilla* (diminutive of *tonada*, a word applied in the sevententh century to a solo song with accompaniment). About the middle of the eighteenth century this finale of the entremés, this tonadilla, began to be expanded to include two or more separate numbers, and even a little dramatic framework. Eventually the tonadilla, thus expanded, was detached from the entremés and launched on a career of its own; it flourished especially at Madrid throughout the second half of the eighteenth century as the national Spanish form corresponding to the English ballad opera or the French opéra comique.[62] One of the earliest composers (though not the originator) of the tonadilla was Luis Misón (d. 1766), who established the independence of the form and the use of the orchestra for accompaniments. The chief later composers were Esteve and Laserna.[63]

The tonadilla was usually performed between the first and second acts of a comedy; it was seldom more than twenty minutes long and consisted almost entirely of solo songs or dialogues, sometimes with dancing, and with occasional short spoken phrases. The later tonadillas became longer and had a larger proportion of spoken parts, though they still kept to the basic plan of a series of songs in contrasting tempos, with occasional duets or ensembles. There were no independent instrumental pieces, though a full orchestra was nearly always used for accompaniments. The cast of singers might comprise one to six persons, or even more in the *tonadilla generale*. The solo tonadillas were mostly on satirical or narrative texts; the others usually consisted of a short comic episode, with scenes and character types from familiar daily life, ending (especially in the later period) with a general moral reflection. In form, the tonadilla was divided

---

61 Cotarelo, *Colección de entremeses, loas, bailes, jácaras y mojingangas desde fines del siglo XVI á mediados del XVII.*

62 The chief study of the tonadilla is Subirá's *Tonadilla escénica*, which contains many musical examples; further examples in the same author's *Tonadillas teatrales inéditas* and *Los maestros de la tonadilla escénica,* also in Nin's modern editions (*Sept Chants lyriques; Sept Chansons picaresques*) and Pedrell's *Cancionero musical popular español* (Vol. IV).

63 Don Pablo Esteve y Grimau produced tonadillas and similar pieces at Madrid 1761–1791. The dates of his birth and death are not known. Don Blas de Laserna (1751–1816) was active as a composer from 1774 to 1810. See biographical study by Gómez.

into three parts, the *introducción, coplas,* and *final,* the last usually consisting of *seguidillas* of various types, which might be both sung and danced; seguidillas were also sometimes inserted in the coplas, the body of the tonadilla, by way of interludes.

The music of the early tonadillas was simple, tuneful, and with marked dancelike rhythms, closely derived from folk song (Example 90). Later it became slightly more sophisticated, often giving evi-

UNA MESONERA Y UN ARRIERO
TONADILLA A DUO (?1757)

Ex.90.

Misón

Vá - mo - nos a la ven - ta, vá - mo - nos a la ven - ta, ca - ri - ño mi - o, ca - ri - ño mi - o.

dence of the popularity of Italian opera at Madrid by the inclusion of recitatives and arias in Italian style and even to Italian texts. By the nineteenth century the national Spanish element had practically disappeared, being replaced by an imitation of Italian opera buffa music. Tonadillas were still produced during the first half of the nineteenth century, but the form finally gave way to a new type of zarzuela about 1850.

17

Mozart [1]

MOST OPERA COMPOSERS HAVE BEEN specialists; Mozart was one of the few whose greatness was manifested equally in opera and in other branches of composition. His genius and training led him to conceive of opera as essentially a musical affair, like a symphony, rather than as a drama in which music was merely one means of dramatic expression. In this conception he was at one with the Italian composers of the day, and his work may be regarded in a sense as the ideal toward which the whole eighteenth-century Italian opera had been striving. He overtopped his predecessors not by a changed approach to the problem of opera but by the superior beauty, originality, and significance of his musical ideas, by his greater mastery of counterpoint, by his higher constructive powers, and by his ability to write music which not only perfectly portrayed a dramatic situation but at the same time could develop freely in a musical sense, without appearing to be in the least hampered by the presence of a text. The variety of musical forms in Mozart's operas, which can only be appreciated by an analysis of the scores, is paralleled by the skill with which these forms are adapted to the dramatic aims. In this rare combination of dramatic truth and musical beauty, there can be no doubt that the music is the important thing. Without it none of the operas, except possibly *Figaro*, would be intelligible; with it, even *The Magic Flute* makes sense. So completely does the music absorb the drama, and so perfect is the music itself, that Mozart today not only holds the stage but offers the phenomenon of one composer whose operas are universally enjoyed, by operagoers and music lovers alike.

It is no disparagement of Mozart to remark that, like many an-

[1] Bibliography: Köchel, *Chronologisch-thematisches Verzeichnis* (3d ed., rev. by A. Einstein); Jahn, *W. A. Mozart* (6th ed., rev. by H. Abert); Wyzewa and Saint-Foix, *W. A. Mozart*; Einstein, *Mozart*; Schiedermair, *Die Briefe W. A. Mozarts*; Anderson, *The Letters of Mozart and His Family*; Keller, *Wolfgang Amadeus Mozart, Bibliographie und Ikonographie*; *Mozart-Jahrbuch*, ed. by Abert; collected edition of Mozart's works, Series V, *Opern* (B&H, 1880–82) also Series XXIV, Nos. 37–38; Dent, *Mozart's Operas*; Lert, *Mozart auf dem Theater*; Conrad, *Mozarts Dramaturgie der Oper*.

other great man, he was born at the right time. Everywhere there were producers ready to stage new operas and audiences ready to listen to them; the classical orchestra and orchestral style were well beyond the experimental stage; the art of singing, though beginning to decline, was still at a high level of virtuosity; the opera itself had the advantage of an established form within which recent developments—the innovations of Gluck, the vitality of opera buffa, and the growing interest in the German Singspiel—offered stimulating possibilities to a composer. Mozart's operas were, on the whole, successful; if they did not obtain for him all the reward or recognition which their merits deserved, and for which he hoped, the fault lay not in the conditions of the time so much as in the fact that Mozart personally was always unfortunate in his adjustments to the patronage system, and that the Viennese public, who might have sustained him, were not yet capable of appreciating those qualities which set him above Dittersdorf and other popular Singspiel composers. In other words, Mozart was slightly in advance of his age; but he was no more a conscious revolutionist in opera than was Handel. His twenty-two dramatic works include school dramas, serenatas, and Italian serious operas, but the important part of his output lies in the two fields most cultivated in the later eighteenth century, the Italian opera buffa and the German Singspiel.

THE ITALIAN OPERAS.—The predominance of Mozart's Italian background is natural, since Italian music was the international standard of his time. The strong early influence of J. C. Bach (London, 1764–1765), the three Italian journeys of his boyhood, and the course of contrapuntal studies with Padre Martini in 1770, all strengthened this tendency. Among Mozart's childhood works was an Italian opera buffa, *La finta semplice* ("The Pretended Simpleton"), composed for Vienna in 1768 but not performed until the following year at Salzburg. At the age of fourteen he composed his first opera seria, *Mitridate re di Ponto* ("Mithridates King of Pontus"), which was performed at Milan in December, 1770. Two years later another work of the same type, *Lucio Silla*, was also produced at Milan. Both are on librettos of the conventional type established by Metastasio and are more remarkable as examples of Mozart's extraordinary precocity than for anything else. His aim, and the aim of his father who still closely supervised his compositions, was to produce successful operas according to the current Italian standard. We marvel at the degree to which Mozart had assimilated the operatic manner of his time, but the whole effect is similar to that produced by any performance of a child prodigy: brilliant but inappropriate coloratura passages abound in these early scores; there is little individuality of melody, nothing of the later variety of forms or, except in a few places, true characterization of the text. One aria in *Mitridate* [2] foreshadows the Mozartian pathetic style; in *Lucio Silla* the ombra scene with chorus (Act I, scenes 7–8) is an imaginative and even powerful treatment of the situation, while Cecilio's aria, "Quest' improvviso tremito" (No. 9), with the preceding accompanied recitative, is an unusually dramatic solo in the grand style. The success of these early works was not great, and, though his interest in the form continued, it was nearly ten years before Mozart had the opportunity to compose another opera seria.

La finta giardiniera ("The Pretended Gardener"), produced at Munich in 1775, was an Italian opera buffa with a libretto (? Calzabigi) which unhappily combined the new sentimental motif of Goldoni's *Buona figliuola* with a complicated and cumbersome array of secondary characters, disguises, mistaken identity, and farcical episodes inherited from the older Italian comedy. The music is only too faithful to the text, with the consequence that it not merely lacks dramatic continuity but presents the same characters at different moments in contradictory aspects. Tragedy and comedy rub shoulders, but there is no sign of the synthesis of the two which is so characteristic of Mozart's later dramatic works. Thus the heroine Sandrina in Act I (No. 4) is presented as a superficial young girl of the usual comic-opera type, but in Act II (Nos. 21, 22) as a tragic figure appropriate to opera seria. Aside from such inconsistencies, which were so common in this period, the score of *La finta giardiniera* is extraordinarily attractive. The musical material is individual and is treated with imagination and humor. The serious portions mark an important advance in Mozart's handling of this type of expression, however out of place they are dramatically. Another notable feature is the finale of Act I, where the development of the action is combined with character differentiation and musical conti-

[2] Aspasia's "Nel sen mi palpitar," No. 4.

nuity, giving a foretaste of the finales of *Figaro* and *Don Giovanni*.[3]

The remaining early Italian works may be briefly noticed here. The serenata *Ascanio in Alba* (Milan, 1771) is notable chiefly for its choruses. The serenata *Il sogno di Scipione* ("The Dream of Scipio," Salzburg, 1772) and the festival opera *Il rè pastore* ("The Shepherd King," Salzburg, 1775) offer nothing of particular interest or significance in Mozart's development. They were occasional pieces composed as part of his duties in the service of the archepiscopal court and (like many of their kind) adequate but uninspired—with the exception of one aria with a solo violin obbligato, "L'amerò, sarò costante," in Act II of *Il rè pastore,* which is a lovely example of Mozart's lyrical genius.

The influence of Italian opera in Mozart's dramatic career was balanced and modified by his interest in symphonic music. Stemming from Italy and based to a large extent originally on the musical idiom and forms of Italian opera, the preclassical German symphony was at a flourishing stage when Mozart visited one of its chief centers, Mannheim, in 1777–1778. Before this date he had already composed many symphonies, two of which especially (K 183, 201) showed a sure grasp of the form; the works of Johann Stamitz and the Mannheim school were among the models which most influenced him in his mature years. His close association with Christian Cannabich (1731–1798), Stamitz's successor as conductor of the famous Mannheim orchestra at the time of Mozart's visit, led to a deeper appreciation of the symphonic style and of the possibilities of orchestral manipulation in general. This is not the place to speak of Mozart as a symphonist, except to point out that his lifelong interest in and mastery of the larger instrumental forms are reflected on every page of his operas—in the way in which voices and instruments are adjusted to one another, in the texture and treatment of the orchestral parts (particularly the independence of the wood winds), in the broadly symphonic overtures, and in the unerring sense of musical continuity extending over long and complex sections of the score.

At Mannheim also Mozart came into contact with German opera

---

[3] *La finta giardiniera* was revised by Mozart in 1780 for a performance in German, and probably again in 1789. It is possible that some of the stylistic inconsistencies in the score as we now have it may be due to these revisions. The autograph ms. of Act I has been lost, and since in the German versions the secco recitatives were replaced by spoken dialogue, the music of these portions cannot be recovered.

—not the Singspiel but the new German opera, raising its head again after a forty years' sleep. In 1773 Wieland's *Alceste,* with music by Anton Schweitzer,[4] was performed at Mannheim and with such success that in January, 1777, a second German opera, this time actually on a subject from German history, was presented: *Günther von Schwarzburg,* composed by Ignaz Holzbauer.[5] Mozart wrote enthusiastically of Holzbauer's music,[6] which is indeed fiery and spirited, though both it and the libretto show all too plainly the outlines of Italian opera seria. Neither Schweitzer nor Holzbauer was able to bring about a permanent awakening in Germany; the time was not ripe, and their works, although performed at Mannheim and in several other cities, remained only an episode in the history of national opera. Yet the ideal persisted; Mozart's *Magic Flute,* which has strains reminiscent of *Günther,* was the first effective step toward its realization.

From Mannheim, Mozart journeyed to Paris, arriving (March, 1778) in the midst of the Gluck-Piccinni controversy. An unknown young foreign musician, he attracted little attention—a disappointing contrast to his reception fifteen years before as a child prodigy. His temperament, coinciding with the anxious advice of his father, kept him aloof from the current quarrel. Moreover, the whole tone of musical life and society in Paris was discouraging to him, with its endless theorizing and debating about matters which he himself either understood quite simply as a musician or else felt to be of no importance. He had no sympathy for French opera and could not abide French singing; the opéra comique apparently did not interest him, and he does not seem to have made the acquaintance of Grétry. Plans for a French opera came to nothing, and the only theatre music of this period was part of a ballet, *Les Petits Riens* (K Suppl. 10), arranged by Noverre and performed in connection with one of Piccinni's operas. Mozart's joy over the success of his

[4] Schweitzer (1735–1787) worked at Weimar and Gotha as conductor and composer. He wrote music for Rousseau's *Pygmalion* and was a very popular composer of Singspiels (*Die Dorfgala,* 1772). A second German opera, *Rosamunde,* was produced at Mannheim in 1780. See Maurer, *Schweitzer als dramatischer Komponist.*

[5] Holzbauer (1711–1783), court chapelmaster at Mannheim from 1753, wrote eleven Italian operas, much church music, symphonies, quartets, and concertos. *Günther,* his only German opera, is published in DdT, Vols. VIII–IX, with introduction by H. Kretzschmar.

[6] Anderson, *Letters* II, 549.

"Paris" Symphony (K 297) was turned to sadness by the death of his mother; he left Paris in September and returned to Salzburg no richer in either money or prospects than when he had left. Yet the Paris visit was not without importance, for it helped to make Mozart for the first time more fully conscious of his own artistic aims and of his position as a composer in relation to the ideals of Gluck and the French school.

In 1780 came a welcome commission to furnish an opera seria for Munich. The result was *Idomeneo, rè di Creta* ("Idomeneus, King of Crete"), the first opera which shows Mozart in the fullness of his powers. The libretto, on a subject first used by the French composer Campra in 1712, was written by the Abbé G. B. Varesco of Salzburg; it is of the old-fashioned Metastasian type, on a classical subject with amorous intrigues, but including some large choral scenes in the newer style of Coltellini and Frugoni. In some external details the music also is old-fashioned: there is the conventional framework of recitatives alternating with arias, one of the principals is a male soprano, and there are many brilliant coloratura songs with improvised cadenzas, such as Idomeneo's comparison aria "Fuor del mar" in Act II or Electra's "Tutte nel cor vi sento" in Act I, which is especially notable for the striking effect made by the return of the first theme in C minor after the original statement in D minor. Ensembles are few: two duets, one trio, and one quartet. In accordance with later eighteenth-century practice, there is relatively little secco recitative but a large number of accompanied recitatives; one of the best of these is the highly dramatic recognition scene between Idomeneo and his son Idamante in Act I ("Spietatissimi Dei"), a masterpiece of psychological perception and effective harmonic treatment. Like the operas of Jommelli, Traëtta, and Gluck, *Idomeneo* is filled with large scene complexes built around recitative, with free musical and dramatic handling, often combined with spectacular effects, for example, the oracle scene in Act III. Many of these scenes introduce ballets,[7] marches, and choruses. The extent and the importance of the choral portions are reminiscent of Gluck and Rameau: the last scene of Act I has a march and chorus (*ciacona*) which is essentially similar to the choral scenes of older French operas, as is also the well-known "Placido è il mar, andiamo" in Act II. More like

[7] Contrary to the usual practice, Mozart himself composed the ballet music for *Idomeneo*.

ancient Greek usage is the scene in Act III between Idomeneo and
the chorus, where the latter comments, warns, and expostulates. The
most dramatic choral scene is that at the end of the second act, where
the repeated cries of the chorus "Il reo qual è?" ("Who is the guilty
one?") with the feeling of terror enforced by the strange, swiftly
changing tonalities of the music, the tumult of the storm in the orchestra, Idomeneo's anguished confession, and the final dispersal
and flight of the people all form a great and powerful finale equal
in force to anything of Gluck and surpassing Gluck in fertility of
musical invention.

Mozart's understanding of the style of opera seria is seen in his
treatment of the most traditional of operatic forms, the aria, of which
we may single out two examples for special mention. Ilia's "Se il
padre perdei" ("Though I have lost my father," Act II) is a splendid
example of Mozart's sensitiveness to details of the text, of his ability
to unite many different aspects of feeling in one basic mood, and of
his imaginative use of orchestral accompaniment for subtle psychological touches.[8] Ilia's third aria, "Zeffiretti lusinghieri" ("Gentle
Zephyrs," Act III) brings a commonplace conceit of eighteenth-
century opera in a setting which simply transfigures the faded sentiments of the poem by the freshness and beauty of the music.

Nowhere in his operas did Mozart lavish more care on the orchestral writing than in *Idomeneo*. This is seen especially in the independence of the wood winds and their frequent employment for
the most subtle touches of color and expression.[9] The overture at
once sets the tone of lofty seriousness which prevails throughout the
opera. At the end, the music dies away with a tonic pedal point, over
which we hear in the wood winds a series of repetitions of a characteristic descending phrase which recurs several times during the
opera, alternating with rising scale-passages; the final chord of D

[8] Cf. the detailed analysis of this aria in Abert, *Mozart* I, 851–54.
[9] See for examples: the recurrent descending fifth in the oboes and bassoons in Ilia's
aria "Padre, germani" (No. 1); the arpeggio figure for the flute in Electra's "Tutte nel
cor vi sento" (No. 4); the many expressive interludes for wood winds in Ilia's "Se il
padre perdei" (No. 11), which seem to envelop the solo as if with phrases of consola-
tion; the spirited interplay of the voice with flutes and oboes in the coloratura passages
of Idomeneo's "Fuor del mar" (No. 12); the repetition of the climactic phrases of the
chorus "Qual nuovo terrore" (No. 17) by the brasses and wood winds; the solemn chords
of the trombones and horns accompanying the voice of the Oracle (No. 28) and the
effective contrast of the dominant seventh chord for flutes, oboes, and bassoons which
introduces the recitative immediately following.

major, owing to the plagal harmonies, has the effect of a dominant in G, thus leading into the G minor accompanied recitative with which the first act opens.

It is perfectly clear that in writing *Idomeneo* Mozart had before his mind not only the most recent developments in the Italian opera seria but likewise the French operas of Gluck. Since *Idomeneo* was Mozart's last opera seria, except for the unfortunate *Clemenza di Tito* of 1791, it is appropriate at this point to establish his position in the history of this form and his relation both to the Italian school and to Gluck.

In many respects *Idomeneo* is the finest opera seria of the late eighteenth century; it shows that Mozart had fully appreciated the advances made by Jommelli, Traëtta, and Sarti and thus marks an important stage in his own development over his youthful dismissal of Jommelli's *Armide* as "too serious and old-fashioned for the theatre." [10] Mozart surpassed Jommelli not only in spontaneity, variety, and richness of invention but even more in his grasp of the emotional content of the text and in his incomparable power of musically characterizing both persons and situations. To the mastery of traditional outward forms he added the quality of psychological insight and the genius for expressing this insight in musical terms. Observing his treatment of the opera seria we are made aware that a miracle is taking place: the plane figures of the old dramma per musica suddenly take on a new dimension, and we see them in depth and perspective. Yet all this did not amount to a fundamental reform. *Idomeneo* was not the starting point of a new evolution in opera seria but rather the last great example of a form which was already on the decline and in which Mozart himself never produced anything more of significance.

The presence of choral scenes in *Idomeneo* does not indicate any acceptance of Gluck's reform theories. Mozart simply adapted for his own purposes certain practices by which the leading Italian composers of the time were seeking to rejuvenate the opera seria. To regard him in any sense as a disciple of Gluck is to misunderstand both men. As a matter of fact, the contrast between two contemporary opera composers could hardly be greater. Gluck, at least so far as *Orfeo* and later works are concerned, was an artist to whom

10 Anderson, *Letters* I, 211; but cf. *ibid.*, p. 208.

the conscious perception of aims and rational choice of means were necessary preliminaries to musical creation; every detail of his scores was the result of a previously thought out plan, and he was always ready to justify his procedures by reference to his intentions. He could claim that when he composed an opera he endeavored before all else to forget that he was a musician. Mozart, on the contrary, was no philosopher; thought and realization were to him indivisible parts of the same creative process; his music was no less logical than Gluck's, but it was the logic of music, not something capable of being detached and discussed in relation to extramusical conceptions. For him, "in an opera poetry must be altogether the obedient daughter of the music." [11] With Gluck the idea of the drama as a whole came first, and the music was written as part of the means through which the idea was realized; with Mozart, the idea took shape immediately and completely as music, the mental steps involved in the process being so smooth and so nearly instantaneous that he has often been called an "instinctive" composer. This is incorrect, unless we choose to denote by the word "instinct" that sureness, clarity, and speed of reasoning which is characteristic of this type of genius.

In addition to this difference of temperament, there was a fundamental difference between Gluck's and Mozart's conceptions of drama. Gluck's characters are generalized and typical rather than individual; they have a certain classic, superhuman stature; and as they are at the beginning of an opera, so they remain to the end. But Mozart's characters are human persons, each uniquely complex and depicted variously in changing moods rather than statically as a fixed bearer of certain qualities. It is for this reason that Mozart's operas seem to us modern while Gluck's seem old-fashioned; Gluck's dramatic psychology is that of the eighteenth century, while Mozart's is that of our own time. The symbols of the contrast are the Gluck chorus, in which the individual is submerged in the typical, and the Mozart ensemble, in which the individual is all the more sharply defined by means of interaction with other individuals.

Finally, Gluck's music, quite apart from its technical inferiority to Mozart's, is intentionally austere. Its appeal is not to the senses and emotions primarily, but to the entire "rational" man as the eighteenth century conceived him. Much of it therefore (though we

11 Anderson, *Letters* III, 1150.

must make important exceptions to this statement, especially in *Orfeo*) lacks those qualities of ease and spontaneity which are never absent from Mozart even in his least inspired moments. To appreciate Gluck, one needs to know something about the eighteenth century, but no comparable background is required in the case of Mozart.

With the exception of two unfinished pieces of 1783,[12] Mozart's next Italian opera was *Le nozze di Figaro* ("The Marriage of Figaro"), performed at Vienna May 1, 1786. During the fifteen years between *Idomeneo* and *Figaro*, Mozart had become acquainted with the music of Bach and Handel; he had written *Die Entführung*, the "Haffner" Symphony, the six "Haydn" quartets, and many of the great piano concertos. He was now a mature artist, at the height of his powers. Moreover, he had a libretto which combined brilliant comedy with excellent possibilities for contrasting character delineation. Lorenzo Da Ponte, who arranged the text from Beaumarchais,[13] was then poet of the Imperial Theatre at Vienna and understood his métier thoroughly. The story is a sequel to Beaumarchais' *Barbier de Seville,* which had been so popular in Paisiello's setting four years previously. It is a rather complicated intrigue comedy, with a strong undercurrent of reference to social abuses in a manner already established in the French opéra comique, though in Beaumarchais the attack was much more pointed and consequently more dangerous. Needless to say, this particular aspect of the plot was not emphasized by Da Ponte or Mozart in an opera intended for Vienna, where Beaumarchais' play was still forbidden. The first performance was a great success,[14] and it was therefore all the more disappointing to Mozart that *Figaro* was soon displaced in the affections of the public by newer works—Dittersdorf's *Doktor und Apotheker* and Martín's *Cosa rara*.[15]

12 *L'oca del Cairo* ("The Goose of Cairo") and *Lo sposo deluso* ("The Deluded Spouse"), both opere buffe.

13 Beaumarchais' play was written in 1778 but, owing to censorship, not publicly performed until 1784. On the checkered career of Da Ponte (1749–1839), including the last thirty-four years of his life in America, see his *Memoirs* (not always reliable) and biographies by Marchesan and Russo; also Livingston, *Lorenzo da Ponte in America*.

14 See Kelly, *Reminiscences* I, 258 ff.

15 Vicente Martín y Soler (1756–1806) was a Spanish composer in the Italian style, whose *Cosa rara* and *Arbore di Diana* (1787) were extremely popular in Germany. He was at St. Petersburg from 1788 to 1801. His name is often Italianized as "Martini," and he should not be confused with other Martinis of the eighteenth century: Padre Giambattisa ("the dry") of Bologna, the famous theorist and teacher, and Jean ("the sweet"), composer of the well-known "Plaisir d'amour," whose real name was Schwarzendorf—not to mention G. B. Sammartini, the symphonist, whose name is correctly San Martini.

No characters in any opera give more the impression of being real persons than do Figaro and Susanna, the Count and Countess, Cherubino, and even the lesser figures of this score. It is therefore important to point out that this vividness of characterization is not due to Da Ponte or Beaumarchais but to Mozart, whose imagination conceived his characters not as stock figures in opera buffa going through a set of conventional antics travestied from the superficial aspects of current daily life, nor yet as social types in an eighteenth-century political pamphlet, but as human beings, each feeling, speaking, and behaving under certain vital circumstances very much as any other human being of like disposition would under similar conditions whether in the eighteenth century or the twentieth. Just how music succeeds in making us aware of this timeless quality is not easy to describe, but no one who has read the libretto and then heard the opera will deny that it does so. It is not merely the fact that the words are sung, or that through his control of tempo, pitch, and accent the composer can suggest the inflections of speech necessary to a given character at a given moment. The secret is rather in the nature of music itself, in the form created by the extension of a melodic line in time, and in the simultaneous harmonic combinations, rhythms, and colors of the supporting instruments—all of which somehow (given a composer like Mozart) convey to us just those things inexpressible in words yet infinitely important which make the difference between a lifeless figure and a living being. Take for example the Countess's "Porgi amor" or Cherubino's "Non so più" or "Voi che sapete": note how little the words alone tell us about the person, and how much the music.

One of the most remarkable things about the character delineation in *Figaro* is the fact that more of it is done in ensembles than in solo arias. Nearly half the numbers in the score are ensembles, a higher proportion than in the usual Italian opera buffa. The technique of differentiating the persons is extremely subtle, depending on details of rhythm, harmony, accompaniment, the register or even the tone of the voice, rather than on obviously contrasting melodic lines. Moreover, it all takes place without causing the slightest impediment to the music, which continues to develop in its natural way all the time while carrying on the drama.

The highest examples of Mozart's skill are to be found in the en-

semble finales, in which no other composer before or since has
equaled him. This characteristic feature of the opera buffa had attained by Mozart's time such a high degree of development that
Da Ponte could describe it quite correctly as "a sort of little comedy
in itself," [16] a section in which all the lines of the action were brought
together and driven more and more swiftly to a climax or to the final
solution of the plot, involving the appearance on the stage of all
the characters, singly and in various combinations, but in increasing
numbers and excitement as the end of the act approached. Mozart's
music appropriately follows the general pattern indicated, but it
differs from that of the typical Italian opera buffa in two important
particulars. Whereas the Italian composers as a rule were concerned
only with suggesting bustle and activity and exploiting in every way
the often crude farcical elements of the finale, Mozart never loses
sight of the individuality of his persons; humor is there in abundance,
but it is a finer, more penetrating humor than that of the Italians,
a humor of character more than of situations, with that intermingling
of seriousness which is the mark of all great comedy. Then too,
Mozart's music in these finales is not merely a succession of pieces in
appropriate tempi but is truly symphonic—that is, a Mozart finale
is a composition for voices and orchestra in several movements, with
variety of texture within each movement, with the musical material
developed by essentially the same technique as in a symphony, with
a definite relation between principal and subordinate elements, and
with continuity and unity arising from an over-all plan of tempo successions and key relationships.

The tonal plan of the finale as a whole in Mozart is an interesting study.
In the first finale of *Figaro* the principal keys are:

$$\overbrace{\text{E-flat}\quad\text{B-flat}}\qquad\overbrace{\text{G C F}}\qquad\overbrace{\text{B-flat}\quad\text{E-flat}}$$

In the last finale, the scheme is:

$$\overbrace{\text{D G}}\qquad\overbrace{\text{E-flat}\quad\text{B-flat}}\qquad\overbrace{\text{G D}}$$

The last finale of *Così fan tutte* is more complicated both dramatically and
tonally; it begins and ends in C, with the tonality strongly enforced by the
dominant-tonic relation of the last two movements, but dwells on the
minor mediant (E-flat) and related keys, with an excursion to E, A, and D

[16] *Memoirs* (Philadelphia, 1929) p. 133. Cf. the tonadilla, which was "a little comedy in
itself," growing out of a finale.

in the middle. The first finale of *Don Giovanni* is tonally in rondo form, thus: Tonic (C)—Subdominant—Tonic—Dominant—Tonic. The second finale is similar: Tonic (D)—Minor Mediants—Tonic (minor → major)—Subdominant—Tonic. The first finale of *The Magic Flute* has the key successions C, G, C, F, C, but with many connecting recitative passages and passing modulations; the second finale (E-flat) is remarkable for having no movement in the dominant, the emphasis instead being on the mediant keys of C and G. Incidentally it may be noted that in every opera of Mozart from *Mitridate* on (with the exception of *Il ré pastore* and *Die Entführung*) the last finale is in the same key as the overture.

The unity within each single movement of a finale comes from its key scheme and from the use of a few simple rhythmic motifs throughout, generally in the orchestra.[17] Forms within these movements are infinitely varied, but each is usually a complete unit; only exceptionally (for example, in the first finale of *Figaro*) is a particular theme or motif carried over from one movement to another. Each finale is a unique form, resulting from the translation of a dramatic action into symphonically conceived music by a master of that style. They are, consequently, invaluable sources for study of the principles (as distinct from the patterns) of symphonic form in the classical period.[18]

Although *Figaro* did not have a long run in Vienna, it met with a very enthusiastic reception at Prague the following winter, which resulted in a commission to Mozart for a new opera for that city. Da Ponte furnished the libretto of *Il dissoluto punito, ossia: Il Don Giovanni* ("The Libertine Punished, or: Don Juan"), a *dramma giocoso* in two acts, performed at Prague October 29, 1787. The ancient Don Juan legends have been used by playwrights and poets since the early seventeenth century;[19] Da Ponte took his version largely from a one-act comic opera *Il convitato da pietra* ("The Stone Guest") by Giovanni Bertati with music by Giuseppe Gazzaniga, which had been first performed at Venice early in 1787.[20] This was the most

[17] This device had been used by earlier buffo composers, notably Piccinni.
[18] This applies only to the Italian operas. The ensembles in *The Magic Flute* are, musically speaking, more in the nature of medleys than symphonic compositions. Cf. Lorenz, "Das Finale in Mozarts Meisteropern," *Die Musik* XIX (June, 1927) 621–32.
[19] E.g., Tirso de Molina, Molière, Shadwell, Goldoni, Byron, Lenau (cf. R. Strauss's tone poem), Shaw.
[20] See Chrysander, "Die Oper *Don Giovanni*," VfMw IV (1888) 351–435, and cf. Heuss, "Mozart's *Idomeneo*," ZfMw XIII (1930–31) 177–99. On what is probably the earliest Don Juan opera, Acciaiuoli's *Empio punito* (Rome, 1669), cf. Engel in MQ XXIX (1943) 527 ff.

recent of some half-dozen musical settings of the story in the eighteenth century before Mozart's.

It may seem strange that an action whose catastrophe shows divine vengeance overtaking a libertine and blasphemer should have been treated as a comedy; the reason lies not only in the obvious comic possibilities of the great lover's adventures but fully as much in the grotesque and fanciful aspects of the statue scenes and the final spectacular punishment of the hero. The legend has a dramatic weakness similar to that of Orpheus in that it is impossible to find a satisfactory ending: moral considerations require that the Don be punished, but unfortunately the spectators either feel so sternly about the matter that the customary lighthearted merrymaking of a closing buffo scene would be improper or else sympathize too strongly with the hero to rejoice at his fate. Da Ponte and Mozart compromised by using a device common in the opéra comique, a "closing moral," sung by the entire surviving cast, to the effect that the death which overtakes the wicked is a fit end to their misdeeds.[21]

Another weakness of the Don Juan subject matter is that the only really necessary scenes are those in which the hero and the Commander are brought together—the duel, the cemetery scene, and the banquet. To fill out the opera the librettist has to bring in a great deal of nonessential material, which, however, Mozart turns to advantage by writing some of his most effective numbers, such as Leporello's "catalogue aria," Don Giovanni's "champagne aria" and serenade ("Deh vieni al finestra"), Ottavio's "Dalla sua pace" (a later addition to the score, which is unfortunately sometimes omitted in performance), Donna Anna's brilliant "Or sai chi l'onore," or Zerlina's "Batti, batti"—to mention only a few of the outstanding arias in a score particularly rich in unforgettable melodies. The ensembles are less important than in *Figaro*. It is significant that not only the duet ("Là ci darem la mano"), the serenade trio ("Ah taci, ingiusto core"), and most of the great sextet in Act II (which Dent conjectures may have been originally intended for one of the finales in a three-act version), but even considerable portions of both actual finales belong to the class of static ensembles; they are like the quintet in the third act of *Die Meistersinger* or the canon in *Fidelio*,

21 On the romantic interpretations of *Don Giovanni* and various "improvements" of the closing scene, see Dent. *Mozart's Operas*, pp. 265 ff.

where the singing, instead of carrying on the action, is devoted to comment on or contemplation of the current situation, developing its significance by means of music in a manner not possible in ordinary drama but eminently suitable to opera.[22] One amusing touch in the last finale, comparable to the practice of representing actual persons among the figures of an imagined group in a painting, is the brief quotation of three melodies from popular operas of the day—Sarti's *Fra i due litiganti il terzo gode*, Martín's *Cosa rara*, and Mozart's own *Figaro*. These inserts, for wind instruments, make a formal counterpart to the little dances in the first finale, which are played by strings.

Although it is misleading to regard *Don Giovanni* as a romantic opera in the nineteenth-century sense, nevertheless we cannot ignore one quality in the music which reveals Mozart in a different light from the all too common misconception of him as a merely elegant and graceful artificer in tones. The very opening measures of the overture—that "sound of dreadful joy to all musicians"—suggest at once the idea of the inexorable, superhuman power which opposes itself to the violent human passion of the hero. The overture does not outline the course of the action, nor does it aim to depict the details of Don Giovanni's character; it simply presents in monumental contrast the two opposing principles whose conflict is the essence of the drama. The daemonic element of Mozart's genius [23] is even more strongly evident in the cemetery scene (where the trombones are heard for the first time) and in the terrifying apparition of the Commander's statue in the last finale.[24] The irruption of this peculiar quality in many of Mozart's late works—it is heard in some scenes of *The Magic Flute* and is even more striking in the *Requiem*—suggests most interesting speculations as to the possible course of his artistic development had he lived long enough to be fully exposed to the forces which brought about the romantic movement in music in the early nineteenth century.

Mozart's last comic opera was *Così fan tutte; osia la Scuola degli amanti* ("Thus Do They All; or the School for Lovers"), on an original libretto by Da Ponte, first performed at Vienna January 26,

22 Cf. Dent, *Mozart's Operas*, pp. 98 f., 239, 248 ff.
23 Cf. Heuss, "Das dämonische Element in Mozarts Werken," ZIMG VII (1906) 175–86.
24 The use of trombones for suggesting the supernatural was, of course, traditional in seventeenth- and eighteenth-century opera.

1790. It is an opera buffa in the Italian manner, with two pairs of lovers, a plot centering about mistaken identities, and a general air of lighthearted confusion and much ado about nothing, with a satisfactorily happy ending. The music is appropriately melodious and cheerful, rather in the vein of Cimarosa, with a large proportion of ensemble numbers. Nowhere does Mozart suggest that he is in the slightest degree constrained by the somewhat commonplace, old-fashioned libretto; rather it is as though he were playing with the traditional types and combinations of the opera buffa, making out of them a masterpiece of musical humor lightly touched with irony, avoiding vapid superficiality but never introducing a tone of inappropriate seriousness. The last finale is an especially fine example of his art, an apotheosis of the whole spirit of eighteenth-century comic opera.

If *Così fan tutte* was the very incarnation of opera buffa, *La clemenza di Tito* was only a shadow of the old opera seria, a form and style which Mozart had long outgrown when he was obliged to compose Metastasio's libretto (with revisions by C. Mazzolà) for the coronation of Leopold II at Prague on September 6, 1791. The first performance was a failure, though the opera later attained a certain degree of popularity. The whole score had been put together within eighteen days, at a time when Mozart was preoccupied with work on *The Magic Flute* and the *Requiem,* when he was suffering under financial distress, worried about the health of his wife, and himself already ill and standing in the shadow of death. The wonder is that under such circumstances he could summon enough of his old powers of adaptability to produce music such as these arias and duets—music which, however lacking in high inspiration, yet has a certain stiff, old-fashioned nobility, appropriate to the formality of the occasion and of the libretto.[25] Of the ensembles (most of which were introduced by Mazzolà) the finale of Act I is the most dramatic and is incidentally interesting on account of the use of the chorus as background for the soloists—a device which Mozart had not hitherto employed.

THE GERMAN OPERAS.—Mozart's first Singspiel was *Bastien und Bastienne,* composed at the age of twelve on a German translation of Favart's vaudeville comedy of 1753 (which in turn had been parodied

---

[25] See for example Sesto's aria "Deh, per questo istante solo" in Act II.

from Rousseau's *Devin du village*) and first performed at Vienna in the garden of Dr. Anton Mesmer, the famous hypnotist. The charming songlike melodies and the simplicity of the style, in which some influence of the French opéra comique composers is discernible, have kept this little work alive, and it is still occasionally heard. Mozart had no further occasion to compose theatre music to German words until 1779, from which year we have an unfinished Singspiel *Zaïde*,[26] evidently intended for performance at Salzburg, and three choruses and five entr'actes for Gebler's play *Thamos, König in Ägypten* ("Thamos, King of Egypt").[27] Both these works are notable for employing the device of melodrama, which Benda had recently introduced in Germany. *Zaïde*, in both subject matter and musical style, is like a preliminary study for *Die Entführung*. Mozart himself was particularly fond of the *Thamos* choruses, which have a dignity comparable to Gluck and Rameau. The same religious and mystical mood is heard again in the second act of *The Magic Flute*, which deals with similar subject matter. *Der Schauspieldirektor* ("The Impresario," Vienna, 1786) was a little one-act comedy with music on the model of some of the early French opéras comiques, in which a rehearsal scene serves as a pretext to show off the paces of two rival women singers, who then fall to quarreling while a tenor tries to make peace. The closing number is a vaudeville final (strophic solos with refrain), like the finale of *Die Entführung*. This piece also is occasionally revived.

That which Mozart had done for the opera seria in *Idomeneo* and for the opera buffa in *Così fan tutte* he did for the German Singspiel in *Die Entführung aus dem Serail* ("The Elopement from the Seraglio"), which was performed at Vienna July 16, 1782, with immediate success. The libretto, arranged by Stephanie the Younger from C. F. Bretzner, makes use of the Turkish background which was so popular in eighteenth-century opera, both serious and comic.[28] It is not remarkable for originality but offers sufficient possibilities for effective musical setting, especially in the character of Osmin, for

---

[26] This title was supplied by André, who completed and published the score in 1838.
[27] Two of the choruses (and possibly the instrumental music also) had been composed in 1773 but were revised in 1779 for Salzburg performances.
[28] E.g., Gluck's *Rencontre imprévue*, the plot of which is almost identical with *Die Entführung*. Cf. Preibisch, "Quellenstudien zu Mozart's *Entführung*," SIMG X (1908–09) 430–76.

whom Mozart wrote two of the best comic bass arias in the whole realm of opera. The music is somewhat inconsistent in style; the hero and heroine sing full-scale arias in Italian fashion, while their two servants have simpler liedlike melodies—a division of labor quite in accordance with the theories of J. A. Hiller. Pedrillo's "romanza" (No. 18), a strophic ballad inserted in the action like "Quand le Sultan Saladin" in Grétry's *Richard,* has curious modulations by which Mozart perhaps intended to suggest oriental atmosphere. Other concessions to local color are found in the theme of the first chorus and in the addition of "Turkish" instruments (that is, piccolo, triangle, cymbals, and bass drum) to the orchestra for the overture, one duet, and the two choruses of Janizaries. The ensembles are not to be compared in either dramatic or musical importance with those of the later Italian comic operas, which is partly owing to the fact that the action takes place almost entirely in spoken dialogue. On the whole, the melodic line is less ornate than in the Italian operas, and the phrases are noticeably shorter and more regular, in conformity with the less flexible construction of the German poetry.

What Mozart accomplished in *Die Entführung* was to raise the Viennese Singspiel at one stroke from a comparatively amateur level to a many-sided work of dramatic art, taking in (though, to be sure, not always fully assimilating) elements of Italian serious and comic opera and of French opéra comique, as well as the warmth and earnestness of German song. Moreover he created a work which, whatever its stylistic inconsistencies, is fresh and youthful in inspiration, filled with vitality and beauty which have not faded to this day.

We come now to Mozart's last dramatic composition, that sphinx among operas, *Die Zauberflöte* ("The Magic Flute"), first performed on September 30, 1791. It was an immediate and lasting success in Vienna, thus realizing one of Mozart's deepest desires; unfortunately he did not live to enjoy the triumph for long. The libretto at first sight presents probably the most extraordinary jumble of persons and incidents ever brought together on the operatic stage since the days of the seventeenth-century Venetians. The explanation of this circumstance is complicated and not clear in all details, but the main outlines are as follows.

The author (even this point has been disputed) was Emmanuel

Schikaneder, an actor and manager whom Mozart had met at Salzburg in 1780.[29] Schikaneder was in charge of a small theatre (the Theater auf der Wieden) just outside the city walls of Vienna, specializing in popular farces with music, of a sort calculated to satisfy the public demand for homemade entertainment—fairy-tale plays in oriental backgrounds, with improvised dialogue, gross farcical episodes, spectacular scenic effects, and tableaux with live animals, the whole spiced with allusions to current events and personalities. Schikaneder proposed to Mozart the general subject of *The Magic Flute,* and Mozart, with some misgivings, agreed to write the music. Why did he, who had seen his operas triumph at the large established theatres of Vienna and Prague, consent to furnish a work for such a troupe as Schikaneder's? Partly because he needed money; partly out of friendship for Schikaneder; and partly, no doubt, because he wanted to try his hand once more at a German opera. Work proceeded in close collaboration throughout the summer of 1791, interrupted only by the composition of *Titus* and the mysterious commission for the *Requiem.* According to Schikaneder's idea, the story was about a good fairy whose daughter was to be rescued from the power of a wicked magician by a hero whose chief weapon was a magic flute. The opera goes on in this way up to the final scene of Act I.[30] At this point Schikaneder and Mozart decided to change the plot altogether—for just what reason we do not know. But since so much of the music was completed, and time was pressing, they did not go back and change everything from the beginning but started off suddenly on a new tack, making only such minor alterations as were absolutely necessary in the parts already written. Moreover, the whole aim of the opera became different: instead of a fairy tale, it was to be a vehicle for the glorification of Freemasonry, to which order both Mozart and Schikaneder belonged. Masonry was a force of great influence and considerable political importance in eighteenth-century Europe, counting among its members such distinguished men as Frederick the Great, Voltaire, Goethe, and Haydn. There is evidence both in Mozart's correspondence and in his music of the deep impression its teachings had made upon him.[31] We may

[29] On Schikaneder (1748–1812) see biography by Komorzynski.
[30] References are to the original two-act version.
[31] K 468, 471, 477, 483, 484, 619, 623. Anderson, *Letters* III, 1351. See also Abert, *Mozart* II, 69–79; Deutsch, *Mozart und die Wiener Logen.*

guess that he and Schikaneder saw in *The Magic Flute* a further opportunity to celebrate Masonry and at the same time increase the
theatrical effectiveness of the opera, and that this was the reason for
the change in the plot. At any rate, the introduction of the new idea
necessitated a reorientation of the personages: the villain Monastatos
became merely a wicked servant of Sarastro, now transformed into a
benevolent High Priest; the good fairy was unmasked as the "Queen
of the Night," always trying to injure Sarastro and his brother priests
—an obvious allusion to Maria Theresa's persecution of the Free-
masons; the original hero, Tamino, remained, as did also the original heroine, Pamina; comic relief was afforded chiefly by the figure
of Papageno, the bird catcher (played by Schikaneder himself), whose
magic chime of bells matched Tamino's magic flute. The second
act carries Tamino and Pamina, as well as Papageno and his mate
Papagena, through various solemn ordeals, undoubtedly veiled representations of the degrees of Masonic initiation, which they un-
dergo successfully with the help of the priests, and they are finally
happily united. The action is further complicated by the introduction of all sorts of comic scenes and spectacular stage effects.

One cannot hope to understand entirely the libretto of *The Magic
Flute* unless he is willing to accept its externals as in some sense
symbolical of profounder meanings. Just what those meanings are
it is difficult, perhaps impossible, to say. That they exist, however,
is suggested by the respect this opera has always claimed from poets
and philosophers as well as musicians. Goethe, for example, not
only praised its theatrical effectiveness but also compared it with the
second part of his *Faust* as a work "whose higher meaning will not
escape the initiated." [32] Was this a reference simply to its Masonic
features? Attempts have been made to interpret it in detail as representing not merely Masonic doctrines but actual persons and events
associated with the lodges of Vienna at Mozart's time.[33] But such an
interpretation, even if true, would not by itself account for the
peculiar quality of the music. Equally inadequate is the assumption

[32] Eckermann, *Gespräche* I, 175; II, 18. Goethe's "Second Part" of *The Magic Flute* was
left unfinished for lack of a suitable composer; many of the ideas it contains reappear
in Part II of *Faust*, which, itself strongly influenced by the form and style of opera,
may be regarded historically as the link between *The Magic Flute* and Wagner's music
dramas.
[33] Zille, *Die Zauberflöte*. Cf. Nettl, *Mozart und die königliche Kunst*.

that Mozart simply poured forth great music in serene disregard of the inconsistencies and silly details of the libretto. Such a view can only ignore his whole career as an opera composer, for he was never uncritical of his texts and was always making changes suggested by his own dramatic instinct or experience of the theatre. It is more reasonable to conclude that he saw in *The Magic Flute* an expression, partly in the guise of a fairy story and partly by means of Masonic or pseudo-Masonic symbols, of the same great ethical ideal of human ennoblement through enlightened striving in brotherhood which exercised such power over men's minds at the time of the French Revolution and which later inspired the Ninth Symphony and the second part of *Faust*. The exact interpretation of the significance of each person and event of the opera in this general plan must be largely an individual matter.[34] What concerns us here is that the idea itself operated so powerfully on Mozart that it not only enabled him to fuse all sorts of contradictory elements into unity—a trait which has always been fundamental to his genius—but furthermore compelled him to seek a new musical language for the stage. With the creation of that language, modern German opera was born. The way lay open to *Fidelio, Der Freischütz,* and the *Ring*.

When we look over the score of *The Magic Flute* we are struck by the variety of musical types: simple, folklike, strophic songs, elaborate coloratura arias, ensembles, choruses, a chorale, and long accompanied recitatives—a diversity corresponding to the diversity of characters and scenes in the story. Yet in hearing the opera we are conscious that it is a unit. This homogeneity results not only from the fundamental dramatic idea but also from musical factors. If one excepts the two arias for the Queen of the Night (in which the style of opera seria is adopted for dramatic reasons) the music is essentially German rather than Italian. Little attention is paid to merely picturesque details of the text, and sensuous appeal is treated not as an end in itself but as a means of expression. German folk-song quality is most apparent in the solos of Papageno (Nos. 2, 20), in his duet with Pamina (No. 7), in the dance of the slaves (Finale I) and in the duet ("Wir wandelten durch Feuergluten") sung by Pamina and Tamino in the last finale. Less naïve in language, more varied in form, richer in harmony, and filled with that combination of German

34 In this connection Dent's *Mozart's Operas,* pp. 396 ff., is particularly suggestive.

fervor and Italian melodic charm which we recognize as peculiarly
Mozartean are airs like Tamino's "Dies' Bildnis ist bezaubernd schön"
(No. 3),[35] Sarastro's "In diesen heil'gen Hallen" (No. 15), and Pamina's "Ach, ich fühl's" (No. 17). The dignified, earnest mood is
especially felt in the march at the opening of Act II, the immediately
following aria "O Isis und Osiris" with its choral refrain, and above
all the choruses of the priests, to which the trombones lend a characteristic somber color. The dark tone-color of the trombones and
bassett horns (tenor clarinets) is a striking feature of this score. A
contrasting, though equally original, color effect is heard in the trios
for boys' voices at the beginning of each finale and in No. 16. In the
duet of the armed men in the second finale we have the chorale "Ach
Gott vom Himmel sieh' darein" sung in octaves and in a strict contrapuntal setting—a style unheard in opera since Fux and producing
here a climax of solemnity. In the recitatives Mozart attacked a
problem which the Singspiel had hitherto avoided, namely that of
finding an appropriate musical declamation for German dialogue. In
the long scene between Tamino and the High Priest in the first finale
we hear how the melodic line—now declamatory, now breaking forth
in arioso phrases—is fitted to the accents and rhythm of the language
and at the same time suggests most vividly the contrasted feelings of
the two interlocutors. Not a note is wasted; there are no meaningless
formulae; every phrase plays its part in the dramatic structure of the
dialogue, to which the harmonic progressions also contribute a significant share.[36] Such recitative had not been heard in Germany since
the time of Bach.

The unity arising from the pervasive national quality of the music is
reinforced by various technical means, chief among which is the key
scheme. The tonality of the opera as a whole is E-flat, and the principal
related keys are the dominant, its dominant, and the two mediants. The
first act begins and ends in C, with the middle section (Nos. 3–7) in E-flat;
the second act is divided, tonally, into three parts: Nos. 9–13, C and its
dominants; Nos. 14–18, distant keys; Nos. 19–21, returning to E-flat. The

[35] An instructive comparison may be made between this aria and one in the same key
on a similar text in La finta giardiniera, "Welch ein Reiz in diesem Bilde" (Act I, No. 6).
The resemblance of melodic outline in the themes makes the contrast in treatment all
the more striking—superficial Italian-style coloratura against simple, expressive German
melody.
[36] This recitative may be compared with that preceding the Queen of the Night's first
aria (No. 4), which is in the conventional Italian style.

second finale is almost an epitome of the whole tonal plan: E-flat—c—F—C —G—C—G—c—E-flat.

Abert's ascription of a particular significance to each key (*Mozart* II, 833, note 5) must be taken with reservations. E-flat is consistently the tonality of the basic dramatic idea of the opera, G major that of the "comic persons," and G minor of the expression of pain. But F, which he calls the tonality of "the world of the priests," is also that of Papageno's "Vogelfänger" aria, and C minor is the key of the chorale as well as of the "inimical dark powers."

There are several motifs which recur at different places in the opera and thus contribute to the effect of unity. Most conspicuous is the symbolic "threefold chord" of the overture, which we hear again at particularly solemn moments in connection with Sarastro and the ceremonies of initiation. The dotted rhythm of these chords in some form or other is always associated with the priests. Phrases from Sarastro's "O Isis und Osiris" appear in the Quintet No. 5 (at "O Prinz, nimm dies' Geschenk" and "Zauberflöten sind zu eurem Schutz vonnöthen") and in the Duet No. 7 (at "wir leben durch die Lieb' allein"). The opening phrase of "Dies' Bildnis ist bezaubernd schön" turns up at a half-dozen unexpected places in the second finale. These and similar melodic reminiscences are not to be regarded as leitmotifs in the Wagnerian sense but for the most part as probably unconscious echoes of musical ideas which were in Mozart's mind throughout the composition of the opera. Certain stylistic details—the large proportion of themes built on notes of the triad, the frequent use of first inversions, deceptive cadences, and the melodic interval of the seventh—may be mentioned as also characteristic of this score.

In Mozart's operas the eighteenth and nineteenth centuries meet. He brought into the inherited traditions, forms, and musical language a new conception, that of the individual as the proper subject for operatic treatment. His characters are viewed from the point which most strongly emphasizes their individuality, namely their love relationships. No composer has ever sung of human love in such manifold aspects or with such psychological penetration. Yet in every instance it is the person, not the abstract emotion, that is central,[37] and it is this fact which separates Mozart from the earlier opera composers of the eighteenth century and establishes his kinship with the romantics. When finally, as in *The Magic Flute,* sexual love is subordinated to a mystic ideal and the individual begins to be a symbol as well as a person, we may well feel that a path has been opened which will lead ultimately to the music drama of Wagner.

[37] The shift in emphasis from the expression of an affect to the portrayal of a person is symbolized in the disappearance of the castrato, in the replacement of this impersonal instrument by the natural human voice.

Part 4

Romantic Opera

18

The Turn of the Century

D
URING THE FIRST HALF OF THE NINE-
teenth century Paris was virtually the
European capital of opera. Not only
did many composers of eminence live there, but even those residing
elsewhere did not feel they had arrived until they had had a Paris
success. The origin of this dominance goes back to the time of Gluck.
Although Gluck's later operas had but a slow success in Germany
and none at all in Italy, their style was so congenial to the French that
it attracted disciples, through whom this style of opera maintained
itself through the Revolutionary period and blossomed anew in the
days of the First Empire.

FOLLOWERS OF GLUCK.—The first of these disciples was Gluck's erst-
while rival, Piccinni, whose *Roland* (1778) was followed by an *Iphigénie en Tauride* (1781) and two years later by *Didon,* his greatest
triumph, a work which infused Italian melodiousness into a massive
framework of choruses and recitatives reminiscent of Rameau and
which remained in the repertoire at Paris until 1826. Even more
popular was Sacchini,[1] whose *Dardanus* (1784) and *Oedipe à Colone*
(1786) show the influence of Gluck in their many choruses and
accompanied recitatives and in their well-managed effects of grandeur
and solemnity. The latter work, his masterpiece, was revived at Paris
as late as 1843. Salieri,[2] whose name is remembered at the present day

[1] Antonio Maria Gaspere Sacchini (1734–1786), a pupil of Durante at Naples, wrote
about fifty Italian operas, principally for Rome and Venice, before 1771. After ten
years in London he came to Paris in 1782. His *Colonie* (1766) and *Olympiade* (1767) had
already been performed there at the Italian Theatre. Piano-vocal scores of French versions of two other earlier works performed at Paris (*Renaud,* 1783; *Le Cid,* 1784) are in
C.F. See Jullien, *La Cour et l'opéra sous Louis XVI.*

[2] Antonio Salieri (1750–1825) received his first training in Italy but went to Vienna under the protection of Gassmann at the age of sixteen and remained there the rest of his
life, being for many years conductor of the Opera and court chapelmaster. He was a
friend of Haydn, and gave lessons to Beethoven, Schubert, and Liszt. He wrote thirty-
seven Italian, three French, and three German operas; a conservative musician, he dis-
approved of nineteenth-century innovations in operatic style and after 1804 wrote only
church music. *La Grotta di Trofonio* (Vienna, 1785) was his best-known Italian opera.
Les Danaïdes and *Tarare* are in C.F. See Jullien, *La Cour et l'opéra,* and biographies by
von Mosel (1827) and Magnani (1934).

chiefly because of his suspected intrigues against Mozart at Vienna, was introduced at Paris by Gluck himself; Gluck recommended him to Marie Antoinette and further allowed his own name to be announced as joint composer of Salieri's first Paris opera, *Les Danaïdes* (1784), until its success had been assured. A later Paris work, *Tarare* (1787), was performed at Vienna in 1788 in a revised version as *Axur, re d'Ormus.*

The traditional French fondness for display was gratified during the Revolution by the inauguration of magnificent national festivals, for which music was provided by composers such as Gossec, Méhul, Catel, Lesueur, and Cherubini, largely in the form of huge choral numbers and "hymns" to be sung by the entire populace.[3] These spectacles kept alive the demand for operas with similar large-scale musical numbers and in this way formed a historical connecting link between old French opera and the grand opera of the nineteenth century. Interest in classical subjects did not wane during the Revolution and is manifest in the operas of still another Italian composer resident at Paris, Luigi Cherubini,[4] who first attracted attention with *Lodoiska* (1791). His *Médée* (1797) is strongly reminiscent of Gluck in its general plan and treatment, though in a musical idiom which is on the dividing line between classicism and romanticism, often suggesting the early style of Beethoven. Cherubini was one of the most influential composers of the early nineteenth century; a conservative by nature, an admirer of Mozart, distrusting Weber, and having apparently no understanding whatever for the later Beethoven, he was nevertheless almost universally praised by nineteenth-century musicians. His importance for the history of opera rests largely on *Les Deux Journées* ("The Two Days," 1800),[5] one of the most famous examples of the rescue opera (of which we have already met one instance in Grétry's *Richard*). The popular taste for this type of plot was strengthened in the disturbed times of the Revolution, when hairbreadth escapes through the loyalty of friends or servants were of frequent actual occurrence. The violent events and feelings of this period naturally stimulated the demand for plays and operas exploiting danger, suspense, and the thrilling last-minute

---

[3] Pierre, *Hymnes et chansons de la révolution.*
[4] See biographies by Bellasis, Hohenemser, and Schemann.
[5] This opera is known in Germany as *Der Wasserträger* ("The Water Carrier"). Like *Médée*, it has spoken dialogue and is thus technically an opéra comique.

rescue. Such a formula had assured the success of Lesueur's *Caverne* [6] in 1793, the most terrible year of the Revolution. *Les Deux Journées* added still another emotional element in the form of frequent outbursts of the most exemplary sentiments of loyalty, kindness, and general devotion to the ideals of "humanity," with which the "good" characters of the libretto are fully identified. The music consists mostly of ensemble numbers, which are developed usually at some length with more regard for musical than dramatic considerations. The chorus of soldiers at the beginning of Act II was one of the favorite numbers of the opera, and the bridal chorus in Act III has a folklike quality similar to the bridal chorus in Weber's *Freischütz*. The principal solo is the romance of Anton in Act I ("Un Pauvre Petit Savoyard"), the refrain of which (Example 91) recurs several

LES DEUX JOURNÉES, Act I

Ex. 91.   Cherubini

times in the course of the opera like Blondel's song in *Richard Coeur-de-Lion*. This song is a forerunner of numberless romances and ballads in nineteenth-century opera, including Senta's ballad in *The Flying Dutchman*, which is clearly modeled on it, even to being in

---

[6] Jean-François Lesueur (1760–1837) was one of many opera composers in Paris during the Revolutionary period. His other principal works were *Paul et Virginie* and *Télémaque* (both 1794), and he also wrote a large amount of church music. He was the teacher of Berlioz and the latter's forerunner in introducing monumental and sensational effects in program music. Other distinguished pupils of Lesueur were Ambroise Thomas and Gounod. See Fouque, "Le Sueur comme prédécesseur de Berlioz" in *Les Révolutionnaires de la musique*, pp. 1–183; also biographies by Buschkötter and Lamy.

the same key (G minor-major). The overture, like most of Cherubini's, is a full movement in sonata form with a slow introduction. The device of melodrama is effectively used in several scenes. The appeal of the libretto, together with the tunefulness and romantic charm of the music, procured for *Les Deux Journées* a long run at Paris; its success was equally great in 1803 at Vienna, where it made a strong impression on Beethoven. Cherubini's last important opera, *Faniska*, which resembles *Les Deux Journées*, was produced at Vienna in 1806, just three months after Beethoven's *Fidelio*. The last part of Cherubini's life was spent in teaching at the Paris Conservatoire and in the composition of the church music by which he has been longest remembered.

Another composer of the Revolutionary period was Etienne Nicolas Méhul (1763–1817),[7] who first turned to dramatic composition on the advice of Gluck. During the two decades 1790–1810 he produced about twenty-five opéras comiques which show a wide variety of styles and many interesting experiments in orchestration. His *Euphrosine et Coradin* (1790) was highly praised by Grétry; this work and *Stratonice* (1792) were important in establishing the type of opéra comique on serious subjects, approaching the musical style of ordinary opera in all respects save for the use of spoken dialogue. Méhul's most celebrated work in this form was *Joseph* (1807), one of the rare examples in the history of opera of a biblical subject treated with good taste and at the same time with real dramatic force. It has no feminine characters, though the part of Benjamin is sung by a soprano and women's voices are heard in many of the choruses. The most noticeable characteristic of the music is the happy combination of classical severity, as in the overture and the chorus "Dieu d'Israël" (on a plainsong motif), with a simple and touching melodic expressiveness in the solos, especially in the two romances of Joseph and Benjamin. Many of the harmonic and rhythmic patterns recall the style of Gluck, but there is throughout a certain personal, direct quality, a rather naïve appeal to the tender emotions, which makes this score an interesting example of the transitional period between classicism and romanticism in music.

Opera in the grand manner attained a climax under the First Em-

7 Biographies by Pougin and Brancoeur; Strobel, "Die Opern von E. N. Méhul," ZfMw VI (1923–24) 362–402.

pire with the works of Napoleon's favorite composer, Gasparo Spontini,[8] whose masterpiece, *La Vestale* ("The Vestal"), triumphed at Paris in 1807 and has remained in the repertoire of opera companies almost to the present day. The success of *La Vestale* was due in part to a brilliant libretto by Etienne Jouy, which combined the old rescue motive and a passionate love story with the solemnity of the tragédie lyrique on a huge scale, adding a strong touch of the melodramatic. The many spectacular crowd scenes are climaxed in the third act, where a bolt of lightning rekindles the fire on the altar of Vesta to establish the innocence of Julia, the heroine, and lead to the happy ending. The music, which Spontini revised many times during the rehearsals, was at first condemned by the Opéra jury as "bizarre, defective, and noisy," and the personal intervention of the Empress Joséphine was required to bring about the performance. It is one of the most effective operas ever written from the theatrical point of view, every opportunity offered by the libretto being exploited to the utmost. The score abounds in beautiful solos and ensembles, the choral numbers are built on a massive scale, and the orchestration is full of fine details. That the music now seems so old fashioned may be explained in part by the rather stodgy harmonic structure, ponderously swinging between tonic and dominant, while the melodic line flows above in regular, often singsong rhythms, dividing by triplets or dotted figures, with a strong beat at the beginning of each measure. "Expressive" appoggiaturas, often on chromatic tones, are a constant feature. Even where the harmonic rhythm is quickened, as in passages of excitement, the rising sequential phrases and the usual diminished seventh chord at the climax are devices which have lost much of their effect for modern ears.

The second act of *La Vestale* contains the most celebrated numbers of the opera, among which may be mentioned especially Julia's aria "Impitoyables Dieux" (No. 9), Licinius' "Les Dieux prendront pitié" (No. 10), and Julia's solo at the beginning of the finale, "O des Infortunés." The finale itself attains a thrilling climax by sheer weight of numbers and volume of sound, intensified at the close by a stretto, that is, an acceleration of the tempo [9]—an effect then new, though later overworked in the operas of Meyerbeer.

[8] Biography by Bouvet; Wagner, "Erinnerungen an Spontini," in *Gesammelte Schriften* V, 86–104; "Lettere inedite di G. Spontini," *Note d'archivio* IX (1932) 23–40.
[9] Cf. the ending of Beethoven's Fifth Symphony.

The success of *La Vestale* was not equaled two years later by *Fernand Cortez,* which Spontini revived with important changes in 1817. The libretto is not so good as that of *La Vestale,* and the musical style is less even; there are some passages of real distinction (Example 92) but also many trivial tunes where the poverty of melodic and harmonic invention suggests nineteenth-century Italian opera at its worst. A third work, *Olympie* (1819), long in composition and subjected to many revisions, was slow in making its way at Paris, though it found some favor at Berlin, where Spontini was conductor of the Opera and a consequential figure in German musical life from 1819 to 1841. During this time his only important dramatic composition was *Agnes von Hohenstaufen* (1827, revised 1837), his last completed opera.

FERNAND CORTEZ, Act III

Ex. 92.   Spontini

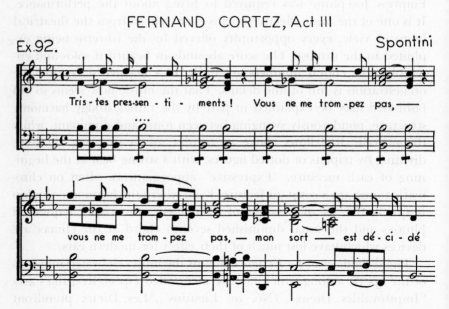

Tris - tes pres-sen - ti - ments ! Vous ne me trom-pez pas,

vous ne me trom - pez pas, mon sort est dé - ci - dé

Spontini was the last of the great opera composers in whose music the dramatic methods of Gluck were still of living force. Although his works, particularly *Fernand Cortez,* may be regarded as the starting point of the Meyerbeer type of grand opera, Spontini has by comparison a certain restraint, an artistic integrity which keeps sensational elements within bounds and never allows the dramatic purpose to be overwhelmed by irrelevant theatrical or musical effects.

His style, despite its pompous rhetoric, has a unity, massiveness, and fundamental simplicity which is closer to the classic than to the romantic spirit.

BEETHOVEN'S "FIDELIO." [10] When Cherubini's operas came to Vienna Beethoven was, as usual, in search of a libretto for himself. There was, in fact, hardly a year between 1800 and 1815 that he did not dally with some operatic proposal. In 1803 he had begun work on a libretto by Schikaneder, *Vestas Feuer* ("The Vestal Fire"), some of the music of which he later incorporated in *Fidelio*. His continued interest in the theatre is evidenced not only by this and other abortive projects but also by such works as the ballet *Prometheus* (1801) and the incidental music to plays (*König Stephan, Egmont, Coriolanus*). His aptitude for dramatic writing was proved in the oratorio *Christus am Ölberg* (1803). But Beethoven was a difficult man to please. He could not bring himself to compose music to the usual buffo libretto and constantly refused any drama which did not conform to his own high standards of the proper subject matter for serious works. He rejected in principle all "magic" subjects and condemned on moral grounds the texts of *Don Giovanni* and *Figaro*. In his opinion the two best opera librettos were *La Vestale* and *Les Deux Journées*.

This preference brings into relief one characteristic of Beethoven's which is important for the understanding of *Fidelio*. We have already mentioned among the effects of the French Revolution on opera the popularization of the grand style and the demand for dramatic tension, suspense, and strong feeling which brought the typical rescue plot into such favor. But another, even more far-reaching effect came from the tremendous liberation of humanitarian idealism all over Europe at this period. The theories of the eighteenth-century Enlightenment suddenly ceased to be playthings of philosophers, orators, and dramatists and became explosive realities of life, ideas to which powerful emotions were attached, capable of inspiring enthusiasm. Their effect on the music of the early nineteenth century in general and that of Beethoven in particular cannot possibly be ignored. *Fidelio*, with its themes of unselfish love, loyalty, courage, sacrifice, and heroic endurance, appealed so strongly to the idealism of Beethoven that he was perhaps blind to the technical faults of the drama.

[10] Bibliography: Thayer, *Life of Ludwig van Beethoven;* Braunstein, *Beethoven's Leonore-Ouvertüren;* Kufferath, *Fidelio.* See further Kastner, *Bibliotheca Beethoveniana;* monographs in *Neues Beethoven-Jahrbuch.*

The original French libretto, by Jean Nicolas Bouilly (author of *Les Deux Journées*), under the title *Léonore, ou l'Amour conjugale* ("Leonora, or Married Love"), was composed by Pierre Gaveaux in 1798.[11] The German version for Beethoven was prepared by Joseph Ferdinand Sonnleithner and was first performed November 20, 1805, at Vienna. It was a comparative failure, partly owing to disturbed political conditions and partly because it was too long and not well arranged. Beethoven was persuaded to make some cuts and changes, and the opera was produced again the following spring, but the composer withdrew it after only a few performances. In 1814 the libretto was completely revised by G. F. Treitschke, and in this final setting began its successful career.

The outline of the plot, said to be based on an actual event of the French Revolution, is as follows: Florestan has been unjustly imprisoned. His wife Leonora, disguised as a man under the name of Fidelio, obtains the post of assistant to Rocco, the jailer. There are two subsidiary characters: the jailer's daughter Marzelline and her lover, the porter Jaquino. Pizarro, governor of the prison, has been warned that Don Fernando, the minister of state, is coming to investigate the cases of the prisoners. Pizarro therefore determines to murder Florestan, but Leonora prevents him. At that instant Don Fernando arrives, sets Florestan free, and punishes Pizarro.

Fidelio is thus a rescue opera, and the customary touch of horror is introduced by means of an episode where Rocco and Fidelio are depicted digging a grave for the doomed prisoner (Beethoven opens this scene very effectively with a melodrama). The whole of the dungeon scene in which Leonora saves Florestan's life, with the superbly theatrical detail of the trumpet call announcing the arrival of Fernando, realizes to the full the suspense and excitement which all opera composers of the time sought. Even the spoken dialogue, so often a stumbling block, is turned to good account. The entrance of Jaquino, the porter, at the climax of this scene, with his excited words, provides an element of almost comic relief after the unbearable tension of the preceding action—one of Beethoven's Shakespearean effects, comparable to the introduction of the Turkish music in the finale of the Ninth Symphony. The characters of Marcelline and Jaquino are descendants of the servant lover pair of eighteenth-century comic operas, and in Fernando we have an echo of the

11 There were also settings in Italian by Paër (1804) and Simon Mayr (1805).

magnanimous king of Metastasio. The significant characters are three: Pizarro, the thoroughly wicked man; Florestan, the just man suffering undeserved cruelty; and above all Leonora, the devoted and courageous wife, one of the truly great heroines of opera. It is obvious from the music that it was these three persons, and the situations rising from their interrelations, that chiefly fired Beethoven's imagination.

The music of *Fidelio* is unique in opera. Every measure bears the stamp of Beethoven's high purpose and painstaking care in composition. The score was a labor of love, but a labor nonetheless, as the four overtures and the endless revisions testify; the introduction to Florestan's aria at the beginning of Act II, for example, was changed at least eighteen times before reaching its final form. All this is a striking contrast to the facility of a composer like Mozart, not to mention the Italian opera composers of both the eighteenth and nineteenth centuries. To be sure, Beethoven was notorious for revising and working over his material, and the composition of any important work was a struggle with him, but *Fidelio* gave him even more trouble than usual. Part of the difficulty was no doubt due to Beethoven's lack of experience with opera; still more rose from the fact that he was not a natural opera composer. It was only by an effort that his mind could concern itself with details of action or characterization that did not form part of the larger ethical and musical plan of the work. Take for example Rocco's aria in Act I, "Hat man auch nicht Geld beineben," the burden of which is that money is more necessary than love for a happy marriage. To this banal proposition Beethoven did his best to write a comic bass aria in the general style of the Viennese Singspiel. It cannot be denied that he succeeded, but the effect on the listener is, in a peculiar way, painful, like the spectacle of a profound thinker with no gift of small talk trying to enter cheerfully into a conversation on trivial topics. To save himself from boredom, and because he cannot help it, he pursues and develops ideas in a manner so superior to that of the company in which he finds himself that he remains, despite the most conscientious effort, an outsider. Thus the music of Rocco's aria, with its fine rhythmic details, its individual harmonic scheme, its masterly welding of three short movements into the strophe, and the little canon between voice and violins in the coda, is perfectly good

Beethoven, and much too good for the commonplace text, which could have been better suited by someone like Dittersdorf. The case is much the same with the famous quartet "Mir ist so wunderbar" (No. 3). Here, where the dramatic situation is not significant, Beethoven simply writes a four-part canon in G major which is so beautiful that the words are quite superfluous.

The whole approach changes, however, when the drama really gets under way. In the arias of Pizarro, Florestan, and Leonora, the ensembles of Act II, and both finales, Beethoven wrestles with the text, using it as a springboard for the loftiest flights of imagination, setting to music not so much the actual words as their implications, the abstract ideas of wickedness, devotion, endurance, courage, and the final triumph of right. It is in these numbers that we are aware of Beethoven the poet, the idealist, the musician for whom opera is only a vehicle for expression of his own towering conceptions, in comparison with which the outward dramatic form is of only secondary importance. In all this music Beethoven, as usual when his "raptus" was upon him, is merciless in his demands on the singers.[12] The thought simply transcends complete expression, and the glory of the music lies not so much in what it says as in its suggestion of things too great for utterance. In *Fidelio* as in the Mass and the Ninth Symphony, there are passages which cannot be adequately sung by human beings, though they are nonetheless worthy to be sung by the angels. *Fidelio* is not merely an opera—and this "not merely" is the source of its defects—but, in the last analysis, a hymn to the heroism of Leonora, and (like the Third Symphony, which was composed about the same time) to heroism in general.

12 There are precedents for Beethoven's cruel treatment of the voice in French opera (Rameau), in the opéra comique, and in Cherubini (*Médée*).

19

Grand Opera

DURING THE EIGHT YEARS AFTER SPON-
tini's *Olympie* (1819) no significant
new works were produced at the Paris
Opéra. In 1828 occurred the first performance of Auber's serious
opera *La Muette de Portici* ("The Dumb Girl of Portici," known
also as *Masaniello,* after the name of its hero). This was followed less
than a year later by Rossini's French opera, *Guillaume Tell.* In 1831
appeared Meyerbeer's *Robert le Diable* ("Robert the Devil"), in
1835 Halévy's *La Juive* ("The Jewess"), and the following year
Meyerbeer's *Huguenots.* These works established a new type of
musical drama which has come to be generally known under the
name of "grand opera." Before considering specific examples, let us
attempt to define the essential features of this style.

The term "grand opera" was originally used in contrast to "opéra
comique," and involved the technical distinction already mentioned,
namely that in the former the musical numbers were connected by
recitatives and in the latter by spoken dialogue. But the adjective
"grand" had other obvious implications: such works were on serious
subjects of a heroic nature, treated on a large scale, and employing
the utmost resources of singing, orchestral music, and staging. Grand
opera was in the line of descent from Lully, Rameau, Gluck, and
Spontini, but in its most flourishing period—the 1830's and 40's—
the traditional features were infused with romantic conceptions in
such a way as to give it a special character. Subjects were chosen
no more from classical antiquity, but from medieval or modern history, with strong emphasis on local color and often with pointed
application to contemporary issues (*Guillaume Tell*); religious motifs were introduced (*Les Huguenots*), and actions of violence and
passion were favored (*La Juive*). The whole treatment aimed at
rousing emotion by means of sudden, grotesque contrasts and huge
displays.[1] Such dramas were well adapted for music and indeed re-

[1] Some parallels in the field of literature may be briefly indicated: the romantic treatment of religious themes by Chateaubriand; the historical novels of Scott and Dumas

quired it for their full realization. Scores became longer and more complex than ever before in the history of opera. All kinds of novel orchestral effects were exploited. Ballets became larger and more elaborate. Choruses and crowd scenes abounded. The Mozartean ensemble, with its careful preservation of the individuality of each character, was transformed into a brilliant chorus for solo voices. Solo parts expanded in range, tone color, and expression; coloratura arias, impassioned dramatic outbursts, appeared side by side with simple ballads and romances. Musical forms and idioms were mingled in a confused eclecticism, the sole object of which was to dazzle the great mixed popular audiences of the time, who demanded thrills and for whom the aristocratic restraints of the eighteenth century had no meaning. The inevitable result was an inflated style of effects without causes,[2] of striking and brilliant musical numbers inadequately motivated by the dramatic situation. In short, composers and librettists acted on three principles which are still perfectly familiar to a certain class of musicians: (1) give the public what it wants; (2) if a little is good, more is better; and (3) the whole (that is, the complete opera) is equal to the sum of its parts (that is, the several musical styles of which the opera is composed).

Auber's *Muette* is his only work in the serious style of grand opera. The plot is based on a historical event, the revolution at Naples in 1647 which was led by Masaniello, a fisherman; for good measure, another event—the eruption of Mt. Vesuvius in 1631—is brought in at the climax of the opera. This work has the distinction of having started a revolution; a performance of *La Muette* at Brussels on August 25, 1830, touched off the popular uprising which resulted the next year in the constitution of Belgium as an independent state. A novelty in the score is that the heroine is a mute personage, who expresses herself only in pantomime to orchestral accompaniment —an interesting and possibly unique use of the melodrama technique. The music is on a typical grand-opera scale, filled with choruses, crowd scenes, processions, ballets, and huge finales. There are a few lighter numbers for contrast, such as the barcarole in the

---

père; the romantic dramas of Dumas (*Henri III et son cour,* 1829) and Victor Hugo (*Hernani,* 1830; *Le Roi s'amuse,* 1832; *Ruy Blas,* 1838; *Les Burgraves,* 1843). Cf. the chapter "Grand Opera" in Láng, *Music in Western Civilization,* pp. 825–34; Abry, *Histoire illustrée de la littérature française,* chaps. 51–58.

2 Wagner, *Oper und Drama,* Pt. I, chap. VI.

finale of Act II and the vivacious market-place chorus in Act III, but the mood is for the most part serious, pervaded with vital rhythms and romantic enthusiasm, rising to patriotic fervor in the celebrated duet of Act II, "Mieux vaut mourir" (Example 93).

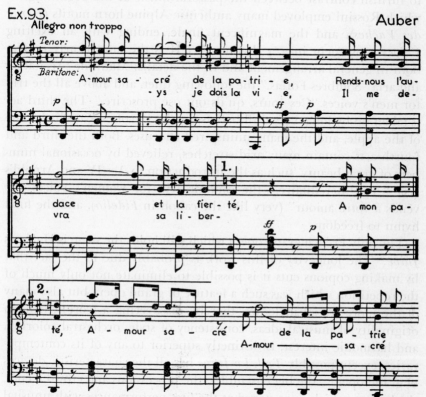

Ex. 93.

LA MUETTE DE PORTICI, Act II, no. 8

Auber

Allegro non troppo

Tenor:

Baritone: A-mour sa - cré de la pa-tri - e, Rends-nous l'au-
- ys je dois la vi - e, Il me de-

dace et la fier - té, A mon pa -
vra sa li - ber-

té, A - mour sa - cré de la pa - trie
A-mour sa - cré

In spite of its grandiose qualities, the music of *La Muette* seems appropriate to and justified by the libretto; Auber does not fall into the error of striving after effects merely for their own sake. The same observation holds for Rossini's *Guillaume Tell*, which exploits a similar patriotic-revolutionary theme in a spectacular, though dramatically weak, arrangement of Schiller's drama by Etienne Jouy and Hippolyte Bis (with revisions by Rossini himself). The success of *Guillaume Tell* was not great at first, but the work has remained in the repertoire almost to the present day, and the score, the masterpiece of one of the most original geniuses of nineteenth-century opera, has always held the respect of musicians. Undoubtedly it is uneven in quality and, by modern standards, too long. The overture has a vitality which years of playing by military bands and radio studio orchestras has failed to quench. The first act is well planned to furnish contrast between the pastoral music at the beginning, in which Rossini employed many authentic Alpine horn motifs (*Ranze des Vaches*), and the magnificent finale, ending with an exciting *Veloce* movement in 3/4 rhythm. Act II is the most nearly perfect both in general arrangement and in the details: Mathilde's recitative and aria "Sombres Forêts," the following duet, and above all the trio for men's voices "Ces Jours, qu'ils ont osé proscrire." The third act is taken up by long, very dull ballets, by the too-often-parodied scene of the apple, and the many uninspired choruses. Both the third and fourth acts contain many arid stretches, relieved by occasional numbers of great beauty, such as the introduction to Act IV and Arnold's aria "Asile héréditaire," the canonic trio for women's voices "Je vends à votre amour" (very like the canon in *Fidelio*), and the final hymn to freedom.

The only French grand opera which still holds the stage is Halévy's *Juive*.[3] The longevity of this work is probably due to the fact that by making copious cuts it is possible to eliminate not only much of the repetition which was such a feature of grand opera but also many of the more trivial melodies, thereby discovering a score which, in originality of musical ideas, consistency of style, orchestral coloring, and harmonic interest, is distinctly superior to any of its contemporaries, except possibly *Tell*. *La Juive* has all the characteristic devices of grand opera—the big ensembles, the processions and crowd scenes, the ballets (which were staged at the first performances with unusual magnificence), and the emotional tension. Among the many effects may be mentioned the use of church style in the Te Deum of Act I (with organ accompaniment) and in the striking choral prayer of the last finale—typical examples of the common practice in romantic

[3] Jacques-François-Fromental-Elie Halévy (1799–1862) studied at the Conservatoire under Berton and Cherubini and won the Prix de Rome in 1819. From 1827 he was a teacher at the Conservatoire, and from 1836 a member of the Academy. Of his thirty-seven comic and serious operas, the most successful were *La Juive*, *L'Eclair* (1835, comic) and *La Reine de Chypre* (1841). The funeral orations which he delivered as secretary of the Academy were published as *Souvenirs et portraits* (1861) and *Derniers Souvenirs et portraits* (1863). The most recent biography of Halévy is by A. Pougin (1865).

opera of employing religious ceremonial for sentimental or theatrical purposes. All the solo roles are expertly written to display the best qualities of the singers. The chief fault of this opera is its monotony of mood, owing to the succession of melodramatic situations almost unrelieved by lighter touches; the choruses and ballets which offer variety in this respect are musically among the weakest numbers of the score. Halévy's style in this and other operas was often criticized as too heavy and learned for the theatre, but it has been admired and studied by musicians.

The leading composer of grand opera was Giacomo Meyerbeer,[4] in whose works all the best and worst features of the type were concentrated. A German by birth, and in his youth a fellow pupil with Weber of the Abbé Vogler, Meyerbeer had already written two German operas and achieved a facile success in Italy when he came to Paris in 1826 to witness a performance of his *Crociatto in Egitto* ("The Crusade in Egypt"), which had been first performed in Venice two years earlier. With tenacious cosmopolitanism he set himself to assimilate the French style as he had earlier mastered the German and Italian. After many years of preparation he produced in 1831 his first French opera, *Robert le Diable,* the sucess of which was only eclipsed by that of *Les Huguenots,* his masterpiece, in 1836. His other two grand operas were *Le Prophète* (first performed at Paris, after many revisions, in 1849) and *L'Africaine,* posthumously produced in 1865. Other notable works of Meyerbeer include two opéras comiques, *L'Etoile du nord* ("The North Star," 1854)[5] and *Le Pardon de Ploermel* ("The Pardon of Ploermel," also known as "Dinorah," 1859). The librettos of all except the last-named work were by Eugène Scribe.

It is not easy at this date to do justice to Meyerbeer. The extraordinary fascination which he exercised over many generations of opera audiences has led with the passage of time to a reaction, so that the

---

4 Meyerbeer's (1791–1864) real name was Jakob Liebmann Beer. In addition to his operas he wrote incidental music for plays (including that for his brother's drama *Streuensee,* 1846), cantatas, songs, and many works for the pianoforte, on which he was a virtuoso performer. The most recent full-length biography is by J. Kapp. See also Abert, "Giacomo Meyerbeer," in his *Gesammelte Schriften,* pp. 397–420; H. Heine, "Über die französische Bühne . . . neunter Brief," in his *Sämtliche Werke* (Leipzig, Insel-Verlag, 1913) VIII, 99–116.
5 Much of the music of this opéra comique was taken from Meyerbeer's German opera *Das Feldlager in Schlesien* (Berlin, 1843).

very qualities which led to his success are those for which he is now most strongly condemned. He was an exceptionally gifted and versatile composer, one who as a dramatic craftsman has had few equals in the history of opera. A master of effect, he labored conscientiously to realize to the uttermost limits all the scenic and emotional possibilities of his librettos. His music is tuneful and highly competent technically, his rhythms vigorous, his harmony often original, his orchestration, choral writing, and treatment of the solo voices uniformly brilliant. Moreover his operas are not lacking in numbers which are beautiful, moving, sincere, and worthy of respect.[6] Why, then, have they fallen out of favor? Partly because of that nemesis of all opera, changes in fashion. Meyerbeer's very opulence is repellent to modern taste, and the same may be said of Scribe's subject matter. The story of *Robert le Diable*, for example, is a jumble of medieval legend, romantic passion, grotesque superstition, and general lunacy which could be appreciated only by a generation nourished on the novels of Mrs. Anne Radcliffe and the tales of E. T. A. Hoffmann. As for *Les Huguenots*, which has been acclaimed "the most vivid chapter of French history ever written," [7] and *Le Prophète*, which deals with the career of John of Leyden (d. 1536), one can only say charitably that their "history" is on a par with that of the average Hollywood historical film. Such considerations, however, are of little importance in accounting for the fate of operas. The real cause of Meyerbeer's decline is his music; and here again change in fashion is to some extent responsible. The very length of the scores, the superfluous ballets and irrelevant spectacular scenes, the wearisome repetitions, the monotony of the phrase structure, the frequently trivial or bombastic melodies, the overworked device of the sequence, the unmotivated coloratura passages, the inappropriate, sugary cadenzas—in short, all those features which were practically obligatory in an opera of this period have become stale through familiarity, mere conventional, outmoded musical gestures. Furthermore, it cannot be denied that very many of Meyerbeer's themes are, not to put too fine a point upon it, vulgar; and it is not the lusty, unin-

---

[6] For example: in *Robert le Diable*, the aria "Robert, toi que j'aime"; in *Les Huguenots*, the duet in Act IV (particularly the portion from the words "Tu m'aimes?" to the final stretto) and the *scena* and trio in Act V; in *Le Prophète* the famous aria "Ah! Mon Fils"; and in *L'Africaine*, the entire finale of Act II.

[7] Mrs. Julian Marshall in *Grove's Dictionary*.

hibited vulgarity of the younger Verdi (a relish for which may be
part of any healthy musical taste) but a calculated solicitation of
unmusical ears in the audience. The key to Meyerbeer's success was
his ability to meet the demands of the public at every level, and in
abandoning himself to this aim he abandoned the possibly higher
aim of leading popular taste instead of following it. His striving after
effects at any cost led him to choose his means without discrimination; an opera of his is like a department store where everything
may be found displayed in the most tempting manner to the prospec-
tive buyer. Only in his last work, *L'Africaine,* is there evident a
higher degree of artistic integrity and a more consistent and continuous musical style, despite the fact that its composition extended
over a period of twenty years; yet the music of this opera lacks those
brilliant strokes which made *Robert le Diable* and *Les Huguenots*
so popular. Its score remains an example of the composer's mature
style, purged of many earlier excesses, rich in melodic beauties, and
containing some interesting harmonic refinements (Example 94); its
musical exoticism was not without influence on Verdi when he undertook the composition of *Aïda* five years later.

For good or ill, the success of Meyerbeer was such as to make him
a powerful influence on operatic composition in the 1830's and 40's,

L'AFRICAINE, Act II, finale

Ex.94.

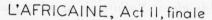

Meyerbeer

and, in Paris at least, even until 1870. Halévy tried to imitate him, to the detriment of his own gifts. Verdi's *Vêpres siciliennes, Don Carlo,* and *Aïda* were in the grand-opera tradition. The most notable disciple, however, was Wagner, whose *Rienzi* (Dresden, 1842), originally designed for Paris audiences, frankly aimed to surpass Meyerbeer and Scribe on their own ground. All the familiar dramatic and scenic apparatus of grand opera was employed in Wagner's libretto, and the music, with its tunes so often repeated, its monotony of phraseology, its massive choruses and ensembles, and its generally inflated proportions, is startlingly like Meyerbeer's. Thus Wagner, like Gluck, began his career by demonstrating his mastery of a style of which he later became the most determined opponent.

Though he cannot be regarded as in any sense a follower of Meyerbeer, the contributions of Hector Berlioz [8] to opera may be considered here, since his chief work, *Les Troyens* ("The Trojans," composed 1856–1858), is in form a grand opera and in content and spirit a worthy successor to the musical dramas of Gluck and the romantic operas of Lesueur. Berlioz wrote a few other operatic works: *Benvenuto Cellini* (1838) is a robust comic opera in the general manner of Auber, but with more variety of musical style and a more original treatment. The overture is one of Berlioz's best short instrumental pieces. *Béatrice et Bénédict* (1862), based on Shakespeare's *Much Ado about Nothing,* is in many places rather lyrical, almost melancholy in mood; it is full of the most exquisite detail, though perhaps too fine in its workmanship for the requirements of the theatre.[9] *La Damnation de Faust* (1846), often given as an opera, is in reality a dramatic cantata, composed of a number of unconnected episodes from Goethe's poem. Here Berlioz's fantastic imagination and orchestral virtuosity are at their height, and it is these things rather than any specifically dramatic qualities which have made this one of his most successful and best-known works.

[8] The tempestuous life and opinions of Berlioz (1803–1869) can best be followed in his own *Mémoires* (translated into English and annotated by Ernest Newman, 1932), supplemented by his letters and other writings (the only complete single edition is the German one of B&H). There is an edition of his music in 20 volumes (B&H), still lacking, however, the two most important operas, *Benvenuto Cellini* and *Les Troyens.* The principal French biographers of Berlioz are Jullien and Boschot; there are recent studies in English by Turner, Wotton, and Elliott. See also A. Ernst, *L'Œuvre dramatique de Berlioz.*
[9] See especially the duet "Vous soupirez, Madame" (Act I) and Beatrice's recitative and aria "Dieu! Que viens-je d'entendre?" (Act II).

The libretto of *Les Troyens* is by Berlioz himself, after Vergil's *Aeneid*. Part I, comprising the first two acts, is entitled *La Prise de Troie* ("The Capture of Troy") and Part II, comprising the last three acts, *Les Troyens à Carthage* ("The Trojans at Carthage"). The second part was performed exactly twenty-one times at Paris in 1863; the first part never saw the stage until 1890, at Karlsruhe. Few if any complete, unabridged performances of the work have ever taken place.[10] Yet *Les Troyens* is the most important French opera of the nineteenth century, the masterpiece of one of France's greatest composers, the Latin counterpart of Wagner's Teutonic *Ring;* its strange fate is paralleled by nothing in the history of music unless it be the century-long neglect of Bach's *Passion According to St. Matthew*. One can easily account for this in the case of Berlioz's work: it is long, it is extremely expensive to stage, and its musical idiom is so original, so different from the conventional operatic style, that managers (no doubt with reason) have felt unable or unwilling to take the huge risks involved in mounting it on a full scale. But in a country properly appreciative of its cultural monuments it would seem that *Les Troyens* ought to be produced regularly at state expense until singers, conductors, and public are brought to realize its greatness. Of all the works of the French grand-opera school in the nineteenth century, this is the one most worthy of being so preserved.[11]

Even the full score has never been published in authentic form— a serious matter in the case of a composer like Berlioz, whose music is conceived in terms of specific instruments and of whom it may almost be said, as of Delacroix, that "the color creates the design." The piano-vocal reduction is the work of Berlioz himself and is full of almost pathetic suggestions as to how scenes might be cut, the cost of staging and the performance time reduced. How deeply the failure of the work affected him may be seen in his foreword: "O ma noble Cassandre, mon heroïque vierge, il faut donc me résigner, je ne t'entendrai jamais!" [12]

---

[10] There were successful performances of a shortened version at Paris in 1920–21, and sporadically in later years; at Berlin in 1930 (in German); and at Glasgow (in English; complete?) in 1935, under the direction of Edward. J. Dent (Loewenberg, *Annals*, p. 593).

[11] For a different opinion of *Les Troyens,* the reader is referred to Láng, *Music in Western Civilization*, pp. 850–51.

[12] "O my noble Cassandra [the heroine of Part I], my heroic virgin, I must then be resigned, I shall never hear thee!"

In form, *Les Troyens* is a number opera with many large choral and ballet scenes. With these features its resemblance to the typical grand opera ends. Its plot revolves not about individuals' fates but about the great historic-legendary motifs: the fall of Troy, the flight of Aeneas, the sojourn at Carthage, the departure of the Trojans for Italy, and the death of Dido. The individuals appear as agents in a cosmic drama, not (as in Scribe and Meyerbeer) as persons concerned only with dramatizing themselves and posturing before a picturesque historical background. Since the average operagoer is not accustomed to associate dramatic emotion with impersonal issues, he is prone to regard a work like *Les Troyens* as an epic (that is, a long and boring narrative relieved by occasional spectacular interludes), especially since he has never been given the opportunity of realizing that here is the unique opera in which the epic has been successfully dramatized.[13] So strong is this suprapersonal, antique character that the appearance of the god Mercury at the end of Act IV or the specters of Priam, Hector, and other Trojan warriors in Act V seems actually natural and convincing.

Berlioz's melodic line is in the best French tradition of utter fidelity to the text. It contains not a trace of Italian operatic opulence; nothing is brought out merely to gratify the singer or tickle the ear of the listener. The rhythmic patterns are novel, subtle, and extraordinarily varied. Most notable in *Les Troyens* is the quality of classic restraint, that purification and concentration of style characteristic of the maturity of genius (Example 95). The harmony occasionally drops into the commonplace (there is unquestionably too much reliance on the chord of the diminished seventh, for example); one remarkable feature is the almost total absence of suspensions and appoggiaturas, making an extreme contrast with the characteristic later Wagnerian style. The chromaticism is much more restrained than in Berlioz's earlier works. There are occasional dull passages, though certainly no more in proportion to the whole than in Wagner. Yet these are surely redeemed by such places as the lament of Cassandra (Act I), the March of the Trojans (Act III, and recurring at various times), the choruses "Dieux de la ville éternelle" (Act I)

13 The word "unique" is used advisedly. Wagner's music dramas are not epics, but myths. The only comparable work is Milhaud's *Christophe Colomb*, the dramatic technique of which is completely different from that of Berlioz.

LES TROYENS, Act V

Ex. 95.   Berlioz

and "Gloire, gloire à Didon" (Act III), the song of the sailor (Act V, scene 1), and the magnificent final scene of Dido's immolation—all examples of music which can hardly be excelled in beauty and vitality by any score of the nineteenth century.

The principal ballet is the scene of the hunt (Act III), a complete symphonic poem in Berlioz's most brilliant orchestral style, accompanied by a fantastic pantomime on the stage with wordless vocalizing calls and distant cries of "Italie!"—the recurring motif of the drama, the command of the gods to Aeneas to lead his Trojan warriors to Italy and there found the empire destined to rule the world.

Comparison of Berlioz with Wagner is inevitable and leaps to the mind again and again when studying the score of *Les Troyens*. It is well to remember that *Tristan* had not yet been heard when Berlioz wrote the marvellously delicate and sensuous love music at the end of Act IV: the septet and chorus "Tout n'est que paix et charme" and the duet "Nuit d'ivresse et d'extase infinie!", the dialogue form of which is imitated from Act V, scene 1, of the *Merchant of Venice*. The change from G-flat to D at the entrance of Mercury, who strikes Aeneas' shield and utters the solemn warning word "Italie!", and the final dark, unexpected cadence in the remote key of E minor make an effect absolutely unparalleled in tragic power.

In view of the current conception of Berlioz (based on his earlier works and autobiographical writings) as an irrational extremist, a composer who "believed in neither God nor Bach," [14] it should be pointed out that he never ceased to emphasize the independence of music from literary associations and expressed the hope that even his *Symphonie fantastique,* when performed as an orchestral work in the concert hall, would "on its own merits and irrespective of any dramatic aim, offer interest in the musical sense alone." He was no Wagnerian. He cared for none of Wagner's music later than *Lohengrin,* found the *Tristan* prelude incomprehensible, and had only the vaguest notion of Wagner's musico-dramatic theories. He wrote, after outlining what he thought were the doctrines of the "music of the future": "If such is this new religion, I am far from being a devotee; I have never been, I am not, I never shall be. I raise my hand, and I swear: 'non credo.' " [15]

Berlioz had an apostle in Félicien David,[16] one of the earliest orientalists in French nineteenth-century music, whose symphonic ode *Le Desert* caused a sensation at Paris in 1844. His opera *La Perle du Brazil* ("The Pearl of Brazil," 1851) has many points of resemblance to Meyerbeer's *Africaine;* another opera, *Herculanum* (1859), obtained a state prize of 20,000 francs in 1867. But David's most successful stage work was his two-act opéra comique *Lalla-Roukh* (1862), which held the stage in Paris till the end of the century and even received some performances outside France. David's orientalism was an early example of these exotic tendencies in French romanticism which were to become more prominent in opera of the seventies and eighties.

14 F. Hiller, cited in Berlioz, *Mémoires*, p. 103.
15 *A Travers Chants* (1872), p. 315.
16 On David (1810–1876) see biography by Brancour (1911) and Combarieu, *Histoire* III 111–17.

20

Opéra Comique, Operetta, and Lyric Opera [1]

EVEN BEFORE THE FRENCH REVOLUTION, two distinct tendencies had become apparent in the opéra comique. On the one hand there were those works, such as Monsigny's *Déserteur,* Philidor's *Tom Jones,* and Grétry's *Richard,* in which the comic features were secondary to sentimental or romantic elements. Other early composers who contributed pieces of this type were Dezède (*Les Trois Fermiers,* 1777) and Dalayrac,[2] whose *Nina* (1786) was the model for Paisiello's opera buffa of the same title. During the Revolution and afterwards this vein of romantic comedy was still cultivated, but it had a strong rival in the many horror and rescue pieces of the same period, to which allusion has already been made. There were also, of course, many operas and opéras comiques on patriotic subjects which were of only ephemeral interest. To the composers of opéra comique who have already been mentioned we need add only the names of Daniel Steibelt (*Roméo et Juliette,* 1793) and Henri Montan Berton, Sacchini's pupil, who obtained success with his *Montano et Stéphanie* (1799).[3] All these works, while never losing

1 Chouquet, *Histoire de la musique dramatique,* chaps. 8–9; Pougin, "La Première Salle Favart," *Ménestrel* LX (1894) and LXI (1895), *passim;* Soubies, *Histoire de l'opéra-comique; la seconde Salle Favart, 1840–[1887]; idem, Histoire du théâtre-lyrique, 1851–1870; idem, Le Théâtre-italien de 1801 à 1913;* "L'Opéra-comique au XIXe siècle," RM XIV (November, 1933), *passim.*

2 Dezède (Dezaides, De Zaides, given name unknown, *ca.* 1740–1792) produced about fifteen opéras comiques at Paris between 1772 and 1787. See biography by Pougin (*Musiciens français du XVIIIe siècle*).

Nicolas Dalayrac (1753–1809), who changed his name from D'Alayrac during the Revolution, was one of the most fertile and popular Parisian composers of the late eighteenth century; he wrote about sixty opéras comiques, beginning in 1781. See biography by Pougin; also Cucuel, *Les Créateurs de l'opéra-comique,* chap. 8, and Lavignac, *Encyclopédie,* Pt. I, Vol. III, pp. 1600–1604.

3 Steibelt (1765–1832) was a well-known concert pianist and composed many sonatas and concertos for that instrument. Born at Berlin, he was in Paris from 1790 to 1797; from 1808 to his death he was active as conductor at St. Petersburg.

Berton (1767–1844) was a teacher at the Conservatoire (harmony and composition). Of his forty-seven operas, the most celebrated were *Montano et Stéphanie, Le Délire* (1799), and *Aline, reine de Golconde* (1803); he was also a prolific composer of romances.

the popular touch or pretending to be as grand and formal as the regular opera, cultivated a more or less serious attitude toward the subject matter, which in turn was reflected in the style of the music. Cherubini's *Médée* and Méhul's *Joseph* are examples of this combination of serious themes with the old opéra comique practice of alternating singing with spoken dialogue, a combination which we find likewise in Germany with Mozart's *Magic Flute* and Beethoven's *Fidelio.* Thus the opéra comique approached more and more closely the style of the regular opera, and the distinction between the two in many cases rested almost entirely on the mere technical point of spoken dialogue in the one as against continuous music (with recitatives) in the other.

The *rapprochement* between the two forms is illustrated by the fact that practically all the opera composers were at least equally active in the field of opéra comique. The old Academy of Music, founded under Lully and made illustrious in the eighteenth century by the productions of Rameau and Gluck, was maintained as a national institution by the Revolutionary governments and strongly supported by Napoleon. Its leading composers during this period were Cherubini, Lesueur, Méhul, and Spontini. Lesser figures included Gossec, Lemoyne, R. Kreutzer (*Abel,* 1810), Catel (*Les Bayadères,* 1810), and Persuis, all of whose dramatic works have long been forgotten.[4]

Along with the opera and the serious opéra comique there continued a lighter type of comic opera with librettos based on amusing intrigues or developments of improbable farcical situations, coupled with music of extreme simplicity and popular appeal, largely in the

[4] François-Joseph Gossec (1734–1829), a Belgian by birth, is better known as a conductor and composer of symphonies and quartets. His operas and opéras comiques, about seventeen in number, were composed between 1765 and 1803. There are biographies by Hédouin (1852), Hellouin (1903), and Dufrane (1927).

Jean-Baptiste Lemoyne (1751–1796) composed sixteen operas at Paris, imitating the styles of Piccinni and Sacchini.

Rodolphe Kreutzer (1766–1831), the violinist to whom Beethoven dedicated the "Kreutzer" Sonata, was the composer of forty-three operas and opéras comiques, as well as many works for the violin and a famous set of studies ("caprices") for that instrument. See biography by H. Kling.

Charles-Simon Catel (1773–1830) was a teacher at the Conservatoire and author of a textbook on harmony. He wrote eleven operas. See biographies by Carlez and Hellouin.

Louis Luc Loiseau de Persuis (1769–1819) composed eleven operas, some in collaboration with other composers. His best known work appears to have been *Jérusalem délivrée* (1812). He was manager of the Academy of Music from 1817 to 1819.

style of the vaudevilles and romances. Among the specialists in this field we may mention Devienne (*Les Visitandines,* 1792), Solié (*Le Secret,* 1796), Della Maria (*Le Prisonnier,* 1798), and especially Isouard,[5] a composer endowed not only with facility but also with a remarkable instinct for effective theatre music. Isouard excelled in ensemble writing; his style gradually developed along more serious lines, and his best works (*Cendrillon,* 1810; *Joconde,* 1814; *Jeannot et Colin,* 1814) were composed under the stimulus of rivalry with Boieldieu, of whom he was the principal forerunner.

François Adrien Boieldieu [6] represents the French opéra comique of the nineteenth century in what may be termed its classical phase. Inadequately trained in youth, he nevertheless attracted favorable attention with some of his early opéras comiques. After a sojourn in St. Petersburg (1803–1811) he returned to Paris where *Jean de Paris* (1812) established his fame. Later works included *Le Petit Chaperon rouge* ("Little Red Riding Hood," 1818) and his masterpiece, *La Dame blanche* ("The White Lady," 1825), which had a thousand performances within forty years. To Boieldieu is due the merit of having upheld the national French comic opera almost singlehanded for a long time against the blandishments of the Italian opera buffa of Rossini. His music is neither learned nor brilliant; it may easily be criticized for its frequent monotony of phraseology and excessive text repetition. But withal it has to a superlative degree the characteristic French traits of clarity, restraint, and simplicity, "de la grâce, de l'esprit, des motifs charmants, une harmonie élégante." [7] In *La Dame blanche* these qualities are applied to a libretto (by Eugène Scribe) [8] with incidents borrowed from Scott's *Monastery* and *Guy*

---

5 François Devienne (1759–1803), flutist and bassoonist, a prolific composer of concerted pieces for wind instruments, wrote ten opéras comiques.

Jean-Pierre Solié, or Soulier (1755–1812), a singer at the Opéra-comique, composed about twenty-five works for this theatre between 1792 and 1811.

Dominique Della Maria (1769–1800), born at Marseilles of Italian parents, studied for a time with Paisiello and produced an Italian opera at Naples in 1792. A composer of extraordinary facility, he wrote *Le Prisonnier* in eight days and completed six more operas in the remaining four years of his life.

Niccolò Isouard, known also as Niccolò or Niccolò de Malte (1775–1818), studied with Guglielmi at Naples and had several operas performed before he came to Paris in 1799. He wrote altogether thirty-three French operas and opéras comiques. See biography by Wahl.

6 On Boieldieu (1775–1834) see biographies by Pougin, Augé de Lassus, and Favre.

7 Clément, *Dictionnaire lyrique,* p. 375.

8 Scribe (1791–1861) was one of the most prolific writers of all times; the 76-volume edi-

Mannering, combining a long-lost hero, a haunted castle, buried treasure, and similar appurtenances in the best romantic tradition. In honor of the Scottish background of the story the composer introduced the tune "Robin Adair" in the last act. The choral theme which is associated with this air, and which recurs in the finale, is typical of the rather sweet, sentimental tone of Boieldieu (Example 96).

With the works of Daniel F. E. Auber [9] we enter a new phase of the opéra comique, a phase marked by greater sophistication in the librettos instead of the earlier naïve romantic fantasy and by the increasing presence of Italian characteristics in the melodies. The latter may undoubtedly be traced from the performance at Paris in 1828 of Rossini's *Comte Ory,* a work which was very influential on French composers of comic opera. Both Auber and his usual librettist, Scribe, were thorough Parisians, and their work has a certain smartness, an air of the boulevards, an alert, nervous, often lightly mocking quality which is one of its principal charms. Their first pronounced success was *Le Maçon* ("The Mason," 1825), followed by a long series of works of which *Fra Diavolo* (1830) and *Le Domino noir* ("The Black Domino," 1837) were especially popular. Auber's musical style

tion of his dramatic works (Paris, 1874–85, 1899) includes 6 volumes of operas and ballets, and 20 of comic operas. He was the outstanding representative of French middle-class drama in the first half of the nineteenth century. As a librettist, his influence was comparable to that of Metastasio in the eighteenth century. His chief composers were Auber (*La Muette de Portici, Fra Diavolo, Le Domino noir, Les Diamants de la couronne*) and Meyerbeer (*Robert le Diable, Les Huguenots, Le Prophète, L'Africaine*), but he also wrote for Boieldieu (*La Dame blanche*), Halévy (*Manon Lescaut, La Juive*), Verdi (*Les Vêpres siciliennes*), and others.

9 On Auber (1782–1871) and his forty-seven dramatic compositions see biographies by Pougin (1873), Kohut (1895), and Malherbe (1911).

is well suited to comic opera, being essentially light-textured, tuneful, piquant, and unpretentious. The most characteristic melodies are built on one salient motif in dotted or 6/8 rhythm, which is repeated over and over without undergoing anything like a musical development (Example 97). Less common are lyrical melodies of

LES DIAMANTS DE LA COURONNE (1841)

Ex.97.   Auber

elegant contour, lightly seasoned with chromatics (Example 98). The favorite solo forms are strophic (as in the frequent couplets, romances, and the like), two-part cavatina, or three-part single movement. There are many duets and trios, though the larger ensembles (for example, the finales) are not so extensively developed

LA PART DU DIABLE, Act III (1843)

Ex.98.   Auber

Re - viens, ma no - ble pro - tec - tri - ce, ai - der ton pau - vre ser - vi - teur: du sort dont je crains le ca - pri - ce pour moi dé - tour- ne la ri - gueur _____ , pour moi dé - tour- ne le ri - gueur !

either musically or dramatically as in Boieldieu. The chorus is used freely, most often in combination with soloists. Instrumental numbers are relatively unimportant, consisting only of the overtures (generally a mere medley of tunes from the opera), entr'actes, and occasional dances or marches.

With Ferdinand Herold [10] the Italian traits evident in Auber's music become more conspicuous. Herold was a brilliant young composer who won the Prix de Rome in 1812 and produced an opera buffa, *La gioventù di Enrico Quinto* ("The Youth of Henry V"), at Naples in 1815. Endowed with a real gift for theatrical style, he nevertheless had no enduring success in French opera until toward the end of his short life, with *Zampa* (1831) and *Le Pré aux clercs* ("The Field of Honor," 1832). The former work, on a melodramatic and confused libretto, and with a wide variety of musical expression, was long a favorite in Germany. *Le Pré aux clercs,* more consistent and unified in both text and music, equaled the popularity of Boieldieu's *Dame blanche,* with a thousand performances at Paris in the first forty years of its existence. Herold's style is a good illustration of his own axiom: "Remember that *rhythm* does everything." [11] His music is more virile than that of Auber; the melodies, most of which begin on the first beat of the measure, are strongly accented and abound in syncopations, chromatic appoggiaturas, and sudden shifts to the minor submediant or even remoter keys (Example 99). Every effect is repeated many times, as if to make sure that the listener shall not possibly miss it. There is some coloratura writing. A common device (found also in Rossini [12]) is for the voice to declaim rapid syllables on a single tone while the melody is heard in the orchestra. Lyrical melodies are exceptional in Herold, though a beautiful example is found in the duet in Act III of *Zampa,* in the form of a barcarole, a type of song almost as popular in early nineteenth-century opera as the siciliano had been a century previous.

THE OPERETTA.—The works of Adolphe Adam (*Le Postillon de Longjumeau,* 1836) [13] continued the trend toward a more frivolous

[10] Louis Joseph Ferdinand Herold (1791–1833; according to Pougin, the name should be spelled without an accent on the "e") was a concert pianist and composed much music for that instrument, in addition to his twenty-nine dramatic works. See biographies by Jouvin (1868) and Pougin (1906).
[11] Pougin, *Herold,* p. 32.
[12] See for example the aria with chorus "Dans ce lieu solitaire" in Act II of *Le Comte Ory.*
[13] Adam (1803–1856) was a pupil of Boieldieu. His fifty-three stage works were pro-

type of opéra comique which, growing in popularity during the next
two decades, prepared the way for the flourishing of the operetta in
the favorable atmosphere of the Second Empire (1852–1870). It is

LE PRÉ AUX CLERCS, Act I

Ex. 99.   Herold

difficult to draw a sharp dividing line between the lighter opéra
comique and the operetta: both have spoken dialogue, both deal with
pleasant subjects and have comic elements, both cultivate a comparatively restricted and simple musical style, and both aim at charm,

duced between 1829 and 1844 at Paris. See his *Souvenirs d'un musicien* and *Derniers
Souvenirs d'un musicien*, also biography by Pougin.

elegance, and *esprit*. If there is any principle of difference, it is that in the opéra comique the audience is expected to lend a certain amount of credence and sympathy to the story; there is some appeal to the feelings of the spectators, some trace of sentiment. In the operetta and similar genres, on the other hand, the aim is simply to amuse, and the means are wit, parody, and satire. Opéra comique, as we have already seen, is a very broad and ambiguous term, admitting at one extreme frivolous, operetta-like pieces, but at the other extreme admitting sentimental and serious works which in some cases cannot be called "comic" at all. The mid-nineteenth-century version of this serious opéra comique in France is exemplified by such composers as A. Thomas and Gounod, with whom we shall deal later. Meanwhile the composers of lighter types, in France and elsewhere, claim our attention.

Among the many forgotten French composers of popular stage works in the 1850's we may recall the names of Albert Grisar (*Bonsoir, M. Pantalon,* 1851) and Antoine Louis Clapisson (*La Fanchonnette,* 1856).[14] A longer day of fame was allotted to Victor Massé [15] for his sentimental *Galatée* (1852) and *Les Noces de Jeannette* ("Jeannette's Wedding," 1853); the latter had received a thousand performances by 1895, and is still given occasionally. A more serious work, *Paul et Virginie,* was produced in 1876 with some success. Maillart's *Dragons de Villars* and Bazin's *Maître Pathelin* (both 1856) were other popular opéras comiques of this decade, though Bazin's greatest success came with *Le Voyage en Chine* in 1865. The works of Hervé represent the French operetta of the 1860's in characteristic fashion (*L'Oeil crevé,* 1867; *Chilpéric,* 1868; *Le Petit Faust,* 1869, a parody of Gounod's opera).[16] But the figure which overshadows all

[14] Grisar (1808–1869) was of Belgian birth; after producing some early opéras comiques at Paris he studied for a time in Naples with Mercadante. Nineteen stage works of his were performed, and he left twelve others, some uncompleted. See Pougin, *Albert Grisar.*
Clapisson (1808–1866) was known as a violinist, a composer of romances, and a collector of musical instruments. Fétis (*Biographie universelle* and *Supplément*) lists twenty-one stage works by him performed between 1838 and 1860.
[15] Felix-Marie (called Victor) Massé (1822–1884) was a pupil of Halévy, and later professor of counterpoint at the Conservatoire. He wrote fifteen stage works.
[16] Louis Aimé Maillart (1817–1871) was the winner of the Prix de Rome in 1841 and composed six operas. François Bazin (1816–1897) was A. Thomas's successor as professor of composition at the Conservatoire. Florimond Ronger, called Hervé (1825–1892), was a church organist, actor, manager, conductor, and tenor singer, as well as the composer of over fifty operettas.

others in this field is Jacques Offenbach, whose witty, melodious, and cleverly orchestrated operettas had a tremendous vogue in the Paris of the Second Empire and have in large part maintained their popularity to this day (*Orphée aux enfers*, 1858, revised 1874; *La Belle Hélène*, 1864; *La Vie parisienne*, 1866; *La Grande Duchesse de Gérolstein*, 1867; *Madame Favart*, 1878; and his masterpiece, posthumously produced, *Les Contes d'Hoffmann*, 1881).[17] In these works Offenbach revived the gay spirit of the eighteenth-century vaudeville comedies and Italian buffo operas, signalizing the connection by using the designation *opéra bouffe*.

The influence of French opéra comique was felt in other countries, setting the tone for light opera everywhere for a long period. It was reflected in Germany in the works of C. Kreutzer, Lortzing, and Flotow, and in England in the sentimental operas of the Irish composers Michael William Balfe (*The Bohemian Girl*, 1843) and William Vincent Wallace (*Maritana*, 1845).[18] The immortal operettas of Gilbert and Sullivan[19] were to London of the eighties what Offenbach's works had been to Paris twenty years earlier (*H.M.S. Pinafore*, 1878; *The Pirates of Penzance*, 1880; *The Mikado*, 1885).

Other composers of English opera in the middle nineteenth century were John Barnett (1802–1890), whose *Mountain Sylph* (1834) was sung throughout, thereby earning the distinction of being the "first English opera since Arne's *Artaxerxes*"; Edward James Loder (1813–1865), whose *Night Dancers* (1846) was highly praised by Hogarth;[20] Sir George Alexander Macfarren (1813–1887), with twelve operas of which the most successful was *Robin Hood* (1860); and Sir Julius Benedict (1804–1885), whose *Lily of Killarney* (1862) is still remembered.

17 Offenbach (1819–1880) was born at Cologne, the son of a Jewish cantor. At Paris he managed his own theatre, the *Bouffes-Parisiens*, from 1855 to 1866 and was later (1872–1876) manager of another theatre. He toured America in 1877 (see his *Offenbach en Amérique; notes d'un musicien en voyage*). See Kracauer, *Orpheus in Paris;* Rieger, *Offenbach und seine Wiener Schule*.
18 Balfe (1808–1870) studied in Italy, and sang in Italian theatres until 1835. Of his twenty-eight operas, four were written to Italian and two to French texts, the remainder to English. See biography by Barrett and *Memoir* by Kenney.
     Wallace (1812–1865) wrote six operas and left a seventh uncompleted. See biography by Pougin and the *Memoir* by W. H. Grattan Flood, and cf. the article in *Grove's Dictionary* (4th ed.).
19 Sir Arthur Seymour Sullivan (1842–1900) composed operas, cantatas, songs, and other serious works, most of which (except for some church music) are now nearly forgotten while his fame rests securely on his comic operas. See Dunhill, *Sullivan's Comic Operas;* Goldberg, *The Story of Gilbert and Sullivan;* Pearson, *Gilbert and Sullivan*.
20 *Memoirs of the Opera* II, 375–76.

A distinct branch of the operetta stemmed from Offenbach and flourished at Vienna from about 1870.[21] The leading composers of this school were Suppé (*Boccaccio*, 1879); Johann Strauss the Younger (*Die Fledermaus* ["The Bat"], 1874); Millöcker (*Der Bettelstudent* ["The Beggar Student"], 1882); Genée (*Der Seekadett* ["The Naval Cadet"], 1876); K. Zeller (*Der Vogel-händler* ["The Bird Dealer"], 1891); and Heuberger (*Der Opernball* ["The Opera Ball"], 1898).[22]

THE LYRIC OPERA.—If the opéra comique turned on the one hand in the direction of the operetta, there were still not lacking composers who, in the middle decades of the nineteenth century, preferred to cultivate the more serious and lyrical aspects of this characteristic French form of dramatic music and thereby continue the tradition of Cherubini and Boieldieu. Between the pompous grand opera of Meyerbeer and the trifling prettiness of the operetta there was room for a type of piece which should be less heavy and pretentious than the former and yet avoid the shallowness of the latter; which should give scope to the national genius for measured and refined lyrical expression of serious (or, at all events, not exclusively comic) subject matter, combined with a certain amount of ballet and similar stage entertainment. This type, although it grew up within the fold of the opéra comique with spoken dialogue, is nevertheless better described by the term "lyric opera." [23] Its chief composers in the period before 1870 were Ambroise Thomas and Charles Gounod.

Thomas [24] began his career auspiciously with an opéra comique *La Double Echelle* ("The Double Ladder") in 1837, but his subsequent works obtained no success until *Le Caïd* (1849), followed by *Le Songe d'une nuit d'été* (a fantastic adaptation of Shakespeare's *Midsummer Night's Dream*) in the following year. His master-

---

[21] See Keller, *Die Operette in ihrer geschichtlichen Entwicklung*.

[22] On Franz von Suppé see monograph by O. Keller; on Strauss ("The Waltz King," 1825–1899), studies by Decsey, Jaspert, and Jacob; for Millöcker, Moser (*Musiklexikon*) lists a biography by C. Preiss (1905); there seem to be no separate studies of Richard Genée (1823–1895), Karl Zeller (1842–1898), or Richard Heuberger (1850–1914).

[23] In one sense, of course, all opera is lyric, in that it is sung. But the word is especially appropriate to this type which is, as compared with the grand opera of Meyerbeer, more subjective in expression (cf. Hegel's distinction between lyric and epic poetry, *Aesthetik*, in *Sämtliche Werke* XIV, 419 ff.), more intimate in scale, and more unified in mood.

[24] Charles Louis Ambroise Thomas (1811–1896) was a pupil of Lesueur, winner of the Prix de Rome in 1832, teacher of Massenet in composition, and successor of Auber as director of the Conservatoire in 1871.

piece, *Mignon* (derived from Goethe's *Wilhelm Meister*), was produced in 1866. Thomas's music is elegant, clear, correct, and melodious, and *Mignon* represents in its own way these estimable French qualities as descended from the eighteenth century through the line of Monsigny, Grétry, and Boieldieu. Thomas's talents were hardly equal to the exigencies of tragic drama, and although his opera *Hamlet* (1868) has remained in the repertoire, it is rather for the sake of its lyrical music than for its adequacy to the Shakespearean subject. His later opera *Françoise de Rimini* (1882) was comparatively unsuccessful.

The most important French dramatic composer of the middle nineteenth century was Charles Gounod,[25] an eclectic, many-sided, and yet individual genius, an ingratiating melodist, capable of a certain profundity, endowed with a fine ear for the effects of harmony and color in music, and exceptionally sensitive to the qualities of a text. Familiarity has tended to breed contempt for Gounod's music, which is sometimes unfairly compared with that of later nineteenth-century composers; it is amusing to note that after the production of *Faust* Gounod was accused of Wagnerism and of obscurity traceable to his fondness for the later Beethoven quartets, "that muddy spring whence have issued all the bad musicians of modern Germany." [26] Such criticisms can be understood only when we remember the opera music to which the Parisians were accustomed from their own countrymen in 1860. Gounod's style is in fact admirably logical and well proportioned, truly French but tinged to some degree by Italianate feeling, and with occasional touches of solemnity which remind us that he was a composer for the church as well as the theatre. His dramatic masterpiece, *Faust,* was staged as an opéra comique in 1859. Recitatives were soon substituted for spoken dialogue, and in the new form *Faust* became the most popular French opera ever written, attaining its two-thousandth Paris performance in 1934 and having been given besides in at least forty-five different countries and twenty-four different languages.[27] The

25 On Gounod (1818–1893) see his own *Autobiographie* and *Mémoires,* and the standard biography by Prod'homme.

26 See quotations in Combarieu, *Histoire* III, 371.

27 See Loewenberg, *Annals,* pp. 481–82. There had been numerous musical treatments of the Faust legend in the nineteenth century, including Spohr's (1816) and Berlioz's (1846); Schumann's *Szenen* (1844–50), Liszt's "Faust" Symphony (1855), and Boïto's *Mefistofele* (1868) included the second part of Goethe's drama. The principal later Faust

Germans quite rightly insist on calling this work *Margarethe*, since it is concerned only with the love affair which is found in the first part of Goethe's drama. Gounod and his librettists did well to limit the subject in this way, for it is not imaginable that he could have risen to the heights necessary for an appropriate treatment of the second part. Berlioz, unusually for him, highly praised Gounod's music, singling out especially Faust's aria "Salut, demeure chaste et pure" and the closing portion of the love duet (Act III); yet nearly every number of the score is famous.

Of Gounod's other operatic works the most popular were *Mireille* (1864) and *Roméo et Juliette* (1867), though the latter called down renewed criticisms of lack of tunefulness (!) and undue subjection to the influence of Meyerbeer and Wagner. A word should be added about the lighter comic operas of Gounod (especially *Philémon et Baucis*, 1860); these are filled with charming and graceful melodies which it would be a pleasure to hear more often on concert programs.

Whatever the present verdict on the music of Gounod, it must be remembered that in the decade before the Franco-Prussian War it was he who, almost alone, successfully maintained characteristic French qualities in serious dramatic music. Maurice Ravel has thus estimated his importance for the modern French school: "The musical renewal which took place with us towards 1880, has no more weighty precursor than Gounod." [28]

---

opera is Busoni's *Doktor Faust* (1925). On Gounod's opera see Chorley, *Recollections*, pp. 302–307 (the impressions of a cultivated contemporary); Soubies, *Documents inédits sur le Faust de Gounod;* and Landormy, *Faust de Gounod.*

[28] Quoted in Hill, *Modern French Music*, p. 45.

21

Italian Opera: Verdi

ALTHOUGH GLUCK'S REFORM OPERAS NEVER made headway in Italy, that country could not escape the forces which were bringing about changes in opera all over Europe at the turn of the eighteenth century. These changes had to do with both subject matter and musical style. They were fulfilled in two distinct lines of development: the international grand opera, centered at Paris, stemming from Gluck and reaching its zenith under the July Monarchy with Meyerbeer; and the various national schools, already begun before the Revolution, taking on new life everywhere beginning about 1815 and destined for an honorable growth during the remainder of the nineteenth century. Italy was affected less than any other country by the international movement; Italian composers of serious opera, at least as long as they stayed at home, remained free of that pronounced eclecticism which characterized Meyerbeer and the grand-opera school. But the opera seria in Italy, though resisting any fundamental change throughout all the latter part of the eighteenth century, finally began to feel the effects of new ideas. The decisive figure in this change was a Bavarian composer, Simon Mayr,[1] who, arriving in Italy at an early age, became as thoroughly Italianized as Hasse or J. C. Bach and produced about seventy Italian operas, most of them between 1800 and 1815. Mayr was able to do what Jommelli had vainly attempted, namely persuade Italian audiences to accept more flexibility of form in the opera seria as well as greater participation of the orchestra in the whole scheme. His melodic style was similar to Mozart's, and it was doubtless by the example of Mo-

---

1 Johann Simon Mayr (1763–1845) studied under Bertoni at Venice and there brought out his first opera in 1794. In 1802 he became chapelmaster at the church of Santa Maria Maggiore at Bergamo and in 1805 the first director of the conservatory in that city, where later Donizetti was one of his pupils. His most successful operas were *Lodoïska* (1800), *Ginevra di Scozia* (1801), *La rosa rossa e la rosa bianca* (1813), and *Medea* (1813). In later life he composed only church music. See Kretzschmar, "Die musikgeschichtliche Bedeutung Simon Mayrs," JMP XI (1904) 27–41 (also in his *Gesammelte Aufsätze* II, 226–41), and Schiedermair's very thorough study, *Beiträge zur Geschichte der Oper um die Wende des 18. und 19. Jahrhunderts*, Vols. I–II, *Simon Mayr*.

zart and other German symphonists that he was led to give the wood-
winds and horns a much more prominent function in his orchestra
than any previous Italian composer had done. Like Traëtta, he drew
often on French sources for his librettos, and his operas showed another French trait in the frequent dramatic use of the chorus. Perhaps more than any other single composer Mayr was responsible for
the fundamental nineteenth-century type of Italian opera. His principal disciples were Mercadante [2] and Donizetti, but his influence is
still noticeable in the works of Meyerbeer and Verdi. It is felt in
Rossini's two early serious operas, *Tancredi* (1813) and *Otello* (1816),
the latter of which uses the orchestra for all the recitatives—a reform
generally followed by later Italian composers. Though now superseded by Verdi's great work, Rossini's *Otello* was his masterpiece in
the field of opera seria, and the third act contains some of the most
beautiful music he ever wrote.

In the opera buffa the leading figures at the end of the eighteenth
century were Cimarosa, the Neapolitan Zingarelli, and Ferdinando
Paër.[3] Paër composed and conducted at Vienna, Dresden, and Paris
after his early successes in Italy. His best work was *Camilla, ossia
il Sotteraneo* ("Camilla, or the Tunnel," Vienna, 1799), on a libretto
adapted from one of the favorite French horror operas of the Revolutionary period.

The high point of Italian comic opera is Rossini's *Barbiere di
Siviglia* (Rome, 1816), the only work of his which is still frequently
performed and the very incarnation of the Italian genius of opera
buffa.

---

[2] Giuseppe Saverio Raffaele Mercadante (1795–1870), Neapolitan and pupil of Zingarelli,
composed about sixty operas in addition to Masses and other church music, cantatas,
etc. His masterpiece, *Il giuramento* (1837), was revived in Italy in 1911. He was one of
the most popular composers of Italy between Rossini and Verdi. See De Napoli, *La
triade melodrammatica altamurana.*

[3] Nicola Antonio Zingarelli (1752–1837), one of the last of the eighteenth-century Neapolitans, wrote thirty-four operas; the most successful was *Giuletta e Romeo* (Milan, 1796),
though many others enjoyed immense popularity. He was also a prolific composer of
church music. See Florimo, *La scuola musicale di Napoli* II.

The life of Ferdinando Paër (1771–1839) was typical of many Italian composer-
conductors of the time. He was at Vienna, 1797–1802; Dresden, 1802–1807; and Paris
from 1807 to his death. Here he conducted first at the Opéra-comique, then at the
Italian Opera (1812–1827). Of his forty-three operas only *Le Maître de chapelle* (1821)
survives. See Della Corte, *L'opera comica* II, 199 ff.; Engländer, "Paërs *Leonora* und
Beethovens *Fidelio*," *Neues Beethoven-Jahrbuch* IV (1930) 118–32.

Gioacchino Rossini (1792–1868)[4] is one of the most enigmatic personalities in the history of music. After a brilliant youthful career in Italy and one profitable season in London, he came to Paris in 1824. His *Donna del lago* (from Scott's "Lady of the Lake," 1819) had shown signs of the romantic influence, and in Paris this tendency was strengthened and combined with larger scenic, choral, and orchestral resources in *Le Siège de Corinthe* (1826, revised from *Moametta II,* 1820), and the oratorio-opera *Moïse* (1827, revised from *Mosé in Egitto,* 1818). *Le Comte Ory* (1828) demonstrated his mastery of the opéra comique, and the climax came in 1829 with *Guillaume Tell*. At this point Rossini renounced opera, for reasons which no one has ever fully understood. Whether it was due to indifference, to ill health, to the fact that he was financially independent (having a pension from the French government), to jealousy of Meyerbeer, or to his own hypersensitive fear of criticism and possible failure, at all events he wrote no more operas after *Guillaume Tell,* though the *Stabat Mater* (1842) showed that he had not forgotten how to be dramatic.

Few composers have ever equaled Rossini in the invention of copious and vital melodies. This fundamental trait of his style is most evident in his Italian works, where the chorus is usually quite unimportant and the texture of the music always light and clear. The essential quality of Rossini's melodies eludes analysis, but it will be found that the majority consist of short, regular phrases of limited range, in a major key, on an extremely simple harmonic basis but usually either having some chromatic passing tones or appoggiaturas, or else modulating to the mediant at some point; the basic motif will be a strongly marked, easily remembered figure, often in ⁶⁄₈ or dotted rhythm, and this may be repeated many times without important contrasting material (Example 100). There is some ornamentation of the line, but it is not excessive for the period; Rossini constantly struggled against the old custom of improvised embellishments and wrote out most of the coloratura passages and cadences as he wanted them to be sung. (This has not prevented singers ever since from substituting their own versions for the composer's.) It is im-

4 The principal biography of Rossini is that by Radiciotti; Stendhal's *Vie de Rossini* (1822) is valuable, as is also the recent biography in English by Toye (1934). See also Moutoz, *Rossini et son Guillaume Tell;* Gatti, *Le Barbier de Seville de Rossini.*

portant to remember that in Italian serious operas of the nineteenth
century such passages were not intended to be taken at high speed
by a light voice but were to be sung rather slowly and expressively
by a dramatic coloratura—a type of singer with which the present
generation is not familiar. Rossini was the last important composer

Aria "Di tanti palpiti," TANCREDI, Act I

Ex.100.   Rossini

to write castrato roles, and one of the first to appreciate the value of
the contralto or mezzo-soprano voices in leading parts.[5] In his ensemble finales Rossini is always lively, realistic, and full of contrasts;
musically they are kaleidoscopic rather than symphonic as in Mozart. Their principle of unity is merely that of steadily mounting
excitement, sometimes assisted by the famous Rossinian crescendo.
This is a simple device (and one easily abused), consisting in many
repetitions of a passage, each time at a higher pitch and with fuller
orchestration; the classic example is the "Calunnia" aria in *Il barbiere.*

Rossini's orchestration, though sometimes criticized by his contemporaries as heavy, seems to us a model of clarity, economy, and
deft choice of instrumental color. Whenever the voice is singing a
melody, the orchestra is kept respectfully subordinate. On the other
hand, it is not uncommon for the orchestra to have the principal melody while the voice sings a rapid patter of words on one tone—an
extremely effective device in the comic style. Many of Rossini's over-

5 *L'Italiana in Algeri,* 1813; and *Il barbiere.*

tures—*La scala di seta* ("The Silken Ladder," 1812), *L'Italiana in Algeri* ("The Italian in Algiers," 1813), *La gazza ladra* ("The Thieving Magpie," 1817) and *Semiramide* (1823)—still sound fresh and attractive on our symphony programs.[6]

The art of Rossini is one with that of the eighteenth-century composers, Pergolesi, Paisiello, and Cimarosa, "seldom sublime, but never tiresome."[7] Often careless of details, totally unencumbered by theories, he is always sure, sane, and vital, unsurpassable in comic verve, endlessly melodious, above all a lover of the sound of music and of the human voice as its perfect instrument.

The last echoes of the opera buffa are heard in Donizetti,[8] the gifted and facile pupil of Simon Mayr, who began writing operas in 1818, produced an average of three or four per year for a while, and thought Rossini "lazy" for having taken thirteen days to compose *Il barbiere di Siviglia*. "Writing the music is nothing; it is the rehearsals that are difficult" is a remark which has been attributed to both these composers. Donizetti's earlier works are imitations of Rossini, but after the latter's retirement Donizetti began his rise to fame with *Anna Bolena* (1830). His best comic operas were *L'elisir d'amore* ("The Elixir of Love," 1832), *Don Pasquale* (Paris, 1843) and the French opéra comique *La Fille du régiment* ("The Daughter of the Regiment," Paris, 1840). Of these, *Don Pasquale* is fully in the buffo tradition, a worthy companion to Rossini's *Barbiere*. *L'elisir d'amore* exploits a more sentimental, lyric vein, of which the well-known aria "Una furtiva lagrima" ("A furtive tear") is a good example.

Two of Donizetti's serious operas (*Lucrezia Borgia*, 1833; *Lucia di Lammermoor*, 1835) are still in the repertoire, though more definitely dated than his comic works. Their old-fashioned effect is no doubt due in part to their romantic librettos, but the chief reason is their musical style. Fundamentally, Donizetti derives his idiom from Mayr and Rossini, though he lacks the latter's easy, ironic

---

6 Berlioz reports that the organists at Rome often played Rossini's overtures in church (*Memoirs*, ed. Newman, p. 158).

7 Stendhal, *Vie de Rossini* I, lvii.

8 Gaetano Donizetti (1797–1848) studied at Bergamo under Mayr and produced his first opera in 1818 at Venice, followed by thirty-one more within the next twelve years; his total output reached the figure of sixty-seven, in addition to church music, songs, string quartets, and piano pieces. He was at the height of his European fame in the decade 1833–1843. See the "Prospetto cronologico delle opere," RMI IV (1897) 736–43, and biographies by Donati-Petteni and Zavadini.

touch. His appeal has been summed up as consisting in the qualities of "dramatic interest, effectively colored music, and scope . . . for the development of fine vocal histrionic talent." [9] This is another way of saying that the stories are filled with violent, bloody, and improbable situations, that the music is by a composer who understood his theatre and audiences with cynical clarity, and, above all, that every opportunity is given for the singers both to exploit their voices and to wring the last possible drop of melodramatic agony from their lines. That this music is careless of all but the most superficial aspects of the text, that it suffers moreover from an almost inconceivable poverty of harmonic, rhythmic, and orchestral interest, are matters which disturbed Donizetti's audiences not at all. They wanted tunes and thrills, and these Donizetti gave them, for he had a Midas gift of turning everything into the kind of melody which people could remember and sing, or at least recognize when they heard it sung next day in the streets. His tunes have a robust swing, with catchy rhythms reinforced by frequent sforzandos on the offbeats. Every cavatina ends with a cadenza, and every *cabaletta* bristles with coloratura passages.[10] Duets are for the most part simply arias divided between two singers, who unite in thirds and sixths at the close. The ensemble finales begin always with a few solo voices, add more, and grow louder and faster to the end. The chorus is omnipresent, for no dramatic purpose but simply to add color and volume, like an organ or a second orchestra. Everywhere—in duets, ensembles, and choruses—occurs a device which had been heard with increasing frequency in opera since the time of Spontini, but which Rossini, Donizetti, Bellini, and their Italian successors especially developed, namely the declamation of an outstanding or significant phrase by a couple, or a half dozen, or a whole stageful of singers all in unison or octaves —an effect electrifying in its brilliance and the very apotheosis of the idea of melody as the crown of music.

Donizetti's operas are romantic only in their librettos. With Bellini,[11] however, romanticism pervades the music as well. In the

[9] Anonymous foreword to a mid-nineteenth-century piano-vocal score of *Lucrezia Borgia* (Boston, Ditson, n.d.).
[10] The cabaletta is the fast section following the slow cavatina; this two-section form is typical of early nineteenth-century opera.
[11] Vincenzo Bellini (1801–1835) was trained at Naples under Zingarelli; his models in music were Haydn, Mozart, Jommelli, Paisiello, and Pergolesi. The first of his ten operas was performed in 1825. His principal works were *Il pirata* (1827), *La straniera*

Italian opera of the 1830's, Bellini holds a place apart by reason of a certain purity of style and melodies of incomparable elegance, often filled with elegiac, melancholy expression (Example 101). He is the aristocrat of opera as Chopin is the aristocrat of the piano; the indebtedness of Chopin to Bellini has often been pointed out, and it may be added that the two are alike not only in their melodic style but also in the fact that both are capable on occasion of considerable dramatic power, and that both require a skilled and sympathetic interpreter to do them justice. It must never be forgotten in dealing

LA SONNAMBULA, Act II, finale

Ex. 101.   Bellini
Andante cantabile

Ah! non cre-dea mi-rar-ti, Si pre-sto e-stin-to, o
fio-re, Pas-sa-sti al par d'a-mo-re Che un gior-no so-lo, che un
gior-no sol du-rò Che un gior-no so-lo, ah sol du-rò

with Italian opera of this period that everything depends on the singers. Composers most often wrote their parts with certain singers in mind, and many a melody which looks banal enough on the page becomes luminous with meaning when sung by one who understands the Italian *bel canto* and the traditions of this type of opera. This is especially true of Bellini, in whose works the whole drama is concentrated in melody to a degree surpassing even Rossini, Donizetti,

(1829), *I Capuleti e Montecchi* (1830), *La sonnambula* (1831), *Norma* (1831), and *I Puritani* (1835). Many biographies appeared at the centenary of his death, by Monaldi, Policastro, Reina (*Il cigno catanese*), and Pizzetti (ed.). See also *Epistolario,* ed. Cambi (1943).

and Verdi. Yet his harmony, while never calling attention to itself, is considerably more varied and interesting than that of Donizetti, and his use of the orchestra, particularly in the later works, is by no means negligible. The principal place of instrumental music in the operas of these two composers is in the introduction of a scena, that is, a large accompanied recitative which is usually followed by an important aria or duet. Comparison of any of these orchestral passages in Donizetti with the introduction to the first act of Bellini's *Norma* (1831) will strikingly demonstrate the latter's superiority. In the accompaniments Bellini's orchestra is, of course, completely subordinated to the singer. Like all his contemporaries, he frequently gives the melody to both voice and instruments, ornamented for one and plain for the other; or he may realize the melody in unbroken continuity in the orchestra while the voice joins in with more or less fragmentary phrases—but it is always one and the same melody. Another device, found equally in Rossini, Donizetti, and Verdi, is the announcement of an aria by playing the first phrase or two in the orchestra before the singer begins. This has a superficial resemblance to the false start of seventeenth- and eighteenth-century opera arias, where the voice sings an opening phrase and then breaks off to begin again, but the difference between the two procedures is significant: in Scarlatti or Handel the beginning is like a sonorously proclaimed title; in Donizetti or Bellini it is a seductive appeal for the audience's attention. It has also the practical purpose of giving the singer time to disengage himself from the business of the preceding recitative and come downstage into position for his aria.

Bellini's chorus, like that of Rossini and Donizetti, is frequently in evidence. It is most prominent in *I Puritani* (1835), a work in which Bellini tried to adapt his genius to the style and scale of grand opera. But the comparative restraint and good taste of Bellini is more apparent in the earlier operas, where some of his choral scenes (notably in Act II of *La sonnambula,* 1831) curiously suggest the feeling of Greek drama. In spirit (though not, of course, in technique), he recalls the early Florentine composers, especially Peri. Like them, he was a master of the expressive, finely psychological nuances of recitative.[12] Like them, too, he was scrupulous about the details of his text, maintaining that the first requirement for a good

---

12 See for example *Norma,* opening of Act II ("Dormono entrambi").

opera was a good libretto. His librettist Felice Romani (for all the important operas except *I Puritani*) collaborated loyally with him in this striving for perfection; the words of Norma's cavatina "Casta diva" were revised eight times before Bellini was satisfied. Bellini was the only Italian composer who, both as a man and as a musician, was generally admired by his contemporaries and immediate successors; even Wagner had a good word for his music. It speaks well for modern musical taste that his operas are returning to popular favor. He is to be honored not only as the creator of beautiful melodies but also as a composer who sought in his own way to repair the widening rift between poetry and music in the Italian opera of his time.

VERDI.[13]—Bellini died young, at the full tide of success, in 1835; *Don Pasquale*, Donizetti's last important work, was produced in 1843. For the next fifty years the history of Italian opera was dominated by one figure, that of Giuseppe Verdi,[14] who began where his countrymen left off, brought the older Italian opera to its greatest height, and finally in his own person embodied the change from that style to the more subtle, complex, and sophisticated manner of the later romantic period. An Italian of the Italians, faithful to the instincts of his race, a clear-sighted and indomitable artist, he maintained almost singlehanded the cause of Italian opera against the dangerous tide of enthusiasm for Wagner and in the end vindicated the tradition of Stradella, Scarlatti, and Rossini alongside that of Keiser, Handel, and Weber. The old struggle between Latin and German, southern and northern music in opera—the singer against the or-

---

13 The important literature on Fortunio Giuseppe Francesco Verdi (1813–1901) is listed in F. Toye's biography (1931), which is the principal authority in English; see also the biographies of Bonaventura (2d edition, 1930) and Bonavia (1930), and the *Copialettere*, edited by Cesari and Luzio (1913). The following have appeared since 1931: Unterholzner, *Giuseppe Verdis Opern-typus;* Berl, "Die Opern Giuseppe Verdis in ihrer Instrumentation"; Loschelder, *Das Todesproblem in Verdis Opernschaffen;* Mila, *Il melodramma di Verdi;* Roncaglia, *Giuseppe Verdi.* The RMI published a special Verdi issue, Vol. VIII, No. 2 (1901). Recent revivals of Verdi operas have called forth many articles, some of which are listed in the bibliography.

14 Lists of Italian opera composers of the early and middle nineteenth century may be found in Adler, *Handbuch* II, 908, 912–14. The most important are: P. A. Coppola, 1793–1877 (*La pazza per amore*, 1835); G. Pacini 1796–1867 (*Saffo*, 1840); the brothers L. and F. Ricci (1805–1859, 1809–1887), whose best work was the jointly composed *Crispino e la comare*, 1850; A. Cagnoni, 1828–1896 (*Don Bucefalo*, 1847); E. Petrella, 1813–1877 (*Marco Visconti*, 1854; *Jone*, 1858); F. Marchetti, 1831–1902 (*Ruy Blas*, 1869); and Amilcare Ponchielli, 1834–1886, whose *Giaconda* (1876) still holds the stage, at least in Italy.

chestra, melody against polyphony, simplicity against complexity—was incarnate in the nineteenth century in the works of Verdi and Wagner, who represented the two ideals in all their irreconcilable perfection.

With the exception of *Falstaff* (1893) and one very early unsuccessful work, all Verdi's operas are serious. His first triumph was achieved at Milan in 1842 with the biblical opera *Nabucodonosor* (generally known as *Nabucco*), followed a year later by *I Lombardi alla prima crociata* ("The Lombards at the First Crusade")—both works which in their large choruses and melodramatic situations recall Meyerbeer's *Robert le Diable*. European fame came with *Ernani* (1844), on a libretto arranged by Francesco Piave from Victor Hugo's drama. The music of these early operas showed Verdi as a composer with a sure feeling for the theatre and a melodic gift in which the facility of Donizetti and Bellini was combined with greater breadth of phrase and ferocious energy of expression (Example 102). The immense popularity he enjoyed in Italy was due in part to the fact that he brought to the accepted forms and idiom of opera just that touch of dynamic individuality which was needed; but there was a further reason which was only indirectly connected with the music itself. Italy during the *risorgimento* (1820–1870) was seething with revolution, and Verdi's operas came to play an important part in the patriotic movements of the 1840's and 50's. Though their scenes and characters ostensibly had no connection with contemporary events, the librettos were filled with conspiracies, political assassinations, appeals to liberty, and exhortations against tyranny, all of which were easily interpreted in the obviously intended sense by sympathetic audiences. *Nabucco, I Lombardi, Ernani, I due Foscari* ("The Two Foscari," 1844), *Giovanna d'Arco* (1845), and especially *Attila* (1846) and the occasional opera *La battaglia di Legnano* ("The Battle of Legnano," Rome, 1849) all gave rise to fervent demonstrations and made Verdi's name a rallying-cry for Italian patriots. Even *Rigoletto* (1851), based on a very good adaptation by Piave of Victor Hugo's *Le Roi s'amuse,* was attacked by the censorship, and the names of historical characters (especially King Francis I of France) as well as several other details had to be changed before production was permitted. A similar situation arose with regard to *Un ballo in maschera* ("A Masked Ball") at Naples in 1859, where the authorities insisted

ERNANI, Act III

Ex.102.   Verdi

on the transformation of the original Gustavus III of Sweden into
an imaginary Earl of Warwick and the locale of this fantastic and
bloody melodrama to the Puritan city of Boston in New England!
It was during the popular demonstrations which attended the prepa-

ration of this opera that crowds in front of his hotel shouted "Viva
Verdi"—a cry of double meaning, for the letters of the composer's
name formed the initials of "Vittorio Emanuele Re D'Italia," and
thus he came to be identified with the cause of Italian national unity
as a symbol.

With the production of *Il trovatore* ("The Troubadour") and
La traviata ("The Erring Woman") in 1853 a climax of Verdi's work
in the purely Italian opera was reached. We may therefore pause here
to indicate some of the essential characteristics of the style by which
Verdi was known and loved in his own land at this time.

Verdi's principal librettists were T. Solera (*Oberto, Nabucco, I Lombardi,
Giovanna d'Arco, Attila*), Francesco Piave (*Ernani, I due Foscari, Macbeth,
Il corsaro, Stiffelio, Rigoletto, La traviata, Aroldo, Simon Boccanegra,* and
La forza del destino), and Cammarano (*Luisa Miller, Il trovatore*). The
literary sources of the librettos were various: from Schiller came *Luisa
Miller* (*Kabale und Liebe*), *I masnadieri* (*Die Räuber*) and *Don Carlo;*
from Victor Hugo, *Ernani* and *Rigoletto;* from Dumas the Younger, *La
traviata* (*La Dame aux camélias*); from Scribe, *Les Vêpres siciliennes* and
Un ballo in maschera; from Byron, *I due Foscari* and *Il corsaro;* from the
Spanish dramatist Gutierrez came *Il trovatore* and *Simon Boccanegra,* and
from another Spaniard, the Duke of Rivas, *La forza del destino;* from
Shakespeare Verdi took *Macbeth, Otello,* and *Falstaff* (the last two arranged by Arrigo Boïto), as well as the projected, but never completed,
King Lear and *Hamlet. Aïda* was first sketched by the French Egyptologist
Mariette Bey and put into final shape by Ghislanzoni, with much assist-
ance from Verdi himself.

The plots (except for *Falstaff*) are all serious, gloomy, and violent;
the earlier works especially are typical examples of the blood-and-
thunder romantic melodrama,[15] marked by situations of strong passion in rapid succession, giving vivid contrasts and a theatrically
effective sweep to the action, however questionable the details may
be from a dramatist's viewpoint. Much of their obscurity is due to
the extreme condensation upon which Verdi insisted, and often a
careful reading of the libretto is necessary in order to understand the
action. Whatever one may think of the subject matter, it cannot be
denied that it always offers the kind of opportunity which Verdi
needed to exercise his special gifts.

[15] The ancestor of this type of plot is the Revolutionary horror opera, the influence of
which may be traced through Meyerbeer in France and through Simon Mayr, Mercadante, and Donizetti in Italy.

The essence of his early style is a certain primitive directness, an uninhibited vigor and naturalness of utterance. This results often in melodies of apparent triviality, which are nevertheless patently sincere and almost invariably appropriate to the dramatic situation. His effects are always obtained by means of voices. His orchestration grew constantly more expert and original from the earliest to the latest operas, but the orchestra never has the symphonic significance or the polyphonic texture of Wagner's. Only two of the overtures (*Luisa Miller* and *Les Vêpres siciliennes*) are important, and many operas begin with only a short orchestral prelude. The ballet music is seldom distinguished, and most of the instrumental music for ball scenes, marches, and the like (often performed by a military band on the stage) is trite. Nature painting and the depiction of the fantastic, so important in contemporary German romantic opera, find little place in Verdi.[16] His interest is in the expression of human passions in song, to which all else is subordinated; and through that medium he creates a musical structure of sheer sensuous beauty and emotional power, basically simple and uncomplicated by philosophical theories, with an appeal so profound, so elemental, that it cannot be conveyed or even intelligibly discussed in any other language than that of music itself.

The heart of the melodramatic, romantic Verdi is to be found in three works: *Ernani, Rigoletto,* and *Il trovatore.* The last is particularly rich in traits which mark the composer's works of this period: the roaring unison of the "anvil chorus"; the unbelievable contrast of moods in the "miserere" scene; the nostalgic sentiment of Azucena's "Ai nostri monti"; Manrico's lusty bravura aria "Di quella pira"—these and other melodies from this opera are so well known that citation or comment is superfluous. *Rigoletto,* almost equally agonizing in its plot and situations, is a more unified whole and superior in character delineation, besides containing the famous quartet, one of the finest serious dramatic ensembles in all opera.

Beside the naked brutality of *Rigoletto, Il trovatore,* and some of the other early works, *La traviata* is a refined drawing-room tragedy; its more restrained, almost intimate, musical style had

---

[16] Some notable exceptions—e.g., the ballet music for the Paris version of *Il trovatore,* the ball scene in Act I of *La traviata,* the storm music in Act III of *Rigoletto*—do not invalidate the general statements made above.

already been foreshadowed in *Luisa Miller* (1849). Several details in *La traviata* are significant in the light of Verdi's future development. The orchestra is of relatively greater dramatic importance: in the ballroom scene of Act I it furnishes a continuous background of dance music against which a conversation is carried on;[17] the opening strain of the prelude, with its pathetic minor harmonies in the divided violins,[18] recurs most effectively at the beginning of Act III to set the mood for the closing scenes of the opera. Then, too, there is an occasional vocal phrase which demonstrates a greater freedom in the melodic line, a beginning of emancipation from the usually all-too-regular patterns of the early Verdi (Example 103); the reci-

LA TRAVIATA, Act II

Ex.103.   Verdi

tative-arioso scene which culminates in this beautiful passage is a fine example of moving dramatic declamation.

Many of Verdi's early operas make systematic use of recurring themes; this procedure is not the same as Wagner's leitmotif system but consists merely in the introduction of a previously heard theme when there is in the action an obvious reminiscence of the earlier situation with which the theme is associated.[19] Thus in *Ernani* the

---

[17] Cf. also the last scene of *Un ballo in maschera,* and the waltzes in Strauss's *Rosenkavalier.*

[18] Cf. the divided violins in the prelude to *Aïda* and in Wagner's *Lohengrin* prelude.

[19] The reminiscence motif is not at all uncommon in operas during the first half of the nineteenth century, and we have already noted instances in even earlier periods (Mozart, Grétry, Monteverdi).

motif of the pledge, and in *Rigoletto* that of Monterone's curse, recur at appropriate moments in the opera; *I due Foscari* offers further examples, as do also *Il trovatore* and *La traviata*. The use of this device in *Aïda* is therefore merely a continuation of Verdi's earlier practice and not necessarily a result of Wagnerian influence.

With regard to the ensembles in Verdi, one can do little but refer the reader to the scores. Telling declamation, perfect dramatic timing, and an infallible sense of climax mark them all; perhaps the most remarkable feature is the composer's endless inventiveness in sound combinations, his sheer reveling in sweet and powerful sonorities. The *sotto voce* ensembles [20] have an indescribably mysterious, suggestive quality.

Verdi was not a composer who studied the scores of his rivals; secure in his own musical and dramatic instincts, he pointedly avoided too close acquaintance with other composers' music. Almost the only specific non-Italian influence which can be traced in his works is that of Meyerbeer, for whom he had considerable admiration. The magic attraction of Paris for Italian composers was still strong, and it is not surprising that Verdi should have aspired, like Cherubini, Spontini, Rossini, Bellini, and Donizetti before him, to the satisfaction of a Paris success. He had made some essays in the grand-opera style in his early career, especially in *Giovanna d'Arco*. *I Lombardi* had been adapted and successfully performed at Paris in 1847, under the title *Jérusalem*. *Il trovatore,* in its bewildering richness of incident and musical effects, is very reminiscent of Meyerbeer, and the character of Azucena, the gypsy mother, has often been compared to that of Fidès, the mother of John of Leyden in Meyerbeer's *Prophète*. Verdi's full capitulation to grand opera, however, came in 1855, when he composed a five-act libretto by Scribe, *Les Vêpres siciliennes* ("The Sicilian Vespers"), on the historical subject of the massacre of the French by the Sicilians in 1282. The story reads almost like a travesty of all the devices for which Verdi's operas were famous; the music, with the exception of the overture, is in general inferior to Verdi's usual style. A better success was obtained with *Don Carlo* (Paris, 1867), another work along grand-opera lines, excessively long [21] but containing many fine individual numbers.

20 See many examples in the Paris version of *Macbeth*.
21 It was considerably shortened in Verdi's revision of 1884.

The other operas of the period between *La traviata* and *Aïda* include *Simon Boccanegra,* which failed at its first appearance (1857) but was successful in a thoroughly revised version in 1884.[22] *Un ballo in maschera* (1859) is remarkable both for certain experimental details in the instrumental writing (for example, the canonic treatment of one of the themes in the prelude) and for the beginning of Verdi's later buffo style in the music given to Oscar, the page—a new idiom which is carried through the role of Fra Melitone in *La forza del destino* and reaches full fruition in the pages of *Falstaff*. *La forza del destino* ("The Power of Destiny," St. Petersburg, 1862) is a somber melodrama distinguished by a score in which we can trace still further the progress of Verdi toward that long-breathed, broadly rhythmed, infinitely expressive melody, sustained by the simplest yet most strikingly effective harmony, which we associate with the composer's later style.

Aïda (Cairo, 1871) was in every respect the culmination of Verdi's art up to that time, uniting the melodic exuberance, the warmth and color of the Italians with the pageants, ballets, and choruses of grand opera. *Aïda* is Italian opera made heroic, grand opera infused with true human passion, a masterwork of two representative nineteenth-century styles. Verdi here surpassed himself in his own domain: he had never written better solo arias than Radames' "Celeste Aïda" or Aïda's soliloquy "Ritorna vincitor"; the finale of Act II excels in splendor anything from the earlier operas; and the closing scene is a climax in the expression of that mood of tragic poignancy of which Verdi had always been a master. But beyond such matters as these are still more significant advances. The libretto, while no less effective theatrically than the earlier ones, is more straightforward in action and clearer in details. The music is more conscientiously and fully devoted to the dramatic requirements, and this in turn affects the form of the opera as a whole: for while *Aïda* is still a number opera, the score possesses more continuity than any of Verdi's previous works. This is due in part, but not entirely, to two devices: (1) the use of recurring themes, more extensively and systematically than in any of the other operas; and (2) a pervasive, subtle exoticism. The latter is not the product of borrowed Egyptian native tunes but of Verdi's own sensitiveness to color, expressed not only in melodies of modal turn,

[22] See Toye's *Verdi*, pp. 342–49, for many interesting details of the composer's revisions.

with chromatic intervals, but also in original harmonies and many details of instrumentation (see for example the introduction to Act III). Even the ballet music, usually rather perfunctory with Verdi, here has a richness of harmony and scoring, a freshness of melodic and rhythmic invention, which make it of equal interest with the rest of the opera.

In a word, the production of *Aïda* saw Verdi, then aged fifty-eight, at the summit of his career, wealthy, successful, the acknowledged master of Italian opera, the idol of his countrymen, a world-famous figure. Had he never written another note, his high position in the history of opera would have been secure. After the triumphal reception of the *Requiem* (1874) he himself felt that his active days as a composer were over. A mood of depression gripped him in the years around 1880, due to both political and musical conditions in Italy at the time. Wagnerian music and Wagnerian philosophy were threatening the very foundations of Italian art, and while Verdi was far from feeling envy toward Wagner, he could not but be alarmed at what he felt was a false course on the part of many of his countrymen. "Our young Italians are not patriots," he wrote. "If the Germans, basing themselves on Bach, have culminated in Wagner they act like good Germans, and it is well. But we, the descendants of Palestrina, commit a musical crime in imitating Wagner, and what we are doing is useless, not to say harmful." [23] Although Verdi sensed the "irrepressible conflict" between German and Italian opera, he hesitated long before committing himself to battle. He was weary, haunted with distrust of his own powers, and apprehensive of public failure. For sixteen years after *Aïda* no new opera came from his pen. It was not until 1887, when the composer was over seventy years old, that *Otello* appeared, the greatest Italian tragic opera of the nineteenth century and the triumphant answer of Italian art to the threat of German domination.

Verdi chose to counter the Nordic myth as operatic subject matter with a return to purely human drama, and from his favorite dramatist, Shakespeare, he chose the subjects of *Otello* and *Falstaff*. The actual arrangement of the librettos was the work of Arrigo Boïto,

---

[23] Letter to Franco Faccio, 1889, quoted in Toye, *Verdi*, pp. 196 f. The sentiments here expressed dated from many years previous. See also Franz Werfel's novel, *Verdi*, for an imaginative treatment of this phase of the composer's life.

a poet, novelist, and composer of distinction, to whose literary skill and devotion to Verdi much of the credit for both works must be given.[24] Boïto's adaptations of Shakespeare are masterly. In *Otello*, especially, the delicate problem of shortening the poetry so as to leave scope for the development of the music is handled with skill, and the action of the original is followed closely. Boïto altered only a few details and added only the verses of Iago's "Credo" in Act II.

As to the music of *Otello*, we must beware of regarding it as a complete break with Verdi's earlier style. It is rather the culminating point of an evolution. Not all the older practices are abandoned: there are precedents for the storm at the opening of Act I (compare *Rigoletto*); the drinking song and chorus in the same act; the serenade in the garden scene of Act II, with its accompaniment of bagpipes, mandolins, and guitars; the duets, conventional enough in their placing at the end of Acts I and II; the ensembles, especially the magnificent one at the end of Act III; and the superb theatrical close of this act, with Iago's melodramatic "Ecco il Leone!", which is in the best tradition of Italian opera. There are recitatives and arias (for example, Iago's "Credo," Otello's "Ora e per sempre addio!", Desdemona's "Salce" and "Ave Maria"). But all these forms and styles in *Otello* have a finish and perfection, a close connection with the drama, surpassing anything previous. Moreover, there are certain procedures which are definitely new in this work. Perhaps the most obvious of these is the continuity of the music throughout each act, that is, the absence of separate numbers as in the earlier operas. But closer attention shows that this does not involve a radical change in structure: the divisions are still there, only their boundaries are a little less distinct; instead of a double bar, there is an interlocking or a transition. Much of the continuity of style in *Otello* must be attributed to the libretto, which offers few opportunities for numbers of the traditional sort, being made up for the most part of scenes of

[24] Boïto had been an ardent disciple of Wagner in Italy; he was converted to Verdi by the music of *Aïda* and the *Requiem*. Boïto's own opera *Mefistofele* (1868, revised 1875), though necessarily episodic in character, is perhaps the most successful dramatic setting of Goethe's *Faust*, far closer to the spirit of the original than either Berlioz's or Gounod's version; it is accompanied in the score by many notes and philosophical disquisitions, *à la* Wagner, on the characters and events of the drama. On Boïto (1842–1918) see biographies by F. Ballo (1938) and P. Nardi (1942); new edition of his *Lettere* by De Rensis (1932). Cf. also Macchetta, *Verdi: Milan and "Othello"*; Baumann, "The Change of Style in Verdi's Operatic Work . . . between *Aida* and *Otello*" (Cornell University Master's Thesis, 1945).

continuing action which are more appropriately set to a different kind of music—a flexible, dramatically powerful, sensitive, and infinitely varied melody, supported by the orchestra and organized in long periods by means of the rhythmic and harmonic structure: "dramatic declamation in strict time substituted for classical recitative on the one hand and Wagnerian polyphony on the other." [25] This declamation includes both strict recitative (used especially effectively for the dialogue between Otello and Emilia at the end of the scene of Desdemona's murder in Act IV) and (on the other hand) short melodic phrases of the most pronounced arioso character, with extreme compression of emotion. No such free, passionate, long-spun melodic line had been heard in Italian opera since Monteverdi's *Poppea*. It is clearly enough the model for Puccini and other later Italian composers, who constantly aimed at, but seldom attained, the pathos of Verdi in this style (Example 104).

Even where there are more or less formal arias, the melody is a

OTELLO, Act IV

25 From a criticism of the first performance in *Secolo*, quoted in Toye, *Verdi*, p. 191.

long way removed from the singsong, patterned, hand-organ tunes of some of the early operas. It is no less expressive than these, no less vocal, but nobler, more plastic, more richly interwoven with the orchestra, more intimately wedded to the harmony. In the harmonic idiom itself, Verdi never went to Wagnerian lengths of chromaticism, though no composer was more alive to the effectiveness of a few judicious chromatic alterations. He was aware of the broadening conceptions of tonality which prevailed at this time, as witness the freedom of his harmonic vocabulary and the range of his modulations.[26]

Inasmuch as it has been claimed that Verdi in his later operas was imitating the Wagnerian music drama, it may be well not only to emphasize again the continuity of the musical style of *Otello* with that of Verdi's preceding works but also to point out certain fundamental differences which remain between the two composers. In the first place, *Otello* and *Falstaff* are both singer's operas; in spite of the greater independence of the orchestra, it is never made the center of the picture, and the instrumental music does not have either the self-sufficiency or the symphonic range of development that it has in Wagner. Second, Verdi never adopted a system of leading motifs; the formal unity of his operas is like that of the classical symphony rather than the romantic tone poem, that is, a union of relatively independent individual numbers with themes recurring only in a few exceptional cases. Third, Verdi's operas are human dramas, not myths. Their librettos have no hidden world, no symbolism, no set of meanings below the surface. They are free of any trace of the *Gestamtkunstwerk* or other theories. And finally, there is about Verdi's music a simplicity, a certain Latin quality of serenity, which the complex German soul of Wagner could never encompass. It is in essence a classic, Mediterranean art, self-enclosed within limits which by their very existence make possible its perfection.

As *Otello* was the climax of tragic opera, so *Falstaff* (1893) is the transfiguration of opera buffa. Written on a libretto arranged from Shakespeare's *Merry Wives of Windsor,* it is not only a remarkable achievement for an octogenarian but a magnificent final crescendo of a great career. Excelling all earlier works in brilliancy of orchestration, wealth of spontaneous melody, and absolute oneness of text

[26] Cf. for example the tonal scheme of the duet at the end of Act I: G-flat– F– C– E– D-flat.

and music, it is a technical masterpiece, abounding in the most subtle beauties which often pass so quickly that only a close acquaintance with the score enables the listener to perceive them all. Because of this very fineness of workmanship and perhaps also because of the profound sophistication of the ideas underlying the music, *Falstaff* has never become as popular with the public as any of the other three comic operas with which alone it can be compared—Mozart's *Figaro*, Rossini's *Barbiere*, and Wagner's *Meistersinger*. *Falstaff* is the kind of comedy which can be imagined only by a man who is mature enough to know human life and still be able to laugh. Verdi not only parodied himself (compare the conspiracy scene at the end of the first part of Act III) but also took his last leave of opera with a jest at the whole world, including the art of music: *Falstaff* ends with a fugue, that most learned of all forms of composition, to the words "Tutto nel mondo è burla"—"All the world's a joke."

22

The Romantic Opera in Germany[1]

IN THE SERIOUS OPERA OF THE EIGHTEENTH century national differences were of little importance. Italian was not only the well-nigh universal language of the libretto but also of the music as well. The blending of Italian and French characteristics in the later works of Gluck led to an international style which continued into the nineteenth century and found its last manifestation in grand opera of the Meyerbeer school. Along with this international opera, as we have seen, various national types flourished, such as the opéra comique in France and the operas of Bellini, Donizetti, and Verdi in Italy. While these were not without mutual influence, it must be noted that as the century wore on, national distinctions came to be more and more marked. The rise of nationalism in music is one of the outstanding features of the romantic period and is nowhere more striking than in the rapid growth of the romantic opera in Germany. Before 1820 German national opera was known outside its own country only through *The Magic Flute* and a few works of the Singspiel type.[2] The performance of Weber's *Freischütz* at Berlin in 1821 began a development which led within fifty years to a virtual dictatorship of European opera by the music drama of Wagner. Since Germany displays more clearly and completely than any other country

---

[1] The fullest and most valuable study of this subject is Edward J. Dent's "The Rise of Romantic Opera" (The Messenger Lectures at Cornell University, 1937–38), which shows how romantic opera is rooted in both comic and serious opera of the late eighteenth century and makes clear the debt of the German romanticists to their French predecessors. Unfortunately, these lectures have not been published, but it is to be hoped that they soon will be. See also Istel, *Die Blütezeit der musikalischen Romantik in Deutschland*, chap. V; Kraus, "Das deutsche Liederspiel in den Jahren 1800–1830"; Goslich, *Beiträge zur Geschichte der deutschen romantischen Oper; Almanach der deutschen Musikbücherei auf das Jahr 1924/25;* Schmitz, "Zur Geschichte des Leitmotivs in der romantischen Oper," *Hochland* IV, No. 2 (1907) 329–43; Daninger, *Sage und Märchen im Musikdrama;* Ehrenhaus, *Die Operndichtung der deutschen Romantik.*
[2] Beethoven's *Fidelio* is not a national opera either in subject or (except to a very slight degree) in music.

the effects of the romantic doctrines on opera, it will be convenient
to summarize here those features of romanticism which are most
important for the study of our subject.

If we were to search for the most general principle of difference
between the opera of the eighteenth and that of the nineteenth century, we should probably find it in the contrast between the idea of
distinctness on the one hand and that of coalescence on the other.
The contrast begins with the relation of the composer to his music.
The eighteenth-century composer was a craftsman who stood outside
the art works which he created; the nineteenth-century composer
thought of music rather as a means of self-expression, a projection
of his own feelings and ideas. His music has consequently a certain
subjective quality which demands that the hearer shall place himself
in sympathy with the composer, failing which he may fail to understand the music. Moreover, the music itself is directed more to the
listener's emotions and less to his intellect than in the eighteenth
century. The horror and rescue operas, the works of Weber, Meyerbeer, Donizetti, Verdi, and Wagner, all make a direct assault on the
nerves and feelings of the audience in a manner which to Handel,
Hasse, Gluck, or Mozart would have been inconceivable. In pursuit
of this aim, and emancipated by the authority of individual freedom
from the old restrictions, the nineteenth century proceeded to create
a new aesthetic and a new set of musical procedures for opera, all of
which, as said before, were dominated by the idea of coalescence as
against the eighteenth-century idea of distinctness.

Let us look for example at the relation between libretto and music
in each of the two periods. We have already seen how in the Neapolitan opera seria these two elements were harnessed together in a kind
of marriage of convenience which, provided certain conventions were
observed, left each to a great extent free and unimpeded; the same
libretto might receive many different musical settings, and the same
music might be used for different words. This conception was foreign
to the nineteenth century, which had as its ideal a complete union
of words and music in one perfect work. The nineteenth century did
not stop here but went on to advocate generally the amalgamation of
music, poetry, and all the other arts in one superart which should be
greater than the sum of its individual parts. The ideal took various
and sometimes fantastic forms; thus Schlegel: "The arts should be

brought together again, and bridges sought from one to another. Perhaps columns shall come to life as paintings, paintings become poems, poems become music." [3] Poets and painters saw in music the ideal toward which the other arts were striving—immediate in its expression of feeling, limited in its power to depict the world of objects, and by this very indefiniteness supporting all the more strongly that flight from the outer to the inner world, toward those "somber longings, depressions and joyous elation without any recognizable cause" [4] which are typical of the romantic mood. The arts were united not only in ideal but also in practice: poets and painters composed music, musicians wrote essays, novels, and poetry. The climax came with Wagner's complete theory and realization of the Gesamt-kunstwerk.

In the librettos of the romantic operas we find also that the eighteenth-century distinction between man and nature, and between nature and the supernatural, is broken down. In the eighteenth century, nature appears in opera only as a background or embellishment, leading to music of a merely imitative or externally descriptive sort, such as bird-song arias, the comparison arias, orchestral storms, and the like. The supernatural in eighteenth-century opera is either a dramatic convention (as in Rameau and Gluck) or else a source of farce (Dittersdorf) or pageantry (*The Magic Flute*). In the nineteenth century, both nature and the supernatural are closely identified with the moods of man, becoming a great soundingboard for the murmurings of the subconscious. The storms in Mozart's *Idomeneo* are only

---

[3] Quoted in Adler, *Handbuch* II, 865. Cf. Schelling's well-known definition of architecture as "frozen music" (*Philosophie der Kunst*, pp. 576, 593), and Goethe's similar statement (Eckermann, *Gespräche* I, 261, March 23, 1829). Such conceptions were not peculiar to the nineteenth century. In 1643 Harsdörffer, at the end of his "Spiel von der Welt Eitelkeit" (*Frauenzimmer Gesprechspiele* III. Theil, p. 242), wrote: "Hieraus erhellet wie alle Künste gleichsam als in einer Ketten aneinander hangen / deren ein Glied in das andere geschlossen / und absonderlich zwar ihre volkommene Rundungen / jedoch ohne so dienstliche Stärkleistung / haben. Die Reimkunst ist ein Gemälde / das Gemälde eine ebenstimmige Music / und diese gleichsam eine beseelte Reimkunst."

This may be compared with an eighteenth-century view (Mattheson, *Neueste Untersuchung der Singspiele,* 1744, pp. 86–87) which notably does not assert the identity of the arts but only their co-operation: "Meines wenigen Erachtens ist ein gutes Operntheater nichts anders, als eine hohe Schule vieler schönen Wissenschaften, worinn zusammen und auf einmal Architectur, Perspective, Mahlerey, Mechanik, Tanzkunst, *Actio oratoria,* Moral, Historie, Poesie, und vornehmlich Musik, zur Vergnügung und Erbauung vornehmer und vernünftiger Zuschauer, sich aufs angenehmste vereinigen, und immer neue Probe geben."

[4] Berlioz, program of *Symphonie fantastique.*

incidental; the storm in Wagner's *Fliegende Holländer* is the whole mood of the drama. In Weber's *Freischütz* both the natural background and the supernatural happenings must be accepted at face value or the opera is meaningless; yet here we are still in the fairy-tale stage. In *Tannhäuser* and *Lohengrin* the supernatural begins to have importance in a symbolic sense. Finally, in the *Ring,* both nature and humanity have become absorbed into the supernatural and the superhuman, and the whole action is on a symbolic, mythical plane.

All this fairy tale, legend, and myth in German romantic opera is national in character, as opposed to the earlier use of Greek mythology, medieval epic, or Roman history. The emphasis on national subject matter in opera followed the movement in literature which had begun in England with the publication of Macpherson's "edition" of Ossian and Percy's *Reliques of Ancient English Poetry* in the 1760's. In Germany Herder's cosmopolitan *Stimmen der Völker in Liedern* (1778–1779) was followed in the years 1805–1808 by an exclusively German collection, Arnim and Brentano's *Des Knaben Wunderhorn.* Interest in German legends and medieval literature was revived by the brothers Grimm (*Kinder- und Hausmärchen,* 1812–1815; *Deutsche Mythologie,* 1835). Folk tales, fairy tales, patriotic odes, historical novels and dramas were produced by many authors. Much of this literature was not only national but also popular, that is, "of the folk"; the glorification of "the folk," and of folk art, was characteristic of the early romantic period. The influence of all these ideas remained in German opera even after 1830, when new influences were at work in literature itself.

Turning now to the music of romantic opera, we find likewise a coalescing of formerly distinct factors. Thus in the eighteenth century the functions of voice and orchestra were clearly defined. The orchestra accompanied the singers; it was heard by itself only on specified occasions, as in the overture, the ritornellos, and the ballets, marches, or descriptive pieces. In the nineteenth century the orchestra enters intimately and continuously into the pattern of the drama: it provides an unbroken background of sound and thereby frees the voice for more realistic, varied, and pointed declamation of the text; it creates moods and provides exotic suggestion. The overture achieves a close connection, not only thematically but also in structure, with the opera itself. Improvement of the brass and wood-wind instruments, and the introduction of new instruments, make possible an enormously enlarged and variegated color scheme in operatic as well as in symphonic music. With increasing importance of the inner voices and increasing chromaticism in the harmony, the orchestra becomes more and more important in the musical texture of opera. Curt Sachs has pointed out how this growth in importance of the orchestra in opera coincides with the rise of non-Italian schools—"the eternal antithesis between the playing North and the singing South." [5] The climax comes in Wagner's music dramas, in which the orchestra develops the entire action in a polyphonic tissue of sound.

Still another contrast between eighteenth- and nineteenth-century opera is seen with respect to musical forms. The older opera consisted of a series of distinct numbers, without thematic interconnection. The tendency throughout the romantic period is for the separate numbers to coalesce until the music is continuous throughout each act; this may be merely a concealing of the joints (as in late Verdi) or it may be a more organic unity, as in Wagner, with a number of musical themes used systematically throughout an entire act, a whole opera, or even several different operas. What is true of the form as a whole is true also of the details: melodies conceal their former distinct phrasing and rhythmic patterns and approach more nearly the free character of recitative or arioso, with numerous short motifs (rather than themes) irregularly combined. Recitatives and choruses do not merely alternate with the aria but are heard simultaneously with it as background or quasi-ensemble. In harmony, the boundaries of tonality become less definite; modulations are more frequent and to more distant keys; chromatic alterations, progressions motivated by chromatically moving inner voices, become characteristic. Distinct cadences are avoided, so that the music seems never to come to a full stop but to move on in an endless melody. Finally dissonance, especially in the form of suspension or appoggiatura, takes on new and special importance as a leading means of expression, and the indefinite postponement of its final resolution becomes a symbol of the eternal romantic longing after the unattainable.

5 "The Road to Major," MQ XXIX (1943) 403.

It must be acknowledged that the original inspiration of German romantic opera, both for the poetry and for the music, came from France—in part directly from late eighteenth- and early nineteenth-century French opera and opéra comique and in part at secondhand through the Singspiel, which, as we have seen, was largely dependent in the beginning on French models. Romantic subject matter came into German opera long before the composers had evolved a fully corresponding language in the music. The titles of some of the most popular Singspiels of the late eighteenth and early nineteenth centuries show their interest in fairy and legendary subjects: P. Wranitzky's *Oberon* (Vienna, 1790); Kauer's *Donauweibchen* (Vienna, 1795; on the same subject as several "Melusine" and "Undine" operas in this period, the marriage of a nixie with a mortal); Ignaz Walter's *Doktor Faust* (1797; the first "Faust" opera on Goethe's poem, and one of a half-dozen on this subject in this period); Grosheim's *Titania* (Cassel, 1801); and Friedrich Himmel's *Sylphen* (Berlin, 1806) and *Der Kobold* (Vienna, 1811) are typical instances of the romantic spirit at work in the libretto while the music remained in the idiom of the eighteenth-century Singspiel.[6] Peter von Winter imitated Mozart with *Die Pyramiden von Babylon* ("The Pyramids of Babylon"), *Das Labyrinth* (a continuation of *The Magic Flute*), and his most successful work, *Das unterbrochene Opferfest* ("The Interrupted Sacrifice," Vienna, 1796). Joseph Weigl's *Schweitzerfamilie* ("The Swiss Family," Vienna, 1809) was a sentimental Singspiel with some romantic orchestral coloring, Swiss themes, and reminiscence motifs, which remained popular in Germany for many years.[7] The romantic

---

[6] Paul Wranitzky (1756–1808) became chapelmaster at the Imperial Theatre, Vienna, in 1785. Besides operas he composed a large quantity of symphonic and chamber music.

Ferdinand Kauer (1751–1831) composed over one hundred stage pieces, in addition to church music, symphonies, and songs.

Ignaz Walter (1759–1822) and Georg Christoph Grosheim (1764–1841) were writers on musical theory as well as composers. The latter left an autobiography (publ. 1925). See also Spitta, "Die älteste Faust Oper," in his *Zur Musik*, pp. 199–234.

Friedrich Heinrich Himmel (1765–1814) was active chiefly at Berlin. He studied in Italy and wrote a few Italian operas, but his most popular work was the Singspiel *Fanchon das Leiermädchen* (1804). See Odendahl, *Friedrich Heinrich Himmel*.

[7] Peter von Winter (1754–1825) was attached to the Munich court from 1778 until his death, but brought out many operas in other European cities. He also composed church music, nine symphonies, and other orchestral and chamber works. See Moser, *Geschichte der deutschen Musik* III, 5 f., and Frensdorf, *Peter Winter als Opernkomponist*.

Joseph Weigl's (1766–1846) thirty operas (German and Italian) were composed before 1825, in which year he succeeded his former teacher, Salieri, as second conductor at the Vienna court. See De Eisner-Eisenhof, "Giuseppe Weigl," RMI XI (1904) 459–83.

writer and poet E. T. A. Hoffmann [8] is of importance in the history of German opera both for his writings and for his music. His best opera is *Undine* (Berlin, 1816). The earlier merely fanciful play with fairy elements in the Singspiel is here given a feeling of human significance, thus achieving some dramatic force in spite of a complex and fantastic plot. The music suffers from some technical faults, but the romantic mood of Weber's *Freischütz* is distinctly foreshadowed, especially in the scenes depicting supernatural beings and in the many folklike melodies and choruses. The more ambitious arias are less successful. Hoffmann shows a sensitiveness for the effect of key contrasts, though the actual results do not always come up to his evident intentions.

The year 1816 also saw the first performance (at Prague) of Spohr's *Faust*. Ludwig Spohr [9] has been remembered longest as a composer of oratorios and violin works, but his operas, especially *Jessonda* (Cassel, 1823), are typical examples of the early romantic school. His music, though less masculine and forceful than that of Weber, is interesting for its freedom of key relationships and chromatic progressions; expressive suspensions and upward-resolving appoggiaturas often suggest the style of Wagner,[10] although it must be confessed that the romanticism of Spohr is mostly a matter of such details as these rather than of a fundamentally new approach. It is somewhat surprising that Spohr was unsympathetic to the music of Beethoven and Weber, but he was one of the earliest champions of Wagner in Germany, and in his own *Kreuzfahrer* ("The Crusaders," 1845) attempted to write a national romantic opera after the model of *Der fliegende Holländer* and *Tannhäuser*.

A word must be said about the dramatic music of Schubert,[11] of which there have been preserved three operas, five Singspiels, and

[8] Ernst Theodor Amadeus Wilhelm Hoffmann (1776–1822) combined the career of a lawyer with writing, conducting, and composing. He produced ten operas and some other works. (The "complete" edition, ed. by G. Becking, does not include the operas.) The comple:e literary works are published in an edition by Griesebach, and the writings on music separately, ed. by Istel. See Kroll, *Ernst Theodor Amadeus Hoffmann,* and further bibliography in Moser, *Geschichte* III, 79, note 2.

[9] On Spohr (1784–1859) see his *Selbstbiographie* (to 1838); Wassermann, *Ludwig Spohr als Opernkomponist*; Salburg, *Ludwig Spohr*; Spitta, "Jessonda," in his *Zur Musik*, pp. 237–66.

[10] See for example the passages quoted in Moser, *Geschichte* III, 107 ff., and the Andante of the first finale in *Jessonda* (quoted in Bücken, *Die Musik des 19. Jahrhunderts*, p. 88).

[11] Krott, *Die Singspiele Schuberts*.

one melodrama, in addition to four or five incomplete works. The two chief operas, *Alfonso und Estrella* (1822–1823) and *Fierrabras* (1823), were not performed until long after the composer's death (1854 and 1897 respectively). A Singspiel, *Die Zwillingsbrüder* ("The Twins"), was performed at Vienna in 1820, and the incidental music to *Rosamunde* in 1823, both with only slight success. In spite of the considerable amount of his dramatic music, therefore, Schubert had no influence on the history of opera. His larger works failed of performance partly because the orchestral parts were adjudged too difficult and noisy (!) and partly because the librettos were insufferably bad, Schubert's notorious lack of discrimination in literary matters betraying him. Moreover the music itself, though beautiful in many details,[12] is essentially no different from that of the lieder and choral works: melodious, interesting in harmony, strong in rhythm, unmistakably Schubertian but fundamentally lyrical and unsuited to the stage, lacking that spark of dramatic life which is the one inescapable necessity for opera.

Two other romantic composers attempted opera without success: Mendelssohn's *Hochzeit des Camacho* ("Camacho's Wedding") was withdrawn after a few performances at Berlin in 1827; he composed a half-dozen smaller stage pieces (of which only the one-act Singspiel *Son and Stranger* was published) and left unfinished a large opera, *Lorelei*.[13] Schumann's *Genoveva* was performed at Leipzig in 1850 under the composer's direction, but neither then nor since has it obtained enduring public favor.[14] Its libretto is poorly constructed and the music lacks genuine dramatic directness and characterizing power, though there are many beautiful passages (see for example near the beginning of Act IV, Genoveva's recitative and aria from the words "Die letzte Hoffnung schwindet"). Schumann's *Szenen aus Goethes Faust,* for chorus, soloists, and orchestra, is an exceptional work, being intended for concert performance; it is perhaps, of all *Faust* music, the most appropriate to Goethe's drama and ranks equal with the composer's better-known cantata *Paradise and the Peri.*

The founder and hero of German romantic opera was Carl Maria von Weber.[15] Weber's father was a theatre director and the boy was

---

12 See for example the melodrama at the end of Act II of *Fierrabras*.
13 Schünemann, "Mendelssohns Jugendopern," ZfMw V (1922–23) 506–45.
14 See Abert, "Robert Schumann's *Genoveva,*" ZIMG XI (1909–10) 277–89.
15 On Weber (1786–1826) see his own writings (ed. Kaiser, 1908) and the biographies by M. M. von Weber and E. Kroll. The Stebbins's *Enchanted Wanderer* is (despite its title)

reared in an atmosphere of the stage. His own experience as impresario and conductor at Breslau (1804–1806) and Prague (1813–1817) [16] gave him a still firmer knowledge of the essentials of dramatic style. The influence of his principal teacher, the Abbé Vogler, as well as the whole intellectual *milieu* of his life, inclined him strongly toward romanticism, and in 1814 his settings of ten songs from Körner's *Leyer und Schwert* ("Lyre and Sword") made him the idol of the patriotic youth of Germany. Weber's first dramatic work has not been preserved; the second was a Singspiel, *Das stumme Waldmädchen* ("The Dumb Girl of the Forest," 1800), which was not successful; parts of the music were incorporated in *Silvana* (1810, revised 1812). Two comic Singspiels, *Peter Schmoll und seine Nachbarn* ("Peter Schmoll and His Neighbors," 1803) and *Abu Hassan* (1811), and an unfinished romantic work, *Rübezahl*,[17] complete the list of Weber's earlier dramatic compositions. Though he showed in these works an original talent for instrumentation, a certain gift for comic writing and characterization, and a natural feeling for the quality of German folk melody, there is comparatively little in the music to suggest the romantic power which was later to be unloosed in *Der Freischütz. Abu Hassan* may be regarded as a forerunner of *Oberon,* and the medieval-romantic *Silvana* anticipates certain features of *Euryanthe.*

Early in the year 1817 [18] Weber persuaded his friend Friedrich Kind to write for him a libretto based on a story by Johann August Apel, *Der Freischütz,* which had been published at Leipzig seven years earlier.[19] Weber's music was not completed until 1820, and still

the best life of Weber in English and contains a copious and well-organized bibliography. A complete edition of Weber's works was begun in 1926, of which only two volumes have so far appeared, containing the operas *Das Waldmädchen, Peter Schmoll* (Vol. I), *Rübezahl* and *Silvana* (Vol. II).

16 At Prague he staged works by Spontini, Méhul, Cherubini, Grétry's *Richard,* Mozart's *Figaro, Don Giovanni,* and *Titus,* Beethoven's *Fidelio,* and other leading operas of the current repertoire.

17 "Rübezahl" is the name of a mountain spirit of the Riesengebirge, a prominent figure in the folklore of Silesia, the subject of many folk tales, plays, and operas. Weber's music was composed at Breslau, *ca.* 1805. The overture is still occasionally played, in a revised form, under the title "The Ruler of the Spirits."

18 Weber at this time had just been appointed director of the German opera at Dresden, a post which he held until his death.

19 The legend itself was at least a hundred years older, and some of its motives belong to even more ancient folklore. The title is practically impossible to translate. It means literally "The Free Marksman," but the subject is better described by the usual English title "The Magic Bullet." The Stebbins in their book on Weber, leaving no room for misunderstanding, render it as "The Marksman Using Charmed Bullets."

another year elapsed before the first performance, at Berlin, on June 18, 1821. The work was fabulously successful from the start and spread like wildfire all over Germany. After Weber had conducted it in Vienna, he wrote in his diary, "Greater enthusiasm there cannot be, and I tremble to think of the future, for it is scarcely possible to rise higher than this." [20] His words were unconsciously prophetic, as the fate of *Euryanthe* was to prove; but with *Der Freischütz*, he had set German romantic opera on its road and dealt the deathblow to the century-long Italian reign in the German theatres. The popularity of *Der Freischütz* was due not only to the music but also to the libretto which, for Germany in the early romantic period, literally had everything.[21] Most of its elements were inherited from the late eighteenth-century Singspiel: a background of nature and a foreground of humble and happy village life; a pure heroine and a well-intentioned but easily misled hero; a villain caught in his own trap; the supernatural in many picturesque and shuddery forms; and finally the time-tested figure of the magnanimous prince as righteous judge and father of his people. But though the ingredients were old, the mixture was new. For the first time in opera all these details were convincingly presented as aspects of something important; the trial of marksmanship took on the character of Armageddon, the ultimate battle of good against evil, one sustained by the power of the church and the other aided by the maleficent spirits of ancient heathendom, and the triumph of good was felt as the triumph of the German soul. Thus the national appeal of *Der Freischütz* was not limited to the romantic period but has remained equally strong to this day. "There never was an opera, and there is no likelihood that there ever will be one, so intimately bound up with the loves, feelings, sentiments, emotions, superstitions, social customs, and racial characteristics of a people." [22]

Weber's overture is a model of its kind. Although made up entirely, except for the opening horn theme, of melodies from the opera, it is not a mere medley but a finished composition in symphonic first-movement form. The mysterious last twelve measures of the intro-

---

20 March 7, 1822. Quoted in *Grove's Dictionary* V, 652.
21 For a synopsis the reader is referred to any opera handbook; many editions of the music do not give the spoken dialogue, which is essential to the understanding of the plot.
22 Krehbiel, *A Book of Operas*, p. 207.

duction (diminished sevenths with low clarinets, strings tremolo, pizzicato basses and kettledrums on the afterbeats) are the quintessence of romanticism in music, and so, in a different way, is the clarinet melody in E-flat of the *vivace* movement. The return of the closing triumph theme in C major, heralded by a recurrence of the last part of the introduction and three impressive "general pauses," is electrifying. In the larger arias the music of *Der Freischütz* approaches grand opera, and it is natural to find in Caspar's "Der Hölle Netz" (end of Act I) a resemblance to Italian style, or in the opening section of Max's "Durch die Wälder" a mild echo of Méhul. Both this aria and Agathe's "Leise, leise" are complex musical structures, splendidly dramatic and of Beethovenian amplitude. Aennchen's "Kommt ein schlanker Bursch gegangen," with its polacca rhythm, is in keeping with the Singspiel tradition of differentiating the social standing of the characters by means of different musical styles and forms. The contrast between Agathe and Aennchen, mistress and maid, so neatly established in their duet at the beginning of Act II. is confirmed and emphasized in their two following arias.

Parts of the score which did much to endear it to the public were those which glorified the songs and dances of the people: the Hunters' and Bridesmaids' choruses, the march and waltzes in Act I, and the shorter pieces (lied, romance, cavatina) in popular form. In *Der Freischütz* Weber succeeded as no other composer had done in raising the music of the folk to the dignity of serious opera and combining it skillfully with more pretentious elements. The most celebrated part of the opera has always been the finale of the second act, the "Wolf's Glen" scene, one of the most effective evocations of supernatural thrills ever created for the stage. Among the many devices which Weber uses may be pointed out the mysterious harmonies (tremolo strings) at the beginning, the monotone choruses of the spirits (note the unison of tenors, altos, and sopranos on a′), the dialogue between the singing Caspar and the speaking Samiel, and the melodrama for the casting of the magic bullets, a real Walpurgisnacht of legendary phantoms of the dark forest. The C minor themes of the overture, associated throughout the opera with the demonic powers, are much in evidence. The systematic recurrence of these motifs and others, especially the triumph motif (overture, in E-flat and C major; Agathe's aria, E major; last finale again in C major), contributes much to the feeling of unity which is one of the outstanding qualities of the work. The overture gives the musical plan of the whole as it were in embryo, and the structure thus sketched is fully expanded in the course of the three acts.

Weber's incidental music to P. A. Wolff's play *Preciosa* (adapted from a novel by Cervantes) was composed immediately after *Der Freischütz* and came sooner to performance (Berlin, March 14, 1821). At about the same time he started, but did not finish, a comic opera on another Spanish subject, *Die drei Pintos* ("The Three Pintos").[23] The *Preciosa* music is an example of Weber's skill in the use of local color; it includes an "authentic" gypsy tune, which Bizet later used in the Smuggler's March in *Carmen*.

Euryanthe was first performed at Vienna October 25, 1823.[24] In it Weber, in accordance with his lifelong habit, deliberately tried to correct the faults which critics had found in *Der Freischütz*. The criticisms had been mainly to the effect that the work was deficient in large, highly developed musical forms; that is, that it was too much of a Singspiel and not enough of an opera. Spontini, whose *Olympie* had been thrown into the shade by *Der Freischütz*, was particularly bitter, and even Weber's friend, the romantic poet Tieck, was not persuaded. *Euryanthe,* therefore, Weber set to music throughout (it is the only opera of his which does not have spoken dialogue), and on a greater scale than any of the composer's other works. However, he did not wish to make the music dominant as in Italian opera, but conceived rather a kind of Gesamtkunstwerk, "a purely dramatic attempt, aiming to create its effect by means of the combined effects of all the sister arts." [25] Unfortunately the results did not correspond to this ideal, nor did the success of the opera come up to Weber's hopes and expectations. It has never become a public favorite, but its interest for musicians is shown by the numerous attempts which

---

23 It was completed, partly from Weber's sketches and partly from other works of the composer, by Gustav Mahler and performed at Leipzig in 1888.

24 The source of the libretto was a medieval French romance which had been employed by Boccaccio (*Decameron,* Day II, Story 9) and Shakespeare (*Cymbeline*). Schlegel published a version in a collection at Leipzig in 1804, under the title "Die Geschichte der tugendsamen Euryanthe von Savoyen." Frau Helmine von Chézy, the translator of this tale, undertook to adapt it as a libretto for Weber. There were many revisions (in which Weber took some part) but the final result has always been much criticized. Méhul's *Euphrosine et Coradin* (1790) and *Ariodant* (1798), and Berton's *Montano et Stéphanie* (1799), are on a similar subject.

25 Quoted in Moser, *Geschichte der deutschen Musik* III, 73, note 1.

have been made to promote it in revised forms. There can be no doubt that it includes some of Weber's greatest music (for example, the overture); the arias are broad and powerful,[26] and the effective use of the chorus in the drama reminds one of Gluck. There is evident Weber's usual clever handling of the orchestra, as well as the same tasteful use of folklike motifs as in *Der Freischütz*. Contrast of key is used as an aid to characterization, and there is a significant employment of reminiscence motifs. All in all, *Euryanthe* is a grand opera in form and in loftiness of conception, a landmark in the history of German opera between *Fidelio* and *Lohengrin,* and one of those works which deserve to be performed more frequently.

Weber's last opera, *Oberon,* was composed to an English libretto by J. F. Planché and first performed under the composer's direction at London, April 12, 1826.[27] In some ways it was a backward step: the story, a rambling oriental fantasy with numberless scene changes, gave only limited occasion for development of character or genuine human emotion; there were many nonsinging actors, and so much of the action took place in spoken dialogue that the music was reduced almost to an incidental position. Weber intended to rearrange the work for German theatres, and though he did not live long enough to do so, many more or less thoroughgoing revisions and additions have been made (some in accordance with Weber's plan) by later musicians. *Oberon* is historically important chiefly because of its fairy music, such as the opening chorus of Act I, the finales of the second and third acts, and above all the beginning of the overture, with its magic horn call, muted strings, and sixteenth-note figure in the wood winds. Such music was in the air: Mendelssohn's octet with its scherzo had appeared the year before, and the *Midsummer Night's Dream* overture was composed in the summer of 1826. The more vigorous, ardent, stormy romanticism of Rezia's aria "Ocean, thou mighty monster" (the closing theme of which had appeared in the overture) is also well represented in *Oberon*.

Weber died in mid-career. Had he lived to complete his work, perhaps the history of German opera for the next twenty years would have been one of steady development. As it was, although *Der*

---

26 See especially Lysiart's aria at the beginning of Act II and Euryanthe's aria with chorus "Zu ihm, und weilet nicht" in Act III.

27 The fatigue of the journey and labor of the production hastened Weber's death, which occurred at London on June 4.

Freischütz continued its triumphal course, no German work was produced for nearly a generation which could match it either in popularity or in musical worth. If Weber can be said to have had a successor, it was Heinrich Marschner,[28] who continued to exploit the supernatural, mingling it with an undoubted gift for the comic. His first success was obtained in 1828 with *Der Vampyr,* an opera now remembered mainly because it was one of Wagner's models for *Der fliegende Holländer* (compare especially the ballade in Act III). Marschner's *Templer und Jüdin* ("The Templar and the Jewess," 1829) was adapted from Scott's *Ivanhoe.* His masterpiece, *Hans Heiling* (1833),[29] was on a libretto by Eduard Devrient from a story by Körner, originally intended for Mendelssohn. Just as the central situation of *Templer und Jüdin* is similar to that of *Lohengrin,* so the figure of Hans Heiling, half man and half earth spirit, in love with a mortal woman, has many points of resemblance to Wagner's Dutchman. Yet in the working out of the story as well as in the music much of the trivial is mingled with the serious. The style in general is that of the popular Singspiel, with simple tunes in symmetrical patterns, interspersed with spoken dialogue. Echoes of Weber, Italian opera, and Meyerbeer's *Robert le Diable* are heard. In some respects the music looks ahead to Wagner: the frequent chromatic passing tones in the melody, especially at cadences; the use of modulating sequences; and occasionally a passage of grimly powerful declamation.[30] Many of the choruses are interesting, and the finales of the first and third acts are well constructed and effective. The most original number, and one which shows Marschner's gifts to best advantage, is the melodrama and lied at the beginning of the second scene of Act II. Yet on the whole, his talent was of second rank, the Biedermeir spirit in music. His later works, in which there are many traces of the fashionable Italian and French opera of the time, contributed nothing to his fame.

Along with the specifically romantic traits of Marschner there lived in German opera a strong current of lighter, entertaining, comic

---

[28] On Heinrich August Marschner (1795–1861) see Münzer, *Heinrich Marschner;* G. Fischer, *Musik in Hannover* (2d ed.) and *Marschner-Erinnerungen;* Gaartz, *Die Opern Heinrich Marschners;* Gnirs, *Hans Heiling.*

[29] New edition by Hans Pfitzner, 1923.

[30] See for example the ensemble No. 9 in Act II; the melody at the words "Sonst bist du verfallen" is the original of Wagner's death-announcement theme in *Die Walküre.*

popular music inherited from the Singspiel of the eighteenth century. Thus Conradin Kreutzer's *Nachtlager in Granada* ("The Night-Camp at Granada," Vienna, 1834; libretto by Karl Johann Braun Ritter von Braunthal, from Friedrich Kind's drama of the same title),[31] with the old motif of the good prince in disguise conferring rewards on humble virtue and innocent young love, offers occasion for musical numbers of a melodious sort (romances, hunting choruses, conspirators' chorus, prayer, airs and ensembles) somewhat in the manner of Auber and Donizetti—light, sometimes vulgar, but on the whole pretty and pleasing in a harmless way. A more spirited comic vein was worked by Gustav Albert Lortzing [32] in his *Zar und Zimmermann* ("Czar and Carpenter," 1837), *Der Wildschütz* ("The Poacher," 1842), and *Der Waffenschmied* ("The Armorer," 1846), which abound in humorous situations like those of the older Viennese Singspiel, with a fresh, pleasant, and often witty melodic style. Some of the ensembles recall the spirit of Mozart. Most characteristic are the simple songs in folk idiom, reminiscent of the tunes of J. A. Hiller.[33] In *Undine* (1845) Lortzing ventured on the ground of romantic opera, with its supernatural beings and theme of redemption through love. Lortzing was hardly capable of composing music equal to the emotions and characters of this libretto, but his systematic use of leitmotifs and his powers of musical description (especially the water-sprites music, which is first heard in Act II, scene 5) are interesting both in themselves and as predecessors of the music of Wagner's *Ring*. Another of Lortzing's comic operas, *Hans Sachs* (1840), is one of the numerous sources of *Die Meistersinger*.

Other composers of German opera toward the middle of the nineteenth century must be only briefly mentioned. Otto Nicolai's [34]

---

[31] Conradin Kreutzer (1780–1849) studied under Albrechtsberger at Vienna. He was chapelmaster at Stuttgart (1812), Donaueschingen (1817) and Vienna (irregularly, 1825–1840). Of his thirty operas the most successful were *Jery und Bätely* (1810), *Das Nachtlager in Granada,* and *Der Verschwender* ("The Spendthrift," 1836). Cf. Riehl, *Musikalische Charakterköpfe* I.

[32] On Lortzing (1801–1851) see biographies by Kruse and E. Killer, also his own *Briefe,* ed. Kruse; Laue, *Die Operndichtungen Lortzings.*

[33] See for example in *Der Waffenschmied,* " 'Smag freilich nicht so übel sein" (near the end of Act I).

[34] Nicolai (1810–1849) brought out several Italian operas in Italy before going to Vienna to succeed C. Kreutzer as court chapelmaster in 1841. He became director of the opera at Berlin in 1847. See his *Tagebücher* (ed. by B. Schröder, 1892; by W. Altmann, 1937); Kruse, *Otto Nicolai; idem,* "Otto Nicolai's italienischen Opern," SIMG XII (1910–11) 267–96.

Lustigen Weiber von Windsor ("The Merry Wives of Windsor,"
Berlin, 1849) is a fine comic work in which Italian and German characteristics are blended. Its cosmopolitan style contrasts with the simple homemade quality of Flotow's *Martha* (1847),[35] a sentimental,
old-fashioned piece which has inexplicably survived while many better operas have been forgotten. Most important in this period is Peter
Cornelius,[36] whose masterpiece is *Der Barbier von Bagdad* (1858,
dedicated to Franz Liszt). This wholly delightful oriental comedy
is in a sophisticated musical idiom obviously influenced by Wagner,
especially with respect to its harmony and melodic line. The rhythms,
deriving in part from oriental verse forms, are particularly varied
and interesting.[37] Each of the two acts runs continuously, without
marked division into numbers. The orchestra has an important role
not only in the formal scheme but also in the providing of many humorous details in the accompaniments. A half-dozen recurring motifs
are used systematically. This work is not high comedy like *Die Meistersinger* but a farce, cleverly using every resource of music for farcical
purposes (see for example the canonic duet "Wenn zum Gebet" in
Act I). The freedom of rhythm, the declamatory melodies, the frequent wide intervals and chromatic harmonies often foreshadow the
style of Strauss's *Rosenkavalier*. There is also some parody of Italian
opera, especially in the sentimental unison love duet "So mag kein
anders Wort erklingen" in the second scene of Act II. (This scene
is also an unconscious parody of the love duet in the second act of
Tristan, with the Barber filling the role of Brangäne).

During the 1830's and 40's it seemed almost as if the Italians had

---

[35] Friedrich von Flotow (1812–1883) studied as a young man in Paris, where his earliest
operas were performed. He first won popularity in Germany with *Alessandro Stradella*
(1844). Many of his twenty-nine operas were performed in translation all over Europe,
but only *Stradella* and *Martha* are still remembered. See R. Flotow, *Friedrich von Flotow's Leben von seiner Witwe;* Dent, "A Bestseller in Opera," M&L XXII (1941) 139–54.
[36] Cornelius (1824–1874) was known as poet and composer, friend of Liszt, and champion
of Wagner in Germany. His only other completed opera was *Der Cid* (Weimar, 1865), but
he composed many songs and choruses. A complete edition of his literary works was
published in 1904–1905 (4 vols.) and of his musical works in 1905–1906 (5 vols.), both
by B&H. Max Hesse's biography *Der Dichtermusiker Peter Cornelius* (1922) has been
criticized as "reliable, but over-laudatory and without orientation in the history of music"
(Moser, *Geschichte der deutschen Musik* III, 210). See also the biography by his son, Carl
Maria Cornelius, *Peter Cornelius der Wort- und Tondichter;* Hasse, *Peter Cornelius
und sein Barbier von Bagdad.*
[37] See for example the aria "O holdes Bild" (Act II, sc. 2) which is in alternate 4/4
and 3/4 measures. Five-measure phrases are also very common throughout the score.

been driven from German opera houses only to be replaced by the French. The works of Herold and Adam were particularly popular, while the equally gifted native composers Marschner and Lortzing were often neglected. The final triumph of German nationalism came with Wagner, whose *Fliegende Holländer, Tannhäuser,* and *Lohengrin* made a new epoch in the history of romantic opera.

23

Wagner[1]

FROM TIME TO TIME IN THE HISTORY OF music there have been composers whose works summed up the achievement of a whole epoch, making the final synthesis of a style: Palestrina and

[1] Wagner's complete musical works have been published in a Collected Edition by Breitkopf & Härtel. There is as yet no comprehensive bibliography of the enormous Wagner literature. (Oesterlein's *Katalog*, limited to items published during Wagner's lifetime, lists over 10,000 titles.) The primary sources are: Wagner, *Mein Leben; idem, Gesammelte Schriften und Dichtungen* (6th ed.); *idem, Briefe in Originalausgaben;* for other principal sources, see Newman's *Life.* The standard biography for many years was that of Glasenapp (*Das Leben Richard Wagners*), now superseded for critical purposes by Ernest Newman's *Life of Richard Wagner.* Koch's *Richard Wagner* emphasizes the literary side of Wagner's production; the most popular short German biography is Julius Kapp's (32d ed., 1929). The "orthodox" Wagner gospel will be found expounded in the official periodical *Bayreuther Blätter* (from 1878, ed. for many years by Hans von Wolzogen) and in the works of Houston Stewart Chamberlain (*Richard Wagner* and *Das Drama Richard Wagners.* Cf. also his *Grundlagen des neunzehnten Jahrhunderts*). The following books may be found useful by the beginning student: Newman, *Stories of the Great Operas* I; Gilman, *Wagner's Operas;* Shaw, *The Perfect Wagnerite;* Mann, "Leiden und Grösse Richard Wagners," in his *Leiden und Grösse der Meister;* A. E. F. Dickinson, *The Musical Design of "The Ring";* Hutcheson, *A Musical Guide to the Ring.* Paul Bekker's *Richard Wagner* is diffuse and involved but worth reading for its many insights. The most important works dealing specifically with Wagner's music are: Adler, *Richard Wagner, Vorlesungen;* Lorenz, *Das Geheimnis der Form bei Richard Wagner* (4 vols.); and Kurth, *Romantische Harmonik und ihre Krise in Wagners "Tristan."*

For convenience, a tabular list of Wagner's operas and music dramas is given here:

TITLE	DATE OF COMPOSITION (incl. scoring)	FIRST PERFORMANCE
Die Feen	1833	Munich, 1888
Das Liebesverbot	1835	Magdeburg, 1836
Rienzi	1838–1840	Dresden, 1842
Der fliegende Holländer	1841	Dresden, 1843
Tannhäuser	1843–1845	Dresden, 1845
Lohengrin	1846–1848	Weimar, 1850
Der Ring des Nibelungen	Poem begun 1848, completed 1852	First complete performance, Bayreuth, 1876
I. Das Rheingold	1853–1854	Munich, 1869
II. Die Walküre	1854–1856	Munich, 1870
III. Siegfried	1856–1857, 1865–1871	Bayreuth, 1876
IV. Götterdämmerung	1869–1874	Bayreuth, 1876
Tristan und Isolde	1857–1859	Munich, 1865
Die Meistersinger von Nürnberg	1862–1867	Munich, 1868
Parsifal	1877–1882	Bayreuth, 1882

Bach are the outstanding examples. There have been other composers whose work incorporated not only the end of one style but the beginning of another: to this group belong Beethoven and Wagner. Wagner's operas, to and including *Lohengrin,* were the consummation of German romantic opera of the nineteenth century; the later music dramas were in a style which, although retaining many features of what had gone before, nevertheless introduced innovations in both theory and practice. These innovations were not confined to the music but embraced the whole drama, and in working them out Wagner, who perceived all the implications of his ideas and developed them with typical German thoroughness, touched on many issues that were fundamentally involved with nineteenth-century thought. He is the only eminent composer whose writings have been considered important outside the conventional limits of the field of music. For him, indeed, these conventional limits hardly existed; consequently, in order to understand his music, it is necessary to take into account his views on other subjects, including his philosophy of art in general and of the drama in particular. Whether one agrees or disagrees with these views is a question of the same order as whether one likes or dislikes the music: in either case it is desirable to comprehend as well as judge.

In music, Wagner was for the most part self-taught. During his student days at Leipzig he became acquainted with some of Beethoven's works and heard at the theatre the plays of Schiller and Shakespeare, as well as the operas of Weber and Marschner. He wrote dramas and some instrumental music, including a Symphony in C major which was performed in 1833. During two seasons as chorus trainer at Würzburg (1833–1834) he became familiar with many more works of the current opera repertoire and composed his own *Feen* ("The Fairies"), his first completed opera (never performed during Wagner's lifetime). This is a long work, with the usual subdivision into recitatives, arias, ensembles, and the like. A few traits of the music suggest the later composer of *Rienzi,* but the style on the whole is modeled after Beethoven and Weber. The romantic idiom of the period is handled with great energy and sincerity, aiming at big theatrical effects by conventional means. There is no technical reason why this opera could not have been performed; it is by no means an inexpert work, only it lacks individuality. Wagner's libretto, based on a fairy tale of Carlo Gozzi (1720–1806), introduces all the fantastic and decorative apparatus of romantic opera in great profusion, but without the unifying power of a really significant dramatic idea.

If *Die Feen* may be regarded as an essay in German romantic opera, *Das Liebesverbot* ("The Ban on Love") showed Wagner eagerly assimilating the Italian style. Bellini's *Montecchi e Capuletti* had aroused great enthusiasm at Leipzig in 1834, and Wagner was temporarily in reaction against the alleged heaviness, lack of dramatic life, and unvocal quality of the typical German operas. His libretto for *Das Liebesverbot* was based on Shakespeare's *Measure for Measure;* it is full of comic scenes and there is some spoken dialogue. The music is a blend of Auber, Rossini, and Donizetti, with distinct traces of Meyerbeer in the finales, which often seem to strain terribly for effect. Like *Die Feen,* this work is very long. The melodies are florid, often with typically Italian cadenzas. Everything is repeated at great length. The best quality of the score is its liveliness and obvious enthusiasm, though even this becomes wearisome after a time. There is not one really distinguished theme in the whole work; the duet in bolero rhythm in the first scene of Act II may be taken as typical of the style (Example 105). Some of the crowd scenes faintly foreshadow the ending of Act II of *Die Meister-*

DAS LIEBESVERBOT, Act II, no. 7

Ex. 105.   Wagner

singer; the duet of Isabella and Marianna and the latter's aria in the last act have a sultry erotic quality which looks forward to Richard Strauss. *Das Liebesverbot* was performed only once, and then very badly, at Magdeburg in 1836, with the composer conducting. In the autumn of that year Wagner was married to the singer Christine Wilhelmine (Minna) Planer.

From 1837 to 1839 Wagner was music director of the theatre at Riga. Here he began the composition of *Rienzi,* based on Bulwer-Lytton's novel and inspired by a performance of Spontini's *Cortez* which Wagner had witnessed at Berlin in 1836. In the summer of 1839 he went to Paris; the first stage of the trip was the memorable stormy sea voyage to London, the impressions of which later influenced him in the composition of *Der fliegende Holländer* ("The Flying Dutchman"). The two and a half years in Paris were a nightmare of failure, disappointment, and poverty. Even the efforts of Meyerbeer on his behalf did not avail to obtain him a hearing. Yet during this time Wagner completed *Rienzi* and wrote *Der fliegende Holländer,* finishing the latter at the suburb of Meudon in August, 1841 "in need and care," as he wrote at the end of the score. At last *Rienzi* was accepted by the Opera at Dresden, where the first performance took place October 20, 1842. Wagner had come from Paris in the summer to supervise the rehearsals. The success of the work was immediate and overwhelming and led to a demand for *Der fliegende Holländer,* which was produced in January, 1843. A month later Wagner was appointed chapelmaster for life of the Dresden opera.

Rienzi, as we have already seen (p. 318), was a grand opera in the fashion of the time, with just enough novelty to make it extremely popular. The reception of *Der fliegende Holländer* was less flattering; in externals this work was less brilliant than *Rienzi,* and its inner dramatic significance went for the most part unperceived or unappreciated. This was not altogether the fault of the audiences, for Wagner himself had not yet perfected his technique. *Der fliegende Holländer* is essentially a German romantic opera in the tradition of *Der Vampyr* or *Hans Heiling,* and is divided into the customary numbers. Some of these numbers are quite successful, while others seem mechanical and forced, monotonous in rhythm and without marked originality of melody or harmony. Wagner took his version of the medieval legend of the Flying Dutchman from a tale by Heinrich Heine, adding features suggested by Marschner's *Vampyr*. As in *Der Freischütz*, nature, animated by supernatural forces, is all pervasive. This time it is not the forest but the sea; in the storm music, the steersman's song in Act I, and the sailors' choruses in Act III, Wagner set forth with all his power the impressions gathered in the voyage from Riga to London. These portions are not mere musical descriptions of the sea but are filled with symbolic meaning for the human drama. In the story of the redemption of the Dutchman from the curse of immortality by Senta's love Wagner for the first time clearly worked out the idea of salvation through love [2] which became fundamental in his later dramas. It is stated in Senta's Ballad (Act II), the central number of the opera and the one first composed. The ballad, a type of song which in earlier nineteenth-century opera had been as a rule only a set piece, here becomes the pivot of the whole dramatic and musical development, and its traditional two-part form is used to contrast the ideas of curse and salvation. The themes chosen are good examples of Wagner's characteristic procedure of representing basic dramatic ideas by appropriate, specific musical formulae: the opening motif forming an empty fifth, the stormy chromatics, and diminished sevenths [3] are set against the calm diatonic major melody of the second section. The ultimate salvation—already prophesied at the end of the overture—is symbolized in the finale of the opera by using the latter theme for an extended plagal cadence in D major. These two themes (or rather theme groups) and their derivatives are used systematically in many other parts of the opera; Wagner has already adopted the leitmotif technique, but he has not yet extended it to every portion of the work. The historical interest of *Der fliegende Holländer* lies not so much in this technique— which, as we have seen, was not new with Wagner—as in the quality of the themes themselves, in the individuality of their harmonies, and the way they seem actually to embody the essential dramatic idea, completing its expression and giving it depth and emotional power.

Another important number in *Der fliegende Holländer* is the C minor recitative and aria of the Dutchman in Act I ("Die Frist ist

[2] The same idea was present, though not so distinctly, in *Die Feen*.

[3] The first motif has an obvious resemblance to the beginning of Beethoven's Ninth Symphony, which Wagner had heard for the first time adequately played by the Paris Conservatoire orchestra under Habeneck. For the orchestration here, as elsewhere in this opera and also in *Tannhäuser*, Wagner had learned much from Berlioz.

um"), ending with his pathetic appeal for death ("Ew'ge Vernichtung, nimm mich auf!") which is echoed mysteriously in E major by the voices of the unseen crew—a momentary shift of tonality made more striking by the immediate, implacable return to C minor in the orchestral coda. The long duet of Senta and the Dutchman in the finale of Act II is the climax of the drama, but its operatic style is an unfortunate lapse into an earlier and less individual musical idiom. Of the remaining numbers it is necessary to mention only the popular Spinning Song which opens the second act, with the women's voices in A major offering a pleasant contrast to the dark colors of Act I and making an ideal prelude to Senta's Ballad.

In *Tannhäuser* (1845) Wagner aimed to unite the two elements which he had developed separately in *Der fliegende Holländer* and *Rienzi,* to clothe the dramatic idea of redemption in the garments of grand opera. His poem combined materials from a number of different sources, treating of the medieval legend of the knight Tannhäuser,[4] who sojourned with Venus in her magic mountain and later went on a pilgrimage to Rome to obtain absolution, which was refused him: "Sooner will the dry staff in your hand blossom than your sins be forgiven," he was told by the Pope. But the staff miraculously blossomed, in sign of God's mercy. To this story Wagner added the episode of the Song Contest and the figure of Elizabeth, through whose pure love and intercession the miracle of salvation was effected. All this is cast in the traditional outlines of an opera with the customary theatrical devices. The division into numbers is still clear, though with more sweep and less rigidity than in the earlier works. There are solos (for example, Tannhäuser's song in praise of Venus, Elizabeth's "Dich, teure Halle," her Prayer, Wolfram's song to the Evening Star), ensembles (especially the end of Act II), choruses (for example, the Pilgrims' Choruses for men's voices,[5] a favorite medium in nineteenth-century opera), the Venusberg ballet, and the brilliant crowd scene of the Entrance of the Knights and the Song Contest in Act II. Numbers such as these, treated with Wagner's mastery of stage effect and in a style which audiences could easily understand, assured the success of *Tannhäuser,* though the new work did not arouse enthusiasm equal to that which had greeted *Rienzi.* Yet even

4 There was also a real Tannhäuser, a minnesinger of the thirteenth century.
5 Sopranos and altos are added for climactic effect at the end of Act III.

where *Tannhäuser* is most operatic, it does not sacrifice the drama to outward show. The spectacular scenes not only are connected with the action but also have a serious dramatic purpose in themselves. Indeed, there are few operas in which form and content are so well balanced.

The portions of *Tannhäuser* that listeners failed to comprehend were just those which were most important in Wagner's estimation, and most significant in view of his later development, namely the recitatives, of which Tannhäuser's narrative of his pilgrimage to Rome (Act III) is the principal example. Here is a long solo containing some of the central incidents of the drama; it is certainly not an aria with regular melody and balanced phrases, but neither is it recitative of the neutral, purely declamatory type familiar in earlier opera. It is a melody strictly molded to the text, a semirealistic declamation of the words combined with expression of their content by means of a flexible line supported by an equally important harmonic structure. In addition to providing the harmony, the orchestra has certain musical motifs which, by reason of their character and their association with the text, are heard as a commentary on the words, or as a further and purely musical expression of their meaning (Example 106). This is the style which came to prevail almost exclusively in Wagner's later works, and to which he gave the name *Sprechgesang,* that is, "speech song." It was not entirely new with Wagner (compare Weber's *Euryanthe*), but he used it so extensively, wielded it so effectively, and built it so firmly into his whole theory of the music drama that he perhaps rightly ranks as its discoverer. To the original singers of *Tannhäuser,* as well as to the audience, it was a mystery. Even the famous soprano Wilhelmine Schröder-Devrient, Wagner's staunch friend from the beginning and one from whom he received much inspiration, confessed that she could not make head or tail of her role of Venus; and the tenor Tichatschek, though equally devoted to the composer, had not the slightest perception of his new dramatic aims. Little by little, however, a small section of the Dresden public began to sympathize; this group—which, significantly, included few professional musicians—was the nucleus of the future Wagner cult.

The essential dramatic idea in *Tannhäuser* is, of course, the opposition of the world of sensual ecstasy and the world of ascetic re-

nunciation, the former represented by Venus and her court, the latter by Elizabeth and the Pilgrims.[6] Wagner's music embodies the
character of each of these worlds with an imaginative grasp and in-

tensity of utterance which is more remarkable than anything else
in the whole score. His greatness as a composer lies just in this power
of evoking in the listener's mind such conceptions, in all their emo-

[6] Both Wagner's expansion of the Venusberg ballet for the disastrous Paris performances
of 1861 and his revision of the last finale to include the actual appearance of Venus
served to accentuate the contrast between the two basic ideas of the opera.

tional depth and complexity, by means of music in which every detail is consciously or unconsciously directed toward the expressive purpose. In pursuit of his aims, Wagner found it necessary to rely more and more on the resources of harmony and instrumental color; as the aria diminished in importance, the orchestra rose correspondingly. This is evident in *Tannhäuser* both in the thematic importance of the accompaniments and in the separate orchestral pieces. The introduction to the third act, depicting Tannhäuser's pilgrimage, is one of those short symphonic poems of which there were to be more in the later works—Siegfried's Rhine Journey in *Gotterdämmerung*, for example, or the Good Friday music in *Parsifal*. The overture to *Tannhäuser* is a complete composition in itself, and, like those of *Der fliegende Holländer* or *Die Meistersinger*, a synopsis of the larger dramatic and musical form to follow.

It has been noted [7] that the first six completed operas of Wagner are grouped in pairs, and that within each pair, each member is in many ways complementary to the other. This is especially noticeable with *Tannhäuser* and *Lohengrin*. The latter was composed in the years 1846–1848, though not performed until 1850 at Weimar, under Liszt's direction. Like *Tannhäuser*, its sources are found in folklore and medieval Germanic legend, but the treatment is considerably different. In *Lohengrin* there is less concern with the tale itself or the external historical scene and more emphasis on the timeless, symbolic significance of the events portrayed. The characters, though adequately depicted as human, are at the same time agents or personifications of forces the conflict of which makes the drama. Thus Lohengrin may be said to represent divine love and its longing for reciprocal love and faith from mankind, while Elsa represents human nature incapable of the necessary unquestioning trust. Whatever meaning one may see in the story, the necessity of some interpretation in the sense suggested is practically unavoidable. In keeping with this view of the drama, the musical setting of *Lohengrin* is altogether less spectacular than that of *Tannhäuser;* there are no sharp, unexpected contrasts, and an extraordinary unity of mood prevails throughout. The system of leitmotifs is still further developed, not only in extent but also in the changed function of the motifs themselves: they are no longer used simply to recall earlier scenes and

[7] See Chamberlain, *Das Drama Richard Wagners*.

actions but to symbolize situations or abstract ideas. For example, the motif which some analysts label "the forbidden question," first sung by Lohengrin as he lays the command on Elsa never to inquire his name or country, is a complete, periodic, eight-measure theme (Example 107). It recurs, in whole or in part, wherever throughout the opera the situation touches pointedly on this prohibition: in the introduction to Act II, during the dialogue between Ortrud and Friedrich in the first scene, in the second scene at Ortrud's hypocritical warning to Elsa against the "unknown" knight, at Elsa's sign of doubt in the last scene of the act, and in the closing orchestral cadence; it comes into the duet of Act III, rises to full force as Elsa's fatal question is asked, echoes again at the end of this scene, and is heard once more at Elsa's entrance in the last finale. Many other characteristic motifs are used in a similar way. The principle is not yet that of the *Ring,* where the motifs are shorter, essentially harmonic and rhythmic rather than melodic, and employed continuously in a symphonic web; nevertheless, *Lohengrin* carries the practice further than any preceding opera and clearly points the way to Wagner's later style.

LOHENGRIN, Act I

Ex.107. Wagner

Nie sollst du mich be-fra-gen, noch Wi-ssens Sor-ge tra-gen, wo-her ich kam der Fahrt, noch wie mein Nam' und Art!

From the formal point of view *Lohengrin* has shed almost all traces of the traditional division into numbers, as well as of the distinction between aria and recitative. The new free declamation is the normal style in this work, except in a few places like Elsa's "Einsam in trüben Tagen" (Act I),[8] Lohengrin's narrative (Act III), the Bridal Chorus, and the lovely duet which follows this. The brilliant orchestral prelude to Act III is often played as a separate concert number. The prelude to the opera, unlike the overture to *Tannhäuser,* is in one

[8] Even here three strophes of the song are separated by choruses and recitatives.

mood and movement, representing (according to Wagner's statement) the descent and return of the Holy Grail, the type of Lohengrin's own mission, as we hear when the same themes and harmonies accompany his narrative in Act III. The A major tonality of the prelude is associated with Lohengrin throughout the opera, just as the key of F-sharp minor is assigned to Ortrud and (as a rule) the flat keys to Elsa. The harmony of *Lohengrin* is remarkably diatonic; there is very little chromaticism of the sort found in the middle section of the Pilgrims' Chorus or the Evening Star aria in *Tannhäuser*. The orchestration likewise is in contrast to that of *Tannhäuser:* instead of treating the instruments as a homogeneous group, Wagner by preference divides them into antiphonal choirs, often with the violins subdivided and the wood-wind section expanded so as to make possible a whole chord of three or four tones in a single color. The effect, while less brilliant than in *Tannhäuser,* is fuller, richer, and more subtle. Even in the last scene of Act II, showing the dawn of day heralded by trumpet fanfares, and the procession to the minister, the sonority is very restrained in comparison with the usual grand-opera treatment of such places.

The skillfully written choruses in *Lohengrin* are an important musical and dramatic factor. For the most part the chorus is treated either as realistically taking part in the action, or else as an "articulate spectator" in the manner of Greek tragedy (see especially the second scene of Act I and the finale of Act III). The prominence of the chorus may have been suggested to Wagner by his study of Gluck's *Iphigénie en Aulide,* which he revised for performances at Dresden in 1847.

Lohengrin is generally regarded as the last of the German romantic operas. It has many resemblances to Weber's *Euryanthe,* not only in the plot and characters [9] but also in the continuity of the music, the style of declamation, and the use of leitmotifs. It was Wagner's last dramatic composition for five years, or until he began to work on the music of *Das Rheingold* in 1853.[10] In 1849, as a result of quarrels

[9] The basic plot—the trial of a wife's love—is common to the two works. The character of Elsa corresponds to Euryanthe, Telramund and Ortrud to Lysiart and Eglantine; the figure of the good king is also in both. Act I of *Lohengrin,* as Bekker points out (*Richard Wagner,* chap. 6), was doubtless also influenced by Marschner's *Templer und Jüdin.*

[10] The short musical sketches made in 1850 for *Siegfrieds Tod* are similar in style to the *Lohengrin* music. See Newman, *Wagner* II, 159–61.

with his superiors and a multitude of other difficulties climaxing in his active participation in the revolutionary uprising of May of that year, Wagner was obliged to flee from Dresden. He sought refuge at Weimar with Liszt, who aided him to escape to Switzerland. Settled at Zürich, Wagner found leisure to clarify in his own mind the new ideas on music and the theatre which had already been occupying him at Dresden, and of which some intimations may be found in his earlier operas, *Lohengrin* especially. The result of these cogitations was a series of essays, including the important *Oper und Drama* ("Opera and Drama," published in 1851), a systematic account of the philosophy and technical methods by which all his subsequent works were to be governed. A knowledge of *Oper und Drama* is indispensable for anyone who seriously desires to understand these works—the *Ring, Tristan, Die Meistersinger,* and *Parsifal*—even though Wagner's practice is not always consistent with his theories.[11]

The doctrines of *Oper und Drama* are best exemplified in *Der Ring des Nibelungen* ("The Ring of the Nibelungs"), which consists of four consecutive music dramas: *Das Rheingold* ("The Rhine Gold"), shorter than the others, and a prelude to them; *Die Walküre* ("The Valkyrie"); *Siegfried;* and *Götterdämmerung* ("The Twilight of the Gods"). Altogether, the composition of the *Ring* occupied twenty years of Wagner's life. Its subject combines two distinct Germanic myth cycles, the story of Siegfried and that of the downfall of the gods. Wagner in 1848 wrote a drama, *Siegfrieds Tod* ("The Death of Siegfried"), which he expected to set to music at once; but as the subject grew in his mind, he felt the need for another drama to precede this, and wrote *Der junge Siegfried* ("Young Siegfried") in 1851. The work expanded still further: *Die Walküre* was required to lead up to *Der junge Siegfried,* and *Das Rheingold* as a general prelude to the whole. These two poems, in this order, were written in 1852, after which *Der junge Siegfried* and *Siegfrieds Tod* were revised as the present *Siegfried* and *Götterdämmerung* respectively, the whole text being completed by the end of 1852.[12] Meanwhile some sketches for the music had been made; actual composition was begun in 1853, and by 1857 the setting was completed through the second

[11] The English translation of *Oper und Drama* by Edwin Evans is recommended. There is a good summary in G. Abraham, *A Hundred Years of Music*, pp. 116–39.
[12] On the changes made in the earlier poems, and some resulting inconsistencies in the present text, see Newman, *Wagner* II. chap. 17.

act of *Siegfried*. After an interim during which he composed *Tristan* and *Die Meistersinger*, Wagner resumed work on the *Ring* in 1865, though *Götterdämmerung* was not finished until nine years later. The first performances of the whole tetralogy took place at Bayreuth in 1876.

The story of the *Ring* is so familiar—or, at least, is so easily accessible in popular books of all sorts, not to mention the scores themselves—that there is no need to recapitulate it here. The material is taken not from history (as in *Rienzi*), or folklore (as in *Die Feen*), or even legend (as in *Der fliegende Holländer* and *Tannhäuser*), but from mythology. The reason is not primarily that the myth is entertaining, but that it is meaningful. According to Wagner the myth presents, in the simplest, most inclusive, and most concentrated form imaginable, the interplay of eternal forces affecting the relation of men to God, to nature, and to each other in society—in other words, living, eternal issues of religious, social, and economic importance, with which it is the duty of art consciously to deal. These issues are set before us in the myth, and consequently in Wagner's *Ring*, by means of symbols, either objects (the Gold, Valhalla, the Sword) or persons (Wotan, Siegfried, Brünnhilde). Now it is the nature of a symbol to be capable of various interpretations; and although Wagner labored hard, both in the poem itself and in other writings, to make clear his own interpretation of the *Ring*, he did not fully succeed—partly because of some inconsistencies in his thinking and the obscurity of his literary style, but more because the symbols were so many sided that it was impossible to make a single definitive explanation of them. Many writers have tried to do so, and have argued vehemently, each according to his own convictions, for or against the doctrines conceived to be embodied in the *Ring*. Still others regard any intentional preaching in art as either of no importance or else downright vicious and inartistic. It is not our intention to add any further than necessary to the enormous mass of controversial literature about Wagner. It is not within the scope of a book like this to investigate the alleged effects of his teaching, in the *Ring* or elsewhere, on European politics.[13] That he did teach—that his views of art and the theatre impelled him in his operas to assume the role of

[13] An introduction to this subject, with bibliographies, may be found in Viereck's *Metapolitics from the Romantics to Hitler*.

prophet as well as musician—is a fact, whether one approves it or not; but all that concerns us here is the consequences of that fact in his art work itself.

It is not easy to dramatize abstractions. In the *Ring,* Wagner felt obliged to introduce some explanatory passages which slow down or interrupt the action of the play.[14] For the benefit of opera audiences, who are not particularly interested in metaphysics, these passages are often cut or shortened in performance. The same is true of the many repetitions of the story which occur from time to time, and other apparent digressions. All these matters have their justification, however, in Wagner's theories; moreover, the leisurely pace of the action suggests the tempo of the long medieval epic poems from which the incidents were taken. Another interesting reminiscence of these poetic models is Wagner's employment of *Stabreim,* or alliteration, instead of the more modern device of end rhymes:

> Gab sein Gold mir Macht ohne Mass,
> nun zeug' sein Zauber Tod dem der ihn trägt!

> (As its gold gave me might without measure,
> Now may its magic deal death to him who wears it!)
>
> *Das Rheingold,* scene 4

The relation of music to the drama is one of the subjects on which Wagner discourses in much detail in his writings. The first proposition of *Oper und Drama* is: "The error in opera hitherto consisted in this, that a means of expression (the music) has been made an end, while the end itself (the drama) has been made the means." [15] It does not follow, however, that now poetry is to be made primary and music secondary, but that both are to grow organically out of the necessities of dramatic expression, not being brought together, but existing as two aspects of one and the same thing. Other arts as well (the dance, architecture, painting) are to be included in this union, making the music drama a Gesamtkunstwerk, that is, a composite or total art work. This is not, in Wagner's view, a limitation of any of the arts; on the contrary, only in such a union can the full possibilities of each be realized. The "music of the future," then, will exist not in isolation as heretofore, but as one aspect of the Gesamtkunstwerk, in

---

[14] E.g., the conversation between Wotan and Brünnhilde in Act II, sc. 2 of *Die Walküre.*
[15] "Oper und Drama," in *Ges. Schriften* III, 231.

which situation it will develop new technical and expressive resources and will progress beyond the point to which it has now arrived, a point beyond which it cannot materially progress in any other way.

This view was the consequence of a typical nineteenth-century philosophy. Wagner regarded the history of music as a process of evolution which must inevitably continue in a certain direction. The theory that the line of progress involved the end of music as a separate art and its absorption into a community of the arts is not without analogy to the communistic and socialistic doctrines of the period, with their emphasis on the absorption of the interests of the individual into those of the community as a whole.[16] It is not surprising that some such view of the future of music should have arisen in the second half of the nineteenth century. It is plain enough to us now that the resources of music—that is, of the kind of music which had been growing up since Beethoven—were approaching their utmost limits at this time, and that these limits were in fact reached in the works of Wagner, Brahms, R. Strauss, and Mahler. It has been the mission of twentieth-century composers to recognize this situation and to create a new musical style, much as the composers of the seventeenth century had to do after the culmination of sixteenth-century polyphony in the works of Palestrina, Byrd, and Lassus. In discerning the approaching end of a musical style, therefore, Wagner was right. His error was in postulating the Gesamtkunstwerk as the only possible road for the future.

Wagner held that music in itself was the immediate expression of feeling, but that it could not designate the particular object toward which feeling was directed. Hence, for him the inner action of the drama existed in the music, while the function of word and gesture was to make definite the outer action.[17] This aesthetic is the theoretical basis of many features of the *Ring* and later works. For example, since the inner action is regarded as being always on a plane of feeling where music is appropriate and necessary, there is no spoken dialogue or recitative. Moreover, the inner action (unlike the outer) is continuous; hence the music is continuous.[18] Transitions from one scene to the next are made by means of orchestral interludes when necessary, and within each scene the music has a continuity of which the most obvious technical sign is the avoidance of perfect cadences.

16 Cf. Barzun, *Darwin, Marx, and Wagner.*
17 Cf. Schopenhauer, *Die Welt als Wille und Vorstellung* I, Bk. III, sec. 52; and Vol. II ("Ergänzungen"), chap. 39.
18 In this theory, intermissions between the acts and the performance of the *Ring* on four separate evenings instead of all at once can be regarded only as one of Wagner's reluctant concessions to human frailty.

Continuity in music, however, is more than avoidance of perfect cadences. It is a result of the musical form as a whole, and since form in Wagner (as in any composer) is partly a function of harmonic procedure, this is an appropriate place to consider these two subjects together.

The statements most frequently made about Wagner's harmony are (1) that it is "full of chromatics," and (2) that the music "continually modulates." Both statements are true but superficial. Much of the chromaticism in the earlier works (for example, in the original version of *Tannhäuser*) is merely an embellishment of the melodic line or occurs incidentally in the course of modulating sequences. Many of the chromatic passages in the *Ring*, such as the magic sleep motif, are found in the midst of long diatonic sections.[19] The impression that Wagner continually modulates is due in part to a short-breathed method of analysis based on a narrow conception of tonality, which tends to see a modulation at every dominant-tonic progression and, preoccupied with such details, overlooks the broader harmonic scheme. A more comprehensive and illuminating view is set forth by Alfred Lorenz in his four studies entitled *Das Geheimnis der Form bei Richard Wagner* ("The Secret of Form in Richard Wagner"). Lorenz shows that all the music dramas are cast in definite musical forms, and that the formal clarity is evident not only in each work as a whole but also in the constituent sections, down to the smallest. The structure of the music is inseparable from that of the drama, and one of its fundamental elements is the key scheme. *Das Rheingold,* for example, is a large a b a form in D-flat, with an introduction in E-flat (dominant of the dominant); D-flat is also the tonality of the *Ring* as a whole.[20] *Tristan* is likewise in three-part form, Acts I and III corresponding, and Act II being the "b" section—though here the correspondence is one of themes and dramatic action, not of tonality. The three acts of *Die Meistersinger* in the same way make a huge a a b form, the first two being equal in length and the third as long as the first two together. These two forms, the *Bogen* (a b a, literally "bow") and *Bar* (a a b),[21] are frequently exemplified

[19] See *Die Walküre*, Act III, G. Schirmer piano-vocal score, pp. 297–98.
[20] Cf. the ending of *Götterdämmerung.*
[21] The Bar, consisting of two Stollen (a a) and an Abgesang (b), was the favorite form of the German minnesinger. It is well illustrated in both versions of Walther's "Preislied," and explained by Hans Sachs (see *Die Meistersinger,* Act III, sc. 2).

also in the structure of the scenes and smaller subdivisions: thus the fifteenth "period" of Act II of *Siegfried* (three measures before "Noch einmal, liebes Vöglein" to change of signature to four sharps "nun Sing") is an a b a or Bogen in E minor (18 + 30 + 21 measures) and the introduction to Act II of *Die Walküre* is a Bar in A minor (introduction, 14 measures; two *Stollen*, 20 + 19 measures; *Abgesang*, 20 measures). Other form types (strophic, rondo) also appear, and many units are composed of two or more of the basic types in various modifications and combinations.[22] One may not choose to follow Lorenz in every detail, and it would certainly be in order to question some of his interpretations of the basic formal schemes; but taken as a whole, it is impossible in the face of his demonstration not to be convinced of the essential orderliness, at once minute and all embracing, of the musical cosmos of the *Ring*, as well as of *Tristan*, *Die Meistersinger*, and *Parsifal*. It is an orderliness not derived at second hand from the text but inhering in the musical structure itself. Was Wagner fully aware of it? One is tempted to think not, in view of the fact that he says almost nothing about it in his writings. Yet whether conscious or unconscious, the sheer grasp and creation of such huge and complex organisms is a matter for wonder.[23]

Within such frameworks of order, and subsidiary to them, take place the various harmonic procedures which have given rise to Wagner's reputation: modulations induced by enharmonic changes in chromatically altered chords and forwarded by modulating sequences; the interchangeable use of major and minor modes and the frequency of the mediants and the flat supertonic as goals of modulation; the determination of chord sequences by chromatic progression of individual voices; the presence of "harmonic parentheses" within a section, related to the tonality of the whole as auxiliary notes or appoggiaturas are related to the fundamental harmony of the chord with which they occur; the systematic treatment of sevenths (and even ninths) as consonant chords; the resolution of dominants to chords other than the tonic; the combination of melo-

---

[22] Lorenz's system of analysis cannot be adequately illustrated without going into greater detail than is possible here. See his outline of Act I of *Die Walküre* in Abraham, *A Hundred Years of Music*, pp. 145–53.

[23] It may be unnecessary to remark that the fact (if it is a fact) that Wagner's creative processes were largely instinctive or unconscious does not of itself invalidate any analysis of his music. It is no essential part of a composer's business to be aware, in an analytical sense, of everything he is doing.

dies in a contrapuntal tissue; and finally, the frequent suspensions and appoggiaturas in the various melodic lines, which contribute as much as any single factor to the peculiar romantic, Wagnerian, "longing" quality of the harmony—a quality heard in perfection in the prelude to *Tristan und Isolde*.

While the musical forms of Wagner's dramas are determined in part by the harmonic structure, a more conspicuous role is played by the recurrence and variation of a limited number of distinct musical units generally known as leitmotifs or leading motifs.[24] Different analysts distinguish, and variously name, seventy to two hundred such motifs in the *Ring*. Each is regarded as the focal point of expression of a certain dramatic idea, with which it remains associated throughout the whole tetralogy. The clue to the association of motif and idea is to be found at the first appearance of the former; for example, the Valhalla motif is first heard at the opening of the second scene of *Das Rheingold* as the curtain rises to reveal the castle of Valhalla.[25] The motifs are short and of pronounced individual character; they are often suggested by a pictorial image (as the fire motifs), or by association (as the trumpet figure for the sword motif), but each aims to convey not merely a picture but also the whole essence of the idea for which the visible symbol stands. In this capacity the motifs may recur, not simply as musical labels, but whenever the idea recurs or is suggested in the course of the drama, forming a symphonic web which corresponds exactly (at least in theory, and generally also in fact) to the dramatic web of the action. The connection between the musical forms so evolved and the dramatic forms is thus complete. The motifs may be contrapuntally combined, or varied, developed, and transformed in accordance with the changing fortunes of the

[24] The term *"leitmotif"* (or leitmotiv) is not Wagner's, but he did use the synonymous word *Hauptmotiv*. It is likely that Wagner himself suggested this word, as well as the whole system of analyzing his music dramas in terms of motifs, to Heinrich Porges, whose book on *Tristan und Isolde* (written 1866–67 but not published before 1902) uses this method. The leitmotif analysis of Wagner's music was first popularized by Hans von Wolzogen (1848–1938), first editor of the *Bayreuther Blätter* and author of many "Guides" to the music dramas, beginning with his *Thematischer Leitfaden durch die Musik zu R. Wagners "Ring des Nibelungen,"* 1876. See further on this subject Newman, *Wagner* III, 382–83.

[25] Here, as usual at the first statement of a motif, Wagner repeats and spins out the phrase so as to impress it on the memory; it is like the first statement of a theme in a symphony (cf. also the premonition of the Valhalla motif at the end of the preceding scene, where its derivation from the ring motif is obvious).

idea with which they are associated. Relationship of ideas may be shown by thematic relationships among the motifs (Example 108), though probably some of the resemblances are not intentional. Altogether, the statement, recurrence, variation, development, and transformation of the motifs is not essentially different from the working out of musical material in a symphony or other work of absolute music.

Motifs from the RING

Since the inner meaning of the drama is found in music, it follows in Wagner's theory that the orchestra is the basic medium rather than the voices. In his phrase, the words "float like a ship on the sea of orchestral harmony." Only rarely are the leitmotifs sung. As a rule, the voice will make a free counterpoint to the instrumental melody. The voice part, however, is always itself melodic, never merely declamatory as in recitativo secco; its line is so arranged as not only to give the correct declamation but also to reproduce the accent, tempo and inflections appropriate to each character.[26] Text repetition is avoided. In theory there are to be no ensembles, especially in the old-fashioned sense where some voices are used only to supply a harmonic background; but this rule Wagner eventually relaxed on occasion, as in the finale of Act II of *Götterdämmerung,* the duet in Act II of *Tristan,* or the quintet in *Die Meistersinger.*[27] Of Wagner's genius as an orchestrator there is no need to speak here. His music is the realization of the full, rich, romantic sound ideal of the latter nineteenth century. Its peculiar texture is determined in large part by the nature of the melodic lines: long phrased, avoiding periodic cadential points (this in contrast to *Lohengrin* and earlier works), so designed that every note tends to move on without ever quite coming to rest.[28] The full resources of symphonic style— counterpoint, orchestral color, and formal structure—are invoked. This in itself was not new in the history of opera, for many earlier composers (for example, Monteverdi in *Orfeo* and Rameau in his tragédies lyriques) had done the same. But Wagner had the immensely developed instrumental resources of the nineteenth century at his disposal; moreover, he was conscious as no earlier composer had been of the drama as the generating force in the whole plan; and he was original in placing the orchestra at the center, with the essential drama going on in the music, while words and gesture furnished only the outer happenings. From this point of view his music dramas may be regarded as huge symphonic poems, the program of which, instead of being printed and read, is explained and acted out by persons on the stage.

Wagner despised "opera," yet his music dramas have been as popular as any operas. What is the source of their appeal? Primarily, of course, the music itself. Yet there are certain other factors which have at different times made for popular success in opera. One of these factors in the nineteenth century was the appeal to national pride

[26] See for example the conversation of Wotan, Loki, and Alberich in sc. 3 of *Das Rheingold.*
[27] The trio of the Rhine maidens might be justified on the ground that the three beings are not really three personalities, but only one.
[28] This is one meaning of Wagner's term "unending melody"; it has other meanings as well. See Lorenz, *Geheimnis der Form* I, 61–70; Kurth, *Romantische Harmonik* (2d ed.), Part 7.

(as in some of Weber's and Verdi's works). Such an appeal is indirectly present in most of Wagner's operas insofar as they are founded on Germanic myths or legends; but this kind of nationalism is of little importance, since Wagner thought of his dramas as universal, dealing with what he called the "purely human," not limited to Germans in the sense in which *Der Freischütz* was. Even *Die Meistersinger,* with all its reference to "holy German art," and regardless of the uses to which it was put by Nazi propaganda, is not narrow in its patriotism or jingoistic in spirit.

Another and more general means of popular appeal in opera is stage spectacle. Wagner availed himself of this resource unstintedly, though always maintaining that every one of his effects grew of necessity out of the drama itself. It would be difficult to think of any beguiling, eye-catching, fanciful, sensational device in the whole history of opera from Monteverdi to Meyerbeer which Wagner did not appropriate and use with expert showmanship somewhere in his works. One has only to look at the poem of the *Ring* to see how prominent is this element; it has a large place also in *Parsifal.* In *Tristan* and *Die Meistersinger,* however, it is less in evidence, for these are dramas of human character and as such appeal directly to fundamental human emotions with less need of spectacular stage effects. This quality of direct, human appeal is heard at only a few places in the *Ring,* as in the love scenes of Siegmund and Sieglinde (*Die Walküre,* Act I), of Siegfried and Brünnhilde (*Siegfried,* Act III), or in the scene of Wotan's farewell to Brünnhilde (*Die Walküre,* Act III); and when Wagner, like Wotan in this scene, put aside his concern with godhood to create the truly memorable characters of Walther, Eva, Hans Sachs, Isolde, and Tristan, he created two works which are likely to outlive in popularity all the showy pageantry and involved symbolism of the *Ring.*

The poem of *Tristan und Isolde* was begun at Zurich in 1857, and the score was finished in 1859. It is often regarded as a monument to Wagner's love for Mathilde Wesendonck, the wife of one of his most devoted friends during his years of exile. Newman sensibly points out, however, that this view probably confuses cause and effect, that Wagner did not compose *Tristan* because he was in love with Mathilde, but rather that he was in love because he was composing *Tristan.* Either way, the matter is not important. In 1857–58 Wagner composed five songs to poems by Mathilde; two of these (*Träume* and *Im Treibhaus*) are made up of thematic material used in *Tristan*, and Wagner later described them as "studies" for the opera. *Tristan* was undertaken at a time when there appeared no prospect of ever bringing the *Ring* to performance, and it was Wagner's hope that a less exacting music drama might have a better prospect of success. But by now his ideas of what constituted a practicable work had so far outgrown the actual practice of the theatres that *Tristan* for many years could not be produced. After many rehearsals at Vienna in 1862–1863 it was abandoned as impossible. Finally in 1864 the young king Ludwig of Bavaria summoned Wagner to Munich and placed almost unlimited resources at his disposal. After careful preparation, the first performance took place at Munich on June 10, 1865, under the direction of Hans von Bülow.

The legend of Tristan and Isolde is probably of Celtic origin. In the early thirteenth century it was embodied by Gottfried of Strassburg in a long epic poem, which was Wagner's principal source for his drama. Wagner's changes consisted in compressing the action, eliminating nonessential personages (for example, the original second Isolde, "of the white hands"), and simplifying the motives. Some details were doubtless borrowed from other sources: the extinction of the torch in Act II from the story of *Hero and Leander,* the dawning of day at the end of the love scene from Shakespeare's *Romeo and Juliet,* and Tristan's delirium in Act III from Matthew Arnold's poem; the love duet in the second act has some points reminiscent of a dialogue between Faust and Helena in the second part of Goethe's drama and the figure of Brangäne as watcher on the tower was perhaps suggested by Goethe's Lynceus.[29] The prominence of the motif of death, the yearning for fulfillment of love in release and annihilation which broods over the whole drama, were at least partly due to Wagner's absorption in the philosophy of Schopenhauer, with whose works he had first become acquainted in 1852.[30] But whatever the contributions of others, *Tristan und Isolde* is Wagner's own. It is

[29] *Faust,* Part II, lines 9372–9418; 11288–11337. These literary derivations are suggested with some diffidence. The torch episode is found in Méhuls *Mélidor et Phrosine;* the watcher is a common figure in German medieval love poems. Cf. Loomis, ed., *The Romance of Tristram and Ysolt by Thomas of Britain,* introduction.

[30] There are echoes here also of Novalis and F. von Schlegel. Cf. Mann, "Leiden und Grösse Richard Wagners" in his *Leiden und Grösse der Meister,* pp. 130–32.

owing to him, and to him alone, that this is now one of the great
love stories, living in the imagination of millions along with the tales
of Romeo and Juliet, Paolo and Francesca, Launcelot and Guinevere;
for Wagner's Tristan is Everyman, his Isolde Everywoman.

The peculiar strength of the drama arises from the fact that external events are simplified to the utmost, so that the action is almost
all inner, and consequently expressed wholly in the music. The words
themselves often melt into music, losing their very character as intelligible language, almost superfluous in many places where the
plane of expression is purely that of the emotions—as, for example, in
Isolde's "Liebestod" at the end of Act III. "Every theory was quite
forgotten," wrote Wagner; "during the working out I myself became
aware how far I had outsoared my system." [31]

The three leading ideas of the drama—love, night, and death—
are really intermingled and inseparable, but each one in turn is
especially emphasized in each of the three acts. The magic potion
of Act I is, in Wagner's version, purely a symbol, figuring forth the
moment of realization of a love already existing but unacknowledged.
Isolde's extinction of the torch is the symbol of Act II; the ecstatic
greeting of the lovers leads into the duet "Descend upon us, night of
love," followed by the love-death music with the words "O could we
but die thus together, endless, never to awaken!" The climax of the
whole scene is in the song of Brangäne, off stage: "Lonely I watch in
the night; you that are lost in the dream of love, heed the lonely one's
call: sorrow comes with awakening. Beware! O beware! For the night
soon passes." Few places in art have so poignantly expressed what
many human beings have experienced, the unutterably sorrowful
realization in the midst of happiness that this moment is unique,
that it cannot last. There is a comparable passage in the *Arabian
Nights:* "Presently one of them arose and set meat before me and I
ate and they ate with me; whilst others warmed water and washed my
hands and feet and changed my clothes, and others made ready sher-
bets and gave us to drink; and all gathered round me being full of
joy and gladness at my coming. Then they sat down and conversed
with me till night-fall, when five of them arose and laid the trays and
spread them with flowers and fragrant herbs and fruits, fresh and
dried, and confections in profusion. At last they brought out a fine

31 "Zukunftsmusik," in *Ges. Schriften* VII, 119.

wine-service with rich old wine; and we sat down to drink and some sang songs and others played the lute and psaltery and recorders and other instruments, and the bowl went merrily round. Hereupon such gladness possessed me that I forgot the sorrows of the world one and all and said, 'This is indeed life; O sad that 'tis fleeting!' " [32]

The doom fated from the beginning is fulfilled. Tristan, reproached by King Mark, mortally wounded by Melot, is carried home to his castle of Kareol and dies as Isolde comes to him bringing Mark's forgiveness. The love-death of Isolde herself brings the tragedy to an end.

Volumes could be, and have been, written about the music of *Tristan und Isolde*. The extreme simplification and condensation of the action, the reduction of the essential characters to only two, and the treatment of these two as bearers of a single all-dominating mood conduce to a complete unity of musical effect and at the same time permit the greatest possible freedom for development of all the musical elements, unchecked by elaborate paraphernalia or the presence of antimusical factors in the libretto. There are comparatively few leitmotifs, and many of the principal ones are so much alike that it is hard to distinguish and label them clearly. The dominant mood is conveyed in a chromatic style of writing which is no longer either a mere decorative adjunct to, or a deliberate contrast with, a fundamentally diatonic idiom, but which is actually the norm, so much so that the few diatonic motifs are felt as deliberate departures, "specters of day" intruding into the all-prevailing night of the love drama. It is impossible here to enter into a comprehensive examination of the technical aspects of this chromaticism; [33] we can only note that history has shown the "*Tristan* style" to be the classical example of the use of a consistent chromatic technique within the limits of the tonal system of the eighteenth and nineteenth centuries. It was not only the climax of all romantic striving in this direction but also the point of departure for Wagner's own later experiments in *Parsifal,* for the more sophisticated, external, ironic chromaticism of Richard Strauss, and for the twelve-tone system of Schönberg, the logical *reductio ad absurdum* of the whole style. The power of the

---

[32] *Tale of the Third Kalendar* (Burton's translation).
[33] This task has been performed, with great thoroughness and insight, by E. Kurth in his *Romantische Harmonik und ihre Krise in Wagners "Tristan."*

Tristan chromaticism comes from its being founded in tonality. A feature of it is the ambiguity of the chords, the constant, immanent, felt possibility that almost any chord may resolve in almost any one of a dozen different directions. Yet this very ambiguity could not exist except for underlying tonal relations, the general tendencies of certain chord progressions within the tonal system. The continuous conflict between what *might be,* harmonically, and what actually *is,* makes the music apt at suggesting the inner state of mingled insecurity and passionate longing which motivates the drama. This emotional suggestiveness is accompanied throughout by a luxuriance of purely sensuous effect, a reveling in tone qualities and tone combinations as if for their own sake, evident in both the subdued richness of the orchestration and the whole harmonic fabric.

Such matters as these are felt by even the casual listener to *Tristan und Isolde.* What is less obvious, though it may be dimly sensed, is the complete formal perfection of the work. Here again the reader must be referred for details to the epoch-making study of Lorenz.[34] The close correspondence of Acts I and III, with the resulting Bogen form of the opera as a whole, has already been mentioned. As to the tonality, Lorenz holds it to be E major—beginning in the subdominant (A minor) and ending in the dominant (B major). The tonic itself, in this view, is almost never sounded, this being at the same time an instance of the persistent avoidance of resolution in the harmony and a symbol of the nature of the love of Tristan and Isolde which attains its satisfaction only in the ideal, not the actual world.[35] The complete first theme as announced in the prelude (measures 1–17) recurs only three times in the course of the opera, once at the climax of each act: at the drinking of the potion in Act I, after Mark's question near the end of Act II, and at Tristan's death in Act III;[36] its function is thus that of a refrain for the whole work. The continuity and formal symmetry, demonstrable in full only by a detailed analysis, are neatly epitomized by the fact that the opening chromatic motif of the prelude receives its final resolution in the closing measures of the last act (Example 109).

The score of *Tristan* was completed in 1859. After an unhappy

---

34 *Das Geheimnis der Form,* II.

35 The only extended E major portion of the opera is the scene of Tristan's vision of Isolde in Act III (pp. 261–63 in the G. Schirmer piano-vocal score).

36 Pages 90–91, 208–209, 276–77 respectively in the Schirmer piano-vocal score.

season in Paris, marked by the scandalous rejection of the revised *Tannhäuser* at the Opéra (March, 1861), Wagner lived for a year and a half in Vienna. With the failure of prospects for performing *Tristan* there, his fortunes reached their lowest ebb. His dramatic rescue by the enthusiastic King Ludwig of Bavaria brought happier times, but

TRISTAN UND ISOLDE

Ex.109.

a) Prelude   *b) End of Act III*   Wagner

six months after the successful first performance of *Tristan* Wagner was compelled to leave Munich, owing largely to political jealousies on the part of the king's ministers. He found a home at Hof Trieb-schen near Lucerne, where he remained from 1866 to 1872. His first wife having died in 1866, he married in 1870 Cosima von Bülow, daughter of Liszt and former wife of Hans von Bülow, the pianist and conductor. Wagner's chief activity in the early years at Triebschen was the composition of *Die Meistersinger*.

Die Meistersinger von Nürnberg ("The Mastersingers of Nurem-berg") had been sketched in 1845, as a kind of comic pendant to *Tannhäuser*. Toward the end of 1861 Wagner planned the work anew,[37] writing some parts of the music before the words. The score was completed in 1867 and first performed at Munich the following year. The story has for historical background the Mastersinger Guilds of sixteenth-century Nuremberg and their song contests, bound about with traditional rules and customs. Wagner not only incorpo-rated many of these points but also borrowed several names and characters of real Mastersingers, notably Hans Sachs, the cobbler-poet-composer who lived 1494–1576.[38] Likewise of historical interest is Wagner's use of an actual Mastersinger melody (the march theme

[37] On the differences between the two versions, and some minor inconsistencies in the final draft, see Newman, *Wagner* III, 156–64; the various sources of the play are studied in Roethe, "Zum dramatischen Aufbau der Wagnerschen *Meistersinger*," *Akademie der Wissenschaften, Berlin, Sitzungberichte* (Jahrgang 1919) pp. 673–708. Cf. also Rayner, *Wagner and Die Meistersinger*; H. Thompson, *Wagner and Wagenseil*.

[38] Many of Sachs's melodies may be found in *Das Singebuch des Adam Puschmann,* ed. by G. Münzer, 1906.

which begins at measure forty-one of the overture), the parody of the Mastersingers' device of *Blumen* or melodic ornaments (literally "flowers") in Beckmesser's songs, and the paraphrase of a poem by the real Hans Sachs (the chorale "Wach' auf!" in Act III). Yet *Die Meistersinger* is not a museum of antiquities; it is a living, sympathetic re-creation in nineteenth-century terms of an important epoch of German musical history, with the literal details of the past illuminated by reference to an ever timely issue, the conflict between tradition and the creative spirit in art. Tradition is represented by the Mastersingers' Guild; the deadly effect of blind adherence to the rules is satirized in the comic figure of Beckmesser, a transparent disguise for the Viennese critic Eduard Hanslick,[39] whose aesthetic views and influence had made him one of the most persistent and conspicuous of Wagner's opponents. The impetuous, innovating drive of the young artist, impatient of all restraints, is incarnated in the person of Walther von Stolzing, whose conflict with the Mastersingers is finally resolved by the wisdom of Hans Sachs, the artist grown wise through experience. Sachs shows that neither tradition nor novelty can suffice by itself; they are reconcilable by one who understands the living spirit behind all rules of art and hence realizes that the new must constantly learn from the old, the old constantly absorb the new. It is probably not fanciful to suggest that in Walther and Hans Sachs Wagner has drawn idealized portraits of two aspects of himself, and that the views of Sachs represent his own mature philosophy of art, set forth with deep insight and poetic beauty. One feature of this philosophy is the professed reliance on the judgment of "the people" as final arbiter in artistic matters. *Das Volk* was one of Wagner's most loved abstractions, one which he always carefully distinguished from *das Publikum*. There is sometimes a temptation to believe that the distinction in his mind was simply between those who liked Wagner's music dramas and those who preferred Rossini or Meyerbeer: the former comprising all the unspoiled virtues and sound instincts of the race, while the latter were unhealthy, misled, or corrupt. Yet there is fundamental truth in the doctrine of the sovereignty of the people in art which *Die Meistersinger* pro-

---

[39] Hanslick (1825–1904) was author of an important work in musical aesthetics, *Vom Musikalisch-Schönen* (1854), and several volumes of essays, mostly collections of his journalistic writings. Cf. Tovey, *Essays in Musical Analysis* II, 71.

claims, so long as we understand "the people" in the democratic sense
of the word, not as a mob but as the bearers of a profound, partly
unconscious instinct which—in the long run—is apt to perceive and
judge rightly.

In the last analysis, however, *Die Meistersinger* is not to be regarded as a treatise on the philosophy of art or anything else. It has
no symbolism, and its teachings are of little importance in comparison to the drama and music themselves. It is by far the most human,
the most easily accessible, of all Wagner's works; for this reason, it
is the one by which every student should be initiated in the knowledge of Wagner as poet and composer. It has every requirement of
good comedy: the simple love story of Walther and Eva, the charming scenes of David and the apprentices, the broadly comic strokes
of Beckmesser's serenade and his ridiculous attempt to steal Walther's
song for the contest. Above all is to be noted the character of Hans
Sachs, Wagner's greatest dramatic figure, who surveys the whole
drama from the standpoint of one who through suffering has attained
to calm resignation, having learned to find joy in the happiness of
others and the triumph of principles.

It is interesting to note that, with such a play as this, Wagner was
led to compose a score which more nearly approaches the traditional
outlines of opera than any of his works since *Tannhäuser*. To be
sure, the principle of symphonic development of a set of leitmotifs
is maintained, and there is no return to the old-fashioned recitative;
but withal there is an amount of formalization of which the listener
is, perhaps, hardly aware, since it fits so well with the dramatic requirements. Like the Orpheus legend, the *Meistersinger* story is
essentially musical in conception. Within its framework fall perfectly
naturally the four "arias" of Walther, the serenade of Beckmesser,
Pogner's "Address," David's song in Act III, and Sach's two monologues, as well as the formal overture and the chorale at the beginning
of Act I. Even more operatic, though no less appropriate for that,
are the apprentice choruses and the huge final ensemble in Act I, the
comic crowd scene at the end of Act II, and the glorified mass finale
with a ballet and choruses in Act III. Then, too, there is the quintet
in the third act, which is as much pure opera as anything in Donizetti
or Verdi: an interpolated number in closed form (a b a) and a remote
key (G-flat), which does not directly further the action and has only

a slight thematic connection with the rest of the work—a number which, in a word, would be out of place in the strict theoretical form of the music drama, but is justifiable here on the same grounds that justify the canonic quartet in *Fidelio* or some of the ensembles of *Don Giovanni*.[40]

It is a sign of Wagner's versatility that, at the same period of his life, he could compose two works which differ so much not only in dramatic plan but also in musical style as do *Die Meistersinger* and *Tristan*. Both the historical background and the nature of the subject matter of *Die Meistersinger* are reflected in the diatonic quality of most of the music, in a certain squareness of rhythmic structure and essential simplicity of idiom. The chorales, the many melodies of folklike cast, the fugal section and contrapuntal combination of three principal themes in the overture, as well as the contrapuntal style of the finale and of many other passages—all seem to contain or suggest the very traits and forms which have always been most typical of German music. By contrast the freer, more chromatic individual Wagnerian touch is heard in the love scenes and the monologues of Hans Sachs. The beautiful orchestral prelude to the third act is not only the quintessence of the musical style but also the high point of the drama, the complete, living description of the noble character of Sachs; there is no better example of music as the very heart of dramatic life, the true carrier of the inner action of the play.

The essentially musical character of the drama in both *Tristan* and *Die Meistersinger* is shown very significantly by the fact that in both these works the musical forms are more clear and comprehensive than anywhere else in Wagner. This is, of course, only another way of saying that in these two works we come as close as possible to the ideally perfect union of music and drama within the Wagnerian system. The form type most prevalent in *Die Meistersinger* is, as we have already mentioned, the Bar, of which five examples should be especially noted: (1) Beckmesser's serenade (pp. 299–318) [41] is a pedantically correct example of two identical Stollen and an Abgesang, the whole being twice repeated to make a song of three strophes. (2) Walther's first song before the Mastersingers, "Am stillen Herd"

---

40 See above, pp. 288–89.
41 Page numbers here refer to the Klindworth piano-vocal score published by G. Schirmer, N.Y., cop. 1904.

(pp. 126–34), is a Bar in which the two Stollen are almost, but not quite, identical. (3) Walther's trial song, "So rief der Lenz" (pp. 144–86), is a more extended Bar with two distinct themes in each Stollen, carried on grimly to the end in spite of the uproar of opposition from his audience. (4) In Walther's dream song, the first version of the Prize Song (pp. 389–93, 395–97, 440–42), the two Stollen are not identical, the second being altered so as to cadence in the dominant. (5) In the final version of the Prize Song (pp. 538–49) the melody is further extended and the differences between the two Stollen are likewise greater, though still without loss of the essential felt likeness. In addition to many other instances of Bar form, some shorter and some longer than the above, the opera as a whole exemplifies the same structure: anyone who will take the trouble to compare Acts I and II, either with or without the help of Lorenz's outline,[42] will discover that there is a detailed parallelism of the action, and that furthermore in most cases each scene in the second act is a parody of the corresponding scene in Act I—a relationship already foreshadowed by the overture, in which the themes of the middle section parody those of the first. Acts I and II thus form two Stollen, of which Act III is the Abgesang. The whole opera is rounded off by the thematic and tonal correspondence of the beginning and the ending; Lorenz notes that the entire finale, from the entrance of the Mastersingers on, is an expanded and varied reprise of the overture.[43]

The principal events in Wagner's life after *Die Meistersinger* were the completion of the *Ring*, the removal to Bayreuth in 1872, and the first full performance of the *Ring* at the new theatre there in 1876. *Parsifal*, his last music drama, was composed between 1877 and 1882, and first performed at Bayreuth January 13, 1882, exactly a year and one month before Wagner's death. The sources of the *Parsifal* drama are even more varied than those of the earlier works. The convergence of many lines of philosophic thought, the complex and often obscure symbolism of the persons and events, make this the most difficult of all Wagner's music dramas to comprehend, even though the outer action is comparatively simple. The legend of the Holy Grail (already touched upon in *Lohengrin* and some other uncomposed dramatic sketches) is combined with profound speculations on the role of suffering in human life, and the central idea is

[42] *Das Geheimnis der Form* III, 11–13.   [43] *Ibid.*, p. 171.

again that of redemption—this time not through love, but by the
savior Parsifal, the Pure Fool, the one "made wise through pity."
The solemnity of this theme, as well as the use of the Christian symbol
of the Eucharist, justify the designation of Parsifal as a "religious
festival-play," a character which is carefully maintained in performances and makes the work unique in the present-day opera
theatre.

No doubt the complexity of the poem is responsible for the fact
that the music of *Parsifal* is less clear in its formal outlines than that
of either *Tristan und Isolde* or *Die Meistersinger*. There is sufficient
resemblance between the first and third acts to delineate a general
a b a structure, but neither the key scheme nor other details of the
various scenes are as amenable to analysis as in the case of the other
two works. The music, like that of *Tannhäuser*, depicts different
worlds of thought and feeling in sharpest possible contrast; but
whereas in *Tannhäuser* there were two such worlds, in *Parsifal* there
are three. Least important, being merely a foil for the other two, is
the realm of sensual pleasure exemplified in the second act: the
Magic Garden and the Flower Maidens of Klingsor's castle, and
Kundry as seductress under the power of evil magic. If we compare
the music of these scenes with the ebullient eroticism of the Venusberg music or the glowing ardors of the *Siegfried* finale, we may be
aware of a slight falling off in Wagner's earlier elemental power,
perhaps a trifle of oversophistication in the technical means. Not so,
however, in the first and third acts. Here are opposed and intermingled the worlds of Amfortas and of the Grail, the agonizing peni-
tent and the mystical heavenly kingdom of pity and peace. The
Amfortas music is of the utmost imaginable intensity of feeling,
expressed in richness of orchestral color, plangency of dissonance,
complexity and subtlety of harmonic relationships, and a degree of
chromaticism which carries it more than once to the verge of atonality. The Grail music, on the other hand, is diatonic and almost
churchlike in style. The very opening theme of the prelude (the
Last Supper motif), a single-line melody in free rhythm, is reminiscent of Gregorian chant; the Grail motif is an old Amen formula in
use at the Dresden Royal Chapel when Wagner conducted there. One
feature of the Grail scenes in *Parsifal* deserves special emphasis,
namely the expertness of the choral writing. One does not ordinarily

look to opera composers for excellence in a field of composition which has always been chiefly associated with the church, and the peculiar technique of which has not always been grasped by even some of the greatest composers. Wagner's distinguished choral writing in *Lohengrin, Die Meistersinger,* and above all in *Parsifal* is therefore of interest; [44] in particular, the closing scenes of Acts I and III of *Parsifal,* with their fine choral effects and the device of separated choirs, with the high and low voices giving an impression in music of actual space and depth, recall the Venetian composers of the later sixteenth century.

In attempting to estimate the significance of Wagner in the history of opera one must first of all acknowledge the man's unswerving idealism and artistic integrity. However open to criticism some aspects of his personal conduct may have been, as an artist he stood uncompromisingly for what he believed to be right. He fought his long battle with such courage and tenacity that his final success left no alternative for future composers but to acknowledge the power of the Wagnerian ideas and methods, whether by imitation, adaptation, or conscious rebellion. His form of the music drama did not, as he had expected, entirely supersede all earlier operatic ideals, but certain features of it were of permanent influence. Chief among these was the principle which lay at the basis of the Gesamtkunstwerk idea, namely that every single detail of a work must be directly connected with the fundamental dramatic purpose and must serve to further that purpose. Wagner is to be numbered among those composers who have seriously maintained the importance and dignity of drama in their works. In addition, many of his procedures left their mark on the next generation or two of composers, for example, the parallel position of voice and orchestra, the orchestral continuity, and the symphonic treatment of leitmotifs. Other matters, however, were less capable of being imitated. Wagner's use of Nordic mythology as subject matter, and his symbolism, were so individual that most attempts to copy them have resulted only in unintended parody.[45] The qualities of his poetry, though appropriate enough in connection with his own music, are not those of the highest literary

[44] It is not always remembered that Wagner greatly admired the music of Palestrina and had made an arrangement of his *Stabat Mater* for a concert in 1848.

[45] E.g., Mangold's *Tanhäuser* (1846), Doss's *Percifal* (1883), and Reyer's *Sigurd* (1884); but Chabrier (*Gwendolyn,* 1886) and D'Indy (*Fervaal,* 1897) were more successful.

art. Likewise the whole structure of aesthetic, economic, historical, and other doctrines by which Wagner sought to give theoretical support to his artistic aims is no longer regarded as generally valid or applicable, though it is none the less valuable for the sake of the light it sheds on his own artistic practice.

In the last analysis, the important thing about Wagner is his music. It would not have been his wish to be remembered primarily as a musician, but the world has so chosen, and the world in this case has probably understood the genius better than he understood himself. The quality of Wagner's music which has been the cause of its great popularity has been equally the cause of the severest attacks upon it by musicians, namely that it is not pure, absolute, spontaneous music, created for music's sake and existing in a realm governed only by the laws of sound, rhythm, and musical form. Wagner is not, like Bach or Mozart, a musician's musician. There is about him in music, as in literature and philosophy, something of the nature of an amateur, though on a gigantic scale and an intellectual level which make the word seem ridiculous.[46] For him no art was self-sustaining. Music, like poetry and gesture, was but one means to a very comprehensive end which can perhaps best be defined as "great theatre." Granted this end (which may or may not be conceived as a limitation), it is hardly possible to deny the adequacy of Wagner's music in relation to it. Not only does the music possess sensuous beauty. It can suggest, depict, and characterize a whole universe of the most diverse objects and ideas. Above all is its power—by whatever aesthetic theory one seeks to explain it—of embodying or evoking feeling, with a purity, fullness, and intensity surely not surpassed in the music of any other composer who has ever lived. Such emotion is justified by the grandiose intellectual conceptions with which it is connected and by the monumental proportions of the musical forms in which it is expressed. In this monumental quality, as well as in the characteristic moods, aspirations, and technical methods of his music, Wagner is fully representative of the time in which he lived. "Feeling" as an attitude is not fashionable in the twentieth century as it was in the nineteenth. Moreover, the ideas toward which Wagner's feeling was directed are not those which appeal most strongly to our own age, and modern composers obviously cannot occupy themselves

46 Mann, *Leiden und Grösse*, p. 104, *et passim*.

in imitating the musical style of late romanticism. Under the circumstances, a certain reaction of distrust, even of depreciation, is inevitable. Whether this will in time be modified cannot be foretold, but it is hardly possible that Wagner's art will ever again hold the dominating position it enjoyed in the generation following his own lifetime. No music is immortal. Sooner or later dusk falls even on the gods.

Part 5

From Romanticism to Modernism

24

French Opera from 1870 to 1914[1]

THE STATE OF MUSICAL TASTE IN PARIS (that is to say, in France) from 1840 to 1870 is sufficiently illustrated by three facts: the adoration of Meyerbeer, the neglect of Berlioz, and the craze for Offenbach. The disaster of the Franco-Prussian War was a salutary shock to both public and musicians. In 1871 the Société Nationale de Musique was founded, with the device *Ars gallica*. The rise of the modern French school dates from this event. Undiscriminating acceptance of incongruous musical styles on the one hand, and a frivolous addiction to the trivialities of operetta on the other, were succeeded by a conscious and strenuous effort to restore in modern terms the great musical individuality which had belonged to France in the sixteenth, seventeenth, and eighteenth centuries. The range of creative activity was widened. Whereas before 1870 composers had centered nearly all their efforts on opera, now choral, symphonic, and chamber music began to be important; higher standards of musical education were introduced, and a more cultivated and exacting public gradually came into being. This renewal of national musical life made the opera more vital, original, and adventurous. And although the highest rewards of popular success still went to those composers who were able and willing to bend their talents to the public fancy, nevertheless the best work found hearing and appreciation; there were no scandals like those of the Second Empire, when *Tannhäuser* was hissed off the stage and *Les Troyens* was closed after only twenty-one performances. It is worthy of remark that almost every important new operatic work in Paris after 1870

[1] *Almanach des spectacles*, Paris 1874–1913; *Cinquante Ans de musique française*, ed. Rohozinski; Bruneau, *La Musique française*; Rolland, *Musiciens d'aujourd'hui*; Seré, *Musiciens français d'aujourd'hui* (contains excellent bibliographical lists); Hill, *Modern French Music*; Coeuroy, *La Musique française moderne*; Jullien, *Musiciens d'aujourd'hui*, 2 vols. (1892–1894); Tiersot, *Un Demi-siècle de musique française* [1870–1917]; Aubry, *La Musique française d'aujourd'hui*.

was produced not at the Opéra but at the more enterprising and progressive Opéra-comique. The old distinction between the forms of opera and opéra comique had practically disappeared by the end of the nineteenth century, for the latter had by then largely abandoned the traditional spoken dialogue; so the repertoire of the two theatres contrasted simply as large-scale, established, conventional works in the one, and new, often experimental works in the other—alternating, of course, with the light, operetta-like pieces, which continued to flourish. Composers of large serious operas which should have been produced at the Paris Opéra frequently had recourse to the Théâtre de la Monnaie at Brussels for the first performances. Monte Carlo was also the scene of some notable premières. How little the term "opéra comique" in this period had to do with "comic" opera will be realized by recalling that Bizet's *Carmen,* Delibes' *Lakmé,* Lalo's *Roi d'Ys,* Massenet's *Manon,* Bruneau's *Attacque du moulin,* D'Indy's *Fervaal,* Charpentier's *Louise,* and Debussy's *Pelléas et Mélisande* were all staged, originally or eventually, at the Théâtre de l'Opéra-comique in Paris.

One of the first new operas of distinction to be produced in Paris after 1870 was Bizet's *Carmen* (1875).[2] The success of this work at Paris did not begin until some eight years after its composer's death, but it stands today as the most popular and vital French opera of the later nineteenth century. Its Spanish subject was a reflection of the exotic trend in French music which had begun a generation earlier with David; but more important than this feature was the realism with which scenes and characters were depicted, a realism which the librettists had somewhat toned down from Mérimée's original story (especially with respect to Carmen herself), but which still was strong enough to scandalize Paris in the seventies. The tragic ending of this opéra comique was also a novelty. As to the music, Bizet had formed his style from many sources. Probably the least important feature is the mild Spanish local color evident in such numbers as the Habañera, the Toreador Song, and the seguidilla "Près des ramparts de Seville" (Act I). Many of the choruses and ensembles are in characteristic operetta style. Fundamental, however, is the clear, firm, concise, and exact musical expression of every situation

2 The most recent biography of Georges Bizet (1838–1875) is by Martin Cooper (1939); see also special Bizet number of RdM (November, 1938).

in terms of which only a French composer would be capable: the typical Gallic union of economy of material, perfect grasp of means, and an electric vitality and rhythmic verve, together with a completely objective, cool, yet passionate sensualism. This opera contains some spoken dialogue and is otherwise divided into the conventional arias, ensembles, and other numbers. So far as Bizet was concerned, Wagner's music dramas and theories might never have existed. The occasional repetition of certain motifs is of no more significance in *Carmen* than in Verdi's *Rigoletto* a quarter of a century earlier. The whole structure and aesthetic of *Carmen* was such that Nietzsche, after he had become disgusted with Wagner, might point to it as the ideal opera according to the principles of a properly "Mediterraneanized" European art.[3] It is hard to imagine what was in the minds of those contemporary critics who found the music untuneful, lacking in definite outlines, and overpowered by a too rich orchestration—charges, in a word, of Wagnerianism, such as had been leveled earlier at Gounod. But "Wagnerian" was a convenient word at this time for damning anything a critic disliked or could not understand. The styles of Gounod and Bizet do, indeed, have much in common, but the affinity is much more apparent in Bizet's earlier operas *Les Pêcheurs de perles* ("The Pearl Fishers," 1863) and *Djamileh* (1872). Both these works are still occasionally given in France and Italy, but they have less musical individuality and interest than *Carmen;* in fact, the only other work of Bizet's which compares with this opera is his incidental music to Daudet's play *L'Arlésienne* (1872).

The slight exotic flavor of *Carmen* and *Les Pêcheurs de perles* is found again in *Lakmé* (1883), the best opera of Léo Delibes,[4] with a Hindu locale and a tragic plot faintly reminiscent of Meyerbeer's *Africaine* and more than faintly foreshadowing Puccini's *Butterfly*. Delibes' music is elegant, graceful, and well orchestrated but lacks the intense quality of Bizet's. In *Lakmé* the oriental perfume is blended with an otherwise conventional idiom. Delibes' amusing and tuneful opéra comique *Le Roi l'a dit* ("The King Said So," 1873)

---

[3] "Der Fall Wagner," ¶3; "Jenseits von Gut und Böse," Pt. VIII *passim*.
[4] Delibes (1836–1891) wrote a dozen operettas before making a hit with his opéra comique *Le Roi l'a dit* in 1873. He was at his best as a composer of ballets: *La Source* (1866), *Coppélia* (1870) and *Sylvia* (1876). He became professor of composition at the Conservatoire in 1881. See biography by H. de Curzon.

is still remembered; a more serious work, *Jean de Nivelle* (1880), was almost equally successful at first but has not remained in the repertoire.

A more substantial figure than Delibes in French nineteenth-century opera was Ernest Reyer.[5] Reyer belongs with those composers whose music often compels more respect for its intentions than admiration for its actual sound. He had "genius without talent," [6] that is, lofty and ideal conceptions without the technique for realizing them fully in an attractive musical form. This incapacity may have been due in part to his defective early training, but it was also partly a matter of temperament; as a critic he was a despiser of mere prettiness, a rebel against the superficial, snap judgments of the Paris public,[7] and an early defender of Berlioz and Wagner. Reyer was influenced by the fashionable orientalism in his choice of subjects, as seen in his symphonic ode *Sélam* (1850) and a ballet-pantomime *Sacountala* (1858). His first important operatic work, *La Statue* (1861), is also an oriental story. A similar background is found in his last opera, *Salammbô* (1890), taken with few alterations from Flaubert's novel and treated in an austere oratorio-like style, yet with a grandeur of line recalling the spirit of Berlioz's *Troyens;* the plot in general and the closing scene in particular are reminiscent of Verdi's *Aïda.* The most successful of Reyer's operas was *Sigurd* (composed in the 1870's, first performed 1884); the subject is almost identical with that of Wagner's *Siegfried* (Act III) and *Götterdämmerung,* with a touch of *Tannhäuser* in the shape of a seductive ballet, with a wordless chorus of elves, in Act II. But the resemblance to Wagner is only skin-deep, even in the libretto: Sigurd talks in the accents of Quinault's Renaud rather than like the great blond lad of the *Ring;* and the rest of the personages likewise somehow seem more Gallic than Teutonic. In the music there is no sign whatever of Wagner; we find the old separate numbers of grand opera, a distinctly periodic melody, and very little chromaticism. There is some recurrence of motifs, but this is not a distinctly Wagnerian

---

[5] Reyer (1823–1909) was mostly self-taught in music, the principal influence on his style being that of Berlioz. He wrote little except dramatic music but was active as journalist and critic. See his *Notes de musique* and *Quarante Ans de musique;* also biography by De Curzon and the same author's *Légende de Sigurd.*

[6] Alfred Bruneau, quoted in Combarieu, *Histoire* III, 389.

[7] See Lavignac, *Encyclopédie,* Pt. I, Vol. III. pp. 1727–28.

trait. The musical style is serious and even has a certain nobility; [8] its model, clearly enough, is *Les Troyens*.

Parisian journalists had been crying "Wolf! wolf!" for years before any serious reflection of Wagner's ideas or musical style became apparent in French music. The bitterness of the Franco-Prussian War, aggravated by Wagner's silly gibes in his playlet *Eine Kapitulation*, delayed his acceptance still longer. Yet by the early eighties apparently all was forgiven, and Wagner became the rage in Paris for some ten or twelve years. "From 1885 Wagner's work acted directly or indirectly on the whole of artistic thought, even on religious and intellectual thought of the most distinguished people of Paris. . . . Writers not only discussed musical subjects, but judged painting, literature, and philosophy, from a Wagnerian point of view. . . . The whole universe was seen and judged by the thought of Bayreuth." [9] A remarkable evidence of this enthusiasm was the flourishing periodical *La Revue Wagneriénne* (1885–1888), contributors to which included Verlaine, Mallarmé, Huysmans, and practically every other important writer in Paris (Baudelaire had been converted already in 1861). One effect of all this was to introduce the subject of music to many people who would otherwise not have taken an interest in it; another was to stimulate symphonic composition. In opera, the risks involved in the magic garden of Wagnerism were so patent that the composers for the most part withstood temptation, though not always without effort. It is sometimes difficult to decide what is to be called imitation of Wagner and what is simply acceptance of new ideas, such as the abolition of formal separate arias and recitatives. Taken altogether, however, the direct influence of Wagner on French opera, in both literary and musical treatment, is seen most strongly in works by three composers: Chabrier, D'Indy, and Chausson.[10]

Chabrier [11] seems at first an unlikely person to be an apostle of Wagner, for the pieces by which he is best known (the orchestral

---

8 See example in OHM VII, 339–42.   9 Rolland, *Musicians of Today*, p. 253.

10 Cf. D'Indy, *Richard Wagner et son influence sur l'art musical français.*

11 Alexis Emanuel Chabrier (1841–1894) was one of the most important composers in the development of the modern French school, as well as a pianist of exceptional ability. He was trained for the law; during fifteen years of service in the Ministry of the Interior he cultivated music as an amateur and kept abreast of contemporary movements in painting and literature. See Hill, *Modern French Music*, chap. IV, and the separate studies by Martineau and Servières.

rhapsody *España*, the *Bourrée Fantasque*) show him as a composer
of typical Gallic vivacity, wit, and rhythmic exuberance. It is these
qualities which are uppermost in his first important comic opera
L'Etoile ("The Star," 1877), [12] and in his best-known stage work, *Le
Roi malgré lui* ("The King in Spite of Himself," 1887), harmonically
one of the most original *opéras comiques* of this period. But in 1879
Chabrier heard a performance of *Tristan und Isolde* at Munich
which made a strong impression on him, reinforced by his experience
shortly afterwards in directing rehearsals of *Lohengrin* and *Tristan*
for performances at Paris. His opera *Gwendoline* (first performed at
Brussels in 1886) is obviously influenced by Wagnerian elements:
in the libretto there are echoes of *Der fliegende Holländer*, of the
Valhalla mythology, and above all of *Tristan*, even to a love duet in
the second act and a love-death at the end of the third. The form is
a compromise between continuous drama and the older number
opera. The music shows more than a trace of Wagner in its systematic
use of leitmotifs, chromatics, chords of the seventh and ninth, and
the characteristic appoggiaturas and suspensions. However, this must
not be taken to mean that it is a mere copy of Wagner's idiom.
Chabrier had a very individual harmonic style, one which was extremely advanced for his time; and as a second facet of his musical
personality he had a genuine and sometimes profound gift of serious
expressiveness. The most interesting portions of *Gwendoline* are
the Spinning Song in Act I (incorporating an air from Moore's *Irish
Melodies*), the love duet (strongly reminiscent of *Tristan*), and the
orchestral prelude to Act II, the style of which has been well described
as one of the links between Wagner and Debussy.[13] The skillful voice
writing and the highly colorful and poetic orchestration of this opera
should also be noted. But the uneven quality of the music as a whole,
together with the rather dull and awkwardly proportioned libretto,
have worked against its success. In his unfinished opera *Briseïs* (Act I
performed 1899) Chabrier demonstrated even more daring harmonies than in *Gwendoline*.

Somewhat similar in subject matter to *Gwendoline*, and likewise
tinctured with Wagnerian conceptions, is César Franck's opera

[12] This work was produced in America as *The Merry Monarch* and elsewhere under
various titles. See Loewenberg, *Annals*, p. 551.
[13] Abraham, *A Hundred Years of Music*, p. 238.

Hulda (first performed in 1894).[14] But the most thorough, and at the same time the most individual, adaptation of Wagner's methods to French opera was brought about by Franck's pupil Vincent d'Indy in his *Fervaal* (1897) and *L'Etranger* ("The Stranger," 1903).[15] Like Wagner, D'Indy wrote his own librettos. The background of *Fervaal* is vaguely mythological, and the action in both operas is treated as symbolic of broad moral issues—the conflict between pagan religion and sacrificial love in *Fervaal,* and the expiation of unlawful love through death in *L'Etranger.* But whereas Wagner's symbolism is nearly always in practice subordinated to the aim of theatrical effect, with D'Indy there is evident a purpose to make art a vehicle for essentially religious teachings and to use every possible artistic means consistently for this end. The almost medieval combination of this austere ideal with a catholic breadth of resource, welded into unity by superb technical skill, is the clue to D'Indy's style.[16] It explains how he was able to take over many features of Wagner's music dramas without sacrificing his own individuality: pseudo mythology, symbolism, continuity of the music, harmonic sophistication, the symphonic orchestral texture with cyclical recurrence of motifs, free arioso treatment of the voice line, Wagnerian instrumental sonorities, even (in the love music of the first and third acts of *Fervaal*) actual reminiscences of *Tristan.* Indebtedness to Wagner is much less apparent in *L'Etranger* than in the earlier opera. The profound suggestiveness of the musical landscape in the introduction to Act II of *Fervaal* and the uniquely somber, mysterious poetry of the following scene are especially noteworthy. The third scene of Act II of *L'Etranger* is remarkable for imaginative and pictorial power (Example 110). As in his dramatic choral works, *Le Chant de la cloche* ("The Song of the Bell," 1879–1883) and *La Légende de St. Christophe* (composed 1908–1915), in the operas too D'Indy has effective

14 This opera was composed 1882–1885. The plot is similar to that of Lalo's *Roi d'Ys.* On Franck (1822–1890) see the biography by D'Indy and other works listed in Lynn's *Bio-bibliography.* Franck's other operas, less dramatic on the whole than his oratorios and of little importance in his total work, are: *Le Valet de ferme,* opéra comique, composed 1851–1852; and an unfinished lyric opera *Ghiselle,* performed in 1896 with the orchestration completed by Franck's pupils.
15 The most recent study of D'Indy (1851–1931) is by De Fraguier (1933). There are the following special studies: Bréville, *Fervaal;* Calvocoressi, *L'Etranger;* Destranges, *Le Chant de la cloche; idem, Fervaal; idem, L'Etranger.* See also D'Indy's own *Wagner et son influence sur l'art musical français.*
16 Rolland, chapter on D'Indy in *Musiciens d'aujourd'hui.*

L'ÉTRANGER, Act II, sc.3

Ex.110.

D'Indy

choral treatments of Gregorian melodies, notably the "Pange lingua"
in the transcendently beautiful closing scene of *Fervaal*.[17] That
neither of these operas has become popular may be owing in part to
the unusual character of their librettos but more to the music, which
lacks the simple, salient, easily perceived qualities apparently necessary for success on the stage. One cannot help feeling that, for the
theatre, the music has many of the defects of Wagner without the latter's constant, compelling emotional power. Yet *Fervaal* in particular
deserves respect as one of the outstanding French operas of the later
nineteenth century in the noble tradition of Berlioz's *Troyens*. If
musicians alone could dictate the repertoire of opera houses, *Fervaal*
would be more often performed.

The influence of Wagner is still noticeable in Chausson's *Roi
Arthus* (1903), a curious and not very successful combination of old
grand-opera formal elements with the new Wagnerian idiom, including the inevitable Tristanesque love duet in Act I. Neither

17 Cf. also the quotation of the intonation of the "Credo" in Act II, sc. 1 of the same
opera; and in Bruneau's *Messidor* (also 1897) the plainsong passage from the litany in
the finale.

libretto nor music offers any passages of real distinction.[18] The composer himself regarded *Le Roi Arthus* as only an experiment. This is perhaps the final word for all the attempts by French composers to assimilate Wagner's methods in the nineteenth century, since no consistent or historically important school grew from them. Along with these experiments the natural line of French lyric opera in descent from Gounod continued to flourish. We now turn our attention to the composers of this distinctively national group.

The first is Camille Saint-Saëns,[19] whose *Princesse jaune* ("The Yellow Princess," 1872) set the fashion for Japanese subjects in comic opera. Saint-Saëns' most famous dramatic work is the biblical *Samson et Dalila* (1877), half opera and half oratorio, like Liszt's *Legende von der heiligen Elisabeth* or D'Indy's *St. Christophe*. Saint-Saëns was not by nature a dramatic composer, but his technical facility and knowledge of many different musical styles enabled him to construct smooth and competent, though not exciting, works in the dramatic field. Of his sixteen stage works the most successful (next to *Samson et Dalila*) were *Henri VIII* (1883), *Ascanio* (1890), and the opéra comique *Phryné* (1893). Another composer of conservative national tendency was Edouard Lalo [20] with *Le Roi d'Ys* (1888), based on a Breton legend. The music of this opera is original in style, of remarkable rhythmic vitality, varied in color, and admirably adapted to the stage—qualities which have assured its survival to the present day. Three other French composers of the late nineteenth century should be mentioned in passing, though their work is less important than that of Saint-Saëns or Lalo: Emile Paladilhe (*Patriel*, 1886), Benjamin Godard (*La Vivandière*, 1895), and Isidore De Lara (*Messaline*, 1899).[21]

18 Ernest Chausson (1855–1899) was a pupil of Massenet and César Franck. *Le Roi Arthus* was his only opera ever to be performed. (It was not performed at Karlsruhe in 1900, as most books of reference say. See Loewenberg, *Annals*, p. 654.)

19 The most recent book on Saint-Saëns (1835–1921) is by Langlois (1934); cf. also his own writings, especially *Portraits et souvenirs*. See bibliography in Baker's *Dictionary* (4th ed., 1940) p. 946, and add: Du Tillet, "A propos du *Drame lyrique*," *Revue politique et littéraire* (July 3, 1897) pp. 27–30.

20 Lalo (1823–1892) had established his reputation as a symphonist before completing his only successful opera; the latter had been sketched as early as 1878. See Servières, *Edouard Lalo*.

21 Paladilhe (1844–1926) was a pupil of Halévy and winner of the Prix de Rome in 1860; Godard (1849–1895) was a composer of facile and pleasing melodic gifts, of which the well known "Berceuse" from his opera *Jocelyn* (1888) furnishes a good example. De Lara (1858–1935) was born in London and lived there chiefly, but most of his operas

The most representative and successful French opera composer of the late nineteenth and early twentieth centuries was Jules Massenet.[22] Massenet was an exceptionally productive worker, whose music is marked by characteristic French traits that we have already had occasion to notice in earlier composers such as Monsigny, Auber, Thomas (Massenet's teacher), and Gounod. First among these is the dominance of melody. Massenet's melody is of a highly personal quality: lyrical, tender, penetrating, sweetly sensuous, rounded in contours, exact but never violent in interpreting the text, sentimental, often melancholy, sometimes a little vulgar, and always charming. This melody determines the whole texture; the harmonic background is sketched with delicacy and a fine sense of instrumental color. Every detail of the score shows smooth craftsmanship and unhesitating choice of means. There is no commitment to particular theories of opera, Wagnerian or otherwise, but within the limits of his own style Massenet never hesitated to make use of any new device which had proved effective or popular, so that his works are not free of eclecticism and mirror in their own way most of the successive operatic tendencies of his lifetime. The subjects and their treatment also show the composer's sensitiveness to popular taste. Thus *Le Roi de Lahore* (1877) is an oriental story, *Le Cid* (1885) is in the manner of grand opera, *Esclarmonde* (1889) is Wagnerian, *La Navarraise* (1894) shows the influence of Italian *verismo,* and *Cendrillon* (1899) recalls Humperdinck's *Hänsel und Gretel;* but *Le Jongleur de Notre Dame* (1902) is a miracle play for which there could have been no public demand, but which the composer treated with special affection and thereby produced one of his best and most enduring operas. The suspicion is sometimes aroused that Massenet's choice of subjects, as well as his use of certain fashionable musical devices, was due to a desire to give his audiences what he knew they wanted rather than to any impulsion of his own. But there is no sacrifice of musical individuality in all this; and in the case of a composer whose instincts were so completely of the theatre, who always succeeded in achieving so neatly and spontaneously just the effect he intended, it seems a little ungracious to insist too strongly on an issue of artistic

were to French texts and were performed in France; his style was based on that of Massenet.

[22] The principal biography of Massenet (1842–1912) is by L. Schneider. See also the study by Bruneau (1934) and the composer's own *Mes Souvenirs.*

sincerity. Massenet excelled in the musical depiction of passionate love, and most of his best works are notable for their heroines— unforgettable ladies all, of doubtful virtue perhaps, but indubitably alive and vivid. To this gallery belong Salomé in *Hérodiade* (1881), the heroines of *Manon* (1884), *Thaïs* (1894), *Sapho* (1897), and Charlotte in *Werther* (1892). With these works should also be mentioned *Thérèse* (1907), one of the last operas of Massenet to obtain general success.

Massenet traveled the main highway of French tradition in opera and his natural gifts so corresponded to the tastes of his day that success seemed to come almost without effort. Nor was his style without influence, direct or indirect, on later French composers. But he was the last to produce operas so easily. Changing musical idioms and new literary movements had their effect on the next generation, giving its work a less assured, more experimental character. Only two French serious operas so far in the twentieth century have even begun to equal the popularity of Massenet's: Charpentier's *Louise* (1900) and Debussy's *Pelléas et Mélisande* (1902). Each represents a characteristic operatic school of the period: the former that of naturalism, the latter that of symbolism.

The word "naturalism" and the related word "realism," however useful they may be in the study of literature or the graphic arts, are exceedingly vague when applied to music. Unless they refer to the obvious and unimportant practice of imitating everyday sounds by voices or instruments in a musical composition (as, for example, the bleating of sheep in Strauss's *Don Quixote*), it is difficult to see what meaning they can have that is related directly to music itself. What some writers call "realistic" or "naturalistic" music is simply, in effect, a certain kind of program music; the realism is deduced not from the music but from an extramusical fact (such as a title) about the composition in question. When we speak of realistic or naturalistic opera, therefore, we have reference primarily to the libretto; we mean that the opera presents persons, scenes, events, and conversations which are recognizably similar to the common daily experience of its audience, and that these things are treated seriously, as becomes matters of real moment, not with persiflage or fantasy as in an operetta. It goes without saying that such tendencies in opera grew out of earlier tendencies in literature. Thus Bizet's *Car-*

men, the first important realistic opera in France and one of the principal sources of the Italian verismo, was based on Mérimée's story. The chief disciples of realism in later nineteenth-century French literature were Guy de Maupassant (1850–1893) and Emile Zola (1840–1902). The latter found a musical interpreter in Alfred Bruneau,[23] the librettos of whose most important operas were either adapted from Zola's books or written especially for the composer by Zola himself; to the former class belong *Le Rêve* ("The Dream," 1891) and *L'Attacque du moulin* ("The Attack on the Mill," 1893), to the latter *Messidor* (1897), *L'Ouragan* ("The Hurricane," 1901), and *L'Enfant roi* ("The Child King," 1905). These works were concerned with current social and economic problems, presented in compact, tense dramatic situations, with symbolical additions. Another realistic detail was the prose form of the text instead of the customary verse. Unfortunately, this did not always inspire the composer to achieve a plastic musical rhythm; the regular accentuation indicated by the bar lines often becomes monotonous. The melodic line is declamatory rather than lyrical. The music is austere; it is especially apt in the creation of moods through reiterated motifs, but with all its evident sincerity and undoubted dramatic power, the important quality of sheer sensuous charm is often lacking. Bruneau is significant as a forerunner of some modern experiments in harmony [24] and as an independent, healthy force in the growth of modern French opera, counterbalancing to some extent the romanticism of D'Indy and the frank hedonism of Massenet.

A fuller measure of success in the field of operatic naturalism was granted to another pupil of Massenet, Gustave Charpentier.[25] *Louise,* a "musical novel," is his only important work, a strange but effective combination of several distinct elements. In scene, characters, and plot it is realistic; Charpentier, writing his own libretto, has almost gone out of his way to introduce such homely details as a bourgeois family supper, the reading of a newspaper, and a scene in a dressmak-

---

[23] Bruneau (1857–1934) was a pupil of Massenet and winner of the Prix de Rome in 1881. He was active not only as a composer of operas (thirteen) and ballets but also as a critic and writer (cf. the works listed in bibliography). See Boschot, *La Vie et les œuvres d'Alfred Bruneau.*

[24] An example from *L'Attaque du moulin* is found in OHM VII, 337–38.

[25] Charpentier (b. 1860) won the Prix de Rome in 1887. His only other opera is *Julien* (1913), a sequel to *Louise* but comparatively unsuccessful. See Delmas, *Gustave Charpentier et le lyrisme français;* Himonet, *Louise.*

ing shop; many of the minor personages are obviously taken "from life," and sing in a marked Parisian dialect. The crude melodrama of the closing scene recalls the mood of the Italian verismo composers. There is also, as in Bruneau, some touching on social questions: the issue of free love, the obligations of children to their parents, the miseries of poverty. But along with realism there is symbolism, especially in the weird figure of the Noctambulist, personification of "the pleasure of Paris." Paris itself is, as Bruneau remarked,[26] the real hero of this opera. Behind the whole action is the presence of the great city, seductive, mysterious, and fatal, enveloping persons and events in an atmosphere of poetry like that of the forest in Weber's *Freischütz*. Its hymn is the ensemble of street cries, running like a refrain through the first scene of Act II and echoing elsewhere throughout the opera. To realism and symbolism is added yet a third factor: sentiment. The dialogue between Louise and her father in Act I is of a convincing tenderness, while the love music of Act III, with the often-heard "Depuis le jour," is not only a great scene of passion but also one of the few of its kind in late nineteenth-century French opera which is never reminiscent of *Tristan und Isolde*—or hardly ever. It was the achievement of Charpentier to take all this realism, symbolism, and sentiment, holding together only with difficulty in the libretto itself, and mold it into one powerful whole by means of music. The score reminds one in many ways of Massenet: there is the same spontaneity and abundance of ideas, the same simple and economical texture, obtaining the maximum effect with the smallest apparent effort. The harmonic idiom is more advanced than Massenet's but not so daring or experimental as Bruneau's. The orchestral music is continuous, serving as background for spoken as well as sung passages,[27] and organized by means of a set of leitmotifs. A number of standard operatic devices are cleverly adapted to the libretto: Julien's serenade with accompaniment of a guitar, the ensemble of working girls in Act II (where the tattoo of the sewing machine replaces the whirr of the old romantic spinning wheel), and the grand ballet-like scene where Louise is crowned as the Muse of Montmartre in Act III. On the whole, it will be seen that when

---

26 *Musiciens d'aujourd'hui*, p. 154.
27 Both orchestrally accompanied spoken dialogue and the use of Parisian street cries are found in Massenet's *Manon;* there are street cries also in Puccini's *Bohème* (1896).

this opera is cited as an example of naturalism, the word needs to be taken with important qualifications. In any case it is not the naturalism which has caused it to survive, for this was but a passing fashion. *Louise* remains in the repertoire for the same reasons as other successful operas: because it has tuneful and moving music, wedded to a libretto which permits the music to operate as an effective partner in the creation of an interesting drama.

Beyond question, the most important French opera of the early twentieth century was Debussy's *Pelléas et Mélisande,* first performed at the Opéra-comique on April 30, 1902, "one of the three or four red-letter days in the history of our lyric stage" as Romain Rolland said.[28] The first sketches for this work are dated 1893, and Debussy revised it continually up to the time of performance. It is customary, and in the main correct, to regard *Pelléas et Mélisande* as a monument to French operatic reaction from Wagner. It is at the same time a focal point of French dramatic music, gathering up many essential national traits and giving them exceptionally clear and perfect expression, though colored by the individual genius of Debussy. The personal qualities of the music are so evident that they tend to usurp attention, and it is therefore well to emphasize that *Pelléas* is not only characteristic of Debussy but also of France.

There are four things which have marked French opera from the beginning of its history. The first is the belief that an opera is fundamentally a drama in words, to which music has been added; from this doctrine comes the insistence on clear and realistic declamation of the text. Both the contemporary admiration for Lully's recitative and Rousseau's later objections to it as "mannered" came from the same interest in the text as basic to the drama and hence to the opera. In no other country has so much attention been given to this issue. The flourishing of the opéra comique with its spoken dialogue was a constant witness that the French were willing to do without music rather than let it interfere with the understanding of the words. *Pelléas et Mélisande* conforms to this ideal. It is one of the rare in-

28 *Musiciens d'aujourd'hui,* essay on Debussy. The standard books on Debussy (1862–1918) in English are those of Vallas (first publ. in French, 1932), Lockspeiser (1936), Thompson (1937), and Dumesnil (1940). See also the volume of Debussy's essays published under the title *Monsieur Croche, anti-dilettante.* There are special studies of *Pelléas et Mélisande* by Gilman, Jardillier, and M. Emmanuel. Debussy's only other stage work was the miracle drama *Le Martyre de Saint-Sebastien* (1911), based on D'Annunzio's play.

stances where a long play, not expressly made for music, has been turned into an opera with practically no rearranging.[29] In most places the music is no more than an iridescent veil covering the text; the orchestral background is shadowy, evanescent, almost a suggestion of sound rather than sound itself; and the voice part, with its independence of the bar line, narrow range, small intervals, and frequent chanting on one tone, adheres as closely as possible to the melody of French speech. Only in a few places, as in Mélisande's song at the beginning of Act III or in the love duet (Act IV, scene 4), does the melody become really lyric. How typical this narrow melodic line is of French music may be realized by comparing the contours of French folk-song melodies with those of German, English, or Italian folk songs, the instrumental themes of Saint-Saëns or César Franck with those of a German like Richard Strauss, or French nineteenth-century recitative in general with the wide-sweeping arioso of Verdi or Wagner. The use of the Wagnerian type of melody with French words, such as we find in the operas of Chabrier and D'Indy (and, to a lesser extent, in Bruneau and Charpentier) was soon felt to be unnatural. In the return to a more natural declamation and in the damping of orchestral sonorities, therefore, Debussy was in accord not only with the traditional French practice but with an even more ancient ideal, that of the early Florentine founders of opera, Peri, Caccini, and Gagliano.

The second historical feature of French opera is its tendency to center the musical interest not in the continuous orchestra or in the solo aria but in the divertissements, that is, interludes in the action where music might be enjoyed without the attention being divided by the necessity of following the drama at the same time. In early French opera and through the nineteenth century the common form of divertissement was the ballet with choruses. There are no ballets in *Pelléas,* and only one quite unimportant chorus, but the function of the divertissement is fulfilled by the orchestral preludes and the interludes which are played for changes of scene. Here, and here only, music has the foreground and the full symphonic resources are employed. But the interludes are not independent of the action;

[29] The following scenes in the play are omitted in the opera: Act I, sc. 1; Act II, sc. 4; Act III, sc. 1; and Act V, sc. 1. There are very many other small omissions ranging from a single phrase to a dozen lines, and numerous alterations in wording. Some words have been added: see especially Act III, sc. 1 of the opera.

rather, they resume in wordless and concentrated form what has just passed and, by gradual transition, prepare for what is to come. Thus Debussy combines the Lullian form of opera with the new nineteenth-century practice of treating every detail as a means toward the central dramatic purpose.

Still another constant feature of French opera has been the deliberate choice of measured, objective, well-proportioned, and rational dramatic actions. The French have not been misled, except momentarily, either by the desire to be forceful at any cost or by the attractions of the world of metaphysical speculation. Not that French opera is as direct and uninhibited in its approach as the Italian; but the French prefer to suggest a hidden meaning by subtle juxtaposition of facts, trusting to stimulate the imagination rather than overwhelm it with exhaustive details, as Wagner tends to do. Now the quintessence of this subtle, indirect, and suggestive method in literature is found in the movement known as symbolism, of which Maeterlinck's five-act drama *Pelléas et Mélisande* is an outstanding example. The story is purposely vague and seems slight indeed when reduced to a bare summary. But the whole effect is in the manner, not the matter. As Edmund Gosse has said: "Maeterlinck is exclusively occupied in revealing, or indicating, the mystery which lies, only just out of sight, beneath the surface of ordinary life. In order to produce this effect of the mysterious he aims at an extreme simplicity of diction, and a symbolism so realistic as to be almost bare. He allows life itself to astonish us by its strangeness, by its inexplicable elements. Many of his plays are really highly pathetic records of unseen emotion; they are occupied with the spiritual adventures of souls, and the ordinary facts of time and space have no influence upon the movements of the characters. We know not who these orphan princesses, these blind persons, these pale Arthurian knights, these aged guardians of desolate castles, may be; we are not informed whence they come, nor whither they go; there is nothing concrete or circumstantial about them. Their life is intense and consistent, but it is wholly of a spiritual character; they are mysterious with the mystery of the movements of a soul." [30]

The mysterious, spiritual character of the drama is perfectly sup-

[30] "Maeterlinck," in *Encyclopædia Britannica* (11th ed.) XVII, 299a. Quoted by permission.

plemented by the music. The latter does everything by understatement, by whispered suggestion. The full orchestra is hardly ever heard outside the interludes. Instrumental doubling is avoided; solo timbres and small combinations are the rule. Strings are often muted and divided. There are only four fortissimos in the whole score. Debussy's almost excessive "genius for good taste" [31] is apparent if we contrast the wild greeting of the lovers in the second act of *Tristan* with the meeting of Pelléas and Mélisande in Act IV (Example 111),

PELLÉAS ET MÉLISANDE, Act IV, sc.4

or the simple and touching scene of Mélisande's death in Act V with Isolde's Liebestod.

However, soft music is not of necessity better than loud music; restraint is of no artistic value unless we are made aware that there is something to be restrained. And here we come to the fourth and last quality characteristic of French opera, which Debussy carries to the ultimate degree, namely a capacity for the appreciation of the most refined and complex sensory stimuli. In the quality of its acceptances as well as of its refusals, French opera has always tended to be aristocratic. The style of musical impressionism which *Pelléas et Mélisande* exemplifies is essentially one of aristocratic sensualism, treating sounds as of primary value for themselves irrespective of accepted grammatical forms, and creating moods by reiterated minute impacts

[31] Rolland, *Musiciens d'aujourd'hui,* essay on Debussy.

of motifs, harmonies, and timbres. These elements in *Pelléas* sounded so completely unprecedented in themselves, and so completely detached from the familiar system of musical progressions, that audiences were at first bewildered; but they soon learned to associate the musical moods with those of the poetry and discovered a marvelous correspondence between the two. For as Maeterlinck's drama moved in a realm outside ordinary time and space, so Debussy's music moved in a realm outside the then known tonal system; lacking any strong formal associations within the field of music itself, his harmonies were irresistibly attracted to the similarly free images of the poet. Never was a happier marriage of music and verse. The technical methods of Debussy are familiar to all students of music and will be only briefly indicated here.[32] Modal, whole-tone, or pentatonic melodies and harmonies suggest the far-off, dreamlike character of the play. The free enchainment of seventh and ninth chords, often in organum-like parallel movement, and the blurring of tonality by complex harmonic relationships are also typical. There are definite leitmotifs which recur and are transformed and harmonically varied, but they are not treated in the continuous symphonic manner of Wagner. D'Indy has well expressed their function by the term "pivot themes." [33]

The influence of Wagner on Debussy is to be felt chiefly in a negative fashion, that is, by the care Debussy took to avoid writing like Wagner. In those days it was not easy. Debussy complained of his first draft of the duet in Act IV that "the ghost of old Klingsor, alias R. Wagner, keeps peeping out." [34] But the final score cannot be said to owe anything to Wagner beyond the orchestral continuity, the use of leitmotifs, and the exclusion of all merely ornamental details; in technique, idiom, feeling, and declamation it is Debussy's own. Whatever he had learned from *Tristan* or from Mussorgsky's *Boris Godunov,* from Massenet, Grieg, or from oriental music had been completely assimilated. So peculiarly was the musical style fitted to Maeterlinck's drama that it is no wonder Debussy was never able to find another suitable libretto. *Pelléas et Mélisande,* like *Fidelio,* remains an isolated masterpiece of its composer in the field of opera.

[32] See further M. Emmanuel, *Pelléas et Mélisande,* pp. 97–114 *et passim.*
[33] *Richard Wagner et son influence sur l'art musical français,* p. 81.
[34] Letter to Chausson, quoted in Abraham, *A Hundred Years of Music,* p. 278.

The next notable French opera of the twentieth century was Dukas' [35] *Ariane et Barbe-Bleue* ("Ariadne and Bluebeard," 1907); like *Pelléas,* it is the composer's only opera, and its libretto is likewise a symbolist drama by Maeterlinck. The influence of Debussy is apparent in the declamation and in some details of the harmony, but the recitative is less supple and poetic than Debussy's. The orchestration is very sonorous, using the brasses with brilliant effect, and the musical style on the whole is anything but impressionistic. Dukas was a composer of great technical attainment whose strong point was the development of ideas in large symphonic forms. Unfortunately, his themes are too often undistinguished in themselves, and their development marked less by inspiration than by system and perseverance; for example, the constant practice of repeating the exposition of a theme immediately in a new key (compare the exposition in the first movement of César Franck's symphony) becomes almost a mannerism. Dukas' harmony is very subtle, but here again one sometimes feels the absence of any compelling musical or dramatic reason for some of his complicated chord progressions. Another defect is the excessive reliance on the augmented triad in association with the whole-tone scale, a device which has lost the attraction of novelty since 1907. So much must be stated by way of negative criticism of *Ariane et Barbe-Bleue.* On the other hand, its many excellences must be emphasized. The work is less an opera than a huge symphony with the addition of choruses (essential to the drama, not mere embellishments) and solo voices. Cyclical recurrence and transformation of themes are used to create an architectural structure of grand and satisfying proportions. The great coda which forms the end of Act III is particularly impressive, summing up with Beethovenian finality all the principal themes of the opera and rounding off the whole with the theme which was first heard in the opening measures of the prelude to Act I. Among the many fine details of the score is the song of the "five daughters of Orlamonde," a striking folk-songlike melody and a source from which many of the leitmotifs of the opera are derived (Example 112). Altogether, *Ariane et Barbe-Bleue* is the most important French lyric drama of the early twentieth

---

35 Paul Dukas (1865–1935) is best known for his orchestral scherzo *L'Apprenti sorcier.* His pianoforte Sonata in E-flat minor is an important work. See study by Samazeuilh and special Dukas issue of RM (May–June, 1936).

century next to *Pelléas et Mélisande*—important, that is, if measured in terms of artistic qualities rather than popular following. It is none the less significant musically for lacking those traits which made the success of Massenet and Charpentier.

There are four more operas of this period which merit special mention, each being in its own way a distinctive contribution. Déodat de Sévérac's *Coeur du moulin* ("The Heart of the Mill,"

1909),[36] a simple and poignant love story in a pastoral setting, has a musical score in which the influence of Debussy is modified by an original gift for direct, spontaneous expression and a charming regional flavor of southern France, evident especially in the choruses. Although its individual features were acclaimed by critics, *Le Coeur du moulin* has not had any popular success. Ravel's *L'Heure espagnole* ("The Spanish Hour," 1911),[37] on the contrary, has been widely performed. It is a one-act opera buffa in French, a tour de force of rhythm and orchestration, varied and witty in declamation, with a libretto in which the art of the *double-entendre* is carried to a height worthy of Favart. The vocal lines are suggestive of Richard Strauss, while under them the orchestra carries on a suite of Spanish dances ending with a mock-grand "scena and habañera." The scene being laid in a clockmaker's shop gives occasion for many charming and clever sound effects, among which the cuckoo motif is, of course, prominent. The strength of this opera is in just those qualities which Dukas' *Ariane* lacks, namely piquant details and a sense of lightness, gaiety, and improvisation. *Le Pays* ("The Country," 1912), by Guy Ropartz,[38] is a dramatic, solid, and well-proportioned score, with symphonic treatment of the orchestra, original in inspiration, evidencing the sound classical training its composer received from César Franck. One can detect a modified Wagnerianism (via D'Indy) in the melody and harmony, as well as the then fashionable obsession with the sound of the augmented fifth chord. Fauré's *Pénélope* (1913) [39] is a beautiful example of the composer's exquisite harmonic style, which lends to the classical subject matter an appropriate atmosphere of repose and remoteness, evoking the feeling of the antique world as no more common idiom could. From the viewpoint of theatrical

36 De Sévérac (1873–1921) was a pupil of D'Indy. Besides *Le Coeur du moulin* he composed two other operas (not produced), incidental music to plays, symphonic poems, and pianoforte pieces. The most recent study is by Selva (1930).

37 On Maurice Ravel (1875–1937) see Manuel, *Maurice Ravel et son œuvre dramatique;* special numbers of RM (April, 1925; December, 1938). Ravel's opera ballet *L'Enfant et les sortilèges* ("The Child and the Sorceries"), first performed in 1925, is simpler in style than *L'Heure espagnole*, with the orchestra subordinated to the voice parts, and some traces of jazz idiom.

38 J. Guy Ropartz (b. 1864) was director of the conservatories at Nancy (1894–1919) and Strasbourg (1919–29). His chief musical works are orchestral (four symphonies, two suites).

39 On Gabriel Urbain Fauré (1845–1924) see biographies by Bruneau (1925), Koechlin (1927), and Servières (1930); special number of RM (October 1922). Fauré's opera *Prométhée* was performed in 1900.

effectiveness, however, *Pénélope* is perhaps too refined; the slow tempo of the action (in Acts I and II especially) emphasizes the statuesque quality which is both the greatest musical beauty and the most serious dramatic weakness of this opera.

The dominant tendency of late nineteenth- and early twentieth-century French opera was idealistic; the noble, if somewhat vague, striving of *Fervaal* and *L'Etranger*, the mood of meditation on destiny in *Pelléas* and *Ariane*, the naïve religious faith of *Le Jongleur de Notre Dame*, the moral earnestness of *Le Coeur du moulin* and *Le Pays*, the serene, contemplative beauty of *Pénélope*—all show this. Even the so-called "naturalistic" operas of Bruneau and Charpentier used realism largely as a means of calling forth idealistic sentiment. Thus motivated, composers sought to bring into the theatre the most subtle and comprehensive resources of a highly developed musical art, aspiring toward universality of expression, freely using any and all means to which they found themselves attracted. Viewed from a later age, it seems an art of leisure and luxury, such as is possible only in a time of prosperity and peace. But leisure gave time for the unfolding of ideals, while luxury provided the material means for their realization on a scale which we have not seen since and probably shall not in this generation.

Among the minor composers of serious opera in this period were Gabriel Pierné (*La Fille de Tabarin*, 1901), Alexandre Georges (*Charlotte Corday*, 1901), Xavier Leroux (*La Reine Fiamette*, 1903, influenced by Puccini and Massenet; *Le Chemineau*, 1907), Henri Février (*Monna Vanna*, 1909), and Jean Noguès, whose *Quo Vadis* (1909) is a mild blend of Massenet and Fauré.[40] Distinguished especially for works in a lighter vein were the French-Venezuelan composer Reynaldo Hahn (1875–1946; *La Carmélite*, 1902), and Camille Erlanger (1863–1919; *Le Juif polonais*, 1900; *Aphrodite*, 1906). More individual in style was Raoul Laparra (1876–1943) with his operas on Spanish subjects; the most popular were *La Habanera* (1908) and *L'Illustre Fregona* (1931). Ernest Bloch's (b. 1880) opera *Macbeth*, composed in 1903, was given at the Opéra-comique in 1910. The music is strongly influenced by Debussy, with declamatory vocal lines, much parallelism in the orchestral texture, and a monotonously constant use of the augmented 5-7 chord, which seems to have fascinated opera composers of this period as much as the diminished seventh had fascinated their predecessors a hundred years earlier. *Macbeth* was severely criticized on account

[40] Pierné's dates are 1863–1937; Georges, 1850–1938; Leroux, 1863–1919; Février, b. 1875; Noguès, 1876–1932.

of its modernistic harmonies and rhythms [41] and soon dropped out of the repertory; in spite of much favorable comment, it has not yet been revived. Silvio Lazzari (1857–1944) with *La Lépreuse* (1912) and Louis Aubert (b. 1877) with *La Forêt bleue* (Geneva, 1913) had no great success, but Henri Rabaud's (b. 1873) oriental *opéra comique Mârouf, savetier de Caire* ("Marouf, Cobbler of Cairo," 1914), witty, modern in harmony, and brilliantly scored, has become a favorite both in Paris and abroad. It is undoubtedly one of the finest modern comic operas, a worthy descendant of the long French line of works in this style and on similar subjects. Another oriental opera was Gabriel Dupont's (1878–1914) *Antar*, finished in 1914 but not performed until 1921.[42] The Belgian Albert Dupuis (b. 1877; *La Passion*, Monte Carlo, 1916) in his operas reverted to the style of Massenet.

It must be remembered that throughout the period we have been considering the semidramatic form of the ballet occupied much of the attention of French composers. Lalo's *Namouna* (1882) never received the recognition it merited, but in the early twentieth century the performances of such works as Florent Schmitt's mimodrama *La Tragédie de Salomé* (1907), Ravel's *Daphnis et Chloé* (1912), and Stravinsky's *Firebird, Petrouchka,* and *The Ceremonial of Spring* (1910, 1911, and 1913 respectively) were very important musical events.

Fashions in opera might come and go, but the operetta and kindred forms went their way unperturbed. The line of French light opera, established in the nineteenth century by Auber, Adam, and Offenbach, was continued after 1870 by Alexandre Charles Lecocq (*La Fille de Madame Angot,* 1872), Robert Planquette (whose sentimental, fantastically successful *Cloches de Corneville* came out in 1877), Edmond Audran (*La Mascotte,* 1880), and Louis Varney (*Les Mousquetaires au couvent,* 1880).[43] Somewhat later began the long and popular series of operettas by André Messager (1853–1929), distinguished conductor and facile composer in a straightforward, attractively melodious vein (*La Basoche,* 1890; *Les P'tites Michu,* 1897; *Monsieur Beaucaire,* 1919). At the beginning of the twentieth century appeared the operettas of Claude Terrasse (1867–1923; *Le Sire de Vargy,* 1903; *Monsieur de la Palisse,* 1904).

[41] See Slonimsky, *Music Since 1900,* p. 106; Cohen, "Ernest Bloch's *Macbeth,*" M&L XIX (1938) 143–48; Hall, "The Macbeth of Bloch," MMus XV, No. 4 (May–June, 1938) 209–15.

[42] See Dumesnil, "Gabriel Dupont," MQ XXX (1944) 441–47.

[43] On Lecocq (1832–1918) see Schneider, *Les Maîtres de l'opérette;* Planquette (1848–1903), Audran (1840–1901), and Varney (1844–1908) have not yet been subjects of separate studies.

25

Italian Opera after Verdi

As Italians in the eighteenth century would have nothing to do with Gluck, so in the nineteenth they cared little for Wagner. It was not until the eighties that even *Lohengrin* began to be accepted. With the exception of Boïto there were no important out-and-out Wagner disciples in Italy. There was considerable talk about Wagner and considerable skepticism as to the future of Italian opera, but the only result of any consequence was to call forth a vigorous national reaction of which the greatest monument is Verdi's *Otello*. Italian opera was too secure in its tradition and methods, too deeply rooted in popular life, to be susceptible to radical experiments, especially experiments resulting from aesthetic theories of a sort in which Italians were temperamentally uninterested. A mild influence of German romanticism, but hardly more, may be found in a few composers of the late nineteenth century. Alfredo Catalani with *Loreley* (1890, a revision of his *Elda,* 1880) and *La Wally* (1892) is the most distinguished of this group. His melodies are refined and musical, nearly always free of exaggerated pathos, supported by interesting and original harmony in a varied texture and with excellent balance of interest between voice and orchestra. Along with some curious traces of "Tristan chromaticism" there are experiments in modern devices (parallelism, augmented triads) which anticipate many of the characteristics of Puccini. The robust and vital rhythms are notable, especially in the choruses and dances of *La Wally.* Unfortunately, Catalani appeared just at a time when the Italian public was being seduced by Mascagni and Leoncavallo, so that his reserved and aristocratic music was drowned by the bellow of realism. With Antonio Smareglia (*Nozze istriane,* "Istrian Wedding," 1895), the influence of Wagner is apparent in the harmonic idiom and relative importance of the orchestra, but he lacked the popular touch in the lyrical parts, and his operas were not favorably received in his own country. Alberto Franchetti has been called "the Meyerbeer of Italy" because of his fondness for massive scenic effects (*Asrael,* 1888; *Cristo-*

foro Colombo, 1892; *Germania,* 1902), but the music is, on the whole, undistinguished. None of these composers [1] was attracted by the verismo movement of the 1890's, which was the popular trend in Italy at that time.

The most explosive reaction against Wagner, and the typical Italian adaptation of late nineteenth-century literary and dramatic movements, was launched with the performance of Mascagni's *Cavalleria rusticana* ("Rustic Chivalry," 1890) and Leoncavallo's *Pagliacci* ("The Clowns," 1892).[2] These two one-act operas are the classics of the school of verismo, or realism. The Italian verismo resembles the French naturalism in the use of scenes and characters from common life; but the naturalists use these materials as a means for the development of more general ideas and feelings, idealizing both scene and music, whereas the goal of the verists is simply to present a vivid, melodramatic plot, to arouse sensation by violent contrasts, to paint a cross section of life without concerning themselves with any general significance the action might have. Verismo is to naturalism what the "shocker" is to the realistic novel. The music corresponds to this conception. It aims simply and directly at the expression of intense passion through melodic or declamatory phrases of the solo voices, to which the orchestra contributes sensational harmonies. Choral or instrumental interludes serve only to establish a mood which is to be rent asunder in the next scene. Everything is so arranged that the moments of excitement follow one another in swift climatic succession. Now it cannot be denied that there was plenty of precedent

---

[1] Catalani (1854–1893) studied at Paris and Milan and was successor to Ponchielli as professor of composition at the Milan conservatory. See Klein, "Alfredo Catalani," MQ XXIII (1937) 287–94.

Smareglia (1854–1929) studied at Vienna and Milan; he became professor of composition at the Tortini Conservatory, Trieste, in 1921. See studies by Nacamuli, M. Smareglia, and A. Smareglia.

Franchetti (b. 1860) studied at Dresden and Munich. The most recent of his nine operas is *Glauco* (Naples, 1922).

[2] Pietro Mascagni (1863–1945) became famous overnight with *Cavalleria rusticana,* which remained his one big success, though *L'amico Fritz* (1891) and the romantic operas *Guglielmo Ratcliff* (1895) and *Iris* (1898) have been widely performed. His last operas were *Il piccolo Marat* (1921), *Nerone* (1935), and *I bianchi ed i neri* (1940). See studies by De Donno and biography by Pompei (1912).

Ruggiero Leoncavallo (1858–1919) is another one-opera composer. A projected early trilogy, *Crepusculum,* was left uncompleted after the failure of the first part. *La Bohème* (1897) suffered by comparison with Puccini's more popular work of the same title, but *Zaza* (1900) was fairly successful. Neither of these is of the verismo type.

On the aesthetic of verismo in general, see Rinaldi, *Musica e verismo.*

in Donizetti and the earlier works of Verdi for melodramatic situations in opera. But by comparison the action of the veristic operas takes place as in an atmosphere from which the nitrogen has been withdrawn, so that everything burns with a fierce, unnatural flame, and moreover quickly burns out. The one-act form is due not so much to concentration as to rapid exhaustion of the material. Much the same is true of the verismo movement as a whole, historically considered. It flared like a meteor across the operatic sky of the 1890's, but by the end of the century it was practically dead, for it had no possibilities of growth. Neither Mascagni nor Leoncavallo, nor any of their imitators in that style, were able to repeat the sensational success of *Cavalleria rusticana* and *Pagliacci*.

The chief figure in Italian opera of the late nineteenth and early twentieth centuries was Giacomo Puccini,[3] who resembles Massenet in his position of mediator between two eras, as well as in many features of his musical style. Puccini's rise to fame began with his third opera, *Manon Lescaut* (1893), which is less effective dramatically than Massenet's opera on the same subject (1884) but rather superior in musical interest—this despite occasional reminiscences of *Tristan*,[4] which few composers in the nineties seemed able to escape. Puccini's world-wide reputation rests chiefly on his next three works: *La Bohême* (1896), *Tosca* (1900), and *Madama Butterfly* (1904). *La Bohême* is a sentimental opera with dramatic touches of realism, on a libretto adapted from Henri Murger's *Scènes de la vie de Bohême* ("Scenes of Bohemian Life");[5] *Tosca*, taken from Victorien Sardou's drama of the same name (1887), is "a prolonged orgy of lust and crime"[6] made endurable by the beauty of the music; and *Madama Butterfly* is a tale of love and heartbreak in a Japanese setting. (In 1904 it was customary to regard the Japanese as a lovable, somewhat fragile, and altogether quaint set of people.) The musical characteristic of Puccini which stands out in all these operas is the intense, concentrated, melting quality of expressiveness in the vocal melodic

[3] Puccini (1858–1924) studied under Ponchielli at Milan and made his debut as an opera composer with *Le Villi* in 1884. By the early years of the twentieth century he had become the most successful and popular Italian composer since Verdi. See biographies by Fraccaroli and Specht; Puccini's letters, ed. by Adami; Gatti, "The Works of Giacomo Puccini," MQ XIV (1928) 16–34.
[4] E.g., the love duet in Act II, from the words "è fascino d'amor."
[5] Dramatized successfully as *La Vie de Bohême* in 1849.
[6] R. A. Streatfeild, in *Grove's Dictionary* (4th ed.) IV, 282.

line. It is like Massenet without Massenet's urbanity. It is naked emotion crying out, and persuading the listener's feeling by its very earnestness. For illustrations the reader need only recall the aria "Che gelida manina" and the ensuing duet in the first scene of *La Bohême*, the closing scene of the same work, or the familiar arias "Vissi d'arte" in *Tosca* and "Un bel di" in *Butterfly*. The history of this type of melody is instructive. It will be remembered that in Verdi we encountered from time to time a melodic phrase of peculiar poignancy which seemed to gather up the whole feeling of a scene in a pure and concentrated moment of expression, such as the "Amami, Alfredo" in *La traviata* (Ex. 103), the recitative "E tu, come sei pallida" of *Otello* (Ex. 104), or the kiss motif from the same work. For later composers, lacking the sweep and balance of construction found in Verdi at his best but perceiving that the high points of effectiveness in his operas were marked by phrases of this sort, naturally became ambitious to write operas which should consist entirely (or as nearly so as possible) of such melodic high points, just as the verismo composers had tried to write operas consisting entirely of melodramatic shocks. Both tendencies are evidence of satiety of sensation. These melodic phrases in Verdi are of the sort sometimes described as "pregnant"; their effect depends on the prevalence of a less heated manner of expression elsewhere in the opera, so that they stand out by contrast. But in Puccini we have, as an apparent ideal if not always an actuality, what may be called a kind of perpetual pregnancy in the melody, whether this is sung or entrusted to the orchestra as a background for vocal recitative. The musical utterance is kept at high tension, almost without repose, as though it were to be feared that if the audiences were not continually excited they would go to sleep. This tendency toward compression of language, this nervous stretto of musical style, is characteristic of the *fin de siècle* period. We shall find it once more, in the realm of harmonic procedure, when we come to the operas of Richard Strauss.

The sort of melody we have been describing runs through all of Puccini's works. In the early operas it is organized in more or less balanced periods, but later it becomes a freer line, often skillfully embodying a series of leitmotifs. The leitmotifs of Puccini are admirably dramatic in conception and effectively used either for recalling earlier moments in the opera or, by reiteration, to establish a mood, but they do not serve as generating themes for musical development.

Puccini's music was enriched by the composer's constant interest in the new harmonic developments of his time; he was always eager to put current discoveries to use in opera. One example of striking harmonic treatment is the series of three major triads (B-flat, A-flat, E-natural) which opens *Tosca* and is associated throughout the opera with the villainous Scarpia. The harmonic tension of the augmented fourth outlined by the first and third chords of this progression is by itself sufficient for Puccini's purpose; he has created his atmosphere with three strokes, and the chord series has no further use but to be repeated intact whenever the dramatic situation requires it. There is no use in making comparisons between Puccini's procedure and that, for example, of D'Indy in *Istar* or Sibelius in the Fourth Symphony, both of which works are developed largely out of the same augmented-fourth interval; but no contrast could show more starkly the difference between good opera music on the one hand and good symphonic music on the other. One common trait of Puccini's, found in all his operas from the early *Edgar* (1889) down to his last works, is the "side-slipping" [7] of chords (Example 113); doubtless this de-

MADAMA BUTTERFLY, Act II

Ex.113.   Puccini

vice was learned from Verdi (compare the passage "Oh! come è dolce" in the duet at the end of Act I of *Otello*) or Catalani, but it is based on a practice common in much exotic and primitive music and going back in European music history to medieval organum and fauxbourdon. Its usual purpose in Puccini is to break a melodic line into a number of parallel strands, like breaking up a beam of white light by

[7] Abraham, *A Hundred Years of Music*, p. 222.

a prism into parallel bands of color. In a sense it is a complementary effect to that of intensifying a melody by duplication at the unison and octaves—an effect dear to all Italian composers of the nineteenth century and one to which Puccini also frequently resorted. Parallel duplication of the melodic line at the fifth is used to good purpose in the introduction to scene 3 of La Bohême to suggest the bleakness of a cold winter dawn; at the third and fifth, in the introduction to the second scene of the same opera, for depicting the lively, crowded street scene (a passage which may or may not have been in the back of Stravinsky's mind when he wrote the music for the first scene of Petrouchka); and parallelism of the same sort, extended sometimes to chords of the seventh and ninth (compare Debussy), is found at many places in the later operas.

The most original places in Puccini, however, are not dependent on any single device; take for example the opening scene of Act III of Tosca, with its broad unison melody in the horns, the delicate descending parallel triads over a double pedal in the bass, the Lydian melody of the shepherd boy, and the faint background of bells, with the veiled, intruding threat of the three Scarpia chords from time to time—an inimitably beautiful and suggestive passage, technically perhaps owing something to both Verdi and Debussy, but nevertheless thoroughly individual.

An important source of color effects in Puccini's music is the use of exotic materials. Exoticism in Puccini was more than a mere borrowing of certain details but rather extended into the very fabric of his melody, harmony, rhythm, and instrumentation.[8] It is naturally most in evidence in the works on oriental subjects, Madama Butterfly and Turandot (1926). Turandot, based on a comedy of the eighteenth-century Carlo Gozzi, was completed after Puccini's death by Franco Alfano; it is "so far the last world success in the history of opera." [9] It shows side by side the most advanced harmonic experimentation (compare the bitonality at the opening of Acts I and II), the utmost development of Puccinian expressive lyric melody, and the most brilliant orchestration of any of his operas.

Puccini did not escape the influence of verismo, but the realism

[8] See the excellent study (with musical examples) by Carner, "The Exotic Element in Puccini," MQ XXII (1936) 45–67.
[9] Loewenberg, Annals, p. 727.

in his operas is always tempered by, or blended with, romantic and exotic elements. In *La Bohême,* common scenes and characters are invested with a romantic halo; the repulsive melodrama of *Tosca* is glorified by the music; and the few realistic details in *Madama Butterfly* are unimportant. A less convincing attempt to blend realism and romance is found in *La fanciulla del West* ("The Girl of the Golden West"), taken from a play by David Belasco and first performed at the Metropolitan Opera House in 1910. Though enthusiastically received by the first American audiences, *La fanciulla* did not attain as wide or enduring popularity as the preceding works. The next opera, *La rondine* ("The Swallow," 1917), was even less successful. A return was made, however, with the *trittico,* or triptych, of one-act operas performed at the Metropolitan in December 1918: *Il tabarro* ("The Cloak"), a veristic melodrama; *Suor Angelica* ("Sister Angelica"), a miracle play; and *Gianni Schicchi,* the most popular of the three, a delightful comedy in the spirit of eighteenth-century opera buffa. Puccini's comic skill, evidenced also in some parts of *La Bohême* and *Turandot,* is here seen at its most spontaneous, incorporating smoothly all the characteristic harmonic devices of his later period. Only the occasional intrusion of sentimental melodies in the old vein breaks the unity of effect.

Puccini was not one of the great composers, but within his own limits (of which he was perfectly aware) he worked honorably and with mastery of his technique. Bill Nye remarked of Wagner's music that it "is better than it sounds"; Puccini's music, on the contrary, often sounds better than it is, owing to the perfect adjustment of means to ends. He had the prime requisite for an opera composer, an instinct for the theatre; to that he added the Italian gift of knowing how to write effectively for singers, an unusually keen ear for new harmonic and instrumental colors, a receptive mind to musical progress, and a poetic imagination excelling in the evocation of dreamlike, fantastic moods. Even *Turandot,* for all its modernistic dissonance, is essentially a romantic work, an escape into the exotic in both the dramatic and the musical sense.

A younger contemporary of Puccini was Umberto Giordano,[10] whose *Andrea Chénier* (1896) is like a rescue opera of the French Revolution period, but without the rescue; both plot and music show

[10] Giordano (1867–1948) studied at the Naples Conservatory. See Galli, *Umberto Giordano.*

the influence of verismo in the exaggerated emphasis on effect at all costs (Example 114). Apart from its undoubted dramatic qualities, the score offers little of interest; the harmonies are heavy and old-fashioned, and there are few notable lyric passages in the voice parts. Some local color is provided by the use of revolutionary songs ("Ça

ANDREA CHÉNIER, sc. 2

Ex.114. Giordano

ira," "La Carmagnole," "La Marseillaise"). *Fedora* (1898) and *Siberia* (1903) are in the same style, with Russian instead of French background. In *Madame Sans-Gêne* (New York, 1915) the composer's skill at producing effective theatre music is brilliantly applied in a vivacious and tuneful comedy drama. Of Giordano's later operas, *La cena delle beffe* ("The Feast of Jests," 1924), a lurid four-act melo-drama, has been the most successful. None of these are of much sig-nificance musically; they are the work of a gifted but not profound composer, operating within the framework of traditional Italian opera and skillfully adapting it to the current fashion of orchestral continuity. A similar, but less conspicuous, position must be assigned to Francesco Cilèa;[11] his *Adriana Lecouvreur* (1902) is an involved drama of the age of Louis XV, with expertly contrived music of a lyrical-tragic sort obviously influenced by Puccini, unadventurous harmonically or rhythmically, but good theatre and grateful for the singers.

One of the most popular composers of the early twentieth century was the German-Italian Ermanno Wolf-Ferrari,[12] who has specialized in comedy operas on librettos either adapted from the eighteenth-century Goldoni or of a similar type: *Le donne curiose* ("The Curious Ladies," 1903); *Il segreto di Susanna* ("The Secret of Suzanne," 1909), his most famous work; and *Sly* (1927), a comic opera distantly reminiscent of Verdi's *Falstaff*, and likewise on a Shakespearean subject (prologue to *The Taming of the Shrew*). His only tragic opera, an experiment with some of the methods of verismo, is *I gioielli della Madonna* ("The Jewels of the Madonna," 1911), a work strongly suggestive of Donizetti with modern trimmings in harmony and rhythm. The Serenade in Act II, perhaps the best-known number in the opera, is a good illustration of the vivacity and rather superficial harmonic cleverness of the style. One of the last composers of the verismo school, whose work is full of the old traditional Italian opera devices, was Mascagni's pupil Riccardo Zandonai (1883–1944); his most important opera is *Francesca da Rimini* (1914), based on D'Annunzio's tragedy of the same name—a smoothly contrived score with a pleasant tincture of late romantic harmony.

The decline of verismo and the effort to combine some of its features with a neoromantic or exotic type of opera, which we find in Puccini, Giordano, and others, is one symptom of a new spirit rising in Italian musical life in the early years of the twentieth century. By comparison with the previous period, this was a time of internationalism and even a certain amount of eclecticism. After Wagner, came

[11] Cilèa (b. 1866) likewise studied at Naples. He is one of the first Italian opera composers of this period to have busied himself with music in other forms (orchestral and chamber works). See *Bollettino bibliografico musicale* VII (June, 1932) 5–16.
[12] Wolf-Ferrari (b. at Venice, 1876, of a German father and an Italian mother) studied under Rheinberger at Munich, and all but the first of his operas up to 1914 were first performed in Germany. See De Rensis, *Ermanno Wolf-Ferrari, la sua vita d'artista;* Grisson, *Ermanno Wolf-Ferrari*.

Strauss, Debussy, and Stravinsky in turn to make their impress on Italian composers. Interest was aroused in symphonic and chamber music (Martucci, Sgambati); an important renewal of church music was led by Don Lorenzo Perosi and Enrico Bossi. Evidence of this broadened outlook is found in the neoromantic operas of Italo Montemezzi,[13] especially *L'amore dei tre re* ("The Love of the Three Kings," 1913) and *La nave* ("The Ship," 1918), where the influence of both Wagner and Debussy is blended with a native Italian lyricism to produce music sound in workmanship, rich in instrumental color, conservative in idiom though not merely imitative, and of enduring beauty. *L'amore dei tre re* is without doubt the greatest Italian tragic opera since Verdi's *Otello*. Its most notable quality is the refinement of the style; the chromaticism of the period is treated with intelligence and restraint, intensifying the expression of feeling by the very refusal to dwell on obvious tricks of theatrical effect. There are memorable moments of classic breadth, as at the end of the love duet in Act II (Example 115). The voice line is an admirable ad-

L'AMORE DEI TRE RE, Act II

Ex. 115.   Montemezzi

[13] Montemezzi (b 1875) studied at the Milan Conservatory. His first two operas were *Giovanni Gallurese* (1905) and *Hellera* (1909). His most recent opera, *La notte di Zoraima* (1931), has been widely performed in Italy.

justment of vocal melody to a continuous symphonic texture; recurring motifs and a carefully worked out key scheme make a formal whole of satisfying proportions. Altogether this opera, with its night-shrouded castle, its lovers swooning in sensual ecstasy, and the tragic figure of the blind Archibaldo, with its music which seems from beginning to end one low cry of voluptuous pain, of delicately scented agony and hopeless fatalism, is an appropriate work with which to close our contemplation of the course of Italian opera at the end of the romantic period: the ripe and languid fruit of a dying age, the sunset of a long and glorious day.

26

German Opera after
Wagner [1]

WAGNER AFFECTED THE COURSE OF LYRIC drama like a new planet hurled into a solar system. The center of the operatic universe shifted; all the old balances were disturbed; regroupings took place, accompanied by erratic movements. These consequences were least marked in Italy, more so in France, and most of all, naturally, in Germany. Yet even there they did not appear quickly. Most of Wagner's contemporary rivals [2] either ignored him or fondly hoped to patch selected details from his system onto the old structure of grand opera. Only Peter Cornelius, with his comic *Barbier von Bagdad* and epic *Cid* (1865), combined a full appreciation of Wagner's achievements with a discriminating independence. Max Bruch's *Loreley* (1863) was a romantic opera of the old nineteenth-century type. [3] Karl Goldmark's *Königin von Saba* ("The Queen of Sheba," 1875), [4] one of the most popular German works of the later nineteenth century, is an agreeable but old-fashioned grand opera in the heavy manner of Meyerbeer, complete with set numbers, ballets, pageantry, and some conventional strokes of oriental color. Goldmark had obviously accepted Wagner as far as *Tannhäuser*, but

1 General bibliography: Schiedermair, *Die deutsche Oper;* R. Louis, *Die deutsche Musik der Gegenwart* (1909); Istel, "German Opera Since Richard Wagner," MQ I (1915) 260–90; *idem, Die moderne Oper* (2d ed., 1923); Bitter, *Die deutsche komische Oper der Gegenwart* (1932); Korngold, *Deutsches Opernschaffen der Gegenwart* (1922); *Monographien moderner Musiker,* ed. Segnitz; Pisk, "Die Moderne: Deutsche: Die Oper," in Adler, *Handbuch* II, 1029–38; Moser, *Geschichte der deutschen Musik* III, 351–451, *passim;* Wellesz, "Opera in the Twentieth Century," in *Grove's Dictionary* (4th ed.), *Supplementary Volume,* pp. 477–88.

2 A list of these forgotten men will be found in Adler, *Handbuch* II, 883–87.

3 Bruch (1838–1920) is best known as a composer of secular oratorios and for his two violin concertos. He wrote two other operas. The libretto of *Die Loreley* was originally intended for Mendelssohn, who apparently composed only three numbers from it.

4 Goldmark (1830–1915) wrote five more operas after *Die Königin von Saba,* but only *Das Heimchen am Herd* ("The Cricket on the Hearth," 1896, after Dickens) was successful. See biographies by Keller and L. Koch, also the composer's own *Erinnerungen.*

he was evidently not acquainted with, or at any rate not at all influenced by, the later style of *Tristan* and the *Ring*.

The composers of comic and popular opera concerned themselves even less with Wagner's dramatic and musical reforms. Thus Hermann Goetz [5] seems to ignore the existence of *Die Meistersinger* in his *Der Widerspenstigen Zähmung* ("The Taming of the Shrew," 1874). This work, like Cornelius' *Barbier*, has never had the wide public success that the clever libretto and Mozartean humor of the music would seem to deserve. Greater popularity was achieved by two other comic operas of the same period: Ignaz Brüll's *Das goldene Kreuz* ("The Golden Cross," 1875),[6] a harmless and pleasant comic opera slightly reminiscent of Auber; and Nessler's *Trompeter von Säckingen* ("The Trumpeter of Säckingen," 1884),[7] an example of *Volksoper,* or "people's opera," with men's choruses, arias, and dances all in the simple, tuneful, sentimental style of nineteenth-century German popular music.

The direct influence of Wagner on German opera began to be felt in the 1880's. It was evidenced by the choice of Germanic, Greek, or Hindu myths as subject matter (often with symbolical overtones and a redemption motive), and in music by the cultivation of the leitmotif system, emphasis on the orchestra, and a harmonic and melodic idiom of an obviously Wagnerian type. (Heinrich Dorn [8] had composed a five-act *Niebelungen* opera in 1854, but neither the poem nor the music had any resemblance to Wagner's *Ring*.) The principal composers of the Wagnerian school in the late nineteenth century were Felix von Weingartner (*Sakuntala,* 1884; *Genesius,* 1892; *Orestes,* a trilogy, 1902), Heinrich Zöllner (*Faust,* 1887; *Der Überfall,* 1895; *Die versunkene Glocke,* "The Sunken Bell," a fairy-tale opera, 1899), and especially August Bungert, whose *Homerische Welt* ("The Homeric World"), consisting of two cycles of six operas in all, was the most ambitious musico-dramatic undertaking since the *Ring* but nevertheless failed to make its way with the public

[5] On Goetz (1840–1876) see biographies by Kreuzhage and Kruse.

[6] Brüll (1846–1907), a close friend of Brahms, studied and taught at Vienna. He composed ten stage works in all.

[7] Viktor Nessler (1841–1890), Alsatian composer and conductor, was active at Strasbourg and Leipzig.

[8] Dorn (1804–1892) composed fourteen stage works and many songs. See his autobiography, *Aus meinem Leben.*

because of appallingly uninteresting music.[9] These composers for the most part followed Wagner in writing their own librettos. Among other Wagnerian works of this period may be mentioned some early operas by composers who later developed a more personal style: Kienzl's *Urvasi* (1886), Schillings' *Ingwelde* (1894), R. Strauss's *Guntram* (1894), Pfitzner's *Arme Heinrich* (1896), and D'Albert's *Kain* (1900).

The inevitable consequence of all this imitation of Wagner was a reaction. Both public and composers, growing tired of more or less feeble repetitions of a style in which Wagner had already said the definitive, final word, were ready for something new, and a way out was discovered quite inadvertently. In 1885 Alexander Ritter [10] had produced a one-act opera *Der faule Hans* ("Lazy Hans"), of a type known in Germany as a *Märchenoper*, that is, a fairy-tale opera. Though this work had no immediate successors, it is of interest as the forerunner of a most important fairy-tale opera which came out in 1893: Humperdinck's *Hänsel und Gretel*.[11] Humperdinck first wrote this music for a play which his sister's children performed at home; made into a full opera, it caught the public fancy to such a degree as to start a whole new school in Germany. People turned with relief from the misty heights of mythology to the homely, familiar, enchanted world of the fairy tale, to subjects like those which their grandparents had enjoyed in the days of Marschner and Lortzing.

---

[9] Weingartner (1863–1942) was known principally as a conductor but was also a prolific composer. His later operas include *Kain und Abel* (1914); *Dame Kobold* (1916); the veristic *Dorfschule* (1920); the comic *Meister Andrea* (1920), with spoken dialogue and separate numbers in early nineteenth-century style; and *Der Apostat* (1938). See his own writings, especially *Die Lehre von der Wiedergeburt des musikalischen Dramas* (1895) and *Lebenserinnerungen*.

Zöllner (b. 1854) was a choral conductor and teacher at Cologne, New York, and Leipzig. He composed ten operas. See essay in Vol. II of Segnitz's *Monographien moderner Musiker*.

Bungert (1845–1915) studied at Cologne and Paris. Besides the operas mentioned (the first cycle, two operas, was not completed) he wrote orchestral and choral works. See Chop, *August Bungert*.

[10] Ritter (1833–1896) was a friend of von Bülow, and married Wagner's niece in 1854. In music he was a disciple of Liszt, his symphonic poems marking a stage between that master and R. Strauss; he is also of importance as a song composer. See von Hausegger, *Alexander Ritter*.

[11] Engelbert Humperdinck (1854–1921) was a pupil of F. Hiller and Rheinberger, a friend of Wagner's, and teacher of many noted opera composers. His most important later works were *Königskinder* ("The Royal Children"), written first in 1898 as incidental music to a play and recast as an opera ten years later, and the comedy opera *Die Heirat wider Willen* ("The Reluctant Marriage," 1905). See biography by O. Besch.

The transition was made easier for intellectuals by the fact that Humperdinck kept up an appearance of loyalty to Wagner. The music of *Hänsel und Gretel* is, in fact, a peculiar mixture of German folk melody and Wagnerian polyphony. Perhaps the texture is too complicated for the subject matter, but if this be a fault, it is one easy to forgive in view of the many musical beauties and the heart-felt, simple emotion of the work. The music brings together many qualities rooted in the affections of Germans over generations: the delightful songs and dances of the children, the idyllic forest scenes, just enough of the supernatural (but with a comic touch), and the chorale-like feeling of the "Evening blessing" melody, which recurs in the finale to the words

> When past bearing is our grief,
> God himself will send relief.

Among the many fairy-tale operas which followed the successful appearance of *Hänsel und Gretel* were Thuille's *Lobetanz* (1898) and *Gugeline* (1901), Klose's *Ilsebill* (1903), Sommer's *Rübezahl* (1904), and two works by Humperdinck's pupil Leo Blech: *Alpenkönig und Menschenfeind* ("Alpine King and Man's Enemy," 1903; revised in 1917 under the title of *Rappelkopf*) and *Aschenbrödel* ("Cinderella," 1905).[12] Here in varying degrees the post-Wagnerian musical idiom was adapted to popular subjects. To this group of composers belongs also Richard Wagner's son Siegfried Wagner,[13] another Humperdinck pupil, whose *Bärenhäuter* (1899) was the first and best of a long series of fairy-tale operas to his own texts, attempt-

[12] Ludwig Thuille (1861–1907) was a pupil of Rheinberger and taught piano and theory at the Munich Conservatory. See biography by Munter.

Friedrich Klose (1862–1942) was Thuille's successor at Munich. A composer in the tradition of Liszt and Wagner, his principal works are choral and orchestral. See biography by Knappe.

Hans Sommer (1837–1922), originally a professor of physics, resigned in 1884 to devote himself to music. He is known as a song composer as well as for his operas. See essay by Stier in Segnitz's *Monographien* I.

Leo Blech (b. 1871) has had a long career as opera conductor in Germany. He composed seven stage works, the best of which was the comedy *Versiegelt* (1908; see below). See biography by W. Jacob.

[13] Siegfried Wagner (1869–1930) was active as conductor and supervisor of the Bayreuth festivals. He composed twelve operas. See his *Erinnerungen;* letters, ed. by Rebois; Glasenapp, *Siegfried Wagner und seine Kunst;* Du Moulin-Eckart, *Wahnfried;* other studies by Pretsch and Daube. (*Der Bärenhäuter* is untranslatable. The story on which it is based will be found under the title "Des Teufels russiger Bruder" in Grimm, *Kinder- und Haus-Märchen* [Berlin, 1815] II, 100–105.)

ing to combine legend, symbolism, and humor in a popular style. None of these composers equaled Humperdinck in either merit or public favor. A genuine school of people's opera appeared in Austria, stemming from Wilhelm Kienzl's *Evangelimann* (1895).[14] Kienzl, like Humperdinck, founded his appeal on the application of the Wagnerian technique to nonheroic subjects, but his texture is less complex than Humperdinck's, and some of his musical material has an equal or even greater folklike flavor (Example 116). *Der Evange-*

DER EVANGELIMANN, Act I

Ex.116.   Kienzl

O Zit-ter-bart, o Zit-ter-bart, o Franz Xa-ve-rius Zit-ter-bart! Du
triffst ja nicht den La-den mehr; die Ku-gel ist für dich zu schwer.

limann is, in fact, a kind of anthology of popular dance and song types, together with sentimental melodies in the style of Nessler, and amusing reminiscences of *Lohengrin, Tristan, Die Meistersinger,* and *Hänsel und Gretel*—all attached to a libretto of the most unashamedly melodramatic-romantic sort. Its popularity in Germany and Austria may be judged by the fact that *Der Evangelimann* had over 5,300 performances in the first forty years of its existence. Closely related to Kienzl's work is that of another Austrian, Julius Bittner,[15]

14 Kienzl (1857–1941) composed songs and chamber music as well as ten operas. His most successful work after *Der Evangelimann* was *Der Kuhreigen* (1911, on a French Revolution subject). He was also noted as an essayist and scholar. Two *Festschriften* (1917, 1937) have been dedicated to him. See his autobiography, *Meine Lebenswanderungen,* and essay by Morold in Segnitz's *Monographien* III (1909). (The personage of the "Evangelimann" has no English equivalent; he is a wandering mendicant who receives alms in return for reading and telling stories from the Scriptures.)

15 Bittner (1874–1939), a graduate in law and for many years a magistrate in Vienna, composed over seventeen stage works (the last in 1935), also orchestral and choral music. See Specht, *Julius Bittner.*

whose operas (to his own texts) are based on a folklike type of melody, alternating closed numbers with declamatory passages and combining sentiment with humor. *Die rote Gred* ("Red-headed Gred," 1907) and *Der Musikant* ("The Musician," 1910) show his characteristic style in purest form; *Der Bergsee* ("The Mountain Lake," 1911) has curious post-Wagnerian reminiscences. *Das höllisch Gold* ("The Infernal Gold," 1916), a humorous miracle play, was his most varied and most popular work. Likewise in the field of people's opera must be noted the Viennese Heuberger's *Barfüssele* (1905) and the Czech Karel Weis's *Polnische Jude* ("The Polish Jew," 1901),[16] both of which were very popular in their day. Finally, we may mention the Viennese operetta in the early twentieth century, represented by Franz Lehár (*Die lustige Witwe*, "The Merry Widow," 1905), Oskar Straus (*Ein Walzertraum*, "A Waltz Dream," 1907; *Der tapfere Soldat*, "The Chocolate Soldier," 1908), and Leo Fall (*Die Dollarprinzessin*, "The Dollar Princess," 1907).[17]

Meanwhile there developed in Germany a more sophisticated type of comic opera, less national in subject matter and going back for musical inspiration either to Cornelius' *Barbier* or Wagner's *Meistersinger*. The most celebrated example of this school, though seldom performed, is Hugo Wolf's *Corregidor* (1896),[18] a sincere and in many respects inspired attempt to create a gay, original German comic opera "without the gloomy, world-redeeming ghost of a Schopenhaurian philosopher in the background." [19] This laudable intention was frustrated by Wolf's long-standing admiration for Wagner's music: the orchestra of *Der Corregidor* is as heavily polyphonic as that

[16] Richard Heuberger (1850–1914) composed three operas, six operettas, two ballets, and numerous choral and orchestral works. See his collected essays, *Musikalische Skizzen* and *Im Foyer*.

Karel Weis (1862–1937) studied and worked chiefly at Prague. Of his many operas and operettas (some in Czech), only *Der polnische Jude* won wide acclaim.

[17] Lehár (b. 1870) was born in Hungary but has lived mostly in Vienna. See biographies by Decsey and Czech.

Straus (b. 1870) studied under Bruch, conducted at many German theatres, and has written much music for Hollywood films. See R. Bizet, *Une Heure . . . avec Oskar Straus*.

Fall (1873–1925) is musically the most interesting of these three composers.

[18] On Wolf (1860–1903) see biographies by Decsey and Newman; also Hellmer, *Der Corregidor*. This, Wolf's only completed opera, was based on a story *El sombrero de tres picos* by P. A. de Alarcón; the same subject was used by Manuel de Falla for a ballet (1919) and by Zandonai for his opera *La farsa amorosa* (1933).

[19] Letter of Wolf to Grohe, 1890. See Istel, "German Opera Since Wagner," MQ I (1915) 278–79.

of *Die Meistersinger,* and the music is full of leitmotifs—a style completely unsuited to Wolf's libretto. Moreover Wolf, like Schubert and Schumann, was not at home in the theatre: his invention seems to have been paralyzed by the requirements of the stage; the music goes from one song to the next like a Liederspiel; neither persons nor situations are adequately characterized. This composer, "who could be so dramatic in the lied, here in the drama remained above all a lyricist." [20] *Der Corregidor,* though not lacking in finely wrought details,[21] was a failure as an opera. Another Spanish subject, from Lope de Vega, was treated by Anton Urspruch in his comic opera *Das Unmöglichste von allem* ("The Most Impossible of All," 1897), with light parlando dialogue and intricate contrapuntal ensembles derived from the style of Mozart. A more spirited and dramatic composer in this field was von Reznicek,[22] whose *Donna Diana* (1894; another Spanish subject) gave promise of a future which was not realized in his next few operas; but with *Ritter Blaubart* ("Knight Bluebeard," 1920), "an eclectic score embodying elements of Italian cantilena style and the technique of French impressionism," [23] he renewed his reputation.

One of the best German comic operas of the later nineteenth century was D'Albert's *Abreise* ("The Departure," 1898), a fine example of swift-moving dialogue with a tuneful, spontaneous, and deftly orchestrated score, somewhat reminiscent of Cornelius. More in the *Meistersinger* idiom were Blech's comic operas *Das war ich* ("That was I," 1902) and the more ambitious *Versiegelt* ("Sealed," 1908); but these, like Wolf's *Corregidor,* suffered from the music being, as a rule, too heavy and polyphonic for the simple librettos. Two other similar comic operas of this period were Schillings' *Pfeifertag* ("The Parliament of Pipers," 1899), and R. Strauss's *Feuersnot* ("The Fire Famine," 1901), the latter an extraordinary combination of humor, eroticism, and autobiography, with music which shows the composer

---

[20] Moser, *Geschichte der deutschen Musik* III, 397.
[21] For instance: the duet "In solchen Abendfeierstunden," Act II; Frasquita's "In dem Schatten meiner Locken" (Act I), a charming song taken from Wolf's earlier *Spanisches Liederbuch;* Lukas's monologue (Act III, sc. 3), the most nearly dramatic music in the opera.
[22] Urspruch (1850–1907) was a pupil of Raff and Liszt. The Austrian Emil Nikolaus Freiherr von Reznicek (1860–1945), an esteemed conductor, wrote eleven operas, nine major symphonic works, a violin concerto, and smaller pieces. See studies by Chop and Specht.
[23] Slonimsky, *Music Since 1900,* p. 209.

in transition from his early Wagnerian style to that of *Salome* and *Elektra*.

Altogether, German comic opera in the late nineteenth- and early twentieth-century period, apart from folk opera, is disappointing. No unified authoritative tradition was evolved, and individual works of talent remained isolated experiments which their composers seemed unable to repeat. The only exceptions, other than Strauss's *Rosenkavalier*, were the comic operas of Wolf-Ferrari, but he was half Italian by birth and more than half Italian by temperament.

One of the most esteemed German opera composers of this period is Hans Pfitzner,[24] a confessed romantic and explicit antimodernist, in whom a musical language deriving fundamentally from Wagner is modified by a more diatonic melody, a certain asceticism of feeling, long dwellings on mystical, subjective moods, and frequently dissonant contrapuntal texture with long-breathed melodic lines (Example 117). Pfitzner's masterpiece, the "musical legend" *Palestrina* (1917), is a romanticized version of the well-known story of the composition of Palestrina's "Pope Marcellus" Mass,[25] motifs from which are incorporated in the score. It does not require any great penetration to perceive that Pfitzner (who in this one instance was his own librettist) has treated the legend with reference to his own position as defender of the ancient, good tradition of music against the modernists and Philistines. This implication, which is not unrelated to the dramatic idea of Wagner's *Meistersinger*, has doubtless been responsible in part for the success which *Palestrina* has had with a large public in Germany—a success which has found little or no echo elsewhere. A more advanced harmonic style and partial return to the form of separate numbers is seen in Pfitzner's most recent opera, *Das Herz* ("The Heart," 1931).

A composer of somewhat similar romantic tendencies, though on a more modest scale, was the Swiss Hans Huber (1852–1921), whose

---

[24] Pfitzner (b. 1869) has composed many songs and choral works as well as operas and has also written many essays on musical subjects (*Gesammelte Schriften*, 3 vols.). The most recent biographies and studies are by Abendroth, Valentin, and Müller-Blattau. See also Dent, "Hans Pfitzner," M&L IV (1923) 119–32; Riezler, *Hans Pfitzner und die deutsche Bühne;* Halusa, *Pfitzners musikdramatisches Schaffen;* studies of separate operas by R. Louis (*Die Rose vom Liebesgarten,* 1901), Hirtler, and Berrsche (*Der arme Heinrich*).
[25] This legend is due to Baini, a nineteenth-century historian. See summary of the historical evidence in *Grove's Dictionary*, art. "Palestrina," and cf. Jeppeson, "Marcellus-Probleme," *Acta Musicologica* XVI/XVII (1944/45) 11–38.

romantic operas had considerable popularity in his own country
(*Die schöne Bellinda,* 1916).

Although the principal musical influence on German opera composers in the early twentieth century was still that of Wagner, there

PALESTRINA, prelude

Ex.117.   Pfitzner

were some reflections of foreign trends. The methods of Italian
verismo and French naturalism are apparent in *Tiefland* ("The Low-
lands," 1903) by Eugen d'Albert,[26] a brutal, realistic drama with an

[26] D'Albert (1864–1932) was born at Glasgow, studied piano under Pauer and Liszt, and
as a virtuoso was famous for his Beethoven interpretations. In addition to twenty operas

extremely effective musical score in which Italian-style parlando recitative alternates with a Puccinian leitmotif technique and Wagnerian harmonies. This was D'Albert's most successful opera, though among his later works the extravagantly theatrical *Die toten Augen* ("The Dead Eyes," 1916), with its cleverly eclectic music, was widely performed. Another German veristic work was Max von Schillings' *Mona Lisa* (1915),[27] murder and melodrama against a Renaissance background, with a modern frame of prologue and epilogue, one of the most popular German operas of the present century. The music lies strongly under the influence of Puccini in melody and instrumentation, and apparently also of early Debussy in the harmony; the score shows a slight tendency toward closed numbers in place of the symphonic continuity of von Schillings' early Wagnerian operas, but the leitmotif still flourishes. Another opera of the German realist school was Waltershausen's *Oberst Chabert* ("Count Chabert," 1912),[28] written in a nonmelodic declamatory style with the dramatic situations underlined by rapidly fluctuating harmonies; the constant alternation of two triads at the interval of an augmented fourth has the effect of a leitmotif.

Impressionism made its mark in Germany with Franz Schreker,[29] whose first opera, *Der ferne Klang* ("The Distant Tone"), was composed 1903–1909, though not performed until 1912. The first notable feature of Schreker's music is the harmony, which basically is like that of Debussy (seventh and ninth chords as consonant units; free use, singly or in combination, of chromatic alteration, pedal points, and organum-like parallel progressions; treatment of sensuous effect as an end for itself). But it is the Debussy of *L'Après-midi*, the *Nocturnes*, and *La Mer* rather than of the subdued *Pelléas et Mélisande* who is Schreker's model. The texture is exceedingly full, often

he composed concertos, orchestral works, piano and chamber music, and songs. See study by Raupp; also Schmitz, "Eugen d'Albert als Opernkomponist," *Hochland* VI, No. 2 (1909) 464–71.

[27] Von Schillings (1868–1933) was assistant conductor at Bayreuth from 1892 and conducted at many other theatres. He composed four operas and a number of choral and orchestral works. See study by Raupp.

[28] Hermann Wolfgang von Waltershausen (b. 1882) composed five operas, but has been most influential in German musical life as a teacher and writer. Some of his writings are listed in the bibliography.

[29] Schreker (1878–1934) was also influential as a teacher (Křenek, Haba, and others). See studies by Bekker, Kapp, and R. S. Hoffmann, also numerous articles in *Anbruch* (especially Jahrg. II, VI, X).

with complicated decorative rhythmic motifs within the beat, or making use of several separated tone masses (as in the opening of Act II of *Der ferne Klang*). All this is, of course, supported by an orchestration of corresponding richness, in which harps, muted strings and horns, glissandi, tremolos, and similar effects are prominent. The feeling of tone impressions (*Klang*) in Schreker's operas is so strong as to lead naturally to a symbolism in which sounds become the embodiment of ideal, mystic forces. There are other signs of the late romantic period as well: occasional Straussian storm and stress in the harmony, reminiscences of Verdi in a melodic line, and traces of Puccini's declamation and orchestral treatment.

The whole, nevertheless, is not mere patchwork but an original and very effective theatrical style which made Schreker, during the war and postwar years, one of the most highly regarded opera composers in Germany. His librettos (written by himself) have been criticized for awkwardness of language and for their preoccupation with sex in exaggerated, pathological forms. *Die Gezeichneten* ("The Stigmatized Ones," 1918), a Renaissance subject, has this feature to an extreme degree. His chief work, *Der Schatzgräber* ("The Treasure Digger," 1920), shows a tendency toward more triadic harmony (with much parallelism) and a somewhat less complicated texture. The leitmotif system is much less prominent here, and in *Irrelohe* (1924) it was abandoned altogether. Meanwhile *Das Spielwerk und die Prinzessin* ("The Playthings and the Princess"), considerably revised in 1920 from its original 1913 form, experimented with pandiatonism and other modern harmonic devices. An even more advanced harmonic idiom is found in the postwar operas of Zemlinsky,[30] though his most important influence has been indirect, through his pupils Arnold Schönberg and E. W. Korngold.

A unique figure in music of the early twentieth century was Ferruccio Busoni,[31] of mixed German and Italian ancestry, one of the

---

[30] Alexander von Zemlinsky (1872–1942) had a distinguished career as conductor and teacher. See special number of *Der Auftakt* (Prague, 1921).

[31] The main biography of Busoni (1866–1924) is by Edward Dent. See also Bekker, *Klang und Eros;* Gatti, "The Stage Works of Ferruccio Busoni," MQ XX (1934) 267–77; "Nota bio-bibliografica su Ferruccio Busoni," RassM XIII (1940) 82–88; and Busoni's *Entwurf einer neuen Aesthetik der Tonkunst, Von der Einheit der Musik* (collected essays), and *Über die Möglichkeiten der Oper.* Busoni wrote all his own librettos. *Turandot* (1917), his only opera not mentioned in the text, was arranged from his earlier incidental music to Gozzi's play.

greatest pianists of his day, a scholar, philosopher, and international figure, reminding one of an artist of the Renaissance in his breadth and clarity of outlook. In his thoroughgoing rejection of Wagner and adherence to the operatic ideals of Mozart, Busoni was an important influence in the neoclassic movement. His first opera, *Die Brautwahl* ("The Bridal Choice," 1912), revives the old principle of set numbers, though the libretto and music still retain many romantic traits. The one-act *Arlecchino* (1917) is an ironical comedy making use of the old commedia dell' arte masks and including some spoken dialogue. Busoni's masterpiece, *Doktor Faust* (completed by Jarnach and posthumously produced in 1925), is, from both the literary and the musical viewpoint, the most significant treatment of this subject in the twentieth century. The highly mystical and symbolical libretto is joined to a score conceived in the same spirit, realized in large forms, worked out with uncompromising musical idealism and logic, but—by reason of these very qualities—lacking the emotional dramatic force which is necessary for wide popular appeal in opera. Professor Dent has said that "one cannot apply to *Doctor Faust* the ordinary standards of operatic criticism. It moves on a plane of spiritual experience far beyond that of even the greatest of musical works for the stage." [32] This may be true; indeed, the more carefully one studies the score the greater his respect for the composer. But, like many another high plane of "spiritual experience," it is sometimes dull for outsiders. The fact remains that the music is so condensed, so completely objective, unromantic, and contrapuntal, so complex and varied in its harmonic tendencies,[33] so remote from the familiar notions of tonality, in short, so remote from all common musical experience, as to prove a stumbling block for any listener who has not prepared himself by a long education in Busoni's peculiar style and aesthetic. Unless this idiom, or one similar to it, becomes an important part of our general musical background, *Doktor Faust* is all too likely to remain a book of wisdom written in a language few can understand and none translate.

[32] *Ferruccio Busoni,* p. 304.
[33] The music is not atonal, but tonality is nearly always blurred by one or more of the following devices: pandiatonic chords, parallelism, dissonances against pedal points or ostinato motives, linear dissonant counterpoint, modality and organum-like chords, cross relations, atonal melodies (often including octave transposition of single notes in the line), and polytonal chord combinations.

If we now summarize the course of German opera from the death of Wagner to the end of the First World War, we find that the period begins with imitations of the master in almost every detail; but soon there appear various branches, in which the basic Wagnerian musical idiom, the leitmotif technique, and the Gesamtkunstwerk aesthetic are still for the most part retained but applied to different subject matters: the fairy-tale (Humperdinck), realistic drama (D'Albert, von Schillings), or comedy (Wolf, Blech). A modification of the harmonic idiom comes with Schreker's impressionism, while Pfitzner continues in the romantic path. There is a more or less unconscious revolt against Wagner in the Volksoper and operetta, a revolt manifest in both subjects and musical style. As we approach the 1920's, we note that the gradual emancipation from Wagner is marked by one or more of the following signs: (1) thoroughgoing adoption of a neoclassical or other antiromantic idiom, (2) abandonment of the leitmotif system, and (3) return to the old principle of the number opera with set musical forms (Busoni, and the later works of von Schillings, Pfitzner, and Schreker). We now turn our attention to the composer in whose works this entire evolution is embodied, the most important representative of German opera in the early twentieth-century period, Richard Strauss.[34]

Strauss was already famous for his symphonic poems before he attracted world-wide notice with his third opera, Salome (1905), the libretto of which is a German translation of Oscar Wilde's drama (written originally in French). The peculiar blend of oriental sensuousness and decadent luxuriance of horror offered by this text has been perfectly caught in Strauss's music. The power of emotional expressiveness shown by Wagner in depicting the agonies of Amfortas is displayed to an equal degree by Strauss in the final scene of Salome in the musical treatment of a form of sexual perversion (necrophilism) not commonly found in opera. There is no need either to apologize for or to condemn the subject; in a work of art, morality is a matter of taste. The only relevant point is that Strauss deals with the scene successfully. It is but one instance of his amazing skill in musical characterization. Formally, Salome is in the Wag-

34 The principal biography of Richard Strauss (b. 1864) is by R. Specht. There are biographies in English by Newman (1908) and Finck (1917). On the operas more particularly see E. Schmitz, Richard Strauss als Musikdramatiker; Hübner, Richard Strauss und das Musikdrama; and Gregor, Richard Strauss.

nerian style: the orchestra is dominant, the music is continuous (in one act), there is a system of leitmotifs, the texture is uniformly thick and polyphonic, the rhythms are nonperiodic, and the voice parts are mostly of an arioso character. Strauss's mastery of orchestral effect, the individuality and variety of his instrumental coloring, are as evident in the operas as in the symphonic poems. His harmony, which sounded so daring and dissonant at the turn of the century, is no longer novel, but just for this reason we can now better appreciate how appropriate it is for the dramatic purposes. Technically it may be regarded as a continuation of Wagner, with progressions generally conditioned by chromatic voice leading but less bound up with romantic expressiveness, more remote and sudden in its modulations, and much more dissonant. It is a type of harmony which assumes a familiarity with Wagner on the listener's part, and which as it were telescopes the characteristic Wagner progressions in a manner analogous to the treatment of a fugue subject in stretto. (We have already noticed a similar evolution from the Verdi melodic style in Puccini's operas.) The melodies in *Salome* are of two sorts: either declamatory, with many unusual intervals rising out of the harmonic progressions, or else long-sustained, impassioned outpourings, marked by a very wide range and wide leaps. Strauss has managed to combine the characteristics of the music drama with the striking dramatic quality of the Italian verismo and to introduce also some features of grand opera (for example, the Dance of the Seven Veils).

All the characteristics of *Salome* are pushed to an extreme in *Elektra* (1909, with libretto by von Hofmannsthal [35]). Here the central passion is Elektra's insane thirst for vengeance on the murderers of her father, and here again Strauss has matched the somber horrors of the libretto with music of fearful dissonance, lurid melodramatic power, and a harmonic idiom in which for long stretches polytonality is the normal state, becoming at times in effect completely atonal. Perhaps the most noticeable feature of the score is the contrast between this dissonant idiom and the occasional stretches of lush, late-romantic sentimentality, with cloying sevenths, ninths, chromatic alterations,

[35] Hugo von Hofmannsthal (1874–1929) also wrote for Strauss the librettos of *Der Rosenkavalier, Ariadne auf Naxos, Die Frau ohne Schatten* (1921) and *Die aegyptische Helena* (1928). See F. Strauss, *Richard Strauss Briefwechsel mit Hugo von Hofmannsthal;* Holländer, "Hugo von Hofmannsthal als Opernlibrettist," *Zeitschrift für Musik* XCVI (1929) 551–54; Krüger, *Hugo von Hofmannsthal und Richard Strauss.*

and suspensions. Whatever the composer's intentions may have been, these portions give the final dreadful touch of spiritual abnormality to the whole action; they are like something familiar suddenly seen in a ghastly, strange light.

Der Rosenkavalier ("The Cavalier of the Rose," 1911), Strauss's best and most successful opera, is a pleasant comedy of Viennese life in the time of Maria Theresa (*ca.* 1750). It is an ideal libretto, with humor, farce, sentiment, swiftly moving action, variety of scenes, and superb characterizations. The music is as varied as the drama. In some portions it is no less complex (though considerably less dissonant) than that of *Salome* and *Elektra*. The erotic quality of the love music in the first part of Act I is equal to Strauss's best in this familiar vein. For the most part, however, the style of *Der Rosenkavalier* is relatively simple and tuneful. The famous waltzes are anachronistic; the waltzes of Schubert, Lanner, and J. Strauss, which these imitate, were not, of course, a feature of eighteenth-century Vienna. But this is of little importance, and it is still less important that Strauss has seen fit to decorate the waltz themes with some of his own characteristic harmonic twists. The best musical characterizations are those of the Princess, a near-tragic figure, and Baron Ochs, the perfect type of comic boor. The music of Octavian and Sophie is music of situations and general sentiment rather than of personalities, but it is none the less fine on that account. The scene of the presentation of the silver rose and the following short duet (near the beginning of Act II) is one of the most beautiful passages in all opera. It is remarkable that here Strauss writes in an almost purely diatonic idiom, even emphasizing the triads by outlining them in the melodies; one of the composer's happiest inspirations, the theme of the silver rose (high, dissonant appoggiatura triads with celesta, flutes, harps, and three solo violins), tinkles against this background. The ensembles are virtuoso creations, particularly the scene of the levee in Act I: a dissolution and at the same time an apotheosis of the eighteenth-century opera buffa ensemble, bringing together all the elements of this form in seeming confusion and with complete realism. The introduction of a stylized Italian aria (compare the old interpolated number in opera) is accomplished in the spirit of sporting with the formal technique. The ensemble of Act II is less elaborate, but the first two-thirds of Act III is really one long ensemble of broad farcical nature, laid on musically with a rather heavy hand perhaps, but of an irresistible comic dash which can only be compared to the similar scenes in *Die Meistersinger* (end of Act II) and *Falstaff* (end of Act III). After all this hurly-burly follows one of those transformations of mood which are so characteristic of *Der Rosenkavalier*. The trio for three soprano voices (Sophie, Princess, Octavian) [36] is another superlative number, a luxurious and melting texture of long-spun, expressive, interweaving lines above a comparatively simple harmonic basis. The long decrescendo continues: the last song is a duet in G major, two strophes of a simple lyric melody in thirds and sixths, in the style of the old German Singspiel. The themes of the silver rose and the lovers' first meeting sound once more. The opera closes with a pantomime of the Princess's little negro pageboy, to the same music which was heard at his first appearance near the beginning of Act I.[37]

Der Rosenkavalier was hardly finished before Strauss and von Hofmannsthal were at work on their next collaborative effort, *Ariadne auf Naxos* (1912), designed as a pendant to a German version of Molière's *Bourgeois Gentilhomme*. This one-act piece, which von Hofmannsthal considered one of his "most characteristic productions," [38] is a profoundly poetic and sensitive treatment of the myth of Ariadne and Bacchus, in form and spirit suggesting the pastorales and ballets of Lully and Molière, which were likewise usually enclosed within a comedy; [39] like these models, it introduces comic-satirical elements through personages borrowed from the Italian commedia dell' arte. Strauss's music continues the trend toward diatonism and simplicity already evident in *Der Rosenkavalier;* harmonically, it starts from the point which the composer had reached in the silver-rose scene of the earlier opera and becomes progressively less and less chromatic. There is a trio in scene 3 for three sopranos,

[36] Octavian's part is a "trouser role"—a man's part sung by a woman; this practice, fairly frequent in nineteenth-century opera, is an interesting historical survival of the castrato hero roles of earlier days.

[37] The whole masterly finale of Act III was largely shaped by Strauss's suggestions. Von Hofmannsthal at one time feared it would be feeble in effect, but Strauss wrote "It is precisely at the end that the composer, when he has found the right idea, can get his best and loftiest effects—on a matter of this kind you may safely leave it to me to judge. . . I will guarantee the end of the act . . . if you will be answerable for the other portions." (Letter, Sept. 7, 1910; in *Correspondence*, pp. 86–87.)

[38] Letter of Dec. 18, 1911 (*Correspondence*, p. 144).

[39] The analogy will be seen most clearly by comparison with the following works of Molière: *La Princesse d'Elide* (1664), *Psyché* (a *tragédie-ballet*, 1671), the pastorale in *La Comtesse d'Escarbagnas* (1671) and the pastoral *intermèdes* in *Georges Dandin* (1668) and *Le Malade imaginaire* (1673), music by M.-A. Charpentier.

similar to the trio in the last act of *Der Rosenkavalier* and likewise followed by a simple folklike song. A new element is the light, swift, parlando style of the comic scenes and of the prologue which was added in 1916 when *Ariadne* was taken out of its original setting in the Molière play. One role (Zerbinetta) is especially written for a high coloratura soprano. The leitmotif technique is used to a slight extent, but the orchestra (only thirty-six players) is subordinated to the voices, and there is a distinct tendency toward division into separate numbers.

Ariadne auf Naxos is the definitive stage of Strauss's conversion to a Mozartean style, an intimate opera in which the musical idiom is refined to classic purity in comparison with the earlier works. From this point on, Strauss became musically conservative. He had summed up in his own creative career the transition from Wagnerian music drama to the postwar, anti-Wagnerian opera. "I give you my word I have now definitely cast off the whole armour of Wagner forever more." [40] But the flame of inspiration no longer burned so brightly; most of his later operas had little more than a *succès d'estime,* even in Germany. Perhaps the best of them are the comedies *Intermezzo* (1924, text by the composer) and *Arabella* (1933). The former is notable for Strauss's conscious attempt to lighten the orchestral texture and make a precise distinction between recitative and cantilena styles in the singing in order to make the words clearer; perhaps by way of compensation, there are important symphonic interludes. *Arabella* combines an operetta-like libretto with attractive and melodious music which is more than once reminiscent of *Der Rosenkavalier.* *Die Frau ohne Schatten* ("The Woman without a Shadow," 1919) and *Die aegyptische Helena* ("The Egyptian Helen," 1928) are serious works, though less complex musically than *Salome* or *Elektra. Die schweigsame Frau* ("The Silent Woman," 1935, libretto by Stefan Zweig) [41] is in the manner of Italian opera buffa. There is not one of these works but has its moments of genius; any of them might have been hailed with applause in the composer's earlier days, but they had nothing new to say to the postwar generation. The same holds even more strongly for *Friedenstag, Daphne* (both 1938), and *Das Liebe der Danae* (1945).

40 Letter to von Hofmannsthal, August, 1916; *Correspondence,* p. 291.
41 See Mathis, "Stefan Zweig as Librettist," M&L XXV (1944) 163–76, 226–45.

27

National Opera in Russia and Other Countries

THE SECOND HALF OF THE NINETEENTH century saw the rise of independent schools of composition in many coun-tries which had previously been only tributary to the chief musical nations of Europe, or which, like Spain and England, had been for a long time in an inferior position. In the growth of musical national-ism opera played an important part. The use of characteristic na-tional subjects, often from patriotic motives, stimulated composers to seek an equally characteristic national expression in their music. National operas, as a rule, were not exportable; only exceptionally (as in the case of some Russian operas) did these works make their way into foreign countries. Nevertheless, they are an important fea-ture of the history of opera in the late nineteenth- and early twentieth-century period. It is the purpose of the present chapter to survey the development of these national schools.

RUSSIA.[1]—There was no native opera in Russia before the end of the eighteenth century. In the late medieval period there were reli-gious mystery plays, and in the seventeenth-century biblical school dramas with incidental music. The first public theatre was opened at St. Petersburg in 1703, giving for the most part foreign plays brought in by way of Germany, with some use of incidental music. There are records of Italian opera at the court from 1735, but the

---

[1] Bibliography (chief works in English): Newmarch, *The Russian Opera;* Montagu-Nathan, *History of Russian Music;* Sabaneiv's *History of Russian Music* is available in German; his *Modern Russian Composers* (tr. Joffe) contains little that bears directly on opera but is nevertheless valuable. See also Mooser, *L'Opéra-comique français en Rus-sie au XVIIIᵉ siècle.* Most important are the following recent books: Calvocoressi and Abraham, *Masters of Russian Music* (1936; contains bibliography of Russian periodicals and books); Abraham, *Studies in Russian Music* and *On Russian Music.*

Titles in this section are given only in English translation. Transliteration of names and titles usually follows that of Baker's *Biographical Dictionary of Musicians,* 4th ed. (1940). Works in Russian are not included in the bibliographies unless translations in English, French, German, or Italian exist.

heyday of Italian opera in Russia came under Catherine II ("The Great," reigned 1762–1796) when Galuppi, Paisiello, Cimarosa, Salieri, and others sojourned at St. Petersburg for varying lengths of time. Already in the eighteenth century a few native composers had begun to write operas on national subjects and occasionally introduced national melodies, but these were amateur affairs of no importance. The upsurge of national spirit under Alexander I (reigned 1801–1825), imbued in Russia as elsewhere with the spirit of Byron's romanticism, encouraged such productions. Curiously, one of the earliest composers of national Russian opera was a versatile Neapolitan, Catterino Cavos (1776–1840), who same to St. Petersburg near the end of the eighteenth century and remained for the rest of his life. He composed, to Russian, French, or Italian texts, over forty operas, including *Ivan Susanin* (1815; same subject as Glinka's *Life for the Czar*) and *The Firebird* (1822). Among the Russian composers of this period was A. N. Verstovsky,[2] some of whose operas (*Askold's Grave*, 1835; *Thunder*, 1857) held the stage in Russia almost to the end of the century.

Essentially in the same native dilettante tradition was Glinka's *Life for the Czar* (1836),[3] from which the Russian national school of opera is usually dated. It is on account of its story, which became a focal point for patriotic feeling, and on account of its immense popularity that *A Life for the Czar* holds this position. Its music is unexpectedly lacking in strongly national qualities; the material for the most part is as much French or Italian as Russian. The melody of the Bridal Chorus in Act III (Example 118) is as close as Glinka

A LIFE FOR THE CZAR, Act III

Ex.118.   Glinka

2 Alexiey Nikolaievitch Verstovsky (1799–1862) was inspector and later manager of the imperial theatres in Moscow, where all of his eight operas were first produced. See Findeisen, "Die Entwickelung der Tonkunst in Russland," SIMG II (1900–1901) 279–302.

3 On Michail Ivanovich Glinka (1804–1857) see biographies by Calvocoressi and Montagu-Nathan, also von Riesemann's *Monographien zur russischen Musik;* bibliography by Inch.

comes to the folk-song idiom in this opera,[4] though the choral theme
of the epilogue so took hold of popular fancy as to become almost a
second national anthem. There is compensation for the undistinguished quality of much of the music in the clear and varied
orchestration, which was a model for all the later Russian nationalists,
including Rimsky-Korsakov. Moreover, in the extensive use of leitmotifs Glinka was far in advance of any opera composer before
Wagner. The Polish soldiers, for example, are characterized by
themes in the national dance rhythms of polonaise and mazurka,
which, first heard in the ball scene of Act II, recur in Act III at the
entrance of the Poles, and the mazurka rhythm again at their appearance in Act IV. The quasi-folk-song theme of the opening chorus
is used as a leitmotif of Russian heroism, sung by the hero Susanin
in Act III as he defies the Polish conspirators; the opposing national
motifs are again contrasted in the orchestral introduction to the
epilogue. Susanin's last aria (Act IV) is to a large extent made up
of previously heard themes, the recurrences here producing a pur-
poseful dramatic effect. The theme of the final chorus, repeated again
and again with cumulative power, has been subtly prepared by two
or three statements earlier in the opera. This brilliant epilogue is
not only the climax of patriotic emotion but also of the highly colored
mass effect of sound and spectacle so beloved in Russian opera.

Although *A Life for the Czar* was more popular, the real musical
foundations for the future were laid in Glinka's second and last
opera, *Russlan and Ludmilla* (1842). The libretto, a fantastic and
incoherent fairy tale, is adapted from a poem of Pushkin. In spite
of some traces of Weber, the music is much more original than in
Glinka's earlier opera, and the musical characterizations are more
definite. The leitmotif system is abandoned; almost the only recurring motif is the descending whole-tone scale associated with the
wicked magician Chernomor.[5] There are at least five distinct styles
or procedures characteristic of all later Russian music which appear
in *Russlan and Ludmilla:* (1) the heroic, broad, solemn, declamatory
style, with modal suggestions and archaic effect (introduction and
song of the Bard, Act I); (2) the Russian lyrical style, with expressive
melodic lines of a folkish cast, delicately colored harmony featuring

---

[4] There are folk-song quotations in the opening of Susanin's aria, No. 3, and in the
accompaniment to Susanin's last two solo passages at the end of Act IV.
[5] This is said to be the earliest use in European music of the whole-tone scale.

the lowered sixth or raised fifth, and chromatically moving inner voices (Fina's ballad and Russlan's first aria in Act II); (3) expression of fantastic occurrences by means of unusual harmonies, such as whole-tone passages or chord progressions pivoting about one note (scene of Ludmilla's abduction, toward the end of Act I); (4) oriental atmosphere, sometimes using genuine oriental themes (Persian chorus at opening of Act III), sometimes manufactured melodies (Ratmir's romance, Act V), but always characterized by fanciful arabesque figures in the accompaniment and a languorous harmony and orchestration; (5) the vividly colored choruses and dances, with glittering instrumentation and often daring harmonies (chorus in honor of Lel, finale of Act I; Chernomor's march and following dances, especially the *lezginka*, finale of Act IV)—models for such scenes in Borodin's *Prince Igor,* Rimsky-Korsakov's *Sadko,* and even Stravinsky's *Sacre du Printemps.*

Almost the only Russian opera of any importance for twenty years after *Russlan and Ludmilla* was Dargomyzhsky's *Russalka* (1856),[6] likewise on a text from Pushkin and somewhat similar in subject to Glinka's work. Musically, however, it was inferior to *Russlan;* its best feature was the realistic declamation of the recitative, which Dargomyzhsky proceeded to develop to the highest degree in his last opera, *The Stone Guest.* This work (a setting of Pushkin's Don Juan drama) was completed after Dargomyzhsky's death by Cui, orchestrated by Rimsky-Korsakov, and first performed in 1872. It is no masterpiece and never had a popular success, but it was influential on later Russian opera because of the composer's attempt to write the entire work (except for some songs near the beginning of Act II) in a melodic recitative, a vocal line which should be in every detail the equivalent of the words. The result, though accurate in declamation and dramatic in some places, lacks sharp characterization or melodic interest, and there is no compensation for the melodic poverty in the orchestral part, which is conceived as accompaniment rather than a continuous symphonic tissue. In his repudiation of set musical forms and high respect for the words, Dargomyzhsky may have been influenced to a slight degree by Wag-

6 Alexander Sergievitch Dargomyzhsky (1813–1869) wrote four operas (one uncompleted) and numerous minor works, as well as several orchestral pieces which were very popular in Russia. See works mentioned in general bibliography above; there are no separate studies in English.

ner's theories, though there is no trace of Wagner in the musical substance itself. Harmonically there is some interest in Dargomyzhsky's use of whole-tone scale fragments as leitmotifs for the Statue (Example 119), and some passages constructed entirely on this scale.

Dargomyzhsky had arrived in his own way at certain features of the

THE STONE GUEST, Act II

Ex.119

Allegro molto

Dargomyzhsky

Wagnerian music drama. The most explicit and self-conscious disciple of Wagner in Russia was Serov,[7] whose first opera, *Judith* (1863), shows the composer's admiration for all the methods of grand opera of the Meyerbeer and early Wagner type. In his third and last opera, *The Power of Evil* (completed by N. T. Soloviev and first produced in 1871), Serov aimed "to embody the Wagnerian theories in a music drama written in Russian, on a Russian subject," and to keep "more closely than has yet been done [sic] to the forms of Russian popular music, as preserved unchanged in our folksongs." [8] The result, however, was a disappointing hybrid, full of striking but superficial effects. Serov's operas received little regard from musicians but were nevertheless popular enough with the public to remain in the repertory of Russian opera companies until the First World War.

From about the middle of the nineteenth century, Russian musicians were sharply divided into two groups. In one were the professional, foreign-trained, and officially supported composers who were not primarily interested in musical nationalism but wished to see Russian musical life develop along the same lines as in western Europe, particularly Germany. The head of this school was Anton Rubinstein,[9] founder and first director (1862–1867) of the Imperial Conservatory at St. Petersburg. Of Rubinstein's nineteen operas (eight on Russian and eleven on German texts), *The Demon* (1875) had a considerable success, both in Russia and abroad. It is on a libretto which strongly recalls Wagner's *Fliegende Holländer*, but the forms are conventional and the musical style is that of pre-Wagnerian romanticism mingled with some oriental elements. A more vital and varied, though less popular, opera was *The Merchant Kalashnikov* (1880). Rubinstein's biblical operas, or rather stage oratorios (for example, *Die Makkabäer*, "The Maccabees," 1875), are remembered now only for a few separate numbers.

The leading opera composer of the nonnationalist school in Russia in the late nineteenth century was Tchaikovsky,[10] in whom Slavic

7 Alexander Nikolaievitch Serov (1820–1871) was a lecturer, teacher, and essayist as well as a composer. See von Riesemann, *Monographien* I.

8 Quoted in Newmarch, *The Russian Opera*, p. 157.

9 Rubinstein (1829–1894) was a celebrated concert pianist and prolific composer (orchestral, chamber, piano, and vocal music). See his Memoirs (in German translation by E. Kretschmann as *Erinnerungen*); Bowen, *Free Artist* (life of A. Rubinstein and his brother Nikolai).

10 On Peter Ilyitch Tchaikovsky (1840–1893) see his *Diaries* (English tr., 1945), biographies by Newmarch and Evans, also Bowen and von Meck, *"Beloved Friend."*

temperament and German training were leavened by a distinct lyrical gift and a lively appreciation of Italian opera and French ballet. Reckoned by bulk, if not also by musical excellence, Tchaikovsky's achievement is as important in the field of opera as in that of the symphony. After two early works [11] in which he experimented with the then fashionable nationalism, he produced his masterpiece, *Eugen Onegin,* at Moscow in 1879. In both the libretto (after Pushkin) and the musical style this is an old-fashioned romantic opera, but the music is in Tchaikovsky's happiest vein, with lyrical, graceful melodies, expressive harmonies, transparent and imaginative orchestration—true and living in expression without any of the hysterical emotionalism of some of the later works (such as the Fifth and Sixth symphonies). The character of the heroine, Tatiana, is delineated with especial sympathy, and that of Onegin himself is scarcely less vivid. The ballet music (particularly the waltz in Act II) is tuneful and charming, as are also the choruses in Act I. Tchaikovsky's next three operas were in a more heavily dramatic style. *The Maid of Orleans* (1881, libretto after Schiller) was less successful than *Mazeppa* (1884, from a poem of Pushkin), which contains two of the composer's finest dramatic moments: the monologue of Kochubey and the extremely pathetic final scene. *The Enchantress* (1887) had such a disappointing reception that Tchaikovsky returned to his more characteristic lyrical medium for his last two operatic works: *The Queen of Spades* (1890), his most popular opera next to *Onegin,* and *Iolanthe* (1892). In *The Queen of Spades,* based on a melodramatic tale of Pushkin, Tchaikovsky attained a more nearly perfect balance than in any of his other operas between dramatic declamation, lyrical expressiveness, and divertissement music (see especially the ballets in Act II).

The struggle for Russian national music, begun by Glinka and Dargomyzhsky, was carried on after 1860 by a group of five composers: Balakirev, Cui, Mussorgsky, Borodin, and Rimsky-Korsakov. All were amateurs; only Rimsky-Korsakov—and he only at a comparatively late stage of his career—ever had a thorough conventional technical training in composition. Balakirev wrote no operas. Cui [12]

---

[11] *The Guardsman* (1874) and *Vakula the Smith* (1876); the latter is known in a later version as *The Little Slippers* and also as *Oxana's Caprice.* There were two still earlier operas which Tchaikovsky destroyed.

[12] Cesar Antonovitch Cui (1835–1918) was a military engineer by profession. He studied

wrote ten, but most of them are not Russian in subject, none are Russian in musical style, and, with the possible exception of *William Ratcliffe* (1869) they are unimportant from any point of view. The Russian national opera in its highest development, therefore, is the work of the remaining three composers of the "mighty five."

The lack of the usual technical musical education (which meant, at this time, a German conservatory training) had the advantage of turning the nationalist composers to the resources of their own country for dramatic and musical material, and to their own instincts and national traditions for the means of shaping this material into operatic form. These conditions were especially important for Mussorgsky,[13] the most individual genius of the group. In *Boris Godunov* (1874) Mussorgsky created one of the great masterpieces of nineteenth-century opera, a monument of much that is most typical in Russian musical drama and at the same time an absolutely personal, inimitable work. *Boris Godunov* was first composed in 1868–1869 and rewritten in 1871–1872. In 1896 Rimsky-Korsakov prepared a thoroughly revised version, with "corrections" of the harmony, improvements in the orchestration, a different order of scenes, and many cuts; the deleted portions were restored in a second revision (1908), and in this form the opera made its way into the repertory of all foreign opera houses. After the revolution of 1918 the composer's own score was revived for performances in Russia, and both his original and recast versions were published in 1928. In 1941 another revision, with new orchestration, was made by Shostakovitch.

The libretto of *Boris Godunov* was prepared by Mussorgsky himself; its sources were Pushkin's drama of the same title and N. M. Karamzin's *History of the Russian Empire*. The character of the half-mad emperor Boris (reigned 1598–1605), especially as sung and acted by the late Feodor Chaliapin, is one of the most vivid and moving in all opera. Yet an equally potent force in the action is the cruel, anonymous mass of the Russian people—a force visibly present in

---

music with the Polish composer Moniuszko and with Balakirev. In addition to operas he wrote many orchestral suites, chamber works, and short pianoforte pieces. He completed Mussorgsky's opera *The Fair at Sorochinsk* in 1917. His *Musique en Russie* (publ. 1880) is the source of many errors concerning the Russian national school.
[13] On Mussorgsky (1839–1881) see biographies by Calvocoressi, Montagu-Nathan, and von Riesemann; also Godet, *En Marge de Boris Godounof*; Abraham, "Moussorgsky's *Boris* and Pushkin's," *M&L* XXVI (1945) 31–38.

the mighty crowd scenes but also invisibly working like the relentless pressure of Fate at every step toward the catastrophe of the drama. With grim poetic vision Mussorgsky set this primeval force in the closing scene of the opera [14] over against the figure of the Idiot Boy, who, left alone at the last on a darkened stage, keens his lament: "Weep, ye people; soon the foe shall come, soon the gloom shall fall; woe to our land; weep, Russian folk, weep, hungry folk!" One senses in such scenes the influence of the democratic ideals prevalent in Russia during the sixties and seventies in the period after the liberation of the serfs under Alexander II, ideals so eloquently expounded in the writings of Tolstoy. In comparison to the elemental power of most of Mussorgsky's opera, the love episode (Act III) seems both dramatically and musically a pale diversion (as does most of the love interest in Russian opera generally). In form, *Boris Godunov* is a series of detached scenes rather than a coherently developed plot; it thus illustrates the Russian habit, in both musical and literary creation (compare Tolstoy's *War and Peace*), of complete absorption in the present moment, leaving the total impression to be achieved by the cumulative impact of many separate effects.

The most striking feature of Mussorgsky's music is the way in which, in the declamation, the melodic line always manages to convey the emotion of the text in the most direct, compressed, and forcible manner imaginable. Perhaps the best examples of this are the two most familiar scenes of the opera, the last part of Act II (including the "clock scene") and the farewell and death of Boris in Act IV.[15] Here Mussorgsky realized the supreme ideal of dramatic, semi-melodic recitative, which Glinka had foreshadowed in *Russlan and Ludmilla* and which Dargomyzhsky had sought in *The Stone Guest*. Much of the same gloomy power, though with less violence, is displayed in the monastery scene at the beginning of Act I. A more songful idiom, equally characteristic of the composer, is heard in the first part of the Inn scene (Act I, scene 2). Still more characteristic are the children's songs in the first part of Act II—examples of a psychological insight and musical style in which Mussorgsky is almost unique, and which he had demonstrated in his song cycle *The*

<hr>

[14] References are to Mussorgsky's 1874 version, piano-vocal score published by J. & W. Chester, Ltd., London, cop. 1926.

[15] The music of the latter scene, like several other numbers in *Boris*, was adapted from an early opera of Mussorgsky's, *Salammbô* (composed 1863–1865).

Nursery (composed 1870–1872). It is to be noted that in all these songs—declamatory or lyrical—the melodic line is the guiding factor. It is a style of melody which, with its peculiar intervals (especially the falling fourth at cadences), monotonous reiteration of patterns, irregularity of phrase structure, and archaic, modal basis, has grown most intimately out of Russian folk-song. To this melodic line the harmony is generally a mere added support, but it is likewise of a strongly personal type,[16] blended of modal feeling, impressionistic (often childlike) fondness for the mere sound of certain combinations, an unconventional harmonic training, and (at least, so one suspects) the happy outcome of improvisation at the piano. While it remains relatively consonant, and far from any suspicion of atonality, nevertheless any effort to analyze a really typical passage of Mussorgsky according to the principles of textbook harmony will show how completely foreign his methods were to the conventional practice of the nineteenth century. Not unrelated to the naïveté of his harmonic effects is Mussorgsky's reveling in brilliant, crude, and massive effects of color. This trait is seen most clearly in the great crowd scene of the coronation, the orchestral introduction of which is also an example of the frequent Russian mannerism of alternating chords pivoting on one common tone (in this case A-flat^7 and D^7 on the common tone G-flat = F-sharp). The chorus itself in this scene is built on the same folk tune which Beethoven used in his second "Razumovsky" Quartet.

Of Mussorgsky's other operas the principal one is *Khovantchina* (1896, libretto by Strassov). This work is, if possible, even more intensely national in subject and musical style than *Boris Godunov* but less concentrated dramatically and less unified in total musical effect. Its finest numbers are the orchestral prelude, the aria of Shaklovity in Act III, and some of the choruses of the Old Believers, in which Mussorgsky has distilled the whole spirit of the ancient Russian church style (Example 120).

The cardinal aesthetic principle of Mussorgsky was the search for realistic expression at any cost: "truth before beauty." To this end, he avoided conventional formulae, evolving a style which is as restrained, economical, and as incapable of successful imitation as that of Debussy. By temperament, he was led to depict predominantly

[16] Cf. Calvocoressi, "Moussorgsky's Musical Style," MQ XVIII (1932) 530–46.

that side of the Russian character which gives itself over to gloom and mysticism, to the emotions of violence, brutality, and madness which dominate *Boris Godunov*. A totally different, though no less normal,

KHOVANTCHINA. Act V

Ex.120   Mussorgsky

aspect of the national personality comes to life in Borodin's *Prince Igor* (1890).[17] The libretto is by the composer, after a plan by Stassov;

[17] Alexander Porfirievitch Borodin (1833–1887) was a professor of chemistry; his principal teacher in music was Balakirev. He wrote two operas, three symphonies, chamber music, and songs. See Habets, *Borodin and Liszt;* Abraham, *Borodin*.

the score, unfinished at Borodin's death, was completed by Glazounov and Rimsky-Korsakov and orchestrated by the latter. The story is taken from a medieval Russian epic (apparently genuine, though long suspected to be an eighteenth-century forgery), but the central plot is of little importance except to give occasion for the many episodic scenes which make up most of the opera. Some of these scenes are comic in style, others are love scenes, but an exceptionally large place is reserved for spectacle, dances, and choruses (for example, the well-known Polovtsian ballets in Act II). The musical ancestor of *Prince Igor* is Glinka's *Russlan and Ludmilla,* and its principal descendant is Rimsky-Korsakov's *Sadko.* The style of *Prince Igor* is predominantly lyric, with many of the arias in conventional Italian forms; there is some arioso writing, but little dramatic recitative in the manner of Dargomyzhsky. Indeed, the music is not dramatic at all in the sense in which *Boris Godunov* is dramatic; it does not so much embody a drama as present a series of musical tableaux to accompany and complete the stage pictures.[18] In technical details also it is less unconventional than Mussorgsky; the most original portions are the oriental scenes, for which Borodin evolved an idiom partly based on Central Asiatic themes but fundamentally an outgrowth of his eighteen-year-long absorption in the subject and study of all available musical and historical material. His ancestry (he was the illegitimate son of a Caucasian prince) may also have given him a particular bent toward this style which, with its persistent rhythmic patterns, chromatic intervals, and melodic arabesques, dominates the second and third acts of the opera. *Prince Igor,* like *Boris Godunov,* makes some use of leitmotifs, but a more important source of unity is the derivation, unobtrusive but unmistakable, of many of the themes of Acts II and III from phrases in the melody of the first Polovtsian chorus.[19]

If *Boris Godunov* represents a darkly fanatical aspect of the Russian character and *Prince Igor* a cheerful, hearty one, then the picture is completed by Rimsky-Korsakov,[20] whose most characteristic operas

[18] Abraham, *Studies in Russian Music,* p. 128.   [19] *Ibid.,* pp. 132–41.
[20] Nikolai Andreyevitch Rimsky-Korsakov (1844–1908) served as an officer in the Russian Navy before devoting himself entirely to music. He studied counterpoint by himself after his appointment as professor of instrumentation and composition at the St. Petersburg Conservatory in 1871. See his memoirs, *My Musical Life,* one of the principal sources of our knowledge about the Russian nationalists. His *Principles of Orchestration* is a standard treatise. See also Gilse van der Pals, *N. A. Rimsky-Korssakow, Opernschaffen.*

reflect a fairy-tale world of fantasy, romance, and innocent humor. This individual musical and dramatic style of Rimsky-Korsakov was not arrived at without some experimentation, and even after it had been achieved, he still continued to experiment. His first two operas, *The Maid of Pskov* (1873) and *May Night* (1880), showed the influence of Dargomyzhsky and Glinka. *The Snow Maiden* (1882) was more spontaneous and original, based on a fairy legend with vaguely symbolic touches. *Mlada* (1892), in which some traces of Wagner may be seen, was adapted from a libretto which was to have been collectively composed by Cui, Mussorgsky, Rimsky-Korsakov, and Borodin twenty years before (this joint undertaking was never completed). *Christmas Eve* (1895) was, like *May Night,* taken from a story by N. V. Gogol (1809–1852). Both these works are village tales, with love stories and comic-supernatural additions; the subject of *Christmas Eve* is the same as that of Tchaikovsky's *Vakula the Smith.* In 1898 appeared Rimsky-Korsakov's masterpiece, *Sadko,* an "opera legend," a typical combination of the epic and fantastic in a libretto adapted jointly by the composer and V. I. Bielsky from an eleventh-century legend and drawing much of the musical material from Rimsky-Korsakov's early symphonic poem (1876) of the same title. Then followed several experimental works: *Mozart and Salieri, Boyarinya Vera Sheloga* (both 1898), and *The Czar's Bride* (1899), the last a real tragedy with arias and concerted numbers in the old Italian style, "the old operatic convention of the first half of the nineteenth century decked out with Wagnerian leit-motives and Dargomïzhskian 'melodic recitative' and mildly flavoured here and there with the Russian folk-idiom." [21] *Czar Saltan* (1900), another fairy tale, returned to distinctive national traits in both libretto and music. *Servilia* (1902) and *Pan Voyevode* (1904) were unsuccessful essays in more dramatic plots with Wagnerian influence in the music. *Kaschey the Immortal* (1902) was also Wagnerian in technique with declamatory lines and constant use of leitmotifs, as well as the redemption idea woven into the legendary story; the music represents Rimsky-Korsakov's extreme excursion in the direction of chromaticism and dissonance. The last two operas were, with *Sadko,* the most important: *The Legend of the Invisible City of Kitezh* (1907) and *The Golden Cockerel* (1909). *Kitezh* has been called "the Russian Parsi-

21 Abraham, *Studies in Russian Music,* p. 248.

fal" because of its mystical and symbolical story, based on two ancient legends. But beyond an evident aspiration to combine the best features of pagan pantheism and orthodox Christianity in the figure of the heroine Fevronya, the symbolism is vague and not of fundamental importance. *The Golden Cockerel,* from a humorous-fantastic tale of Pushkin, is more objective and ironic, even satirical, but equally unclear as to the detailed application of its moral.

Other than a gradual growth in complexity of idiom and an increasing skill in the fabrication of piquant harmonic and coloristic effects, there is little that can be called an evolution in Rimsky-Korsakov's musical style through these fifteen operas—nothing remotely comparable to the change in Wagner from *Die Feen* to *Parsifal.* Rimsky-Korsakov was a lyrical and pictorial composer, resembling Mendelssohn in exquisiteness of detail as well as in the absence of strongly emotional and dramatic qualities. The realism of Mussorgsky was not for him: art, he once said, was "essentially the most enchanting and intoxicating of lies" [22]—no doubt an extreme statement, but one which explains much in his own music. The dramatic force of the last act of *The Maid of Pskov* and the serious musical characterization of Fevronya in *Kitezh* are exceptional in his work; his original, personal contribution lies in another realm. "[He] must be granted the quite peculiar power of evoking a fantastic world entirely his own, half-real, half-supernatural, a world as limited, as distinctive and as delightful as the world of the Grimms' fairy-tales or as Alice's Wonderland. It is a world in which the commonplace and matter-of-fact are inextricably confused with the fantastic, naivete with sophistication, the romantic with the humorous, and beauty with absurdity. He was not its inventor, of course; he owed it in the first place to Pushkin and Gogol. But he gave it a queer touch of his own, linking it with Slavonic antiquity and hinting at pantheistic symbolism, which makes it peculiarly his. And musically, of course, he reigns in it undisputed. He invented the perfect music for such a fantastic world: music insubstantial when it was matched with unreal things, deliciously lyrical when it touched reality, in both cases coloured from the most superb palette musician has ever held." [23]

[22] Quoted in Calvocoressi and Abraham, *Masters of Russian Music,* p. 411.
[23] *Ibid.,* p. 422. Quoted by permission of the publisher.

For Rimsky-Korsakov an opera was primarily a musical rather than a dramatic-literary work; hence the importance of musical design, which frequently dominates both the poetry and the scenic plan (for example, the rondo form in the fourth tableau of *Sadko*). Along with this there is usually a definite association of certain keys with certain moods. In most of the operas there is a consistent use of leitmotifs. These are not, as in Wagner, the material out of which a symphonic fabric is developed but are rather melodic fragments (sometimes only a phrase from a large theme) or even inconspicuous harmonic progressions, woven into the opera in a kind of mosaic pattern; they are as often given to the voices as to the orchestra.[24] In the harmony, there are as a rule two distinct idioms in each opera: one chromatic, fanciful, cunningly contrived, for the imaginary scenes and characters (Example 121), and the other diatonic, solid,

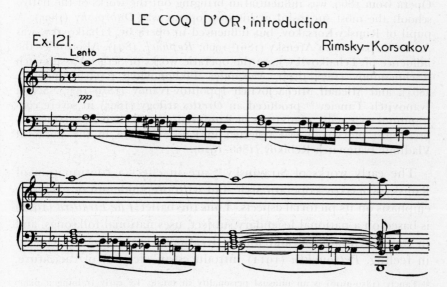

LE COQ D'OR, introduction

Ex.121.
Lento

Rimsky-Korsakov

often modal, for the "real" world. The vocal parts, as usual in Russian opera, alternate between melodic recitative and closed aria-like forms. In his lyrical melodies, Rimsky-Korsakov owes much to the model of Glinka; his own melodies are elegant and graceful, though marked by certain persistently recurring formulae. An important factor in his style is the extensive use of folk tunes, and of original

[24] Cf. Rimsky-Korsakov, *My Musical Life*, p. 204.

tunes of the folk-song type; the source or inspiration for many of these was his own collection of Russian folk songs, made in 1876. Church melodies are also occasionally used, notably in *Kitezh*. The oriental idiom, however, is much less extensive and less significant in Rimsky-Korsakov's music than in that of either Balakirev or Borodin. Like all Russian opera composers, he excelled in the depiction of crowd scenes, especially in *The Maid of Pskov* (Act II), *Sadko, Kitezh* (Act II and finale), and the humorous ensembles in *May Night, Christmas Eve,* and *Sadko.* Above all, of course, he is distinguished for his mastery of orchestral effects, a virtuosity in the treatment of instrumental color such as few composers in history have equaled.

A number of minor Russian opera composers of the late nineteenth- and early twentieth-century period can be only briefly mentioned. Eduard Frantsovitch Napravnik (1839–1916), as conductor of the St. Petersburg Opera from 1869, was influential in bringing out the works of the native school; the most successful of his own operas was *Dubrovsky* (1895). A pupil of Rimsky-Korsakov, but influenced in opera by Tchaikovsky, was Anton Stepanovitch Arensky (1861–1906; *Raphael,* 1894). Also under the influence of Tchaikovsky were the operatic works of Sergei Vassilievitch Rachmaninov (1873–1943), Alexander Tikhonovitch Gretchaninov (b. 1864), and Michail Michaelovitch Ippolitov-Ivanov (1859–1935). Sergei Ivanovitch Taneiev [25] produced an *Orestes* trilogy (1895) in severe contrapuntal style with admixtures of Rubinstein and Tchaikovsky. The impressionist movement was reflected in Russian opera in the works of Vladimir Ivanovitch Rebikov (1866–1920).

The early works of Stravinsky [26] are in effect a continuation of Rimsky-Korsakov's operatic style, but with preponderant or exclusive emphasis on its pictorial aspects. Thus the ballet *The Firebird* (1910) is based on a national legendary subject, uses national folksongs, and in both orchestration and formal treatment is thoroughly Russian in feeling. *Petrouchka* (1911) introduces an element of caricature,

[25] Taneiev (1850–1918) is an unusual personality in music. By early training a piano virtuoso (pupil of N. Rubinstein), he became interested in the study of counterpoint and brought out in 1909 a two-volume treatise on the subject, the result of nearly twenty years' work. His later compositions were chiefly chamber music. He lived the life of an ascetic, caring little for recognition or even publication of his work. See Sabaneiev, *Modern Russian Composers.*

[26] On Igor Stravinsky (b. 1882) see his autobiography and his *Poétique musicale,* also studies by Schloezer, Schaeffner, and Handschin; Blitzstein, "The Phenomenon of Stravinsky," MQ XXI (1935) 330–47: Armitage (ed.), *Stravinsky;* special Stravinsky issue of RM (1939); Sternfeld, "Some Russian Folk Songs in Stravinsky's *Petrouchka,*" *Music Library Association Notes, Second Series* II, No. 2 (March, 1945) 95–107.

and *The Ceremonial of Spring* (1913) exaggerates the neoprimitive —departures from the pure nationalist tradition which are reflected in the novel, experimental features of the music of both works. In the opera *The Nightingale* (1914) the Russian elements begin to have the character of exotic material. So far as national qualities are concerned, the burlesque chamber opera *Renard* (composed 1916–1917) and the one-act opera buffa *Mavra* (1922) are wholly satirical in spirit, while in *The Story of the Soldier* (1918) and *The Wedding* (1923) the national subject matter as well as the musical idiom has become stylized. The neoclassic ballet *The Fairy Kiss* (1928), on themes from Tchaikovsky, may be regarded as the last faint echo of Russian nationalism in Stravinsky's work.

CENTRAL AND SOUTHEASTERN EUROPE.[27]—Although there were Polish operas as early as 1778 by Matthias Kamienski (1734–1821), the real founder of Polish national opera was Stanislaw Moniuszko,[28] a contemporary of Chopin and a song composer of undoubted lyric gifts. His *Halka* (1854) is still performed in Poland. Other works in a similar romantic vein, some of which are still revived, include *The Raftsman* (1858), *The Countess* (1860), and especially a comic work, *The Haunted Castle* (1865), next to *Halka* his most popular opera. Conditions in Poland were not favorable to native opera during the latter part of the nineteenth century, and therefore the promising work begun by Moniuszko did not come to full fruition.

The principal composers and works of this period were: Ludwik Grossman, 1835–1915 (*The Ghost of the Voyvod,* 1873); Adam Minhejmer, 1831–1904 (*Mazeppa,* composed before 1875 but not performed until 1900); Ladislas Zelenski, 1873–1921, a composer of chamber and orchestral music influenced by Brahms, and who in opera remained faithful to the pre-Wagnerian form and style (*Goplana,* 1896); Sigismund Noskowski, 1846–1909 (*Livia Quintilla,* 1898); Roman Statkowski, 1860–1925, whose two operas won prizes in international competitions, their style being in transition between the pre-Wagnerian and the music drama (*Philaenis,* 1904; *Marya,* 1906); [29] Ignace Jan Paderewski, 1860–1941 (*Manru,* 1901);

[27] Bibliography: Opieński, *La Musique polonaise;* Newmarch, *The Music of Czechoslovakia;* Nosek, *The Spirit of Bohemia;* Haraszti, *La Musique hongroise;* Adorján, "L'Opérette hongroise," *Revue de Hongroie* VI (1910) 269–80; Dobronic, "A Study of Jugoslav Music," MQ XII (1926) 56–71.
[28] Moniuszko's dates are 1819–1872. See Jachimecki, "Moniuszko," MQ XIV (1928) 54–62.
[29] The text of *Marya* is from a poem by A. Malczewski; there are other operas on this subject by Melcer, Soltys, W. Gawronski, and H. Opienski (Loewenberg, *Annals,* p. 663).

Miecyslaw Soltys, 1863–1929 (*Panie Kochanku,* 1924); and Felician Szopski, b. 1865 (*Lilje,* 1917, in Wagnerian style).

A new generation whose music showed more progressive tendencies came to recognition in opera for the most part only after the restoration of Polish nationality in 1919.

This group included the pianist Henrik Melcer, 1869–1928 (*Marya,* 1904); the conductor Emil Mlynarski, 1870–1935 (*Summer Night,* composed 1915, performed 1923); the musicologist Henrik Opieński, 1870–1942 (*Marya,* 1924; *Jacob the Lutenist,* 1927); Taddeusz Joteyko, 1872–1932, the most successful of the group (*Sigmund August,* 1925); Felix Nowowiejski, 1877– ca. 1945, choral composer, conductor, winner of many prizes, whose *Baltic Legend* (1924) abounds in massive effects; and Adam Táddeusz Wieniawski, b. 1879, pupil of D'Indy and Fauré, a more subtle talent (*Megae,* 1912; *Wyzolony,* 1928).

The most productive and most naturally dramatic modern Polish opera composer is Ludomir Rózycki (b. 1883), whose works include *Boleslav the Bold* (1909), *Eros and Psyche* (1917, and winning the Polish state prize in 1931), the comic opera *Casanova* (1923), and the tragic *Beatrice Cenci* (1927). Karol Szymanowski (1883–1937),[30] by common consent the greatest Polish composer of the present century, was primarily interested in other than operatic forms. His *Hagith* (composed 1912) was influenced by Strauss's *Elektra. King Roger* (1926) is an outstanding modern opera. Its libretto, on a subject perhaps suggested by Schreker's *Der ferne Klang,* is exceptionally well constructed; the music is rich, sonorous, and original, deriving some of its material from Greek church modes (parallel-organum choruses in Act I) and oriental motifs (ballets in Act II).

The father of Bohemian music and opera was Bedřich Smetana,[31] whose first great success came with *The Bartered Bride* in 1866. This melodious comic opera, so permeated with the rhythms and spirit of national music, has become famous all over the world. Two other comic operas of Smetana, *The Kiss* (1876) and *The Secret* (1878),

---

30 Jachimecki, "Szymanowski," *Slavonic . . . Review* XVII (July, 1938) 174–85.

31 There were a few operas with Bohemian texts before Smetana, notably several by František Škroup (1801–1862) produced at Prague from 1826. Other early composers were František Skuherský (1830–1892), Karel Šebor (1845–1903; *The Hussite Bride,* 1868), Karel Bendl (1838–1897), and Vilém Blodek (1834–1874; especially noted for comic operas); one of the first Slovenian opera composers was Anton Foerster (1837–1909). For other names in this early period see Adler, *Handbuch* II, 925. On Smetana (1824–1884) the principal biography is that of Nejedlý, which has not been translated; there is a smaller work on Smetana by Nejedlý in English translation (London, 1924).

showed advances in technical skill and were almost as successful in the composer's own country as *The Bartered Bride*. Smetana's serious operas, especially *Dalibor* (1868) and *Libussa* (composed 1872, performed 1881), were attacked by patriotic critics because of their use of certain procedures associated with Wagner, such as leitmotifs and the declamatory character of the vocal parts. But the alleged Wagnerisms hardly ever penetrated to the substance of the music, which remained stoutly individual. The leader of the next generation of Bohemian composers, Antonin Dvořák,[32] was primarily a symphonic rather than a dramatic musician, though several of his nine operas were successful at Prague. *The Cunning Peasant* (1878) was inspired by Smetana's *Bartered Bride*. *The Devil and Kate* (1899) was Dvořák's most popular work in the comic style. In serious opera, he underwent the influence first of Meyerbeer and then of Wagner; the height of his achievement in this field was attained in a late work, *Rusalka* (1901), the libretto of which was well adapted to his lyrical powers. A third early figure in Bohemian music was Zdenko Fibich,[33] a prolific composer who, more internationally minded than either Smetana or Dvořák, came fully under the influence of romanticism and the Wagnerian music drama. He was noted especially for the classical trilogy *Hippodameia* (1890–91), set entirely as a melodrama —that is, orchestral music accompanying a spoken text—a form established by the eighteenth-century Bohemian composer Georg Benda. Fibich's best opera was *Šarka* (1897), based on a story from Czech mythology.

Other composers of this generation were Adalbert Hřimalý, 1842–1908 (*The Enchanted Prince*, 1872), Joseph Nešvera, 1842–1914 (*Woodland Air*, 1897), and Hanuš Trneček, 1858–1914.

An important Bohemian composer of the late nineteenth-century was Joseph Bohuslav Foerster,[34] whose most successful operas were *Eva* (1889) and *Jessika* (1905). Four pupils of Fibich also made their mark in Bohemian opera: Karel Kovařič, 1862–1920 (*On the Old*

[32] On Dvořák (1841–1904) see Hadow, *Studies in Modern Music, Second Series*, 10th ed. There are biographies in English by Paul Stefan (based on the monumental Czech biography by Otakar Šourek) and Karel Hoffmeister.

[33] Fibich (1850–1900) composed five overtures, three symphonies, five symphonic poems, some chamber music, songs, and piano pieces, in addition to his six operas and eight melodramas. See study by C. L. Richter.

[34] Foerster (b. 1859) is notable for choral works as well as for his seven operas. See biography by Nejedlý.

Bleaching Ground, 1901), Karel Weis (1862–1937), Antonín Horák (1875–1910), and Otakar Ostrčil, 1879–1935 (*The Bud,* 1911). An influential composer and teacher was Vitěslav Novák,[35] with four operas of which the most important was *The Imp of Zvikov* (1915). The Moravian Leoš Janáček [36] in his operas cultivated an intense style based on the rhythms of Czech speech, with a varied harmonic vocabulary influenced by Mussorgsky and the French impressionists, though modern in its primitive directness of expression and economy of resource (*Her Foster Daughter,* 1904, better known under the title *Jenufa; Káta Kabanová,* 1921; *The Sly Vixen,* 1924; *The Makropulos Case,* 1926).

Modern Czechoslovak composers of opera are: Otakar Zich, 1879–1934 (*The Sin,* 1922); Rudolf Karel, 1880–1945, a pupil of Dvořák (*Godmother Death,* 1933); Jaroslav Křička, b. 1882; Alois Haba, b. 1893 (*Die Mutter,* Munich 1931, the first quarter-tone opera); Marij Kogoj, b. 1895 (*Black Masks,* 1929); and Jaromir Weinberger, b. 1896, whose folk opera *Schwanda the Bagpiper* (1927) is one of the only two Czech operas that have become widely known outside their own country. Weinberger's *Outcasts of Poker Flat* (1932, from Bret Harte's story) shows American jazz influence. Bohuslav Martinu, b. 1890, better known for his symphonic and chamber music, is also the composer of six operas.

The founder of opera in Hungary was Ferencz Erkel (1810–1893), whose works have been performed more often than those of any other Hungarian composer (*Hunyady László,* 1844; *Bánk-Bán,* 1861). Others of the early nationalist group were András Bartay, 1798–1856 (*The Trick,* 1839, the first Hungarian comic opera); György Czászár, *ca.* 1820–? (*The Cumans,* 1848); Michael Brand, called Mosonyi, 1814–1870 (*Fair Ilonka,* 1861); and August von Adelburg, 1830–1873 (*Zrynyi,* 1868). Later nationalists included Jenö Hubay, 1858–1937 (*The Violin Maker of Cremona,* 1894), and Ede Poldini, b. 1869 (*The Vagabond and the Princess,* 1903). Wagnerian influence came with Ödön Mihalovich, 1842–1929 (*Toldi's Love,* 1893), and a pronounced flavor of late German romanticism is heard in the operas of Géza Zichy [37] and Erno Dohnányi, b. 1877 (*The Tower of the*

---

[35] On Novák (b. 1870) see Newmarch, "New Works in Czechoslovakia," *The Chesterian* XII (1931) 213–19.

[36] Janáček (1854–1928) was an enthusiastic student of folk songs and wrote two books on harmonic theory. See biography by D. Muller; also Holländer, "Leoš Janáček and His Operas," MQ XV (1929) 29–36.

[37] Zichy (1849–1924) has left an autobiography, *Aus meinem Leben.*

Voyvod, 1922). The leading modern Hungarian composer was Béla Bartók,[38] whose only opera, *Duke Bluebeard's Castle* (Budapest, 1918), is a masterpiece of orchestral color and somber dramatic power within the confines of a single act and using only two characters. Less individual but equally nationalistic in his music is Zoltán Kodály (b. 1882), with two Hungarian ballad operas: *Háry János* (1926) and *The Spinning Room of the Szekelys* (1932). Finally to be mentioned is Jenö Zádor, b. 1894 (*The Isle of the Dead,* 1928).

The principal opera composers of Rumania were: Liubicz Skibinski (*Verfel cu Dor,* 1879); Eduard Caudella, 1841–1923 (*Petru Rares,* 1900); Georg Kosmovici (*Marioara,* 1904); Theodor von Flondor, d. 1908 (*Mosul Ciokärlan,* 1901); Sabin Dragoi, b. 1894, a pupil of Dvořák and Janáček, with sophisticated modern use of Rumanian folksong in *Napasta* (1928); and Georges Enesco, b. 1881, with one opera, *Oedipe* (Paris, 1936).

Croatian opera is represented by Vatroslav Lisinski, 1819–1854 (*Ljubav i Zloba,* 1846); Ivan Zajc, 1832–1914 (*Nikola Šubič Zrinski,* 1876); Franjo Serafin Vilhar, 1852–1928 (*Smiljana,* 1892); Petar Konjović, b. 1882 (*Koštana,* 1931); Krešimir Baranović, b. 1894 (*Striženo-Košeno,* 1932); and Jacov Gotovac, b. 1895 (*Morana,* 1930).

In Serbia the only opera composer of importance is Alexander Savin, b. 1881 (*Ksenia,* 1919). Bulgarian opera has two composers: Georgi Athanassov, 1872–1931, a pupil of Mascagni (*Borislav,* 1911), and Pantcho Vladigerov, b. 1899, with the nationalist opera *Czar Kalojan* (1936). The only nationalist opera composer of Greece is Manuel Kalomiris, b. 1883 (*The Master,* 1915; *Mother's Ring,* 1917).

GERMANIC, SCANDINAVIAN, AND BALTIC COUNTRIES.—On the whole, opera found no very congenial ground in these countries, but there are sporadic examples, of which some of the most important will be mentioned.

Holland throughout the nineteenth century was under the musical domination of Germany.[39] Opera composers in this period included Richard Hol, 1825–1904 (*Floris V,* 1892); Cornelis van der Linden, 1842–1908 (*The Relief of Leyden,* 1893); Henry Brandts-Buys, 1850–1905 (*Albrecht Beiling,* 1891); Karl Dibbern, b. 1855 (*Odja,* 1901); Emile van Brucken-Fock, b. 1857 (*Seleneia,* 1895); Cornelis Dopper, 1870–1939 (*The Cross of Honor,* 1903); and Charles Grelinger, b. 1873, with the successful

[38] On Bartók (1881–1945) see biography by Harászti.
[39] Dresden, *Het Muziekleven in Nederland sinds 1880;* Sanders, *Moderne nederlandsche Componisten.* The earliest Dutch opera, *De triomferende Min* ("Love's Triumph"), by Carolus Hacquart (*ca.* 1649–*ca.* 1730), was published in 1680 but not performed until 1920, at Antwerp. (See Loewenberg, *Annals,* p. 36.)

opera *Op Hoop van Zegen* ("On Board the 'Hope of Blessing,' " 1907). Jan Brandts-Buys, 1868–1933, was more German than Dutch (*Die drei Schneider*, Dresden, 1916), but national traits appeared in the realistic-satiric operas of Hol's pupil Johan Wagenaar, b. 1862 (his *Doge van Venetie*, 1904, and *De Cid*, 1916, are serious operas). A modern Dutch opera is *Halewijn* (1933) by Willem Pijper (1894–1947).

Flemish opera composers of the nineteenth and twentieth centuries were: Joseph Mertens, 1834–1901 (*De zwarte Kapitein*, 1877); Jan Blockx (*De Herbergprinses*, 1896);[40] Paul Gilson, 1865–1942 (*Prinses Zonneschijn*, 1903); and Auguste de Boeck, 1865–1937 (*La Route d'Emeraude*, 1921).

Denmark, like Holland, has been to a large extent a musical province of Germany.[41] The earliest national opera composers were Johan Hartmann, 1805–1900 (*Liden Kirsten*, 1846); Henrik Rung, 1807–1871 (*Storm over Copenhagen*, 1845); Siegfried Saloman, 1816–1899 (*The Diamond Cross*, 1847); and Peter Arnold Heise, 1830–1879 (*King and Marshal*, 1878). Four operas by Peter Erasmus Lange-Müller (1850–1926) were produced at Copenhagen (*Spanske Studenter*, 1883). One of the most successful Danish comic operas was Carl August Nielsen's (1865–1931) *Maskarade* (1906). The most prolific recent Danish opera composer was August Enna, 1860–1939 (*The Witch*, 1892; *The Match Girl*, 1897).

The first Norwegian opera was *A Mountain Adventure* by Waldemar Thrane (1790–1828), which was published by 1824 but not performed on the stage until 1850.[42] Twenty years later came *The Knight and the Fluberg Sprite* by Martin Andreas Udbye (1820–1899), and in 1894 the first of Johannes Haarklou's (1847–1925) five operas, *Of Olden Days*. Ole Olsen (1850–1927) wrote four operas, of which *Leila* was performed at Christiana in 1908. Gerhard Schjelderup (1859–1933), though of Norwegian birth, composed most of his operas to German texts; the same is true of Sigwardt Aspestrand (b. 1856). Catherinus Elling (b. 1858) wrote one opera, *Kosakkerne* (1897).

Sweden from the seventeenth century had been in touch with the general development of opera in Europe.[43] Italian, French, and German subjects and musical styles, as might be expected, dominated Swedish opera houses in the late eighteenth and early nineteenth centuries. The earliest attempt at a Swedish historical subject was made by Carl Stenborg with *King Gustavus Adolphus's Hunting Party* (1779).[44] The first grand opera in Swedish was *Thetis och Pelée* (1773), by the Italian composer Francesco

40 Solvay, *Notice sur Jan Blockx* [1851–1912].

41 On the Danish branch of the eighteenth-century Singspiel see above, p. 267. The German composer Franz Gläser (1798–1861) wrote three operas to Danish texts.

42 Loewenberg, *Annals*, p. 448. *See also* Kindem, *Den norske operas historie*.

43 See Moberg, "Essais d'opéras en Suède," in *Mélanges de musicologie*, pp. 123–32; Engländer, *Joseph Martin Kraus*.

44 This "comedy mingled with songs" was imitated from Collet's French opéra comique text, *La Partie de chasse de Henri IV*, part of which had been used by Weisse and J. A. Hiller for their popular Singspiel *Die Jagd* (1770).

Antonio Uttini (1723-1795). Swedish opera composers in the early and middle nineteenth century included J. N. Ahlström (1805-1857), Adolf Lindblad (1801-1878), Siegfried Saloman (1816-1899), and August Johan Södermann (1832-1876). Some German composers in this period also occasionally wrote operas to Swedish texts. A more definitely national type of Swedish opera, using native legends and folk melodies, appeared toward the end of the nineteenth century with the works of Ivar Hallström, 1826-1901 (*The Mountain King*, 1874). Nationalism was temporarily pushed aside, however, by the desire to emulate the Wagnerian music drama, as in the earlier operas of Anders Hallén, 1846-1925 (*Harald the Viking*, Leipzig, 1881), though more independent traits are evident in his *Valdemar's Treasure*, written for the opening of the new Stockholm Opera in 1899. A Wagner propagandist in Sweden was Richard Henneberg (1853-1925), who wrote a comic opera, *Drottningen's Pilgrimage*, in 1882. A combination of the Wagner style with national melodies is found in the operas of Vilhelm Stenhammar, 1871-1927 (*Tirfing*, 1898: *Das Fest auf Solhaug*, Stuttgart, 1899). A more definite step toward national opera, though still on a Wagnerian basis, was *Arnjlot* (1910), by Olof Wilhelm Peterson-Berger.[45] Natanaël Berg (b. 1879) and Kurt Atterberg (b. 1887) are distinguished chiefly in the field of the symphony, though both have produced operas. A contemporary opera composer is Ture Rangström, 1884-1947 (*Die Kronbraut*, Stuttgart 1919; in Swedish, at Stockholm, from 1922; based on Strindberg's drama).

In Finland there was no national opera before the twentieth century. *Kung Carls Jakt* by Fredrik Pacius (1809-1891), performed at Helsinki in 1852 and sometimes called the "first Finnish opera," was by a German-born composer and on a Swedish text.[46] The first opera composed to Finnish words was Oskar Merikanto's (1868-1924) *Pohjan Neiti* ("The Maid of Bothnia"), performed at Viipuri in 1908. Merikanto's subsequent works (*Elinan Surma*, "Elina's Death," 1910; *Regina von Emmeritz*, 1920) were somewhat influenced by Italian verismo methods. Other composers of this period were Erkki Gustaf Melartin, 1875-1937 (*Aino*, 1909), and Selim Palmgren, b. 1878 (*Daniel Hjort*, 1910; Swedish text). A more distinctly national style, with folk melodies and recitative rhythms adapted to the Finnish language, was exemplified by Armas Launis, b. 1884 (*Seitsemän Veljestä*, "Seven Brothers," 1913; *Kullervo*, 1917). Another Finnish folk-song scholar, Ilmari Krohn (b. 1867), produced an opera *Tuhotulva* ("The Deluge") at Helsinki in 1928. The most important modern Finnish operas are by Leevi Madetoja (b. 1887), a pupil of D'Indy: *Pohjalaisia* ("The East Bothnians," 1924) and *Juha* (1935).

A few national operas were produced in the smaller Baltic states after the First World War. In Latvia an opera company was organized at Riga

[45] Peterson-Berger (1867-1942) is the author of several books and a collection of essays published at Stockholm in 1923.
[46] See Loewenberg, *Annals*, p. 458.

in 1919. Native composers include Alfreds Kalnins, b. 1879 (*Banuta*, 1920; *Dzimtenes Atmoda*, "The Country's Awakening," 1933, a historical opera); Jazeps Medins, b. 1877 (*Vaidelote*, "The Virgin," 1927); Janis Medins, b. 1890 (*Uguns un Nakts*, "Fire and Night," 1921); and Janis Kalnins, b. 1904 (*Hamlets*, 1936). A Lithuanian opera house was opened at Kaunas toward the end of 1920, and the first Lithuanian opera, *Birute*, by Petrauskas Miskas, was performed in 1921. Another Lithuanian composer is Jurgio Karnavičius, b. 1885 (*Grazina*, 1933). Estonian operas have been composed by Arthur Lemba, b. 1885 (*Armastus ja Surm*, "Love and Death," Tallinn 1931; *Elga*, 1934).

SPAIN, PORTUGAL, AND LATIN AMERICA.[47]—With the disappearance of the old tonadilla in the first half of the nineteenth century, Spanish national opera went into an eclipse from which it did not emerge until about 1850. The first signs of reaction against the reign of Italian opera and French opéra comique in Spanish theatres appeared, strangely enough, in the works of a resident Italian composer, Basilio Basili, who in the late thirties and early forties brought out at Madrid a number of comic operas in Spanish. The first of these (1837) was labeled a *zarzuela-comedia*, thus reviving the ancient Spanish designation. Within a decade there was a flourishing school of the new zarzuela, a form derived essentially from the eighteenth-century tonadilla, using music of a light, popular, national style with admixture of some French and Italian elements. Many of the early librettos were from French sources—an instance of the influence which France has constantly exerted on the growth of national Spanish music. The leading composer of this first period of the revival was Francisco Asenjo Barbieri (1823–1894), who produced over seventy zarzuelas between 1850 and 1880, including the classic work of this type, *Pan y toros* ("Bread and Bulls," 1864). This and other zarzuelas of Barbieri[48] were long popular and have been influential on the development of national music in both Spain and South America. The principal contemporaries of Barbieri were Rafael José Maria Hernando (1822–1888), Joaquín Gaztambide (1882–1870), Cristóbal Oudrid y

47 See Chase, *The Music of Spain*, for the most recent survey of this subject, with bibliographies. Further consult: Lavignac, *Encyclopédie*, Pt. I, Vol. IV, pp. 2290–2351, 2470–84; Salazar, *La música contemporánea en España*; music dictionaries of Saldoni and Pedrell and the "Espasa" encyclopedia; Trend, *A Picture of Modern Spain*; Peña y Goñi, *La ópera española*. Cf. also titles under early Spanish opera (above, pp. 270 ff.).

48 E.g., *Tramoya* ("The Trick," 1850); *Jugar con fuego* ("Playing with Fire," 1851); *El barberillo de Lavapiés* ("The Little Barber of Lavapiés," 1874).

Segura (1829–1877), and Emilio Arrieta y Corera (1823–1894).[49]

Two distinct types of zarzuela developed at Madrid, corresponding to the two types of French opéra comique which evolved during the nineteenth century. On the one hand was the *genero chico*—comic, popular, informal, often quite ephemeral pieces in one act. These were produced in immense numbers throughout the century and indeed have continued up to the present day. The other type was the *zarzuela grande,* usually in three acts, which might be on a serious subject and even in some cases approach the scale and style of grand opera. Most composers of the later nineteenth century wrote zarzuelas of both kinds. Some of the most popular works of the genero chico were *La gran via* ("The Great Road," 1886) by Federico Chueca (1846–1908), in collaboration with Joaquín Valverde (1846–1910); *La viejecita* ("The Old Woman," 1897) by Manuel Fernández Caballero (1835–1906); *La bruja* ("The Witch," 1887) and *La revoltosa* ("The Revolutionary Girl," 1897) by Ruperto Chapí y Lorente (1851–1909); and above all *La verbena de la paloma* ("The Festival of Our Lady of the Dove," 1894) by Tomas Bretón y Hernández.[50]

Along with the rise of the popular zarzuela there was a growing desire for a national serious opera in Spain. Spanish composers of the earlier nineteenth century had rarely used Spanish texts or national subjects, and their music seldom had anything differentiating it from the contemporary Italian style.[51] A solitary early crusader for Spanish opera was Joaquín Espín y Guillén (1812–1881), one act of whose *Padilla, o el Asedio de Medina* ("Padilla, or the Siege of Medina") was performed at Madrid in 1845. Later in the century, however, the zarzuela composers interested themselves in the task of creating a more permanent and artistic form of national lyric drama than could be made of the genero chico pieces to which they chiefly owed their popular success. Barbieri had definite ideas on the

49 Chief works: Hernando: *Colegiales y soldados* ("College Girls and Soldiers"), 1849; *El duende* ("The Ghost"), 1849. Gaztambide: *La mensanjera* ("The Errand Girl"), 1849. Oudrid: *Buenas noches, Don Simón* ("Good Night, Don Simon"), 1852. Arrieta: *El domino azul* ("The Blue Domino"), 1853; *Marina,* 1855.
50 See biography of Bretón (1850–1923) by Salcedo.
51 Composers of this period were: Ramón Carnicer, 1789–1855 (*Cristoforo Colombo,* 1831); Tomás Genovés y Lapetra, 1806–1861; Baltasar Saldoni, 1807–1889 (*Ipermestra,* 1838); Vicente Cuyas, 1814–1839 (*La Fattuchiera,* 1838); and Miguel Hilarión Eslava, 1807–1878 (*Il solitario del Monte Selvaggio,* 1841).

subject; [52] Arrieta, who had composed a number of Italian operas, expanded his two-act zarzuela *Marina* into a three-act Spanish opera with recitatives (1871). Chapí wrote several serious zarzuelas (*La tempestad* "The Storm," 1882; *Curro Vargas,* 1898) as well as operas (*Margarita la Tornera,* 1909), but his genius was for the comic rather than the serious. Bretón, who had also written Italian operas, composed an important Spanish opera, *La Dolores,* in 1895. Still another composer of this period was Emilio Serrano y Ruiz (1850–1939), with the operas *Irene de Otranto* in 1891 and *Gonzalo de Cordoba* (to his own text) in 1898.

The honorable title of "father of modern Spanish music" belongs to Felipe Pedrell, [53] distinguished scholar, composer, and teacher (or at least mentor) of most of the Spanish composers of the following generation. Pedrell combined a deep feeling for the qualities of Spanish folk-song and the great Spanish music of the past with a romantic-mystical temperament which led him frequently into paths where the general public could not follow. He was a greater idealist than composer, and his beneficent influence on Spanish music is out of all proportion to the very slight outward success of his own works. He was dubbed "the Spanish Wagner"; his most successful opera, *La Celestina* (1904), was called "the Spanish *Tristan.*" These expressions exaggerate the resemblance of his work to Wagner's. That there was some influence is, of course, unquestionable, but the examples of Glinka, Mussorgsky, and the other Russian opera composers were at least equally potent. As a matter of fact, if comparisons must be made, the composer whom Pedrell most closely resembles is D'Indy. The likeness is one of both temperament and musical style: each was irresistibly drawn into the orbit of Wagner; each, being an ardent nationalist and an artist of high ethical purpose, adapted the technique of the music drama for his own aims; and each succeeded in being individual in spite of this debt. D'Indy was a better technician than Pedrell and was more at home in the realm of purely

---

[52] Chase, *Music of Spain,* p. 141.
[53] Pedrell (1841–1922) composed seven operas, several symphonic poems, and choral works. He was editor of the *Hispaniae schola musica sacra* and the Complete Edition of Victoria. See Tebaldini, *Felipe Pedrell ed il dramma lirico spagnuolo;* Curzon, *Felipe Pedrell et Les Pyrénées;* Istel, "Felipe Pedrell," MQ XI (1925) 164–91; Gilbert Chase, "Felipe Pedrell" (unpublished essay); Pedrell's own *Jornadas de arte* (essays and critical writings); and catalogue of works by Reiff, AfMw III (1921) 86–97.

musical expression; Pedrell, on the other hand, drew his musical idiom from more varied sources.

The most important of Pedrell's ten operas is *Los Pirineos* ("The Pyrenees"), a trilogy in three acts with prologue, composed to a Catalan text of Victor Balaguer in 1890–1891 and first performed in Italian translation at Barcelona in 1902.[54] The poem offers a number of effective scenes, but on the whole its nature is more that of an epic than of a dramatic work. Pedrell's setting is unified by the use of leitmotifs. An idea of his style may be gained from Example 122, part of the Funeral March in the second act. The orchestra has a much less conspicuous position than in Wagner, and the voice parts are nearly always melodic. An important proportion of the score is

LOS PIRINEOS, Act II

Ex.122.   Pedrell

Largamente e funebre

---

[54] *Los Pireneos* is itself the first opera of a larger trilogy, of which *La Celestina* is the second number; the third, *Raymond Lully*, was not completed.

given to set pieces, which appear in great variety. The composer's scholarly conscience is shown in his evident care to reproduce as authentically as possible the oriental idiom in the solos of the heroine, "Moon-Ray"; the scene of the Love Court in Act I offers modern adaptations of trouvère and troubadour art forms—*tenso, lai,* and *sirventes.* There are quotations from plainsong and from sixteenth-century Spanish church composers, and the excellent choral writing throughout the opera should be especially mentioned. The prologue in particular should make a very effective concert number for a choral society.

It is too much to claim that Pedrell is to be numbered among the greatest opera composers. His dramatic sense often failed him. Too many pages of *Los Pirineos* are thin in inspiration, repetitious, and lacking in rhythmic vitality and variety. But, out of a sincere artist's soul, enough moments of greatness have emerged to make this work an honor to its composer and country and to entitle it to at least an occasional performance, even if in a shortened version.

The national spirit which Pedrell did so much to inspire achieved world-wide recognition in the piano music of two of his pupils, Albéniz and Granados.[55] Both these composers essayed opera, but without important results. Albéniz, apparently under a mistaken notion of his own gifts, and also instigated by a wealthy English patron who fancied himself a dramatic author, devoted several years to writing operas in a heavy, pseudo-Wagnerian style but finally obtained a moderate success with a comic work, *Pepita Jiménez* (1896). Granados, like many of his contemporaries, was interested in trying to re-create the spirit of Madrid as typified in Goya, and the music of his principal opera, *Goyescas* (New York, 1916), was expanded from a series of piano pieces of the same title. The plot of this opera has a strong tinge of Italian verismo.

The mixture of romanticism and nationalism with a musical idiom related to that of Franck and D'Indy which was so characteristic of Pedrell is found likewise in the operas of Angel Barrios (b. 1862) and Conrado del Campo y Zabalata (b. 1879); their jointly composed *El Avapiés* [56] was performed at Madrid in 1919. Another Pedrell

55 On Isaac Albéniz (1860–1909) see Klein, "Albéniz's Opera, *Pepita Jiménez,*" *Musical Times* LIX (March, 1918) 116–17; Collet, *Albéniz et Granados;* Istel, "Isaac Albéniz," MQ XV (1929) 117–48. On Enrique Granados y Campina (1867–1916) see studies by Boladeres Ibern and Subirá.
56 The title is the name of a quarter in Madrid.

disciple was Amadeo Vives (1871–1932), composer of many zarzuelas and other dramatic works, including the "lyric eclogue" *Maruxa* (1914) and the three-act comic opera *Doña Francisquita* (1923), which has been very successful in both Spain and South America. Joachín Turina (b. 1882) is significant chiefly for his orchestral and pianoforte compositions, though he has produced a few operas (*Margot*, 1914; *La adúltera penitente*, 1917; *Jardín de Oriente*, 1923). A more conservative composer was Vicente Arregui Garay (1871–1925), with his prize-winning opera *Yolanda* (performed 1923). Two of the best known modern Spanish operas are by Manuel de Falla.[57] *La vida breve* ("Life Is Short"; composed 1905, performed 1913) is less notable for its dramatic qualities than for its effective and authentic Andalusian musical background, and especially for the ballets in Act II. The marionette opera, *El retablo de Maese Pedro* ("Master Peter's Puppet Show," 1923), is an interesting dramatic experiment in a more modern idiom, using an orchestra of only twenty-five players. De Falla's ballets *El amor brujo* (1915) and *El sombrero de tres picos* (1919) should also be mentioned as important modern works for the theatre.

In addition to his influence on what may be called the main stream of modern Spanish opera, Pedrell is also the founder of the regional school of Catalonia. The leading figure in this school is Jaime Pahissa (b. 1880), with *La presó de Lleida* ("The Prison of Lérida," 1906; rewritten in 1928 as a three-act opera *La Princèsa Margarida*) and *Gala placidia* (1913). Other Catalan composers are Enric Morera (*Emporium*, 1906),[58] Juan Lamote de Grignon, b. 1872 (*Hesperia*, 1907), and Joan Manén, b. 1883 (*Acté*, 1903). Independent regional development is characteristic of Spanish music, but the only extensive regional opera outside Catalonia is found in the Basque country. The outstanding composer here was José María Usandizaga (1887–1915) with the nationalistic *Mendi-Mendyian* (1910) and the very successful Puccinian melodramatic opera *Las golondrinas* ("The Swallows," 1914). Another Basque composer is Jesús Guridí (b. 1886), whose national folk opera *Mirentxu* (1910) was followed in 1920 by a more ambitious work with some Wagnerian traits, *Amaya*, and a successful zarzuela *El Caserio* ("The Hamlet") in 1926.

The early history of dramatic music in Portugal [59] is similar to that of Spain, except that there was no distinct national form of as great

57 See biography of De Falla (1876–1946) by R. Manuel.
58 See biography of Morera (1865–1942) by Iglesias.
59 Bibliography: Luper, "The Music of Portugal," in Chase, *Music of Spain*, chap. XVIII; Vieira, *Diccionario biographico de musicos portuguezes;* Fonseca Benevides, *O real theatro de S. Carlos de Lisboa;* Lavignac, *Encyclopédie*, Pt. I, Vol. IV, pp. 2422–35, 2447–57.

importance as the tonadilla. The first opera in Portuguese was *La vida do grande D. Quixote de la Mancha* (1733) by Antonio José da Silva (1705–1739), an isolated attempt which led to nothing. Italian opera came to Portugal as early as 1682, but its flourishing period began only about 1720. Of the Portuguese composers who devoted themselves to writing in the Italian style, the chief was Marcos Antonio Portugal,[60] whose thirty-five operas were widely performed in Europe in the late eighteenth and early nineteenth centuries. He was also the composer of twenty-one comic operas to Portuguese texts. Italian and French opera continued to dominate the Portuguese stage throughout the nineteenth century; Miguel Pereira's (1843–1901) opera *Eurico* (1870), with Italian text arranged from a Portuguese novel, is typical of this tendency. Native composers only occasionally adopted their own language or musical idiom, except for comic pieces. In this genre, however, there were successful works by Antonio Luiz Miró, d. 1853 (*A marqueza*, 1848); Guilherme Cossoul, 1828 – 1880 (*A cisterna do diablo*, "The Devil's Cistern," 1850); Francisco Alves Rente, 1851–1891 (*Verde gaio*, "Light Yellow," 1876); and Domingo Cyriaco de Cardoso, 1846–1900 (*O burro do Senhor Alcaide*, "The Mayor's Donkey," 1891). An outstanding nationalist composer was Alfredo Keil, of whose serious Portuguese operas *Serrana* (1899) was most frequently performed. The principal contemporary composer of operas in Portugal is Ruy Coelho, b. 1891 (*Belkiss*, 1938).

Opera in Latin America [61] has been for the most part only an off-

60 M. A. Portugal (1762–1830), after producing some operas at Lisbon, rose to fame in Italy from 1793 to 1799. He was conductor at Lisbon from 1799 to 1810, then fled to Brazil, where he remained the rest of his life.

61 Chase, *A Guide to Latin-American Music* (1945). Publications of the Pan American Union, Washington, D.C.: *Music in Latin America* (1942); *The Music of Argentina*, by Albert T. Luper (1944); *The Music of Brazil*, by Albert T. Luper (1944). Periodicals: *Handbook of Latin American Studies* (Cambridge, Mass., annually from 1935); *Boletín latino-americano de música*, 5 vols. (Montevideo, 1935–1941); *Rivista brasileira de música* (quarterly, from 1934); special number of RM, February–March, 1940 ("La Musique dans les pays latins"). See further: Slonimsky, *Music of Latin America;* Chase, *The Music of Spain; idem*, articles with bibliographies in *Harvard Dictionary of Music* (by countries); Alfredo Fiorda Kelley, *Cronología de las óperas . . . etc. cantados en Buenos Aires* [1825–1933]; Almeida, *História da música brasileira* (2d ed., 1942); Cernicchiaro, *Storia della musica nel Brasile;* Ayesterán, *Crónica de una temporada musical en el Montevideo de 1830;* Abascal Brunet, *Apuntes para la historia del teatro en Chile;* Saldívar, *Historia de la música en México;* Galindo, *Nociones de historia de la música mejicana;* Mayer-Serra, *Panorama de la música mexicana;* Alarcón, "La ópera en Mexico," *Boletín del instituto mexicano de musicología* I (1940) 5–9; Maria y Campos, *Una temporada de opera italiana en Oaxaca* [1874–1875]; Tolón, *Operas cubanas y sus autores.*

shoot of Italian and Spanish opera. In the colonial period the missionaries promoted plays with music, and at larger centers (for example, Lima) there were performances of the works of Calderón and other Spanish dramatists with music. A few tonadillas were imported in the eighteenth century. There is an eighteenth-century opera, La Partenope, composed by Manuel de Sumaya and performed at Mexico City in 1711. Regular performances of opera began in many Latin-American countries during the second quarter of the nineteenth century. Brazil had a national Opera from 1857; a famous Brazilian composer was Antonio Carlos Gomes, some of whose operas used native subjects, though all were in an Italian style of music modeled on Verdi.[62] The same Italianism is found in Henrique Eulalio Gurjão (1833–1885), whose best-known opera was Idalia (1881). Leopoldo Miguez (1850–1902) was influenced by Wagner in Os Saldunes (1901). Even the so-called "nationalist" composer Alberto Nepomuceno (1864–1920) did not develop an independent musical style in his operas.

In Argentina the Italian influence was even stronger, though national subjects were occasionally used, as in La indigena (1862) by Wenceslao Fumi (1823–1880) and in Pampa (1897) and Yupansky (1899) by Arturo Berutti (1862–1938). Justin Clérice (1863–1908) won recognition in Europe for his French comic operas and ballets.

In Mexico, Italian operas were composed by Melesio Morales, 1838–1908 (Ildegonda, 1865), and works in the German romantic style by Ricardo Castro, 1864–1907 (Atzimba; La leyenda de Rudel). A distinguished national one-act opera, using popular melodies, was Guatimotzin (1871) by Aniceto Ortega (1823–1875).

Most of the favorite Spanish zarzuelas were immediately brought to the new world and inspired similar works by local composers in all Latin American countries. Thus the Venezuelan José Angel Montero (1839–1881) produced fifteen zarzuelas as well as an opera, Virginia (1873). In Colombia, zarzuelas and similar pieces were composed by Juan Crisóstomo Osorio y Ricaurte (1863–1887) and Santos Cifuentes (1870–1932); in Mexico there was a popular comic opera, Keofar (1893) by Felipe Villanueva. Other Latin American opera

[62] Gomes (1836–1896) was educated at Rio de Janeiro and Milan. His most famous opera, Il Guarany (1870), is still given in Italy and Brazil. See studies by Seidl, Marchant, and Andrade; also Correa de Azvedo, "Carlos Gomez," Boletín latino-americano de música III (1937) 83–87; Castro, Carlo Gomez.

composers in this period were: in Colombia, Augusto Azzali (*Lhidiac,* 1893) and José María Ponce de León, 1846–1882 (*Ester; Florinda*); in Peru, Daniel Alomias Robles, 1871–1942 (*Illa-Cori*), and Theodoro Valcárcel, 1902–1942 (*Suray-Surita,* ballet opera); in Chile, Eleodoro Ortiz de Zarate, b. 1865 (*La fioraia di Lugano,* 1895; Italian text); and in Cuba, Eduardo Sánches de Fuentes y Peláez, b. 1876 (*Dolorosa,* 1910; *Kabelia,* 1942).[63]

The twentieth-century national musical renaissance in Latin America has not brought forth operas comparable in either numbers or importance to the music produced in other forms. In Argentina, where there is more native opera than anywhere else, the Italian influence is still predominant. This is especially the case with Ettore Panizza (b. 1875), the dean of living Argentine opera composers, whose works include *Il fidanzato del mare* ("The Bridegroom of the Sea," 1897), *Medio evo latino* (1900; three one-act operas, each placed in a different Latin country and a different medieval century), *Aurora* (1908, commissioned for the opening of the new Teatro Colón at Buenos Aires), and *Bisanzio* (composed about 1925). Alfredo Schiuma's (b. 1885) Italian opera *Tabaré* (1925), closely patterned after Verdi's *Forza del destino,* has been very successful; a highly praised recent work of Schiuma is *Las Virgenes del sol* (1939).[64] A more definitely national group is represented by Felipe Boero (b. 1885) with his folk opera *El matrero* ("The Rogue," 1929). Others in this group are Pascual de Rogatis, b. 1881 (*Hemac,* 1916; *La novia del hereje,* "The Heretic's Bride," 1935), Raul Espoile, b. 1889 (*La ciudad roja,* "The Red City," 1938), and Enrique Casella, b. 1891 (*La tapera,* "The Ruin").

In Brazil the new nationalism is evident in the works of Oscar Lorenzo Fernandez, b. 1897 (*Malazarte,* 1941), Francisco Mignone (b. 1897), and Comargo Guarnieri, b. 1907 (one-act comic opera *Pedro Malazarte,* 1942). Heitor Villa-Lobos (b. 1881), the leading present-day South American composer, wrote five operas early in his career, but only one (*Izaht,* composed 1912–1914) has been performed, and that only in a concert version (1940).

63 See Chase, "Some Notes on Afro-Cuban Music and Dancing," *Inter-American Monthly* (Washington, D.C.) I, No. 8 (December, 1942) 32–33.
64 Ferrari Nicolay, "En torno a *Las Virgenes*," *Estudios* (Buenos Aires) Año 29 (1939) tomo 62, pp. 29–46.

A recent Mexican opera is *Tata Vasca* (1941), by Miguel Bernal Jimenez (b. 1910).[65]

THE BRITISH ISLES [66] AND THE UNITED STATES OF AMERICA.—"English Opera—the darkest page of our musical history," wrote Henry Davey.[67] His despairing estimate holds with all force for the nineteenth century, when serious opera in England was universally understood to mean Italian opera, that "exotic and irrational entertainment" which the British had been patronizing ever since the days of Dr. Johnson.[68] Almost the only English musical stage works to have any success at all in the nineteenth century were those of the light variety—Balfe, Wallace, Benedict, and (later) Sullivan. The Carl Rosa Opera Company, beginning in 1875, commissioned a few English works, including some from Arthur Goring Thomas, 1851–1892 (*Esmeralda*, 1883; *Nadeshda*, 1885) and the zealous Wagner apostle Frederick Corder (1852–1932). Sullivan's *Ivanhoe* made a great stir at its first production in 1891 but has long since disappeared from the stage. Other operas of a romantic cast were produced by Cowen, Mackenzie, and Stanford.[69] Mackenzie's most popular opera was *The Cricket on the Hearth* (composed about 1900, performed 1914). Stanford attempted to create an English *Meistersinger* in *The Canterbury Pilgrims* (1884), but is best known for his comic opera *Shamus O'Brien* (1896); his *Much Ado about Nothing* made a favorable impression at its first performance in 1901 and was revived in 1935. A later work, *The Critic* (1916), is said to be equally deserving. One of the best English opera composers in the early twentieth century was Dame Ethel Smyth (1858–1944), whose *Wreckers* (first given at Leipzig in 1906 in German as *Strandrecht*) is a very effective work;

65 See Barros Sierra, "*Tata Vasco* y su partitura," *Romance* II (April, [1941]) 23.

66 Streatfeild, *Musiciens anglais contemporains* (1913); Holbrooke, *Contemporary British Composers* (1925).

67 *History of English Music*, 2d ed., p. 442.

68 Cf. Mapleson, *Memoirs,* and Carlyle, "The Opera," in *Critical and Miscellaneous Essays* IV, 397–403.

69 Sir Frederic Hymen Cowen (1852–1935) wrote four operas and two operettas, as well as many symphonies and oratorios, but is remembered chiefly for some of his shorter pieces. See his memoirs, *My Art and My Friends.*

Sir Alexander Campbell Mackenzie (1847–1935), noted conductor and educator, wrote four operas and an operetta, as well as many orchestral pieces.

Sir Charles Villiers Stanford (1852–1924) wrote seven operas and many orchestral works and edited several volumes of Irish folk songs. See studies by Fuller-Maitland (*The Music of Parry and Stanford*, chap. 9) and H. P. Greene.

a comic opera in the tradition of Sullivan, *The Boatswain's Mate* (1916), has been frequently performed in England.[70]

Frederick Delius [71] composed six operas, the best of which is *A Village Romeo and Juliet,* first performed (in German) at Berlin in 1907. This work, which from its story might almost have been entitled "A Village Tristan and Isolde," is full of lovely music in a late romantic style somewhat influenced by impressionism—rich textured, chromatic, with long expressive melodic lines for the solo voices and some fine choral scenes. The use of Celtic folk-song idiom, as in Vreli's song at the opening of scene 4, is also worthy of remark. The popular orchestral selection *"The Walk to Paradise Gardens"* (from the end of scene 5) may be taken as typical of the general style.

The revival of Celtic literature in the late nineteenth and early twentieth centuries led to a number of operas on Celtic legends. Most notable among these was Josef Holbrooke's mythological Welsh trilogy *The Cauldron of Anwen,*[72] broadly conceived along Wagnerian lines and written in a neo-romantic musical style strongly influenced by that of Wagner. Welsh subjects have also attracted Joseph Parry (1841–1903), Granville Bantock, 1868–1946 (*Caedmar,* 1892; *The Seal Woman,* 1924), and George Lloyd (b. 1913). Scottish stories or legends have been used by Hamish MacCunn, 1868–1916 (*Jeanie Deans,* 1894; *Diarmid,* 1897), and Irish by Robert O'Dwyer, b. 1860 (*Eithne,* 1910), and Geoffrey Palmer, b. 1882 (*Sruth na Maoile,* "The Sea of Moyle," 1923).

English operetta and light opera of this period were represented by Alfred Cellier (1844–1891); Edward Soloman (1853–1895); George H. Clutsam (b. 1866); Sidney Jones 1869–1946 (*The Geisha,* 1896); Edward German, 1862–1936 (*Merrie England,* 1902); Ivan Caryll, 1861–1921 (*The Duchess of Dantzic,* 1903); Edward Naylor, 1867–1934 (*The Angelus,* 1909); and Hubert Bath, 1883–1945 (*Bubbles,* 1923). Recent comic operas by English composers are Lord Berners's (b. 1883) *Carosse du Saint-Sacrament* (1923) and Arthur Benjamin's (b. 1893) *The Devil Take Her* (1931)—both witty one-act pieces in a fluent modern style.

In the present century many serious operas have been written for the English stage, though most have met with only indifference from the general public. Nearly all these works are distinguished by good

[70] See Capell, "Dame Ethel Smyth's Operas at Covent Garden," *Monthly Musical Record* LIII (1923) 197–98; also the composer's own writings, especially *Impressions That Remained* (1919).

[71] See biography of Delius (1862–1934) by Heseltine.

[72] See G. Lowe's biography of Holbrooke (b. 1878). The three operas of his trilogy were performed as follows: *The Children of Don,* 1912; *Dylan, Son of the Wave,* 1914; *Bronwen,* 1929.

literary quality and patent artistic sincerity in the musical settings, and the composers deserve recognition for having labored in the face of such discouraging conditions. John Edmund Barkworth's (1858–1929) *Romeo and Juliet* (1916) is the most important of his three operas. Alick Maclean's (1872–1936) *Quentin Durward,* published in 1894, was produced in 1920, and Robert Ernest Bryson's (1867–1942) *The Leper's Flute* in 1926. Philip Napier Miles [73] was active in organizing opera productions in England and wrote two operas (*Markheim,* 1924; *Westward Ho,* 1913). Effective in performance, though simple and conservative in musical style, are the operas of Nicholas Comyn Gatty (b. 1874): *Duke or Devil* (1909), the three-act romantic Shakespearean *Tempest* (1920), and the charming fairy opera *Prince Ferelon* (1919–1921). Eugène Goossens (b. 1893) has had considerable success with two operas in modern idiom, both to librettos by Arnold Bennett: *Judith* (1929) and *Don Juan de Mañera* (1937).

Other composers in this group are Sir Donald Francis Tovey, 1875–1940 (*The Bride of Dionysus,* 1929); Colin Macleod Campbell, b. 1890 (*Thais and Talmaae,* 1921); Lawrance Arthur Collingwood, b. 1887 (*Macbeth,* 1934); and the distinguished conductor Albert Coates, b. 1882 (*Samuel Pepys,* 1929; *Pickwick,* 1936.)

A recent movement has developed from interest in a type of opera adapted to limited conditions of performance and aiming to revive the chamber-opera spirit of Blow and Purcell. The leader of this revival was a disciple of Wagner's theories of the music drama, and one who in his own music followed a frankly romantic line during a period when romanticism was decidedly unfashionable. Rutland Boughton [74] dreamed of founding a British Bayreuth at Glastonbury, where festivals were organized in 1914 and for several years after the First World War. The project was finally abandoned, but its influence remained. Of Boughton's own nine operas, the most successful was *The Immortal Hour* (1914); many of his librettos were based on Arthurian legend. Equally national in subject, but of less heroic scope, were chamber operas by such composers as Charles Wood (1866–1926), Cyril Bradley Rootham (1875–1938), Martin Shaw

---

[73] On Napier Miles (1865–1935) see a study by Colles, M&L XVII (1936) 357–67.
[74] On Boughton (b. 1878) see his own books listed in bibliography, and Antcliffe, "The British School of Music-Drama," MQ IV (1918) 117–27.

(b. 1876), and Cecil Armstrong Gibbs (b. 1889). To these may be added from a younger generation the name of Benjamin Britten (b. 1913), whose *Paul Bunyan* was produced at Columbia University, New York, in 1941. Performances of his *Peter Grimes* at Tanglewood in 1946 have attracted much attention; his most recent opera is *The Rape of Lucretia* (1946).

The two most notable English composers of the early twentieth century, Gustav Holst and Ralph Vaughan Williams,[75] have made significant contributions to opera. Holst's *Savitri* (composed 1908, performed 1916) is a chamber opera of exquisite tenderness and simple emotion, in a musical style which suggests the Eastern setting of the story without attempt at literal imitation of Hindu melodies, and which contains some beautiful writing for women's chorus. Holst's principal opera, a one-act comedy *The Perfect Fool,* had very successful performances at Covent Garden in 1923; the music shows the composer fully emancipated from the neo-Wagnerian tendencies of his earlier dramatic works. *At the Boar's Head* (1925) is a Shakespearean intermezzo for *Henry IV,* a jolly work made up very largely of traditional English tunes, somewhat in the manner of ballad opera. The influence of these works is not to be reckoned so much by their outward success as by the fact that they represent the serious, original, and uncompromising efforts of a first-rank English composer in the restricted and thankless field of native opera. Much the same may be said of Vaughan Williams' dramatic works. *The Shepherds of the Delectable Mountains,* a pastoral episode after Bunyan, has been frequently revived in England since its first performance in 1922. *Hugh the Drover, or Love in the Stocks* (1924) is a ballad-type opera with continuous music, containing allusions to a number of traditional tunes without direct quotation, and as thoroughly English in spirit as any of Gilbert and Sullivan. *Sir John in Love* (1929), based on Shakespeare's *Merry Wives of Windsor,* is the composer's biggest work for the stage (four acts); the music is similar to that of *Hugh the Drover,* but more highly developed both formally and harmonically—a truly English *Falstaff* not unworthy of comparison with Verdi's Italian one. The Gilbert and Sullivan tradition

---

75 On Holst (1874–1934) see biography by his daughter, Imogen Holst; on Vaughan Williams (b. 1872) see Howes, *The Dramatic Works of Ralph Vaughan Williams.*

is carried on in *The Poisoned Kiss* (1936), a tuneful comic opera with spoken dialogue. *Riders to the Sea* (1937) is a restrained but moving setting of Synge's play, in neomodal style with much parallel chord progression and with a subdued intensity of feeling reminiscent of the composer's well-known song cycle, *On Wenlock Edge.*

The early history of opera in the United States of America [76] is similar to that in the other nations of the Western Hemisphere. It begins in colonial times with the importation of comic operas from Europe (in this case English ballad opera instead of the Spanish zarzuela); during the nineteenth century fashion favors alternately Italian opera, French grand opera, and German music drama. Tentative and unsuccessful efforts are made by native composers to imitate the musical style currently in vogue, sometimes applying it to "American" subjects, the Indians and the Puritan colonists being the two commonest sources of material for librettos. Prizes are offered and awarded; new operas by American composers are produced with great fanfare, given a few performances, then shelved and forgotten. There is no continuously subsidized theatre specifically for American opera, and in the absence of any assurance of adequate performance no first-rate composer will undertake to write one unless he is motivated by an irresistible inner urge or is an inveterate optimist. A few experimental works on a small scale are produced, but the American public at large shows little interest in them, preferring to hear *La Bohême* or *Die Walküre* in sumptuous settings and sung by expensive stars. In a word, American opera at the present time is in much the same state as English opera: an unrealized ideal. All the more honor, then, to those composers who have essayed this difficult field without much hope of reward or recognition. It must be added, unfortunately, that in many cases the honor is due for good intentions rather than actual results, though one should not too severely reproach American opera composers for shortcomings rising only out of their lack of experience and limited opportunity to hear their own works in performance.

[76] General bibliography: histories of American music by Ritter (to 1880), Elson, and Howard; *Dictionary of American Biography;* Howard, *Our Contemporary Composers:* Hipsher, *American Opera and Its Composers;* Graf, *The Opera and Its Future in America;* Mattfeld, *A Hundred Years of Grand Opera in New York;* Mapleson, *Memoirs;* Kolodin, *The Metropolitan Opera;* Gatti-Casazza, *Memories of the Opera;* Moore, *Forty Years of Opera in Chicago;* Carson, *St. Louis Goes to the Opera.*

It is possible that the first opera performance in the United States took place as early as 1703, but the earliest date which can yet be substantiated is 1735, when *Flora, or Hob in the Well,* a ballad opera, was presented at Charleston, South Carolina. *The Begger's Opera* and several similar works were played in New York in 1750–1751, and a like repertoire was heard in Annapolis and Upper Marlborough, Maryland, in 1752. In the same year ballad operas were given at Williamsburg, Virginia. Philadelphia followed two years later. All during the latter half of the eighteenth century there were seasons of opera, fairly regularly at New York and sporadically at other places; the total number in proportion to the population was actually greater than at any period since. Most of the works so presented were English comic operas (Shield, Storace, Dibdin, and others), but there were also a few French opéras comiques (Grétry, Monsigny, Philidor), usually in translation and with the music more or less extensively altered and adapted by English and American arrangers, besides many pantomimes and ballets. French opera, both grand and comic, flourished at New Orleans from 1791 until the Civil War and even afterwards. The first season of regular Italian opera in New York was in 1825. From that time on, the uneven career of foreign opera in the United States becomes too complicated to follow here even in outline, the more since our chief concern is not with "opera in America" but "American opera."

The known American operas of the eighteenth century have been thoroughly studied by Oscar G. T. Sonneck.[77] Many of these were of the type of *The Beggar's Opera,* with characters and dialects appropriate to the American locale. Toward the end of the century there were imitations and adaptations of popular plays, such as *The Archers* (1796), with music by the English-born composer Benjamin Carr (1769?–1831), which plainly was inspired by Schiller's *Tell;* in 1797 there was a melodrama, *Ariadne Abandoned,* probably imitated from Benda. Still other "operas" were on patriotic themes, with battle scenes and allegorical tableaux. None of these pieces had continuous music; most, in fact, were merely plays with incidental songs. The composers (or arrangers) included Francis Hopkinson (*The*

---

[77] "Early American Operas," SIMG VI (1904–1905) 428–95; also in his *Miscellaneous Studies,* pp. 16–92. See also Sonneck's *Bibliography of Early Secular American Music* (new ed., 1945); *Early Concert Life in America; Early Opera in America;* and further, Wegelin, *Micah Hawkins; idem, Early American Plays;* Seilhamer, *History of the American Theatre.*

Temple of Minerva, 1781),[78] James Hewitt (*Tammany*, 1794),[79] and Victor Pelissier (*Edwin and Angelina*, 1796).[80]

So little is known about the history of American music in the first half of the nineteenth century that it is impossible to make any definitive statement about American opera in this period. So far as present information goes there were no operatic works by American composers, except for the plays-with-incidental-music type, until 1845. In that year was produced at Philadelphia "the first publicly performed grand opera written by a native American," *Leonora*, by William Henry Fry [81]—a work of considerable competence and musical interest, modeled on the styles of Donizetti and Meyerbeer. Fry's next opera, *Notre-Dame de Paris*, was given at Philadelphia in 1864. Another American composer of this period was George Frederick Bristow,[82] whose *Rip Van Winkle* (New York, 1855) is arranged from Irving's tale with added love scenes and other episodes. There is some spoken dialogue; the music, unfortunately, is completely conventional and undistinguished, a lame imitation of the fashionable European light-opera style.

Of the many German-descended or German-trained American composers in the later nineteenth century, the most important in the field of opera was Walter Damrosch,[83] whose first success with *The Scarlet Letter* (1896) was hardly equaled by his two later works, *Cyrano* (1913) and *The Man without a Country* (1937). Damrosch's music is pleasantly put together, technically well fashioned, but does not depart from the style of late nineteenth-century German romanticism. A rather more original score, though one still strongly suggestive of Wagner, is John Knowles Paine's *Azara* (published 1901; performed only in concert version, 1907).[84]

[78] On Hopkinson (1737–1791) see study by Sonneck.
[79] Hewitt (1770–1827) was born in England and came to New York in 1792. He wrote music (almost none preserved) for at least seven operas. See Howard, "The Hewitt Family in American Music," MQ XVII (1931) 25–39.
[80] The dates of Pelissier's birth and death are not known. He was undoubtedly a native of France, coming to America in 1792 or earlier.
[81] Fry (1813–1864) was one of the earliest active propagandists for American music. He composed four program symphonies and several choral works in addition to his two operas. See Upton, *The Musical Works of William Henry Fry*.
[82] Bristow (1825–1898) wrote several large choral and symphonic works, two quartets, and many smaller pieces.
[83] Damrosch was born in Germany in 1862 but has lived most of his life in the United States. See his autobiography, *My Musical Life*.
[84] Paine (1839–1906), the first professor of music in an American university (Harvard, 1875), composed many choral, symphonic, and chamber works.

Two earlier opera composers of German birth were Eduard Sobolewski, 1808–1872 (*Mohega,* Milwaukee, 1859) and Johann Heinrich Bonawitz, 1839–1917 (*Ostrolenka,* Philadelphia, 1874). With this group may also be listed the Americans Frederick Grant Gleason, 1848–1903 (*Otho Visconti,* Chicago, 1907) and Louis Adolphe Coerne, 1870–1922, of whose three operas only *Zenobia* was ever performed (Bremen, 1905). To the same generation as Coerne belong Arthur Finley Nevin, 1871–1943 (*Poia,* Berlin, 1910; *The Daughter of the Forest,* Chicago, 1918), Joseph Carl Breil, 1870–1926 (*The Legend,* New York, 1919), and John Adam Hugo, b. 1873 (*The Temple Dancer,* New York, 1919).

The German influence was still preponderant in American music in the early part of the twentieth century, but by this time composers were more thoroughly trained, more ambitious, versatile, and productive and spoke a more authoritative musical language. Nevertheless it is significant that neither of the two leading figures in this generation, Loeffler and MacDowell, composed an opera. The most important dramatic composers were Converse, Hadley, and Parker.[85] Converse's *The Pipe of Desire* (Boston, 1906) was the first American opera ever to be produced at the Metropolitan (1910); it is a pleasant and tuneful score showing some impressionist influence. Another opera, *The Sacrifice,* was presented at Boston in 1911. Hadley's chief successes, in a sound conservative style, were *Azora, Daughter of Montezuma* (Chicago, 1917) and *Cleopatra's Night* (New York, 1920).

Horatio Parker's *Mona* (New York, 1912) and *Fairyland* (Los Angeles, 1915), each of which won a ten-thousand-dollar prize, are still regarded by many as the most significant American operas, important works which have been unjustly neglected. The neglect is certainly not due to any technical shortcomings of the scores, which are sound in craftsmanship, large in conception, distinguished in musical ideas, and excellent in theatrical effects. But the librettos are definitely dated: *Mona,* a sufficiently good drama in essence, is markedly romantic in plot and language, with the scene laid in ancient

---

[85] Frederick Shepherd Converse (1871–1940) wrote four operas (two not performed) and much orchestral and choral music.

Henry Kimball Hadley (1871–1937) wrote six operas, four symphonies, many overtures, and other orchestral and choral works. See biography by Boardman, and study by Berthoud.

Horatio William Parker (1863–1919) was, like Paine, Converse, and Hadley, of New England birth and training and studied in Germany. Most of his music is choral (oratorio. *Hora Novissima,* 1893). See Chadwick, *Horatio Parker;* Smith, "A Study of Horatio Parker." MQ XVI (1930) 153–69; and memoir by Semler.

Britain and the whole obviously owing much to *Tristan und Isolde.*
Fairyland is one of those combinations of whimsy, symbolism, and
vague pantheistic aspiration such as are found in the fairy operas of
Rimsky-Korsakov or in Converse's *Pipe of Desire.* Parker's music is
likewise typical of the late romantic period. *Mona* is a slightly modernized *Tristan,* with the same sort of continuous symphonic structure, system of leitmotifs, opulent harmony, chromatic melody, and
avoidance of perfect cadences which characterize its model; *Fairyland* is somewhat lighter in texture and more diatonic in harmony
—Wagner leavened by a dash of late Strauss. Musically, the gravest
accusation that can be made against either opera is that the same
things had been said before; and it may be regretted that these works
had the misfortune to come at a moment when tastes in musical matters were on the verge of a radical change.

Of later American operas in a conservative style, designed for full-
scale production, the most successful were two by Deems Taylor: [86]
The King's Henchman (New York, 1927) and *Peter Ibbetson* (New
York, 1931), smooth, expert works in a mild late-romantic style with
modern trimmings, well molded to the taste of that large majority
of the opera-going public who are pleased with expressive melodies
and sensuous harmonies which pleasantly stimulate without disturb-
ing. Other American operas at the Metropolitan have been much
less enthusiastically received (for example, Richard Hageman's
Caponsacchi, 1937).[87] A brief popular success was obtained by the
Italian-born Gian-Carlo Menotti's opera buffa *Amelia Goes to the
Ball* (1937).[88] Among the American operas which have been produced under respectable auspices and gone their way without leaving
a mark may be mentioned Ernest Carter's *The White Bird* (Chicago,
1930), Forrest Hamilton's jazzy *Camille* (Chicago, 1930), and John

[86] Joseph Deems Taylor (b. 1885) is known for his orchestral suite *Through the Looking
Glass* (1922) and for cantatas, as well as his operas which have received more performances
at the Metropolitan than those of any other American composer. See study by J. T.
Howard.

[87] Hageman was born in Holland in 1882 and has been active in the United States as
accompanist and opera conductor since 1906. *Caponsacchi* was first performed in German
translation as *Tragödie in Arezzo* at Freiburg in 1932. The libretto is from Browning's
The Ring and the Book.

[88] Menotti was born in Italy in 1911. *Amelia,* his first opera, was performed in Philadelphia and at the Metropolitan in 1938. He composed a similar work for radio (*The Old
Maid and the Thief,* 1939), a serious grand opera, *The Island God* (1942), and a chamber
opera, *The Medium* (1946).

Laurence Seymour's prize-winning *In the Pasha's Garden* (New York, 1935).[89]

National scenes and subjects, as might be expected, have been frequently tried by composers. Charles Wakefield Cadman's *The Robin Woman (Shanewis)*,[90] given at the Metropolitan in 1918, uses a number of authentic Indian tunes and has an attractive, if superficial, melodic vein, but is very slight in substance and awkward in dramatic details. The same composer's *A Witch of Salem* (Chicago, 1926) has been frequently given in the United States.

The best American historical opera to date is Hanson's *Merry Mount* (New York, 1934),[91] a work incorporating many ballets and choruses in a wild, implausible story of Puritan New England. It may be the extravagance of the libretto which has interfered with the full success of *Merry Mount*, or it may be a somewhat stiff, oratorio-like, undramatic quality in much of the music. The harmonic style is generally static; the chords are built on pandiatonic principles (with occasional bitonality) and there is much use of modal effects and parallel progressions. The melodies likewise are often static, consisting of reiterated phrases within a narrow range. There are four distinct idioms: the psalmlike choruses of the Puritans; the madrigalesque worldly songs of the revelers (beginning of Act II); the beautifully sensuous love music of Bradford's aria "Rise up, my love" and the duet which is its continuation; and the bacchanalian strains for the evil spirits of the "Walpurgisnacht" ballet in Act II. The music is able, serious, and sincere; there is no compromise of principle, no writing down to a supposed lower taste of an opera audience. The whole is good enough to make one sad at the thought of what American composers might do in opera if they had more incentive to produce and more opportunity to try out their works in actual performance.

In the period following the First World War American composers, in common with those of other nationalities, produced many operas which, for lack of a better common descriptive term, may be called

[89] For fuller lists see Hipsher, *American Opera*, or Howard, *Our Contemporary Composers*.

[90] Cadman (1881–1946) wrote six operas and seven operettas, numerous orchestral suites, cantatas, songs, etc.

[91] Howard Hanson (b. 1896), director of the Eastman School of Music, is widely known for his symphonies, choral works, and chamber music. *Merry Mount* is his only opera. See Tuthill, "Howard Hanson," MQ XXII (1936) 140–53.

"experimental." Such a work was George Antheil's *Transatlantic* (Frankfurt, Germany, 1930),[92] which uses jazz tunes and odd mechanical effects in a fantastic, satirical plot similar to Křenek's *Jonny spielt auf*. Louis Gruenberg's *Emperor Jones* (New York, 1933),[93] based on Eugene O'Neill's play, cleverly exploits a neoprimitive orchestra with percussive drum rhythms and choral interludes in an exciting drama. Perhaps the most publicized of all American experimental operas is Virgil Thomson's *Four Saints in Three Acts* (Hartford, 1934),[94] on a libretto by Gertrude Stein, in a sophisticatedly simple musical style and with the melodic lines fitted to the text with exceptional sensitivity.

In view of the very limited opportunities for the production of large operas it is natural that in America, as in England, there is considerable interest in chamber opera of various kinds. An early work in this field is Lazare Saminsky's *Gagliarda of a Merry Plague* (New York, 1925).[95] Marc Blitzstein [96] has also produced a number of chamber operas in New York. The first of these to attract wide notice was *The Cradle Will Rock* (1937), a leftist propaganda play, alternating spoken dialogue, recitatives, and singable tunes in a cultured and clever jazz idiom. *No for an Answer* (1941) has relatively more music (including some very effective choral portions) and a wider range of characterization and feeling, though still based for the most part on the popular song style. The Juilliard Music School in New York has sponsored several chamber operas, including works by Gruenberg (*Jack and the Beanstalk,* 1931), Antheil (*Helen Retires,* 1934), Robert Russell Bennet (*Maria Malibran,* 1935), Albert Stoes-

[92] Antheil (b. 1900) has written much music for the stage and screen, three symphonies, and other orchestral and chamber works. See Pound, *Antheil and the Treatise of Harmony;* Thompson, "George Antheil," MMus VIII, No. 4 (May–June, 1931) 17–27; Wiesengrund-Adorno, critical review of *Transatlantic,* MMus VII, No. 4 (June–July, 1930) 38–41.
[93] Gruenberg (b. 1884) has written much orchestral and chamber music, but is best known for his stage works and the cantata *Daniel Jazz* (1923).
[94] Virgil Thomson (b. 1896) has written many articles and reviews and two books: *The State of Music* (1939) and *The Musical Scene* (1945): *Four Saints* is his best known composition. See Seldes, "Delight in the Theatre," MMus XI, No. 3 (March–April, 1934) 138–41.
[95] Saminsky (b. 1882) has composed five symphonies and other orchestral works; he has written many articles and two books (*Music of Our Day,* 1932). See Pisk, "Lazare Saminsky," *The Chesterian* XX (1938–39) 74–78.
[96] Blitzstein (b. 1905) has written six stage works and a number of songs and chamber pieces, besides many articles for periodicals. See Barlow, "Blitzstein's Answer," MMus XVIII, No. 2 (January–February, 1941) 81–83.

sel (*Garrick,* 1937), and Beryl Rubinstein (*The Sleeping Beauty,* 1938). Still other "school operas," suitable for use by semiprofessional or amateur groups, are Aaron Copland's *The Second Hurricane* (New York, 1937), Douglas Moore's *The Devil and Daniel Webster* (New York, 1939), Randall Thompson's *Solomon and Balkis* (Cambridge, 1942), Ernst Bacon's *A Tree on the Plains* (1942), and Normand Lockwood's *The Scarecrow* (1945).[97] As long as present conditions prevail it seems likely that the best possibilities for both the development of American opera composers and the education of audiences will be found in works of the chamber-opera type.

American operetta and comic opera may be traced from the works of the German-born Julius Eichberg, 1824–1893 (*The Doctor of Alcantara,* Boston, 1862) through Dudley Buck, 1839–1909 (*Deseret,* New York, 1880), Edgar Stillman Kelley, 1857–1944 (*Puritania,* Boston, 1892), George Whitefield Chadwick, 1854–1931 (*Tabasco,* Boston, 1894), and John Philip Sousa, 1854–1923 (*El Capitan,* Boston, 1896) to a climax in the works of Reginald de Koven, 1859–1920 (*Robin Hood,* Chicago, 1890) and Victor Herbert, 1859–1924 (*Babes in Toyland,* 1903). Both De Koven and Herbert attempted grand opera, but comparatively without success in either case (De Koven's *The Canterbury Pilgrims,* New York, 1917, and *Rip van Winkle,* Chicago, 1920; Herbert's *Natoma,* Philadelphia, 1911, and *Madeleine,* New York, 1914).

In light opera and musical comedy after the First World War the two leading figures were Jerome Kern, 1885–1945 (*Sally,* 1920) and George Gershwin, 1898–1937 (*Of Thee I Sing,* 1931). Each of these composers has written one distinguished work in more serious style: Kern's *Showboat* (1928) and Gershwin's *Porgy and Bess* (1935).[98] These widely popular works are practically American folk operas.

[97] Copland (b. 1900) is one of the best known contemporary American composers. His book *Our New Music* (1941) has a very discerning chapter on the opera music of Thomson and Blitzstein.

Moore (b. 1893) is the composer of three chamber operas and several symphonic works which have been frequently performed.

Thompson (b. 1899) is a distinguished composer of choral and symphonic music. *Solomon and Balkis* is his only opera.

Bacon (b. 1898) is a pianist, conductor, and the composer of several symphonic works.

Normand Lockwood (b. 1906) is particularly noted in the field of vocal and choral music.

[98] See review by Virgil Thomson, MMus XIII, No. 1 (November–December, 1935) 13–19.

28

Opera between Two Wars

T HE MOST RECENT EVENTS ARE NOTORI-
ously the most difficult to set in historical order. This is especially the
case with music in the period from the end of the First to the beginning of the Second World War, when so many apparently immutable
principles were being called in question and when for a time it
seemed almost incumbent on every composer to invent a new style
before he could begin to write music. It was only natural that the
opera, like all other forms, should be strongly affected by these new
currents, and that a great many works of an experimental nature
should be produced, particularly where economic and social conditions were favorable for such experimental work on a full scale, as in
Germany during the 1920's and in France for a somewhat longer
period. The revival of chamber opera was also a potent factor in
encouraging new dramatic and musical devices, since chamber operas
could be produced at less financial risk, and thus serve as a kind of
laboratory for new ideas. On the other hand, there are many forces
which always tend to make opera conservative, chief of which is the
cost of production (as compared with solo, chamber, or even symphonic music) and the consequent necessity of appealing to a large
public. Though it may be true that opera is the ideal medium through
which to introduce new musical ideas to the masses.[1] yet in practice
it has usually been found that during an unsettled era the masses are
uninterested in advanced notions and prefer their opera in a more
familiar idiom. Thus during the period under consideration there
was a considerable proportion of opera in musical and dramatic
styles which did not pretend to be radical in any respect, and which
advanced beyond the styles of the immediately preceding decade
either not at all, or else only slightly and in a direction easily to be
understood by the public. Some such works we have already noticed,
such as those of Deems Taylor in the United States, Richard Strauss

[1] Cf. George Antheil, MMus VII, No. 4 (June–July 1930) 11–16, and XI, No. 2 (January–
February, 1934) 89–94.

in Germany, and in general the later operas of established older composers. But there were other men, some old, some young, who of deliberate choice wrote conservatively; and not all these are negligible figures. Let us therefore first turn our attention to the progress of what may be called "orthodox" opera in the three principal operatic countries, Italy, France, and Germany.

One of the leading composers in Italy is Franco Alfano,[2] the choice of whom to complete Puccini's *Turandot* is significant of his historical position as a continuator of the main Italian opera tradition. Alfano had become known as early as 1904 with his *Risurrezione* ("Resurrection"), but his two principal works are the heavily tragic *Leggenda di Sakuntala* (1921) and the lyrical comedy *Madonna imperia* (1927). The latter may be taken as an example of his style. It is on a charming Boccaccio-like libretto (by Arthur Rossato) with neo-Puccinian music. The voice lines alternate smoothly between melodic phrases and a most flexible, lively, and expressive arioso, supported by luscious and delicate harmonies not unlike Ravel in many respects (complex key relationships, continual chromaticism, parallelism) and with beautiful impressionistic orchestration—a perfect match for the refinedly voluptuous text (Example 123). Alfano's *L'ultimo Lord* ("The Last Lord," 1930) is in a light, vivacious comic style, with a modern scene.

The operas of Ildebrando Pizzetti[3] are less conventional than those of Alfano but nevertheless do not attempt any radical reforms. One of Pizzetti's salient characteristics is his extensive use of polyphonic choruses, especially at the dramatic climaxes. This is seen already in his first opera *Fedra* (1915; text by D'Annunzio) and likewise in *Dèbora e Jaéle* (1922). These are his two most important stage works. The solo singing in both is in a close-packed, tense recitative, with occasional short melodic fragments closely molded to the text. The orchestra furnishes continuous musical support, full textured and expertly varied in color, a mosaic of motifs but without the systematic recurrences characteristic of the old leitmotif system. The

2 Alfano (b. 1876) has composed little except opera music. See Gatti, "Franco Alfano," MQ IX (1923) 556–77; *idem*, "Recent Italian Operas," MQ XXIII (1937) 77–88; Della Corte, *Rittrato di Franco Alfano*.
3 Pizzetti (b. 1880) has composed principally choral works and incidental music for plays in addition to his eight operas. See study by Gatti; also De'Paoli, "Pizzetti's Fra Gherardo," MMus VI, No. 2 (January–February, 1929) 39–42.

MADONNA IMPERIA

Ex.123.

Alfano

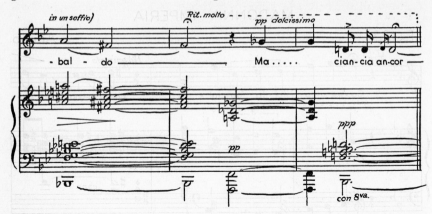

harmonies are late romantic rather than modernistic, with impressionist touches, strongly dramatic and always at high emotional tension. In *Fra Gherardo* (1928) Pizzetti attempted to introduce lyrical portions in the manner of nineteenth-century opera, but the result (perhaps partly due to the weak libretto) was a comparatively uninteresting hybrid. Of Pizzetti's later works *Orsèolo* (1935) has had some success in Italy, but not elsewhere.

A composer of decidedly prewar style was Ottorino Respighi,[4] though his best stage works were composed in the postwar period: the comic, colorful *Belfagor* (1923), *La campana sommersa* ("The Sunken Bell," 1927), the spectacular biblical ballet *Belkis, regina di Saba* (1930), the mystery play *Maria Egiziaca* (New York, 1932), and especially *La fiamma* ("The Flame," 1934) with its sumptuous orchestral texture. Ricardo Pick-Mangiagalli (b. 1862) has had some successful opera performances at Rome. The operas of Felice Lattuada (b. 1882) are conventional in the main, though the composer "distinguishes himself by an exuberance which sometimes attains its effect."[5] His *Preziose ridicole* (after Molière) was heard at the Metropolitan in 1930. Adriano Lualdi (b. 1887), experienced conductor and important musical official in Fascist Italy, wrote his most popular opera, *La figlia del re* ("The King's Daughter"), in 1922. The most prolific of younger Italian opera composers seems to be

4 Respighi (1879–1936) is best known for his symphonic poems and other instrumental works, also a few songs. He was the greatest master of orchestral color of his generation in Italy. He composed eight operas and several ballets. See biography by De Rensis.
5 G. Gatti, MMus XI, No. 4 (May–June, 1934) 216.

Lodovico Rocca (b. 1895); his best-known work, *Il dibuc* (1934), contains important choral sections.

In France the line of demarcation between prewar and postwar opera is much more clearly drawn than in either Italy or Germany. Strictly speaking, there are no important operas of a genuinely conservative type in France after the war, with the possible exception of Marcel Delannoy's (b. 1898) *Poirier de misère* (1927); there are, however, some works of a neoclassical nature which have a deceptive old-fashioned appearance, such as Henri Sauget's operetta *Le Plumet du colonel* (1925) and his opera *La Chartreuse de Parme*. Continuity with the past is generally most apparent in comic opera; some successful composers in this field were Alfred Bachelet (1864–1944) with *Quand le cloche sonnera* ("When the Clock Strikes," 1922); Charles Gaston Levadé (b. 1869) with *La Rôtisserie de la reine Pédauque* ("Queen Pédauque's Cook Shop," 1920) and *Le Peau de chagrin* ("The Shagreen Pelt," 1929); Marcel Samuel-Rousseau (b. 1882) with *Le Hulla* (1923) and *Le Bon Roi Dagobert* ("Good King Dagobert," 1927); and Arthur Honegger with *Les Aventures du roi Pausole* (1930). Perhaps the best comic operas of this period are by Jacques Ibert.[6] His *Angélique* (1927) is a witty one-act farce with spoken dialogue. The music is unpretentious, frankly of the entertainment variety, and very well adapted to this aim; it is in Ibert's scintillating epigrammatic manner, using polytonal effects, dance rhythms, and banal melodies dressed up with dissonant chords or skeleton-like harmonies, as in the chanson "Pauvre Madame Boniface" (Example 124), which is in the never-dying spirit of the old Paris vaudevilles. Ibert's later operatic works include *Le Roi d'Yvetot* (1930) and *L'Aiglon* (1937, in collaboration with Honegger).

Opera in Germany during the interwar years was strongly affected by the economic collapse of the late 1920's and the rise to power of the National Socialist regime in 1933; the former event put an end to a lush era of experimenting, and the latter officially discouraged all types of "modern" music. Therefore, German conservative composers in this period tend to divide into two groups: the first, which may be called "conservative by conviction," is made up of composers like Pfitzner, Strauss, and Schreker, whose style had already been

---

[6] Ibert (b. 1890) is noted especially for his ballets, cinema music, chamber works, and songs, as well as some half-dozen operas.

established earlier in the century; the younger group, "conservative with the blessing of the government," seems, on the basis of information at present available, to be of little importance. It includes Rudolf Wagner-Régeny (b. 1903), with two operas: *Der Günstling* ("The Favorite," 1935), a neo-Handelian work with choruses and

ANGÉLIQUE

Ex.124.   Ibert

arias, spiced with "a nice admixture of Kurt Weill"; [7] and *Die Bürger von Calais* ("The Citizens of Calais," 1939). The principal other member of this group is Werner Egk (b. 1901) with *Die Zaubergeige* ("The Magic Fiddle," 1935), a folk-opera plot with intricately rhythmed, sometimes polytonal, music; and *Peer Gynt* (1938). Among the older composers who may be said to belong to the conservative

[7] MMus XVI, No. 4 (May–June, 1939) 210.

party in this period are a few who have not been mentioned earlier. Paul Graener (1872–1944) had become known as conductor and composer before the war; his most popular opera was *Friedemann Bach* (1931). The distinguished Swiss composer Othmar Schoeck [8] is best known in opera for *Penthesilea* (1927). Paul von Klenau (b. 1883) produced a neo-Wagnerian work *Rembrandt von Rijn* in 1937. The most talented of this group is doubtless Walter Braunfels (b. 1882), whose operas, while not adventurous, have attractive melodies, good workmanship, charm, and a sense of the theatre. His best work, *Die Vögel* ("The Birds"), to his own libretto after Aristophanes, was first given in 1920. Braunfels' activity was suppressed during the Nazi regime, but for racial, not musical, reasons. The operas of Max Ettinger (b. 1874) continued the tradition of the Munich school of Thuille, Braunfels, and Waltershausen (*Frühlings Erwachen*, "Spring's Awakening," 1928). A brilliant younger composer of essentially conservative style, influenced by Strauss, Schreker, and Puccini, was Erich Wolfgang Korngold (*Die tote Stadt*, "The Dead City," 1920).[9]

We now turn to the consideration of those operas produced during the interwar period which may fairly be called modern in musical style.[10] There is no completely satisfactory method of classification in this field. Modernity may be evident to varying degrees in the different aspects of an opera: in the choice and treatment of subject, in the extent to which current social, economic, or political events are consciously reflected, in the relation between composer and audience, in the musical style itself, and in the relation between music and text. Despite the difficulties, however, some classification must be attempted unless we are willing to produce a mere chronology.

[8] On Schoeck (b. 1886) see essays by W. Schuh and H. Corrodi.
[9] Korngold (b. 1897) has produced some instrumental works, arrangements of operettas, much incidental music for plays and films, and the following operas: *Violante* and *Der Ring des Polykrates* ("Polykrates' Ring"; both 1916), *Das Wunder der Heliane* ("The Miracle of Heliana," 1927), and *Die Katrein* (1937). He is now living in the United States.
[10] Bibliography: Copland, *Our New Music* (1941); Slonimsky, *Music Since 1900* (1937); Istel, "For a Reversion to Opera," MQ X (1924) 405–37; Prunières, "The Departure from Opera," MMus III, No. 2 (January–February, 1926) 3–9; Bekker, "The Opera Walks New Paths," MQ XXI (1935) 266–78; Křenek, *Music Here and Now* (1939); idem, "Opera between the Wars," MMus XX, No. 2 (January–February, 1943) 102–11; Gatti, *Musicisti moderni d'Italia e di fuori* (1920); Saint-Cyr, *Musicisti italiani contemporanei* (1932); *Annuario del teatro lirico italiano*, 1940–; Bekker, *Neue Musik* (1920); Heinsheimer, "Die Umgestaltung des Operntheaters in Deutschland," *Anbruch* XV (August–September, 1933) 107–13.

Without aiming at undue rigidity, therefore, we shall consider modern opera under the following heads: (1) opera which seeks to appeal to a broad public by means of music in a popular style, subjects of topical interest, or both. (2) Opera which, to varying degrees, revives the musical forms and aesthetic of the eighteenth century or earlier periods and, in some cases, combines hitherto conventionally distinct musical forms in a modern idiom of antiromantic tendency. (3) Opera which, while in many respects similar to the preceding type, is in a more radical or unfamiliar (for example, atonal) musical style.

1. The most striking examples of popularized modern opera are two extremely successful works produced in Germany in the late 1920's: Ernst Křenek's *Jonny spielt auf* ("Johnny Strikes Up," 1927) and Kurt Weill's *Dreigroschenoper* ("The Threepenny Opera," 1928).[11] The plot of the former work is a combination of gross realism and fantasy. The music undoubtedly owed its popularity to the exuberant rhythms and catchy tunes of the then novel jazz style which prevails throughout, spiced with enough dissonance to give audiences the comfortably superior sensation of listening to something really modernistic and daring. Viewed in cold blood nearly twenty years later, it is astonishing to realize what variety of effect was possible within the restrictions of this idiom, from the gaudily vulgar tunes of a restaurant orchestra to the moving, almost romantically conceived scene 7, and the final apotheosis of Johnny, the Negro band leader, incarnation of the vigorous new world "conquering old Europe with the dance." Needless to say, the jazz is about as genuinely American in flavor as a French ice-cream soda, but the German audiences were not aware of this, and the work altogether did not pretend to be much more than a revue, frankly aiming at popular success and deservedly enjoying it for a few years.

11 Křenek (b. 1900), a pupil of Schreker, has composed at least twelve operas and a large quantity of other music in all forms. He is now living in the United States. His opera *Tarquin* was performed at Vassar College in 1941. See his book *Music Here and Now;* also "The New Music and Today's Theatre," MMus XIV, No. 4 (May–June, 1937) 200–203; Stuckenschmidt, "Ernst Křenek," MMus XVI, No. 1 (November–December, 1938) 41–44; Weissmann, "Germany's Latest Music Dramas," MMus IV, No. 4 (May–June, 1927) 20–26.

Weill (b. 1900), after a successful career in Germany, was compelled to emigrate when the Nazis came to power. He is now living in the United States. He has written about a dozen operas and ballets, incidental music for plays, and some choral and orchestral works.

Křenek, one of the most gifted and productive of modern German opera composers, was already known to the public by three earlier works: *Der Sprung über den Schatten* ("The Leap over the Shadow," 1924), a farce operetta of variegated musical styles; and *Zwingburg* ("Dungeon Castle," 1924) and *Orpheus und Euridike* (1926), both in a dissonant, linear idiom. Three one-act operas produced at Wiesbaden in 1928 did not attain the popularity of *Jonny*. Křenek's subsequent operas come within the orbit of the Vienna school of composers and will be noticed later.

Weill's *Dreigroschenoper* makes even less pretension to eternal significance than does *Jonny*. A modern version of Gay's *Beggar's Opera*, the music consists only of a succession of German-American jazz songs, one would-be *Schlager* after another, unbearably monotonous now that the shine of novelty has worn off. Some of Weill's other stage works are more interesting and historically of greater importance. *Der Protagonist* (1926) and *Der Zar lässt sich photographieren* ("The Czar Permits Himself to Be Photographed," 1928), both surrealistic in technique, show skillful craftsmanship but lack the melodic inventiveness of *Die Dreigroschenoper*. *Aufstieg und Fall der Stadt Mahagonny* ("The Rise and Fall of the City of Mahogany," 1927, 1930) is a bitterly satirical picture of degenerate modern life, which attempts to extend the basic style of *Die Dreigroschenoper* to a longer work with continuous music. In both *Mahagonny* and *Die Bürgschaft* ("The Surety," 1932) the note of warning and revolt against evil social conditions is sounded. Weill, more than any other composer, is the inspiration of many modern American operatic works of a socially critical, satirical, or topical nature: not only Antheil's *Transatlantic,* but also the operas of Blitzstein and even Gershwin's *Of Thee I Sing* and *Porgy and Bess*. Weill, moreover, in a delicate balance between banality and poignancy, caught the mood of life at a moment in Germany when economic disaster was preparing the way for the Hitler regime which was to put a violent end to all such sensitive expression.[12] Finally, he exemplifies in his most characteristic operas the modern aesthetic view expressed by Bert Brecht, the librettist of *Mahagonny:* "Opera should be a spectacle made up of clearly definable components, rather than an illusory image of a magic super-world, and that spectacle should con-

---

[12] Virgil Thomson writes of Weill's "tearful but elegant ditties about the Berlin ghetto," and claims that "Weill did for Berlin what Charpentier did for Paris." See "Most Melodious Tears," MMus XI, No. 1 (November–December, 1933) 13–17.

vey an explicitly demonstrated meaning for those beholding it, instead of being merely expensive entertainment or glorified dope." [13]

Another modern German opera may be listed here, although it is not by any means a pure example of the popular type. Max Brand's *Maschinist Hopkins* (1929; libretto by the composer) [14] is obviously influenced in its text by Eugene O'Neill and in the music to some extent by Berg's *Wozzek*. It is a realistic-expressionistic play of murder, lust, and revenge, with references to actual factory working conditions, a kind of modernized Zola-Bruneau opera. The music is extremely percussive and dissonant, underlaying dialogue of an intense, declamatory nature. In addition to ordinary spoken declamation, three distinct types of delivery are indicated: the Sprechstimme, as in Schönberg and Berg (words half sung in varying but not exactly notated pitch with exactly notated rhythm); rhythmic declamation of words on one tone level; and unarticulated vowel sounds of indefinite pitch in exactly notated rhythm. Sensational novelties of this opera were the choruses of the machines, in which these three techniques are combined. The prevailing percussive style of music gives way in the love scene (scene 5, end of Act I) to long, lyrical, neo-Straussian melodic lines, though the harmonies remain dissonant as ever. The current fad for American jazz is recognized particularly in scenes 4 and 10; the former has a song in English (words by George Antheil) by a six-man Negro jazz band; the latter makes use, among other effects, of an out-of-tune electric piano.[15] *Maschinist Hopkins* was altogether too much of its own day to have remained permanently in the repertoire, even without the "purifying" influence of National Socialism; it is interesting chiefly as being symptomatic of this peculiar period in German opera, specializing in the depiction of restless, pathological states of suffering and situations calling forth extravagantly bitter emotions.

13 Quoted in Křenek, "Opera between the Wars," MMus XX, No. 2 (January–February, 1943) 108. See also Einstein, "German Opera, Past and Present," MMus XI, No. 2 (January–February, 1934) 65–72; and Gutman, "*Mahagonny* and Other Novelties," MMus VII, No. 4 (June–July, 1930) 32–36.
14 Brand (b. 1892) was a pupil of Schreker. See his essay " 'Mechanische' Musik und das Problem der Oper," *Musikblätter des Anbruch* VIII (1926) 356–59. Articles on *Maschinist Hopkins* in *Signale für die musikalische Welt* LXXXVII (1929) 136–65, 1075–78; LXXXVIII (1930) 395–99; see also Thompson, "Fly-Wheel Opera," MMus VII, No. 1 (December–January 1929–30) 39–42.
15 Cf. *Wozzek*, Act III sc. 3. Is the taste for off-pitch effects in music comparable to the taste for ripe game and certain kinds of cheese?

The minor operas of Paul Hindemith [16] well illustrate the popular satirical tendencies fashionable in Germany in the late 1920's. The most notable of these operas are *Hin und zurück* ("There and Back," 1927) and *Neues vom Tage* ("News of the Day," 1929). *Hin und zurück* [17] is a one-act tour de force in which the second half exactly reverses the action of the first, so that at the end the situation is exactly the same as at the beginning; the music correspondingly reverses the order of its themes and movements, but without going into the intricacies of an academic crab canon. The work is scored for an orchestra of seven wind instruments and two pianos; the music is in various styles by turns but triumphantly unified in effect nevertheless, and decidedly clever and successful in performance. *Neues vom Tage,* Hindemith's last opera to be produced in Germany, is a larger work, a witty revue about a married couple who, through their efforts to obtain evidence for a divorce, become "the news of the day," with characters so firmly established in the minds of their public that they no longer have any right of private action and cannot even drop their divorce proceedings, although they wish to. On this plot are strung several amusing episodes, including a chorus of stenographers to the rhythmic accompaniment of clacking typewriters and a bathroom scene which attracted the august disapproval of Dr. Goebbels himself. The music, like most of Hindemith in this period, is linear in texture and strongly rhythmic, well suited to the lively action. There is, of course, a jazz scene, and the final chorus is a fugue. It is unfortunate that the text is so full of topical references which have long since lost their timeliness as to make revivals of the work difficult if not impossible. One of Hindemith's most charming examples of *Gebrauchsmusik* is a children's opera, *Wir bauen eine Stadt* ("We Build a Town"), in straightforward simple melodic style, first performed at Oxford in 1931.

[16] Hindemith (b. 1895), the foremost modern German composer, has produced a dozen stage works, as well as a large quantity of other music in all forms. See his *Craft of Musical Composition,* 2 vols. (New York, Associated Music Publishers [1937–1945]); biography by H. Strobel (3d ed., 1937); Epstein, "Hindemiths Theatermusik," *Die Musik* XXIII (1931) 582–87; Blitzstein, *"Hin und Zurück* in Philadelphia," MMus V, No. 4 (May–June, 1928) 34–36; Gutman, "Tabloid Hindemith" [on *Neues vom Tage*], MMus VII, No. 1 (December, 1929–January, 1930) 34–37; Reich, "Paul Hindemith," MQ XVII (1931) 486–96.

[17] This was originally produced at Baden-Baden on the same program as Ernst Toch's *Die Prinzessin auf der Erbse* ("The Princess and the Pea"), Weill's *Mohagonny,* and Milhaud's *Enlèvement d'Europe* ("The Rape of Europa").

In the Soviet Union [18] an effort has been made, nation-wide in scope, long continued, and sponsored by official government agencies, to bring art to the masses of the people. This is an experiment which, considering all its aspects, is perhaps unique in modern times. It has definite results in all forms of music written by Soviet composers and especially in the musical and dramatic content of recent operas. One effect has been to extend the nationalist musical movement to new peoples within the orbit of Soviet Russia: thus Reinhold Glière (b. 1875), a composer of the older generation, produced at Baku in 1926 (revised version, 1934) *Shah-Senem,* an opera based on Caucasian legends and including musical elements from Turkish, Arabian, and Persian sources; Sergei Vassilenko's (b. 1872) *Son of the Sun* (Moscow, 1929), based on a story of the Boxer Rebellion, uses Chinese and Mongolian themes; Michail Gnessin (b. 1883) has spoken for the Jewish population of Russia in *The Maccabeans* and *The Youth of Abraham* (1921); Andrei Pashtchenko's *Eagles in Revolt* (Leningrad, 1923) is a revolutionary opera employing Kirghiz, Russian, and Tartar melodies; and other national groups are represented by V. A. Uspensky's *Farkhad and Shirin* (Tashkent, 1936; national Uzbek tunes),[19] S. A. Balasanian's *Revolt of Vose* (Stalinabad, 1939; Tadzik folk melodies), and Nazib Zhiganov's *The Deserter,* the "first nationalist Tartar opera." [20]

The Russian Revolution, like the French Revolution, called forth a large number of musical works on patriotic themes. Practically every Soviet composer has written program symphonies, symphonic poems, oratorios, choral odes, or the like glorifying different phases of life under the new regime. Naturally opera has not been neglected as a means for promoting Soviet ideology. Russian history has been operatically reinterpreted in the light of new doctrines; satirical, moral, or didactic dramas have condemned the abuses of the old order; life under the Marxian dispensation has been idyllically represented and the hardier revolutionary virtues glowingly extolled. The music in these works is, of course, uneven in quality; most are fundamentally conservative in style. Few, probably, are of per-

18 Bibliography: Sabaneiev, *Modern Russian Composers;* Braudo, "The Russian Panorama," MMus X, No. 2 (January–February, 1933) 79–86; *idem,* "Concerts, Opera, Ballet in Russia Today," MMus X, No. 4 (May–June, 1933) 213–19; Keefer, "Opera in the Soviet," *Music Library Association Notes, Second Series* II, No. 2 (March, 1945) 110–17.
19 Slonimsky, *Music Since 1900,* p. 406.   20 *Ibid.,* p. 117.

manent value. So far the most enduringly popular Soviet opera, and one which apparently fully meets the ideal official requirements. is *The Quiet Don,* based on Sholokhov's novel with music by Ivan Dzerzhinsky, first performed at Leningrad in 1935.[21] The music is nationalistic, inspired by Russian folk melody (though without obvious citation of particular tunes), fairly simple in texture, and slightly modernist in some of its harmonies and rhythms.

Since his return to Russia in 1934, Sergei Prokofiev [22] has become an important influence in Soviet music. Prokofiev's early opera, *Love for Three Oranges* (Chicago, 1921), written in his facile, rhythmic, brilliant manner of those days, was very successful. A still earlier opera, *The Gambler,* prepared for performance at Petrograd in 1917, was not performed until 1929, at Brussels. As a Soviet composer, Prokofiev has produced his two most important operas: *Simeon Kotko* (Moscow, 1940), based on scenes from the life of one of the leaders in the Russian civil war and revolution; and *War and Peace,* an epical setting of Tolstoy's epical novel, completed in 1941, consisting of arias, duets, important choral sections, and mass battle scenes, in the grand tradition of old Russian opera.

Probably the best-known Soviet opera is Shostakovitch's *Lady Macbeth of Mzensk District* (Moscow, 1934), which was at first accepted by the Russian critics, made its way to the United States for a few sensational performances, and a year later was suddenly and savagely condemned in an official article in *Pravda* as "a leftist mess instead of human music . . . fidgety, screaming, neurasthenic." [23] *Lady Macbeth* has no connection with Shakespeare. Its heroine is Ekaterina, an adulterous wife who first murders her father-in-law and then collaborates with her lover in murdering her husband. The

21 See Slonimsky, *Music Since 1900,* p. 397, for a translation of interesting analytical comments on this work by A. Ostertzov. Dzerzhinsky (b. 1909) has written other operas: *Soil Upturned* (Moscow, 1937); *Volatchaevko Days; Nadeshda Svetlova* (1944).
22 Prokofiev (b. 1891), one of the best known abroad of all Soviet Russian composers, has written much music in nearly all instrumental and choral forms. See Slonimsky, "Sergei Prokofiev," *American Quarterly on the Soviet Union* II, No. 1 (1939) 37–44; Prokofiev, "The War Years," MQ XXX (1944) 421–27; Schlifstein, "On *War and Peace,*" MMus XX, No. 3 (March–April, 1943) 185–87; biography by Nestyev.
23 Quoted in Slonimsky, *Music since 1900,* p. 403; see also *ibid.,* pp. 372, 389. Cf. also Shostakovitch, "My Opera. Lady Macbeth," MMus XII, No. 1 (November–December, 1934) 23–30; Rosenfeld, *Discoveries of a Music Critic.* There is a biography in English of Shostakavitch (b. 1906) by V. I. Seroff (1943). Shostakovitch's earlier satirical opera, *The Nose* (1930), was not successful.

pair is arrested and sent to Siberia with a convict gang; the lover deserts Ekaterina for another of the women convicts; Ekaterina murders her rival by pushing her off a bridge and commits suicide by jumping off the bridge herself. It is hard to say how much of this story is intended to satirize bourgeois society—the scene is nineteenth-century Russia under the Czarist regime—and how much is mere pornography (the love scenes) and perversion (the whipping scene). The music is well suited to the action, being brutal, lusty, strong in the suggestion of horror, cruelty, and suffering, full of tremendous rhythmic drive and willful dissonance. There are many distinct arias, some duets, and a few passages of straight recitative, as well as the more typical long sections where the voice parts are freely woven into a continuous orchestral texture. As in the old Russian opera, choruses and crowd scenes are prominent. The work is divided into four acts, with nine scenes. Within each act the scenes are connected by means of orchestral interludes which continue and develop the preceding musical material. Very little use is made of motifs recurring from one scene to another, but within each scene the music is organized as a clearly planned formal unit. Moreover, the four acts are designed like the four movements of a symphony: I. Alternating slow and fast tempi, and ending in F major. II. Adagio, with a few interludes in fast tempo, centering about the key of G minor but ending on a C major chord with an added flat seventh (that is, the dominant seventh of F); the climax of this long act is the powerful orchestral interlude between scenes 4 and 5. III. Scherzo: comic drunken solo and a Gilbert-and-Sullivan-esque policemen's chorus; the tonalities are varying, but prominence is given to the key of F-sharp minor, in which the act ends. IV. Finale: Adagio, F minor, framed by gloomy Mussorgsky-like choruses of convicts.

As in his other music of this period, Shostakovitch excels in two idioms: the nervously energetic presto, thin textured, erratic in tonality, rhythmically irregular, conveying an inimitable and positively physical sensation of excitement; and the perfectly objective, long-spun adagio, mounting with clashing contrapuntal lines to sonorous climaxes of elemental grandeur. There is no subjective feeling in this score; indeed, the libretto makes no place for any, except for an occasional touch of sneering satire. The only use of national material is in Act IV, where Ekaterina sings a grotesquely distorted version of a folk song. The music is vivid and theatrical; to hear it must be an experience one would be equally sorry either to miss or to be often obliged to repeat.

Outside Soviet Russia there appears to have been but little significant operatic composition inspired by the ideals or achievements of governments. Exception may be made, perhaps, of two Italian works glorifying the ill-fated imperialism of Mussolini. Alfredo Casella's *Il deserto tentato* ("Conquest of the Desert," 1937), a "mystery in one act," presents the adventures of a crew of a wrecked bombing plane who brave the dangers of the wilderness and eventually gain the respect and loyalty of the natives. It endeavors "to evoke the Ethiopian war, transfiguring it on an altogether unreal and mythical plane. It reflects a poetic exaltation of the civilizing mission of a great nation." [24] The music is in a rather simple oratorio-like style with many choral sections.

Another work which was conceived at least in part as a gesture of acclaim to Mussolini is Francesco Malipiero's *Giulio Cesare* (1936), based on Shakespeare's play. The vocal parts of this opera are all robust declamation of the recitativo secco type, supported by a continuous orchestral ground with distinct leading motifs. Each scene is developed over a few such motifs, woven into a texture of comparatively static harmony (slow-changing basses, frequent ostinato figures, short motifs canonically in a pandiatonic web, parallelism). The effect therefore depends on the vividness of the declamation, the directness and economy of the dramatic details, the strikingly pictorial or expressive character of the motifs themselves, and the admirable dramatic quality of the infrequent harmonic changes, which follow and underline the action most effectively. It is a style, for example, which permits a really successful musical setting of Anthony's funeral oration. The dramatic choruses in this scene and the temple chorus in Act I (with percussion accompaniment) are also excellent writing. Altogether, this is a stageworthy work, good theatre, though possibly a trifle monotonous in musical texture.

2. The second main current in modern opera may be called, in contrast to all the foregoing, neoclassical. In this type of opera, the

[24] From a letter of the composer, quoted in Slonimsky, *Music Since 1900*, p. 426. See also review by Einstein, MMus XV, No. 1 (November–December, 1937) 41.

subjects are generally timeless rather than timely; or if the latter, their topical significance is not stressed. The action is likely to be condensed, simplified, even stylized, so that a comparatively few significant moments stand out, with the essential interconnecting material reduced to the minimum. Composers are not inclined to appeal to their audience by recalling effects familiar in common musical experience but rather tend to pile up subtlety, novelty, and complexity. Although there are many varieties of musical style, the prevailing tone in these operas is antiromantic; the music may be pathetic or objective, intense or indifferent, monumental and stark or witty and satirical, but it is seldom sentimental. In form, these operas tend toward the eighteenth-century ideal of distinct units, the number opera. Many are in the typically modern compressed form of chamber opera; others must be designated as opera oratorio or opera ballet; still others resemble in form the medieval mystery plays.

The founders of neoclassicism were Busoni and Stravinsky. Busoni's *Doktor Faustus* (1925) is the earliest opera which exemplifies the neoclassic principles on a large scale. Stravinsky, however, had already begun a characteristic development of similar principles in three short stage works which had considerable influence. *L'Histoire du soldat* ("Story of the Soldier," Lausanne, 1918) is a ballet the action of which is explained by a narrator, with dry, percussive, metrically complex music for an orchestra of only seven players. Two burlesque one-act chamber operas, *Renard* and *Mavra,* were produced at Paris in 1922. The latter is a particularly good modern example of opera buffa; it is a farce based on a story by Pushkin, with artificially simplified characters (almost like puppets), a continuously developing symphonic background of nimble rhythm, and vocal declamation similar to that in the cantata *Les Noces* (1923). Repose and classical proportions are evident in Stravinsky's later ballet *Apollon Musagète* (1928) and the opera ballet *Persèphone* (1934). His greatest neoclassic dramatic work is the monumental Latin opera-oratorio *Oedipus Rex* (1927; original French text by Jean Cocteau, after Sophocles) for chorus, soloists, and narrator, in which the stylized, completely impersonal character of the action, words, and music often produces sublime effects. (Similar means are employed even more fittingly in the oratorio *Symphony of Psalms,* 1930.)

An important work in this period of the Paris lyric theatre is the opera ballet *Padmâvati,* words by Louis Laloy and music by Albert Roussel,[25] produced in 1923. The ancient French genius for this type of spectacle—slender plot with a large proportion of choruses and ballets—is here realized in modern style. The variety and splendor of the rhythms, the great individuality of the harmony, the exquisite finesse and good taste of the whole, are remarkable. The ballets often include wordless choruses, and this peculiar technique is developed here to a point which has probably never been excelled (see especially the Funeral Ceremony at the end of Act II). Slonimsky's notation on this work—"free from pseudo-exoticism" [26]—is ambiguous. Does it mean "having genuine exoticism"? What is genuine exoticism? If it is the free, striking, individual use of themes and harmonies which may perhaps have been suggested by hearing oriental music, and the employment of these in such a way as to create a definite feeling of the Hindu background without anywhere giving the impression of merely quoting oriental melodies for the sake of factitious local color—then the music of *Padmâvati,* like that of Roussel's earlier orchestral-choral *Evocations,* is genuinely exotic. Whether or not it is pedantically authentic is of no importance. There is no composer who more than Roussel gives the impression of complete originality. The dissonances of his music are never arbitrary, but always vital and logical. He is able to make an extremely complex and refined harmonic idiom really sound. He is a true disciple of D'Indy, but no mere copyist; in line of descent from Dukas, but with greater imaginative fire and poetic genius. One feels that here is the revelation in music of something always existing but hitherto veiled, and now made known with perfect assurance and clarity.

Another major composer of French neoclassical opera is the Swiss Arthur Honegger,[27] who became famous after his *Roi David* was

---

25 Roussel (1869–1937) also composed a one-act opera *La Naissance de la lyre* to a text by Théodore Reinach after Sophocles' *Ichneutai* (Paris, 1925); a comic opera *Le Testament de la tante Caroline* ("Aunt Caroline's Will," Bergamo, 1936); several ballets, incidental music, and many orchestral and chamber works. See special Roussel issue of RM (1929); Hill, *Modern French Music,* pp. 314–26; and Hoérée, *Albert Roussel.*
26 Slonimsky, *Music since 1900,* p. 236.
27 Honegger (b. 1892) is distinguished for his symphonic poems and other orchestral and chamber works, as well as for ballets, incidental music, and operas. His most recent opera is *L'Aiglon* (in collaboration with Ibert, 1937). See Tappolet, *Honegger;* review of *Judith* by Prunières, MMus III, No. 4 (May–June, 1926) 30–33.

presented, in the original dramatic version, in 1921. In *Judith* (1926), rewritten as an opera from the incidental music to René Morax's biblical drama produced in 1925, the style of *Le Roi David* was continued; fervid declamatory phrases in incisive rhythms over percussive harmonies, the progressions of which are actuated by contrapuntal, chromatically moving lines generally in contrary motion, with much use of ostinato figures. In both works the chorus is extensively used; in *Judith* it functions chiefly as a background for the soloists' singing, except for the last scene, with its strong closing fugue "Gloire au dieu tout puissant Jehovah des armées." Honegger's *Antigone* (1927) is his most important opera, to a text by Jean Cocteau "freely adapted from Sophocles." It is a continuous symphonic setting of the drama without word repetitions, arias, ballets, or any other diversionary matter. The vocal lines are constantly in a type of recitative analogous to that of Lully (that is, deriving its pace, accent, and contour immediately and in detail from the words), but of course much more varied in rhythm and melodic pattern than Lully's. An unusual feature of the declamation is the placing of first syllables on the accented beat instead of treating them in the usual way as anacruses, resulting in a singular vehemence of expression (Example 125).[28] The orchestral part is, as usual in Honegger,

ANTIGONE, sc. 4

Ex. 125.   Honegger

la jus-ti-ce non plus n'im-po-se pas des lois de ce gen-re et je ne croy-ais pas que ton de-cret put fai-re pré-va-loir le ca-pri-ce d'un hom-me sur la ré-gle des im-mor-tels sur ces lois qui ne sont pas é-cri-tes

strongly dissonant and percussive; the effect is altogether stark, quite in keeping with the grim, tragic, swift-moving text.

The leading composer of French opera during the interwar period, one of the most productive of contemporary musicians, is Darius

[28] Cf. Honegger's foreword to the score.

Milhaud.[29] Milhaud's first big success was *Le Pauvre Matelot* ("The Poor Sailor," 1927), a short three-act play by Jean Cocteau about a sailor who, returning home rich after an absence of many years, decides to test his wife's fidelity by telling her he is a rich friend of her husband who, he says, is about to return home in utter poverty; the wife, not recognizing him, murders the supposed stranger in order to get his money for her husband. The peculiar unreality of the action is heightened by Milhaud's music, which is in a playful, intentionally banal manner, with jazzy tunes and sophisticated, dissonant harmony. Much of the same mocking spirit and the same musical characteristics are found in the three one-act *opéras minutes* composed in 1927, parodies of Greek myths in the fashion of the early eighteenth-century Théâtre de la Foire. Another comic opera, *Esther de Carpentras* (composed in 1925, produced in 1938), a modern, lightly satirical version of the biblical Esther story, is especially remarkable for the comic ensembles of Act I and the vivid crowd scenes of Act II.

[29] Milhaud (b. 1892) studied at the Paris Conservatory and has composed a large amount of music in all instrumental and vocal forms. He is now living in the United States. The following is a complete list of his operas:

TITLE AND LIBRETTIST	COMPOSED	PERFORMED
La Brebis egarée Francis Jammes	1910–1915	Opéra-Comique, December, 1923
Les Euménides Aeschylus, tr. Claudel	1917–1922	———————
Les Malheurs d'Orphée Armand Lunel	1924	La Monnaie (Brussels), 1926
Esther de Carpentras Armand Lunel	1925	Opéra-Comique, February, 1938

Three opéras minutes:
  L'Enlèvement d'Europe
  L'Abandon d'Ariane
  La Delivrance de Thesée
  Henri Hoppenot
	1927	Wiesbaden, April, 1928
		(*L'Enlèvement d'Europe* had been performed at Baden-Baden, July, 1927)

Le Pauvre Matelot Jean Cocteau	1926	Opéra-Comique, December, 1927
Christophe Colomb Paul Claudel	1928	Berlin, May, 1930
Maximilien Werfel-Hoffmann-Lunel	1930	Paris Opéra, January, 1932
La Sagesse Paul Claudel	1935	———————
Médée Madeleine Milhaud	1938	Paris Opéra, May, 1940
Bolivar Supervielle—Madeleine Milhaud	1943	———————

Milhaud's first serious opera was *Les Euménides,* composed in the years 1917–1922 to the text of Aeschylus translated by Claudel, a massive work with huge choruses, constantly polytonal in an extremely dissonant texture of blended ostinato figures. Similar technical procedures are found in *Christophe Colomb* (composed 1928),[30] one of Milhaud's principal operas. It is interesting to note the position of this work in the history of French opera. Having in mind the music of such composers as Gounod, Massenet, and Debussy, one is inclined to think of French opera music as marked chiefly by the qualities of economy, elegance, and restraint; yet it must also be remembered that Berlioz's *Troyens,* the outstanding French musical drama of the nineteenth century, was not distinguished alone by these qualities but rather by what seem to be their opposites: expansiveness, grandeur, and (on occasion) lavish expenditure of resources. *Christophe Colomb* belongs in this "grand" tradition of French opera, in the line reaching back through Berlioz to Spontini, Gluck, Rameau, and Lully. It is on a large scale: two acts and twenty-seven scenes, with ten principal soloists, thirty-five other solo parts, three speaking parts, a chorus, and orchestra reinforced by a special battery of percussion instruments. The drama is conceived in epic-allegorical form, with a Narrator and other external personages, presented in a series of tableaux which are explained, commented on, and connected by choral and spoken interludes with percussion accompaniment. There is no English term which fits this kind of work so well as the French designation *opéra sacrale;* an idea of the method will be best obtained from the Prayer of the Narrator in the prologue (spoken in rhythm, with words murmured by the chorus as a background, to a rhythmical accompaniment of percussion instruments, softly): " 'I pray to the God of all power to give me light and strength to open and explain to you the Book of the Life and Voyages of Christopher Columbus who discovered America and that land which lies beyond. For it is he who has brought together the whole Catholic world and made it one globe under the Cross. I set forth the life of this chosen man whose name signifies the Dove and the Christ-bearer, as it passed not only in time but in eternity. For it is not he alone but all men who hear the call to the other world and to that farther shore whither may it please the Divine Grace to bring us all.' Chorus (shout): 'So mote it be!' "

30 Lopatnikoff, "*Christophe Colomb,*" MMus VII, No. 4 (June–July, 1930) 36–38.

This mystical interpretation of Christopher Columbus is always at the forefront as the various scenes in his career are unfolded. The climax of Act I is the scene of the mutiny on board Columbus' ship; this act ends with a gigantic setting (in Latin) of the Sanctus. Part II finally takes us back to the Inn at Valladolid, the exact point at which the action began after the prologue, and there is an epilogue ending with a choral Alleluia.

The music is in planar polytonal harmony, that is, with free dissonance arising from superposing motifs (often chord streams) in different tonalities, though as a rule no one motif is completely in a single key. The usual method of construction, except in the longest scenes, is to introduce one theme, establish it by ostinato-like repetition, then add successively one, two, or more themes, each of which is also usually treated in ostinato fashion. For example, scene 8 (orchestra alone) consists of three different motifs over sustained bitonal chords: the first motif is in the Aeolian mode on G-sharp with parallel sevenths and ninths, the second a chromatic series of six-four chords, and the third a melody in F-sharp minor fluctuating to F minor, while the sustained chords consist of the G major and C-sharp major triads. In the following scene there is added to all this a wordless chorus in the Hypodorian mode on E-flat with conflicting major-minor thirds in the sustaining chords (for tenors and basses). Some scenes are simpler than this, others more complex. Of course the various planes of harmony are kept distinct to some degree by the use of contrasting orchestral color, but nevertheless the total effect is one of practically unmitigated dissonance, so that the harmony is consequently static. To be sure, there is some contrast between the amount of dissonance produced by, say, two conflicting keys and that produced by a half-dozen; but these are contrasts within what is to the ordinary ear a very limited harmonic range: it is extremely difficult, if not actually impossible, to perceive distinct degrees in dissonance beyond a certain point of harmonic complexity. Compensation for all this is found, however, in the variety and vitality of Milhaud's rhythmic patterns and in the completely impersonal, spectacular, monumental effect of this type of musical construction. Moreover, when the long-continued dissonance finally resolves to a simple chord at the end of a section, the intensity of the resolution is magnified. An example of this is the great mutiny scene in Act I, where after a climax of four tonalities in the chorus and four in the orchestra (a total of seven different keys at once, one being reduplicated), the whole resolves on a closing climactic triad of B-flat major with a perfectly electrifying result. The motifs themselves, the units of the structure, are mostly short and in strongly marked rhythm. The voice lines are treated more freely as longer melodic phrases, never in the style of recitative. On occasion, special rhythmic patterns may be used, as in the Spanish dances in the scene at Queen Isabella's court (Act I, scene 7).

In 1930 Milhaud applied a similar technique to a historical opera, *Maximilien*, based on a drama by Franz Werfel. Here, however, the degree of stylization surpasses that of any previous works: action, melodies, rhythms, all are ritualistic; even church hymns and military marches are indicated in formal, antirealistic outline as parts of a tonal design rather than representations of actual happenings. But in *Médée* (composed 1938) there is less of the monumental, less dissonance, more lyricism, and more interest in the individual figures of the drama. The restrained dramatic force of the scene of the preparation of the enchantments is remarkable. Most expressive are the slow, melismatic, long lines in the soprano role of the suffering Creusa, innocent victim of Medea's cruelty (Example 126).

It appears, then, that Milhaud has recapitulated the typical course of development of composers of his generation, from the flippant-satirical (rococo) through the grandiose-formal (baroque) to the more equable and balanced (classical) style of *Médée*. It is to be hoped that his recent *Bolivar* (1943) may be widely performed, and that still other operas may be forthcoming.

One of the outstanding German serious operas of a neoclassical type is Hindemith's *Cardillac* (1926),[31] on an excellent tragic libretto by Ferdinand Lion. This is one of the best examples in this period of the revival of the principle of separate musical numbers in opera. Not only is each number a distinct, clearly organized musical unit, but the music is constructed purely according to its own laws, the themes being straightforwardly developed in the manner of a concerto, undeflected by any attempt to illustrate mere details of the text. Music and drama run parallel, but without interpenetration. The absolute, instrumental character of the music is aided by the

31 See Willms, *Führer zur Oper Cardillac.*

prevailing texture, which is highly rhythmic and contrapuntal; the voice is treated in the eighteenth-century way as one contrapuntal line among concertizing instruments. In addition to this typical

MÉDÉE, Act III

Ex.126.   Milhaud

Créuse:

Ah!— Ah!— Ah! ——— É-tei-gnez cet-te flam-me qui me con-

-su-me.   Ah! —— Ah!— Ah ! —— É-tei-gnez-

-la de grâ-ce. Ah! ——————— Ah!

Hindemith linear style, two other idioms are occasionally used: a kind of accompanied recitative in which the vocal declamation is set against a single rhapsodic line in the orchestra (for example, p. 131 of the piano-vocal score); and a quieter, chordal, neoromantic style which foreshadows some of Hindemith's characteristic later development (for example, the recitative and aria "Die Zeit vergeht" in Act I, scene 2). The chorus writing is vigorous, idiomatic, and effective, especially in the closing scene. Hindemith's latest dramatic work, *Mathis der Maler* ("Mathias the Painter"), was performed at Zurich in 1938.[32] It is an oratorio opera on the subject of Matthias Grünewald, the sixteenth-century German painter. In its original form it is a long, complex work holding much the same position in Hindemith's dramatic production as *Christophe Colomb* in Milhaud's and embracing a great variety of musical styles, among which suggestions of medieval modality are prominent. *Mathis* has been given a few times in concert form; the most familiar portions of the music are those arranged by the composer as an orchestral suite, which is frequently heard.

Another German work of large size, combining characteristics of both oratorio and opera, is Kaminski's *Jürg Jenatch* (1929),[33] a historical drama from the period of the Thirty Years' War. The most striking feature of this work is the extensive choral writing in very intricate polyphony, often with special acoustical and polychoral effects. The action is carried on by means of spoken dialogue combined with vocal numbers, massive tableaux, and orchestral numbers.

In Italy the distinctive modern trend is not toward opera of gigantic size but rather toward a revival of classical subjects, light ballet-like pieces, or eighteenth-century opera buffa. Thus the Orpheus theme, one of the earliest and best opera subjects, has been recently used by Malipiero (*L'Orfeide*, trilogy, 1925), Rieti (1928), and Casella (1932).[34] Malipiero's trilogy is most interesting formally:

[32] See Huth, "Forbidden Opus—Protestant," MMus XVI, No. 1 (November–December, 1938) 38–41.

[33] Heinrich Kaminski (b. 1886) is known chiefly as a choral composer. See Krieger, "Heinrich Kaminski's Drama *Jürg Jenatsch*," *Zeitschrift für Musik* C (1933) 992–95; Saminsky, "*Jürg Jenatch*," MMus VII, No. 1 (December, 1929–January, 1930) 37–39.

[34] Gian Francesco Malipiero (b. 1882), one of the most celebrated modern Italian composers, has written (in addition to many stage works) symphonies, suites, chamber music, and oratorios. His own style has doubtless been influenced by his studies of old Italian

it consists of seven short detached scenes (*sette canzone*) with a prologue and semisatirical epilogue, in which a puppet show is introduced (compare De Falla's *Retablo de Maese Pedro*, 1923). A similar technique of short, concentrated action is found in Malipiero's *Tre commedie goldoniani* ("Three Goldonian Comedies") of 1926, the *Komödie des Todes* ("Comedy of Death," Munich, 1931), which comprises seven scenes called by the composer "nocturnes," and *Mysterium Venedigs* ("Mystery [in the medieval sense] of Venice," 1932), another trilogy. Heroic subjects and longer continuous structure are found in his more recent operas *Giulio Cesare* (1936), *Antonio e Cleopatra* (1938), and *Ecuba* (1941; based on Euripides). Casella has produced an excellent comedy in *La donna serpente* ("The Serpent Lady," 1932).

There are two Italian operas of an experimental type which have attracted some attention, though they have had only a few performances: *L'aviatore Dro* ("Aviator Dro," 1920) by the futurist composer Francesco Balilla Pratella (b. 1880), and *Mirra* (1920) by Domenico Alaleona (1881–1928). The former is harmonically based on the whole-tone scale, and the latter uses "novel non-tempered scales such as a 'pentafonia' of five equal intervals." [35]

3. **The** third and last principal group of modern operas might almost be considered as a subdivision of the neoclassical school. Like the latter, its dramatic themes are mostly nontopical and their treatment nonrealistic and nonpopular. It is set apart by the two circumstances that all its composers stem from central Europe (principally Vienna) and that all are to a greater or lesser degree committed to the twelve-tone (or so-called "atonal") technique of composition.[36] There are only a few composers in this group, but their influence and importance are great in proportion to their numbers.

---

music; he is editor of the Collected Edition of Monteverdi. For a bibliography of the numerous articles relating to Malipiero's dramatic music see Baker's *Biographical Dictionary* (4th ed.) and add: Labroca, "The Rebirth of Italian Opera," MMus IV, No. 4 (May–June 1927) 8–14; De'Paoli, "Italy's New Music of the Theatre," MMus VIII, No. 1 (November–December, 1930) 21–26.

Vittorio Rieti (b. 1898) is best known for his chamber music; he has written a chamber opera *Teresa nel bosco* (1933) and several ballets which have been produced by Diaghilev.

Alfredo Casella (1883–1947), distinguished as conductor and editor, has written orchestral, chamber, and piano music. See study by L. Cortese.

35 Slonimsky, *Music Since 1900*, pp. 207, 204.

36 Cf. R. Hill, "Schoenberg's Tone-Rows and the Tonal System of the Future," MQ XXII (1936) 14–37.

The founder and head of the school is Arnold Schönberg,[37] who has composed three operas. Two of these, *Erwartung* ("Expectation") and *Die glückliche Hand* ("The Lucky Hand"), were composed before the First World War (1909 and 1913 respectively), though not performed until 1924. Both call for a very large orchestra, usually subdivided with only a few instruments playing at any one time, and both are in the extremely dissonant, peculiar, thick Schönbergian harmonic style of the prewar period. The voice lines are wide ranged, with large, ultraexpressive intervals, occasionally going over into the Sprechstimme.[38] Both dramas are essentially subjective, and the outward scenery and action are largely symbolical; both are, in scale, rather cantatas than operas. The only character in *Erwartung* is a woman who, seeking her lover, finds only his dead body, over which she sings a long monologue, a kind of modernistic Liebestod. *Die glückliche Hand* has three soloists with a chorus of twelve voices, and uses colors symbolically in scenery, costumes, and lighting. Both in the music and in the dramatic technique, these two pieces may be regarded as forestages of Berg's *Wozzek*. Schönberg's later one-act opera, *Von Heute auf Morgen* ("From Today until Tomorrow," 1930), is completely in the twelve-tone technique, with distinct recitatives and arias, thus following the general trend of the postwar period toward the number opera.

The two operas of Schönberg's distinguished pupil Alban Berg [39] are among the most discussed works of modern times. *Wozzek*, composed in the years 1914–1922 and first performed at Berlin in December of 1925, is based on a "dramatic fragment" by Georg Büchner (1813–1837), the original twenty-five scenes being reduced by Berg to fifteen and grouped in three acts of five scenes each. Wozzek, the hero, is a representative of what he himself calls "Wir arme Leut' "

37 Schönberg (b. 1874) has been influential as a theorist and teacher as well as through his compositions. He is now living in the United States. See Armitage (ed.), *Arnold Schoenberg;* also Stefan, "Schoenberg's Operas," MMus II, No. 1 (January, 1925) 12–15, and VII, No. 1 (December, 1929–January, 1930) 24–28; Pisk, "Schoenberg's Twelve-Tone Opera," MMus VII, No. 3 (April–May, 1930) 18–21.
38 See musical excerpt from *Erwartung* in *Grove's Dictionary, Supplementary Volume*, p. 480.
39 On Berg (1885–1935) see the standard biography by W. Reich and others (1937); also Berg, "A Word about *Wozzek*," MMus V, No. 1 (November–December, 1927) 22–24; Reich, "Alban Berg's *Lulu*," MQ XXII (1936) 383–401; *idem*, "*Lulu*—the Text and Music," MMus XII, No. 3 (March–April, 1935) 103–11; List, "*Lulu*, after the Premiere," MMus XV, No. 1 (November–December, 1937) 8–12.

("We poor people"), tormented by circumstances, suffering through no fault of his own, finally murdering his mistress and killing himself, driven always by forces incomprehensible to him and too strong for him to resist. Despite the date of Büchner's drama, *Wozzek* is a thoroughly typical opera of the postwar period in Germany—expressionistic, morbid, neurotic, hysterical, "charged with passionate bitterness, the fruit of shock." [40] Yet it is not merely topical; Wozzek is a universal figure, a symbol of the oppressed. All the characters and events of the opera have an unearthly quality, like a tragic puppet show, and the music supports this impression, being for the most part systematically atonal with multiple orchestras and many unusual tone effects, giving an unreal, unhuman feeling through the very strangeness of the idiom. The music is continuous throughout each act, changes of scene being accompanied by orchestral interludes. The voice parts are in flexibly rhythmed declamatory style, with exaggerated intervals; in some scenes the Sprechstimme is used, and also ordinary speech. There are leitmotifs for the principal characters, but the chief means of unity is the organization of each act in strict forms derived mostly from absolute music. Thus the five scenes of Act I are respectively a suite, rhapsody and hunting song, military march and cradlesong, passacaglia (twenty-one variations on a tone row), and rondo; Act II is a symphony in five movements: sonata form, fantasia and fugue on three themes, largo for chamber orchestra, scherzo, and rondo; Act III consists of six "inventions": on a theme (variations), a tone (pedal point), a rhythm, a six-note chord (A-sharp, C-sharp, E-sharp, G-sharp, E-flat, F-flat), a tonality (D minor), and an equal movement in eighth notes (quasi toccata).[41] Of course it is not intended that these forms shall be perceived as such during the performance of the opera; they are primarily for musical rather than dramatic purposes. In principle, the music, like that of Hindemith's *Cardillac,* runs generally parallel to the action but takes much more account of detailed nuances. However, the relation is not altogether one of details; there is a grim appropriateness, for example, in the choice of the learned passacaglia (or chaconne) form for the scene (Act I, scene 4) in which Wozzek, desperately seek-

40 Lazare Saminsky in MMus VIII, No. 4 (May–June, 1931) 37.
41 See W. Reich, *A Guide to . . . Wozzek.* The author is indebted also to Dr. Karl H. Eschman for additional information on this topic.

ing to earn more money for the support of his mistress and their child, submits himself to a doctor as a subject for scientific experiments. In this scene, as throughout the opera, there is a special quality of poignancy, an emotional tension, which is unmistakable though impossible to explain. All in all, *Wozzek* deserves its reputation as one of the most remarkable operas of the twentieth century, perhaps the most profound musico-dramatic creation rising out of its own peculiar moment of history.

Berg's second opera, *Lulu,* was completed in substance before the composer's death, but the orchestration had been finished only through the first two acts and a small part of the third. The first two acts, and two fragments of the third, were performed with great success at Zurich in 1937. The libretto is taken, with some cuts, from a drama in two parts by Frank Wedekind (1864–1918). The central personage, Lulu, is conceived as the incarnation of the "primal woman-spirit," and the drama is concerned with the fatal effects of her attraction for various lovers, finally ending with her own doom. Although externally occupied with the most realistic details, the work is not essentially realistic but rather an example of symbolism in modern accoutrements, often grotesque and extravagantly expressionistic, but never as abstract as Schönberg's operas. This symbolic, universal character, which *Lulu* shares with *Wozzek,* is the justification for setting such a work to a long and highly complex musical score. It is nearly impossible to form an opinion as to the effect of this opera without having actually heard and seen it on the stage. The jagged, overrealistic declamation, the alternation of singing, Sprechstimme, and spoken dialogue, the use of a silent film accompanied by orchestral music to carry on the central episode of the action, the unusual but perfectly appropriate instrumentation, and especially Berg's characteristic use of the twelve-tone technique, all over and above the strange qualities of the drama itself, make an accumulation of impressions which it is difficult to summarize. Be it said, however, that the fundamental impression is one of monumental dramatic strength, intensity of emotion controlled by form-creating intellectual power. It is all too easy to be repelled by the apparently rigid mathematical character of Berg's principles of construction. The entire music of *Lulu,* for example, is founded on a single tone row; from this are derived various themes associated with individuals of the drama in the manner of leitmotifs. The row in its primitive form (transposed) gives the opening phrase of Lulu's aria in Act II, scene 1 (Example 127). Some other principles of structure

LULU, Act II

Ex.127.   Berg

Wenn sich die Men-schen um mei-net-wil-len um-ge-bracht ha-ben

in *Lulu* have been stated by the composer: musical form types are associated with certain characters (instead of with specific scenes as in *Wozzek*); the two scenes of the second act are rigidly symmetrical and are connected by an interlude built on the principle of a crab canon, with the second half recapitulating the first half in reverse. Do such things, it may be asked, make great music? Neither their presence nor their absence does so. The issue is whether they are used as means or as ends. If they are means which effectually help to accomplish the desired end of making a musical drama, their use is justified. Whether or not this is the case with *Lulu* can be decided only when there has been more opportunity to hear and understand the work. Meanwhile, and irrespective of theoretical explanations, there can be no doubt that the music of *Lulu* owes part of its variety and effect to the manipulation of the tone row in such a way as to give at times the impression of orthodox tonality—an agreeable contrast among the multitude of other harmonic impressions.

Another opera composer of the Vienna school is Egon Wellesz.[42] His *Alkestis* (1924) is a one-act opera to a text by von Hofmannsthal, from Euripides, in which the death of Alkestis, the funeral ceremonies, the arrival of Herakles, Admetus' hospitality, and the restoration of Alkestis to life are presented in a series of broad tableaux without any unessential connecting material. The music, while it does not break entirely with conventional tonality, shows the Schönberg influence in its wide-sweeping melodic lines and dissonant harmonies. Lacking almost all dominant-tonic or other tension-release

[42] Wellesz (b. 1885) is a distinguished scholar and teacher as well as a composer (principally operas, ballets, and choral works). See Beer, "Egon Wellesz und die Oper," *Die Musik* XXIII (1931) 909–12; Redlich, "Egon Wellesz," MQ XXVI (1940) 65–75; review of *Die Bakchantinnen* by Paul Pisk, MMus IX, No. 1 (November–December, 1931) 44–45; Wellesz, "The Return to the Stage," MMus IV, No. 1 (November–December, 1926) 19–24.

patterns, it does not always escape the peril of harmonic monotony; the whole setting is, perhaps intentionally, oppressive, monolithic, of an almost forbidding austerity. The important position of the chorus in *Alkestis* is even more emphasized in *Die Bakchantinnen* (1931; text by the composer after Euripides).

The later operas of Křenek may also be numbered among the productions of the Vienna school. His *Leben des Orest* (1930),[43] a half-satirical, surrealistic treatment of the whole Orestes myth cycle, shows Křenek in a stage of transition between the early jazzlike manner of *Jonny* and a serious classical style. *Karl V*, composed before 1933 and first performed at Prague in 1938, is entirely in the twelve-tone system. The nobility of style is remarkable in this work, well fitting the epic treatment of the subject. The music is somewhat similar to Wellesz's *Alkestis* but less uncompromising in its dissonances and often very expressive in melodic line.

This concludes our survey of the history of opera. As we look back over the past there is borne in upon us with irresistible force a certain feeling of futility. The thought of so much buried beauty is saddening; for it is buried for the most part beyond recall, with even less hope of resurrection than old poems or old paintings, which can at least be enjoyed without a complex mediating apparatus in the shape of instruments and performers to create the art work anew each time. We have tried to bring to the reader some idea of how these operas of the past sounded and why they were written as they were. But none of this can be more than a simple introduction. All descriptions, all analyses of forms, music, or poetry, make only a flat picture, a map, a mere diagram. The real living art can be glimpsed through the music, vividly enough perhaps in the case of a few works which still hold a place on our stage, but for all the rest only in moments of insight, and only then if we are able to cast ourselves back in imagination to the times when these operas were part of the life of men now passed away, "faded into impalpability through death, through absence, through change of manners." [44]

[43] Cf. Stuckenschmidt, "Hellenic Jazz," MMus VII, No. 3 (April–May, 1930) 22–25.
[44] James Joyce, *Ulysses* (New York, Random House, 1934) p. 186.

Bibliography

Bibliography

I

Bibliographies, Lexicons, Guides, Histories,
and Other Works Dealing with
the Opera in General

Aber, Adolf. Die Musik im Schauspiel, Geschichtliches und Aesthetisches. Leipzig, M. Beck, 1926.

Abert, Hermann. Grundprobleme der Operngeschichte. Leipzig, B&H, 1926.

Ademollo, Alessandro. Bibliografia della cronistoria teatrale italiana. Milano, Ricordi, 1888.

Albinati, Giuseppe. Piccolo dizionario di opere teatrali, oratori, cantati, ecc. Milano, Ricordi, 1913.

Allacci, Leone. Drammaturgia . . . accresciuta e continuata fino all' anno MDCCLV. Venezia, G. Pasquali, 1755. First published Rome, 1666.

Altmann, Wilhelm. Führer durch die einaktigen Opern, Operetten und Singspiele des Verlages Ed. Bote und G. Bock. Berlin, Bote & Bock, 1919.

—— Katalog der seit 1861 in den Handel gekommenen theatralischen Musik (Opern, Operetten, Possen, Musik zu Schauspielen, usw.); ein musikbibliographischer Versuch. Wolfenbüttel, Verlag für musikalische Kultur und Wissenschaft, 1935.

Annesley, Charles (pseud. of Charles and Anna Tittman). Home Book of the Opera, Including the Standard Opera Glass; Detailed Plots of the Celebrated Operas. New York, Tudor, 1937.

Apthorp, William Foster. The Opera Past and Present. London, John Murray, 1901.

Arnals, Alexander d'. Der Operndarsteller; Lehrgang zur musikalischen Darstellung in der Oper. Berlin, Bote & Bock, [1932].

Arundell, Dennis. "Operatic Ignorance," PMA LI (1924–25) 73–96.

Associazione dei musicologi italiana. Bolletino: catalogo delle opere musicali sino ai primi decenni del secolo XIX, Parma, 1910–11.

Catalogues of music collections by cities, under each city by libraries, under each library by forms and media, e.g. "opere teatrali."

Austin, Cecil. "Cinema Music," M&L V (1924) 177–91.

Barrenechea, Maríano Antonío. Historia estética de la música, con dos estudios mas sobre consideraciones historicas y tecnicas acerca del canto y la obra maestra del teatro melodramatico. Buenos Aires, Editorial Claridad, 1941.

Bekker, Paul. Das Operntheater. Leipzig, Quelle & Meyer, 1931.

—— Wandlungen der Oper. Zürich and Leipzig, Orell Füssli, [1934]. Translated as: The Changing Opera. [New York], W. W. Norton, [1935].

Bertrand, Paul. "Pure Music and Dramatic Music," MQ IX (1923) 545–55.

Bibliographie für Theatergeschichte 1905–1910, bearbeitet von Paul Alfred Merbach. Berlin, Selbstverlag der Gesellschaft für Theatergeschichte, 1913.

Bie, Oskar. Die Oper. Berlin, S. Fischer, 1913.

Bologna. Liceo musicale. Biblioteca. Catalogo della biblioteca del Liceo musicale di Bologna, compilato da Gaetano Gaspari. Bologna, Libreria romagnoli dell' acqua, 1890–1905. 4 vols.

Bonaccorsi, Alfredo. "L'opera in musica," RMI XXXVI (1929) 594–99.

Boston. Public Library. Allen A. Brown Collection. A Catalogue of the Allen A. Brown Collection of Books Relating to the Stage. Boston, 1919.

—— Catalogue of the Allen A. Brown Collection of Music. Boston, 1910–16. 4 vols.

British Museum. Department of Manuscripts. Catalogue of Manuscript Music in the British Museum, by Augustus Hughes-Hughes. London, 1906–1909. 3 vols.

British Museum. Department of Printed Books. Catalogue of Printed Music Published between 1487 and 1800 Now in the British Museum, by W. Barclay Squire. [London], 1912. 2 vols. The Second Supplement (1940) lists all acquisitions from 1912 to 1940 and makes corrections of the 1912 catalogue.

British Museum. Department of Printed Books. King's Music Library. Catalogue of the King's Music Iibrary, by William Barclay Squire. London, 1927–29. 3 vols.

Brockway, Wallace, and Herbert Weinstock. The Opera; a History of Its Creation and Performance, 1600–1941. New York, Simon & Schuster, 1941.

Brussels. Bibliothèque royale de Belgique. Catalogue de la bibliothèque de F. J. Fétis acquise par l'état belge. Gand, J. S. Van Doosselaere; Bruxelles, C. Muquardt; Paris, Firmin-Didot, 1877.

Brussels. Conservatoire royal de musique. Bibliothèque. Catalogue de la bibliothèque du Conservatoire royal de musique de Bruxelles . . . par Alfred Wotquenne. Bruxelles, J.-J. Coosemans, 1898– . 4 vols. Annexe[s] I, Bruxelles, O. Schepens, 1901, contains: Libretti d'opéras et d'oratorios italiens du XVIIe siècle.

Bulthaupt, Heinrich Alfred. Dramaturgie der Oper. Leipzig, B&H, 1887. 2 vols.

Bustico, Guido. Bibliografia delle storie e cronistorie dei teatri italiani. Milano, Bollettino bibliografico musicale, 1929.

Cambridge. University. Fitzwilliam Museum. Library. Catalogue of the Music in the Fitzwilliam Museum, Cambridge, by J. A. Fuller-Maitland. London, C. J. Clay, 1893.

Capell, Richard. Opera. London, E. Benn, [1930].

Capri, Antonio. Il melodramma dalle origini ai nostri giorni. Modena, Guanda, 1938.

Carducci, Edgardo. "The Tenor Voice in Europe," M&L XI (1930) 318-23.

Challis, Bennett. "The Technique of Operatic Acting," MQ XIII (1927) 630-45.

Cheney, Sheldon. The Theatre. New York, Longmans, Green, 1929.

Child, Harold. "Some Thoughts on Opera Libretto," M&L II (1921) 244-53.

Clayton, Ellen Creathorne. Queens of Song. London, Smith, Elder, 1863. 2 vols.
 Contains a (worthless) "chronological list of all the operas that have been performed in Europe [!]."

Clément, Félix. Dictionnaire des opéras (dictionnaire lyrique), rev. et mis à jour par Arthur Pougin. Paris, Larousse, [1905].

Closson, Hermann. Musique et drame. Bruxelles, [Institut national belge de radiodiffusion], 1939.

[Conti, Armand de Bourbon, prince de.] Traité de la comédie et des spectacles selon la tradition de l'église, tirée des conciles & des saints pères. Paris, L. Billaine, 1669.

Curzon, Henri de. L'Evolution lyrique au théâtre dans les differents pays; tableau chronologique. Paris, Fortin, 1908.

Czech, Stany. Das Operettenbuch; ein Wegweiser durch die Operetten und Singspiele der deutschen Bühne. Dresden, E. Wulffen, [1939]. 2d ed.

Dassori, Carlo. Opere e operisti (dizionario lirico 1541-1902); elenco nominativo universale dei maestri compositori di opere teatrali, col prospetto cronologico dei lori principali lavori e catalogo alfabetico generale delle opere . . . coll' indicazione di data e di luogo della prima rappresentazione, avuto speciale reguardo al repertorio italiano. Genova, R. Istituto sordomuti, 1903.

Davidson, Gladys. Standard Stories from the Operas. London, T. W. Laurie, 1935-[40]. 2 vols.

Deditius, Annemarie. Theorien über die Verbindung von Poesie und Musik. Liegnitz, Seyffarth, 1918.

Denkmäler des Theaters; Inszenierung, Dekoration, Kostüm des Theaters. Wien, Nationalbibliothek; München, R. Piper, [1925?-30]. In twelve parts; plates (some colored) in portfolios, with explanatory text laid in. Also published as: Monumenta scenica: The Art of the Theatre. London, Batsford, 1925-31.

Dent, Edward J. "The Nomenclature of Opera," M&L XXV (1944) 132-40, 213-26.

—— Opera. New York, Penguin Books, [1940].

—— "The Translation of Operas," PMA LXI (1934-35) 81-104.

Dilla, Geraldine P. "Music Drama: An Art Form in Four Dimensions," MQ X (1924) 492-99.

Dittmar, Franz. Opernführer, ein unentbehrlicher Ratgeber für den Besuch der Oper. Leipzig, Hachmeister & Thal, [1919].

Dubech, Lucien, J. de Montbrial, and Hélène Horn-Monval. Histoire générale illustrée du théâtre. Paris, Librairie de France, 1931–34. 5 vols.

Edwards, [Henry] Sutherland. History of the Opera from Monteverdi to Donizetti. London, W. H. Allen, 1862. 2d ed.

Einstein, Alfred. "The Mortality of Opera," M&L XXII (1941) 358–66.

Eisenmann, Alexander. Das grosse Opernbuch. Stuttgart and Berlin, Deutsche Verlagsanstalt, 1923.

Elson, Arthur. A Critical History of Opera; Giving an Account of the Rise and Progress of the Different Schools, with a Description of the Master Works in Each. Boston, L. C. Page, 1901.

Elson, Louis C. "Atrocities and Humors of Opera," MQ VI (1920) 206–13.

England, Paul. Fifty Favourite Operas; a Popular Account Intended as an Aid to Dramatic and Musical Appreciation. London, G. G. Harrap, [1925].

Fink, Gottfried Wilhelm. Wesen und Geschichte der Oper; ein Handbuch für alle Freunde der Tonkunst. Leipzig, G. Wigand, 1838.

Frankenfelder, August. Historische Elemente in der Oper und ihre ästhetische Bedeutung. Würzburg, Becker, 1896.

Freedley, George, and John A. Reeves. A History of the Theatre. New York, Crown Publishers, [1941].
Includes a bibliography of 433 works, cross-indexed by country and special topics.

Fürst, Leonhard. Der musikalische Ausdruck der Körperbewegung in der Opernmusik. Miesbach, Mayr, 1932.

Galli, Amintore. Estetica della musica ossia del bello nella musica sacra, teatrale, e da concerto in ordine alla sua storia. Torino, Bocca, 1899.

Galloway, W. Johnson. The Operatic Problem. London, Long, 1902.

Gavazzeni, Gianandrea. "La poesia dell' opera in musica," RassM XI (1938) 137–62.

Gloggner, Carl. "Oper und Gesangskunst," Musikalisches Wochenblatt I (1870) 65–67, 81–82, 97–98, 113–14.

Goddard, Joseph. The Rise and Development of Opera. London, W. Reeves, 1912.

Götze, Willibald. Studien zur Formbildung der Oper. Frankfurt a.M., Brönner, 1935.

Goode, Gerald. The Book of Ballets. New York, Crown Publishers, [1939].

Grabbe, Paul. Minute Stories of the Opera. New York, Grosset & Dunlap, [1932].

Grand-Carteret, John. "Les Titres illustrés et l'image au service de la musique," RMI V (1898) 1–63, 225–80; VI (1899) 289–329; IX (1902) 557–635; XI (1904) 1–23, 191–227.

Gregor, Hans. Die Welt der Oper—die Oper der Welt. Berlin, Bote & Bock, [1931].

Gregor, Joseph. Kulturgeschichte der Oper. Wien, Gallus, 1941.

Hagemann, Carl. Oper und Szene; Aufsätze zur Regie des musikalischen Dramas. Berlin, Schuster & Loeffler, 1905.

Hansemann, Marlise. Der Klavier-Auszug von den Anfängen bis Weber. Borna, Meyen, 1943.

Hatton, A. P. "Personality in Opera," M&L XII (1931) 164–69.

Heseltine, Philip. "The Scope of Opera," M&L I (1920) 230–33.

Hirsch, Paul. Katalog der Musikbibliothek Paul Hirsch . . . Band II: Opern-Partituren. Berlin, Breslauer, 1930.

Howes, Frank. A Key to Opera. London and Glasgow, Blackie, [1939].

—— "Professor Wellesz on Opera," M&L XV (1934) 120–27.

Hussey, Dyneley. Euridice; or The Nature of Opera. London, K. Paul, 1929.

Istel, Edgar. Das Buch der Oper. Berlin, M. Hesse, [1920]. 2d ed.

—— Das Libretto; Wesen, Aufbau und Wirkung des Opernbuchs. Berlin and Leipzig, Schuster & Loeffler, 1914. Translated (revised) as: The Art of Writing Opera Librettos. New York, G. Schirmer, [1922].

—— Revolution und Oper. Regensburg, G. Bosse, 1919.

Kapp, Julius. Das Opernbuch; eine Geschichte der Oper und ein musikalisch-dramatischer Führer. Leipzig, Hesse & Becker, 1935.

Kinsky, Georg. [Geschichte der Musik in Bildern.] A History of Music in Pictures. London, J. M. Dent, [1937].

Kobbé, Gustav. The Complete Opera Book; the Stories of the Operas, together with 400 of the Leading Airs and Motives in Musical Notation. New York and London, G. P. Putnam's Sons, [1932].

Köhler, Louis. Die Melodie der Sprache in ihrer Anwendung besonders auf das Lied und die Oper. Leipzig, Weber, 1853.

Kraussold, Max. Geist und Stoff der Operndichtung; eine Dramaturgie in Umrissen. Leipzig, Strache, 1931.

Krehbiel, Henry Edward. A Book of Operas. New York, Macmillan, 1928. 2 vols. in one, combining "A Book of Operas" and "A Second Book of Operas."

Kretzschmar, Hermann. "Für und gegen die Oper," JMP XX (1913) 59–70.

—— Geschichte der Oper. Leipzig, B&H, 1919.

Kruse, Georg Richard. Reclams Opernführer. Leipzig, P. Reclam, [1937]. 7th enlarged ed. 1942, 13th ed.

Kunath, Martin. "Die Charakterologie der stimmlichen Einheiten in der Oper," ZfMw VIII (1925–26) 403–10.

—— Die Oper als literarische Form. Leipzig Dissertation, 1925.

La Laurencie, Lionel de. Inventaire critique du fonds Blancheton de la Bibliothèque du Conservatoire de Paris. Paris, E. Droz, 1930–31. 2 vols.

Loewenberg, Alfred. Annals of Opera, 1597–1940. Cambridge, W. Heffer, 1943.

Loschelder, Josef Die Oper als Kunstform. Wien, A. Schroll, [1941].

McSpadden, Joseph Walker. Light Opera and Musical Comedy. New York, Thomas Y. Crowell, [1936].

—— Opera Synopses. New York, Thomas Y. Crowell, [1934]. 5th ed.

—— Operas and Musical Comedies. New York, Thomas Y. Crowell, 1946. A rearrangement and expansion of his two earlier books above.

Madrid. Biblioteca nacional. Departmento de manuscritos. Catálogo de las piezas de teatro. Madrid, Blass, 1934–35. 2 vols.

Manners, Charles. "The Financial Problems of National Opera," M&L VII (1926) 93–105.

Mantzius, Karl. A History of Theatrical Art in Ancient and Modern Times. London, Duckworth, 1903–21. 6 vols.

Martens, Frederick Herman. The Book of the Opera and the Ballet and History of the Opera. New York, C. Fischer, [1925].

—— A Thousand and One Nights of Opera. New York, D. Appleton, [1926].

Matthews, Brander. "The Conventions of the Music Drama," MQ V (1919) 255–63.

Mayer, Anton. Die Oper; eine Anleitung zu ihrem Verständnis. Berlin, K. Wolff, [1935].

Mayer, Ernesto Rodolfo. "Verso quali mète è diretta l' 'opera'?" RMI XLII (1938) 363–67.

Melitz, Leo L. The Opera Goers' Complete Guide. New York, Dodd, Mead, 1924.

[Mendelssohn, Felix.] The Story of a Hundred Operas. New York, Grosset & Dunlap, [1940].

Mengelberg, Curt Rudolf. "Das Musikdrama als Kunstform," Die Musik XIII (1913–14) 288–99.

Mila, Massimo. "Il concetto di musica drammatica," RassM IV (1931) 98–106.

Mnilk, Walter. Reclams Operettenführer. Leipzig, Reclam, [1937].

Neitzel, Otto. Der Führer durch die Oper des Theaters der Gegenwart. Leipzig, A. G. Liebeskind, 1890–98. 3 vols.

Newman, Ernest. More stories of Famous Operas. New York, Knopf, 1943.

—— Stories of the Great Operas and Their Composers. New York, Garden City Publishing Company, [1928]. 3 vols. in one. Both the above titles reprinted, 1946.

New York. Public Library. The Development of Scenic Art and Stage Machinery; a List of References in the New York Public Library. New York, 1920.

Nicoll, Allardyce. The Development of the Theatre. London, George C Harrap, 1927.

O'Neill, Norman. "Music to Stage Plays," PMA XXXVII (1911) 85–102.

"Opera," in Enciclopedia universal ilustrada europea-americana ("Espasa") XXXIX, 1360–94; XXI, 1297–1300.

Ordway, Edith Bertha. The Opera Book. New York, Sully & Kleinteich, [1915].

Paris. Bibliothèque nationale. Département des imprimés. Catalogue du fonds de musique de la Bibliothèque nationale, par J. Ecorcheville. Paris, 1910–14. 8 vols.

Paris. Conservatoire national de musique et de déclamation. Bibliothèque. Catalogue bibliographique . . . avec notices et reproductions musicales des principaux ouvrages de la réserve, par J. B. Weckerlin. Paris, Firmin-Didot, 1885.

Peltz, Mary Ellis. The Metropolitan Opera Guide. New York, The Modern Library, [1939].

Percival, Robert. "Can Opera Be Made to Pay?" M&L VII (1926) 114–19.

[Pereira Peixoto d'Almeida Carvalhaes, Manoel.] Catálogo da importante biblioteca que pertencen ao . . . erudito e bibliofilo ilustre Manuel de Carvalhaes . . . organisado par Augusta Sâ da Costa. Lisboa, 1928.

Peyser, Herbert F. "Some Observations on Translation," MQ VIII (1922) 353–71.

Prod'homme, Jacques Gabriel: "Etat alphabétique sommaire des archives de l'opéra," RdM XIV (1933) 193–205.

Rabich, Ernst. Die Entwicklung der Oper. Langensalza, Beyer, 1926.

Radford, Maisie. "A Comparative Study of Indigenous Forms of Opera," M&L VII (1926) 106–13.

Radio Listener's Book of Operas. Boston, Lothrop, Lee & Shepard, [1926]. 2 vols. in one.

Refardt, Edgar. Verzeichnis der Aufsätze zur Musik in den nichtmusikalischen Zeitschriften der Universitätsbibliothek Basel abgeschlossen auf den 1. Januar 1924. Leipzig, B&H, 1925.

Renner, Hans. Die Wunderwelt der Oper; der grosse Führer durch die Oper und die klassische Operette. Berlin, Vier Falken Verlag, [1938].

Riemann, Hugo. Opern-Handbuch; Repertorium der dramatisch-musikalischen Litteratur. Leipzig, H. Seemann Nachfolger, [published in parts; 1881–1900?].

Rinaldi, Mario. L'opera in musica; saggio estetico. Roma, "Novissima," [1934].

Sanborn, Pitts. The Metropolitan Book of the Opera; Synopses of the Operas. Garden City, N.Y., Garden City Publishing Co., [1942].

Sauerlandt, Max. Die Musik in fünf Jahrhunderten der europäischen Malerei etwa 1450 bis etwa 1850. Leipzig, Langewiesche Verlag, 1922.

Schiedermair, Ludwig. "Ueber den Stand der Operngeschichte," in International Music Society, Second Congress Report (Leipzig, B&H, 1907) pp. 212–16.

Schladebach, Julius. "Geschichte der Oper bis auf Gluck," Die Wissenschaft im 19. Jahrhundert I (1856) 361.

Scholze, Johannes. Vollständiger Opernführer. Berlin, S. Mode, 1919. 4th ed. 5th ed., S. Mode, 1921. 7th ed. under the title "Opernführer," Leipzig, J. Dörner, 1935.

Schumann, Otto. Meyers Opernbuch. Leipzig, Bibliographisches Institut, [1938]. 4th ed.

Sear, H. G. "Operatic Mortality," M&L XXI (1940) 60–74.

Small, Herbert F. "On Opera," MQ IV (1918) 37–49.

Sonneck, Oscar George Theodore. "Noch etwas über Opernlexika," *Die Musik* XIII (1913–14) Qt. 4, 140–43.

Steidel, Max. Oper und Drama. Karlsruhe, G. Braun, 1923.

Stieger, Franz. "Opernkomponistinnen," *Die Musik* XIII (1913–14) Qt. 4, 270–71.

Storck, Karl G. L. Das Opernbuch. Stuttgart, Muth, 1929. 33–34th ed.

[Strangways, A. H. Fox.] "Opera and the Musician," M&L XIII (1932) 119–25.

Strantz, Ferdinand von. Opernführer. Berlin, A. Weichert, [1931].

Streatfeild, Richard Alexander. The Opera. London, G. Routledge, 1925. 5th ed.

Theatrical Designs from the Baroque through Neo-Classicism; Unpublished Material from American Private Collections. New York, H. Bittner, 1940. 3 vols.

Thompson, Oscar. Plots of the Operas, as Compiled for the International Cyclopedia of Music and Musicians. New York, Dodd, Mead, 1940.

Tommasini, Vincenzo. "Del drama lirico," RMI XXXIX (1932) 73–113.

Towers, John. Dictionary-Catalogue of Operas and Operettas Which Have Been Performed on the Public Stage. Morgantown, W. Va., Acme, [1910].

Turin. Biblioteca civica. Sezione teatrale. [Letteratura drammatica. Torino, G. B. Vassallo, 1912, 1911. 2 vols.]

United States Library of Congress. Division of Music. Catalogue of Opera Librettos Printed before 1800, prepared by Oscar George Theodore Sonneck. Washington, Government Printing Office, 1914. 2 vols.

—— Dramatic Music (Class M 1500, 1510, 1520); Catalogue of Full Scores, Compiled by E. G. T. Sonneck. Washington, Government Printing Office, 1908.

Upton, George Putnam. The Standard Light Operas. Chicago, A. C. McClurg, 1902.

—— The Standard Operas. Chicago, A. C. McClurg, 1928. New ed.

Valentin, Erich. "Dichtung und Oper; eine Untersuchung des Stilproblems der Oper," AfMf III (1938) 138–79.

Watkins, Mary Fitch. First Aid to the Opera-Goer. New York, F. A. Stokes, 1924.

Welter, Friedrich. Führer durch die Opern. Leipzig, Hachmeister & Thal, [1937].

Wichmann, Heinz. Der neue Opernführer, mit einem Anhang, Klassische Operetten. Berlin, P. Franke, 1943.

Wossidlo, Walter. Opern-Bibliothek; populärer Führer durch Poesie und Musik. Leipzig, Rühle & Wendling, [1919?].

Zopff, Hermann. Grundzüge einer Theorie der Oper. Leipzig, Arnold, 1868.

II

Works Dealing with Particular Operas, Composers, Schools, Regions, or Periods

Abascal Brunet, Manuel. Apuntes para la historia del teatro en Chile; la zarzuela grande. Santiago de Chile, Imprenta universitaria, 1940.

Abendroth, Walter. Hans Pfitzner. München, A. Lagen & G. Müller, 1935.

Abert, Hermann. "Die dramatische Musik," in Herzog Karl Eugen von Württemberg und seine Zeit I (Esslingen a. N., 1907) 555–611.

—— Gesammelte Schriften und Vorträge. Halle an der Saale, M. Niemeyer, 1929.
Contains essays on Gluck, Handel, Meyerbeer, Mozart, Noverre, Paisiello, Piccinni, Wagner, Weber, and eighteenth-century opera.

—— "Gluck und unsere Zeit," Die Musik XIII (1913–14) Qt. 4, 3–9.

—— "Glucks Alkestis im Stuttgarter Landestheater," ZfMw VI (1923–24) 353–61.

—— "Händel als Dramatiker," in Haendelfestspiele (Göttinger, 1922). Göttingen, Turm-Verlag, 1922.

—— "Herzog Karl von Württemberg und die Musik," in Süddeutsche Monatshefte V (1908) Bd. 1, 548–54.

—— "Johann Christian Bach's italienische Opern und ihr Einfluss auf Mozart," ZfMw I (1918–19) 313–28.

—— "Mozart and Gluck." M&L X (1929) 256–65.

—— Niccolo Jommelli als Opernkomponist, mit einer Biographie. Halle an der Saale, M. Niemeyer, 1908.

—— "Robert Schumann's Genoveva," ZIMG XI (1909–10) 277–89.

—— W. A. Mozart: neubearbeitete und erweiterte Ausgabe von Otto Jahns Mozart. Leipzig, B&H, 1923–24. 6th ed. 2 vols.

—— "Zur Geschichte der Oper in Württemberg," in III. Kongress der Internationalen Musikgesellschaft . . . Bericht (Wien, Artaria; Leipzig, B&H, 1909) pp. 186–93.

Abraham, Gerald. "The Best of Spontini," M&L XXIII (1942) 163–71.

—— Borodin, the Composer and His Music. London, Wm. Reeves, [1927].

—— "The Flying Dutchman: Original Version," M&L XX (1939) 412–19.

—— A Hundred Years of Music. New York, Knopf, 1938.

—— "The Leitmotif since Wagner," M&L VI (1925) 175–90.

—— "Moussorgsky's Boris and Pushkin's," M&L XXVI (1945) 31–38.

—— "Nietzsche's Attitude to Wagner; a Fresh View," M&L XIII (1932) 64–74.

—— On Russian Music. New York, Scribner, 1939.

—— Studies in Russian Music. New York, Scribner, 1936.

Abry, Emile. Histoire illustrée de la littérature française . . . par E. Aubry, C. Audic, P. Crouzet. Paris, Didier, 1935. Nouvelle éd.

Achenwall, Max. Studien über die komische Oper in Frankreich im 18. Jahrhundert und ihre Beziehungen zu Molière. Eilenburg, Offenhauer, 1912.

Adaiewsky, E. "Glinka; études analytiques," RMI XI (1904) 725–60; XVII (1910) 113–29.

Adam, Adolphe. Derniers souvenirs d'un musicien. Paris, Michel Levy frères, 1859.

—— Souvenirs d'un musicien . . . précédés de notes biographiques écrites par lui-même. Paris, Calmann-Lévy, 1884.

Adam de la Halle. Œuvres complètes du trouvère Adam de la Halle, poésies et musique; publiées . . . par E. de Coussemaker. Paris, A. Durand & Pedone-Lauriel, 1872.

Adami, Giuseppe. Puccini. Milano, Fratelli Treves, [1935].

Ademollo, Alessandro. La bell' Adriana ed altre virtuose del suo tempo alla corte di Mantova; contributo de documenti per la storia della musica in Italia nel primo quarto del seicento. Città di Castello, Lapi, 1888.

—— I primi fasti del teatro di via della Pergola in Firenze (1657–1661). Milano, Ricordi, [etc., 1885].

—— I teatri di Roma nel secolo decimosettimo. Roma, L. Pasqualucci, 1888.

Adimari, Lodovico. "Satira quarta; contro alcuni vizi delle donne, e particolamente contro le cantatrice," in Satire del marchese Lodovico Adimari (Londra, Si vende in Livorno presso T. Masi e comp., 1788) pp. 183–253.

Adler, Guido. "Einleitung [to Cesti's Pomo d'oro]," DTOe, Jahrg. III, Pt. 2 (1896) v–xxvi.

—— "Euryanthe in neuer Einrichtung [von Gustav Mahler]," ZIMG V (1903–1904) 269–75.

—— Handbuch der Musikgeschichte unter Mitwirkung von Fachgenossen. Frankfurt am Main, Frankfurter Verlags-Anstalt, 1924.

—— "Die Kaiser Ferdinand III., Leopold I., Joseph I. und Karl VI. als Tonsetzer und Förderer der Musik," VfMw VIII (1892) 252–74.

—— Richard Wagner, Vorlesungen gehalten an der Universität zu Wien. München, Drei Masken Verlag, 1923. 2d ed. (first publ. 1904).

Adorján, Andor. "L'Opérette hongroise," Revue de Hongrie VI (1910) 269–80.

Alaleona, Domenico. Studi su la storia dell' oratorio musicale in Italia. Torino, Bocca, 1908.

—— "Su Emilio de' Cavalieri," La nuova musica, Nos. 113–114 (1905) 35–38, 47–50.

Alarcón, Esperanza. "La ópera en México, sus comienzos y los mexicanos autores de óperas," Boletín del instituto mexicano de musicología y folklore I (1940) 5–9.

Albert, Maurice. Les Théâtres de la foire (1660–1789). Paris, Hachette, 1900.

—— Les Théâtres des boulevards (1789–1848). [Paris?], Lecène et Oudin, 1902.

Alberti, C. E. R. Ludwig van Beethoven als dramatischer Tondichter. Stettin, 1859. ("Für Freunde der Tonkunst.")

Albrecht, Otto E. Four Latin Plays of St. Nicholas from the 12th Century Fleury Play-Book; Text and Commentary, with a Study of the Music of the Plays, and of the Sources and Iconography of the Legends. Philadelphia, University of Pennsylvania Press; London, Oxford University Press, 1935.

Aldrich, Putnam C. The Principal Agréments of the Seventeenth and Eighteenth Centuries; a Study in Musical Ornamentation. Harvard Dissertation, 1942.

Alfieri, Pietro. Notizie biografiche di Niccolò Jommelli di Aversa. Roma, Tip. delle belle arte, 1845.

Algarotti, Francesco, conte. Saggio sopra l'opera in musica. Livorno, Coltellini, 1763.

Almanach der deutschen Musikbücherei auf das Jahr 1924/25. Regensburg, Gustav Bosse, 1924.

Almanach des Spectacles. Paris, Nos. 1–43, 1874–1913.

Almeida, Renato. História da música brasileira. Rio de Janeiro, F. Briguiet, 1942. 2d. ed.

Altmann, Charlotte. Der französische Einfluss auf die Textbücher der klassischen Wiener Operette. Vienna Dissertation, 1935.

Altmann, Wilhelm. "Lortzing als dramaturgischer Lehrer," *Die Musik* XIII (1913–14) Qt. 4, 157–58.

—— "Meyerbeer-Forschungen; archivalische Beiträge aus der Registratur der Generalintendantur der Königlichen Schauspiele zu Berlin," SIMG IV (1902–1903) 519–34.

—— "Spontini an der Berliner Oper; eine archivalische Studie." SIMG IV (1902–1903) 244–92.

—— "Ur- und Erstaufführungen von Opernwerken auf deutschen Bühnen in den letzten Spielzeiten 1899/1900 bis 1924/25," in *Jahrbuch der Universal-Edition* (1926).

Altucci, Carlo. Le origini del teatro comico in Francia. Aversa, Tip. R. Catoggio, 1931.

Ambros, August Wilhelm. Geschichte der Musik, Bd. IV. Leipzig, Leuchart, 1909. 3d ed., rev. and enl. by Hugo Leichtentritt.

Anderson, Emily, ed. The Letters of Mozart and His Family Chronologically Arranged, Translated and Edited with an Introduction, Notes and Indices . . . with Extracts from the Letters of Constanze Mozart to Johann Anton André Translated and Edited by C. B. Oldman. London, Macmillan, 1938. 3 vols., paged continuously.

Andeutungen zur Geschichte der Oper. Marienwerder, A. Baumann, 1845. "Besonderer Abdruck aus dem ersten Hefte des Archivs für vaterländische Interessen pro 1845."

Andrade, Mário de. Carlos Gomez. Rio de Janeiro, Pongetti, 1939.

Anecdotes dramatiques; contenant toutes les pièces de théâtre . . . joués à Paris . . . jusq'à l'année 1775. Paris, Duchesne, 1775. 3 vols.

Anheisser, Siegfried. Für den deutschen Mozart. Emsdetten i. Westf., H. & J. Lechte, 1938.

—— "Die unbekannte Urfassung von Mozarts Figaro," ZfMw XV (1932–33) 301–17.

—— "Das Vorspiel zu Tristan und Isolde und seine Motivik," ZfMw III (1921) 257–304.

Annuario del teatro lirico italiano, 1940—. [Milano], Edizioni Corbaccio, [1940–   ].

Antcliffe, Herbert. "The British School of Music-Drama; the Work of Rutland Boughton," MQ IV (1918) 117–27.

Antheil, George. "Opera—a Way Out," MMus XI, No. 2 (January–February, 1934) 89–94.

—— "Wanted—Opera by and for Americans," MMus VII, No. 4 (June–July, 1930) 11–16.

Anthon, Carl Gustav. Music and Musicians in Northern Italy during the Sixteenth Century. Harvard Dissertation, 1943.

Anticlo, —— "Gli spiriti della musica nella tragedia greca," RMI XX (1913) 821–87.

Antonini, G. "Un episodio emotivo di Gaetano Donizetti," RMI VII (1900) 518–35.

Appia, Adolphe. La Mise en scène du drame Wagnérien. Paris, L. Chailley, 1895.

—— Die Musik und die Inscenierung; aus dem Französischen übersetzt. München, Bruckmann, 1899.

Arend, Max. "Gluck, der Reformator des Tanzes," Die Musik XIII (1913–14) Qt. 4, 16–22.

—— Gluck, eine Biographie. Berlin, Schuster & Loeffler, 1921.

—— "Die Ouvertüren zu Glucks Cythère assiégée," ZfMw IV (1921–22) 94–95.

—— "Die unter Gluck's Mitwirkung, verschollene älteste deutsche Übersetzung der Iphigenia auf Tauris," ZIMG VII (1905–1906) 261–67.

Arger, Jane. Les Agréments et le rhythme; leur représentation graphique dans la musique vocale française du XVIIe siècle. Paris, Rouart, Lerolle, [pref. 1917].

—— "Le Rôle expressif des 'agréments' dans l'école vocale française de 1680 à 1760," RdM I (1917–19) 215–26.

Aristotle. Aristotle's Treatise on Poetry, translated . . . by Thomas Twining. London, Payne and Son [etc.], 1789.

Armitage, Merle, ed. Arnold Schoenberg. New York, G. Schirmer, 1937.

—— ed. Igor Stravinsky; Articles and Critiques. New York, G. Schirmer, 1936.

Arnaldi, Enea, conte. Idea di un teatro nelle principali sue parte simile a' teatri antichi. Vicenza, A. Veronese, 1762.

Arnaudiès, Fernand. Histoire de l'opéra d'Alger; épisodes de la vie théâtrale algéroise, 1830–1940. Alger, V. Heintz, [1941].

Arnheim, Amalie. "Ein Beitrag zur Geschichte des einstimmigen weltlichen Kunstliedes in Frankreich im 17. Jahrhundert," SIMG X (1908–1909) 399–421.

—— "Le Devin du village von Jean-Jacques Rousseau und die Parodie Les Amours de Bastien et Bastienne," SIMG IV (1902–1903) 686–727.

Arnold, Franck T. The Art of Accompaniment from a Thorough-Bass as Practiced in the XVIIth and XVIIIth Centuries. London, Oxford University Press, 1931.

Arnold, Robert F. Das deutsche Drama. München, C. H. Beck, 1925.

Arnoldson, Mrs. Louise Parkinson. Sedaine et les musiciens de son temps. Paris, l'Entente linotypiste, 1934.

Arteaga, Stefano. Le rivoluzioni del teatro musicale italiano, dalla sua origine fino al presente. Venezia, C. Palese, 1785. 2d ed. 3 vols.

Arundell, Dennis. Henry Purcell. London, Oxford University Press, 1927.

Asenjo y Barbieri, Francisco. Cancionero musical de los siglos XV y XVI. Madrid, Tip. de los huérfanos, [1890].

Aubignac, François Hédelin, abbé d. La Pratique du théatre. Amsterdam, J. F. Bernard, 1715. New ed. Alger, J. Carbonel, 1927.

Aubin, Léon. Le Drame lyrique; histoire de la musique dramatique en France. [Tours, édition de l' "Echo littéraire et artistique"], 1908.

Aubry, Georges Jean. La Musique française d'aujourd'hui. Paris, Perrin, 1916. Translated as: French Music of Today. London, K. Paul [etc.], 1919.

Augé-Chiquet, Mathieu. La Vie, les idées et l'œuvre de Baïf. Paris [etc.], Edouard Privat Hachette, 1909.

Augé de Lassus, Lucien. Boieldieu . . . ; biographie critique illustree. Paris, H. Laurens, [1908].

Auriac, Eugène d'. Théâtre de la foire; recueil de pièces représentées aux foires St.-Germain et St.-Laurent, précédé d'une essai historique sur les spectacles forains. Paris, Garnier frères, 1878.

Ayesterán, Lauro. Crónica de una temporada musical en el Montevideo de 1830. Montevideo, Ediciones Ceibo, 1943.

Babbitt, Irving. Rousseau and Romanticism. Boston and New York, Houghton Mifflin, 1919.

Babcock, Robert W. "Francis Coleman's 'Register of Operas,' 1712–1734," M&L XXIV (1943) 155–58. Supplemented and corrected in a letter by O. E. Deutsch, ibid. XXV (1944) 126.

Bacher, Otto. "Die deutschen Erstaufführungen von Mozarts Don Giovanni," Jahrbuch des Freien deutschen Hochstifts Frankfurt a. M. (1926) pp. 338–79. Also separately reprinted.

—— "Ein Frankfurter Szene zu Glucks Don Juan," ZfMw VII (1924–25) 570–74.

Bacher, Otto (*Cont.*). "Frankfurts musikalische Bühnengeschichte im 18. Jahrhundert. Theil I. Die Zeit der Wandertruppen (1700–1786)," *Archiv für Frankfurts Geschichte und Kunst* (1925) pp. 133–206.

—— Die Geschichte der Frankfurter Oper im 18. Jahrhundert. Frankfurt a. M., Englert und Schlosser, 1926.

—— "Ein Mozartfund," ZfMw VIII (1925–26) 226–30.

—— "Zur Geschichte der Oper auf Frankfurter Boden im 18. Jahrhundert," ZfMw VIII (1925–26) 93–102.

Bätz, Rüdiger. Schauspielmusiken zu Goethes *Faust*. Leipzig Dissertation, 1924.

Bagge, Selmar. "Robert Schumann und seine *Faust*-Scenen," in Waldersee, *Sammlung musikalischer Vorträge* (Leipzig, Graf, 1879) I, 121–40.

"Le Ballet au XIXe siècle," RM II (December, 1921; numéro special) 97–231.

Ballo, Ferdinando. Arrigo Boito. Torino, Ed. Arione, [1938].

Bannard, Yorke. "Music of the Commonwealth," M&L III (1922) 394–401.

Bapst, Germain. Essai sur l'histoire du théâtre. Paris, 1883.

Barberet, Vincent. Lesage et le théâtre de la foire. Nancy, 1887.

Barberio, Francesco. "Disavventure di Paisiello." RMI XXIII (1916) 534–58.

—— "Giovanni Paisiello tra le ire di un copista e di un innovatore," RMI XXII (1915) 301–18.

—— "Lettere inedite di Paisiello [1792–1812]," RMI XXIV (1917) 173–88.

—— "I primi dieci anni di vita artistica di Paisiello," RMI XXIX (1922) 264–76.

Barbieri, Francisco. *See* Asenjo y Barbieri.

Barclay Squire. *See* Squire, W. Barclay.

Bardi-Poswiansky, Benno. Flotow als Opernkomponist, Königsberg Dissertation, 1924.

—— Der tolle Kapellmeister; heitere Oper in 3 Akten mit Benutzung Reinhard Keiserscher Melodien. Textbuch. Berlin, Revo-Verlag, [1929].

Barini, Giorgio. "Noterelle Belliniane," RMI IX (1902) 62–71.

Barlow, Samuel. "Blitzstein's Answer," MMus XVIII, No. 2 (January–February, 1941) 81–83.

Baroni, Jole Maria. "La lirica musicale di Pietro Metastasio," RMI XII (1905) 383–406.

Barrett, William. Balfe; His Life and Work. London, Remington, 1882.

Barros Sierra, José. "*Tata Vasco* y su partitura," *Romance*, Vol. II, No. 23 (April [1941]).

Barry, C. A. "Introductory to the Study of Wagner's Comic Opera *Die Meistersinger von Nürnberg*," PMA VII (March 7, 1881) 74–97.

Bartmuss, Arwed Waldemar. Die Hamburger Barockoper und ihre Bedeutung für die Entwicklung der deutschen Dichtung und der deutschen Bühne. Jena Dissertation, 1925.

Bartsch, Karl. Romances et pastourelles françaises des XIIe et XIIIe siècles. Leipzig, F. Vogel, 1870.

Barzun, Jacques. Darwin, Marx and Wagner; Critique of a Heritage. Boston, Little, Brown, 1941.

Bateson, F. W. English Comic Drama, 1700–1750. Oxford, Clarendon Press, 1929.

Batka, Richard. Die alt-italienische Aria; Ida Isori und ihre Kunst des Bel-Canto. Wien, H. Heller, 1912.

—— Aus der Opernwelt; Prager Kritiken und Skizzen. München, Callwey, 1907.

—— Die moderne Oper. Prag, Verlag der Lese- und Redehalle der deutschen Studenten in Prag, 1902.

Bauer, Marion. "Darius Milhaud," MQ XXVIII (1942) 139–59.

Baumann, Ken C. The Change of Style in Verdi's Operatic Work in the Interlude between *Aida* and *Otello*. Cornell A. M. Thesis, 1945.

Beare, Mary. The German Popular Play *Atis* and the Venetian Opera: a Study of the Conversion of Operas into Popular Plays, 1675–1722. Cambridge, University Press, 1938.

Beau, A. Eduard. "Die Musik im Werk des Gil Vicente," *Volkstum und Kultur der Romanen* IX (1936) 177–201.

Beaujoyeulx, Baltasar de. Balet comique de la royne, faict aux nopces de Monsieur le Duc de Ioyeuse & madamoyselle de Vaudemont sa soeur. Paris, LeRoy, Ballard & Patisson, 1682.

Beaulieu, Henri. Les Théâtres du boulevard de Crime . . . de Nicolet à Déjazet (1752–1862). Paris, H. Daragon, 1905.

Beck, Paul. "Oberschwäbische Volkstheater im 18. Jahrhundert," *Alemannia* XX (1892) 73–97.

Becker, Marta. "Der Einfluss der Philosophie Schellings auf Richard Wagner," ZfMw XIX (1931–32) 433–47.

Beckers, Paul. Die nachwagner'sche Oper bis zum Ausgang des 19. Jahrhunderts im Spiegel der Münchener Presse. Bielefeld, Beyer & Hausknecht, 1936.

Beer, Otto Fritz. "Egon Wellesz und die Oper," *Die Musik* XXIII (1931) 909–12.

—— Mozart und das Wiener Singspiel. Vienna Dissertation, 1932.

Behrend, William. "Weyse und Kuhlau; Studie zur Geschichte der dänischen Musik," *Die Musik* III, No. 22 (1904) 272–86.

Bekker, Paul. Franz Schreker; Studie zur Kritik der modernen Oper. Berlin, Schuster & Loeffler, 1919.

—— "Glucks *Alkeste* auf der Bühne," ZfMw I (1918–19) 193–96.

—— Klang und Eros. Stuttgart and Berlin, Deutsche Verlags-Anstalt, 1922.

—— Kritische Zeitbilder. Berlin, Schuster & Loeffler, 1921.

—— Das Musikdrama der Gegenwart. Stuttgart, Strecker & Schröder, 1909.

—— Neue Musik. Berlin, E. Reiss, 1920. 5th ed.

—— "The Opera Walks New Paths," MQ XXI (1935) 266–78.

Bekker, Paul (*Cont.*). Wagner; das Leben im Werke. Stuttgart, Deutsche Verlags-Anstalt, 1924. Translated as: Richard Wagner; His Life in His Works. New York, Norton, [1931].

Belaiev, Victor. Moussorgsky's *Boris Goudonov* and Its New Version. London, Oxford University Press, 1928.

Bellaigue, Camille. "Les Epoques de la musique; le grand opéra français," *Revue des deux mondes* (1906) No. 5, pp. 612–49.

—— "Les Epoques de la musique; l'opéra-comique," *Revue des deux mondes* (1905) No. 5, pp. 177–210.

—— "Les Epoques de la musique; l'opéra mélodique—Mozart," *Revue des deux mondes* (1901) No. 6, pp. 885–907.

—— "Les Epoques de la musique; l'opéra récitatif," *Revue des deux mondes* (1900) No. 6, pp. 608–38.

Bellasis, Edward. Cherubini; Memorials Illustrative of His Life. London, Burns & Oates, 1874.

Bellini, Vincenzo. Epistolario, a cura di Luisa Cambi. Verona, Mondadori, 1943.

Belluci la Salandra, Mario. Opere teatrali serie e buffe di Nicolò Piccinni. Roma, Edizioni Psalterium, 1935. For corrections, etc., see *Note d'archivio* XIII (1936) 55–58.

—— Saggio cronologico delle opere teatrali di Gaetano Latilla. Bari, 1935. Separate from *"Japigia," Rivista di arch., storica e arte.*

—— Triade musicale bitontina; . . . Logroscino, Traetta, Planelli. Bitonto, A. Amendolagene, 1935.

Beloch, Julius. "La populazione d'Italia nei secoli XVI, XVII e XVIII," *Bulletin de l'Institut international de statistique* III (1888) 1–42.

Benham, Evelyn. "A Musical Monopolist [J. B. Lully]," M&L IX (1928) 249–54.

[Benjamin, Lewis Saul.] Life and Letters of John Gay . . . by Lewis Melville [pseud.]. London, D. O'Connor, 1921.

Bennett, Howard G. "Opera in Modern Germany," MTNA XXIX (1934) 65–73.

Benvenuti, Giacomo. "Il manoscritto veneziano della *Incoronazione di Poppea*," RMI XLI (1937) 176–84.

Bérard, Jean Antoine. L'Art du chant. Paris, Dessait & Saillant, 1755.

Berend, Fritz. Nicolaus Adam Strungk. Hannover, E. Homann, [1915].

Berg, Alban. "A Word about *Wozzek*," MMus V, No. 1 (November–December, 1927) 22–24.

Berger, Arthur V. *"The Beggar's Opera,* the Burlesque, and Italian Opera," M&L XVII (1936) 93–105.

Bergmans, Paul. "Une Collection de livrets d'opéras italiens (1669–1710)," SIMG XII (1910–11) 221–34.

Berl, Paul. Die Opern Giuseppe Verdis in ihrer Instrumentation. Vienna Dissertation, 1931.

Berlioz, Hector. A Travers Chants; études musicales. Paris, Michel Lévy, 1872. 2d ed.

—— Les Grotesques de la musique. Paris, A. Bourdilliat, 1854.

—— Mémoires. Paris, Michel Lévy, 1870. Translated as: Memoirs of Hector Berlioz. New York, Tudor, [1935]. Annotated and the translation revised by Ernest Newman.

—— Les Musiciens et la musique. Paris, Calmann-Lévy, [1903].
A selection of articles from the *Journal des débats*, 1835–63.

—— Les Soirées de l'orchestre. Paris, Michel Lévy, 1852. Translated as: Evenings in the Orchestra. New York and London, Knopf, 1924. Introduction by Ernest Newman.

Bernacki, Ludwik. Teatr, dramat i muzyka za Stanislawa Augusta. Lwów, Zaktad Narodowy imiena Ussolínskich, 1925. 2 vols.

Bernet Kempers, Karel P. De Italiaansche Opera, haar Ontstaan en Ontwikkeling van Peri tot Puccini. Amsterdam, H. J. Paris, 1929.

Bernhard, Christoph. Die Kompositionslehre Heinrich Schützens in der Fassung seines Schülers Christoph Bernhard. Leipzig, B&H, 1926. Edited with an introduction by J. M. Müller-Blattau.

Bernstein, Nikolai Davidovich. Russland's Theater und Musik zur Zeit Peters des Grossen. Riga, Gizycko; Leipzig, Pabst, [1904].

Berrsche, Alexander. Kurze Einführung in Hans Pfitzners Musikdrama *Der arme Heinrich*. Leipzig, [1910].

Berthoud, Paul B. The Musical Works of Dr. Henry Hadley. New York, National Association for American Composers and Conductors, 1942.

Bertolotti, Antonio. Artisti francesi in Roma nei secoli XV, XVI e XVII. Mantua, Mondovi, 1894.

—— Musici alla corte dei Gonzaga in Mantova dal secolo XV al XVII; notizie e documenti raccolti negli Archivi Mantovani. Milano, Ricordi, [1890].

Besch, Otto. Engelbert Humperdinck. Leipzig, B&H, 1914.

Bethléem, Abbé L., and others. Les Opéras, les opéras-comiques et les opérettes. Paris, Editions de la Revue des lectures, 1926.
Critical evaluations from the standpoint of historical truthfulness, religion, and morality.

Beyle, Henri. Vie de Rossini, suivi des notes d'un dilettante. Paris, E. Champion, 1922. Preface and annotations by Henry Prunières. Translated as: Memoirs of Rossini. London, T. Hookham, 1824.

—— Vies de Haydn, de Mozart et de Métastase. Paris, H. Champion, 1914. Text established and annotated by Daniel Muller, preface by Romain Rolland.

Bie, Oscar. "Stand der Oper," *Die Neue Rundschau* XLIII, No. 2 (July–December, 1932) 124–31.

Biedenfeld, [Ferdinand, Freiherr von]. Die komische Oper der Italiener, der Franzosen und der Deutschen. Leipzig, Weigl, 1848.

Biehle, Herbert. Musikgeschichte der Stadt Bautzen. Berlin Dissertation, 1923.

Bienenfeld, Elsa. "Verdi and Schiller," MQ XVII (1931) 204–208.

Bilbao, José. Teatro Real; recuerdos de las cinco temporadas del empresario Arana. Madrid, Editorial Norma, 1936.

Billeci, A. La Bohème di Giacomo Puccini; studio critico. Palermo, Vesca, 1931.

Bitter, K[arl] H[ermann]. Die Reform der Oper durch Gluck und R. Wagner's Kunstwerk der Zukunft. Braunschweig, F. Vieweg, 1884. Critical review by H. Kretzschmar, VfMw I (1885) 227–34.

—— Mozart's Don Juan und Gluck's Iphigenia in Tauris; ein Versuch neuer Uebersetzungen. Berlin, F. Schneider, 1866.

Bitter, Werner. Die deutsche komische Oper der Gegenwart; Studien zu ihrer Entwicklung. Leipzig, Kistner & Siegel, 1932.

Bittrich, Gerhard. Ein deutsches Opernballett des siebzehnten Jahrhunderts; ein Beitrag zur Frühgeschichte der deutschen Oper. Leipzig, Frommhold & Wendler, 1931.

[Bizet, Georges.] See RdM XXII (November, 1938), special number devoted to Bizet.

Bizet, René. Une Heure de musique avec Oscar Straus. Paris, Editions cosmopolites, 1930.

Blareau, Ludovic. Histoire de la création et du développement du drame musical particulièrement en Italie, depuis l' Euridice de Peri jusqu'à l' Orfeo de Gluck. Bruxelles, Maurice Lamerten, 1921. Superficial and uncritical.

Blaze, [François Henri Joseph], called Castil-Blaze. L'Académie impériale de musique . . . de 1645 à 1855. Paris, Castil-Blaze, 1855.

—— Chapelle-musique des rois de France. Paris, Paulin, 1832.

—— De l'opéra en France. Paris, Janet et Cotelle, 1820.

—— L'Opéra-Italien de 1548 à 1856. Paris, Castil-Blaze, 1856.

Blaze de Bury, Yetta. "The French Opera," Nineteenth Century (1890) No. 2, pp. 39–53.

Blitzstein, Marc. "Hin und Zurück in Philadelphia," MMus V, No. 4 (May–June, 1928) 34–36.

—— "The Phenomenon of Stravinsky," MQ XXI (1935) 330–47.

Blom, Eric. "The Problem of Don Giovanni," M&L XIII (1932) 381–90.

Blondel, S. "Les Castrats," La Chronique musicale IX (1875) 241–50.

Blümml, Emil Karl, and Gustav Gugitz. Alt-Wiener Thespiskarren; die Frühzeit der Wiener Vorstadtbühnen. Wien, A. Schroll, 1925.

Boardman, Herbert Russell. Henry Hadley, Ambassador of Harmony. Emory University, Georgia, Banner Press, [1932].

Boas, Hans. "Lorenzo da Ponte als Wiener Theaterdichter," SIMG XV (1913–14) 325–38.

[Bobillier, Marie.] Les Concerts en France sous l'ancien régime. Paris, Fischbacher, 1900.

—— "Grétry, sa vie et ses œuvres," in *Mémoires couronnés et autres mémoires publiés par l'Académie royale . . . de Belgique,* Tome XXXVI, 1884.

—— Notes sur l'histoire du luth en France. Turin, Bocca, 1899.

Böhme, Erdmann Werner. "Die frühdeutsche Oper in Altenburg," *Jahrbuch der Theaterfreunde für Altenburg und Umkreis* (1930) pp. 53 ff.

—— Die frühdeutsche Oper in Thüringen. Stadtroda in Thüringen, Richter, 1931.

—— Musik und Oper am Hofe Christians von Sachsen-Eisenberg (1677–1707). Stadtroda in Thüringen, Richter, [1930]. First published in *Mitteilungen des Geschichts- und Altertumsvereins zu Eisenberg in Thüringen,* 41. und 42. Heft (8. Band, 1. und 2. Heft, 1930).

—— "Zur Vorgeschichte der Barockoper in Altenburg," *Jahrbuch der Theaterfreunde für Altenburg und Umkreis* (1931).

Böhme, Franz Magnus. Geschichte des Tanzes in Deutschland. Leipzig, B&H, 1886. 2 vols.

Bötcher, Elmar. Goethes Singspiele *Erwin und Elmire* und *Claudine von Villa Bella* und die "opera buffa." Marburg, Elwert, 1912.

Böttger, Friedrich. Die "Comédie-Ballet" von Molière-Lully. Berlin, Funk, 1931.

Bohe, Walter. Die Wiener Presse in der Kriegszeit der Oper. Würzburg, Triltsch, 1933. Published also with the title: Wagner im Spiegel der Wiener Presse.

Bohn, [Emil?]. "Theophilus; niederdeutsches Schauspiel aus einer Handschrift des 15. Jahrhunderts," MfMg IX (1877) 3–4. Music, pp. 24–25.

Boislisle, Arthur Michel de. "Les Débuts de l'opéra français à Paris," *Mémoires de la Société de l'histoire de Paris* II (1876) 172 ff.

Boïto, Arrigo. Lettere. Roma, Società editrice "Novissima," [1932].

—— "Pensieri critici giovanili," RMI XXXI (1924) 161–98.

Boladeres Ibern, Guillermo de. Enrique Granados. Barcelona, Editorial Arte y letras, [1921].

Bollert, Werner. Aufsätze zur Musikgeschichte. Bottrop, Postberg, 1938. Contains essays on Salieri and Weigl.

—— Die Buffoopern Baldassare Galuppis. Bottrop, Postberg, 1935.

—— "Giuseppe Petrosellini quale librettista di opere," RMI XLIII (1939) 531–38.

—— "Tre opere di Galuppi, Haydn e Paisiello sul' *Mondo della luna* di Goldoni," *Musica d'oggi* XXI (1939) 265–70.

Bolte, Johannes. Die Singspiele der englischen Komödianten und ihrer Nachfolger in Deutschland, Holland und Skandinavia. Hamburg and Leipzig, L. Voss, 1893.

Bonaventura, Arnaldo. "Una celebre cantante livornese del settecento," *Musica d'oggi* VI (1924) 255–58.

—— Giacomo Puccini. Livorno, [1925].

—— "Le maggiolate," RMI XXIV (1917) 272–99.

Bonaventura, Arnaldo (*Cont*.). L'opera italiana. Firenze, Novissima enciclopedia monografia illustrata, [1928].

—— Saggio storico sul teatro musicale italiano. Livorno, R. Giusti, 1913.

—— Verdi. Paris, F. Alcan, 1923.

Bonavia, Ferrucio. Verdi. London, Oxford University Press, 1930.

Bonnefon, Paul. "Les Métamorphoses d'un opéra (lettres inédites d'Eugène
Scribe)," *Revue des deux mondes* (1917) No. 5, pp. 877–99.

Bonnet, George Edgar. Philidor et l'évolution de la musique française au
XVIIIe siècle. Paris, Delagrave, 1921.

[Bonnet, Jacques.] Histoire de la musique, et de ses effets. Paris, J. Cochart,
1715.

Borcherdt, Hans Heinrich. "Beiträge zur Geschichte der Oper und des
Schauspiels in Schlesien bis zum Jahre 1740," *Zeitschrift für die Geschichte Schlesiens* XLIII (1909) 217 ff.

—— "Geschichte der italienischen Oper in Breslau," *Zeitschrift für die
Geschichte Schlesiens* XLIV (1910) 18 ff.

Borland, John E. "French Opera before 1750," PMA XXXIII (1907) 133–
57.

Borrel, Eugène. L'Interprétation de la musique française (de Lully à la
révolution). Paris, F. Alcan, 1924.

——"L'Interprétation de l'ancien récitatif français," RdM XII (1931)
13–21.

—— "Les Notes inégales dans l'ancienne musique française," RdM XII
(1931) 278–89.

—— "Un Paradoxe musical au XVIIIe siècle," in *Mélanges de musicologie*
(Paris, Droz, 1933) pp. 217–21.

Borrelli, E. "Il Wort-Ton-Drama," RassM VII (1934) 333–43, 433–36.

Borren, Charles van den. Alessandro Scarlatti et l'esthétique de l'opéra
napolitain. Paris, Editions de la Renaissance d'occident, 1921.

—— *Il ritorno d'Ulisse in patria* du Claudio Monteverdi. Bruxelles, Weis-
senbruch, 1925.

—— "Roma centro musicale del settecento," RMI XXXI (1924) 69–71.

Bosch, Mariano. Historia de la ópera en Buenos Aires. Buenos Aires, El
Comercio, 1905.

Boschot, Adolphe. "A propos du centenaire de *La Damnation de Faust*,"
RM XXII (February–March, 1946) 11–14.

—— Le *Faust* de Berlioz. Paris, Librairie de France, 1927.

—— Hector Berlioz; une vie romantique. Paris, Plon, [1939]. Published in
1920 under title: Une Vie romantique; Hector Berlioz.

—— L'Histoire d'un romantique: Hector Berlioz. I. La Jeunesse d'un
romantique . . . 1803–1831. Paris, Plon-Nourrit, 1906. II. Un Romantique sous Louis-Philippe . . . 1831–1842. Paris, Plon-Nourrit, 1908.
III. Le Crépuscule d'un romantique . . . 1842–1869. Paris, Plon-Nourrit, 1913.

—— "Sur Gluck et Wagner," *Revue politique et littéraire* XXXVII (1900) 19–23.

—— La Vie et les œuvres de Alfred Bruneau. Paris, Fasquelle, [1937].

Botstiber, Hugo. Geschichte der Ouvertüre und der freien Orchesterformen. Leipzig, B&H, 1913.

Boughton, Rutland. The Death and Resurrection of the Music Festival. London, W. Reeves, [1913].

—— The Glastonbury Festival Movement. London, [Somerset Press], 1922. Reprinted from *Somerset and the Drama* [by S. R. Littlewood and others].

—— Music Drama of the Future; *Uther and Igraine,* Choral Drama . . . with Essays by the Collaborators. London, W. Reeves, 1911.

—— "A National Music Drama; the Glastonbury Festival," PMA XLIV (1917–18) 19–35.

Bourdelot, Pierre. *See* Bonnet, Jacques.

Bouvet, Charles. Spontini. Paris, Rieder, [1930].

Bowen, Catherine D. Free Artist. New York, Random House, [1939].

Bowen, Catherine D., and Barbara von Meck. "Beloved Friend." New York, Random House, 1937.

Brabec, Ernst. Richard Wagner und Friedrich Smetana. Prague Dissertation, 1937.

Brady, William S. "Operatic Opportunities for American Pupils," MTNA XXI (1926) 140–44.

Braga, Theophilo. Historia do theatro portuguez [Vol. III]; a baixa comedia e a opera, secolo XVIII. Porto, Impr. portugueza-editora, 1870–71.

Bragaglia, Anton Giulio. "Celebrazioni Marchigiane; Giacomo Torelli da Fano," *Il giornale di politica e di letteratura* X (1934) 331–62; XI (1935) 69–80.

Brancour, René. Félicien David. Paris, H. Laurens, [190–].

—— Méhul. Paris, H. Laurens, [1912].

Brand, Max. " 'Mechanische' Musik und das Problem der Oper," *Musikblätter des Anbruch* VIII (1926) 356–59.

Brandstetter, Renward. "Musik und Gesang beiden Luzerner Osterspielen," *Der Geschichtsfreund* XL (1885) 145–68.

Braudo, Eugen. "Concerts, Opera, Ballet in Russia Today," MMus X, No. 4 (May–June, 1933) 213–19.

—— "The Russian Panorama," MMus X, No. 2 (January–February, 1933) 79–86.

Braun, Lisbeth. "Die Balletkomposition von Joseph Starzer," SzMw XIII (1926) 38–56.

Braunstein, Josef. Beethovens Leonore-Ouvertüren; eine historisch-stilkritische Untersuchung. Leipzig, B&H, 1927.

—— "Gibt es zwei Fassungen von der Ouvertüre Leonore Nr. 2?" ZfMw IX (1926–27) 349–60.

Bravo, F. Suarez. "La Musique à Barcelone: *Los Pireneos* de F. Pedrell," ZIMG III (1901–02) 231–39.

Brazil. Ministerio da educação e saude. Relação das opéras de autores brasileiros por Luiz Heitor Corrêa de Azevedo. Rio de Janeiro, Serviço gráfico do Ministerio da educação e saude, 1938. (Coleção brasileira de teatro. Série D: Estudos sobre teatro. Vol. II.)

Brenon, Algernon. "Giuseppe Verdi," MQ II (1916) 130–62.

Bréville, Pierre de, and H. Gauthier-Villars. *Fervaal;* étude thématique et analytique. Paris, A. Durand, 1897.

Bricqueville, Eugène de. Le Livret d'opéra français de Lully à Gluck. Bruxelles, 1888.

Brindejont-Offenbach, Jacques. Offenbach, mon grand-père. Paris, Plon, 1940.

Brinkmann, Hennig. Zum Ursprung des liturgischen Spieles. Bonn, F. Cohen, 1929.

Brockt, Johannes. "Verdi's Operatic Choruses," M&L XX (1939) 309–12.

Brosses, Charles de. Lettres familières sur l'Italie. Paris, Firmin-Didot, 1931. Introduction and notes by Yvonne Bezard.

Brown, John. Letters on the Italian Opera. London, T. Cadell, 1791. 2d ed.

Brownlow, Jane. "The Bardi Coterie," PMA XXII (1896) 111–27.

Brück, Paul. "Glucks *Orpheus und Euridike*," AfMw VII (1925) 436–76.

Brückner, Fritz. Georg Benda und das deutsche Singspiel. Leipzig, B&H, 1904. Also SIMG V (1903–04) 571–621.

—— "Zum Thema 'Georg Benda und das Monodram,' " SIMG VI (1904–05) 496–500.

Brüggemann, Fritz. Bänkelgesang und Singspiel vor Goethe. Leipzig, Reclam, 1937.

Bruger, Hans. Glucks dramatische Instrumentationskunst und ihre geschichtlichen Grundlagen. Teil 1: Glucks italienischen Werke (einschliesslich der Wiener Reformopern). Heidelberg Dissertation, 1922.

Brukner, Fr. *Die Zauberflöte;* unbekannte Handschriften und seltene Drucke aus der Frühzeit Mozarts Oper. Wien, Gilhofer & Rauschburg, 1934.

Bruneau, Alfred. Massenet. Paris, Delagrave, 1934.

—— La Musique française; rapport sur la musique en France du XIIIe au XXe siècles; la musique à Paris en 1900. Paris, E. Fasquelle, 1901.

—— Musiques d'hier et de demain. Paris, Bibliothèque Charpentier, 1900.

—— La Vie et les œuvres de Gabriel Fauré. Paris, Charpentier & Fasquelle, 1925.

Brunswick, Mark. "Beethoven's Tribute to Mozart in *Fidelio*," MQ XXXI (1945) 29–32.

Brusa, Filippo. "Il *Nerone* di Arrigo Boito," RMI XXXI (1924) 392–443.

Bruyr, José. Grétry. Paris, Rieder, [1931].

Bücken, Ernst. Der heroische Stil in der Oper. Leipzig, Kistner & Siegel, 1924.

Bukofzer, Manfred. "The *Book of the Courtier* on Music," MTNA XXXVIII (1944) 230–35.

Burckhardt, Jakob. The Civilization of the Period of the Renaissance in Italy. London, C. K. Paul, 1878. 2 vols.

Burney, Charles. A General History of Music from the Earliest Ages to the Present Period. London, Printed for the Author, 1776. Also: 2d ed., with critical and historical notes by Frank Mercer. London, Foulis; New York, Harcourt, Brace, 1935.

—— Memoirs of the Life and Writings of the Abate Metastasio; in Which Are Incorporated Translations of His Principal Letters. London, G. G. and J. Robinson, 1796. 3 vols.

—— The Present State of Music in France and Italy. London, T. Becket, 1771.

—— The Present State of Music in Germany, the Netherlands, and United Provinces. London, T. Becket, 1773. 2 vols.

Buschkötter, Wilhelm. "Jean François Le Sueur; eine Biographie," SIMG XIV (1912–13) 58–154.

Busi, Leonida. Benedetto Marcello. Bologna, N. Zanichelli, 1884.

Busne, Henry de. *"Ariane et Barbe-bleue* de M. Paul Dukas," MM III (1907) 465–71.

Busoni, Ferruccio. Entwurf einer neuen Aesthetik der Tonkunst. Leipzig, Insel-Verlag, [19—]. Translated as: Sketch of a New Esthetic of Music. New York, G. Schirmer, 1911.

[——] "Nota bio-bibliografica su Ferruccio Busoni," RassM XIII (1940) 82–88.

—— Über die Möglichkeiten der Oper und über die Partitur des *Doktor Faust.* Leipzig, B&H, 1926.

—— Von der Einheit der Musik. Berlin, M. Hesse, [1923].

Bustico, Guido. "Un librettista antiromantico (Angelo Anelli)," RMI XXVIII (1921) 53–81.

—— Pier Alessandro Guglielmi, musicista. Massa, Medici, 1898.

—— "Saggio di una bibliografia di libretti musicali di Felice Romani," RMI XIV (1907) 229–84.

—— "Saverio Mercadante a Novara," RMI XXVIII (1921) 361–96.

—— "Gli spettacoli musicali al 'Teatro Novo' di Novara (1779–1873)," RMI XXV (1918) 84–103, 202–48; "Nuovo contributo," RMI XXVI (1919) 615–52.

Caccini, Giulio. Le nuove musiche; riproduzione dell' edizione dell' 1601. Roma, Raccolte Claudio Monteverdi (R. Mezzetti), 1930.

Cahn-Speyer, Rudolf. Franz Seydelmann als dramatischer Komponist. Leipzig, B&H, 1909.

Callegari, Matelda. "Il melodramma e Pietro Metastasio," RMI XXVI (1919) 518–44; XXVII (1920) 31–59, 458–76.

Calmus, Georgy. "Die *Beggar's Opera* von Gay und Pepusch," SIMG VIII (1906–1907) 286–335.

—— "Drei satirisch-kritische Aufsätze von Addison über die italienische Oper in England," SIMG IX (1907–08) 131–45, 448.

—— Die ersten deutschen Singspiele von Standfuss und Hiller. Leipzig, B&H, 1908.

—— Zwei Opernburlesken aus der Rokokozeit. Berlin, Liepmannssohn, 1912. Contents: *Télémaque* (Lesage), *The Beggar's Opera* (Gay and Pepusch).

Calvocoressi, Michel D. "*Boris Goudonov*," MM IV (1908) 61–78.

—— Glinka. Paris, H. Laurens, [1911?].

—— "*Le Mariage*, par Moussorgsky," MM IV (1908) 1284–90.

—— Masters of Russian Music, by M. D. Calvocoressi and Gerald Abraham. New York, Knopf, 1936.

—— Moussorgsky. Paris, F. Alcan, 1921. 3d ed. Translated as: Musorgsky, the Russian Musical Nationalist. London, K. Paul; New York, Dutton, 1919.

—— Moussorgsky. London, Dent, 1946.

—— "Moussorgsky's Musical Style," MQ XVIII (1932) 530–46.

—— "L'orchestrazione autentica dal *Boris Godunof*," RassM I (1928) 633–39.

—— "La vera *Kovanscina* di Mussorgski," RassM V (1932) 166–75.

—— "Il vero e completo *Boris Godunof*," RassM I (1928) 217–25.

—— Vincent d'Indy, *L'Etranger;* le poème, analyse thématique de la partition. Paris, Editions du Courrier musical, [1903].

Cametti, Alberto. "Alcuni documenti inediti su la vita di Luigi Rossi," SIMG XIV (1912–13) 1–26.

—— Christina di Svezia, l'arte musicale e gli spettacoli teatrali in Roma. Roma, Tipografia Romano Mezzetti, 1931.

—— "Critiche e satire teatrali romane del '700," RMI IX (1902) 1–35.

—— "Donizetti a Roma; con lettere e documenti inediti," RMI XI (1904) 761–88; XII (1905) 1–39, 515–54, 689–713; XIII (1906) 50–90, 522–45, 616–55; XIV (1907) 301–32.

—— "Il *Guglielmo Tell* e le sue prime rappresentazioni in Italia," RMI VI (1899) 580–92.

—— "Leonardo Vinci e i suoi drammi in musica al Teatro delle Dame 1724–30," *Musica d'oggi* (1924) No. 10, pp. 297–99.

—— La musica teatrale a Roma cento anni fa: Il *Corsaro* di Pacini. Roma, Mezzetti, 1931.

—— La musica teatrale a Roma cento anni fa: *Olivo e Pasquale* di Donizetti. Roma, A. Manuzio, 1928.

—— Un poeta melodrammatico romano . . . Jacopo Ferretti. Milano, Ricordi, [1898].

—— "Saggio cronologico delle opere teatrali (1754–1794) di Nicolò Piccinni," RMI VIII (1901) 75–100.

—— Il teatro di Tordinona, poi di Apollo. Tivoli, A. Chicca, 1939.

Campardon, Emile. L'Académie royale de musique au XVIIIe siècle. Paris, Berger-Levrault, 1884. 2 vols.

—— Les Comédiens du roi de la troupe italienne. Paris, Berger-Levrault, 1880. 2 vols.

—— Les Spectacles des foires . . . depuis 1595 jusqu'à 1791. Paris, Berger-Levrault, 1877. 2 vols.

Canal, Pietro. Dalla musica in Mantova. Venezia, Presso la segreteria del R. Istituto, 1881.

Cantillon, Arthur. Essai sur les symboles de la tétralogie Wagnerienne. Mons, Imprimerie générale, 1911.

Canudo, Ricciotto. "Le Drame musical contemporain," MM III (1907) 1185–92; IV (1908) 56–60.

—— "L'Esthétique de Verdi et la culture musicale italienne," MM III (1907) 719–37.

Capell, Richard. "Dame Ethel Smyth's Operas at Covent Garden," Monthly Musical Record LIII (1923) 197–98.

Capri, Antonio. Musica e musicisti d'Europa dal 1800 al 1938. Milano, Hoepli, 1939. 2d ed.

—— Il seicento musicale in Europa. Milano, Hoepli, 1933.

—— Il settecento musicale in Europa. Milano, Hoepli, 1936.

—— Verdi, uomo e artista. Milano, Ed. ufficio concerti, 1939.

Carey, Clive. "The Problem of Don Giovanni Again," M&L XIV (1933) 30–35.

Carlez, Jules. Catel. Caen, H. Delesques, 1894.

—— Grimm et la musique de son temps. Caen, Le Blanc-Hardel, 1872.

—— L'Œuvre d'Auber. Caen, Le Blanc-Hardel, 1874.

—— Un Opéra biblique au XVIIIe siècle. Caen, Le Blanc-Hardel, 1879.

—— Pacini et l'opéra italien. Caen, H. Delesques, 1888.

—— Pierre et Thomas Corneille librettistes. N.p., n.d.

—— La Sémiramis de Destouches. Caen, H. Delesques, 1892.

Carlyle, Thomas. "The Opera," in Critical and Miscellaneous Essays (New York, Scribner, 1904) IV, 397–403.

Carmena y Millán, Luis. Crónica de la ópera italiana en Madrid desde el año 1738 hasta nuestros dias. Madrid, M. Minuesa de los Rios, 1878.

Carmody, Francis J. Le Repertoire de l'opéra-comique en vaudevilles de 1708 à 1764. Berkeley, California, University of California Press, 1933.

Carner, Mosco. "The Erotic Element in Puccini," MQ XXII (1936) 45–67.

—— "Puccini's Early Operas," M&L XIX (1938) 295–307.

Carreras y Bulbena, José Rafael. Domenech Terradellas. Barcelona, F. X. Altés, 1908.

Carson, Wm. G. B. St. Louis Goes to the Opera, 1837–1941. St. Louis, The Missouri Historical Society, 1946.

Casella, Alfredo, ed. La favola di Orfeo, opera in un atto di Messer Angelo Ambrogini detto "Poliziano." Milano, Carisch, [1934].

564 Bibliography

Castiglione, Baldassare, conte. Il libro del cortegiano. Firenze, Heredi di Philippo di Giunta, 1528. Translated by Thomas Hoby as: The Courtier. [New York], The National Alumni, [1907].

Castil-Blaze, see Blaze.

Castro, Enio de Freitas e. Carlo Gomes. Pôrto Alegre, A. Nação, 1941.

Catelani, Angelo. Delle opere di Alessandro Stradella esistente nell' archivio musicale della R. Biblioteca Palatina di Modena. Modena, C. Vincenzi, 1866.

Cauchie, Maurice. "The High Lights of French Opéra Comique," MQ XXV (1939) 306–12.

Cavalli, Francesco. Venti arie tratte dai drami musicali di Francesco Cavalli. Wien-Triest, Verlag Schmiedel (Mozarthaus), 1909.

Cecil, George. "Impressions of Opera in France," MQ VII (1921) 314–30.

—— "Monte Carlo: Opéra de Luxe," MQ IX (1923) 65–71.

Celani, Enrico. "Canzoni musicale del secolo XVII," RMI XII (1905) 109–150.

—— "Musica e musicisti in Roma (1750–1850)," RMI XVIII (1911) 1–63; XX (1913) 33–88.

Cellamare, Daniele. Mascagni e la Cavalleria visti da Cerignola. Roma, Filli Palombi, 1941.

Cernicchiaro, Vincenzo. Storia della musica nel Brasile dai tempi coloniali sino ai nostri giorni. Milano, Fratelli Riccioni, 1926.

Cesari, Gaetano, and others. Antonio Bartolomeo Bruni, musicista cuneese (1751–1821). Torino, S. Lattes, 1931.

Chadwick, George. Horatio Parker. New Haven, Yale University Press, 1921.

Challis, Bennett. "Opera Publics of Europe; Impressions and Reminiscences," MQ XII (1926) 564–79.

Chamberlain, Houston Stewart. Das Drama Richard Wagners. Leipzig, B&H, 1921. 6th ed. First published 1892. Translated as: The Wagnerian Drama. London and New York, John Lane, 1915.

—— Die Grundlagen des neunzehnten Jahrhunderts. München, F. Bruckmann, 1912. 10th ed. First published 1900. Translated as: Foundations of the Nineteenth Century. München, F. Bruckmann, 1911.

—— Richard Wagner. München, F. Bruckmann, [1936]. 9th ed. First published 1896. English translation: London, Dent, 1900.

Chambers, E. K. The Medieval Stage. London, Oxford University Press, 1903. 2 vols.

Champigneulle, Bernard. "L'Influence de Lully hors de France," RM XXII (February–March, 1946) 26–35.

Chase, Gilbert. A Guide to Latin-American Music. Washington, D.C., Government Printing Office, 1945.

—— The Music of Spain. New York, Norton, [1941].

—— "Origins of the Lyric Theater in Spain," MQ XXV (1939) 292–305.

—— "Some Notes on Afro-Cuban Music and Dancing," Inter-American Monthly I, No. 8 (December, 1942) 32–33.

Chatfield-Taylor, H. C. Goldoni; a Biography. New York, Duffield, 1913.

Chavarri, Eduardo López. Historia de la música. Barcelona, Imprenta elzeviriana, 1929. 3d ed.

Chevaillier, Lucien. "Le Récit chez Monteverdi," RHCM X (1910) 284–94.

Chop, Max. August Bungert. Leipzig, H. Seemann Nachfolger, 1903.

—— E. N. v. Reznicek. Wien, Leipzig, Universal-Edition, [1920].

Chorley, Henry F. Music and Manners in France and Germany. London, Longmans, 1844.

—— Thirty Years' Musical Recollections. New York, Knopf, 1926.

Chouquet, Gustave. Histoire de la musique dramatique en France. Paris, Firmin Didot, 1873.

Chrysander, Friedrich. "*Adonis;* Oper von Reinhard Keiser," AMZ XIII (1878) 65–70, 81–87, 97–101.

—— "Eine englische Serenata von J. Sigismund Kusser um 1710," AMZ XIV (1879) 408–12, 417–22.

—— "Der erste Entwurf der Bassarie 'Nasce al bosco' in Händel's Oper *Ezio* (1732)," AMZ XIV (1879) 641–46.

—— "Die Feier des zweihundertjährigen Bestandes der Oper in Hamburg," AMZ XIII (1878) 113–15, 129–32, 145–48.

—— "Geschichte der Braunschweig-Wolfenbüttelschen Capelle und Oper vom XVI. bis zum XVIII. Jahrhundert," *Jahrbücher für musikalische Wissenschaft* I (1863) 147–286.

—— ["Geschichte der Hamburger Oper"], AMZ XII–XV (1877–80):
"Die erste Periode," AMZ XII (1877) 369–486 *passim*
"Die zweite Periode," AMZ XIII (1878) 289–442 *passim*
". . . unter . . . J. S. Kusser 1693–1696," AMZ XIV (1879) 385–408 *passim*
". . . vom Abgange Kusser's bis zum Tode Schott's," AMZ XIV (1879) 433–534 *passim*
". . . unter der Direction von Reinhard Keiser (1703–1706)," AMZ XV (1880) 17–87 *passim.*

—— G. F. Händel. Leipzig, B&H, 1858–67. 3 vols.

—— "Ludovico Zacconi als Lehrer des Kunstgesanges," VfMw VII (1891) 337–96; IX (1893) 249–310; X (1894) 531–67.

—— "Mattheson's Verzeichniss Hamburgischer Opern von 1678 bis 1728, gedruckt im *Musikalischen Patrioten,* mit seinen handschriftlichen Fortsetzungen bis 1751, nebst Zusätzen und Berichtigungen," AMZ XII (1877) 198–282, *passim.*

—— "Musik und Theater in Mecklenburg," *Archiv für Landeskunde in den Grossherzogthümern Mecklenburg* IV (1854) 105–25, 258–80, 346–79.

—— "Neue Beiträge zur mecklenburgischen Musikgeschichte," *Archiv für Landeskunde in den Grossherzogthümern Mecklenburg* VI (1856) 666–82.

—— "Die Oper *Don Giovanni* von Gazzaniga und von Mozart," VfMw IV (1888) 351–435.

Chrysander, Friedrich (*Cont.*). "Reinhard Keiser," in *Allgemeine deutsche Biographie* XV (1882) 540–51.

—— "Spontini nach Mitteilungen von Caroline Bauer und H. Marschner," AMZ XIV (1879) 259–64, 274–80, 289–93.

—— "Ueber die Unsittlichkeiten in unseren Operntexten," AMZ XIV (1879) 257–59, 273–74, 305–308.

—— ". . . über Wagners Tannhäuser," ZIMG V (1903–1904) 208–19.

Cinquante Ans de musique française de 1874 à 1925. Paris, Librairie de France, [1925]. Ed. by L. Rohozinski.

Civita, A. Ottavio Rinuccini e il sorgere del melodramma in Italia. Mantova, Manuzio, 1900.

Clark, George Norman. The Seventeenth Century. Oxford, Clarendon Press, 1929.

Clarke, Henry Leland. "Cambert, Lully, and Blow." Unpublished essay.

—— Dr. John Blow (1649–1708), Last Composer of an Era. Harvard Dissertation, 1947.

Clément, Félix. "Liturgie, musique et drama du moyen age," *Annales archéologiques* VII (1847) 303–20; VIII (1848) 36–48, 77–87, 304–11; IX (1849) 27–40, 162–74; X (1850) 154–60; XI (1851) 6–15.

Coeuroy, André. "Further Aspects of Contemporary Music," MQ XV (1929) 547–73.

—— La Musique française moderne. Paris, Delagrave, 1922.

—— "Nouveau Visages de l'opéra," RM (February, 1928) 7–16.

—— *La Tosca* de Puccini. Paris, Mellottée, [1922?].

—— "Wagner et le ballet," RM II (December, 1921) 206–13.

Cohen, Alex. "Ernest Bloch's *Macbeth*," M&L XIX (1938) 143–48.

Cohen, Gustave. Histoire de la mise en scène dans le théâtre réligieux français du moyen age. Paris, Champion, 1926. New ed.

Cohen, Hermann. Die dramatische Idee in Mozarts Operntexten. Berlin, Cassirer, 1916.

Colles, H. C. "Philip Napier Miles," M&L XVII (1936) 357–67.

Collet, Henri. Albeniz et Granados. Paris, F. Alcan, 1929. New ed.

—— *Samson et Dalila* de C. Saint-Saëns. Paris. Mellottée, [1922].

Colombani, A. L'opera italiana nel secolo XIX. Milano, ed. Corriere della Sera, 1900.

Colomb de Batines. Bibliografia delle antiche rappresentazioni italiane sacre e profane, stampate nei secoli XV e XVI. Firenze, Società tip., 1852. Additions by E. Narducci in *Il bibliofilo* III (1882) 73–74, 87–88.

Colson, J. B. Manuel dramatique. Bordeaux, chez l'auteur, 1817.

Combarieu, Jules. Histoire de la musique. Paris, A. Colin, 1920. 3d ed. 3 vols.

—— "Histoire du théâtre lyrique," RHCM VII (1907) 581–97; VIII (1908) 1–594 *passim;* IX (1909) *passim;* X (1910) *passim.*

—— "J.-J. Rousseau et le mélodrame," RHCM I (1901) 273–77.

—— "L'Opéra-comique d'hier et d'aujourd'hui," RHCM VII (1907) 549–63.

Comte, Charles, and Paul Laumonier. "Ronsard et les musiciens du XVIe siècle," *Revue d'histoire littéraire de la France* VII (1900) 341–81.

Conrad, Leopold. Mozarts Dramaturgie der Oper. Würzburg, Triltsch, 1943.

Conrat, Hugo J. "La musica in Shakespeare," RMI X (1903) 646–69; XI (1904) 35–54.

[Contant d'Orville, André Guillaume.] Histoire de l'opéra bouffon. Amsterdam and Paris, Grangé, 1768. 2 vols.

Cooper, Martin. "Charles Gounod and His Influence on French Music," M&L XXI (1940) 50–59.

—— Georges Bizet. London and New York, Oxford University Press, 1938.

—— Gluck. New York, Oxford University Press, 1935.

Coopersmith, J[acob] M[aurice]. [1.] An Investigation of Georg Friedrich Händel's Orchestral Style. [2.] A Thematic Index of the Printed Works of Händel. Harvard Dissertation, 1932. 12 vols.

—— "The Libretto of Handel's *Jupiter in Argos*," M&L XVII (1936) 289–96.

Copland, Aaron. Our New Music. New York, Whittlesey, [1941].

Coradini, Francesco. Antonio Maria Abbatini e d. Lorenzo Abbatini; notizie biografiche. Arezzo, Scuola tipografica aretina, 1922.

—— Brevi notizie sul musicista aretino Giovanni Apolloni. Arezzo, Scuola tipografica aretina, 1922.

—— "P. Antonio Cesti; nuove notizie biografiche," RMI XXX (1923) 371–88.

Corbet, August. Het muziekdrama in de XVIe en XVIIe eeuwen in Italie gezien in het licht van H. Wölfflin's *Kunstgeschichtliche Grundbegriffen;* ein bijdrage tot de theorie van het parallelisme in de kunst. Antwerpen, De Sikkel, 1936.

Corder, Frederick. "The Works of Sir Henry Bishop," MQ IV (1918) 78–97.

Cornelissen, Thilo. C. M. v. Webers *Freischütz* als Beispiel einer Opernbehandlung. Berlin, Matthiesen, 1940.

Cornelius, Carl Maria. Peter Cornelius, der Wort- und Tondichter. Regensburg, G. Bosse, [1925].

Cornelius, Peter. Literarische Werke. Leipzig, B&H, 1904–05. 4 vols.

Cornet, J. Die Oper in Deutschland und das Theater der Neuzeit. Hamburg, O. Meissner, 1849.

Correa de Azvedo, L. H. "Carlos Gomes; sua verdadeira posição no quadro da ópera italiana no sec. XIX e na evolução da musica brasileira," *Boletin latino-americano de música* III (1937) 83–87.

Corrodi, Hans. "Othmar Schoeck's *Massimilla Doni*," M&L XVIII (1937) 391–97.

Cortese, Louis. Alfredo Casella. Genova, Orfini, [1935].

Cortese, Nino. "Un' autobiografia inedita di Giovanni Paisiello," RassM III (1930) 123–35. Following is Paisiello's autobiography.

Cortolezis, Fritz. "Gedanken über eine stilgerechte Aufführung des *Fidelio*," *Neues Beethoven Jahrbuch* III (1926) 93–102.

Costa, Alessandro. "Schopenhauer e Wagner," RMI XXXIX (1932) 1–12.

Cotarelo y Mori, Emilio, ed. Colección de entremeses, loas, bailes, jácaras y mojingangas desde fines del siglo XVI á medíados del XVII. Madrid, Bailly-Baillière, 1911.

—— Historia de la zarzuela o sea El drama lírico en España, desde su origen a fines del siglo XIX. Madrid, Tipografía de Archivos, 1934.

—— Orígenes y establecimento de la ópera en España hasta 1800. Madrid, Tip. de la "Revista de arch.," [etc.], 1917.

Coussemaker, Edmond de. Drames liturgiques du moyen âge. Rennes, H. Vatar, 1860; Paris, Lib. archéologique de V. Didron, 1861.

Cowen, Sir Frederic Hymen. My Art and My Friends. London, E. Arnold, 1913.

Croce, Benedetto. I teatri di Napoli, secolo XV–XVIII. Napoli, L. Pierro, 1891.

Crocioni, Giovanni. L'Alidoro o dei primordi del melodramma. Bologna, L. Parma, 1938.

Crocker, Eunice. The Instrumental Ensemble Canzona. Radcliffe Dissertation, 1943.

Crowder, C. Fairfax. "Neglected Treasures in Handel's Operas," M&L II (1921) 135–48.

Cucuel, Georges. Les Créateurs de l'opéra-comique français. Paris, F. Alcan, 1914.

—— "La Critique musicale dans les 'revues' du XVIIIe siècle," L'Année musicale II (1912) 127–203.

—— "Giacomo Casanova e la musica," RMI XXXVI (1929) 446–65.

—— "Notes sur la comédie italienne de 1717 à 1789," SIMG XV (1913–14) 154–66.

—— "Les Opéras de Gluck dans les parodies du XVIIIe siècle," RM III, No. 5 (1922) 201–21; No. 6, pp. 51–68.

—— "Sources et documents pour servir à l'histoire de l'opéra-comique en France," L'Année musicale III (1913) 247–82.

Cui, César. La Musique en Russie. Paris, Fischbacher, 1880.

Cummings, William H. "The Lord Chamberlain and Opera in London, 1700 to 1741," PMA XL (1914) 37–72.

—— "Matthew Locke, Composer for the Church and Theatre," SIMG XIII (1911–12) 120–26.

Curiel, Carlo Leone. Il teatro S. Pietro di Trieste, 1690–1801. [Milano], Archetipographia di Milano, 1937.

Curzon, Henri de. Ernest Reyer. Paris, Perrin, 1924.

—— Felipe Pedrell et Les Pyrénées. Paris, Fischbacher, 1902.

—— Grétry. Paris, Laurens, [1907].

—— La Légende de Sigurd. Paris, Fischbacher, [1889].

—— Léo Delibes. Paris, G. Legouix, 1926.

—— "L'Opéra en 1843; mémoire du directeur Léon Pillet," RdM II (1920–21) 223–33.

—— "Les Opéras-comiques de Boieldieu," RM XIV (November, 1933) 249–63.

Czech, Stan. Franz Lehár; Weg und Werk. Berlin, Werk-Verlag, 1942.

Dacier, Emile. *"Les Caractères de la danse;* histoire d'un divertissement pendant la première moitié du XVIIIe siècle," RHCM V (1905) 324–35, 365–67.

—— "Une Danseuse française à Londres au début du XVIIIe siècle," MM III (1907) 437–63, 746–65.

—— "L'Opéra au XVIIIe siècle; les premières représentations du *Dardanus* de Rameau," RHCM III (1903) 163–73.

Daffner, Hugo. Friedrich Nietzsches Rundglossen zu Bizets *Carmen.* Regensburg, Bosse. 1938.

Dahms, Walter. "The 'Gallant' Style of Music," MQ XI (1925) 356–72.

Damerini, Adelmo. "Un precursore italiano di Gluck: Tommaso Traetta," *Il pianoforte* (July, 1927).

—— "Tommaso Traetta; cenni biografici," *Bollettino bibliografico musicale* II (July, 1927) 1–13.

Damrosch, Walter. My Musical Life. New York, Scribner, 1923.

D'Ancona, Alessandro. Origini del teatro italiano. Torino, E. Loescher, 1891. 2d ed. 2 vols.

Dandelot, Arthur. Evolution de la musique de théâtre depuis Meyerbeer jusqu'à nos jours. Paris, Flammarion, 1927.

D'Angeli, Andrea. Benedetto Marcello, vita e opere. Milano, Fratelli Bocca, 1940.

—— Commemorazione di Gio. Batta Pergolesi. Padova, L. Penada, 1936.

Daninger, Josef G. Sage und Märchen im Musikdrama; eine ästhetische Untersuchung an der Sagen- und Märchenoper des 19. Jahrhunderts. Prag, Hoffmanns Witwe, 1916.

Da Ponte, Lorenzo. Memorie. Nuova-Jorca, Lorenzo e Carlo Da Ponte, 1823. 2 vols. Translated, with introduction and notes, by L. A. Sheppard, Boston, Houghton Mifflin, 1929. Translated by Elisabeth Abbott, edited and annotated by Arthur Livingston, Philadelphia, J. B. Lippincott, 1929. Other editions: Bari, G. Laterza, 1918 (Italian); Paris, Henri Jonquières, 1931 (French; includes previously unpublished letters to Casanova; preface and notes by Raoul Vèze).

—— Storia compendiosa della vita di Lorenzo Da Ponte scritta di lui medesimo. New York, Riley, 1807.

D'Arienzo, Nicola. "Le origini dell' opera comica," RMI II (1895) 597–628; IV (1897) 421–59; VI (1899) 473–95; VII (1900) 1–33.

Daube, Otto. Siegfried Wagner und die Märchenoper. Leipzig, Deutscher Theater-Verlag, M. Schleppegrell, [1936].

Dauriac, Lionel. "Herbert Spencer et Meyerbeer," ZIMG V (1903–1904) 103–109.

—— "Un Problème d'esthétique Wagnérienne," MM IV (1908) 50–55.

Davari, Stefano. "Notizie biografiche del distinto maestro di musica Claudio Monteverdi," *Atti e memorie della R. Accademia Virgiliana di Mantova* X (1884–85) 79–183.

Davey, Henry. History of English Music. London, Curwen, [1921]. 2d ed., revised.

David, Ernest. Les Opéras du juif Antonio José da Silva. Paris, A. Wittersheim, 1880.

De Angelis, Alberto. "Cantanti italiani del secolo XIX: Erminia e Giuseppe Frezzolini," RMI XXXII (1925) 438–54.

—— "Musica e musicisti nell' opera di G. d'Annunzio," RMI XLIII (1939) 275–301.

—— "Il teatro farnese di Parma," RMI XLIII (1939) 364–82.

Debussy, Claude. Monsieur Croche, anti dilettante. Paris, Dorbon-aîné, 1921.

De' Calzabigi, Ranieri. "Dissertazione . . . su le poesie drammatiche del Sig. Abate Pietro Metastasio," in *Poesie del Signor Abate Pietro Metastasio* (Parigi, Vedova Quillan, 1755–69) I, xix–cciv.

—— Risposta . . . alla critica ragionatissima delle poesie drammatiche del C. de' Calsabigi, fatta del baccelliere D. Stefan Arteaga. Venezia, Curti, 1790.

Decsey, Ernst. Franz Lehár. München, Drei Masken-Verlag, 1930. 2d ed.

—— Hugo Wolf. Berlin, Schuster & Loeffler, [1919]. 3d-6th ed., revised.

—— Johann Strauss. Stuttgart, Berlin, Deutsche Verlags-Anstalt, 1922.

Dedekind, Constantin Christian. Heilige Arbeit über Freud und Leid der alten und neuen Zeit in Music-bekwehmen Schau-Spielen (9) ahngewendet. Dreszden, 1676.

—— Neue geistliche Schauspiele (5) bekwehmet zur Musik. [Dresden], 1670.

De Dominicis, Giulia. "Roma centro musicale nel settecento," RMI XXX (1923) 511–28.

De Donno, Alfredo. Mascagni nel 900 musicale. Roma, Casa del libro, [1935].

—— Modernità di Mascagni. Roma, Pinciana, 1931.

De Eisner-Eisenhof, A. "Giuseppe Weigl; una biografia," RMI XI (1904) 459–83.

Degey, Maurice. Les Echos imprévus de la mort de Grétry. Liège, Editions de la Vie wallonne, 1938.

Della Corte, Andrea. "Appunti sull' estetica musicale di Pietro Metastasio," RMI XXVIII (1921) 94–119.

—— ed. Canto e bel canto (Tosi e Mancini). Torino, G. B. Paravia, [1933].

—— "Cimarosa nel '99 e nella fortuna postuma," RassM IX (1936) 280–83.

—— "La drammaturgia nella *Semiramide* di Rossini," RassM XI (1938) 1–6.

—— Figuras y motivas de lo opera bufa italiano. Buenos Aires, La revista de musica, 1928.

—— Un Italiano all' estero, Antonio Salieri. Torino, G. B. Paravia, [1936].

—— "Nel II centenario della morte di Pergolesi; *Il geloso schernito e Il maestro di musica*," RassM IX (1936) 202–208.

—— "Notizie di Gaetano Pugnani musicista torinese (1731–1798)," *Rassegna mensile municipale "Torino"* (1931) pp. 26–39.

—— L'opera comica italiana nel 1700. Bari, G. Laterza, 1923. 2 vols.

—— Paisiello; con una tavola tematica. L'estetica musicale di P. Metastasio. Torino, Fratelli Bocca, 1922.

—— Piccinni (settecento italiano); con frammenti musicali inediti e due ritratti. Bari, G. Laterza, 1928.

—— Rittrato di Franco Alfano. Torino, G. B. Paravia, [1935].

—— "Tragico e comico nell' opera veneziana della seconda parte del seicento," RassM XI (1938) 325–33.

—— Tre secoli di opera italiana. Torino, Arione, [1938].

Della Torre, Arnaldo. Saggio di una bibliografia delle opere intorno a Carlo Goldoni (1793–1907). Firenze, Alfani e Venturi, 1908.

Delmas, Marc. Gustave Charpentier et le lyrisme français. Paris, Delagrave, 1931.

Demarquez, Suzanne. "Un Voyageur français et la musique italienne au XVIIIe siècle," RM, numéro spécial, "La Musique dans les pays Latins" (February–March, 1940) pp. 125–33.

De Napoli, Giuseppe. "Niccolò Piccinni nel secondo centenario della nascità," RMI XXXV (1928) 209–18.

—— La triade melodrammatica altamurana: Giacomo Tritto, 1733–1824; Vincenzo Lavigna, 1776–1836; Saverio Mercadante, 1795–1870. Milano, Rosio e Fabe, 1932.

Denizard, Marie. "La Famille française de Lully," MM VIII, No. 5 (1912) 1–14.

Dent, Edward J. "Alessandro Scarlatti," PMA XXX (1904) 75–90.

—— Alessandro Scarlatti, His Life and Works. London, E. Arnold, 1905.

—— "The *Amfiparnaso* of Orazio Vecchi," *Monthly Musical Record* XXXVI (1906) 50–52, 74–75.

—— "The Baroque Opera," MA I (1909–10) 93–107.

—— "A Best-Seller in Opera," M&L XXII (1941) 139–54.

—— "Busoni's *Doctor Faust*," M&L VII (1926) 196–208.

—— "Ensembles and Finales in 18th Century Italian Opera," SIMG XI (1909–10) 543–69; XII (1910–11) 112–38.

—— Ferrucio Busoni; a Biography. London, Oxford University Press, 1933.

—— Foundations of English Opera. Cambridge (England), University Press, 1928.

—— "Giuseppe Maria Buini," SIMG XIII (1911–12) 329–36.

—— Handel. London, Duckworth, [1934].

Dent, Edward J. (*Cont.*). "Handel on the Stage," M&L XVI (1935) 174–87.
—— "Hans Pfitzner," M&L IV (1923) 119–32.
—— "Italian Opera in the Eighteenth Century, and Its Influence on the Music of the Classical Period," SIMG XIV (1912–13) 500–509.
—— "Leonardo Leo," SIMG VIII (1906–1907) 550–66.
—— Mozart's Operas; a Critical Study. London, Chatto & Windus; New York, McBride, Nast, 1913.
—— Mozart's Opera *The Magic Flute*; Its History and Interpretation. Cambridge, W. Heffer, 1911.
—— "The Musical Interpretation of Shakespeare on the Modern Stage," MQ II (1916) 523–37.
—— "Notes on Leonardo Vinci," MA IV (1912–13) 193–201.
—— "Notes on the *Amfiparnaso* of Orazio Vecchi," SIMG XII (1910–11) 330–47.
—— "The Operas of Alessandro Scarlatti," SIMG IV (1902–1903) 143–56.
—— The Rise of the Romantic Opera. (The Messenger Lectures at Cornell University, 1937–38.) Typescript, 256 pp.
—— "The Romantic Spirit in Music," PMA LIX (1932–33) 85–102.
—— "Translating *Trovatore*, M&L XX (1939) 7–20.
De' Paoli, Domenico. Claudio Monteverdi. Milano, Hoepli, 1945.
—— *"Diane ed Endimione* di Alessandro Scarlatti," RassM XIII (1940) 139–46.
—— "Italian Chamber Cantatas," MA II (1911) 142–53, 185–99.
—— "Italy's New Music of the Theatre," MMus VIII, No. 1 (November–December, 1930) 21–26.
—— *"Orfeo* and *Pelléas,"* M&L XX (1939) 381–98.
—— "Pizzetti's *Fra Gherardo,"* MMus VI, No. 2 (January–February, 1929) 39–42.
De Rensis, Raffaello. Ercole Bernabei. Roma, tip. Sociale, 1920.
—— Ermanno Wolf-Ferrari, la sua vita d'artista. Milano, Fratelli Treves, 1937.
—— Musica italiana in Francia; la riforma intitolata a Gluck. Roma, Casa editrice "Musica," 1916.
—— "Un musicista diplomatico del settecento: Agostino Steffani," *Musica d'oggi* III, No. 5 (May, 1921) 129–32.
—— Ottorino Respighi. Torino, Paravia, [1935].
—— Primo Riccitelli: *I compagnacci;* guida attraverso la commedia e la musica. Milano, Bottega di poesia, 1923.
Desastre, Jean. Carlo Broschi; kuriose Abenteuer eines Sopranisten. Zürich, Bürdecke & Herwig, 1903.
[Desboulmiers, Jean Auguste Julien.] Histoire anecdotique et raisonée du théâtre italien, depuis son rétablissement en France jusqu'à l'année 1769. Paris, Lacombe, 1769. 7 vols.
—— Histoire du théâtre de l'opéra-comique. Paris, Lacombe, 1769. 2 vols.

Desderi, Ettore. "Le tendenze attuali della musica; il teatro," RMI XXXVIII (1931) 247–77.

Desessarts, Nicolas Toussaint Lemoyne. Les Trois Théâtres de Paris, ou abrégé historique de l'établissement de la Comédie Françoise, de la Comédie Italienne & de l'Opéra, Paris, Lacombe, 1777.

Desnoiresterres, Gustave. Gluck et Piccinni, 1774–1800. Paris, Didier, 1875. 2d ed.

Destranges, Etienne. Le Chant de la cloche, de Vincent d'Indy; étude analytique. Paris, Tresse et Stock, 1890.

—— L'Etranger de M. Vincent d'Indy; étude analytique et thématique. Paris, Fischbacher, 1904.

——L'Evolution musicale chez Verdi; Aida—Othello—Falstaff. Paris, Fischbacher, 1895.

—— Fervaal de Vincent d'Indy: étude thématique et analytique. Paris, A. Durand, 1896.

—— Messidor d'A. Bruneau; étude analytique et critique. Paris, Fischbacher, 1897.

—— L'Œuvre théâtral de Meyerbeer; étude critique. Paris, Fischbacher, 1893.

—— L'Ouragan d'Alfred Bruneau; étude analytique et thématique. Paris, Fischbacher, 1902.

—— Le Rêve d'Alfred Bruneau; étude thématique et analytique. Paris, Fischbacher, 1896.

Deutsch, Otto Erich. Das Freihaustheater auf der Wieden, 1787–1801. Wien-Leipzig, Deutsche Verlag für Jugend und Volk Gesellschaft, [1937].

—— Mozart und die Wiener Logen; zur Geschichte seiner Freimaurer-Kompositionen. Wien, Wiener Freimaurer-Zeitung, 1932.

De Vito, M. S. L'origine del dramma liturgico. Milano, Dante Alighieri, [1939?]

Dickinson, Alan Edgar Frederic. The Musical Design of The Ring. London, Oxford University Press, 1926.

Diderot, Denis. Le Neveu de Rameau; satyre publiée pour la première fois sur le manuscrit original autographe. Paris, Plon, Nourrit, 1891.

Dieckmann, Karin. De Braut von Messina auf der Bühne im Wandel der Zeit. Helsingfors Dissertation, 1935.

Dietz, Max. Geschichte des musikalischen Dramas in Frankreich während der Revolution bis zum Directorium (1787 bis 1795). Wien, Groscher & Blaha, 1885. 2d ed., Leipzig, B&H, 1893.

Di Giacomo, Salvatore. Il conservatorio dei poveri di Gesu Cristo e quello di S. M. di Loreto. Palermo, Sandron, 1928.

—— Il conservatorio di Sant' Onofrio a Capuana e quello di S. M. della Pietà dei Turchini. Napoli, Sandron, 1924. ("I quattro antichi conservatorii di Napoli MDXLIII–MDCCC.")

[Ditters] von Dittersdorf, Karl. Karl von Dittersdorfs Lebensbeschreibung: seinem Sohne in die Feder diktiert. Leipzig, B&H, 1801. Translated as: The Autobiography of Karl von Dittersdorf. London, R. Bentley, 1896. Modern German editions: Leipzig, Reclam, 1909 (Istel); Regensburg, G. Bosse, [ca. 1940] (E. Schmitz); Leipzig, Staackmann, 1940 (Loets).

Dobronić, A. "A Study of Jugoslav Music," MQ XII (1926) 56–71.

"Documents historiques: les origines de l'opéra en France," RHCM VIII (1908) 562–64.

Doebner, Richard, ed. Briefe der Königin Sophie Charlotte von Preussen und der Kurfürstin Sophie von Hannover an hannoversche Diplomaten. Leipzig, S. Hirzel, 1905.
Contains letters to Agostino Steffani.

Donath, Gustav. "Florian Gassmann als Opernkomponist," SzMw II (1914) 34–211.

Donati Petteni, Giuliano. Donizetti. Milano, Fratelli Treves, 1930.

Doni, Giovanni Battista. Compendio del trattato de' generi e de' modi della mvsica. Roma, A. Fei, 1635.
Abstract of a larger work which was never published. Portions of this work are quoted in Solerti's Origini under the title "Trattato della musica scenica."

—— Lyra Barberina ΑΜΦΙΧΟΡΔΟΣ; accedunt eiusdem opera, pleaque nondum edita ad veterem musicam illustrandam pertinentia. Florentiae typis Caesareis, 1763. 2 vols.

Doran, John. 'Mann' and Manners at the Court of Florence, 1740–1786; Founded on the Letters of Horace Mann to Horace Walpole. London, R. Bentley, 1876. 2 vols.

Dorn, Heinrich. Aus meinem Leben. Berlin, B. Behr, 1870–1886. 7 vols.

—— Gesetzgebung und Operntext (eine Schrift für Männer); zeitgemässe Betrachtungen. Berlin, Schlesinger, 1879.

Draper, John W. Eighteenth Century English Aesthetics; a Bibliography. Heidelberg, C. Winter, 1931.

Dresden, Sem. Het Muziekleven in Nederland sinds 1880. Amsterdam, Uitgeversmaatschlappy "Elsevier," 1923.

Du Bled, Victor. "Le Ballet de l'opéra," RM II (December, 1921) 191–205.

DuBos, Jean Baptiste. Critical Reflections on Poetry, Painting and Music. London, J. Nourse, 1748. 3 vols. Translated from the French 5th ed. Originally published anonymously, Paris, 1719.

Ducannès–Duval, G. "L'Opéra à Bordeaux en 1784," RdM XXI (1937) 82–83.

Dufrane, Louis. Gossec. Paris, Fischbacher, 1927.

Du Gérard, N. B. Tables alphabetique & chronologique de pieces representées sur l'ancien Theatre italien, depuis son etablissement jusqu'en 1697. Paris, Prault, 1750.

Duhamel, Raoul. "Eugène Delacroix et la musique," RMI XLIII (1939) 35–54, 333–56.

—— "Ferdinand Herold," RM XIV (November, 1933) 278–90.

—— "Quelques Maîtres de l'opéra-comique au XIXe siècle," RM XIV (November, 1933) 291–302.

[Dukas, Paul.] RM numéro spécial (May–June, 1936) contains articles on Dukas' operas.

Dumesnil, Maurice. Claude Debussy, Master of Dreams. New York, Ives Washburn, [1940].

—— "Gabriel Dupont, Musician of Normandy," MQ XXX (1944) 441–47.

Dumesnil, René. Le Don Juan de Mozart. Paris, Editions musicales de la librairie de France, 1927.

—— "Le Livret et les personnages de Don Giovanni," RM No. 4 (February, 1927) 118–28.

Du Moulin-Eckart, Richard Maria Ferdinand. Wahnfried. Leipzig, Kistner & Siegel, 1925.

Dunhill, Thomas F. Sullivan's Comic Operas; a Critical Appreciation. New York, Oxford University Press; London, Edw. Arnold, 1928.

Dupré, Henri. Purcell. Paris, Alcan, 1927. Translated, New York, Knopf, 1928.

Du Tillet, Jacques. "A propos du drame lyrique; une lettre de M. Camille Saint-Saëns," Revue politique et littéraire (July 3, 1897) pp. 27–30.

"Early Elizabethan Stage Music," MA I (1909–10) 30–40; IV (1912–13) 112–17.

Ebert, Alfred. Attilio Ariosti in Berlin (1697–1703). Leipzig, Giesecke & Devrient, 1905.

Eckermann, Johann Peter. Gespräche mit Goethe. Berlin, Bong, [1916]. 2 vols.

Ecorcheville, Jules. "Corneille et la musique," Courrier musical IX (1906) 405–12, 438–49. Also separate: Paris, Fortin, 1906.

—— De Lulli à Rameau, 1690–1730; l'esthétique musicale. Paris, Fortin, 1906.

—— "Lully gentilhomme et sa descendance," MM VII No. 5 (1911) 1–19; No. 6, pp. 1–27; No. 7, pp. 36–52.

Edgar, Clifford B. "Mozart's Early Efforts in Opera," PMA XXXII (1906) 45–58.

—— "A Résumé of Mozart's Early Operas," ZIMG VII (1905–1906) 460–64.

Edwards, Henry Sutherland. The Life of Rossini. London, Hurst & Blackett, 1869.

—— Rossini and His School. New York, Scribner & Welford, 1881.

Egert, Paul. Peter Cornelius. Berlin, B. Hahnefeld, [ca. 1940].

Ehrenhaus, Martin. Die Operndichtung der deutschen Romantik; ein Beitrag zur Geschichte der deutschen Oper. Einleitung und I. Teil. Breslau, F. Hirt, 1911. (Breslauer Beiträge zur Literaturgeschichte, Heft 29 [New Series 19].)

Ehrhard, Auguste. "La Danse à l'opéra en 1834; les debuts de Fanny Elssler," Bulletin de la société des amis de l'université de Lyon XIX (1906) 61–81.

Ehrichs, Alfred. Giulio Caccini. Leipzig, Hesse & Becker, 1908.

Eichborn, Hermann. Die Trompete in alter und neuer Zeit. Leipzig, B&H, 1881.

Einstein, Alfred. "Agostino Steffani," *Kirchenmusikalisches Jahrbuch* XXIII (1910) 1–36.

—— "Agostino Steffani," *Neue Musik-Zeitung* XLIX (1928) 316–19.

—— "Ein Bericht über den Turiner Mordanfall auf Alessandro Stradella," in *Festschrift Adolf Sandberger* (Müchen, Zierfuss, 1918) pp. 135–37.

—— "Concerning Some Recitatives in *Don Giovanni*," M&L XIX (1938) 417–25.

—— "Das erste Libretto des *Don Giovanni*," *Acta musicologica* IX (1937) 149–50.

—— "Firenze prima della monodia," RassM VII (1934) 253.

—— "German Opera, Past and Present," MMus XI, No. 2 (January-February, 1934) 65–72.

—— Gluck. London, Dent; New York, E. P. Dutton, [1936].

—— "The Greghesca and the Giustiniana of the Sixteenth Century," *Journal of Renaissance and Baroque Music* I (1946) 19–32.

—— "Die mehrstimmige weltliche Musik von 1450–1600," in Adler, *Handbuch der Musikgeschichte* (Frankfurt a.M., Frankfurter Vertags-Anstalt, 1924) pp. 358–73.

—— "Mozart et l'opéra-bouffe à Salzburg," RdM XXI (1937) 1–4.

—— "Mozart e Tarchi; un episodio della storia delle *Nozze di Figaro*," RassM VIII (1935) 269–72.

—— Mozart, His Character, His Work. New York and London, Oxford University Press, 1945.

—— "L'opera tedesca d'oggi," RassM V (1932) 26–37.

—— "Richard Wagners *Liebesverbot;* zur Aufführung am Münchner National-Theater (24. März 1923)," ZfMw V (1922–23) 382–86.

—— "Ein Schüler Gluck's," *Acta musicologica* X (1938) 48–50.

—— "Die Text-Vorlage zu Mozart's *Zaide*," *Acta musicologica* VIII (1936) 30–37.

—— "Eine unbekannte Arie der Marcelline," ZfMw XIII (1930–31) 200–205.

—— "Vincenzo Bellini," M&L XVI (1935) 325–32.

Eisenschmidt, Joachim. Die szenische Darstellung der Opern Georg Friedrich Händels auf der Londoner Bühne seiner Zeit. Wolfenbüttel and Berlin, Kallmeyer, 1940.

Eitner, Robert, ed. "Das älteste bekannte deutsche Singspiel, *Seelewig*, von S. G. Staden, 1644," MfMg XIII (1881) 53–147.

—— "Benedetto Marcello," MfMg XXIII (1891) 187–94, 197–211.

—— "Die deutsche komische Oper," MfMg XXIV (1892) 37–92.

—— "Der Generalbass des 18. Jahrhunderts," MfMg XII (1880) 151–54

—— "Johann Philipp Krieger," MfMg XXIX (1897) 114–17.

[——] "Die Quellen zur Entstehung der Oper," MfMg XIII (1881) 10–15, 21–28.

Ellinger, Georg. "Händel's *Admet* und seine Quelle," VfMw I (1885) 201–24.

Ellinwood, Leonard. "The *Conductus*," MQ XXVII (1941) 165–204.

Ellis, W. Ashton. "Richard Wagner's Prose," PMA XIX (1892) 13–33.

Elson, Louis C. The History of American Music. New York, Macmillan, 1925. Revised to 1925 by Arthur Elson.

Emmanuel, Maurice. *Pelléas et Mélisande* de Debussy; étude et analyse. Paris, Mellottée, [1925?].

Engel, Carl. "Die Wagnerdämmerung," MQ XIV (1928) 438–55.

Engel, Gustav. "Eine mathematisch-harmonische Analyse des *Don Giovanni* von Mozart," VfMw III (1887) 491–560.

Engelfred, Abele. *"Enoch Arden* di Riccardo Strauss," RMI VI (1899) 176–84.

—— "*Hulda* . . . di Cesare Franck," RMI II (1895) 312–23.

Engelke, Bernhard. "Aus den entscheidenden Entwicklungsjahren der Opéra-comique," in *Festschrift Arnold Schering* (Berlin, A. Glas, 1937) pp. 51–60.

—— Musik und Musiker am Gottorfer Hofe. Bd. 1. Die Zeit der englischen Komödianten (1590–1627). Breslau, Hirt, 1930.

Engländer, Richard. "Domenico Fischietti als Buffokomponist in Dresden," ZfMw II (1919–20) 321–52, 399–442.

—— "Dresden und die deutsche Oper im letzten Drittel des 18. Jahrhunderts," ZfMw III (1920–21) 1–21.

—— "Das Ende der *opera seria* in Dresden: Naumanns *Clemenza di Tito* 1769," *Neues Archiv für Sächsische Geschichte und Altertumskunde* XXXIX (1918) 311–29.

—— Johann Gottlieb Naumann als Opernkomponist. Leipzig, B&H, 1922.

—— Joseph Martin Kraus und die Gustavianische Oper. Uppsala, Almqvist & Wiksell; Leipzig, O. Harrassowitz, [1943].

—— "Die Opern Joseph Schusters," ZfMw X (1927–28) 257–91.

—— "Paërs *Leonora* und Beethovens *Fidelio*," *Neues Beethoven Jahrbuch* IV (1930) 118–32.

—— "Il *Paride* in musica (1662) di G. A. Bontempi," *Note d'archivio* XVII (1940) 39–53.

—— "The Sketches for *The Magic Flute* at Upsala," MQ XXVII (1941) 343–55.

—— "Zur Frage der *Dafne* (1671) von G. A. Bontempi und M. G. Peranda," *Acta musicologica* XIII (1941) 59–77.

—— "Zur Musikgeschichte Dresdens gegen 1800," ZfMw IV (1921–22) 199–241.

Engler, Günther. Verdis Anschauung vom Wesen der Oper. Breslau, Stenzel, 1938.

Enzinger, Moriz. Die Entwicklung des Wiener Theaters vom 16. zum 19. Jahrhundert. Berlin, Gesellschaft für Theatergeschichte, 1918–19. 2 vols.

Epstein, Peter. "Dichtung und Musik in Monteverdi's Lamento d'Arianna," ZfMw X (1927–28) 216–22.

—— "Paul Hindemiths Theatermusik," Die Musik XXIII (May, 1931) 582–87.

—— "Zur Rhythmisierung eines Ritornells von Monteverdi," AfMw VIII (1926) 416–19.

Epstein, Th. Don Giovanni von Mozart. Frankfurt a. M., Offenbach a. M., Andre, 1870.

Ernst, Alfred. "Les Motifs du Héros dans l'œuvre de R. Wagner," RMI I (1894) 657–77.

—— L'Œuvre dramatique de Berlioz. Paris, Levy, 1884.

—— "Thaïs . . . de J. Massenet," RMI I (1894) 296–306.

Esbert, C. L. R. "Hans Sachs," M&L XVII (1936) 59–61.

Eschweiler, Hans-Georg. Klara Ziegler; ein Beitrag zur Theatergeschichte des 19. Jahrhunderts. Rostock Dissertation, 1935.

Ettler, Carl. "Bibliographie des œuvres de Meyerbeer," RHCM IV (1904) 436–44.

Euting, Ernst. Zur Geschichte der Blasinstrumente im 16. und 17. Jahrhundert. Berlin, A. Schulze, 1899.

Evans, Edwin. Tchaikovsky. New York, E. P. Dutton, 1935. New ed., revised by E. Blom.

Evans, Herbert Arthur, ed. English Masques. London, Glasgow, Blackie & Son, 1897.

Evans, Willa McClung. Ben Jonson and Elizabethan Music. Lancaster, Pa., Lancaster Press, 1929.

Evelyn, John. Diary. London, J. M. Dent, 1907. 2 vols.

Färber, Sigfrid. Das Regensburger Fürstlich Thurn und Taxissche Hoftheater und seine Oper 1760–1786. [Regensburg], Pustet, 1936.

Faller, H. Die Gesangskoloratur in Rossinis Opern und ihre Ausführung. Berlin, Triltsch & Huther, 1935.

Fano, Fabio, ed. La camerata fiorentina; Vincenzo Galilei. Milano, Ricordi, 1934. (Istituzioni e monumenti dell' arte musicale italiana, Vol. IV.)

—— "Norma nella storia del melodramma italiano," RassM VIII (1935) 315–26.

Fassini, Sesto. "Gli albori del melodramma italiano a Londra," Giornale storico della letteratura italiana LX (1912) 340–76.

—— "Il melodramma italiano a Londra ai tempi del Rolli," RMI XIX (1912) 35–74, 575–636.

—— Il melodramma italiano a Londra nella prima metà del settecento. Turin, Bocca, 1914.

[Fauré, Gabriel Urbain.] See RM, numéro spécial (October, 1922).

[——] "Gabriel Fauré; note biografiche," Bollettino bibliografico musicale V, No. 3 (March, 1930) 5–[17].

Faustini-Fasini, Eugenio. "Gli astri maggiori del 'bel canto' Napoletano," *Note d'archivio* XII (1935) 297–316.

—— "Documenti paisielliani inediti," *Note d'archivio* XIII (1936) 105–27.

—— G. B. Pergolesi attraverso i suoi biografi e le sue opere. Milano, Ricordi, 1900.

—— "Leonardo Leo e la sua famiglia," *Note d'archivio* XIV (1937) 11–18.

—— Opere teatrali, oratori e cantate di Giovanni Paisiello (1764–1808); saggio storico-cronologico. Bari, Laterza, 1940.

Favart, Charles Simon. Memoires et correspondances littéraires, dramatiques et anecdotiques. Paris, L. Collin, 1808. 3 vols.

—— Théâtre. Paris, DuChesne, 1763–[77]. 10 vols.

Favre, G. Boieldieu. Paris, Droz, 1944–45. 2 vols.

Fedeli, Vito. "Dal *Cavaliere Ergasto* alla *Molinarella,*" RMI XVIII (1911) 357–81.

—— "*La Molinarella* di Piccinni," SIMG XIII (1911–12) 302–21, 507.

—— "Un' opera sconosciuta di Pergolesi?" SIMG XII (1910–11) 139–50.

Fehr, Max. Apostolo Zeno, 1668–1750, und seine Reform des Operntextes. Zürich, A. Tschopp, 1912.

—— "Pergolesi und Zeno," SIMG XV (1913–14) 166–68.

—— "Zeno, Pergolesi und Jommelli," ZfMw I (1918–19) 281–87.

Fellerer, Karl Gustav. Beiträge zur Musikgeschichte Freisings. Freising, Freising. Tagbl., 1926.

—— "Max von Droste-Hülshoff," AfMf II (1937) 160–72.

Fellmann, Hans Georg. Die Böhmsche Theatergruppe und ihre Zeit. Leipzig, L. Voss, 1928.

Fellowes, E. H. "The Philidor Manuscripts," M&L XII (1931) 116–29.

Ferand, Ernst. Die Improvisation in der Musik. Zürich, Rhein-Verlag, [1938].

Ferrari, A. Rodigino; le convenienze teatrali; analisi della condizione presente del teatro musicale italiano. Milano, Redaelli, 1843.

Ferrari Nicolay, Mauricio. "En torno a *Las Vírgenes del Sol,* la nueva opera argentina," *Estudios* (Buenos Aires) Año 29, tomo 62 (1939) 29–46.

Fétis, Edouard. Les Musiciens belges, tome premier. Bruxelles, Ajamar, n.d.

Filippi, Joseph de. Parallèle des principaux théâtres modernes de l'Europe et des machines théâtrales françaises, allemandes et anglaises. Paris, Lévy, 1870. 2 vols.

Finck, Henry T. Richard Strauss. Boston, Little, Brown, 1917.

Findeisen, Nicholas. "The Earliest Russian Operas," MQ XIX (1933) 331–40.

—— "Die Entwicklung der Tonkunst in Russland in der ersten Hälfte des 19. Jahrhunderts," SIMG II (1900–1901) 279–302.

—— "Die Oper in Russland," ZIMG I (1899–1900) 367–75.

Finney, Gretchen Ludke. "Chorus in *Samson Agonistes,*" *Publications of the Modern Language Association of America* LVIII (1943) 649–64.

Finney, Gretchen Ludke (*Cont.*). "*Comus,* Dramma per Musica," *Studies in Philology* XXXVII (1940) 483–500; also separate.

Fiorda Kelly, Alfredo. Cronología de las óperas, dramas líricos, oratorios, himnos, etc. cantados en Buenos Aires. Buenos Aires, Riera, 1934.

Fischer, Georg. Marschner-Erinnerungen. Hannover and Leipzig, Hahn, 1918.

—— Musik in Hannover. Hannover, Hahn, 1903. 2d enlarged edition of his Opern und Concerte im Hoftheater zu Hannover bis 1866.

Fleischer, Oskar. "Napoleon Bonaparte's Musikpolitik," ZIMG III (1901–02) 431–40.

Flemming, Willi. Geschichte des Jesuitentheaters in den Landen deutscher Zunge. Berlin, Gesellschaft für Theatergeschichte, 1923.

—— ed. Die Oper. Leipzig, Reclam, 1933. (Deutsche Literatur; Sammlung literarischer Kunst- und Kulturdenkmäler in Entwicklungsreihen . . . Reihe Barock; Barockdrama. Bd. 5.)

Floch, Siegfried. Die Oper seit Richard Wagner. Köln, Fulda, 1904.

Flögel, Bruno. "Studien zur Arientechnik in den Opern Händels," *Händel-Jahrbuch* II (1929) 50–156.

Flood, W. H. Grattan. "The *Beggar's Opera* and Its Composers," M&L III (1922) 402–406.

—— "Quelques Précisions nouvelles sur Cambert et Grabu à Londres," RM IX (August, 1928) 351–61.

—— William Vincent Wallace; a memoir. Waterford, "The Waterford News," 1912.

Florence, Italy. R. Istituto musicale. Atti dell' accademia del R. Istituto musicale di Firenze, Anno XXXIII; commemorazione della riforma melodrammatica. Firenze, Galletti e Cocci, 1895.

Florimo, Francesco. La scuola musicale di Napoli e i suoi conservatori. Napoli, V. Morano, 1880–1882. 4 vols. 2d ed.

Flotow, Rosa. Friedrich von Flotow's Leben von seiner Wittwe. Leipzig, B&H, 1892.

Flower, Newman. George Frederic Handel; His Personality and His Times. Boston and New York, Houghton Mifflin, 1923.

Foerster-Nietzsche, Elizabeth. "Wagner and Nietzsche; the Beginning and End of Their Friendship," MQ IV (1918) 466–89.

Fondi, Enrico. "Il sentimento musicale di Vittorio Alfieri," RMI XI (1904) 484–99.

—— La vita e l'opera letteraria del musicista Benedetto Marcello. Roma, W. Modes, 1909.

Fonseco Benevides, Francisco da. O real theatro de S. Carlos de Lisboa, desde a sua funação em 1793 até á actualidade. Lisboa, Castro Irmão, [1883].

Font, Auguste. Favart, l'opéra-comique et la comédie-vaudeville aux XVIIe et XVIIIe siècles. Paris, Fischbacher, 1894.

Fontana, Francesco. "Vita di Benedetto Marcello," in *Estro poetico-armonico parafrasi sopra le primi venticinque salmi, poesia di Girolamo Asconio Giustiniani, musica di Benedetto Marcello* (Venezia, Sebastiano Valle, 1803), I, 1–48.

Forsyth, Cecil. Music and Nationalism; a Study of English Opera. London, Macmillan, 1911.

Fouque, Octave. "Le Sueur comme prédécesseur de Berlioz," in *Les Révolutionnaires de la musique* (Paris, Calmann-Lévy, 1882) pp. 1–183.

Fraccaroli, Arnaldo. La vita di Giacomo Puccini. Milan, Ricordi, 1925.

Fraguier, Marguerite-Marie de. Vincent d'Indy; souvenirs d'une élève. Paris, Jean Naert, 1933.

Franklin, Benjamin. "The Ephemera; an Emblem of Human Life," in *The Writings of Benjamin Franklin,* edited by Albert Henry Smith (New York, Macmillan, 1907) VII, 206–209.

Frati, Lodovico. "Antonio Bernacchi e la sua scuola di canto," RMI XXIX (1922) 443–91.

—— "Attilio Ottavio Ariosti," RMI XXXIII (1926) 551–57.

—— "Un impresario teatrale del settecento e la sua biblioteca," RMI XVIII (1911) 64–84.

—— "Metastasio e Farinelli," RMI XX (1913) 1–30.

—— "Musica e balli alla corte dei Pico della Mirandola," RMI XXV (1918) 249–58.

—— "Musicisti e cantanti bolognesi del settecento," RMI XXI (1914) 189–202.

—— "Per la storia della musica in Bologna nel secolo XVII," RMI XXXII (1925) 544–65.

—— "Satire di musicisti," RMI XXII (1915) 560–66.

—— "Torquato Tasso in musica," RMI XXX (1923) 389–400.

Freisauff, Rudolf von. Mozart's Don Juan, 1787–1887. Salzburg, H. Kerber, 1887.

"The *Freischütz* in London, 1824," ZIMG XI (1909–10) 251–54.

Fremy, Edouard. Origines de l'Académie française: l'Académie des derniers Valois. Paris, E. Leroux, [1887].

Frensdorf, Victor Egon. Peter Winter als Opernkomponist. Erlangen, Junge, 1908.

Frere, Walter Howard, ed. The Winchester Troper, from Mss. of the Xth and XIth Centuries, with Other Documents Illustrating the History of Tropes in England and France. London, [Printed for the Henry Bradshaw Society by Harrison and Sons], 1894.

Freund, Hans and Wilhelm Reinking. Musikalisches Theater in Hamburg; Versuch über die Dramaturgie der Oper. Hamburg, Hans Christians, 1938.

Friedländer, Max. "Deutsche Dichtung in Beethovens Musik," JMP XIX (1912) 25–48.

Friedländer, Max (*Cont.*). Das deutsche Lied im 18. Jahrhundert. Stuttgart and Berlin, Cotta, 1902. 3 parts in 2 vols.

Friedrich, Gerhard. Die deutsche und italienische Gestaltung des Falstaff-Stoffes in der Oper. Habelschwerdt, Groeger, 1941.

Friedrich, Julius. Claus Schall als dramatischer Komponist. Herchenbach, Wanne-Eickel, 1930.

Fröhlich, Willi. Jean Paul's Beziehungen zur Musik. Frankfurt Dissertation, 1922.

Frost, Henry F. "Some Remarks on Richard Wagner's Music Drama *Tristan und Isolde*," PMA VIII (1882) 147–67.

Fuchs, Albert. "Wieland et l'esthétique de l'opéra," *Revue de littérature comparée* X (1930) 608–33.

Fuchs, Marianne. Die Entwicklung des Finales in der italienischen Opera Buffa vor Mozart. Vienna Dissertation, 1932.

Fürstenau, Moritz. "Maria Antonia Walpurgis, Kurfürstin von Sachsen; eine biografische Skizze," MfMg XI (1879) 167–81.

—— "Die Oper *Antiope* und die Bestellungen des Kurfürstlich Sächsischen Vicekapellmeisters Nicolaus Adam Strunck und des Hofpoeten Stefano Pallavicini," MfMg XIII (1881) 1–6.

—— "Eine theologische Zeitschrift des 17. Jahrhunderts über Castraten und Oper; Johann Samuel Adami," *Musikalisches Wochenblatt* I (1870) 241–43.

—— "Zur Don Juan-Literatur," MfMg II (1870) 41–47.

—— Zur Geschichte der Musik und des Theaters am Hofe zu Dresden. Dresden, R. Kuntze, 1861–62. 2 parts.

Fuller-Maitland, John Alexander. The Age of Bach and Handel. Oxford, Clarendon Press, 1902. 2d ed., London, Oxford University Press, 1931. (Oxford History of Music, Vol. IV.)

—— The Music of Parry and Stanford. Cambridge, W. Heffer, 1934.

Gaartz, Hans. Die Opern Heinrich Marschners. Leipzig, B&H, 1912.

Gagey, Edmond M. Ballad Opera. New York, Columbia University Press, 1937.

Gál, Hans. "A Deleted Episode in Verdi's *Falstaff*," *Music Review* II (1941) 266–72.

Galilei, Vincenzo. Dialogo della musica antica, et della moderna. Fiorenza, G. Marescotti, 1581. Facsimile reprint, Roma, R. Accademia d'Italia, 1934.

Galindo, Miguel. Nociones de historia de la música mejicana, tomo 1. Colima, Tip. de "El dragón," 1933.

Galli, Amintore. Umberto Giordano nell' arte e nella vita. Milano, F. Sonzogno, 1915.

Gallusser, Rita. Verdis Frauengestalten. Zürich Dissertation, 1936.

[Galluzzi, Riguccio.] Istoria del granducato di Toscana sotto il governo della casa Medici. Firenze, Stamperia di R. del Vivo, 1781. 5 vols. New ed., Firenze, 1822. 11 vols.

Gandolfi, Riccardo. "Appunti di storia musicale; Cristofano Malvezzi—Emilio de' Cavalieri," *Rassegna nazionale* XV (November, 1893) 297–306.

—— "Cinque lettere inedite di Giuseppe Verdi," RMI XX (1913) 168–72.

Gaspari, Gaetano. "Dei musicisti Bolognesi al XVII secolo e delle loro opere a stampa," *Atti e memorie della R. R. Deputazione di storia patria per le provincie dell'Emilia, Nuova serie* III (1878) 1–24.

Gastoué, Amadée. "Gossec et Gluck à l'opéra de Paris: le ballet final *d'Iphigénie en Tauride*," RdM XVI (1935) 87–99.

—— "Nicolò Piccinni et ses opéras à Paris," *Note d'archivio* XIII (1936) 52–54.

Gatti, Carlo. Il Teatro alla Scala rinnovato; le prime quattro stagioni. Milano, Fratelli Treves, 1926.

Gatti, Guido Maria. *Le Barbier de Seville* de Rossini; étude historique et critique, analyse musicale. Paris, P. Mellottée, [1924?].

—— "Boito's *Nero*," MQ X (1924) 596–621.

—— "Franco Alfano," MQ IX (1923) 556–77.

—— "Gabriele D'Annunzio and the Italian Opera Composers," MQ X (1924) 263–88.

—— Ildebrando Pizzetti. Torino, G. B. Paravia, [1934].

—— "Ildebrando Pizzetti," MQ IX (1923) 96–121, 271–86.

—— "Malipiero and Pirandello at the Opera," MMus XI, No. 4 (May–June, 1934) 213–16.

—— Musicisti moderni d'Italia e di fuori. Bologna, Pizzi, 1920.

—— "Recent Italian Operas," MQ XXIII (1937) 77–88.

—— "The Stage Works of Ferruccio Busoni," MQ XX (1934) 267–77.

—— "Two *Macbeths*: Verdi—Bloch," MQ XII (1926) 22–31.

—— "The Works of Giacomo Puccini," MQ XIV (1928) 16–34.

Gatti-Casazza, Giulio. Memories of the Opera. New York, Charles Scribner's Sons, 1941.

Gaudier, Charles. *Carmen* de Bizet; étude historique et critique, analyse musicale. Paris, P. Mellottée, [1922].

Gautier, Léon. Histoire de la poésie liturgique au moyen âge: les tropes. Paris, V. Palmé, 1886.

Gautier, Théophile. Les Beautés de l'opéra. Paris, Soulié, 1845.

—— Histoire de l'art dramatique en France depuis vingt-cinq ans. Paris, Magnin, Blanchard, 1858–59. 6 vols.

Gavazzeni, Gianandrea. "Donizetti e l' *Elisir d'amore*," RassM VI (1933) 44–50.

—— "Karol Szymanowski e il *Re Ruggero*," RassM X (1937) 409–15.

Gay, John. The Beggar's Opera. London, De la Mare Press, 1905.

Gaye, Phoebe Fenwick. John Gay; His Place in the 18th Century. London, Collins, 1938.

Gedenkschrift für Hermann Abert. Halle an der Saale, M. Niemeyer, 1928. Contains essays on Sailer, G. C. Wagenseil, and French Opera.

Geffcken, Johannes. "Die ältesten Hamburgischen Opern," *Zeitschrift des Vereines für Hamburgische Geschichte* III (1851) 34–55.

Geiringer, Karl. Haydn; a Creative Life in Music. New York, W. W. Norton, 1946.

—— "Haydn as an Opera Composer," PMA LXVI (1939–40) 23–30.

—— Joseph Haydn. Potsdam, Athenaïon, [1932].

Genest, Émile. L'Opéra-comique connu et inconnu. Paris, Fischbacher, 1925.

Gentili, Alberto. "La raccolta Mauro Foà nella Biblioteca Nazionale di Torino," RMI XXXIV (1927) 356–68.

George, André. Arthur Honegger. Paris, C. Aveline, 1926.

—— *Tristan et Isolde* de Richard Wagner; étude historique et critique, analyse musicale. Paris, Mellottée, [1929].

Georges, Horst. Das Klangsymbol des Todes im dramatischen Werk Mozarts. Wolfenbüttel-Berlin, G. Kallmeyer, 1937.

Gerber, Rudolf. Der Operntypus Johann Adolf Hasses und seine textlichen Grundlage. Leipzig, Kistner & Siegel, 1925.

Gerigk, Herbert. "Das alte und das neue Bild Rossinis," ZfMw XVI (1934) 26–32.

Gérold, Théodore. L'Art du chant en France au XVIIe siècle. Strasbourg, G. Fischbach, 1921.

—— La Musique au moyen age. Paris, Champion, 1932.

Gettemann, H. "*Sniégourotchka* opéra de M. Rimsky-Korsakoff," RHCM VIII (1908) 137–43, 179–87, 213–16.

Geulette, Thomas Simon. Notes et souvenirs sur le théâtre-italien au XVIIIe siècle. Paris, E. Praz, 1938.

Gherardi, Evaristo, compiler. Le Théâtre italien de Gherardi. Amsterdam, M. C. le Cene, 1721. 6 vols. 5th ed.

Ghisi, Federico. I canti carnascialeschi nelle fonti musicali del XV e XVI secolo. Firenze-Roma, L. S. Olschki, 1937.

—— Del "Fuggilotio musicale" di Giulio Romano (Caccini); saggio critico. Roma, De Santis, 1934.

—— Feste musicali della Firenze Medicea. Firenze, Vallecchi, 1939.

Giani, Romualdo. "Il *Nerone* di Arrigo Boito," RMI VIII (1901) 861–1006.

Giazotto, Remo. Il melodramma a Genova nei secoli 17 & 18; con gli elenchi completi dei titoli, dei musicisti, dei poeti e degli attori di quei componomenti rappresentati fra il 1652 e il 1771 ai teatri detti "Del Falcone" e "Da S. Agostino." Genova, A cura dell' ente del Teatro Carlo Felice, 1941.

Gilman, Lawrence. Aspects of Modern Opera. London, John Lane; New York, Dodd, Mead, 1924.

—— Debussy's *Pelléas et Mélisande*, a Guide to the Opera. New York, G. Schirmer, 1907.

—— Wagner's Operas. New York, Toronto, Farrar & Rhinehart, [1937].

Gilse van der Pals, Nikolai van. N. A. Rimsky-Korssakow: Opernschaffen nebst Skizze über Leben und Wirken. Paris-Leipzig, W. Bessel, 1929.

Ginisty, Paul. Le Melodrama. Paris, L. Michaud, [1910].

Giraldi, Romolo. Giovanni Battista Pergolese. Roma, Laziale, 1936.

Glareanus, Henricus. Dodecachordon. Leipzig, B&H, 1888. Translated and transcribed by Peter Bohn. Originally published 1547.

Glasenapp, Carl Friedrich. Das Leben Richard Wagners. Leipzig, B&H, 1904–11. 6 vols. 4th ed. Translated as: The Life of Richard Wagner. London, Paul, Trench & Trübner, 1900–1908. 6 vols.

——— Siegfried Wagner und seine Kunst. Leipzig, B&H, 1911.

——— Siegfried Wagner und seine Kunst. Neue Folge. I. Schwartzschwanenreich (Leipzig, B&H, 1913); II. Sonnenflammen (Leipzig, B&H, 1919).

——— Versuch einer thematischen Analyse der Musik zu Siegfried Wagner's Kobold. Leipzig, M. Brockhaus, 1904.

Gluck, Christoph Willibald, Ritter von. "Correspondance inédite," MM X, No. 11 (1914) 1–16.

——— "Vier Gluck-Briefe," Die Musik XIII (1913–14) Qt. 4, 10–15.

Gluck-Jahrbuch. Jahrgang I–IV (1913, 1915, 1917, 1918). Leipzig, B&H. Ed. by H. Abert.

Gmeyner, Alice. Die Opern M. A. Caldaras. Vienna Dissertation, 1935.

Gnirs, Anton. Hans Heiling. Karlsbad, Heinich, 1931.

Goddard, Scott. "Editions of Boris Goudonov," M&L X (1929) 278–86.

Godet, Robert. En Marge de Boris Godounof; notes sur les documents iconographiques de l'édition Chester. Paris, F. Alcan, 1926.

Goldberg, Isaac. The Story of Gilbert and Sullivan. New York, Simon & Schuster, 1928.

Goldmark, Karl. Erinnerungen aus meinem Leben. Wien, Rikola, 1922. Translated as: Notes from the Life of a Viennese Composer. New York, A. and C. Boni, 1927.

Goldoni, Carlo. Mémoires. Paris, Veuve Duchesne, 1787. 3 vols. Translated as: Memoirs of Goldoni. London, H. Colburn, 1814. 2 vols.

Goldschmidt, Hugo. "Cavalli als dramatischer Komponist," MfMg XXV (1893) 45–48, 53–58, 61–111.

——— "Das Cembalo im Orchester der italienischen Oper der zweiten Hälfte des 18. Jahrhunderts," in Festschrift Liliencron (Leipzig, B&H, 1910) pp. 87–92.

——— "Claudio Monteverdi's Oper: Il ritorno d'Ulisse in patria," SIMG IX (1907–1908) 570–92.

——— "Francesco Provenzale als Dramatiker," SIMG VII (1905–1906) 608–34.

——— "Die Instrumentalbegleitung der italienischen Musikdramen in der ersten Hälfte des XVII. Jahrhunderts," MfMg XXVII (1895) 52–62.

——— Die italienische Gesangsmethode des XVII. Jahrhunderts und ihre Bedeutung für die Gegenwart. Breslau, Schlesische Buchdruckerei, 1890. 2d ed., Breslau, S. Schottlaender, 1892.

Goldschmidt, Hugo (*Cont.*). Die Lehre von der vokalen Ornamentik, erster Band: das 17. und 18. Jahrhundert bis in die Zeit Glucks. Charlottenburg, P. Lehsten, 1907.

—— "Monteverdi's *Ritorno d'Ulisse*," SIMG IV (1902–1903) 671–76.

—— Die Musikästhetik des 18. Jahrhunderts und ihre Beziehungen zu seinen Kunstschaffen. Zürich, Rascher, 1915. *See also* review by A. Schering, ZfMw I (1918–1919) 298–308.

—— "Die Reform der italienischen Oper des 18. Jahrhunderts und ihre Beziehungen zur musikalischen Aesthetik," in *III. Kongress der Internationalen Musikgesellschaft . . . Bericht* (Wien, Artaria; Leipzig, B&H, 1909) pp. 196–207.

—— Studien zur Geschichte der italienischen Oper im 17. Jahrhundert. Leipzig, B&H, 1901–1904. 2 vols. Review by R. Rolland, RHCM II (1902) 20–29.

—— "Verzierungen, Veränderungen und Passaggien im 16. und 17. Jahrhundert," MfMg XXIII (1891) 111–26.

—— "Zur Geschichte der Arien- und Symphonie-Formen," MfMg XXXIII (1901) 61–70.

Gómez, Julio. "Don Blas de Laserna; un capítolo de la historia del teatro lirico español," *Archivo y museo al ayuntamicuto de Madrid* (1925–26).

Gorer, R. "Weber and the Romantic Movement," M&L XVII (1936) 13–24.

Goslich, Siegfried. Beiträge zur Geschichte der deutschen romantischen Oper zwischen Spohrs *Faust* und Wagners *Lohengrin*. Leipzig, Kistner & Siegel, 1937.

Gottsched, Johann Christoph. Nöthiger Vorrath zur Geschichte der deutschen dramatischen Dichtkunst oder Verzeichniss aller deutschen Trauer- Lust- und Sing-Spiele, die im Druck erschienen von 1450 bis zur Hälfte des jetzigen Jahrhunderts. Leipzig, J. M. Teubner, 1757–65. 2 vols.

—— Versuch einer kritischen Dichtkunst vor die Deutschen. Leipzig, B. C. Breitkopf, 1730. 2d ed., 1737.

Goudar, Ange. Le Brigandage de la musique italienne. 1777.

[Goudar, Mme. Sara.] De Venise, remarques sur la musique & la danse. Venise, C. Palese, 1773.

Gounod, Charles François. Autobiographical Reminiscences, with Family Letters and Notes on Music. London, W. Heinemann, 1896.

—— Mémoires d'un artiste. Paris, Calmann Lévy, 1896. 5th ed. Translated as: Memoirs of an Artist. New York, Rand, McNally, 1895.

—— Mozart's *Don Giovanni;* a Commentary. London, R. Cocks, 1895. Translated from the 3d French ed.

Graf, Herbert. The Opera and Its Future in America. New York, W. W. Norton, [1941].

—— Richard Wagner als Regisseur. Vienna Dissertation, 1925.

Gramisch, Lore. Die Erscheinungsformen des melodramatischen Stils im 19. Jahrhundert. Vienna Dissertation, 1936.

Grannis, Valleria Belt. Dramatic Parody in Eighteenth Century France. New York, Institute of French Studies, 1931.

Grattan Flood, *see* Flood, William Henry Grattan.

Gray, Alan. "Purcell's Dramatic Music," PMA XLIII (1916–17) 51–62.

Gray, Cecil. "Pietro Raimondi," *Music Review* I (1940) 25–35.

—— "Vincenzo Bellini," M&L VII (1926) 49–62.

Greene, Harry Plunket. Charles Villiers Stanford. London, E. Arnold, [1935].

Grégoir, Edouard. Bibliothèque musicale populaire. Bruxelles, Schott, 1877–79. 3 vols.

—— Des Gloires de l'opéra et la musique à Paris. Bruxelles, Schott, 1878. 3 vols.

—— Littérature musicale. Bruxelles, Schott, 1872–76. 4 vols.

—— Panthéon musical populaire. Bruxelles, Schott, 1876–77. 6 vols.

Gregor, Joseph. Richard Strauss. München, R. Piper, [1939].

—— Weltgeschichte des Theaters. [Zürich], Phaidon, [1933].

Grétry, André Ernest Modeste. Mémoires, ou essais sur la musique. Paris, Imprimerie de la république, [1797]. 3 vols. First published 1789.

—— Oèuvres complètes; reflexions d'un solitaire. Bruxelles-Paris, Von Oest, 1919–22. 4 vols.

Greulich, Martin. Beiträge zur Geschichte des Streichinstrumentenspiels im 16. Jahrhundert. Saalfeld, Günther, [1934?].

Griepenkerl, Wolfgang Robert. Die Oper der Gegenwart. Leipzig, Hinrich, 1847.

Griggs, John C. "The Influence of Comedy upon Operatic Form," MQ III (1917) 552–61.

Grimm, Friedrich Melchior, Freiherr von. Correspondance littéraire, philosophique et critique. Paris, Garnier, 1877–82. 16 vols. Contains "Lettre sur Omphale," XVI, 287–309.

—— Le Petit Prophète de Boemischbroda. Paris, 1753.

Grisson, Alexandra Carola. Ermanno Wolf-Ferrari, autorisierte Lebensbeschreibung. Regensburg, Bosse, 1941.

Groppo, Antonio. Catalogo di tutti i drammi per musica recitati ne' teatri di Venezia dall' anno 1637 sin all' anno presente 1745. Venezia, A. Groppo, [1745?].

Gros, Etienne. Philippe Quinault. Paris, E. Champion, 1926.

Grosheim, Georg Christoph. Selbstbiographie. Hamburg, Cassel, F. Settnick, 1925. Ed. by Georg Heinrichs.

[Grosley, Pierre Jean.] New Observations on Italy and Its Inhabitants. London, L. Davis & C. Reymers, 1769. 2 vols.

Gross, Rolf. Joseph Hartmann Stuntz als Opernkomponist. Würzburg, Triltsch, 1936.

Grout, Donald J. "German Baroque Opera," MQ XXXII (1946) 574–87.

—— "The 'Machine' Operas," *Bulletin of the Fogg Museum of Art, Harvard University* IX, No. 5 (November, 1941) 100–103.

Grout, Donald J. (*Cont.*). "The Music of the Italian Theatre at Paris, 1682–1697," in *Papers of the American Musicological Society, Annual Meeting, 1941* . . . Edited by Gustave Reese (Printed by the Society [cop. 1946]), pp. 158–70.

—— The Origins of the Opéra-comique. Harvard Dissertation, 1939.

—— "Seventeenth Century Parodies of French Opera," MQ XXVII (1941) 211–19, 514–26.

—— "Some Forerunners of the Lully Opera," M&L XXII (1941) 1–25.

Grovlez, Gabriel. "Jacques Offenbach; a Centennial Sketch," MQ V (1919) 329–37.

Grüel, C. Aufschlüsse über die Bedeutung des angeblich Schikaneder'schen Textes zu Mozart's *Zauberflöte*. Magdeburg, Creutz, 1868.

Güttler, Hermann. Königsbergs Musikkultur im 18. Jahrhundert. Kassel, Bärenreiter, [1929].

Gui, Vittorio. "Arlecchino," RassM XIII (1940) 30–37.

Guiet, René. L'Evolution d'un genre: le livret d'opéra en France de Gluck à la révolution (1774–1793). Northampton, Mass., Smith College, Dept. of Modern Languages, 1936.

Guingené, Pierre Louis. Notice sur la vie et les ouvrages de Nicolas Piccini. Paris, Panckoucke, [1801].

Gutman, Hans. "*Mahagonny* and Other Novelties," MMus VII, No. 4 (June–July, 1930) 32–36.

—— "Tabloid Hindemith," MMus VII, No. 1 (December, 1929–January, 1930) 34–37.

Guy, Henri. Bibliographie critique du trouvère Adan de le Hale. Paris, A. Fontemoing, [1900].

—— Essai sur la vie et les œuvres littéraires du trouvère Adan de le Hale. Paris, Hachette, 1898.

Haas, Robert A. Afführungspraxis der Musik. Wildpark-Potsdam, Athenaion, [1931].

—— "Beitrag zur Geschichte der Oper in Prag und Dresden," *Neues Archiv für Sächsische Geschichte und Altertumskunde* XXXVII (1916) 68–96.

—— "Gioseppe Zamponis *Ulisse nell' isola di Circe*," ZfMw III (1920–21) 385–405.

—— Gluck und Durazzo im Burgtheater. Zürich, Amalthea, 1925.

—— "Josse de Villeneuves Brief über den Mechanismus der italienischen Oper von 1756," ZfMw VII (1924–25) 129–63.

—— Die Musik des Barocks. Potsdam, Athenaion, [1934].

—— "Die Musik in der Wiener deutscher Stegreifkomödie," SzMw XII (1925) 1–64.

—— "Teutsche Comedie Arien," ZfMw III (1920–21) 405–15.

—— "Die Wiener Ballet-Pantomime im 18. Jahrhundert und Glucks *Don Juan*," SzMw X (1923) 3–36.

Bibliography 589

—— "Der Wiener Bühnentanz von 1740 bis 1767," JMP XLIV (1937) 77–93.

—— "Wiener deutsche Parodieopern um 1730," ZfMw VIII (1925–26) 201–25.

—— Die Wiener Oper. Wien-Budapest, Eligius, 1926.

—— "Zur Neuausgabe von Claudio Monteverdis *Il ritorno d'Ulisse in patria*," SzMw IX (1922) 3–42.

—— "Zur Wiener Balletpantomime um den *Prometheus*," *Neues Beethoven Jahrbuch* II (1925) 84–103.

Haberl, Franz X. "Johann Mattheson; biographische Skizze," *Caecilien Kalender* (1885) 53–60.

Habets, Alfred. Alexandre Borodine, d'après la biographie et la correspondance publiées par M. Wladimir Stassof. Paris, Fischbacher, 1893. Translated as: Borodin and Liszt. London, Digby, Long, [1895].

Haböck, Franz. Die Gesangskunst der Kastraten; erster Notenbuch A. Die Kunst des cavaliere Carlo Broschi Farinelli. B. Farinellis berühmte Arien. Wien, Universal, [1923].

—— Die Kastraten und ihre Gesangskunst. Stuttgart, Deutsche Verlags-Anstalt, 1927.

Hackett, Karleton. "The Possibilities of Opera in America," MTNA IV (1909) 52–60.

Hadow, Sir William Henry. Studies in Modern Music, Second Series. New York, Macmillan, [1923]. 10th ed.

Händel-Festspiele . . . 1922; veranstaltet vom Universitätsbund. Göttingen, W. H. Lange, 1922. Contains essays on Handel by H. Abert and O. Hagen.

Händel-Jahrbuch. Leipzig, B&H, 1928–.

Hänsler, Rolf. Peter Lindpainter als Opernkomponist. Stuttgart-Caunstadt, Kirchoff, [1930].

Hagen, Oskar. "Die Bearbeitung der Händelschen *Rodelinde* und ihre Uraufführung am 26. Juni 1920 in Göttingen," ZfMw II (1919–20) 725–32.

Halévy, François. Derniers Souvenirs et portraits. Paris, M. Lévy, 1863.

—— Souvenirs et portraits. Paris, M. Lévy, 1861.

Hall, Raymond. "The *Macbeth* of Bloch," MMus XV, No. 4 (May–June, 1938) 209–15.

Halle. Stadtarchiv. Georg Friedrich Händel, Abstammung und Jugendwelt. Halle, Gebauer-Schwetschke, 1935.

Halusa, Karl. Hans Pfitzners musikdramatisches Schaffen. Vienna Dissertation, 1929.

Hamilton, Edith. "The Greek Chorus, Fifteen or Fifty?" *Theatre Arts Monthly* XVII (1933) 459.

Hamilton, Mrs. Mary (Neal). Music in Eighteenth Century Spain. Urbana, The University of Illinois, 1937.

Hampe, Theodor. Die Entwicklung des Theaterwesens in Nürnberg von der 2. Hälfte des 15. Jahrhunderts bis 1806. Nürnberg, J. L. Schrag, 1900.

Handbook of Latin American Studies. Cambridge, Mass., Harvard University Press, 1936–.

Handschin, Jacques. Igor Stravinsky. Zürich and Leipzig, Hug, 1933.

—— "Das Weinachts-Mysterium von Rouen als musikgeschichtliche Quelle," *Acta musicologica* VII (1935) 97–110.

Hanslick, Eduard. Die moderne Oper; Kritiken und Studien. Berlin, A. Hofmann, 1875. This is also the title of a series of books by Hanslick, the respective subtitles and dates of which are as follows: I. Die moderne Oper, 1875; II. Musikalische Stationen, 1880; III. Aus dem Opernleben der Gegenwart, 1884; IV. Musikalische Skizzenbuch, 1888; V. Musikalisches und Litterarisches, 1889; VI. Aus dem Tagebuche eines Musikers, 1892; VII. Fünf Jahre Musik (1891–1895), 1896; VIII. Am Ende des Jahrhunderts (1895–1899), 1899; IX. Aus neuer und neuester Zeit, 1900.

—— Vom Musikalisch-Schönen; ein Beitrag zur Revision der Aesthetik der Tonkunst. Leipzig, R. Weigel, 1854.

Harászti, Emil. Béla Bartók, His Life and Works. Paris, The Lyrebird Press, [1938].

—— La Musique hongroise. Paris, Laurens, 1933.

—— "Le Problème du Leit-motiv," RM IV (August, 1923) 35–37.

Harcourt, Eugène d'. La Musique actuelle en Allemagne et Autriche-Hongrie. Paris, Durdilly, [1908].

—— La Musique actuelle en Italie. Paris, Durdilly, [1907].

[Harsdörffer, Georg Philipp.] Frauenzimmer Gesprechspiele so bey ehr- und tugendliebenden Gesellschaften mit nutzlicher Ergetzlichkeit beliebet und geübet werden mögen. Nürnberg, W. Endtern, 1643–57. 8 vols.

Hartmann, Fritz. Sechs Bücher Braunschweigischer Theatergeschichte. Wolfenbüttel, J. Zwissler, 1905.

Hasse, Max. Der Dichtermusiker Peter Cornelius. Leipzig, B&H, 1922–23. 2 vols.

—— Peter Cornelius und sein *Barbier von Bagdad*. Leipzig, B&H, 1904.

Hasselberg, Felix. *Der Freischütz;* Friedrich Kinds Operndichtung und ihre Quellen. Berlin, Dom Verlag, 1921.

Hausegger, Siegmund von. Alexander Ritter; ein Bild seines Characters und Schaffens. Berlin, Marquardt, [1907].

Haweis, Hugh Reginald. Music and Morals. New York, Harper, 1872.

Hawkins, John. A General History of the Science and Practice of Music. London, T. Payne, 1776. 5 vols.

[——?] Memoirs of the Life of Sig. Agostino Steffani. [London? 17—.]

Hédouin, Pierre. Gossec, sa vie et ses ouvrages. Paris, Prignet, 1852.

—— Mosaique; peintres—musiciens— . . . à partir du 15e siècle jusqu'à nos jours. Paris, Heugel, 1856.

—— *Richard Coeur-de-Lion* de Grétry. Boulogne, Birlé-Morel, 1842.

Hegel, Georg Wilhelm Friedrich. Sämtliche Werke. Stuttgart, F. Fromann, 1927. Contains (Vols. 12–14): "Vorlesungen über die Aesthetik."

Heger, Theodore E. The Function and Type of Music in the English Dramatic Theater of the Early 18th Century. Michigan A.M. Dissertation 1939.

Heinemann, Franz. "Schillers *Wilhelm Tell* in der Musikgeschichte des 19. Jahrhunderts," *Zeitschrift für Bücherfreunde* XI, No. 2 (1907) 321–38.

Heinichen, Johann David. Der General-Bass in der Composition. Dresden, bey dem Autor, 1728. A revised ed. of his Neu erfundene und gründliche Anweisung (Hamburg, B. Schiller, 1711.)

Heinrich, Viktor. Komik und Humor in der Musik. Vienna Dissertation, 1931.

Heinrichs, Georg. *See* Grosheim, Georg Christoph.

Heinse, Wilhelm. Hildegard von Hohenthal. Berlin, Vossischen Buchhandlung, 1795–96. 3 vols.

Heinsheimer, Hans. "Die Umgestaltung des Operntheaters in Deutschland," *Anbruch* XV (August/September, 1933) 107–13.

Helfert, W. "Zur Geschichte des Wiener Singspiels," ZfMw V (1922–23) 194–209.

Hellberg (-Kupfer), Geerd. Richard Wagner als Regisseur. Berlin, Gesellschaft für Theatergeschichte, 1942.

Hellmer, Elmund, ed. *Der Corregidor* von Hugo Wolf. Wien, Hugo Wolf Verein; Berlin, S. Fischer, 1900.

Hellouin, Frédéric. Gossec et la musique française à la fin du XVIIIe siècle. Paris, A. Charles, 1903.

—— Un Musicien oublié; Catel. Paris, Fischbacher, 1910.

Henderson, William James. "A Note on Floridity," MQ II (1916) 339–48.

—— Some Forerunners of the Italian Opera. London, John Murray, 1911.

Henseler, Anton. Jakob Offenbach. Berlin-Schöneberg, M. Hesse, 1930.

Herford, Charles. "Jonson," in *Dictionary of National Biography* X (1917) 1069–79.

Hernried, Robert. "Hugo Wolf's *Corregidor* at Mannheim," MQ XXVI (1940) 19–30.

—— "Hugo Wolf's 'Four Operas,' " MQ XXXI (1945) 89–100.

Herre, Max. Franz Danzi; ein Beitrag zur Geschichte der deutschen Oper. Munich Dissertation, 1930.

Heseltine, Philip. Frederick Delius. London, John Lane, [1923].

Hess, Heinz. Zur Geschichte des musikalischen Dramas im Seicento; die Opern Alessandro Stradellas. Leipzig, B&H, 1906. (PIMG, 2. Folge, Heft 3.)

Heuberger, Richard. Im Foyer; gesammelte Essays über das Opernrepertoire der Gegenwart. Leipzig, H. Seemann, 1901.

—— Musikalische Skizzen. Leipzig, H. Seemann, 1901.

Heulhard, Arthur. La Foire Saint-Laurent; son histoire et ses spectacles. Paris, A. Lemerre, 1878.

—— Jean Monnet. Paris, A. Lemerre, 1884.

Heuss, Alfred. "Carl Heinrich Graun's *Montezuma*," ZIMG VI (1904–1905) 71–75.

—— "Das dämonische Element in Mozarts Werken," ZIMG VII (1906) 175–86.

—— "Gluck als Musikdramatiker," ZIMG XV (1913–14) 274–91.

—— "Graun's *Montezuma* und seine Herausgabe durch Albert Mayer-Reinach," MfMg XXXVII (1905) 67–71.

—— Die Instrumental-Stücke des *Orfeo* und die venetianischen Opern-Sinfonien. Leipzig, B&H, 1903. (Both parts of this work were published independently in SIMG IV.)

—— "Mozarts *Idomeneo* als Quelle für *Don Giovanni* and *Die Zauberflöte*," ZfMw XIII (1930–31) 177–99.

—— "Verdi als melodischer Charakteristiker," ZIMG XV (1913–14) 63–72.

—— "Zu Umlauf's Singspiel: *Die Bergknappen*," ZIMG XIII (1911–12) 164–71.

Hey, Julius. Richard Wagner als Vortragsmeister 1864–1876; Erinnerungen. Leipzig, B&H, 1911.

Heyden, Otto. Das Kölner Theaterwesen im 19. Jahrhundert. Emsdetten, Lechte, 1939.

Hill, Edward Burlingame. Modern French Music. Boston and New York, Houghton Mifflin, 1924.

Hill, Richard S. "Concert Life in Berlin, Season 1943–44," *Music Library Association Notes, Second Series* I, No. 3 (June, 1944) 13–33.

—— "Schoenberg's Tone-Rows and the Tonal System of the Future," MQ XXII (1936) 14–37.

Hiller, Johann Adam. Johann Adam Hiller. Leipzig, C. F. W. Siegel, [1915].

Hiltebrandt, Philipp. Preussen und die römische Kurie. Berlin, Bath, 1910. Vol. I: Die vorfriderizianische Zeit (1625–1740).

Himonet, André. *Lohengrin* . . . étude historique et critique, analyse musicale. Paris, Mellottée, [1925].

—— *Louise* de Charpentier; étude historique et critique, analyse musicale. Paris, Mellottée, [1922].

Hipsher, Edward E. American Opera and Its Composers. Philadelphia, T. Presser, [1927].

Hirsch, Franz. Die Oper und der Literaturgeist; ein Wort zu Operntextreform. Leipzig, Voigt, 1868.

Hirsch, R. Mozart's *Schauspieldirektor;* musikalische Reminiscenzen. Leipzig, Matthis, 1859.

Hirschberg, Eugen. Die Enzyklopädisten und die französische Oper im 18. Jahrhundert. Leipzig, B&H, 1903. *See also* review by A. Heuss, ZIMG V (1903–1904) 280–87.

Hirschfeld, Robert. "Mozart's *Zaide* in der Wiener Hofoper," ZIMG IV (1902–1903) 66–71.

—— "Oper in Wien [1857–1900]," ZIMG I (1899–1900) 264–67.

Hirt, Giulio C. "Autografi di G. Rossini," RMI II (1895) 23–35.

Hirtler, Franz. Hans Pfitzners *Armer Heinrich* in seiner Stellung zur Musik des ausgehenden 19. Jahrhunderts. Würzburg, K. Triltsch, 1940.

Hirzel, Bruno. "Operatic Italy in 1770—by an Eyewitness," MTNA V (1910) 219–31.

—— "Der Text Wagner's *Liebesverbot* nach der Handschrift in Washington," SIMG XIII (1911–12) 348–82.

Hitzig, Wilhelm. Georg Friedrich Händel, 1685–1759; sein Leben in Bildern. Leipzig, Bibliographisches Institut, [1935].

Hjelmborg, Bjørn. "Une Partition de Cavalli," *Acta Musicologica* XVI–XVII (1944–45) 39–54.

Hodermann, Richard. Georg Benda. Coburg, H. Wechsung, 1895.

—— Geschichte des Gothaischen Hoftheaters 1725–1779. Hamburg, L. Voss, 1894.

Hodik, Fritz. Das Horn bei Richard Wagner. Innsbruck Dissertation, 1937.

Höffding, Harold. Jean Jacques Rousseau and His Philosophy. New Haven, Yale University Press; London, Oxford University Press, 1930. Translated from the 2d Danish ed.

Högg, Margarete. Die Gesangskunst der Faustina Hasse und das Sängerinnenwesen ihrer Zeit in Deutschland. Königsbrück i. Sa., Pabst, 1931.

Hoérée, Arthur. Albert Roussel. Paris, Rieder, 1938.

Hoffmann, Ernst Theodor Amadeus. Sämtliche Werke. Leipzig, M. Hesse, 1900. 15 vols.

—— Musikalische Novellen und Aufsätze; vollständige Gesamtausgabe, herausgegeben und erläutert von Dr. Edgar Istel. Regensburg, G. Bosse, [1921?]. 2 vols.

Hoffmann, Rudolf Stephan. Franz Schreker. Leipzig, E. P. Tal, 1921.

Hoffmann von Fallersleben, August Heinrich. In dulci jubilo . . . ein Beitrag zur Geschichte der deutschen Poesie. Hannover, C. Rümpler, 1854.

—— Unsere volkstümlichen Lieder. Leipzig, W. Engelmann, 1900. 4th ed.

Hoffmeister, Karel. Antonín Dvořák. London, John Lane, 1928. Ed. and translated by Rosa Newmarch.

Hofmannsthal, Hugo von. "Ce que nous avons voulu en écrivant *Ariane à Naxos* et *Le Bourgeois Gentilhomme*," MM VIII, Nos. 9–10 (1912) 1–3.

Hogarth, George. Memoirs of the Musical Drama. London, R. Bentley, 1838. 2 vols. New ed. as: Memoirs of the Opera in Italy, France, Germany, and England. London, R. Bentley, 1851. 2 vols.

Hohenemser, R. Luigi Cherubini. Leipzig, B&H, 1913.

Hol, Joan C. *"L'Amfiparnaso e Le veglie di Siena,"* RMI XL (1936) 3–22.

—— "Horatio Vecchi et l'évolution créatrice," in *Gedenkboek Dr. D. F. Scheurleer* ('s-Gravenhage, Nijhoff, 1925) pp. 159–67.

Hol, Joan C. (*Cont.*). Horatio Vecchi's weltliche Werke. Leipzig, Heitz, 1934.

—— "*Le Veglie di Siena* de Horatio Vecchi," RMI XLIII (1939) 17–34.

Holbrooke, Josef. Contemporary British Composers. London, C. Palmer, [1925].

Holl, Karl. Carl Ditters von Dittersdorfs Opern für das wiederhergestellte Johannisberger Theater. Heidelberg, C. Winter, 1913.

Holländer, Hans. "Hugo von Hofmannsthal als Opernlibrettist," *Zeitschrift für Musik* XCVI (1929) 551–54.

—— "Leoš Janáček and His Operas," MQ XV (1929) 29–36.

Holst, Imogen. Gustav Holst. London, Oxford University Press, 1938.

Holzer, Ludmilla. "Die komische Opern Glucks," SzMw XIII (1926) 3–37.

Hoover, Kathleen O'Donnell. "Gustave Charpentier," MQ XXV (1939) 334–50.

—— "Verdi's *Rocester*," MQ XXVIII (1942) 505–13.

"*Hortus musarum* de Pierre Phalèse, deuxième partie (1553)," in *Chansons au luth et airs de cour français du XVIe siècle* (Paris, E. Droz, 1934).

Howard, John Tasker. "The Hewitt Family in America," MQ XVII (1931) 25–39.

—— Our American Music. New York, Thomas Y. Crowell, [1939]. 3d ed., 1946.

—— Our Contemporary Composers. New York, Thomas Y. Crowell, 1941.

—— Studies of Contemporary American Composers: Deems Taylor. New York, J. Fischer, 1927.

Howes, Frank. The Dramatic Works of Ralph Vaughan Williams. London, Oxford University Press, 1937.

Hübner, O. Richard Strauss und das Musikdrama. Leipzig, [Pabst], 1910. 2d ed.

Hughes, Charles W. "John Christopher Pepusch," MQ XXXI (1945) 54–70.

[Hunold, Christian Friedrich.] Die allerneueste Art, zur reinen und galanten Poesie zu gelangen. Hamburg, G. Liebernickel, 1707.

—— "Gesellschaftliche Verhältnisse in der Oper zu Anfang des achtzehnten Jahrhunderts," AMZ [New Series] XV (1880) 753–58, 769–73, 785–90.

—— Theatralische, galante und geistliche Gedichte. Hamburg, G. Liebernickel, 1706.

Hussey, Dyneley. "Beethoven as a Composer of Opera," M&L VIII (1927) 243–52.

—— "Casanova and *Don Giovanni*," M&L VIII (1927) 470–72.

—— "Nationalism and Opera," M&L VII (1926) 3–16.

Hutcheson, Ernest. A Musical Guide to the Richard Wagner *Ring of the Nibelung*. New York, Simon & Schuster, 1940.

Hutchings, A. J. B. "The Unexpected in Mozart," M&L XX (1939) 21–31.

Huth, Arno. "Forbidden Opus—Protestant," MMus XVI, No. 1 (November–December, 1938) 38–41.

Huygens, Constantijn. Correspondance et œuvre musical. Leyden, W. J. A. Jonckbloet, 1882.

Iacuzzi, Alfred. The European Vogue of Favart; the Diffusion of the Opéra-Comique. New York, Institute of French Studies, 1932.

Iglesias, Ignasi. Enric Morera; estudi biografie. Barcelona, Artis, [1921].

Inch, Herbert Reynolds. A Bibliography of Glinka. [New York, 1935.] Typewritten; available in the Music Division of the New York Public Library.

Indy, Vincent d'. César Franck. Paris, F. Alcan, 1906. Translated: New York, John Lane, 1910.

—— Richard Wagner et son influence sur l'art musical français. Paris, Delagrave, 1930.

Ingegneri, Angelo. Della poesia rappresentativa e del modo di rappresentare le favole sceniche. Ferrara, V. Baldini, 1598.

Irvine, David. Parsifal and Wagner's Christianity. London, H. Grevel, 1899.

Irving, William Henry. John Gay, Favorite of Poets. Durham, N.C., Duke University Press, 1940.

Iselin, Isaak. Pariser Tagebuch 1752. Basel, Benno Schwabe, 1919.

Istel, Edgar. "Act IV of Les Huguenots," MQ XXII (1936) 87–97.

—— "Beethoven's Leonora and Fidelio," MQ VII (1921) 226–51.

—— Bizet und Carmen. Stuttgart, J. Engelhorn, 1927.

—— Die Blütezeit der musikalischen Romantik in Deutschland. Leipzig, B. G. Teubner, 1909. 2d ed., 1921.

—— "Einiges über Georg Benda's 'akkompagnierte' Monodramen," SIMG VI (1904–1905) 179–82.

—— Die Entstehung des deutschen Melodramas. Berlin, Schuster & Loeffler, 1906.

—— "Felipe Pedrell," MQ XI (1925) 164–91.

—— "For a Reversion to Opera," MQ X (1924) 405–37.

—— "Fünf Briefe Spohrs an Marschner," in Festschrift . . . Liliencron (Leipzig, B&H, 1910) pp. 110–15.

—— "A Genetic Study of the Aida Libretto," MQ III (1917) 34–52.

—— "German Opera Since Richard Wagner," MQ I (1915) 260–90.

—— "Gluck's Dramaturgy," MQ XVII (1931) 227–33.

—— "Hermann Goetz," ZIMG III (1901–1902) 177–88.

—— "Isaac Albeniz," MQ XV (1929) 117–48.

—— Die komische Oper; eine historisch-ästhetische Studie. Stuttgart, C. Grüninger, [1906].

—— Das Kunstwerk Richard Wagners. Leipzig, B. G. Teubner, 1918.

—— "Meyerbeer's Way to Mastership," MQ XII (1926) 72–109.

—— Die moderne Oper vom Tode Wagners bis zum Weltkrieg. Leipzig, B. G. Teubner, 1915. 2d ed., 1923.

—— "Mozart's Magic Flute and Freemasonry," MQ XIII (1927) 510–27.

—— "The Othello of Verdi and Shakespeare," MQ II (1916) 375–86.

Istel, Edgar (*Cont.*). "Peter Cornelius," MQ XX (1934) 334–43.

—— "Rossini: a Study," MQ IX (1923) 401–22.

—— Studien zur Geschichte des Melodrams. I. Jean Jacques Rousseau als Komponist seiner lyrischen Szene *Pygmalion.* Leipzig, B&H, 1901. (PIMG, Beihefte, Heft I.)

Jachimecki, Zdzislaw. "Karol Szymanowski," MQ VIII (1922) 23–37.

—— "Karol Szymanowski," *Slavonic and East European Review* XVII (July, 1938) 174–85.

—— "Stanislaus Moniuszko," MQ XIV (1928) 54–62.

Jacob, Heinrich Eduard. Johann Strauss, Father and Son. [New York], Greystone Press, 1940.

—— Johann Strauss und das neunzehnte Jahrhundert. Amsterdam, Querido Verlag, 1937.

Jacob, Walter, ed. Leo Blech; ein Brevier. Hamburg-Leipzig, Prisman-Verlag, [1931].

Jacobs, Reginald. Covent Garden, Its Romance and History. London, Simpkin, 1913.

Jacobsohn, Fritz. Hans Gregors komische Oper, 1905–1911. Berlin, Oesterheld, [1911].

Jäger, Erich. "Gluck und Goethe," *Die Musik* XIII (1913–14) Qt. 4, 131–39.

Jahn, Otto. W. A. Mozart. Leipzig, B&H, 1905–1907. 2 vols. 4th ed. Translated as: Life of Mozart. London, Novello, Ewer, 1882. 3 vols. (From the 2d German ed., 1867.) *See also* Abert, Hermann.

Janowitzer, Erwin. Peter Cornelius als Opernkomponist. Vienna Dissertation, 1921.

Jansen, Albert. Jean-Jacques Rousseau als Musiker. Berlin, Reimer, 1884.

Jansen, Lothar. Studien zur Entwicklungsgeschichte der Oper in Italien, Frankreich, und Deutschland. Bonn Dissertation, 1914.

Jardillier, Robert. Pelléas. Paris, C. Aveline, 1927.

Jaspert, Werner. Johann Strauss. Berlin, Werk Verlag, [1939].

Jean-Aubry, G. "A Romantic Dilettante: Emile Deschamps (1791–1871)," M&L XX (1939) 250–65.

Jenny, Ernst. "Das alte Basler Theater auf dem Blömlein," *Basler Jahrbuch* (1908) 1–68.

Jensen, Wilhelm. Spontini als Opernkomponist. Berlin Dissertation, 1920.

Jeri, A. Mascagni. Milano, Garzanti, 1940. 2d ed.

Jersild, Jorgen. "Le Ballet d'action italien du 18e siècle au Danemark," *Acta musicologica* XIV (1942) 74–93.

Johnson, Harold Edgar. Iphigenia in Tauris as the Subject for French Opera. Cornell Dissertation (A.M.) 1939.

Jouvin, B[enoît Jean Baptiste]. Hérold, sa vie et ses œuvres. Paris, Au Ménestrel, Heugel, 1868.

Jubinal, Achille, ed. Mystères inédits du quinzième siècle. Paris, Téchener, 1837. 2 vols.

Bibliography 597

Jullien, Adolphe. "Ambroise Thomas," RMI III (1896) 358–66.

—— "A Propos de la mort de Charles Gounod," RMI I (1894) 60–67.

—— La Cour et l'opéra sous Louis XVI. Paris, Didier, 1878.

—— "Hector Berlioz," RMI I (1894) 454–82.

—— Hector Berlioz, sa vie et ses œuvres. Paris, Librairie de l'Art, 1888.

—— Musiciens d'aujourd'hui. Paris, Librairie de l'Art, 1892–94. 2 vols.

—— La Ville et la cour au XVIIIe siècle. Paris, E. Rouveyre, 1881.

Jungk, Klaus. Tonbildliches und Tonsymbolisches in Mozarts Opern. Berlin, Triltsch & Huther, 1938.

Junk, Victor. Die Bedeutung der Schlusskadenz im Musikdrama. Leipzig, L. Doblinger, [1926].

—— Goethe's Fortsetzung der *Zauberflöte*. Berlin, Duncker, 1899.

Junker, Hermann. "Zwei 'Griselda'-Opern," in *Festschrift Adolf Sandberger* (München, Zierfuss, 1918) pp. 51–64.

Kaestner, Erwin. Das Opernproblem und seine Lösung bei Mozart. Jena, Neuenhahn, 1932.

Kaestner, Rudolf. Johann Heinrich Rolle. Kassel, Bärenreiter, 1932.

Kalbeck, Max. Opern-Abende. Berlin, "Harmonie," 1898.

—— "Zu Scheidemantels Don Juan-Uebersetzung," Die Musik XIII (1913–14) Qt. 4, 67–72.

Kalisch, Alfred. "Impressions of Strauss's *Elektra*," ZIMG X (1908–1909) 198–202.

Kapp, Julius. Franz Schreker. München, Drei Masken, 1921.

—— 185 Jahre Staatsoper. Berlin, Atlantic-Verlag, 1928.

—— Geschichte der Staatsoper Berlin. Berlin, M. Hesse, 1937. New ed., 1942.

—— Meyerbeer. Berlin, Schuster & Loeffler, [1920]. 8th ed., 1930.

—— Richard Wagner. Berlin, M. Hesse, 1929. 32d ed.

—— Richard Wagner und die Berliner Oper. Berlin-Schöneberg, M. Hesse, 1933.

—— Die Staatsoper Berlin 1919 bis 1925. Stuttgart, Deutsche Verlags-Anstalt, [1925].

—— 200 Jahre Staatsoper im Bild. Berlin, M. Hesse, 1942.

Karasowski, Maurycy. Rys historyczny opery polskiéj. Warszawa, M. Glücksberga, 1859.

Karstädt, Georg. "Zur Geschichte des Zinken und seiner Verwendung in der Musik des 16.–18. Jahrhunderts," AfMf II (1937) 385–432.

Kastner, Emerich. Bibliotheca Beethoveniana; Versuch einer Beethoven-Bibliographie. Leipzig, B&H, 1913.

—— Die dramatischen Werke R. Wagner's; chronologisches Verzeichnis der ersten Aufführungen. Leipzig, B&H, 1899. 2d ed.

Kaul, Oskar. Geschichte der Würzburger Hofmusik im 18. Jahrhundert. Würzburg, Becker, 1924.

—— "Die musikdramatischen Werke des Würzburgischen Hofkapellmeisters Georg Franz Wassmuth," ZfMw VII (1924–25) 390–408, 478–500.

Keefer, Lubov. "Opera in the Soviet," *Music Library Association Notes, Second Series* II, No. 2 (March, 1945) 110–17.

Keeton, A. E. "Elgar's Music for *The Starlight Express*," M&L XXVI (1945) 43–46.

Keller, Otto. Franz von Suppé. Leipzig, R. Wöpke, 1905.

—— "Gluck-Bibliographie," *Die Musik* XIII (1913–14) Qt. 4, 23–37, 85–91.

—— Karl Goldmark. Leipzig, H. Seemann, [1901].

—— Die Operette in ihrer geschichtlichen Entwicklung. Wien, Stein-Verlag, 1926.

Keller, Otto. Wolfgang Amadeus Mozart; Bibliographie und Ikonographie. Berlin, Gebrüder Paetel, 1927.

Kelly, Alfredo. *See* Fiorda Kelly, Alfredo.

Kelly, Michael. Reminiscences of the King's Theatre. London, H. Colburn, 1826. 2 vols.

Kenney, Charles Lamb. A Memoir of Michael William Balfe. London, Tinsley, 1875.

Kidson, Frank. *The Beggar's Opera*, Its Predecessors and Successors. Cambridge, The University Press, 1922.

Kienzl, Wilhelm. Meine Lebenswanderung. Stuttgart, J. Engelhorn, 1926.

Kiesewetter, R[aphael] G[eorg], Edler von Wiesenbrunn. Schicksale und Beschaffenheit des weltlichen Gesanges. Leipzig, B&H, 1841.

Killer, Hermann. Albert Lortzing. Potsdam, Athenaion, 1938.

—— Die Tenorpartien in Mozarts Opern. Kassel, Bärenreiter, 1929.

Kindem, Ingeborg Eckhoff. Den norske operas historie. Oslo, E. G. Mortensen, 1941.

Kinkeldey, Otto. "Luzzasco Luzzaschi's Solo-Madrigale mit Klavierbegleitung," SIMG IX (1907–1908) 538–65.

—— Orgel und Klavier in der Musik des 16. Jahrhunderts. Leipzig, B&H, 1910.

Kinsky, Georg. "Glucks Reisen nach Paris," ZfMw VIII (1925–26) 551–66.

Kirby, Percival R. "The Kettle-drums; an Historical Survey," M&L IX (1928) 34–43.

—— "A 13th Century Ballad Opera," M&L XI (1930) 163–71.

Kisch, Eve. "Rameau and Rousseau," M&L XXII (1941) 97–114.

Kitzig, Berthold. "Briefe Carl Heinrich Grauns," ZfMw IX (1926–27) 385–405.

Klages, Richard. Johann Wolfgang Franck. Hamburg, 1937.

Kleefeld, Wilhelm. "Hessens Beziehungen zur alten deutschen Oper," *Vom Rhein; Monatsschrift des Altertumsvereins für die Stadt Worms* IV (1905) 15.

—— Landgraf Ernst Ludwig von Hessen-Darmstadt und die deutsche Oper. Berlin, Hofmann, 1904.

—— "Das Orchester der Hamburger Oper 1678–1738," SIMG I (1899–1900) 219–89.

Klein, Herman. "Albéniz's Opera *Pepita Jiménez*," *Musical Times* LIX (March, 1918) 116–17.

—— The Golden Age of Opera. London, George Routledge, 1933.

—— "The Vienna Hofoper," M&L XIV (1933) 239–46.

Klein, John W. "Alfredo Catalani," MQ XXIII (1937) 287–94.

—— "Bizet's Early Operas," M&L XVIII (1937) 169–75.

—— "Boito and His Two Operas," M&L VII (1926) 73–80.

—— "Nietzsche and Bizet," MQ XI (1925) 482–505.

—— "Verdi and Boito," MQ XIV (1928) 158–71.

—— "Verdi's Italian Contemporaries and Successors," M&L XV (1934) 37–45.

—— "Wagner and His Operatic Contemporaries," M&L IX (1928) 59–66.

Kling, H. "Caron de Beaumarchais et la musique," RMI VII (1900) 673–97.

—— "Le Centenaire d'un compositeur suisse célèbre: Louis Niedermeyer," RMI IX (1902) 830–59.

—— "Goethe et Berlioz," RMI XII (1905) 714–32.

—— "Helmine de Chézy," RMI XIV (1907) 25–39.

Klob, Karl Maria. Beiträge zur Geschichte der deutschen komischen Oper. Berlin, "Harmonie," [1903].

—— Die komische Oper seit Lortzing. Berlin, "Harmonie," [1905].

—— Die Oper von Gluck bis Wagner. Ulm, H. Kerler, 1913.

Kloiber, Rudolf. Die dramatischen Ballette von Christian Cannabich. Munich Dissertation, 1927.

Knappe, Heinrich. Friedrich Klose. München, Drei Masken, 1921.

Knopf, Kurt. Die romantische Struktur des Denkens Richard Wagners. Jena, G. Neuenhahn, 1932.

Knudsen, Hans. "Das Posener Theater unter Franz Wallner," *Zeitschrift der historischen Gesellschaft für die Provinz Posen* XXVI (1911) 225–42.

[Koch, Lajos.] Karl Goldmark. Budapest, Hauptstädtische Hausdruckerei, 1930.

Koch, Max. Richard Wagner. Berlin, E. Hofmann, 1907–18. 3 vols.

Köchel, Ludwig, Ritter von. Chronologisch-thematisches Verzeichnis sämtlicher Tonwerke Wolfgang Amade Mozarts. Leipzig, B&H, 1937. 3d ed., revised by Alfred Einstein.

—— Johann Josef Fux. Vienna, A. Hölder, 1872.

—— Die kaiserliche Hofmusikkapelle in Wien von 1543 bis 1867. Wien, Beck, 1869.

Koechlin, Charles. Gabriel Fauré. Paris, F. Alcan, 1927. 2d ed.

Kohut, Adolph. Auber. Leipzig, Reclam, 1895.

Kolodin, Irving. The Metropolitan Opera, 1883–1938. New York, Oxford University Press, 1939. Revised ed.

Komorzyński, Egon von. Emmanuel Schikaneder. Berlin, B. Behr, 1901.

Komorzyński, Egon von (*Cont.*). "Lortzings *Waffenschmied* und seine Tradition," *Euphorion* VIII (1901) 340–50.

—— "Streit um den Text der *Zauberflöte*," *Alt-Wiener Kalender* (1922) 79–105.

Korngold, Julius. Deutsches Opernschaffen der Gegenwart. Wien, Rikola, 1922.

—— Die romanische Oper der Gegenwart. Wien, Rikola, 1922.

Kracauer, Siegfried. Orpheus in Paris. New York, Knopf, 1938. First published as: Jacques Offenbach und das Paris seiner Zeit. Amsterdam, de Lange, 1937.

Kramer, Margarete. Beiträge zu einer Geschichte des Affektenbegriffes in der Musik von 1550–1700. Halle Dissertation, 1924.

Kraus, Ludwig. Das deutsche Liederspiel in den Jahren 1800–1830. Halle Dissertation, 1921.

Krause, Christian Gottfried. Abhandlung von der musikalischen Poesie. Berlin, J. F. Voss, 1752.

Krauss, Rudolf. Das Stuttgarter Hoftheater von den ältesten Zeiten bis zur Gegenwart. Stuttgart, J. B. Metzler, 1908.

—— "Das Theater," in *Herzog Karl Eugen von Württemberg und seine Zeit* (Esslingen a. N., 1907) I, 481–554.

Krebs, Carl. Dittersdorfiana. Berlin, Gebrüder Paetel, 1900.

Krehbiel, Henry. Music and Manners in the Classical Period. New York, Scribner, 1899.

Kreidler, Walter. Heinrich Schütz und der Stile concitato von Claudio Monteverdi. Cassel, Bärenreiter, 1934.

Křenek, Ernst. Music Here and Now. New York, W. W. Norton, [1939].

—— "The New Music and Today's Theatre," MMus XIV, No. 4 (May–June, 1937) 200–203.

—— "Opera between the Wars," MMus XX, No. 2 (January–February, 1943) 102–111.

—— "Problemi di stile nell' opera," RassM VII (1934) 199–202.

—— "Zur musikalischen Bearbeitung von Monteverdis *Poppea*," *Schweizerische Musikzeitung* LXXVI (1936) 545–55.

Kretzschmar, Hermann. "Allgemeines und Besonderes zur Affektenlehre," JMP XVIII (1911) 63–77; XIX (1912) 65–78.

—— "Aus Deutschlands italienischer Zeit," JMP VIII (1901) 45–61.

—— "Beiträge zur Geschichte der venetianischen Oper," JMP XIV (1907) 71–81; XVII (1910) 61–71; XVIII (1911) 49–61.

—— "Die *Correspondance littéraire* als musikgeschichtliche Quelle," JMP X (1903) 77–92; also in his *Gesammelte Aufsätze* II, 210–25.

—— "Einige Bemerkungen über den Vortrag alter Musik," JMP VII (1900) 53–68.

—— Gesammelte Aufsätze über Musik und anderes. Leipzig, F. W. Grunow, 1910–[11]. 2 vols.

—— Geschichte des neuen deutschen Liedes; I. Teil: von Albert bis Zelter. Leipzig, B&H, 1911.

—— "Giuseppe Verdi," JMP XX (1913) 43–58.

—— "Hasse über Mozart," ZIMG III (1901–1902) 263–65.

—— "Monteverdi's *Incoronazione di Poppea*," VfMw X (1894) 483–530.

—— "Mozart in der Geschichte der Oper," JMP XII (1905) 53–71.

—— "Die musikgeschichtliche Bedeutung Simon Mayrs," JMP XI (1904) 27–41.

—— "Peter Cornelius," in Waldersee, *Sammlung musikalischer Vorträge* (Leipzig, B&H, 1879–98) II, 225–60.

—— "Ueber das Wesen, das Wachsen und Wirken Richard Wagners," JMP XIX (1912) 49–64.

—— "Ueber die Bedeutung von Cherubinis Ouvertüren und Hauptopern für die Gegenwart," JMP XIII (1906) 75–91.

—— "Die venetianische Oper und die Werke Cavalli's und Cesti's," VfMw VIII (1892) 1–76.

—— "Zum Verständnis Glucks," JMP X (1903) 61–76.

—— "Zwei Opern Nicolo Logroscinos," JMP XV (1908) 47–68.

Kreuzhage, Eduard. Hermann Goetz. Leipzig, B&H, 1916.

Krieger, Erhard. "Heinrich Kaminski's Drama *Jürg Jenatsch*," *Zeitschrift für Musik* C (1933) 992–95.

Krieger, Ludwig. Die sozialische Lage der Theatermusiker. Heidelberg, Schulze, 1913.

Krienitz, Willy. Richard Wagner's *Feen*. München, G. Müller, 1910.

Krogh, Torben Thorberg. "Reinhard Keiser in Kopenhagen," in *Musik-wissenschaftliche Beiträge; Festschrift für Johannes Wolf* (Berlin, Breslauer, 1929).

—— Zur Geschichte des dänischen Singspiels im 18. Jahrhundert. København, Levin & Munksgaard, 1924.

Krohn, Ilmari. "Puccini: *Butterfly*," in *Gedenkboek D. F. Scheurleer* ('s Gravenhage, Nijhoff, 1925) pp. 181–90.

Kroll, Erwin. Carl Maria von Weber. Potsdam, Athenaion, [1934].

—— Ernst Theodor Amadeus Hoffmann. Leipzig, B&H, 1923.

Krone, Walter. Wenzel Müller. Berlin, Ebering, 1906.

Krott, Rudolfine. Die Singspiele Schuberts. Vienna Dissertation, 1921.

Kroyer, Theodor. Anfänge der Chromatik im italienischen Madrigal des XVI. Jahrhunderts. Leipzig, B&H, 1902. (PIMG, Beihefte, IV.)

—— "Die circumpolare Oper," JMP XXVI (1919) 16–33.

Krüger, Karl Joachim. Hugo von Hofmannsthal und Richard Strauss. Marburg Dissertation, 1935.

Krüger, Viktor. Die Entwicklung Carl Maria von Webers in seinen Jugendopern *Abu Hassan* und *Silvana*. Vienna Dissertation, 1907.

Kruse, Georg Richard. Albert Lortzing. Berlin, "Harmonie," 1899.

—— Hermann Goetz. Leipzig, Reclam, [1920].

—— "Meyerbeers Jugendopern," ZfMw I (1918–19) 399–413.

—— Otto Nicolai. Berlin, Verlag "Berlin-Wien," [1911].

Kruse, Georg Richard (*Cont.*). "Otto Nicolai's italienische Opern," SIMG XII (1910–1911) 267–96.

Kuckuk, Ludwig. Peter Winter als deutscher Opernkomponist. Heidelberg Dissertation, 1924.

Kufferath, Maurice. *"Fervaal . . .* di V. d'Indy," RMI IV (1897) 313–27.

—— *Fidelio* de L. van Beethoven. Paris, Fischbacher, 1913.

—— *La Flûte enchantée* de Mozart. Paris, Fischbacher, 1914.

Kuhn, Max. Die Verzierungskunst in der Gesangs-Musik des 16.–17. Jahrhunderts (1535–1650). Leipzig, B&H, 1902. (PIMG, Beiheft 7.)

Kurth, Ernst. "Die Jugendopern Glucks bis *Orfeo*," SzMw I (1913) 193–277.

—— Romantische Harmonik und ihre Krise in Wagners *Tristan*. Berlin, M. Hesse, 1923. 2d ed.

Kutscher, Artur. Vom Salzburger Barocktheater zu den Salzburger Festspielen. Düsseldorf, Pflugscher-Verlag, 1939.

Kuznitzky, Hans. "Weber und Spontini in der musikalischen Anschauung von E. T. A. Hoffmann," ZfMw X (1927–28) 292–99.

Labroca, Mario. "The Rebirth of Italian Opera," MMus IV, No. 4 (May–June, 1927) 8–14.

Lach, Robert. "Das mittelaltleriche Musikdrama im Spiegel der Kunstgeschichte," in *Festschrift Adolph Koczirz* (Wien, Strache, [1930]) pp. 17–20.

—— "Sebastian Sailers *Schöpfung* in der Musik," *Akademie der Wissenschaften in Wien, Denkschriften*, 60. Band, 1. Abhandlung (1917).

Lacroix, Paul. Ballets et mascarades de cour, de Henri III à Louis XIV (1581–1652). Geneva, J. Gay, 1868–70. 6 vols.

Lafontaine, H. C. de. "Richard Wagner," PMA XVI (1890) 63–78.

Lafont du Cujala. "Réflexions sur l'état actuel de la musique dramatique en France," *Mercure de France* (February, 1782) pp. 38–44.

Lajarte, Théodore de. Bibliothèque musicale du théâtre de l'opéra. Paris, Librairie des bibliophiles, 1878. 2 vols.

—— Curiosités de l'opéra. Paris, Calmann Lévy, 1883.

Lalande, Joseph Jérôme Lefrançais de. Voyage d'un françois en Italie, fait dans les années 1765 & 1766. A Venise, et se trouve à Paris chez Desaint, 1769. 8 vols.

La Laurencie, Lionel de. "André Campra, musicien profane; notes biographiques," *Année musicale* III (1913) 153–205.

—— "Une Convention commerciale entre Lully, Quinault et Ballard en 1680," RdM II (1920–21) 176–82.

—— Les Créateurs de l'opéra français. Paris, F. Alcan, 1930. New ed.

—— "Les Débuts de Viotti comme directeur de l'opéra en 1819," RdM V (1924) 110–22.

—— "Deux Imitateurs français des bouffons: Blavet et Dauvergne," *Année musicale* II (1912) 65–125.

—— "Un Emule de Lully: Pierre Gautier de Marseille," SIMG XIII (1911–12) 39–69, 400.

—— "La Grande Saison italienne de 1752; les bouffons," MM VIII, No. 6

(1912) 18–33; Nos. 7–8, pp. 13–22. Also separate as: Les Bouffons (1752–1754). Paris, Publications de la Revue SIM, 1912.

—— "Leclair; une assertion de Fétis; Jean-Marie Leclair l'ainé à l'orchestre de l'Opéra," RHCM IV (1904) 496–503.

—— Lully. Paris, F. Alcan, 1911.

—— "Un Musicien dramatique du XVIIIe siècle français: Pierre Guedron," RMI XXIX (1922) 445–72.

—— "Un Musicien italien en France à la fin du XVIIIe siècle," RdM XII (1931) 268–77.

—— "Notes sur la jeunesse d'André Campra," SIMG X (1908–1909) 159–258. Also separate: Leipzig, B&H, 1909.

—— "L'Opéra français au XVIIe siècle; la musique," RM VI (January, 1925) 26–43.

—— "Un Opéra inédit de M.-A. Charpentier: *La Descente d'Orphée aux enfers*," RdM X (1929) 184–93.

—— "L'*Orfeo nell' inferni* d'André Campra," RdM IX (1928) 129–33.

—— *Orphée* de Gluck; étude et analyse. Paris, Mellottée, 1934.

—— "Les Pastorales en musique au XVIIe siècle en France avant Lully et leur influence sur l'opéra," in *International Musical Society, 4th Congress Report* (London, Novello, 1912) pp. 139–46.

—— "Quelques documents sur Jean-Philippe Rameau et sa famille," MM III (1907) 541–614.

—— "Rameau et les clarinettes," MM IX, No. 2 (1913) 27–28.

—— "Rameau et son gendre," MM VII, No. 2 (1911) 12–23.

Laloy, Louis. "Le Drame musical moderne," MM I (1905) 8–16, 75–84, 169–77, 233–50.

—— "Les Idées de Jean-Philippe Rameau sur la musique," MM III (1907) 1144–59.

Lamm, Max. Beiträge zur Entwicklung des musikalischen Motivs in den Tondramen Richard Wagners. Vienna Dissertation, 1932.

Lamy, Félix. Jean-François le Sueur. Paris, Fischbacher, 1912.

Landi, Antonio. Il commodo, commedia d'Antonio Landi con i suoi intermedi [etc.]. Firenze, I. Giunti, 1566. The intermedi are by G. B. Strozzi the elder. Earlier ed. 1539.

Landormy, Paul Charles René. *Faust* de Gounod. Paris, P. Mellottée, [1922].

—— "Gabriel Fauré," MQ XVII (1931) 293–301.

—— "Maurice Ravel," MQ XXV (1939) 430–41.

—— "Vincent d'Indy," MQ XVIII (1932) 507–18.

Láng, Paul Henry. "Background Music for *Mein Kampf*," *Saturday Review of Literature* XXVIII, No. 3 (January 20, 1945) 5–9.

—— "Haydn and the Opera," MQ XVIII (1932) 274–81.

—— The Literary Aspects of the History of the Opera in France. Cornell Dissertation, 1935.

—— Music in Western Civilization. New York, W. W. Norton, [1941].

Lange, Francisco Curt. "Leon Ribeiro," *Boletin latino-americano de musica* III (1937) 519–36.

Langlois, Jacques. Camille Saint-Saëns. Moulins, Crépin-Leblond, 1934.

[Lardin, Jules.] *Zémire et Azor* par Grétry; quelques questions à propos de la nouvelle falsification de cet opéra. Paris, Moëssard et Jousset, 1846.

La Roche, Charles. Antonio Bertali als Opern- und Oratorienkomponist. Vienna Dissertation, 1919.

La Rotella, Pasquale. Niccolo Piccinni. Bari, Cressati, 1928.

Larsen, Jens Peter. Die Haydn-Ueberlieferungen. Kopenhagen, Munksgaard, 1939.

La Salandra. *See* Belluci La Salandra.

La Tour, Georges Imbart de. "La Mise en scène d' *Hippolyte et Aricie,*" MM IV (1908) 247–71.

Laue, Hellmuth. Die Operndichtung Lortzings. Bonn am Rhein, L. Röhrscheid, 1932.

Lavignac, Albert. Le Voyage artistique à Bayreuth. Paris, C. Delagrave, 1900. 4th ed. Translated as: The Music Dramas of Richard Wagner and His Festival Theatre in Bayreuth. New York, Dodd, Mead, 1904.

Lavoix, Henri. "Les Opéras madrigalesques," *Revue et gazette musicale* XLIV (1877) 307–309, 323–24, 331–32.

Lawrence, William John. "Early Irish Ballad Opera and Comic Opera," MQ VIII (1922) 397–412.

—— "The Early Years of the First English Opera House," MQ VII (1921) 104–17.

—— The Elizabethan Playhouse and Other Studies. Philadelphia, J. B. Lippincott, 1912.

—— "The English Theatre Orchestra: Its Rise and Early Characteristics," MQ III (1917) 9–27.

—— "Foreign Singers and Musicians at the Court of Charles II," MQ IX (1923) 217–25.

—— "Marionette Operas," MQ X (1924) 236–43.

—— "Notes on a Collection of Masque Music," M&L III (1922) 49–58.

Lebègue, Raymond. Le Mystère des Actes des Apôtres. Paris, Champion, 1929.

[Le Blond, Gaspard Michel, ed.] Mémoires pour sevir à l'histoire de la révolution opérée dans la musique par M. le Chevalier Gluck. Naples and Paris, Bailly, 1781.

[Le Cerf de La Viéville, Jean Laurent, seigneur de Freneuse.] Comparaison de la musique italienne et de la musique françoise. Bruxelles, F. Foppens, 1704–1706. 3 vols. Also forms Vols. 2–4 of Jacques Bonnet's Histoire de la musique et de ses effets. Amsterdam, J. Royer, 17—.

[Leclercq, Louis.] Les Décors, les costumes, et la mise en scène au XVIIe siècle, 1615–1680, par Ludovic Celler [pseud.]. Paris, Liepmannssohn & Dufour, 1869.

Lee, Vernon. *See* Paget, Violet.

Lehmann, Lilly. Studien zu *Fidelio*. Leipzig, B&H, 1904.

Lehner, Walter. "Franz Xaver Süssmayr als Opernkomponist," SzMw XVIII (1931) 66–96.

Leib, Walter. Joseph Huber; Beitrag zur Geschichte der circumpolaren Oper. Heidelberg Dissertation, 1923.

Leichtentritt, Hugo. Händel. Stuttgart-Berlin, Deutsche Verlags-Anstalt, 1924.

—— "Handel's Harmonic Art," MQ XXI (1935) 208–23.

—— Music, History, and Ideas. Cambridge, Mass., Harvard University Press, 1938.

—— "On the Prologue in Early Opera," MTNA XXXI (1936) 292–99.

—— Reinhard Keiser in seinen Opern. Berlin, Tessarotypie-Actien-Gesellschaft, 1901.

—— "Schubert's Early Operas," MQ XIV (1928) 620–38.

—— *See also:* Ambros, August Wilhelm. Geschichte der Musik.

Leist, Friedrich. "Geschichte des Theaters in Bamberg bis zum Jahre 1862," *Berichte des historischen Vereins zu Bamberg* LV (1893) 1–283.

Lejeune, Caroline. "Opera in the Eighteenth Century," PMA XLIX (1922–23) 1–20.

Lengl, Georg. Die Genesis der Oper. München, Mössl, 1936.

Lenzewsky, Gustav. "Friedrich der Grosse als Komponist des Singspiels *Il Re pastore*," *Schriften des Vereins für die Geschichte Berlins* XXIX (1912) 20.

Leo, Giacomo. Leonardo Leo, celebre musicista del secolo XVIII, ed il suo omonimo Leonardo Leo di Corrado; nota storica. Napoli, Cozzolino, 1901.

—— Leonardo Leo . . . e le sue opere musicali. Napoli, Melfi & Joele, 1905.

Leo, Sophie Augustine. "Musical Life in Paris (1817–1848)," MQ XVII (1931) 259–71, 389–403.

Leoni, Carlo. Dell'arte e del teatro nuovo di Padova; racconto anecdotico. Padova, Sacchetto, 1873.

Lepel, Felix von. Die Dresdner Oper als Weltkulturstätte. Dresden, Spohr, 1942.

[Le Prévost d'Exmes, François.] Lully, musicien. [Paris, 1779.]

[Léris, Antoine de.] Dictionnaire portatif des théâtres. Paris, C. A. Jombert, 1754. Another ed., 1763.

Leroy, L. Archier. Wagner's Music Drama of *The Ring*. London, N. Douglas, [1925].

Lert, Ernst. Mozart auf dem Theater. Berlin, Schuster & Loeffler, 1918.

Le Sage, Alain René. Le Théâtre de la foire, ou l'Opéra-comique. Paris, P. Gandouin, 1724–37. 10 vols.

Lespês, Léo. Les Mystères du grand-opéra. Paris, Maresq, 1843.

Leti, Giuseppe, and Louis Lachat. L'Esotérisme à la scène; *La Flûte enchantée, Parsifal, Faust.* Annecy, L. Dépollier, 1935.

Leux, Irmgard. Christian Gottlob Neefe. Leipzig, Kistner & Siegel, 1925.

—— "Ueber die 'verschollene' Händel-Oper *Hermann von Balcke,*" AfMw VIII (1926) 441–51.

Levi, Vito. "Un grande operista italiano (Antonio Smareglia, 1854–1929)," RMI XXXVI (1929) 600–15.

Levinson, André. "Notes sur le ballet au XVIIe siècle; les danseurs de Lully," RM VI (January, 1925) 44–55.

Lieboldt, J. "Der Verbleib der alten Hamburger Operndekoration *Der Tempel Salomonis,*" *Mitteilungen des Vereins für Hamburgische Geschichte* XIII (1890) 128–29.

Liliencron, Rochus, Freiherr von. "Die Chorgesänge des lateinischen-deutschen Schuldramas im 16. Jahrhundert," VfMw VI (1890) 309–87.

[Limojon de St. Didier, Alexandre Toussaint.] La Ville et la république de Venise. Paris, G. de Luyne, 1680. Translated as: The City and Republick of Venice. London, C. Brome, 1699.

Lindner, Ernst Otto. Die erste stehende deutsche Oper. Berlin, Schlesinger, 1855. 2 vols.

—— Zur Tonkunst; Abhandlungen. Berlin, I. Guttentag, 1864. Contains essays on the rise of opera, Vittorio Loreto, and *The Beggar's Opera.*

List, Kurt. "*Lulu,* after the Premiere," MMus XV, No. 1 (November–December, 1937) 8–12.

Liuzzi, Fernando. "Drammi musicali dei secoli XI–XIV," *Studi medievali,* nuova serie III (1930) 82–109.

—— "L'espressione musicale nel dramma liturgico," *Studi medievali,* nuova serie II (1929) 74–109.

Livermore, Ann. "The Spanish Dramatists and Their Use of Music," M&L XXV (1944) 140–49.

Livingston, Arthur. Lorenzo da Ponte in America. Philadelphia, Lippincott, 1930.

Lockspeiser, Edward. Debussy. London, J. M. Dent; New York, E. P. Dutton, [1936].

—— "Musorgsky and Debussy," MQ XXIII (1937) 421–27.

Lockwood, Elisabeth M. "Some Old-Fashioned Music," M&L XII (1931) 262–70.

Loëb, Harry Brunswick. "The Opera in New Orleans," *Louisiana Historical Society, Proceedings and Reports* IX (1916) 2941.

Loehner, Ermanno von. "Carlo Goldoni e le sue memorie," *Archivio veneto* XXIII (1881) 45–65; XXIV (1882) 5–27.

Loewenberg, Alfred. "*Bastien and Bastienne* Once More," M&L XXV (1924) 176–81.

—— "Gluck's *Orfeo* on the Stage," MQ XXVI (1940) 311–39.

—— "Lorenzo da Ponte in London," *Music Review* IV (1943) 171–89.

—— "Paisiello's and Rossini's *Barbiere di Siviglia*," M&L XX (1939) 157–67.

Loisel, Joseph. *Manon* de Massenet; étude historique et critique, analyse musicale. Paris, Mellottée, [1922].

Long des Clavières, P. "Lettres inédites de A. E. M. Grétry," RMI XXI (1914) 699–727.

—— "Les *Réflexions d'un solitaire* par A. E. M. Grétry," RMI XXVI (1919) 565–614.

Loomis, Roger Sherman, ed. The Romance of Tristram and Ysolt by Thomas of Britain. New York, Columbia University Press, 1931. Revised ed.

Lopatnikoff, Nikolai. "*Christophe Colomb* [by Milhaud]," MMus VII, No. 4 (June–July, 1930) 36–38.

López Chavarri, *see* Chavarri, Eduardo López.

Lorenz, Alfred Ottokar. Alessandro Scarlatti's Jugendoper. Augsburg, Benno Filser, 1927. 2 vols.

—— "Alessandro Scarlattis Opern und Wien," ZfMw IX (1926–27) 86–89.

—— "Das Finale in Mozarts Meisteropern," *Die Musik* XIX (June, 1927) 621–32.

—— Das Geheimnis der Form bei Richard Wagner. Berlin, M. Hesse, 1924–33. 4 vols.

Lortzing, Gustav Albert. Gesammelte Briefe. Regensburg. G. Bosse, [1913]. New, enlarged ed.

Loschelder, Josef. Das Todesproblem in Verdis Opernschaffen. Stuttgart, Deutsche Verlagsanstalt, 1938.

Lote, Georges. "La Déclamation du vers français à la fin du XVIIe siècle," *Revue de phonétique* II (1912) 313–63.

Lothar, Rudolf, [and Julius Stern]. 50 Jahre Hoftheater; Geschichte der beiden Wiener Hoftheater unter der Regierungszeit des Kaisers Franz Josef I. Wien, Steyermühl, [1898].

Louis, Rudolf. Die deutsche Musik der Gegenwart. München, G. Müller, 1909. 3d ed., 1912.

—— Hans Pfitzners *Die Rose vom Liebesgarten*. München, C. A. Seyfried, 1904.

Lowe, George. Josef Holbrooke and His Work. London, K. Paul [etc.]; New York, E. P. Dutton, 1920.

Lozzi, C. "Brigida Banti, regina del teatro lirico nel secolo XVIII," RMI XI (1904) 64–76.

—— "La musica e specialmente il melodramma alla Corte Medicea," RMI IX (1902) 297–338.

Lualdi, Adriano. "Arrigo Boito, un' anima," RMI XXV (1918) 524–49.

—— "Claudio Debussy, la sua arte e la sua parabola," RMI XXV (1918) 271–305.

—— "Il *Principe Igor* de Borodine," RMI XXIII (1916) 115–39.

Luciani, Sebastiano Arturo. "Domenico Scarlatti," RassM XI (1938) 460–72; XII (1939) 20–31, 61–74.

—— La rinascita del dramma: saggio sul teatro di musica. Roma, Ausonia, 1922.

Lucianus Samosatensis. Lucian; with an English Translation by A. M. Harmon. London, W. Heinemann; New York, Macmillan, 1913–36. Contains "On the Dance," V, 209–89.

Lütge, Wilhelm. "Zu Beethovens Leonoren-Ouvertüre Nr. 2," ZfMw IX (1926–27) 235–36.

Lüthge, Kurt. Die deutsche Spieloper. Braunschweig, W. Piepenschneider, 1924.

Lugli, A. Il melodramma, l'ultima geniale creazione del rinascimento. Milano, A. Ballardi, 1921.

Luin, E. J. "Giovanni Ferrandini e l'apertura del Teatro Residenziale a Monaco nel 1745," RMI XXXIX (1932) 561–66.

Lully et l'opéra français. RM, numéro spécial, Vol. VI (January, 1925).

Lunelli, R. Un' opera in musica, la morte di un vescovo ed una bega consolare nel 1800. Trient, Artigrafiche Tridentum, 1923.

Lupo, Bettina. "Scene e persone musicale dell' Amfiparnaso," RassM XI (1938) 445–59.

Lusson, A. L. Projet d'un théâtre d'opéra définitif pour la ville de Paris en remplacement de l'opéra provisoire. Paris, Gratiot, 1846.

Lutze, G. Aus Sonderhausens Vergangenheit. III. Band. Sonderhausen, Fr. Aug. Eupel, 1919.

Lynn, Thelma. César Franck; a Bio-bibliography. New York, 1934. Typescript. Available at the New York Public Library.

Mably, Gabriel Bonnot de. Lettres à Madame la Marquise de P . . . sur l'opéra. Paris, Didot, 1741.

Macchetta, Mrs. Blanche Roosevelt (Tucker). Verdi: Milan and Othello . . . by Blanche Roosevelt. London, Ward & Downey, 1887.

MacCormack, Gilson. "Weber in Paris," M&L IX (1928) 240–48.

MacFarren, Sir George Alexander. "The Lyrical Drama," PMA VI (1880) 125–40.

Maclean, Charles. "La Princesse Osra [by Herbert Bunning] and Der Wald [by Ethel Smyth]," ZIMG III (1901–1902) 482–88.

McMullen, Edward Wallace. The Earliest Operatic Adaptations of Shakespeare. Columbia Dissertation (A.M.), 1939.

Maddalena, E. "Libretti del Goldoni e d'altri," RMI VII (1900) 739–45.

Maecklenburg, Albert. "Der Fall Spontini-Weber," ZfMw VI (1923–24) 449–65.

—— "Verdi and Manzoni," MQ XVII (1931) 209–18.

Magnani, Giuseppe. Antonio Salieri. [Legnano], Edito a cura del commune di Legnano e di un comitato cittadino, 1934.

Magni-Dufflocq, Enrico. "Domenico Cimarosa, note biografiche," Bollettino bibliografico musicale V (1930) 5–15.

Maier, Johann Christoph. Beschreibung von Venedig. Leipzig, J. A. Barth, 1795. 4 vols. 2d ed.

Maine, Basil. "*Don Juan de Mañara;* Goossens' New Opera," *The Chesterian* XVI (1935–36) 5–10.

[Mainwaring, John.] Memoirs of the Life of the Late George Frederic Handel. London, R. & J. Dodsley, 1760.

Maione, Italo. "Tasso-Monteverdi; *Il combattimento di Tancredi e Clorinda,*" RassM III (1930) 206–15.

Maisch, W. Puccinis musikalische Formgebung, untersucht an der Oper *La Bohême.* Neustadt a. d. Aisch, Schmidt, 1934.

Malherbe, Charles Théodore. Auber; biographie critique. Paris, H. Laurens, [1911].

—— "Le Centenaire de Donizetti et l'exposition de Bergamo," RMI IV (1897) 707–29.

—— "Un Précurseur de Gluck; le comte Algarotti," RHCM II (1902) 369–74, 414–23.

Malipiero, Gian Francesco. Claudio Monteverdi. Milano, Treves, 1929.

—— "Claudio Monteverdi of Cremona," MQ XVIII (1932) 383–96.

—— "Orchestra e orchestrazione," RMI XXIII (1916) 559–69; XXIV (1917) 89–114.

Mandalari, M. T. "Gradi della evoluzione drammatica nel *Ballo in Maschera* di Verdi," RassM XII (1931) 277–87.

Mann, Thomas. Leiden und Grösse der Meister. Berlin, S. Fischer, 1935. A condensed English translation of the essay on Wagner in this volume is found in Mann's *Freud, Goethe, Wagner* (New York, Knopf, 1937).

—— Pfitzners *Palestrina.* Berlin, S. Fischer, 1919.

Manschunger, Kurt. Ferdinand Kauer. Vienna Dissertation, 1929.

Mantica, Francesco, ed. Prime fioriture del melodramma italiano. Roma, Casa editrice Claudio Monteverdi, 1912–30. 2 vols.

Manuel, Roland. Manuel de Falla. Paris, "Cahiers d'art," 1930.

—— Maurice Ravel et son œuvre dramatique. Paris, Librairie de France, 1928.

Mapleson, James Henry. The Mapleson Memoirs, 1848–1888. London, Remington, 1888. 2d ed. 2 vols.

Marangoni, Guido, and Carlo Vanbianchi. "La Scala," studie e richerche; note storiche e statistiche (1906–20). Bergamo, Istituto italiano d'arti grafiche, 1922.

Marcello, ——. "La prima rappresentazione del *Guglielmo Tell* a Parigi," RMI XVI (1909) 664–70.

[Marcello, Benedetto.] Il teatro alla moda, osia metodo sicuro, e facile per ben comporre, & esequire l'Opere Italiane in Musica all' uso moderno. [Venezia], Borghi di Belisania per A. Licante, [ca. 1720]. Among the numerous later editions the following may be cited: Venezia, Tip. dell' Ancora, 1887; Milano, Bottega di Poesia, 1927; French translation ("Le Théâtre à la mode au XVIIIe siècle") Paris, Fischbacher, 1890; German translation ("Das Theater nach der Mode") München and Berlin, G. Müller, [1917].

Marchant, Annie d'Armond. "Carlos Gomes, Great Brazilian Composer," *Bulletin of the Pan American Union* LXX (1936) 767–76.

Marchesan, Angelo. Della vita e delle opere di Lorenzo Da Ponte. Treviso, Turazza, 1900.

Mariani, Renato. "L'ultimo Puccini," RassM IX (1936) 133–40.

Mariani, Valerio. "Ricordando Sabbatini e Torelli scenografi marchigiani," *Rassegna Marchigiana* XII (1934) 193–207.

Maria y Campos, Armando de. Una temporada de opera italiana en Oaxaca. Mexico, Ediciones populares, 1939.

Marix-Spire, Thérèse. "Gounod and His First Interpreter, Pauline Viardot. Part I," MQ XXXI (1945) 193–211.

Mark, Jeffrey. "Dryden and the Beginnings of Opera in England," M&L V (1924) 247–52.

—— "The Jonsonian Masque," M&L III (1922) 358–71.

Marpurg, Friedrich Wilhelm. Anleitung zur Musik überhaupt und zur Singkunst besonders. Berlin, A. Wever, 1763.

—— Historisch-kritische Beiträge zur Aufnahme der Musik. Berlin, G. A. Lange, 1754–62. 5 vols.

Marsan, Jules. La Pastorale dramatique en France à la fin du XVIe et au commencement du XVIIe siècle. Paris, Hachette, 1905.

Martens, Frederick H. "Music Mirrors of the Second Empire," MQ XVI (1930) 415–34, 563–87.

Martens, Heinrich. Das Melodram. Berlin, Vieweg, 1932. (Music.)

Martersteig, Max. Das deutsche Theater im 19. Jahrhundert. Leipzig, B&H, 1924.

Martienssen, C. A. "*Holger Danske,* Oper von Fr. L. Ae. Kunzen," ZIMG XIII (1911–12) 225–32.

Martin, Henriette. "La 'Camerata' du Comte Bardi et la musique florentine du XVIe siècle," RdM XIII (1932) 63–74, 152–61, 227–34; XIV (1933) 92–100, 141–51.

Martineau, René. Emmanuel Chabrier. Paris, Dorbon, [1910].

Marx, Adolf Bernhard. Gluck und die Oper. Berlin, O. Janke, 1863. 2 vols.

Mason, James Frederick. The Melodrama in France from the Revolution to the Beginning of Romantic Drama. Johns Hopkins Dissertation, 1911. Chapter I published: Baltimore, J. H. Furst, 1912.

Massenet, Jules. Mes Souvenirs. Paris, P. Lafitte, [1912]. Translated as: My Recollections. Boston, Small, Maynard, [1919].

Masson, Paul-Marie. "*Les Fêtes vénitiennes* de Campra," RdM XIII (1932) 127–46, 214–26.

—— "Les Idées de Rousseau sur la musique," SIM *Revue musical* VIII, No. 6 (1912), 1–17; Nos. 7–8, pp. 23–32.

—— "Lullistes et Ramistes," *L'Année musicale* I (1911) 187–211.

—— "Musique italienne et musique française," RMI XIX (1912) 519–45.

—— L'Opéra de Rameau. Paris, Laurens, 1930.

—— "Rameau and Wagner," MQ XXV (1939) 466–78.

Mathis, Alfred. "Stefan Zweig as Librettist and Richard Strauss," M&L XXV (1944) 163–76, 226–45.

Mattei, Saverio. Memorie per servire alla vita di Metastasio. Colle, A. M. Martini, 1785.

Mattfeld, Julius. A Hundred Years of Grand Opera in New York, 1825–1925; a Record of Performances. New York, The New York Public Library, 1927.

Matthes, Wilhelm. "Paul von Klenau," Blätter der Staatsoper XX (1940) 5–14.

Mattheson, [Johann]. Grundlage einer Ehrenpforte. Hamburg, In Verlegung des Verfassers, 1740. New ed., Berlin, L. Liepmannssohn, 1910.

—— Mithridat, wider den Gift einer welschen Satyre, genannt: la musica. Hamburg, Geissler, 1749.

—— Der musikalische Patriot. Hamburg, 1728.

—— Das neu-eröffnete Orchestre. Hamburg, B. Schillers Wittwe, 1713.

—— Die neueste Untersuchung der Singspiele. Hamburg, C. Herold, 1744.

—— Der vollkommene Capellmeister. Hamburg, C. Herold, 1739.

Maugars, André. "Response faite à un curieux sur le sentiment de la musique d'Italie, écrite à Rome le premier octobre 1639 . . . in deutscher Uebersetzung mitgetheilt von W. J. von Wasialewski," MfMg X (1878) 1–9, 17–23.

Maurer, Julius. Anton Schweitzer als dramatischer Komponist. Leipzig, B&H, 1912. (PIMG, 2. Folge, Heft XI.)

Maxton, Willy. Johann Theile. Tübingen Dissertation, 1927.

Mayer, Ludwig K. "Eine Vorwebersche 'Preciosa'-Musik," AfMf I (1936) 223–27.

Mayer-Reinach, Albert. "Carl Heinrich Graun als Opernkomponist," SIMG I (1899–1900) 446–529.

—— "Zur Herausgabe des Montezuma von Carl Heinrich Graun in den Denkmälern deutscher Tonkunst," MfMg XXXVII (1905) 20–31.

Mayer-Serra, Otto. Panorama de la música mexicana desde la independencia hasta la actualidad. [México], El Colegio de México, [1941].

Maylender, Michele. Storia delle accademie d'Italia. Bologna, L. Cappelli, [1926–30]. 5 vols.

Medicus, Lotte. Die Koloratur in der italienischen Oper des 19. Jahrhunderts. Zürich, Wetzikon & Rüti, 1939.

Meinardus, Ludwig. "Johann Mattheson und seine Verdienste um die deutsche Tonkunst," in Waldersee, Sammlung musikalischer Vorträge (Leipzig, B&H, 1879–98) I, 215–72.

Meissner, August Gottlieb. Bruchstücke zur Biographie J. G. Naumann's. Prag, K. Barth, 1803–1804. 2 vols.

Menantes (pseud.) *See* Hunold, Christian Friedrich.

Ménestrier, Claude François. Des Ballets anciens et modernes. Paris, R. Guignard, 1682.

Mennicke, Karl. Hasse und die Gebrüder Graun als Sinfoniker. Leipzig, B&H, 1906.

—— "Johann Adolph Hasse; eine biographische Skizze," SIMG V (1903–1904) 230–44, 469–75.

Merbach, Paul Alfred. "Briefwechsel zwischen Eduard Devrient und Julius Rietz," AfMw III (1921) 321–60.

—— "Parodien und Nachwirkungen von Webers *Freischütz*," ZfMw II (1919–20) 642–55.

—— "Das Repertoire der Hamburger Oper 1718–1750," AfMw VI (1924) 354–72.

Mercure de France. Paris. 1672–1820.

Mercure françois, Le. Paris, J. Richer, 1612–48. 25 vols.

Merlo, G. M. "L'arte di Arrigo Boito e il valore di *Nerone*," RassM VIII (1935) 126–32.

Merlo, Johann. "Zur Geschichte des Kölner Theaters im 18. und 19. Jahrhundert," *Annalen des historischen Vereins für den Niederrhein* L (1890) 145–219.

Mersenne, Marin. Harmonie universelle. Paris, S. Cramoisy, 1636–37.

Metastasio, Pietro. Dramas and Other Poems, Translated from the Italian by John Hoole. London, Otridge, 1800.

—— Lettere. Firenze, Della rosa, 1787–89. 4 vols.

—— Lettere disperse e inedite, Vol. I. Bologna, N. Zanichelli, 1883.

—— Opere. Padova, G. Foglierini, 1811–12. 17 vols.

—— *See also* Burney, *Memoirs*.

Mielsch, Rudolf. "*Dafne*, die erste deutsche Oper," *Die Musik* XIX (May, 1927) 586–91.

Mies, Paul. "Ueber die Behandlung der Frage im 17. und 18. Jahrhundert," ZfMw IV (1921–22) 286–304.

Migot, Georges. Jean-Philippe Rameau et le génie de la musique française. Paris, Delagrave, 1930.

Mila, Massimo. "Jacopo Peri," RassM VI (1933) 214–27.

—— Il melodramma di Verdi. Bari, G. Laterza, 1933.

Milizia, Francesco. Trattato completo, formale e materiale del teatro. Venezia, Pasquali, 1794.

Minor, Jakob. Christian Felix Weisse. Innsbruck, Wagner, 1880.

Miragoli, Livia. Il melodramma italiano nell' ottocento. Roma, P. Maglione & C. Strini, [1924].

Mirow, Franz. Zwischenaktsmusik und Bühnenmusik des deutschen Theaters in der klassischen Zeit. Berlin, Gesellschaft für Theatergeschichte, 1927.

Misson, Maximilien. A New Voyage to Italy. London, R. Bonwicke, 1714. 2 vols.

Mitjana y Gordón, Rafael. Histoire du développement du théâtre dramatique et musical en Espagne des origines au commencement du XIXe siècle. Uppsala, Almqvist & Wiksell, 1906.

—— "La Musique en Espagne," in Lavignac, Encyclopédie de la musique (Paris, Delagrave, 1920) Pt. I, Vol. IV, 1913–2351.

Mizler [von Kolof], Lorenz [Christoph]. Neu eröffnete musikalische Bibliothek. Leipzig, Im Verlag des Verfassers, 1739–54. 4 vols.

Moberg, Carl Allan. "Un Compositeur oublié de l'école de Lully: Jean Desfontaines," RdM X (1929) 5–9.

—— "Essais d'opéras en Suède, sous Charles XII," in Mélanges de musicologie (Paris, Droz, 1933) pp. 123–32.

Mohr, Albert Richard. Frankfurter Theaterleben im 18. Jahrhundert. Frankfurt a. M., W. Kramer, 1940.

Moller, Johannes. Cimbria literata. Havniae, G. E. Kisel, 1744. 3 vols.

Molmenti, P[ompeo] G[herardo]. La storia di Venezia nella vita privata dalle origini alla caduta della repubblica. Bergamo, Istituto italiano d'arti grafiche, 1905–1908. 3 vols.

Monaldi, Gino. "A proposito del centenario di Vincenzo Bellini," RMI IX (1902) 72–78.

—— Cantanti evirati celebri del teatro italiano. Roma, Ausonia, 1920.

—— I teatri di Roma negli ultimi tre secoli. Napoli, R. Ricciardi, 1928.

Monaldi, Guido. Vincenzo Bellini. Milan, Sonzogno, [1935].

Mone, Franz Joseph, ed. Altdeutsche Schauspiele. Quedlinburg and Leipzig, G. Basse, 1841.

—— Schauspiele des Mittelalters. Karlsruhe, C. Macklot, 1846. 2 vols.

Monnet, Jean. Mémoires. Paris, Louis-Michaud, [1884].

Monnier, Philippe. Venise au XVIIIe siècle. Paris, Perrin, 1907. Translated as: Venice in the Eighteenth Century. London, Chatto & Windus, 1910.

Monographien moderner Musiker. Leipzig, C. F. Kahnt, 1906–1909. 3 vols.

Montagu, Lady Mary [Pierrepont] Wortley. The Letters and Works of Lady Mary Wortley Montagu. London, Bickers, [1861]. 2 vols.

—— Letters to and from Pope. In Alexander Pope, Works (London, Longman, 1847) VII, 27–119.

Montagu-Nathan, Montagu. Glinka. London, Constable, 1916.

—— A History of Russian Music. London, W. Reeves, [1914]. 2d ed., 1918.

—— Moussorgsky. London, Constable, 1916.

—— Rimsky-Korsakof. London, Constable, 1916.

[Monteverdi, Claudio.] See special number of RassM II (October, 1929).

Moore, Edward C. Forty Years of Opera in Chicago. New York, H. Liveright, 1930.

Moos, Paul. Richard Wagner als Aesthetiker. Berlin and Leipzig, Schuster & Loeffler, 1906.

Mooser, Robert Aloys. Contribution à l'histoire de le musique russe; l'opéra-comique français en Russie au XVIIIe siècle. Genève, L'auteur, 1932.

Mooser, Robert Aloys (*Cont.*). "Un Musicien espagnol en Russie à la fin du XVIIIe siècle [Martin i Soler]," RMI XL (1936) 432–49.

Morgan [Sydney (Owenson)], Lady. The Life and Times of Salvator Rosa. London, 1824. 2 vols.

Morphy, G., compiler. Les Luthistes espagnoles du XVIe siècle. Leipzig, B&H, 1902. 2 vols.

Mortari, Virgilio. "L' *Oca del Cairo* di W. A. Mozart," RMI XL (1936) 477–81.

Mosel, Ignaz Franz, Edler von. Ueber das Leben und die Werke des Anton Salieri. Wien, J. B. Wallishausser, 1827.

—— Versuch einer Aesthetik des dramatischen Tonsatzes. Wien, A. Strauss, 1813. New ed., München, Lewy, 1910, with introduction and notes by Eugen Schmidt.

Moser, Hans Joachim. Christoph Willibald Gluck. Stuttgart, Cotta, 1940.

—— Geschichte der deutschen Musik. Stuttgart and Berlin, J. G. Cotta, 1920–24. 3 vols.

—— "Giuseppe Verdi," RassM XII (1939) 149–58.

—— "Kleine Beiträge zu Beethovens Liedern und Bühnenwerken," *Neues Beethoven Jahrbuch* II (1925) 43–65.

Moser, Max. Richard Wagner in der englischen Literatur des 19. Jahrhunderts. Bern, Stämpfli, 1938.

Mountford, J. F. "Greek Music in the Papyri and Inscriptions," in J. Powell and E. Barber, *New Chapters in the History of Greek Literature, Second Series* (London, Oxford University Press, 1929) pp. 146–83.

Moutoz, A. Rossini et son *Guillaume Tell*. Paris, A. Pilon, 1872.

[Mozart, Wolfgang.] Ausstellung die Zauberflöte; Mozarthaus, Katalog. Salzburg, Mozarteum, 1928.

Mozart-Jahrbuch, ed. by Abert. München, Drei Masken, 1923–29. 3 vols. (suspended 1925–28).

Müller, Erich H. "Isaak Iselins *Pariser Tagebuch* als musikgeschichtliche Quelle," ZfMw VII (1924–25) 545–52.

Müller-Blattau, Joseph. Georg Friedrich Händel. Potsdam, Athenaion, [1933].

—— "Gluck und die deutsche Dichtung," JMP XLV (1938) 30–52.

—— Hans Pfitzner. Potsdam, Athenaion, 1940.

Müller-Hartmann, Robert. "Wieland's and Gluck's Versions of the *Alkestis*," *Journal of the Warburg Institute* II (October, 1938) 176–77.

Münzer, G. Heinrich Marschner. Berlin, "Harmonie," 1901.

Muffat, Georg. Suavioris harmoniae instrumentalis hyporchematicae florilegium I. Augustae Vindelicorum, Typis Jacobi Koppmayr, 1695. Reprinted in DTOe, Vol. 2.

—— Florilegium secundum. Passovii, Typis Georgij Adam Höller, 1698. Reprinted in DTOe, Vol. 4.

Muller, Daniel. Leoš Janáček. Paris, Rieder, [1930].

Munter, Friedrich. Ludwig Thuille. München, Drei Masken, 1923.

Muratori, Lodovico Antonio. Della perfetta poesia italiana, spiegata e dimostrata con varie osservazioni. Venezia, S. Colete, 1724. Contains: Lib. III, Cap. V (Vol. II, pp. 30–45) "De' difetti, che possono osservarsi ne' moderni Drammi." Refutation of Muratori's criticisms is undertaken by Johann Mattheson in his *Neueste Untersuchung der Singspiele.*

Musatti, Cesare. "Drammi musicali di Goldoni e d' altri tratti dalle sue commedie," *Ateneo Veneto* XXI (1898) 51–60. Also separate: Venezia, Fratelli Visentini, 1898.

Musik und Bild; Festschrift Max Seiffert. Kassel, Bärenreiter, 1938.

Myers, Robert Manson. "Mrs. Delany: An Eighteenth-Century Handelian," MQ XXXII (1946) 12–36.

Nacamuli, Guido Davide. Discorso commemorativo su Antonio Smareglia. Trieste, Giuliana, 1930.

Nagel, Willibald. "Die Chöre aus *Philargyrus* von Petrus Dasypodius," MfMg XXI (1889) 109–12.

—— "Daniel Purcell," MfMg XXX (1898) 47–53.

—— "Deutsche Musiker des 18. Jahrhunderts im Verkehr mit J. Fr. A. v. Uffenbach," SIMG XIII (1911–12) 69–106.

—— "Das Leben Christoph Graupner's," SIMG X (1908–1909) 568–612.

—— "Die Musik in den schweitzerischen Dramen des 16. Jahrhunderts," MfMg XXII (1890) 67–83.

Napoli-Signorelli, Pietro. Storia critica dei teatri antichi e moderni. Napoli, V. Orsino, 1787–90. 6 vols. A later ed., 1813, 10 vols.

Narciss, Georg Adolf. Studien zu den Frauenzimmergesprächspielen Georg Philipp Harsdörfers. Leipzig, H. Eichblatt, 1928.

Nardi, Piero. Vita di Arrigo Boito. Verona, Mondadori, 1942.

Nathan, Hans. Das Rezitativ der Frühopern Richard Wagners. Berlin, Dobrin, 1934.

Navarra, Ugo. Nel tricentenario del teatro lirico 1637–1937; grande inchiesta particolare sulle condizioni odierne della scena melodrammatica. Milano, Alba, 1937.

Naylor, Bernard. "Albert Lortzing," PMA LVIII (1931–32) 1–13.

Naylor, Edward Woodall. "Music and Shakespeare," MA I (1909–10) 129–48.

—— Shakespeare and Music. London, J. M. Dent, [1931].

—— "Verdi and Wagner," PMA XX (1893) 1–10.

Nef, Karl. Zur Geschichte der deutschen Instrumentalmusik in der 2. Hälfte des 17. Jahrhunderts. Leipzig, B&H, 1902. (PIMG, Beiheft V.)

—— "Zur Instrumentation im 17. Jahrhundert," JMP XXXV (1929) 33–42.

Negri, Francesco. La vita di Apostolo Zeno. Venezia, Alvisopoli, 1816.

Neisser, Arthur. *Servio Tullio,* eine Oper aus dem Jahre 1685 von Agostino Steffani. Leipzig, C. G. Röder, 1902.

Nejedlý, Zdeněk. Frederick Smetana. London, G. Bles, [1924].

—— J. B. Foerster. V Praze, M. Urbánek, 1910.

Neretti, Luigi. L'importanza civile della nostra opera in musica. Firenze, Tipografia cooperativa, 1902.

Neri, Achille. "Gli intermezzi del Pastor fido," *Giornale storico della letteratura italiana* XI (1888) 405–15.

Nestyev, Israel. Sergei Prokofiev: His Musical Life . . . Translated by Rose Prokofieva. New York, Knopf, 1946.

Nettl, Paul. "Beitrag zur Geschichte des deutschen Singballets," ZfMw VI (1923–24) 608–20.

—— "Casanova and Music," MQ XV (1929) 212–32.

—— "An English Musician at the Court of Charles VI," MQ XXVIII (1942) 318–28.

—— "Exzerpte aus der Raudnitzer Textbüchersammlung," SzMw VII (1920) 143–44.

—— Mozart und die königliche Kunst. Berlin, Wunder, 1932.

—— "Zur Geschichte der kaiserlichen Hofkapelle von 1636–1680," SzMw XVI (1929) 70–85; XVII (1930) 95–104; XVIII (1931) 23–35; XIX (1932) 33–40.

Neues Beethoven Jahrbuch. Augsburg, B. Filser, 1924–. Articles relevant to opera will be found separately listed under the names of the following authors: Cortolezis, Engländer, Haas, Moser, Unger, Waltershausen.

Neuhaus, Max. "Antonio Draghi," SzMw I (1913) 104–92.

Neumann, Egon. Die Operetten von Johann Strauss. Vienna Dissertation, 1919.

Newman, Ernest. Gluck and the Opera. London, B. Dobell, 1895.

—— Hugo Wolf. London, Methuen, [1907].

—— The Life of Richard Wagner. New York, Knopf, 1933–46. 4 vols.

—— Richard Strauss. London and New York, J. Lane, 1908.

Newmarch, Rosa. The Music of Czechoslovakia. London, Oxford University Press, 1942.

—— "New Works in Czechoslovakia; Janáček and Novák," *The Chesterian* XII (July, 1931) 213–19.

—— The Russian Opera. New York, E. P. Dutton, [1914].

—— Tchaikovsky, His Life and Works. New York, J. Lane, 1900.

—— "Tchaikovsky's Early Lyrical Operas," ZIMG VI (1904–1905) 29–34.

Nicolai, Otto. Tagebücher. Leipzig, B&H, 1892. Edited, with biographical notes, by B. Schröder.

—— Tagebücher, soweit erhalten zum ersten Male vollständig herausgegeben von Prof. Dr. Wilhelm Altmann. Regensburg, G. Bosse, 1937.

Nicolai, Paul. Der Ariadne-Stoff in der Entwicklungsgeschichte der deutschen Oper. Viersen, J. H. Meyer, 1919.

Nicoll, Allardyce. A History of Early Eighteenth Century Drama, 1700–1750. Cambridge, The University Press, 1925.

—— A History of Restoration Drama, 1660–1700. Cambridge, The University Press, 1940. 3d ed.

—— "Italian Opera in England; the First Five Years," *Anglia* XLVI (1922) 257–81.

Niecks, Frederick. "Historical Sketch of the Overture," SIMG VII (1905–1906) 386–90.

Nietan, Hanns. Die Buffoszenen der spätvenezianischen Oper (1680 bis 1710). Halle Dissertation, 1925.

Nietzsche, Friedrich. Gesammelte Werke. München, Musarion, 1920–29. 23 vols. Contains: "Die Geburt der Tragödie," Vol. 3; "Jenseits von Gut und Böse," Vol. 15; "Der Fall Wagner," "Nietzsche contra Wagner," Vol. 17.

Niggli, Arnold. "Faustina Bordoni-Hasse," in Waldersee. *Sammlung musikalischer Vorträge* (Leipzig, B&H, 1879–98) II, 261–318.

—— "Giacomo Meyerbeer," in Waldersee, *Sammlung musikalischer Vorträge* (Leipzig, B&H, 1879–98) V, 287–324.

Nilsson, Kurt. Die Rimsky-Korssakoffsche Bearbeitung des *Boris Godunoff* von Mussorgskii als Objekt der vergleichenden Musikwissenschaft. Münster, Buschmann, 1937.

Nin [y Castellano], J[oachin]. Sept Chansons picaresques espagnoles anciennes, librement harmonisées et précédées d'une étude sur les classiques espagnols du chant. Paris, M. Eschig, 1926.

—— Septs Chants lyriques espagnols anciens, librement harmonisés et précédés d'une étude sur les classiques espagnols du chant. Paris, M. Eschig, 1926.

Noack, Friedrich. "Die Musik zu der molièreschen Komödie *Monsieur de Pourceaugnac* von Jean Baptiste de Lully," in *Festschrift für Johannes Wolf* (Berlin, Breslauer, 1929) pp. 139–47.

—— "Die Opern von Christoph Graupner in Darmstadt," in *Bericht über den I. Musikwissenschaftlichen Kongress der Deutschen Musikgesellschaft* (Leipzig, B&H, 1926) pp. 252–59.

Nodot, ——. "Le Triomphe de Lully aux Champs-Elysées," RM VI (January, 1925) 89–106. First printing of Bibliothèque de l'Arsenal ms. 6.542, pp. 260 ff.

Nohl, Ludwig. *Die Zauberflöte;* Betrachtungen über Bedeutung der dramatischen Musik in der Geschichte des menschlichen Geistes. Frankfurt a. M., Schneider, 1862.

Nolhac, Pierre, and Angelo Solerti. Il viaggio in Italia di Enrico III, re di Francia, e le feste a Venezia, Ferrara, Mantova, e Torino. Torino, L. Roux, 1890.

Nordau, Max. Entartung. Berlin, Duncker, 1893. 2 vols. Translated as: Degeneration. New York, D. Appleton, 1895.

Norman, Gertrude. A Consideration of Seicento Opera with Particular Reference to the Rise of the Neapolitan School. Columbia Dissertation (A. M.), 1937.

Nosek, Vladimir. The Spirit of Bohemia; a Survey of Czechoslovak History, Music, and Literature. London, G. Allen & Unwin, [1926].

Nouveau Théâtre italien, Le. Paris, Briasson, 1733-1753. New ed.

Noyes, Robert Gale. Ben Jonson on the English Stage, 1660-1776. Cambridge, Mass., Harvard University Press, 1935.

—— "Contemporary Musical Settings of the Songs in Restoration Dramatic Operas," *Harvard Studies and Notes in Philology and Literature* XX (1938) 99-121.

Nuitter. *See* Truinet.

Nungezer, Edwin. Dictionary of Actors and Other Persons Associated with the Public Representations of Plays in England before 1642. New Haven, Yale University Press; London, Oxford University Press, 1929.

Nuovo, Antonio. Tommaso Traetta. Bitonto, A. Amendolagine, 1938.

Odendahl, Laurenz. Friedrich Heinrich Himmel. Bonn, P. Rost, 1917.

Oesterlein, Nikolaus. Katalog einer Wagner-Bibliothek. Leipzig, B&H, 1882-95. 4 vols.

Offenbach, Jacques. Offenbach en Amérique; notes d'un musicien en voyage. Paris, Calmann Lévy, 1877.

Ohrmann, Fritz. "Max Brands Oper *Maschinist Hopkins*," *Signale für die musikalische Welt* LXXXVIII (1930) 395-99.

Olivier, Jean Jacques (pseud.) Les Comédiens français dans les cours d'Allemagne au XVIIIe siècle. Paris, Société française d'imprimerie et de libraire, 1901-1905. Series 1-4.

Ollone, Max d'. "Gounod et l'opéra-comique," RM XIV (November, 1933) 303-308.

O'Neill, Norman. "Music to Stage Plays in England," SIMG XIII (1911-12) 321-28.

Opel, Julius Otto. "Die erste Jahrzehnte der Oper in Leipzig," *Neues Archiv für sächsische Geschichte und Altertumskunde* V (1884) 116-141.

"Opera as It Is—and May Be," general title of several articles in M&L IV (1923) 85 ff.

"L'Opéra-comique au XIXe siècle," RM XIV (November, 1933) 241-312.

Opieński, Henryk. La Musique polonaise. Paris, Gebethner & Wolff, 1929.

—— "Les Premiers Opéras polonais considérés dans leur rapports avec la musique de Chopin," RdM X (1929) 92-98.

"Origen y progressos de las tonadillas que se cantan en los Coliseos de esta Corte," *Memorial literario, instructivo y curioso de la corte de Madrid* XII (1787) 169-80.

[Origny, Abraham Jean Baptiste Antoine d'.] Annales du théâtre-italien. Paris, Duchesne, 1788. 3 vols.

Orlandini, Giuseppe. "Domenico Cimarosa e la musica nella seconda civiltà latina," *Rivista bolognese* II [?] (1868) 933-47, 1005-24.

Orsini, Giovanni. Pietro Mascagni e il suo *Nerone*. Milano, A.&G. Carisch, 1935.

Ortigue, Joseph Louis d'. Le Balcon de l'opéra. Paris, Renduel, 1833.

—— De l'école musicale italienne. Paris, Au dépot central des meilleures productions de la presse, 1839. Second edition in 1840 entitled: Du théâtre-italien et son influence sur le goût musical français.

Ottzen, Curt. Telemann als Opernkomponist. Berlin, E. Ebering, 1902. 2 vols. See review by Oskar Fleischer, ZIMG III, 497.

Oven, A. H. E. von. "Das erste städtische Theater zu Frankfurt am Main," in Neujahrsblatt des Vereins für Geschichte und Altertumskunde zu Frankfurt am Main (1872).

Pagano, Luigi. "Arrigo Boito: l' artista," RMI XXXI (1924) 199–234.

—— "Dèbora e Jaéle di Ildebrando Pizzetti," RMI XXX (1923) 47–108.

[Paget, Violet.] Studies of the Eighteenth Century in Italy. London, W. Satchell, 1880. "By Vernon Lee" (pseud.).

Pahlen, Kurt. Das Rezitativ bei Mozart. Vienna Dissertation, 1929.

Paisiello, Cavalier Giovanni. "Saggio del corso dei travagli musicali del cavaliere Giovanni Paisiello," RassM III (1930) 124–35.

Palmer, John. "Gesture and Scenery in Modern Opera," MQ II (1916) 314–30.

Pannain, Guido. "Il Dottor Faust," RassM XIII (1940) 20–29.

—— "Rossini nel Guglielmo Tell," RMI XXXI (1924) 473–506.

—— "Saggio sulla musica a Napoli nel secolo XIX," RMI XXXV (1928) 198–208, 331–42; XXXVI (1929) 197–210; XXXVII (1930) 231–42; XXXVIII (1931) 193–206; XXXIX (1932) 51–72.

—— "Vincenzo Bellini," RassM VIII (1935) 1–13, 100–110, 174–88, 237–44.

Panoff, Peter. "Der nationale Stil N. A. Rimsky-Korsakows," AfMw VIII (1926) 78–117.

Pardo Pimentel, Nicolas. La opera italiana. Madrid, Aguado, 1851.

Parente, Alfredo. "Note sull' estetica musicale contemporanea in Italia," RassM III (1930) 289–310.

[Parfaict, François.] Dictionnaire des théâtres de Paris. Paris, Lambert, 1756. 7 vols.

—— Histoire de l'ancien théâtre italien depuis son origine en France, jusqu'à sa suppression en l'année 1697. Paris, Lambert, 1753.

—— Mémoires pour servir à l'histoire des spectacles de la foire. Paris, Briasson, 1743.

Paris, Luis. Museo-archivo teatral (Madrid); catálogo provisional. Madrid, Yagües, 1932.

Parisini, G. Musica e balli in Faenza nel 1745. Faenza, Lega, 1935.

Parker, D. C. "A View of Giacomo Puccini," MQ III (1917) 509–16.

Parodies du nouveau théâtre italien . . . avec les airs gravés, Les. Paris, Briasson, 1738. New ed.

Parolari, Cornelio. "Giambattista Velluti," RMI XXXIX (1932) 263–98.

Parry, Sir C[harles] Hubert H[astings]. The Music of the Seventeenth Century. London, Oxford University Press, 1938. 2d ed. (The Oxford History of Music, Vol. III.)

—— "The Significance of Monteverde," PMA XLII (1915–16) 51–67.

Pastor, Ludwig, Freiherr von. The History of the Popes, from the Close of the Middle Ages. Vols. 29, 30, 31. London, Kegan Paul, 1938–40.

Pastura, Francesco. "Due frammenti della Beatrice di Tenda di Bellini," RassM VIII (1935) 327–34.

Patterson, Frank. "Fifty Years of Opera in America," MTNA XXIII (1928) 176–85.

Paulig, Hans. Peter Cornelius und sein *Barbier von Bagdad;* ein stilkritischer Vergleich der Originalpartitur mit der Bearbeitung von Felix Mottl. Cologne Dissertation, 1923.

Pavan, Giuseppe. Contributo alla storia del teatro musicale; il dramma più musicato; l'*Artaserse* del Metastasio. Cittadella, Tip. Sociale, 1917.

Pearce, Charles E. "Polly Peachum": the Story of *Polly* and *The Beggar's Opera*. London, S. Paul, [1923].

Pearson, Hesketh. Gilbert and Sullivan; a Biography. New York, Harper, 1935.

Pedrell, Felipe. Cancionero musical popular español. Valls, E. Castells, [1918–22]. 4 vols.

—— "L'Eglogue *La Forêt sans amour* de Lope de Vega, et la musique et les musiciens du théâtre de Calderón," SIMG XI (1909–1910) 55–104.

—— "La Festa d'Elche ou le drame lyrique liturgique La Mort et l'assomption de la Vierge," SIMG II (1900–1901) 203–52.

—— Jornadas de arte (1841–1891). Paris, Ollendorf, 1911.

—— "La Musique indigène dans le théâtre espagnol du XVIIe siècle," SIMG V (1903) 46–90.

—— Orientaciones (1892–1902); continuaciò de Jornadas de arte. Paris, Ollendorf, 1911.

—— Por nuestra música; algunas observaciones sobre la magna cuestión de una escuela lírico nacional. Barcelona, Heurich, 1891.

—— Teatro lírico español anterior al siglo XIX. La Coruña, Berea, [1897–] 1898. 5 vols.

Peiser, Karl. Johann Adam Hiller. Leipzig, Gebrüder Hug, 1894.

Pelicelli, Nestore. "Musicisti in Parma dal 1800 al 1860," *Note d'archivio* XII (1935) 213–22, 317–63; XIII (1936) 180–97.

—— "Musicisti in Parma nel secolo XVIII; la musica alla corte di Parma nel 1700," *Note d'archivio* XI (1934); XII (1935) 27–42, 82–92.

Pellisson, Maurice. Les Comédies-ballets de Molière. Paris, Hachette, 1914.

Peña y Goñi, Antonio. La ópera española y la música dramática en España en el siglo XIX. Madrid, El Liberal, 1881.

Pepys, Samuel. The Diary of Samuel Pepys. London, G. Bell; New York, Harcourt, Brace, 1924–26. 8 vols.

Pereira Peixoto d'Almeida Carvalhaes, Manoel. Inês de Castro; na opera e na choregraphia italianas. Lisboa, Castro Irmão, 1908, 1915. 2 vols.

—— Marcos Portugal na sua musica dramatica. Lisboa, Castro Irmão, 1910.

Perinello, C. "L' *Amfiparnaso* di Horatio Vecchi," RMI XLI (1937) 1–23.

Perrault, Charles. Les Hommes illustres qui ont paru en France pendant ce siècle. Paris, A. Dezallier, 1696.

Perrino, Marcello. Nouvelle Methode de chant . . . précédé . . . de la vie de Benedetto Marcello . . . d'une notice sur les usages du théâtre en Italie. Paris, Ebrard, 1839. Originally published as: Osservazioni sul canto. Napoli, Stampa reale, 1810.

Peterson-Berger, Olof Wilhelm. "The Life Problem in Wagner's Dramas," MQ II (1916) 658–68.

—— Peterson-Berger recensioner; glimtar och skuggor ur Stockholms musik värld 1896–1923. Stockholm, Ahlén & Åkerlund, 1923.

—— Richard Wagner als Kulturerscheinung. Leipzig, B&H, 1917. Review by R. Hohenemser ZfMw I, 683–84.

—— "The Wagnerian Culture Synthesis," MQ VII (1921) 45–56.

Petzet, Walter. "Maschinist Hopkins," Signale für die musikalische Welt LXXXVII (1929) 1363–65.

Peyser, Herbert F. "Some Fallacies of Modern Anti-Wagnerism," MQ XII (1926) 175–89.

—— "Tristan, First-Hand," MQ XI (1925) 418–36.

Pfitzner, Hans Erich. Gesammelte Schriften. Augsburg, B. Filser, 1926. 3 vols.

—— Vom musikalischen Drama; gesammelte Aufsätze. München and Leipzig, Süddeutsche Monatshefte, 1915.

Pfordten, Hermann, Freiherr von der. Carl Maria von Weber. Leipzig, Quelle & Meyer, [1918].

Phalèse. See Hortus musarum.

Piccioli, Giuseppe. Composizioni di antichi autori bolognesi. Bologna, Bongiovanni, 1933.

Pierre, Constant. Les Hymnes et chansons de la révolution; aperçu général et catalogue avec notes historiques, analytiques et bibliographiques. Paris, Imprimerie nationale, 1904.

Pincherle, Marc. "Antonio Vivaldi; essai biographique," RdM XI (1930) 161–70, 265–81.

Pinetti, Gian Battista. Teatro Donizetti (già Riccardi); la stagione d'opera alla fiera d'agosto; cronistoria illustrata dal 1784 al 1936. Bergamo, Sesa, 1937.

Piovano, Francesco. "A propos d'une recente biographie de Léonard Leo," SIMG VIII (1906–1907) 70–95, 336.

—— "Baldassare Galuppi; note bio-bibliografiche," RMI XIII (1906) 676–726; XIV (1907) 333–65; XV (1908) 233–74.

—— "Elenco cronologico delle opere (1757–1802) di Pietro Guglielmi," RMI XII (1905) 407–46.

—— "Notizie storico-bibliografiche sulle opere di Pietro Guglielmi (Guglielmini) con appendice su Pietro Guglielmi," RMI XVI (1909) 243–70, 475–505, 785–820; XVII (1910) 59–90, 376–414, 554–89, 822–77. This is about the son, Pietro Carlo Guglielmi, 1763–1817.

—— "Un Opéra inconnu de Gluck," SIMG IX (1907–1908) 231–81, 448.

Pirker, Max. Die Zauberflöte. Wien, Wiener literarischer Anstalt, 1920.

Pirro, André. Descartes et la musique. Paris, Fischbacher, 1907.

—— Schütz. Paris, F. Alcan, 1913.

Pisk, Paul A. "Lazare Saminsky," The Chesterian XX (1938–39) 74–78.

—— "Schönberg's Twelve-Tone Opera," MMus VII, No. 3 (April–May, 1930) 18–21.

Pistorelli, L. "Due melodrammi inediti di Apostolo Zeno," RMI III (1896) 261–74.

—— "I melodrammi giocosi del Casti," RMI II (1895) 36–56, 449–72; IV (1897) 631–71.

Piton, Alexis. "Les Origines du mélodrame français à la fin du XVIIIe siècle," Revue d'histoire littéraire (1911) pp. 256–96.

Pizzetti, Ildebrando. "Ariadne et Barbebleue . . . de Paul Dukas," RMI XV (1908) 73–112.

—— "L'arte di Verdi: spiriti e forme," RassM X (1937) 201–206.

—— "Il Faust della leggenda, del poema e del dramma musicale," RMI XIII (1906) 1–49.

—— "Pelléas et Mélisande . . . Debussy," RMI XV (1908) 350–63.

—— ed. Vincenzo Bellini. Milan, Fratelli Treves, [1936].

Planelli, Antonio. Dell' opera in musica. Napoli, D. Campo, 1772.

Plümicke, Carl Martin. Entwurf einer Theatergeschichte von Berlin. Berlin and Stettin, F. Nicolai, 1781.

Pohl, Karl Ferdinand. Joseph Haydn. Leipzig, B&H, 1878–1927. 3 vols. in 2.

Pohl, Richard. "Richard Wagner," in Waldersee, Sammlung musikalischer Vorträge (Leipzig, B&H, 1879–98) V, 121–98.

Poladian, Sirvart. Handel as an Opera Composer. Cornell Dissertation, 1946.

Policastro, Guglielmo. Vincenzo Bellini. Catania, Studio editoriale moderno, 1935.

Poliziano, Angelo Ambrogini, known as. Le stanze, l'Orfeo e le rime. Firenze, G. Barbèra, 1863.

—— Orfeo. See Casella, Alfred.

Polko, Elise. Die Bettler-Oper. Hannover, Rümpler, 1863. 3 vols.

Pollatschek, Walter. Hofmannsthal und die Bühne. Frankfurt Dissertation, 1924.

Pompeati, Arturo. "Il Parini e la musica," RMI XXXVI (1929) 556–74.

Pompei, Edoardo. Pietro Mascagni. Roma, Editrice nazionale, 1912.

Ponz de Leon, Giuseppe. "Il dramma lirico nell' arte di Pizzetti," RMI XLIII (1939) 539–44.

Potter, John. The Theatrical Review; or, New Companion to the Playhouse; Containing a Critical and Historical Account of Every Tragedy, Comedy, Opera, Farce &c Exhibited at the Theatres during the Last Season. London, S. Crowder, 1772. 2 vols.

Pougin, Arthur. Adolphe Adam. Paris, G. Charpentier, 1877.

—— Auber; ses commencements, les origines de sa carrière. Paris, Pottier de Lalaine, 1873.

—— "Bernardo Mengozzi," RMI XXV (1918) 176–201, 323–44.

—— Boieldieu. Paris, Charpentier, 1875.

—— "Les Dernières Années de Spontini," RMI XXIX (1922) 54–80, 236–63.

—— Un Directeur d'opéra au dix-huitième siècle; l'opéra sous l'ancien régime; l'opéra sous la révolution. Paris, Fischbacher, 1914.

—— F. Halévy, écrivain. Paris, A. Clauden, 1865.

—— "Gounod écrivain," RMI XVII (1910) 590–627; XVIII (1911) 747–68; XIX (1912) 239–85, 637–95; XX (1913) 453–86, 792–820.

—— Herold. Paris, H. Laurens, [1906].

—— Jean-Jacques Rousseau musicien. Paris, Fischbacher, 1901.

—— Madame Favart, étude théâtrale, 1727–1772. Paris, Fischbacher, 1912.

—— "Massenet," RMI XIX (1912) 916–85.

—— Méhul. Paris, Fischbacher, 1893. 2d ed.

—— Molière et l'opéra-comique. Paris, J. Baur, 1882.

—— Monsigny et son temps. Paris, Fischbacher, 1908.

—— Musiciens français du XVIIIe siècle; Dezèdes. Paris, N. Chaix, 1862.

—— "Notice sur Méhul par Cherubini," RMI XVI (1909) 750–71.

—— L'Opéra-comique pendant la révolution de 1788 à 1801. Paris, A. Savine, 1891.

—— "L'Orchestre de Lully," Le Ménestrel LXII (1896) 44–45, 59–60, 67–68, 76, 83–84, 91–92, 99–100.

—— "Les Origines de l'opéra français: Cambert et Lully," Revue d'art dramatique Année 6, tome XXI (1891) 129–55.

—— "La Première Salle Favart et l'opéra-comique 1801–1838," Le Ménestrel LX (1894) and LXI (1895), passim.

—— Les Vrais Créateurs de l'opéra français, Perrin et Cambert. Paris, Charvay, 1881.

—— William-Vincent Wallace. Paris, A. Ikelmer, 1866.

Pound, Ezra Loomis. Antheil and the Treatise of Harmony. Chicago, P. Covici, 1927.

Preibisch, Walter. "Quellenstudien zu Mozart's Entführung aus dem Serail; ein Beitrag zur Geschichte der Türkenoper," SIMG X (1908–1909) 430–76.

Prendergast, Arthur H. "The Masque of the Seventeenth Century," PMA XXIII (1897) 113–31.

Pretzsch, Paul. Die Kunst Siegfried Wagners. Leipzig, B&H, 1919.

Previtali, F. "Turandot [Busoni]," RassM XIII (1940) 38–46.

Pribram, Alfred Francis. Materialen zur Geschichte der Preise und Löhne in Oesterreich. Bd. I. Wien, C. Ueberreuter, 1938.

Prochazka, R. Mozart in Prag. Prag, G. Neugebauer, 1899.

Prod'homme, Jacques Gabriel. "Austro-German Musicians in France in the Eighteenth Century," MQ XV (1929) 171–95.

—— "Chabrier in His Letters," MQ XXI (1935) 451–65.

—— "Les Dernières Représentations du Devin du village (mai–juin 1829)," RM VII (August, 1926) 118–25.

—— "Les Deux Benvenuto Cellini de Berlioz," SIMG XIV (1912–13) 449–60.

—— "Deux Collaborateurs italiens de Gluck: Raniero de Calzabigi e Giuseppe D'Affligio," RMI XXIII (1916) 33–65, 201–18.

—— "The Economic Status of Musicians in France until the French Revolution," MQ XVI (1930) 83–100.

Prod'homme, Jacques Gabriel (*Cont.*). "A French Maecenas of the Time of Louis XV: M. de la Pouplinière," MQ X (1924) 511–31.

—— "Gluck's French Collaborators," MQ III (1917) 249–71.

—— Gounod. Paris, Delagrave, [1911]. 2 vols.

—— "*Léonore ou l'amour conjugal*, de Bouilly et Gaveaux," SIMG VII (1905–1906) 636–39.

—— "Lettres de G. Verdi à Léon Escudier," *Bulletin de la Société union musicologique* V (1925) 7–28.

—— "Lettres de Gluck et à propos de Gluck (1776–1787)," ZIMG XIII (1911–12) 257–65.

—— "Lettres inédites de G. Verdi à Léon Escudier," RMI XXXV (1928) 1–28, 171–97, 519–52.

—— "Marie Fel (1713–1794)," SIMG IV (1902–1903) 485–518.

—— "Miscellaneous Letters by Charles Gounod," MQ IV (1918) 630–53.

—— "A Musical Map of Paris," MQ XVIII (1932) 608–27.

—— "La Musique à Paris de 1753 à 1757, d'après un manuscrit de la Bibliothèque de Munich," SIMG VI (1904–1905) 568–87.

—— "Notes sur deux librettistes français de Gluck: du Roullet et Moline (d'après des documents inédits)," ZIMG VII (1905–1906) 12–15.

—— L'Opéra (1669–1925). Paris, Delagrave, 1925.

—— "*Le Page inconstant;* ballet anacréontique . . . sur la musique de Mozart," RdM XVI (1935) 205–12.

—— "A Pastel by La Tour: Marie Fel," MQ IX (1923) 482–507.

—— "Pierre Corneille et l'opéra français," ZIMG VII (1905–1906) 416–21.

—— "Pierre de Jélyotte (1713–1797)," SIMG III (1901–1902) 686–717.

—— "The Recent Fiftieth Anniversary of the 'New Opera'," MQ XII (1926) 13–21.

—— "Rosalie Levasseur, Ambassadress of Opera," MQ II (1916) 210–43.

—— "Rossini and His Works in France," MQ XVII (1931) 110–37.

—— "Spontini et Ch. Gounod," ZIMG XI (1909–10) 325–28.

—— "Two Hundred and Fifty Years of the Opéra (1669–1919)," MQ V (1919) 513–37.

—— "Unpublished Letters from Verdi to Camille du Locle," MQ VII (1921) 73–103.

—— "Wagner and the Paris Opéra: Unpublished Letters (February–March, 1861)," MQ I (1915) 216–31.

—— "Wagner, Berlioz and Monsieur Scribe; Two Collaborations That Miscarried," MQ XII (1926) 359–75.

—— "The Works of Weber in France (1824–1926)," MQ XIV (1928) 366–86.

Prokofiev, Sergei. "The War Years," MQ XXX (1944) 421–27.

"Prospetto cronologico delle opere di Gaetano Donizetti," RMI IV (1897) 736–43.

Prota-Giurleo, Ulisse. Alessandro Scarlatti, "il Palermitano" (la patria & la famiglia). Napoli, L'autore, 1926.

—— La grande orchestra del Teatro S. Carlo nel settecento (da documenti inediti). Napoli, L'autore, 1927.

—— Musicanti napoletani alla corte di Portogallo nel 700. Napoli, Elzevira, 1925.

—— Nicola Logroscino, "il dio dell' opera buffa." Napoli, L'autore, 1927.

Provenzal, Dino. La vita e le opere di Lodovico Adimari. Rocca S. Casciano, L. Cappelli, 1902.

Prunières, Henry. "L'Académie royale de musique et de danse," RM VI (January, 1925) 3–25.

—— Le Ballet de cour en France avant Benserade et Lully. Paris, H. Laurens, 1914.

—— Cavalli et l'opéra vénitien au XVIIe siècle. Paris, Rieder, [1931].

—— Claudio Monteverdi. Paris, F. Alcan, 1924.

—— "Défense et illustration de l'Opéra-comique," RM XIV (November, 1933) 243–47.

—— "De l'interpretation des agréments du chant aux XVIIe et XVIIIe siècles," RM XIII (May, 1932) 329–44.

—— "The Departure from Opera," MMus III, No. 2 (January–February, 1926) 3–9.

—— "Honegger's Judith," MMus III, No. 4 (May–June, 1926) 30–33.

—— "Jean de Cambefort," Année musicale II (1912) 205–26.

—— "La Jeunesse de Lully (1632–62)," MM V (1909) 234–42, 329–53.

—— "Lecerf de la Viéville et l'esthétique musicale classique au XVIIe siècle," MM IV (1908) 619–54.

—— "Lettres et autographes de Lully," MM VIII (1912) 19–20.

—— "I libretti dell' opera veneziana nel secolo XVII," RassM III (1930) 441–48.

—— Lully. Paris, H. Laurens, 1909.

—— "Lully and the Académie de Musique et de Danse," MQ XI (1925) 528–46.

—— "Lully, fils de meunier," MM VIII (1912) 57–61.

—— "Monteverdi's Venetian Operas," MQ X (1924) 178–92.

—— "Les Musiciens du Cardinal Antonio Barberini," in Mélanges de musicologie (Paris, Droz, 1933) pp. 117–22.

—— "Notes sur la vie de Luigi Rossi (1598–1653)," SIMG XII (1910–11) 12–16.

—— "Notes sur les origines de l'ouverture française," SIMG XII (1910–11) 565–85.

—— "Notes sur une partition faussement attribuée à Cavalli: L'Eritrea (1686)," RMI XXVII (1920) 267–73.

—— L'Opéra italien en France avant Lulli. Paris, E. Champion, 1913. Review by R. Rolland, MM X, No. 5 (1914) 6–15.

—— "Les Premières Ballets de Lully," RM XII (June, 1931) 1–17.

—— "Recherches sur les années de jeunesse de J. B. Lully," RMI XVII (1910) 646–54.

Prunières, Henry (*Cont.*). "Les Représentations du *Palazzo d'Atlante* à Rome (1642) d'après des documents inédits," SIMG XIV (1912–13) 218–26.

—— "Ronsard et les fêtes de cour," RM V (May, 1924) 27–44.

—— "Stendhal and Rossini," MQ VII (1921) 133–55.

—— La Vie et l'œuvre de Claudio Monteverdi. Paris, Librairie de France, 1926. 2d ed., 1931. Translated as: Monteverdi; His Life and Works. London, J. M. Dent, 1926.

—— La Vie illustre et libertine de Jean-Baptiste Lully. Paris, Plon-Nourrit, [1929].

Puccini, Giacomo Epistolario. Milano, A. Mondadori, 1928. Translated as: Letters of Giacomo Puccini. Philadelphia and London, J. B. Lippincott, 1931.

Pültz, Wilhelm. Die Geburt der deutschen Oper; Roman um Carl Maria v. Weber. Leipzig, v. Hase & Koehler, [1939].

Pulver, Jeffrey. "The Intermezzi of the Opera," PMA XLIII (1916–17) 134–63.

Pupino-Carbonelli, Giuseppe. Paisiello. Napoli, Tocco, 1908.

Pure, Michel de. Idée des spectacles anciens et nouveaux. Paris, M. Brunet, 1668.

Puttman, Max. "Zur Geschichte der deutschen komischen Oper von ihren Anfängen bis Dittersdorf," *Die Musik* III (1903–1904) Qt. 4, 334–49, 416–28.

Quadrio, Francesco Saverio, abate. Della storia e della ragione d'ogni poesia. Bologna, F. Pisarri, 1739–49. 4 vols.

Quantz, Johann Joachim. Versuch einer Anweisung die Flöte traversiere zu spielen. Leipzig, C. F. Kahnt, 1906. Originally published Berlin, J. F. Voss, 1752.

Quinault, Philippe. Théâtre. Paris, Compagnie des Libraires, 1739. 5 vols.

Quittard, Henri. "Les Années de jeunesse de J. P. Rameau," RHCM II (1902) 61–63, 100–14, 152–70, 208–18.

—— "*Le Bucheron,* opéra comique de Philidor," RHCM VII (1907) 421–24.

—— "*Ernelinde,* de Philidor," RHCM VII (1907) 469–74.

—— "L' *Hortus musarum* de 1552–53 et les arrangements de pièces polyphoniques pour voix seule et luth," SIMG VIII (1906–1907) 254–85.

—— "L'Orchestre de l' *Orfeo,*" RHCM VII (1907) 380–89, 412–18.

—— "La Première Comédie française en musique," *Bulletin français de la SIM.* IV (1908) 378–96, 497–537.

—— "*Le Sorcier,* opéra comique de Philidor," RHCM VII (1907) 537–41.

—— "Le Théorbe comme instrument d'accompagnement," *Bulletin français de la SIM.* (1910) 221–37, 362–84.

Raab, Leopold. Wenzel Müller. Boden bei Wien, Verein der N.-Oe. Landesfreunde in Boden, 1928.

Raabe, Peter. Kulturwille im deutschen Musikleben. Regensburg, G. Bosse, [1936].

—— Die Musik im dritten Reich. Regensburg, G. Bosse, [1935].

Rabany, Charles. Carlo Goldoni; le théâtre et la vie en Italie au XVIIIe siècle. Paris, Berger-Levrault, 1896.

Rabich, Franz. Richard Wagner und die Zeit. Langensalza, Beyer, 1925.

Raccolta di melodrammi giocosi scritti nel secolo XVIII. Milano, Soc. tip. dei classici italiani, 1826.

Raccolta di melodrammi serj scritti nel secolo XVIII. Milano, Soc. tip. dei classici italiani, 1822. 2 vols.

Radet, Edmond. Lully, homme d'affaires, propriétaire et musicien. Paris, L. Allison, [1891].

Radiciotti, Giuseppe. "L'arte di G. B. Pergolesi," RMI XVII (1910) 916–25.

—— "Due lettere inedite di G. Rossini e la sua definitiva partenza da Bologna," RMI XXXII (1925) 206–12.

—— "La famosa lettera al Cicognara non fu scritta dal Rossini," RMI XXX (1923) 401–407.

—— Gioacchino Rossini. Tivoli, A. Chicca, 1927. 3 vols.

—— Pergolesi. Milano, Fratelli Treves, [1935].

—— "Primi anni e studi di Gioacchino Rossini," RMI XXIV (1917) 145–72, 418–48.

—— "Il Signor Bruschino ed il Tancredi di G. Rossini," RMI XXVII (1920) 231–66.

Raeli, V. "The Bi-Centenary of Tommaso Traetta," The Chesterian VIII (1926–27) 217–23.

—— "Tommaso Traetta," Rivista nazionale di musica (March, 1927).

Raff, Joachim. Die Wagnerfrage. Braunschweig, Vieweg, 1854.

[Raguenet, François.] Défense du parallèle des Italiens et des François en ce qui regarde la musique et l'opéra. Paris, C. Barben, 1705.

—— Paralele des Italiens et des François en ce qui regarde la musique et les opéras. Paris, J. Moreau, 1602 [i.e. 1702]. Translated as: A Comparison between the French and Italian Musick and Opera's . . . to Which Is Added a Critical Discourse upon Opera's in England. London, W. Lewis, 1709. German translation with notes in Mattheson's Critica Musica (Hamburg, 1722).

Raimund, Ferdinand. Die Gesänge der Märchendramen in den urspringlichen Vertonungen. Wien, A. Schrall, 1924. (Vol. VI of his collected works.)

Rau, Carl August. Loreto Vittori. München, Verlag für moderne Musik, [1916].

Rauber, A. Die Don Juan Sage im Lichte biologischer Forschung. Leipzig, Georgi, 1898.

Rauh, Adam. Heinrich Dorn als Opernkomponist. Neustadt a. d. Aisch, Schmidt, 1939.

Raupp, Wilhelm. Eugen d'Albert. Leipzig, Koehler & Amelang, [1930].

—— Max von Schillings. Hamburg, Hanseatische Verlagsanstalt, [1935].

[Ravel, Maurice.] See the two special issues of RM: April, 1925; December, 1938.

Rayner, Robert Macey. Wagner and *Die Meistersinger*. London, Oxford University Press, 1940.

Rebois, Henri. La Renaissance de Bayreuth de Richard Wagner à son fils Siegfried. Paris, Fischbacher, 1933. Contains "Lettres de Siegfried Wagner."

Redlich, Hans F. "Egon Wellesz," MQ XXVI (1940) 65–75.

—— "Monteverdi-Renaissance," *Atlantis* VIII (1936) 768.

—— "Notationsprobleme in Cl. Monteverdis *Incoronazione di Poppea*," *Acta musicologica* X (1938) 129–32.

—— "*L'oca del Cairo*," *Music Review* II (1941) 122–31.

—— "Sull' edizione moderna delle opere di Claudio Monteverdi," RassM VIII (1935) 23–41.

—— "Zur Bearbeitung von Monteverdis *Orfeo*," *Schweizerische Musikzeitung* LXXVI (1936) 37–42, 74–80.

Reese, Gustave. Music in the Middle Ages. New York, W. W. Norton, [1940].

Refardt, Edgar. "Die Musik der Basler Volksschauspiele des 16. Jahrhunderts," AfMw III (1921) 199.

Regli, Francesco. Dizionario biografico dei più celebri poeti ed artisti melodrammatici . . . in Italia dal 1800 al 1860. Torino, E. Dalmazzo, 1860.

Reiber, Kurt. Volk und Oper; das Volkstümliche in der deutschen romantischen Oper. Würzburg, Triltsch, 1942.

Reich, Willi. Alban Berg. Vienna, H. Reichner, [1937].

—— "Alban Berg's *Lulu*," MQ XXII (1936) 383–401.

—— A Guide to Alban Berg's *Wozzek*. [New York, League of Composers, 1931.]

—— "*Lulu*—the Text and Music," MMus XII, No. 3 (March–April, 1935) 103–11.

—— "Paul Hindemith," MQ XVII (1931) 486–96.

Reicha, Antoine. Art du compositeur dramatique. Paris, A. Farrenc, 1832. 2 vols.

Reichardt, Johann Friedrich. Ueber die deutsche comische Oper. Hamburg, C. E. Bohn, 1774.

Reichel, Eugen. "Gottsched und Johann Adolph Scheibe," SIMG II (1900–1901) 654–68.

Reiff, A. "Die Anfänge der Oper in Spanien, mit Textproben," *Spanien, Zeitschrift für Auslandskunde* Jahrgang I, Heft 3 (1919).

—— "Ein Katalog zu den Werken von Felipe Pedrell," AfMw III (1921) 86–97.

Reimers, Dagmar. Geschichte des Rigaer deutschen Theaters von 1782–1822. Posen, A. Meyer, 1942.

Reina, Calcedonio. Il cigno catanese: Bellini. Catania, "Etna," 1935.

Reinach, Théodore. La Musique grècque. Paris, Payot, 1926.

Reipschläger, Erich. Schubaur, Danzi und Poissl als Opernkomponisten. Berlin-Mariendorf, H. Wegner, 1911.

Rellstab, Ludwig. "Die Gestaltung der Oper seit Mozart," *Die Wissenschaft im 19. Jahrhundert* II (1856) 361.

[Rémond de Saintmard, Toussaint.] Reflexions sur l'opéra. La Haye, J. Neaulme, 1741.

Rendell, E. D. "Some Notes on Purcell's Dramatic Music, with Especial Reference to the *Fairy Queen*," M&L I (1920) 135–44.

Reuter, Fritz. "Die Entwicklung der Leipziger, insbesondere italienischen Oper bis zum siebenjährigen Krieg," ZfMw V (1922–23) 1–16.

—— Die Geschichte der deutschen Oper in Leipzig am Ende des 17. und am Anfang des 18. Jahrhunderts (1693–1720). Leipzig Dissertation, 1923.

"Revue der Revueen: zum 200. Geburtstag von Chr. W. Gluck," *Die Musik* XIII (1913–14) Qt. 4, 223–27, 276–78.

Revue Wagnérienne. Paris, 1885–88.

Reyer, i.e., Louis Etienne Ernest Rey. Notes de musique. Paris, Charpentier, 1875. 2d ed.

—— Quarante Ans de musique. Paris, Calmann Lévy, [1909].

Reyher, Paul. Les Masques anglais. Paris, Hachette, 1909.

Ricca, Vincenzo. Il centenario della *Norma;* Vincenzo Bellini. Catania, N. Gianotta, 1932.

Ricci, Corrado. Vita barocca. Milano, L. F. Cogliati, 1904.

Ricci, Vittorio. "Un melodramma ignoto della prima metà del '600: *Celio di Baccio Baglioni e di Niccolò Sapiti*," RMI XXXII (1925) 51–79.

Riccoboni, Luigi. Reflexions historiques et critiques sur les differens théâtres de l'Europe. Paris, J. Guérin, 1738.

Richard, Pierre. "Stradella et les Contarini; épisode des moeurs vénitiennes au XVIIe siècle," *Le Ménestrel* XXXII (1864–65), XXXIII (1865–66). *passim*.

Richebourg, Louisette. Contribution à l'histoire de la "Querelle des Bouffons." Paris, Nizet, 1937.

Richter, Carl Ludwig. Zdenko Fibich. Prag, F. A. Urbánek, 1900.

Riedel, Emil. Schuldrama und Theater. Hamburg, L. Voss, 1885.

Riedinger, Lothar. "Karl von Dittersdorf als Opernkomponist," SzMw II (1914) 212–349.

Rieger, Erwin. Offenbach und seine Wiener Schule. Wien, Wiener literarischer Anstalt, 1920.

Riehl, Wilhelm Heinrich. Musikalische Charakterköpfe. Stuttgart, Cotta, 1899. 2 vols.
Contains essays on Spontini, W. Müller, K. Kreutzer, Lortzing, and other opera composers of the early nineteenth century.

—— Zur Geschichte der romantischen Oper. Berlin, Weltgeist-Bücher, [1928].

Riemann, Hugo. "*Basso ostinato* und *Basso* quasi *ostinato;* eine Anregung," in *Festschrift Liliencron* (Leipzig, B&H, 1910) pp. 193–202.

Riesemann, Oskar von. Monographien zur russischen Musik. München, Drei Masken, 1923–26. 2 vols. Vol. II, Modest Petrowitsch Mussorgski, translated as: Moussorgsky. New York, Tudor, 1935.

Riesenfeld, Paul. "Die Romantik der neuen Sachlichkeit," *Signale für die musikalische Welt* LXXXVII (1929) 1075–78.

Riess, Otto. "Johann Abraham Peter Schulz' Leben," SIMG XV (1913–14) 169–270.

Rietzler, W. Hans Pfitzner und die deutsche Bühne. München, Piper, 1917.

Rimsky-Korsakov, Nikolai. My Musical Life. New York, Knopf, 1923. Translated from the revised second Russian edition.

Rinaldi, Mario. Antonio Vivaldi. Milano, Istituto d'alta cultura, [1943].

—— Musica e verismo. Roma, Fratelli de Santis, [1932].

—— "Valori drammatici e musicali del *Simon Boccanegra* di Verdi," RassM VIII (1935) 42–53.

Rinuccini, Giovanni Battista. Sulla musica e sulla poesia melodrammatica italiana del secolo XIX. Lucca, L. Guidotti, 1843.

Ritscher, Hugo. Die musikalische Deklamation in Lully's Opernrezitativen. Berlin Dissertation, 1925.

Ritter, A. G. "Die musikalischen Chöre des Chr. Th. Walliser zur Tragödie *Andromeda*," MfMg I (1869) 134–41.

Ritter, Frédéric Louis. Music in America. New York, Scribner, 1883.

Rivalta, Camillo. Giuseppe Sarti. Faenza, F. Lega, 1928.

Robert, Paul-Louis. "Correspondance de Boieldieu," RMI XIX (1912) 75–107; XXII (1915) 520–59.

Roberti, Giuseppe. "La musica in Italia nel secolo XVIII secondo le impressioni di viaggiatori stranieri," RMI VII (1900) 698–729; VIII (1901) 519–59.

Robinson, Percy. Handel and His Orbit. London, Sheratt & Hughes, 1908.

—— "Handel up to 1720: a New Chronology," M&L XX (1939) 55–63.

Rockstro, William Smyth. The Life of George Frederick Handel. London, Macmillan, 1883.

Roethe, Gustav. "Zum dramatischen Aufbau der Wagnerschen *Meistersinger*," *Akademie der Wissenschaften, Berlin; Sitzungsberichte* (Jahrgang 1919) pp. 673–708.

Röttger, Heinz. Das Formproblem bei Richard Strauss. Berlin, Junker & Dünnhaupt, 1937.

Rogers, Francis. "Adolphe Nourrit," MQ XXV (1939) 11–25.

—— "America's First Grand Opera Season," MQ I (1915) 93–101.

—— "Handel and Five Prima Donnas," MQ XXIX (1943) 214–24.

—— "Henriette Sontag in New York," MQ XXVIII (1942) 100–104.

—— "The Male Soprano," MQ V (1919) 413–25.

—— "Sophie Arnould (1740–1803)," MQ VI (1920) 57–61.

—— "Victor Maurel," MQ XII (1926) 580–601.

Rogge, Hendrik Cornelis. "De opera te Amsterdam," *Oud Holland* V (1887) 177, 241–62.

—— "De opvoeringen van Mozarts *Don Juan* in Nederland," *Tijdschrift der Vereeniging voor Nord-Nederlands Muziekgeschiedenis* II (1887) 237–77.

Rognoni, Luigi. Un' opera incompiuta di Mozart: *L' oca del Cairo;* a proposito di una ricostruzione. Milano, Bocca, 1937.

Rokseth, Yvonne. "Antonia Bembo, Composer to Louis XIV," MQ XXIII (1937) 147–67.

Rolandi, Ulderico. *"Il Ciclope:* dramma harmonica con musica di D. Lorenzo Ratti (Roma: 1628)," *Note d'archivio* X (1933) 253–60.

—— "Didascalie sceniche in un libretto dell' *Euridice* del Rinuccini (1600)," RMI XXXIII (1926) 21–27.

—— Il librettista del *Matrimonio segreto:* Giovanni Bertati. Trieste, C. Reali, 1926.

—— Quattro poeti ed un compositore alle prese . . . per un libretto d'opera (*Il bravo* di S. Mercadante). Roma, A. Marchesi, 1931.

Roland-Manuel. *See* Manuel, Roland.

Rolland, Romain. "L'Autobiographie d'un illustre oublié: Telemann," in *Voyage musical au pays du passé* (Paris, Eduard-Joseph, 1919).

—— "Le Dernier Opéra de Gluck: *Echo et Narcisse* (1779)," RHCM III (1903) 212–15.

—— *"L'Etranger* de Vincent d'Indy," RMI XI (1904) 129–39.

—— "Gluck, une révolution dramatique," *Revue de Paris* (1904) No. 3, pp. 736–72.

—— Haendel. Paris, F. Alcan, 1910. Translated as: Handel. London, K. Paul, 1916.

—— "Les Maîtres de l'opéra; recueil de musique inédite du XVIIe et du XVIIIe siècle," RHCM III (1903) 40–41, 178–79.

—— "Métastase, précurseur de Gluck," MM VIII, No. 4 (1912) 1–10.

—— Musiciens d'aujourd'hui. Paris, Hachette, 1912. 5th ed. Translated as: Musicians of Today. New York, Holt, 1915. 2d ed.

—— Musiciens d'autrefois. Paris, Hachette, 1924. 9th ed. Translated as: Some Musicians of Former Days. London, K. Paul, 1915.
Contains essays on Gluck, Grétry, Mozart, Lully, L. Rossi, and the beginnings of opera.

—— "Notes sur l' *Orfeo* de Luigi Rossi et sur les musiciens italiens à Paris, sous Mazarin," RHCM I (1901) 225–36, 363–72.

—— "L'Opéra populaire à Venise; Francesco Cavalli," MM II, No. 1 (1906) 61–70, 151–60.

—— "Les Origines de l'opéra et les travaux de M. Angelo Solerti," RHCM III (1903) 127–29, 280–82.

—— Les Origines du théâtre lyrique moderne; histoire de l'opéra en Europe avant Lully et Scarlatti. Paris, E. Thorin, 1895. New ed. Paris, E. de Boccard, 1931.

—— "La Première Représentation du *Sant Alessio* de Stefano Landi en 1632, à Rome, d'après le journal manuscrit de Jean Jacques Bouchard," RHCM II (1902) 29–36, 74–75.

Rolland, Romain (*Cont.*). "La Représentation d' *Orféo* à Paris et l'opposition religieuse et politique à l'opéra," RHCM I (1901) 10–17.

Roncaglia, Gino. L'ascensione creatrice di Giuseppe Verdi. Firenze, G. C. Sansoni, 1940.

—— Le composizioni di Alessandro Stradella esistenti presso la R. Biblioteca Estense di Modena. Milano, Bocca, 1942.

—— Il melodioso settecento italiano. Milano, Hoepli, 1935. Contains examples of music by Galuppi, Paisiello, Cimarosa, A. M. Bononcini, and T. Giordani.

—— La rivoluzione musicale italiana (secolo XVII). Milano, G. Bolla, 1928.

Ronga, Luigi. "Scarlatti fra due epoche," *Musicista* VII (1940) 57–61.

Roosevelt, Blanche. *See* Macchetta.

Rosa, Salvator. "La musica," in Mattheson, *Mithridat* (Hamburg, Geissler, 1749) pp. i–lvi, with German translation.

Roscoe, P. C. "Arne and *The Guardian Outwitted*," M&L XXIV (1943) 237–45.

Rosenfeld, Ernst. Johann Baptist Schenk als Opernkomponist. Vienna Dissertation, 1921.

Rosenfeld, Paul. Discoveries of a Music Critic. New York, Harcourt, Brace, [1936].

Rosenthal, Karl. "Ueber Volksformen bei Mozart; ein Beitrag zur Entwicklung der Vokalformen von 1760 bis 1790," SzMw XIV (1927) 5–32.

Rosenzweig, Alfred. Zur Entwicklungsgeschichte des Strauss'schen Musikdramas. Vienna Dissertation, 1923.

Ross, Erwin. Deutsche und italienische Gesangsmethode; erläutert auf Grund ihrer geschichtlichen Gegensätzlichkeit im achtzehnten Jahrhundert. Kassel, Bärenreiter, 1928.

[Rossi, Bastiano de'.] Descrizione dell' apparato e degli intermedi fatti per la commedia rappresentata in Firenze nelle nozze de' serenissimi Don Ferdinando Medici, e Madama Cristina di Loreno, gran duchi di Toscana. Firenze, A. Padouani, 1589.

Rossi-Doria, Gastone. "Opera," in *Enciclopedia italiana* XXV (1935) 390–404.
Valuable for the sixteenth century and Italian opera generally.

—— "Il teatro musicale di G. F. Malipiero," RassM II (1929) 354–64.

Rossmayer, Richard. Konradin Kreutzer als dramatischer Komponist. Vienna Dissertation, 1928.

Roth, Hermann. "Händels Ballettmusiken," *Neue Musik-Zeitung* XLIX (1928) 245–52.

—— "Händels Ballettoper *Ariodante;* zur deutscher Uraufführung," ZfMw IX (1926–27) 159–67.

—— "Zur Karlsruher Einrichtung von Händels *Tamerlan*," ZfMw V (1922–23) 380–82.

Rothschild, James, Baron de, ed. Le Mistère du Viel Testament. Paris, Firmin Didot, 1878–91. 6 vols.

Rousseau, Jean Jacques. Dictionnaire de musique. Amsterdam, M. M. Rey, 1768. Vol. II, Amsterdam, M. M. Rey, 1779. Translated as: A Complete Dictionary of Music. London, J. Murray, 1779.

—— Œuvres complètes. Paris, P. Dupont, 1823–26. 25 vols. Contains "Confessions," Vols. 14–16; writings on music, Vols. 11–13.

Roustan, Marius. Les Philosophes et la société française au XVIIIe siècle. Paris, Hachette, 1911.

Royer, Louis. Bibliographie stendhalienne. Paris, Champion, 1931.

Rubinstein, Anton. Erinnerungen aus fünfzig Jahren, 1839–1889. Leipzig, B. Senff, 1895. Translated from the Russian.

Rubsamen, Walter. "Political and Ideological Censorship of Opera," in Papers of the American Musicological Society, Annual Meeting, 1941 . . . Edited by Gustave Reese (Printed by the Society [cop. 1946]), pp. 30–42.

Rudhart, Franz Michael. Geschichte der Oper am Hofe zu München . . . Erster Theil: die italienische Oper von 1654–1787. Freising, F. Datterer, 1865.

Rühlmann, Franz. Richard Wagner und die deutsche Opernbuehne. Kiel Dissertation, 1925.

Rusca, Paolo. "Studi critici sul Tristano e Isotta," RMI XIX (1912) 286–314.

—— "Il Tannhäuser nella vita e nell' arte di Riccardo Wagner," RMI XXI (1914) 675–98.

Russo, Joseph Louis. Lorenzo da Ponte, Poet and Adventurer. New York, Columbia University Press, 1922.

Russo, Luigi. Metastasio. Bari, G. Laterza, 1921.

Sabaneiev, Leonid Leonidovitch. Geschichte der russischen Musik. Leipzig, B&H, 1926.

—— Modern Russian Composers. Translated by Joffe. New York, International Publishers, [1927].

—— "Remarks on the Leitmotif," M&L XIII (1932) 200–206.

Sabbatini, Nicola. Pratica di fabricar scene, e machine ne' teatri. Ravenna, Pietro de Paoli, 1638. New ed. German ed. as: Anleitung Dekorationen und Theatermaschinen herzustellen. Weimar, Gesellschaft der Bibliophilen, 1926. Ed. by Willi Flemming.

Sacchi, Giovenale. Vita del cavaliere Don Carlo Broschi. Vinegia, Coleti, 1784.

Sachs, Curt. "Die Ansbacher Hofkapelle unter Markgraf Johann Friedrich (1672–86)," SIMG XI (1909–10) 105–37.

—— Die Musik der Antike. Potsdam, Athenaion, [1928].

—— Musik und Oper am kurbrandenburgischen Hofe. Berlin, J. Bard, 1910.

—— "The Road to Major," MQ XXIX (1943).

Sachs, Edwin O., and E. A. E. Woodrow. Modern Opera Houses and Theatres. London, B. T. Batsford, 1896–98. 3 vols.

Saint-Cyr, Mario. Musicisti italiani contemporanei . . . prima serie. Roma, De Santis, [1932?].

Saint-Evremond, Charles de Marguetel de St. Denis, Seigneur de. Œuvres meslées. Londres, Tonson, 1709. 3 vols. 2d ed. Contains "Sur les opera," II, 214–22; "Les Opera, comedie," II, 223–92; "A Monsieur Lulli," III, 106–107.

Saint-Foix, Georges de. "La Conclusion de l'ouverture de Don Juan," RdM V (1924) 169–72.

—— "Le Livret de Così fan tutte," RdM XI (1930) 43–97.

—— "Les Maîtres de l'opéra bouffe dans la musique de chambre à Londres," RMI XXXI (1924) 507–26.

—— "Le Théâtre à Salzbourg en 1779–80," RdM XVI (1935) 193–204.

—— "Sammartini et les chanteurs de son temps," RMI XLIII (1939) 357–63.

St. John-Brenon, Algernon. "Giuseppe Verdi," MQ II (1916) 130–62.

Saint-Saëns, Charles Camille. Portraits et souvenirs. Paris, Société d'édition artistique, [1900]. Translated as: Musical Memories. Boston, Small, Maynard, [1919].

Salazar, Adolfo. Juan del Encina y la música en el primitivo teatro español. Mexico, D.F., 1940. (Bóletin de musicologia y folklore, January, 1940.)

—— La música contemporánea en España. Madrid, Ediciones La Nave, [1930].

——La música en el primitivo teatro español, anterior a Lope de Vega y Calderón. México, A. Salazar, [1942?].

Salburg, Edith, Gräfin. Ludwig Spohr. Leipzig, Koehler & Amelang, [1936].

Salcedo, Angel S. Tomás Bretón. Madrid, Imprenta clásica española, 1924.

Saldívar, Gabriel. Historia de la música en México (épocas precortesiana y colonial). Mexico, "Cvltvra," 1934.

Saldoni, Baltasar. Diccionario biográfico-bibliográfico de efemérides de músicos españoles. Madrid, D. Antonio Perez Dubrull, 1868–81. 4 vols.

Salerno, F. Le donne Pucciniane. Palermo, A. Trimarchi, 1929.

Salvioli, Giovanni. Bibliografia universale del teatro drammatico italiano. Volume primo. Venezia, [1894–] 1903. A-Czarina only; no more published.

[——] Saggio bibliografico relativo ai melodrammi di Felice Romani [per] Luigi Lianovosani [pseud.]. Milano, Ricordi, [1878].

[——] Serie cronologica delle opere teatrali, cantate ed oratori del maestro Giovanni Comm. Pacini. Milano, Ricordi, 1875.

[——] I teatri musicali di Venezia nel secolo XVII. Milano, Ricordi, [1879].

Salza, Abd-el-kader. "Drammi inediti di Giulio Rospigliosi," RMI XIV (1907) 473–508.

Samazeuilh, Gustave. Paul Dukas. Paris, A. Durand, 1913.

Saminsky, Lazare. *"Jürg Jenatch,"* MMus VII, No. 1 (December, 1929–January, 1930) 37–39.

—— *"More about Faustus,"* MMus V, No. 1 (November–December, 1927) 38–39.

—— Music of Our Day. New York, T. Y. Crowell, [1939]. New ed.

Sandberger, Adolf. "Beziehungen der Königin Christine von Schweden zur italienischen Oper und Musik, insbesondere zu M. A. Cesti; mit einem Anhang über Cestis Innsbrucker Aufenthalt," *Bulletin de la Société union musicologique* V (1925) 121–73.

—— "Rossiniana," ZIMG IX (1907–1908) 336–45.

—— "Tommaso Traëtta," DTB XIV, No. 1 (1913) xii–xc.

—— "Zu den literarischen Quellen von Richard Wagners *Tannhäuser,"* in *Gedenkboek . . . Scheurleer* ('s Gravenhage, Nijhoff, 1925) pp. 267–69.

—— "Zur Geschichte der Oper in Nürnberg in der 2. Hälfte des 17. und zu Anfang des 18. Jahrhunderts," AfMw I (1918) 84–107.

—— "Zur venezianischen Oper," JMP XXXI (1924) 61–70; XXXII (1925) 53–63.

Sanders, Paul F. Moderne nederlandsche Componisten. s'Gravenhage, Kruseman, [1930].

Sartori, Claudio. "Franco Faccio e venti anni di spettacoli di fiera al Teatro Grande di Brescia," RMI XLII (1938) 64–77, 188–203, 350–62.

Sassi, Romualdo. "Lettere inedite di Gaspare Spontini," *Note d'Archivio* XII (1935) 165–83.

Saunders, William. "The American Opera," M&L XIII (1932) 147–55.

—— "National Opera, Comparatively Considered," MQ XIII (1927) 72–84.

Saussine, Henri de. "L'Harmonie Bellinienne," RMI XXVII (1920) 477–82.

Savaron, Jean. Traitté contre les masques. Paris, Perier, 1611. 3d ed.

Saviotti, Alfredo. "Feste e spettacoli nel seicento," *Giornale storico della letteratura italiana* XLI (1903) 542–77.

Scarlatti, Gli: Alessandro, Francesco, Pietro, Domenico, Giuseppe; note e documenti sulla vita e sulle opere. Siena, Ticci Poligrafico, 1940.

Schäfer, Karl. Das Opernschaffen Siegfried Wagners. Vienna Dissertation, 1936.

Schaeffner, André. Igor Stravinsky. Paris, Rieder, [1931].

Schall, Heinrich. Beiträge zur Entwicklungsgeschichte der Oper mit besonderer Berücksichtigung der deutschen in neuerer Zeit. Bonn, J. Bach, 1898.

Schatz, Albert. "Giovanni Bertati," VfMw V (1889) 231–71.

Scheibe, Johann Adolf. Critischer Musikus. Leipzig, B. C. Breitkopf, 1745. New ed.

Schemann, Ludwig. Cherubini. Stuttgart, Deutsche Verlags-Anstalt, 1925.

Schemann, Ludwig (*Cont.*). "Cherubinis dramatisches Erstlingsschaffen," *Die Musik* XVII (June, 1925) 641–47.

Schenk, Erich. Johann Strauss. Potsdam, Athenaion, 1940.

Schenk, Johann Baptist. ["Autobiographische Skizze"], SzMw XI (1924) 75–85.

Scherillo, Michele. L'opera buffa napoletana durante il settecento; storia letteraria. [Milano], R. Sandron, [1917]. 2d ed. First published as: Storia letteraria dell' opera buffa napolitana dalle origini al principio del secolo XIX. Napoli, R. Università, 1883.

—— "La prima commedia musicale a Venezia," *Giornale storico della letteratura italiana* I (1883) 230–59.

Schering, Arnold. Aufführungspraxis alter Musik. Leipzig, Quelle & Meyer, 1931.

—— Geschichte des Instrumentalkonzerts. Leipzig, B&H, 1927. 2d ed.

—— Geschichte des Oratoriums. Leipzig, B&H, [1911].

—— Musikgeschichte Leipzigs. Leipzig, Kistner & Siegel, 1926. 3 vols.

—— "Zur Geschichte des begleiteten Sologesangs im 16. Jahrhundert," ZIMG XIII (1911–12) 190–96.

—— "Zur Geschichte des italienischen Oratoriums im 17. Jahrhundert," JMP X (1903) 31–44.

—— "Zwei Singspiele des Sperontes," ZfMw VII (1924–25) 214–20.

Scheurleer, D. F. "Ein marionetten-theater te Amsterdam 1696," *Tijdschrift der Vereeniging voor Noord Nederlands muziekgeschiedenis* IX, No. 3 (1912) 147–53.

Schiedermair, Ludwig. "Die Anfänge der Münchener Oper," SIMG V (1903–1904) 442–68.

—— "Eine Autobiographie Pietro Generalis," in *Festschrift Liliencron* (Leipzig, B&H, 1910) pp. 250–53.

—— Bayreuther Festspiele im Zeitalter des Absolutismus. Leipzig, C. F. Kahnt, 1908.

—— Beiträge zur Geschichte der Oper um die Wende des 18. und 19. Jahrhunderts. Leipzig, B&H, 1907–1910. 2 vols.

—— "Briefe Johann Philipp Käfers," in *Festschrift Adolf Sandberger* (München, Zierfuss, 1918) pp. 121–28.

—— "Briefe . . . an Simon Mayr," SIMG VIII (1906–1907) 615–29.

—— ed. Die Briefe W. A. Mozarts und seiner Familie. München, G. Müller, 1914.

—— Die deutsche Oper. Leipzig, Quelle & Meyer, 1930. 2d ed., Bonn, Dümmler, 1940.

—— "Die Oper an den badischen Höfen des 17. und 18. Jahrhunderts," SIMG XIV (1912–13) 191–207, 369–449, 510–50.

—— "*I sensali del teatro,*" SIMG VI (1904–1905) 589–94.

—— "Ueber Beethovens *Leonore,*" ZIMG VIII (1906–1907) 115–26.

—— "Ein unbekannter Opernentwurf für Beethoven," *Neues Beethoven Jahrbuch* VII (1937) 32–36.

—— "Zur Geschichte der frühdeutschen Oper," JMP XVII (1910) 29–43.

Schild, M. Die Musikdramen Ottavio Rinuccinis. Würzburg, Mayr, 1933.

Schletterer, Hans Michael. Das deutsche Singspiel von seinen ersten Anfängen bis auf die neueste Zeit. Leipzig, B&H, [1863?].

—— Die Entstehung der Oper. Nördlingen, C. H. Beck, 1873.

—— "Giovanni Battista Pergolesi," in Waldersee, *Sammlung musikalischer Vorträge* (Leipzig, B&H, 1879–98) II, 139–78.

—— "Ludwig Spohr," in Waldersee, *Sammlung musikalischer Vorträge* (Leipzig, B&H, 1879–98) III, 127–62.

—— "Die Opernhäuser Neapels," MfMg XIV (1882) 175–81, 183–89; XV (1883) 12–19.

—— Vorgeschichte und erste Versuche der französischen Oper. Berlin, R. Damköhler, 1885. (Vol. III of his Studien zur Geschichte der französischen Musik.)

—— Zur Geschichte dramatischer Musik und Poesie in Deutschland. Augsburg, Schlosser, 1863.

Schlifstein, S. "On *War and Peace*," MMus XX, No. 3 (March–April, 1943) 185–87.

Schloezer, Boris Fedorovich. Igor Stravinsky. Paris, C. Aveline, 1929.

—— "The Operatic Paradox," MMus IV, No. 1 (November–December, 1926) 3–8.

Schmid, Anton. Christoph Willibald Ritter von Gluck. Leipzig, F. Fleischer, 1854.

Schmid, Otto. Carl Maria von Weber und seine Opern in Dresden. [Dresden?, Selbstverlag des Verfassers, 1922.]

—— Die Heimstätten der sächsischen Landestheater. Dresden, A. Waldheim, [19—?].

—— Richard Wagner; Gedanken über seine Ideale und seine Sendung. Langensalza, Beyer, 1920.

—— Das sächsische Königshaus in selbstschöpferischer musikalischer Bethätigung (Musik am sächsischen Hofe). Leipzig, B&H, 1900.

Schmidt, Friedrich. Das Musikleben der bürgerlichen Gesellschaft Leipzigs im Vormärz (1815–1848). Langensalza, Beyer, 1912.

Schmidt, Gustav Friedrich. "Die älteste deutsche Oper in Leipzig am Ende des 17. und Anfang des 18. Jahrhunderts," in *Festschrift Adolf Sandberger* (München, Zierfuss, 1918) pp. 209–57.

—— Die frühdeutsche Oper und die musikdramatische Kunst Georg Caspar Schürmann's. Regensburg, G. Bosse, 1933. 2 vols.

—— "Johann Wolfgang Francks Singspiel *Die drey Töchter Cecrops*," AfMf IV (1939) 257–316.

—— Neue Beiträge zur Geschichte der Musik und des Theaters am Herzoglichen Hofe zu Braunschweig-Wolfenbüttel. München, W. Berntheisel, 1929.

Schmidt, Gustav Friedrich (*Cont.*). "Zur Geschichte, Dramaturgie und Statistik der frühdeutschen Oper (1627–1750)," ZfMw V (1922–23) 582–97, 642–65; VI (1923–24) 129–57, 496–530.

Schmidt, Heinrich. Johann Mattheson, ein Förderer der deutschen Tonkunst, im Lichte seiner Werke. Leipzig, B&H, 1897.

Schmidt, Immanuel. "Ueber Ben Jonson's Maskenspiele," *Archiv für das Studium der neueren Sprachen* XXVII (1860) 55–90.

Schmidt, Leopold. Zur Geschichte der Märchenoper. Halle a.d.S., O. Hendel, 1895.

Schmidt, Ludwig. "Briefe von und über Carl Maria von Weber," ZIMG III (1901–1902) 93–99.

Schmitz, Arnold. "Monodien der Kölner Jesuiten aus der ersten Hälfte des 17. Jahrhunderts," ZfMw IV (1921–22) 266–85.

Schmitz, Eugen. "Antonio Brunelli als Monodist," ZIMG XI (1909–10) 383–86.

—— "Eugen d'Albert als Opernkomponist," *Hochland* VI, No. 2 (1909) 464–71.

—— Geschichte der weltlichen Solo–Kantate. Leipzig, B&H, 1914.

—— "Louis Spohr's Jugendoper *Alruna*," ZIMG XIII (1911–12) 293–99.

—— Richard Strauss als Musikdramatiker. München, Lewy, 1907.

—— "Zu Mozarts *Bastien und Bastienne*," *Hochland* IX, No. 2 (1912) 607–11.

—— "Zur Frühgeschichte der lyrischen Monodie Italiens im 17. Jahrhundert," JMP XVIII (1911) 35–48.

—— "Zur Geschichte des italienischen Continuo-Madrigals im 17. Jahrhundert," SIMG XI (1909–10) 509–28.

—— "Zur Geschichte des Leitmotivs in der romantischen Oper," *Hochland* IV, No. 2 (1907) 329–43.

—— "Zur musikgeschichtlichen Bedeutung der Harsdörfferschen 'Frauenzimmergesprächspiele'," in *Festschrift . . . Liliencron* (Leipzig, B&H, 1910) pp. 254–77.

Schnapp, Friedrich. "Robert Schumann's Plan for a Tristan-Opera," MQ X (1924) 485–91.

Schneider, Constantin. "Franz Heinrich von Biber als Opernkomponist," AfMw VIII (1926) 281–347.

—— "Die Oratorien und Schuldramen Anton Cajetan Adlgassers," SzMw XVIII (1931).

Schneider, Louis. Les Maîtres de l'opérette française: Offenbach. Paris, Perrin, 1923.

—— Massenet. Paris, L. Carteret, 1908. Revised ed., without illustrations and documents, Paris, Charpentier, 1926.

—— Un Précurseur de la musique italienne aux XVIe et XVIIe siècles: Claudio Monteverdi. Paris, Perrin, 1921.

Schneider, Ludwig. Geschichte der Oper und des königlichen Opernhauses in Berlin. Berlin, Duncker & Humblot, 1852.

Schneider, Max. Die Anfänge des Basso Continuo und seiner Bezifferung. Leipzig, B&H, 1918.

—— "Die Begleitung des Secco-Rezitativs um 1750," *Gluck-Jahrbuch* III (1917) 88–107.

—— "Zur Geschichte des begleiteten Sologesangs," *Festschrift Hermann Kretzschmar zum 70. Geburtstage überreicht von Kollegen, Schülern, und Freunden.* (Leipzig, C. F. Peters, 1918), pp. 138–40.

Schnerich, Alfred. "Wie sahen die ersten Vorstellungen von Mozart's *Don Juan* aus?" ZIMG XII (1910–11) 101–108.

Schoenemann, Otto. "Der Sündenfall und Marienklage; zwei niederdeutsche Schauspiele," MfMg VII (1875) 129–39, 145–57.

Scholes, Percy. The Puritans and Music in England and New England. London, Oxford University Press, 1934.

Scholz, Hans. "Hektor Berlioz zum 50. Todestage," ZfMw I (1918–19) 328–51.

—— Johann Sigismund Kusser. Leipzig, Röder, 1911.

Schopenhauer, Arthur. Sämmtliche Werke. Leipzig, Brockhaus, 1922–23. 6 vols.

Schott, Eberhardt. Zur Soziologie der Bühne; die Oper im Jahrzehnte 1901/02–1910/11. Typescript only.

Schramm, Erich. "Goethe und Diderots Dialog *Rameaus Neffe*," ZfMw XVI (1934) 294–307.

Schreiber, Irmtraud. Dichtung und Musik der deutschen Opernarien 1680–1700. Bottrop i. W., Postberg, 1934.

Schubert, Karl. Spontinis italienische Schule. Strassburg, Heitz, [1932].

Schünemann, Georg. Geschichte der deutschen Schulmusik. Leipzig, Kistner & Siegel, 1928.

—— "Mendelssohns Jugendopern," ZfMw V (1922–23) 506–45.

—— "Eine neue *Tristan*-Handschrift zu Richard Wagners 125. Geburtstag," AfMf III (1938) 129–37.

Schütze, Johann Friedrich. Hamburgische Theatergeschichte. Hamburg, J. P. Treder, 1794.

Schuh, Willi. Othmar Schoeck. Zürich, Hug, [1934].

Schultz, William Eben. Gay's *Beggar's Opera;* Its Content, History, and Influence. New Haven, Yale University Press, 1923.

—— "The Music of the *Beggar's Opera* in Print, 1728–1923," MTNA XIX (1934) 87–99.

Schulze, Walter. Die Quellen der Hamburger Oper (1678–1738). Hamburg-Oldenburg, G. Stalling, 1938.

Schuré, Edouard. Le Drame musicale. Paris, Didier, 1886. 2 vols.

Schwan, Wilhelm Bernhard. Die opernästhetischen Theorien der deutschen klassischen Dichter. Bonn Dissertation, 1928.

Schwartz, Rudolf. "Zur Geschichte der liederlosen Zeit in Deutschland," JMP XX (1913) 13–27.

Schwarz, Max. "Johann Christian Bach," SIMG II (1900–1901) 401–54.

Schwerké, I. "Paul Dukas; a Brief Appreciation," MQ XIV (1928) 403–12.

Schwietering, Julius. "Ueber den liturgischen Ursprung des mittelalterlichen geistlichen Spiels," Zeitschrift für deutsche Altertum LXII (1925) 1–20.

Scudo, Pierre. Le Chevalier Sarti. Paris, Hachette, 1857. (Previously in Revue des deux mondes, 1854–56.)

—— "Pergolèse et La serva padrona," Revue des deux mondes XXXII, No. 41 (September 1, 1862) 226–30.

Scuola veneziana, La (secoli XVI–XVIII), note e documenti. Siena, Libreria editrice Ticci, 1941. Contains articles on Cavalli, G. B. Bassani, Caldara, and Marcello.

Sear, H. G. "Charles Dibdin: 1745–1814," M&L XXVI (1945) 61–65.

Segnitz, Eugen. "Anselmo Feuerbach e Riccardo Wagner," RMI XIII (1906) 437–50.

—— Goethe und die Oper in Weimar. Langensalza, Beyer, 1908.

—— "La musica nel romanticismo tedesco," RMI XV (1908) 500–18.

Seidl, Roberto. Carlos Gomes. Rio de Janeiro, [Imprensa moderna], 1935.

Seiffert, Max. "J.A.P. Schultz' 'dänische' Oper," AfMw I (1918–19) 422–23.

—— "Zur Biographie Joh. Adolph Hasse's," SIMG VII (1905–1906) 129–31.

Seilhamer, George Overcash. History of the American Theatre. Philadelphia, Globe Printing House, 1888–91. 3 vols.

Seldes, Gilbert. "Delight in the Theatre," MMus XI, No. 3 (March–April, 1934) 138–41.

—— "Jazz Opera or Ballet?" MMus III, No. 2 (January–February, 1926) 10–16.

Seligmann, Herbert Wolff. Beiträge zur Geschichte der Bühne der opera seria. Bonn Dissertation, 1924.

Selva, Blanche. Déodat de Séverac. Paris, Delagrave, 1930.

Semler, Isabel Parker. Horatio Parker; a Memoir for His Grandchildren Compiled from Letters and Papers. New York, Putnam, 1942.

Seré, Octave. Musiciens français d'aujourd'hui. Paris, Mercure de France, 1911.

Serov, Victor Ilyitch. Dmitri Shostakovitch. New York, Knopf, 1943.

Servières, Georges. Edouard Lalo. Paris, H. Laurens, [1925].

—— Emmanuel Chabrier. Paris, F. Alcan, 1912.

—— Gabriel Fauré. Paris, H. Laurens, 1930.

—— La Musique française moderne. Paris, G. Havard, 1897.

—— "Le 'Wagnerisme' de C. Saint-Saëns," RMI XXX (1923) 223–44.

Settecento italiano, Il. Milan-Roma, Bestetti & Tumminelli, 1932. 2 vols.

Sharp, Geoffrey. "Don Giovanni: Some Observations," Music Review IV (1943) 45–52.

Shaw, George Bernard. London Music in 1888–89 as Heard by Corno di Bassetto. New York, Dodd, Mead, 1937.

—— The Perfect Wagnerite. New York, Brentano's, 1909.

Shedlock, J. S. "The Correspondence between Wagner and Liszt," PMA XIV (1888) 119–43.

Sherwin, Oscar. Mr. Gay; Being a Picture of the Life and Times of the Author of the *Beggar's Opera*. New York, John Day, 1929.

Shostakovitch, Dmitri. "My Opera, *Lady Macbeth of Mtzensk*," MMus XII, No. 1 (November–December, 1934) 23–30.

Sievers, Heinrich. Die lateinischen liturgischen Osterspiele der Stiftskirche St. Blasien zu Braunschweig. Wolfenbüttel, Georg Kallmeyer, 1936.

—— 250 Jahre Braunschweigisches Staatstheater, 1690–1940. Braunschweig, Appelhans, 1941.

Silbert, Doris. "Francesca Caccini, Called La Cecchina," MQ XXXII (1946) 50–62.

Silin, Charles I. Benserade and His Ballets de Cour. Baltimore, Johns Hopkins Press, 1940.

Silva, G. Silvestri. Illustri musicisti calabresi: Leonardo Vinci. Genova, Tip. Nazionale, [1935].

Silva, Lafayette. Historia do teatro brasileiro. Rio de Janeiro, Ministério da educaçiõ e saude, 1938.

Simon, Alicja. "Grétry au Théâtre national de Varsovie," in *International Society for Musical Research, First Congress, Report* (Burnham, Plainsong and Medieval Music Society, [1930]).

Simon, James. Faust in der Musik. Leipzig, C. F. W. Siegel, [1906].

Sincero, Dino. *"Boris Godounow* al teatro Alla Scala di Milano," RMI XVI (1909) 385–94.

—— "Da *Tannhäuser* a *Parsifal*," RMI XXI (1914) 122–26.

Sittard, Josef. "Gioachimo Antonio Rossini," in Waldersee, *Sammlung musikalischer Vorträge* (Leipzig, B&H, 1879–98) IV, 385–433.

—— "Reinhard Keiser in Württemberg," MfMg XVIII (1886) 3–12.

—— Zur Geschichte der Musik und des Theaters am württembergischen Hofe. Stuttgart, W. Kohlhammer, 1890–91. 2 vols.

Skilton, Charles Sanford. "American Opera," MTNA XX (1925) 112–18.

Slanina, Ernst Alfred. Die Sakralszenen der deutschen Oper des frühen 19. Jahrhunderts. Bochum-Langendreer, Pöppinghaus, 1935.

Slawik, Friedrich. Die Jugendopern Richard Wagners und ihre Beziehungen zu den späteren Meisterwerken. Vienna Dissertation, 1928.

Slonimsky, Nicolas. Music of Latin America. New York, Thomas Y. Crowell, 1945.

—— Music Since 1900. New York, Norton, [1937].

—— "Sergei Prokofiev; His Status in Soviet Music," *American Quarterly on the Soviet Union* II, No. 1 (1939) 37–44.

Smareglia, Ariberto. Vita ed arte di Antonio Smareglia. [Lugano, C. Mazzuconi, 1932.]

Smareglia, Mario, compiler. Antonio Smareglia nella storia del teatro melodrammatico italiano dell' ottocento attraverso critiche e scritti raccolti da Mario Smareglia. Pola, Smareglia, [1934].

Smith, David Stanley. "A Study of Horatio Parker," MQ XVI (1930) 153–69.

Smits van Waesberghe, Jos. Muziek en drama in de Middeleeuwen. Amsterdam, Bigot & Van Rossum, 1942.

Smythe, Dame Ethel. Impressions That Remained; Memoirs. New York, Knopf, 1946. First published London, New York [etc.], Longmans, Green, 1919. 2 vols.

Soleinne, Martineau de. Bibliothèque dramatique. Paris, Administration de l'Alliance des arts, 1843–45. 7 vols. See also: Tableau générale du catalogue (Paris, Administration de l'Alliance des arts, 1845); and Table des pièces du théâtre décrites dans le catalogue . . . par Charles Brunet publiée par Henri de Rothschild (Paris, D. Morgand, 1914).

Solerti, Angelo. Gli albori del melodramma. Milano, R. Sandron, [1905]. 3 vols.

—— "Un balletto musicato da Claudio Monteverdi," RMI XI (1904) 24–34.

—— ed. Ferrara e la corte Estense nella seconda metà del secolo decimosesto; i discorsi di Annibale Romei, gentiluomo ferrarese. Città di Castello, S. Lapi, 1891.

—— "Feste musicale alla Corte di Savoia nella prima metà del secolo XVII," RMI XI (1904) 675–724.

—— Laura Guidiccioni ed Emilio de' Cavalieri; i primi tentativi del melodramma," RMI IX (1902) 797–829.

—— "Lettere inedite sulla musica di Pietro della Valle a G.B. Doni ed una Veglia drammatica-musicale del medesimo," RMI XII (1905) 271–338.

—— Musica, ballo e drammatica alla corte Medicea dal 1600 al 1637. Firenze, R. Bemporad, 1905.

—— compiler and ed. Le origini del melodramma; testimonianze dei contemporanei. Torino, Fratelli Bocca, 1903.

—— "Precedenti del melodramma," RMI X (1903) 207–33, 466–84.

—— "Primi saggi del melodramma giocoso," RMI XII (1905) 814–38; XIII (1906) 91–112.

—— "I rappresentazioni musicali di Venezia dal 1571 al 1605," RMI IX (1902) 503–58.

—— "Un viaggio in Francia di Giulio Caccini," RMI X (1903) 707–11.

—— Vita di Torquato Tasso. Torino, Roma, E. Loescher, 1895. 3 vols.

Solvay, Lucien. L'Evolution théâtrale. Bruxelles and Paris, G. van Oest, 1922. 2 vols.

—— Notice sur Jean Blockx. Bruxelles, Hayez, 1920.

Somerset, H. V. F. "Giovanni Paisiello," M&L XVIII (1937) 20–35.

—— "Jean Jacques Rousseau as a Musician," M&L XVII (1936) 37–46, 218–24.

Somiglio, Carlo. "Del teatro reale d'opera in Monaco di Baviera e del suo repertorio," RMI V (1898) 721–53.

Sommer, Hans. "Die Oper *Ludwig der Fromme* von Georg Caspar Schürmann," MfMg XIV (1882) 48–51, 53–55.

—— "Zur Schürmann'schen Oper *Ludovicus Pius*," MfMg XXIV (1892) 137–39.

Sondheimer, Robert. "Gluck in Paris," ZfMw V (1922–23) 165–75.

Sonette, Jean Jacques, pseud. *See* Goudar, Ange.

Sonneck, Oscar George Theodore. A Bibliography of Early Secular American Music (Eighteenth Century). Washington, D.C., The Library of Congress, Music Division, 1945.

—— "Ciampi's *Bertoldo, Bertoldino e Cacasenno* and Favart's *Ninette à la cour*," SIMG XII (1911) 525–64.

—— "*Dafne*, the First Opera," SIMG XV (1913–14) 102–10.

—— "A Description of Alessandro Striggio and Francesco Corteccia's Intermedi *Psyche and Amore*, 1565," MA III (1911) 40.

—— "Die drei Fassungen des Hasse'schen *Artaserse*," SIMG XIV (1912–13) 226–42.

—— Early Concert Life in America. Leipzig, B&H, 1907.

—— Early Opera in America. New York, G. Schirmer, [1915].

—— "Foot-note to the Bibliographical History of Grétry's Operas," in *Gedenkboek . . . Scheurleer* ('s Gravenhage, Nijhoff, 1925) pp. 321–36.

—— Francis Hopkinson, the First American Poet-Composer. Washington, D.C., Printed for the Author by H. L. McQueen, 1905.

—— "*Il Giocatore*," MA IV (1912–13) 160–74.

—— "Heinrich Heine's Musical Feuilletons," MQ VIII (1923) 119–59, 273–95, 435–68.

—— Miscellaneous Studies in the History of Music. New York, Macmillan, 1921. Contains "*Caractacus* Not Arne's *Caractacus*," "Ciampi's *Bertoldo, Bertoldino e Cacasenno* and Favart's *Ninette à la cour*; a Contribution to the History of the Pasticcio," "A Description of Alessandro Striggio and Francesco Corteggia's Intermedi: *Psyche and Amor*, 1565,' "Early American Opera," and "A Preface."

—— "La nuova rappresentazione del *D. Giovanni* di Mozart a Monaco," RMI III (1896) 741–55.

Sooper, Frances O. "The Music of Dittersdorf," M&L XI (1930) 141–45.

Soriano Fuertes, Mariano. Historia de la musica española. Madrid, Martin y Salazar; Barcelona, Narciso Ramírez, 1856–59. 4 vols.

Soubies, Albert. Histoire de l'opéra-comique; la seconde Salle Favart 1840–[1887]. Paris, E. Flammarion, 1892–93. 2 vols.

—— Histoire du théâtre-lyrique 1851–1870. Paris, Fischbacher, 1899.

—— Le Théâtre-italien de 1801 à 1913. Paris, Fischbacher, 1913.

Soubies, Albert, and Henri de Curzon. Documents inédits sur le *Faust* de Gounod. Paris, Fischbacher, 1912.

Specht, Richard. E. N. v. Reznicek. Leipzig, E. P. Tal, 1923.

—— Giacomo Puccini. Berlin-Schöneberg, M. Hesse, [1931]. English translation: New York, Knopf, 1933.

Specht, Richard (*Cont.*). Julius Bittner. München, Drei Masken, 1921.

—— Richard Strauss, *Die Frau ohne Schatten;* thematische Einführung. Berlin, Fürstner, 1919.

—— Richard Strauss und sein Werk. Leipzig, P. Tal, 1921. 2 vols.

—— Das Wiener Operntheater; von Dingelstedt bis Schalk und Strauss. Wien, P. Knepler, 1919.

Spectator, The (London, 1711–1714). London and Toronto, J. M. Dent, 1919–26. 4 vols.

Speer, Daniel. Grund-richtiger, kurtz, leicht und nöthiger Unterricht der musikalischen Kunst. Ulm, G. W. Kühnen, 1687.

Spencer, H. "Meyerbeer," RMI X (1903) 126–28.

Speziale, G. "Ancora per Paisiello," RassM IV (1931) 1–16.

Spinelli, Alessandro Giuseppe. Bibliografia goldoniana. Milano, Dumolard, 1884.

Spinner, Leopold. Das Rezitativ in der romantischen Oper bis Wagner. Vienna Dissertation, 1931.

Spitta, Philipp. "Die älteste Faust-Oper und Goethe's Stellung zur Musik," in his *Zur Musik* (Berlin, Paetel, 1892) pp. 199–234.

—— "Jessonda," in his *Zur Musik* (Berlin, Paetel, 1892) pp. 237–66.

—— Johann Sebastian Bach. Leipzig, B&H, 1930. 4th ed. 2 vols.

—— "Rinaldo di Capua," VfMw III (1877) 92–121.

Spitz, Charlotte. "Eine anonyme italienische Oper um die Wende des 17. zum 18. Jahrhundert," ZfMw II (1919–20) 232–35.

—— Antonio Lotti in seiner Bedeutung als Opernkomponist. Borna–Leipzig, Noske, 1918.

—— "Die Entwickelung des 'stilo recitativo'," AfMw III (1921) 237–44.

—— "Die Opern *Ottone* von G. F. Händel (London 1722) und *Teofane* von A. Lotti (Dresden 1719); ein Stilvergleich," in *Festschrift Adolf Sandberger* (München, Zierfuss, 1918) pp. 265–71.

Spohr, Louis. Louis Spohr's Selbstbiographie. Cassel and Göttingen, Wigand, 1860–61. 2 vols. English translation: London, Reeves & Turner, 1878.

Spontini, G. "Lettere inedite," *Note d'archivio* IX (1932) 23–40.

Squire, William Barclay. "Gluck's London Operas," MQ I (1915) 397–409.

—— "An Index of Tunes in the Ballad-Operas," MA II (1910–1911) 1–17.

—— "J. W. Franck in England," MA III (1911–1912) 181–90.

—— "The Music of Shadwell's *Tempest*," MQ VII (1921) 565–78.

—— "An Opera under Innocent X," in *Gedenkboek . . . Scheurleer* ('s Gravenhage, Nijhoff, 1925) pp. 65–71.

—— "Purcell's Dramatic Music," SIMG V (1903–1904) 489–564.

Stählin, Karl. Aus den Papieren Jacob von Stählins. Königsberg, Ost-Europa-Verlag, 1926.

Stals, Georgs. Das lettische Ballett der Rigaer Oper. Riga, Kadilis, 1943.

Stanley, Albert Augustus. "Cesti's *Il Pomo d'Oro*," MTNA I (1906) 139–49.

Stasov, Vladimir Vasil'evich. Russkiia i inostrannyia opery ispolniavshiasia na Imperatorskikh Teatrakh v Rosii v XVIII-m'i XIX-m stoletiiakh. St. Petersburg, 1898.

Statisticus [pseud.]. "Notes sur l'histoire de l'Opéra," RHCM III (1903) 277–79.

Stauder, Wilhelm. "Johann André; ein Beitrag zur Geschichte des deutschen Singspiels," AfMf I (1936) 318–60. Also separate: Leipzig, B&H, 1936.

Stebbins, Lucy Poate, and Richard Poate Stebbins. Enchanted Wanderer; the Life of Carl Maria von Weber. New York, G. P. Putnam, [1940].

Stefan, Paul. Anton Dvořák. New York, Greystone, [1941]. Translated and rearranged from the German edition, which was based on the authoritative four-volume biography by Otakar Sourck.

—— Das neue Haus; ein Halbjahrhundert Wiener-Opernspiel und was voranging. Wien and Leipzig, E. Strache, 1919.

—— "Schoenberg's Operas," MMus II, No. 1 (January, 1925) 12–15.

—— "Schönberg's Operas," MMus VII, No. 1 (December, 1929–January, 1930) 24–28.

—— Die Wiener Oper; ihre Geschichte von den Anfängen bis in der neueste Zeit. Wien, Augartenverlag, 1932.

—— Die Zauberflöte; Herkunft, Bedeutung, Geheimnis. Wien, Reichner, 1937.

Steglich, Rudolf. "Das deutsche Händelfest in Leipzig," ZfMw VII (1924–25) 587–92.

—— "Göttinger Händelfestspiele 1924," Zeitschrift für Musik XCI (1924) 496–98.

—— "Göttinger Händel-Opern Festspiele 1927," Zeitschrift für Musik XCIV (1927) 424–26.

—— "Das Händelfest in Münster (2. bis 5. Dezember 1926)," ZfMw IX (1926–27) 290–93.

—— "Die Händel-Opern-Festspiele in Göttingen," ZfMw III (1920–21) 615–20.

—— "Händels Oper Rodelinde und ihre neue Göttinger Bühnenfassung," ZfMw III (1920–21) 518–34.

—— "Händels Saul in szenischer Darstellung," Zeitschrift für Musik XC (1923) Heft XVII, pp. 15–17.

—— "Händels Xerxes und die Göttinger Händel-Opern-Festspiele 1924," ZfMw VII (1924–25) 21–33.

—— "Händel und die Gegenwart," Zeitschrift für Musik XCII (1925) 333–38.

—— "Die neue Händel-Opern-Bewegung," Händel-Jahrbuch I (1928) 71–158.

—— "Schütz und Händel," Zeitschrift für Musik LXXXIX (1922) 478–80.

—— "Ueber die gegenwärtige Krise der Händelpflege," ZfMw X (1927–28) 632–41.

Steigman, B. M. "The Great American Opera," M&L VI (1925) 359–67.

—— " 'Nicht mehr Tristan'," MQ VII (1921) 57–67.

Steinitzer, Max. Zur Entwicklungsgeschichte des Melodrams und Mimodrams. Leipzig, C. F. W. Siegel, [1919].

Stendhal [pseud.]. See Beyle, Henri.

Stenhouse, May. The Character of the Opera Libretto according to Quinault. Columbia Dissertation (A.M.), 1920.

Sternfeld, Frederick W. "Some Russian Folk Songs in Stravinsky's *Petrouchka*," *Music Library Association Notes, Second Series* II, No. 2 (March, 1945) 95–107.

Stier, Ernst. "Georg Caspar Schürmann," *Die Musik* III, No. 2 (1903–1904) 107–11.

Stier-Somlo, Helene. Das Grimmsche Märchen als Text für Opern und Spiele. Berlin and Leipzig, de Gruyter, 1926.

Storz, Walter. Der Aufbau der Tänze in den Opern und Balletts Lully's vom musikalischen Standpunkte aus betrachtet. Göttingen, Dieterischen Universitäts-Buchdruckerei, 1928.

Stoullig, E. Les Annales du théâtre et de la musique. Paris, Ollendorf, 1899.

Strasser, Stefan. "Susanna und die Gräfin," ZfMw X (1927–28) 208–16.

Strauss, Franz, ed. Richard Strauss Briefwechsel mit Hugo von Hofmannsthal. Wien, Zsolnay, 1926. Translated as: Correspondence between Richard Strauss and Hugo von Hofmannsthal 1907–1918. New York, Knopf, 1927.

Stravinsky, Igor. Chroniques de ma vie. Paris, Denoël & Steele, [1935]. Translated as: Chronicles of My Life. London, V. Gollanez, 1936.

—— Poétique musicale sous forme de six leçons. Cambridge, Mass., Harvard University Press, 1942.

—— See RM, numéro spécial (May–June, 1939).

Streatfeild, Richard Alexander. Handel. New York, John Lane, 1909.

—— "Handel, Rolli, and Italian Opera in London in the Eighteenth Century," MQ III (1917) 428–45.

—— Musiciens anglais contemporains. Paris, Editions du temps présent, 1913.

Strelitzer, Hugo. Meyerbeers deutsche Jugend-Opern. Münster Dissertation, 1922.

Strobel, Heinrich. "Die Opern von E. N. Méhul," ZfMw VI (1923–24) 362–402.

—— Paul Hindemith. Mainz, Melosverlag, B. Schotts Söhne, 1937. 3d ed.

Strüver, Paul. Die cantata da camera Alessandro Scarlattis. Munich Dissertation, 1924.

Stuckenschmidt, H. H. "Ernst Křenek," MMus XVI, No. 1 (November–December, 1938), 41–44.

—— "Hellenic Jazz," MMus VII, No. 3 (April–May, 1930) 22–25.

—— "Opera in Germany Today," MMus XIII, No. 1 (November–December, 1935) 32–37.

Subirá, José. Enrique Granados. Madrid, [Z. Ascasíbar], 1926.
—— "Les Influences françaises dans la Tonadilla madrilène du XVIIIe siècle," in *Mélanges de musicologie* (Paris, Droz, 1933) pp. 209–16.
—— Los maestros de la tonadilla escénica. Barcelona, Editorial Labor, 1933.
—— La música en la casa de Alba. Madrid, ["Sucesores de Rivadeneyra"], 1927.
—— El operista español d. Juan Hidalgo. Madrid, Bermejo, 1934.
—— La participación musical en el antiguo teatro español. Barcelona, Disputación provincial, 1930.
—— "Le Style dans la musique théâtrale espagnole," *Acta musicologica* IV (1932) 67–75.
—— La tonadilla escénica. Madrid, Tipografía de archivos, 1928–30. 3 vols.
—— Tonadillas teatrales inéditas. Madrid, Tipografía de archivos, 1932.
Supplément aux parodies du théâtre italien. Paris, Duchesne, 1765. New ed.
Swalin, Benjamin F. "Purcell's Masque in *Timon of Athens*," in *Papers of the American Musicological Society, Annual Meeting, 1941 . . . Edited by Gustave Reese* (Printed by the Society [cop. 1946]), pp. 112–24.
Swan, Alfred J. "Moussorgsky and Modern Music," MQ XI (1925) 271–80.
Swanepoel, Pieter. Das dramatische Schaffen Henry Purcells. Vienna Dissertation, 1926.
Symonds, John Addington. The Renaissance in Italy: Italian Literature. New York, H. Holt, 1882. 2 vols.
Szametz, Ralph. Hat Mozart eine Psychose durchgemacht? Frankfurt Dissertation, 1936.
Tabanelli, Nicola. "Oriani e la musica," RMI XLII (1938) 325–43, 495–505.
Tanner, Richard. Johann David Heinichen als dramatischer Komponist. Leipzig, B&H, 1916.
Tappolet, Willy. Arthur Honegger. Zürich and Leipzig, Gebrüder Hug, 1933. French ed., Neuchâtel, Editions de la Baconnière, [1939].
Tasso, Torquato. Opere. Pisa, Capuro, 1821–32. 33 vols.
Taubert, Otto. "*Daphne,* das erste deutsche Operntextbuch," in *Programm des Gymnasiums zu Torgau* (Torgau, Fr. Lebinsky, 1879).
Taut, Kurt. "Verzeichnis des Schrifttums über Georg Friedrich Händel," *Händel-Jahrbuch* VI (1933).
Taylor, Sedley. The Indebtedness of Handel to the Works by Other Composers; a Presentation of Evidence. Cambridge, University Press, 1906.
Tchaikovsky, Peter Ilyitch. Diaries; Translated from the Russian with Notes by Wladimir Lakond. New York, Norton, 1945.
—— Life and Letters. London, J. Lane, 1906. Ed. from the Russian by Rosa Newmarch.
Teatro italiano antico. Milano, 1808–12. 10 vols.

Tebaldini, Giovanni. "Felipe Pedrell ed il dramma lirico spagnuolo," RMI IV (1897) 267–98, 494–524. Also separate: Torino, Bocca, 1897.

—— "Giuseppe Persiani e Fanny Tacchinardi; memorie ed appunti," RMI XII (1905) 579–91.

—— "Telepatia musicale; a proposito dell' *Elettra* di Richard Strauss," RMI XVI (1909) 400–412.

Teneo, Martial. "Les Chefs-d'œuvre du chevalier Gluck à l'Opéra de Paris," RHCM VIII (1908) 109–16.

—— "Le Chevalier de Malte ou la reine de Chypre," ZIMG VIII (1906–1907) 352–54.

—— "La Détresse de Niccola Piccinni," RHCM VIII (1908) 237–44, 279–81.

—— "Jacques Offenbach d'après des documents inédits," MM VII, No. 12 (1911) 1–35.

—— "Jacques Offenbach: His Centenary," MQ VI (1920) 98–117.

—— "Pierre Montan Bertons," RHCM VIII (1908) 389–97, 416–24, 493.

—— "Un Spectacle à la cour," MM I (1905) 480–86.

Tenschert, Roland. "Die Kadenzbehandlung bei Richard Strauss," ZfMw VIII (1925–26) 161–82.

—— Mozart; ein Leben für die Oper. Wien, Frick, 1941.

—— "Die Ouvertüren Mozarts," *Mozart-Jahrbuch* II (1924).

—— "Versuch einer Typologie der Richard Strausschen Melodik," ZfMw XVI (1934) 274–93.

Ternant, Andrew de. "French Opera Libretti," M&L XI (1930) 172–76.

Terry, Charles Stanford. Johann Christian Bach. London, Oxford University Press, 1929.

Tessier, André. "Berain, créateur du pays d'opéra," RM VI (January, 1925) 56–73.

—— "Les Deux Styles de Monteverdi," RM III, No. 8 (June, 1922) 223–54.

—— "Giacomo Torelli a Parigi e la messa in scena delle *Nozze di Peleo e Teti* di Carlo Caproli," RassM I (1928) 573–90.

—— "L'*Orontée* de Lorenzani et l'*Orontea* du Padre Cesti," RM IX, No. 8 (1928) 169–86.

—— "Quelques notes sur Jean Desfontaines," RdM X (1929) 9–16.

—— "Robert Cambert à Londres," RM IX (December, 1927) 101–22.

Teutsche Arien, welche auf dem Kayserlich-privilegierten Wienerischen Theatro in unterschiedlich producirten Comoedien, deren Titeln hier jedesmahl beygerucket, gesungen worden; Codex ms. 12706–12709 der Wiener Nationalbibliothek. Wien, E. Strache, 1930.

Thayer, Alexander Wheelock. The Life of Ludwig van Beethoven. New York, The Beethoven Association, [1921]. Ed. by H. E. Krehbiel.

Theater-Kalendar auf das Jahr . . . (Reichard). Gotha, Vols. 1–25, 1775–1800.

Theatro comico portuguez, ou Collecção das operas portuguezas, que se representárão na casa do theatro público do Bairro Alto di Lisboa. Lisboa, S. T. Ferreira, 1787–92. 4 vols.

Thomas, Eugen. Die Instrumentation der *Meistersinger von Nürnberg* von Richard Wagner. Wien, Universal, [1907]. 2 vols. 2d ed.

Thomas, L. P. "Les Strophes et la composition du Sponsus," *Romania* LV (1929) 45–112.

—— "La Versification et les leçons douteuses du Sponsus," *Romania* LIII (1927) 43–81.

Thomas of Britain. The Romance of Tristram and Ysolt. *See* Loomis, Roger Sherman, ed.

Thompson, Herbert. Wagner and Wagenseil. London, Oxford University Press, 1927.

Thompson, Oscar. Debussy, Man and Artist. New York, Dodd, Mead, 1937.

—— "Fly-Wheel Opera," MMus VII, No. 1 (December, 1929–January, 1930) 39–42.

—— "If Beethoven Had Written *Faust*," MQ X (1924) 13–20.

Thompson, Randall. "George Antheil," MMus VIII, No. 4 (May–June, 1931) 17–27.

Thomson, Virgil. "George Gershwin," MMus XIII, No. 1 (November–December, 1935) 13–19.

—— "Most Melodious Tears," MMus XI, No. 1 (November–December, 1933) 13–17.

—— The Musical Scene. New York, Knopf, 1945.

—— The State of Music. New York, W. Morrow, 1939.

Thorp, Willard, ed. Songs from the Restoration Theatre. Princeton, Princeton University Press, 1934.

Thouret, Georg. "Einzug der Musen und Grazien in die Mark," *Hohenzollern-Jahrbuch* IV (1900) 192–230.

Thrane, Carl. Danske Komponister. Copenhagen, Forlagsbureaunet, 1875.

—— "Sarti in Kopenhagen," SIMG III (1901–1902) 528–38.

Tibaldi Chiesa, Mary. Cimarosa e il suo tempo. [Milano], A. Garzanti, [1939].

Tiby, Ottavio. *L'incoronazione di Poppea* di Claudio Monteverdi. Firenze, A. Vallecchi, 1937.

Tiersot, Julien. "Auber," RM XIV (November, 1933) 265–78.

—— "Bizet and Spanish Music," MQ XIII (1927) 566–81.

—— "Charles Gounod; a Centennial Tribute," MQ IV (1918) 409–39.

—— "Les Choeurs d' *Esther* de Moreau," RHCM III (1903) 35–40.

—— Un Demi-siècle de musique française. Paris, Alcan, 1918.

—— "Edouard Lalo," MQ XI (1925) 8–35.

—— "Etude sur *Don Juan* de Mozart," *Le Ménestrel* LXII (1896) 399–411 *passim;* LXIII (1897) 1–139 *passim*

—— "Etude sur *Orphée* de Gluck." *Le Ménestrel* LXII (1896) 273–386 *passim*.

—— "Gluck and the Encyclopædists MQ XVI (1930) 336–57.

Tiersot, Julien (*Cont.*). "Gounod's Letters," MQ V (1919) 40–61.

—— "Hector Berlioz and Richard Wagner," MQ III (1917) 453–92.

—— Histoire de la chanson populaire en France. Paris, Plon, Nourrit, 1889. Contains (Part III, Chapter IV) "La Mélodie populaire au théâtre."

—— Jean-Jacques Rousseau. Paris, Alcan, 1912.

—— "Lettres de musiciens écrites en français du XVe au XXe siècle," RMI XVII (1910)–XXI (1914); XXIII (1916); XXIX (1922)–XXX (1923); XXXIII (1926)–XXXIV (1927); XXXVI (1929)–XXXVIII (1931), *passim.*

—— La Musique dans la comédie de Molière. Paris, La Renaissance du livre, [1922].

—— "La Musique de J.-J. Rousseau," MM VIII, No. 6 (1912) 34–56.

—— "La Musique des comédies de Molière à la Comédie-française," RdM VI (1922) 20–28.

—— "Rameau," MQ XIV (1928) 77–107.

—— "Ronsard et la musique de son temps," SIMG IV (1902–1903) 70–142.

—— "L'ultima opera di Gluck, *Eco e Narciso,*" RMI IX (1902) 264–96.

Till, Theodor. Die Entwicklung der musikalischen Form in Richard Wagners Opern und Musikdramen, von der Ouvertüre (Vorspiel) und deren Funktionsvertretern aus betrachtet. Vienna Dissertation, 1930.

Tintelnot, Hans. Die Entwicklungsgeschichte der barocken Bühnendekoration in ihren Wechselbeziehungen zur bildenden Kunst. Berlin, Mann, 1938.

Tirabassi, Antonio. "The Oldest Opera: Belli's *Orfeo Dolente,*" MQ XXV (1939) 26–33.

Tirabassi, M. A. "Introduction à l'étude de la parabole des vierges sages et des vierges folles," *Annales de la Société R. d' archéologie de Bruxelles* XXXII (1926) 15.

Tiraboschi, Girolamo. Storia della letteratura italiana. Roma, L. P. Salvioni, 1782–97. 10 vols.

Titon du Tillet, [Evrard]. Le Parnasse françois. Paris, J. B. Coignard, 1732–[43]. 2 vols., paged continuously.

Tittmann, Julius. Kleine Schriften zur deutschen Literatur und Kulturgeschichte. Göttingen, Dieterischen Buchhandlung, 1847.

Törnblom, Folke H. "Opera [in Sweden]," *Theatre Arts* XXIV (1940) 597–600.

Toffani, Giuseppe, ed. Storia letteraria d'Italia: il cinquecento. Milano, Vallardi, 1929. 3d ed.

Tolksdorf, Cäcilie. John Gays *Beggar's Opera* und Bert Brechts *Dreigroschenoper.* Rheinberg, Rhl., Sattler & Koss, 1934.

Tolón, Edwin T., and Jorge A. González. Operas cubanas y sus autores. Habana, [Imprenta Ucar, García], 1943.

Tommasini, Oreste. "Pietro Metastasio e lo svolgimento del melodramma italiano," in *Scritti di storia e critica* (Roma, E. Loescher, 1891) pp. 153–222.

Tommasini, Vincenzo. "L'opera di Riccardo Wagner e la sua importanza nella storia dell' arte e delle cultura," RMI IX (1902) 113–47, 422–41, 694–716.

Tonelli, Luigi. Il teatro italiano dalle origini ai giorni nostri. Milano, Modernissima, 1924.

Toni, Alceo. "Sul basso continuo e l'interpretazione della musica antica," RMI XXVI (1919) 229–64.

Torchi, Luigi. "L'accompagnamento degli istrumenti nei melodrammi italiani della prima metà del seicento," RMI I (1894) 7–38; II (1895) 666–71.

—— "Canzoni ed arie italiane ad una voce nel secolo XVII," RMI I (1894) 581–656.

—— "Consuelo di A. Rendano," RMI X (1903) 564–80.

—— "L'esito del concorso Sonzogno; le tre opere rappresentate al 'Teatro Lirico' di Milano," RMI XI (1904) 516–49.

—— "Germania, di G. Franchetti," RMI IX (1902) 377–421.

—— "Ghismonda, opera in tre atti di Eugenio D'Albert," RMI III (1896) 526–61.

—— "Guglielmo Ratcliff . . . di Pietro Mascagni," RMI II (1895) 287–311.

—— "Iris . . . di Pietro Mascagni," RMI VI (1899) 71–118.

—— "Oceana di A. Smareglia," RMI X (1903) 309–66.

—— "L'opera di Giuseppe Verdi e i suoi caretteri principali," RMI VIII (1901) 279–325.

—— "The Realistic Italian Operas," in Famous Composers and Their Works, New Series (Boston, J. B. Millet, [1900]) I, 183.

—— "R. Schumann e le sue 'Scene tratte dal Faust di Goethe'," RMI II (1895) 381–419, 629–65.

—— "Salome di Riccardo Strauss," RMI XIV (1907) 113–56.

—— "Studi di orchestrazione; l' Anello del Nibelunge di Riccardo Wagner," RMI XX (1913) 347–53; XXI (1914) 509–12, 768–75.

—— "Tosca, di G. Puccini," RMI VII (1900) 78–114.

—— "La vita nuova di E. Wolf-Ferrari," RMI X (1903) 712–36.

Torrefranca, Fausto. "Arrigo Boito," MQ VI (1920) 532–52.

—— "Il 'grande stregone' Giacomo Torelli e la scenografia del seicento," Scenario III (1934) 473–80.

—— "La nuova opera di Riccardo Strauss," RMI XIX (1912) 986–1031.

—— "L'officina dell' opera," RassM III (1930) 136–46.

—— "Opera as a 'Spectacle for the Eye'," MQ I (1915) 436–52.

—— "La prima opera francese in Italia? (l'Armida di Lulli, Roma 1690)," in Festschrift für Johannes Wolf (Berlin, Breslauer, 1929) pp. 191–97.

—— "Il Rosencavalier di R. Strauss," RMI XVIII (1911) 147–79.

—— "R. Strauss e l' Elektra," RMI XVI (1909) 335–84.

Torri, Luigi. "Il primo melodramma a Torino," RMI XXVI (1919) 1–35.

—— "Saggio di bibliografia Verdiana," RMI VIII (1901) 379–407.

Tosi, Pietro Francesco. Opinioni de' cantori antichi, e moderni, o sieno Osservazioni sopra il canto figurato. [Bologna, L. dalla Volpe, 1723.] Translated as: Observations on the Florid Song; or, Sentiments on the Ancient and Modern Singers. London, J. Wilcox, 1742. Later English editions: 1743, 1906, 1926.

Tottmann, Albert. Mozart's *Zauberflöte*. Langensalza, Beyer, 1908. Makes use of C. Grüel's "Aufschlüsse über die Bedeutung des angeblich Schikanederschen Textes zu Mozart's Zauberflöte," Magdeburg, 1868.

Touchard-Lafosse, G. Chroniques secrètes et galantes de l'opéra depuis 1667 jusqu'en 1845. Paris, Lachapelle, 1846. 4 vols.

Tovey, Donald Francis. "Christopher Willibald Gluck (1714–1787) and the Musical Revolution of the Eighteenth Century," in *The Heritage of Music,* ed. Hubert J. Foss (London, Oxford University Press, 1934) II, 69–117.

—— Essays in Musical Analysis, III: The Concerto. London, Oxford University Press, 1936.

Toye, Francis. Giuseppe Verdi. London, W. Heinemann; New York, Knopf, 1931.

—— "Is Musical Reservation Justifiable?" MQ I (1915) 118–28.

—— Rossini, a Study in Tragi-Comedy. New York, Knopf, 1934.

—— "Verdi," PMA LVI (1929–30) 37–53.

Trend, John Brande. "The Mystery of Elche," M&L I (1920) 145–57.

—— A Picture of Modern Spain. New York, Houghton Mifflin, 1921.

Trenkle, J. B. "Ueber süddeutsche geistliche Schulkomödien," *Freiburger Diöcesan-archiv* II (1866) 131–76.

Trilogia *Los Pireneos* y la critica, La. Barcelona, Oliva, 1901.

Trocki, Ladislas von. Die Entwickelung der Oper in Polen. Leipzig, Voigt, 1867.

[Truinet, Charles Louis Etienne, and A. E. Roquet (Thoinan).] Les Origines de l'opéra français. Paris, Plon-Nourrit, 1886.

Tufts, George. "Ballad Opera; a List and Some Notes," MA IV (1912–13) 61–86.

Turrini, G. "De Vlaamsche Componist Giovanni Nasco te Verona (1547–1551)," *Tijdschrift der Vereeniging voor Nederl. Muziekgeschiedenis* XIV, No. 3 (1935) 132–59; XV, No. 2 (1937) 84–93. Also in Italian, *Note d'archivio* XIV (1937) 180–225.

Tutenberg, Fritz. "Moderne schwedische Musik und Musiker im Umriss, II: die schwedische Oper," *Zeitschrift für Musik* CVI (1939) 930–34.

—— "Die *opera-buffa* Sinfonie und ihre Beziehungen zur klassischen Sinfonie," AfMw VIII (1926–27) 452–72.

Tuthill, Burnet C. "Howard Hanson," MQ XXII (1936) 140–53.

Tutti i trionfi, carri, mascherate, o Cante carnascialeschi andati per Firenze dal tempo del magnifico Lorenzo de' Medici fino all' anno 1559. Cosmopoli [i.e. Lucca], 1750. 2d ed.

"Ueber das Rezitativ," *Bibliothek der schönen Wissenschaften* XI, No. 2 (1764) 209; XII, No. 1 (1765) 1; XII, No. 2 (1765) 217.

Uffenbach, Johann Friedrich von. Pharasmen; ein Singspiel. Berlin, O. Elsner, 1930.

Uhlenbruch, Fritz. Herforder Musikleben bis zur Mitte des 18. Jahrhunderts. Münster Dissertation, 1926.

Ulibishev, Aleksandr Dmitrievich. Mozart's Opern; kritische Erläuterungen. Leipzig, B&H, 1848. Originally in French.

Unger, Max. "Beethoven und das Wiener Hoftheater im Jahre 1807," *Neues Beethoven Jahrbuch* II (1925) 76–83.

Unterholzner, Ludwig. Giuseppe Verdis Opern-typus. Hannover, A. Madsack, [1933].

Untersteiner, Alfredo. "Agostino Steffani," RMI XIV (1907) 509–34.

Upton, William Treat. The Musical Works of William Henry Fry in the Collections of the Library Company of Philadelphia. Philadelphia, The Free Library of Philadelphia, 1946.

—— "Secular Music in the United States 150 Years Ago," in *Papers of the American Musicological Society, Annual Meeting, 1941 . . . Edited by Gustave Reese* (Printed by the Society [cop. 1946]), pp. 105–11. Contains a list of "certain operas whose librettos were published in the United States before 1800 and which received at least fifteen performances in Philadelphia and New York during that period."

Ursprung, Otto. "*Celos* usw., Text von Calderón, Musik von Hidalgo,— die älteste erhaltene spanische Oper," in *Festschrift Arnold Schering* (Berlin, A. Glas, 1937) pp. 223–40.

—— "Das Sponsus-Spiel," AfMf III (1938) 80–95, 180–92.

—— "Ueber die Aufführung von Monteverdis *Combattimento* und von Peris *Euridice* durch das musikwissenschaftliche Seminar der Universität München," ZfMw XVI (1934) 188–90.

Valdrighi, Luigi Francesco, conte. I Bononcini da Modena. Modena, G. T. Vincenzi, 1882.

Valentin, Caroline. " 'Ach wie ist's möglich dann' von H. von Chézy und seine erste Melodie," in *Festschrift Liliencron* (Leipzig, B&H, 1910) pp. 358–86.

Valentin, Erich. Georg Philipp Telemann. Burg b.M., A. Hopfer, [1931].

—— Hans Pfitzner. Regensburg, G. Bosse, 1939.

Vallas, Léon. Claude Debussy et son temps. Paris, F. Alcan, 1932. Translated as: Claude Debussy, His Life and Works. London, Oxford University Press, 1933.

—— "The Discovery of Musical Germany by Vincent d'Indy in 1873," MQ XXV (1939) 176–94.

—— "Jacques-Simon Maugot," RdM V (1924) 123–26.

—— Un Siècle de musique et de théâtre à Lyon (1688–1789). Lyon, P. Masson, 1932.

Van Vechten, Carl. "Back to Delibes," MQ VIII (1922) 605–10.

Van Vechten, Carl (*Cont.*). "Notes on Gluck's *Armide*," MQ III (1917) 539–47.

—— "Shall We Realize Wagner's Ideals?" MQ II (1916) 387–401.

Vatielli, Francesco. "Le opere comiche di G. B. Martini," RMI XL (1936) 450–76.

—— "Operisti-librettisti dei secoli XVII e XVIII," RMI XLIII (1939) 1–16, 315–32, 605–21.

—— "Riflessi della lotta Gluckista in Italia," RMI XXI (1914) 639–72.

Vautier, Gabriel. "Le Jury de lecture et l'opéra sous la restauration," RHCM X (1910) 13–25, 44–49, 75–78.

Vené, Ruggero. "The Origin of *Opera Buffa*," MQ XXI (1935) 33–38.

Verdi, Giuseppe. I copialettere. [Milano, Stucchi Ceretti, 1913.] Ed. by G. Cesari and A. Luzio, preface by M. Scherillo.

Vetter, Walther. Die Arie bei Gluck. Leipzig Dissertation, 1921.

—— "Georg Christoph Wagenseil als Vorläufer . . . Glucks," ZfMw VIII (1925–26) 385–402.

—— "Gluck's Entwicklung zum Opernreformation," AfMw VI (1924) 165–212.

—— "Glucks Stellung zur tragédie lyrique und opéra comique," ZfMw VII (1924–25) 321–55.

—— "Gluck und seine italienischen Zeitgenossen," ZfMw VII (1924–25) 609–46.

—— "Stilkritische Bemerkungen zur Arienmelodik in Glucks *Orfeo*," ZfMw IV (1921–22) 27–49.

—— "Zur Entwicklungsgeschichte der opera seria um 1750 in Wien," ZfMw XIV (1931–32) 2–28.

Viardot-Garcia, Pauline. "Pauline Viardot-Garcia to Julius Rietz (Letters of Friendship)," MQ I (1915) 350–80, 526–59; II (1916) 32–60.

Vicentino, Nicola. L'antica musica ridotta alla moderna prattica. Roma, A. Barre, 1555.

Vieira, Ernesto. Diccionario biographico de musicos portuguezes; historia e bibliographia da musica em Portugal. Lisboa, M. Moreira & Pinheiro, 1900. 2 vols.

Vienna. Internationale Ausstellung für Musik- und Theaterwesen, 1892. Fach-Katalog der Abtheilung des Königreiches Italien. Wien, [J. N. Vernoy], 1892.

Viereck, Peter. Metapolitics from the Romantics to Hitler. New York, Knopf, 1941.

Villalba, L. "La cuestión de la ópera española; carta abierta," *La Ciudad de Dios* XXXIII, No. 2 (1913) 204–11.

Villarosa, Carlo Antonio de Rosa, Marchese de. Memorie dei compositori di musica del regno di Napoli. Napoli, Stamperia reale, 1840.

[Villeneuve, Josse de.] Lettre sur le méchanisme de l'opéra italien. Ni Guelfe, ni Gibelin; ni Wigh, ni Thoris. Paris, Duchesne; Florence and Paris, Lambert, 1756. German translation by R. Haas, ZfMw VII (1924–25) 129–63. *See also* Bédarida, Henri. "L'Opéra italien jugé par un amateur français en 1756," in *Mélanges de musicologie* (Paris, Droz, 1933) pp. 185–200.

Viollier, Renée. "Les Divertissements de J.-J. Mouret pour la 'Comédie italienne' à Paris," RdM XXIII (1939) 65–71.

—— "Un Opéra-ballet au XVIIIe siècle: *Les Festes ou le triomphe de Thalie,*" RdM XVI (1935) 78–86.

Viotta, H. A. "Richard Wagner's verhouding tot die muziekgeschiedenis," in *Gedenkboek . . . Scheurleer* ('s Gravenhage, Nijhoff, 1925) pp. 359–65.

Virella Cassañes, Francisco. La ópera en Barcelona. Barcelona, Redondo y Zumetra, 1888.

Virgilio, Rudolph. Development of Italian Opera in New York. New York, Italian Library of Information, 1938.

Visetti, Albert. "Tendencies on the Operatic Stage in the Nineteenth Century," PMA XXII (1896) 141–51.

Vitale, Roberto. Domenico Cimarosa. Aversa, Noviello, 1929.

Vittadini, Stefano. Il primo libretto del Mefistofele di Arrigo Boito. Milano, Gli amici del museo teatrale alla scala, 1938.

Vivaldi, Antonio; note e documenti sulla vita e sulle opere. Roma, Sansaini, 1939.

Vogel, Emil. Bibliothek der gedruckten weltlichen Vokalmusik Italiens aus den Jahren 1500–1700. Berlin, A. Haack, 1892. New ed. serially in *Music Library Association Notes, Second Series* II, No. 3 (June, 1945) and later numbers.

—— "Claudio Monteverdi; Leben, Werken im Lichte der zeitgenössischen Kritik," VfMw III (1887) 315–450.

—— "Marco da Gagliano," VfMw V (1889) 396–442, 509–68.

Voigt, F. A. "Reinhard Keiser," VfMw VI (1890) 151–203.

Volbach, Fritz. Die Praxis der Händel-Aufführung, 2. Theil: das Händel-Orchester . . . I. Das Streichorchester. Charlottenburg, "Gutenberg," 1899.

Volkmann, Hans. "Domenico Terradellas," ZIMG XIII (1911–12) 306–309.

Wachten, Edmund. "Der einheitliche Grundzug der Straussschen Formgestaltung," ZfMw XVI (1934) 257–74.

Wagner, Richard. Briefe in Originalausgaben. Leipzig, B&H, [1911–1913]. 17 vols.

—— Gesammelte Schriften und Dichtungen. Leipzig, B&H, n.d. 12 vols. 5th ed.

—— Mein Leben; Volks-Ausgabe. München, Bruckmann, 1914.

—— Opera and Drama. New York, C. Scribner; London, W. Reeves, [1913]. Translated by Edwin Evans.

Wagner, Rudolf. "Beiträge zur Lebensgeschichte Johann Philipp Kriegers und seines Schülers Nikolaus Deinl," ZfMw VIII (1925–26) 146–60.

Wagner, Siegfried. Erinnerungen. Stuttgart, J. Engelhorn, 1923.

Wahl, Eduard. Nicolo Isouard. München, C. Wolf, 1906.

Wahle, Werner. Richard Wagners szenische Visionen und ihre Ausführung im Bühnenbild. Munich Dissertation, 1937.

Waldersee, Paul. "Robert Schumann's *Manfred*," in Waldersee, *Sammlung musikalischer Vorträge* (Leipzig, B&H, 1879–98) II, 1–20.

Walker, Ernest. A History of Music in England. London, Oxford University Press, [1924]. 2d ed.

Wallaschek, Richard. Das K. k. Hofoperntheater. Wien, Gesellschaft für vervielfältigende Kunst, 1909. ("Die Theater Wiens. 4. Band.")

Walter, Friedrich. Geschichte des Theaters und der Musik am kurpfälzischen Hofe. Leipzig, B&H, 1898.

Waltershausen, Hermann Wolfgang Karl Sartorius, Freiherr (von). Der Freischütz; ein Versuch über die musikalische Romantik. München, Bruckmann, 1920.

—— *Orpheus und Eurydike;* eine operndramaturgische Studie. München, Drei Masken, 1923.

—— Das Siegfried-Idyll, oder, Die Rückkehr zur Natur. München, H. Bruckmann, 1920.

—— *Die Zauberflöte;* eine operndramaturgische Studie. München, H. Bruckmann, 1920.

—— "Zur Dramaturgie des *Fidelio*," *Neues Beethoven Jahrbuch* I (1924) 142–58.

Wang, Kwang-chi. Ueber die chinesische klassische Oper. Genf, 1934.

Wassermann, Rudolf. Ludwig Spohr als Opernkomponist. München, Huber, 1909.

Weber, Carl Maria, Freiherr von. Sämtliche Schriften. Berlin and Leipzig, Schuster & Loeffler, 1908.

Weber, Max Maria von. Carl Maria von Weber. Leipzig, E. Keil, 1864–66. 3 vols.

Weckerlin, Jean Baptiste. L'Ancienne Chanson populaire en France. Paris, Garnier, 1887.

Wegelin, Oscar. Early American Plays 1714–1830. New York, The Dunlap Society, 1900.

—— Micah Hawkins and the Saw-Mill; a Sketch of the First Successful American Opera and Its Author. New York, privately printed, 1917.

Weigl, Bruno. Die Geschichte des Walzers nebst einem Anhang über die moderne Operette. Langensalza, Beyer, 1910.

Weil, Rudolf. Das Berliner Theaterpublikum unter A. W. Ifflands Direktion (1746–1814). Berlin, Gesellschaft für Theatergeschichte, 1932.

Weilen, Alexander von. Geschichte des Wiener Theaterwesens von den ältesten Zeiten bis zu den Anfängen der Hoftheater. Wien, Gesellschaft für vervielfältigende Kunst, 1899. ("Die Theater Wiens, Bd. I.")

—— Zur Wiener Theatergeschichte; die vom Jahre 1629 bis zum Jahre 1740 am Wiener Hofe zur Aufführung gelangten Werke theatralischen Charakters und Oratorien. Wien, A. Hölder, 1901.

An important supplement to Köchel's *Kaiserliche Hofmusikkapelle;* see corrections in Nettl, "Exzerpte aus der Raudnitzer Textbüchersamm-lung," SzMw VII (1920) 143–44.

Weingartner, Felix. Bayreuth (1876–1896). Leipzig, B&H, 1904.

—— Lebenserinnerungen. Zürich and Leipzig, Orell Füssli, [1928–29]. 2 vols. Translated as: Buffets and Rewards. London, Hutchinson, [1937].

—— Die Lehre von der Wiedergeburt des musikalischen Dramas. Kiel and Leipzig, Lipsius & Fischer, 1895.

Weissmann, Adolph. "Germany's Latest Music Dramas," MMus IV, No. 4 (May–June, 1927) 20–26.

—— "Richard Wagner; Constructive and Destructive," MQ XI (1925) 138–56.

Wellesz, Egon. "Die Aussetzung des Basso Continuo in der italienischen Oper," in International Musical Society, Fourth Congress Report (London, Novello, 1912) pp. 282–85.

—— Der Beginn des musikalischen Barock und die Anfänge der Oper in Wien. Wien and Leipzig, Wiener literarische Anstalt, 1922.

—— "Ein Bühnenfestspiel aus dem 17. Jahrhundert," Die Musik LII (1914) Qt. 4, pp. 191–217.

—— "Cavalli und der Stil der venetianischen Oper von 1640–1660," SzMw I (1913).

—— "Don Giovanni and the 'dramma giocoso'," Music Review IV (1943) 121–26.

—— "Einige handschriftliche Libretti aus der Frühzeit der Wiener Oper," ZfMw I (1918–19) 278–81.

—— "Francesco Algarotti und seine Stellung zur Musik," SIMG XV (1913–14) 427–39.

—— "Giuseppe Bonno," SIMG XI (1909–10) 395–442.

—— "Die Opern und Oratorien in Wien von 1660–1708," SzMw VI (1919) 5–138.

—— "The Return to the Stage," MMus IV, No. 1 (November–December, 1926) 19–24.

—— "Zwei Studien zur Geschichte der Oper im 17. Jahrhundert," SIMG XV (1913) 124–54.

Welti, Heinrich. "Gluck und Calsabigi," VfMw VII (1891) 26–42.

Wendschuh, Ludwig. Ueber Jos. Haydns Opern. [Halle a. S.], 1896.

Werckmeister, Andreas. Der edlen Music-Kunst Würde, Gebrauch und Missbrauch. Franckfurt, Calvisius, 1691.

Werfel, Franz. Verdi; Roman der Oper. Berlin, Zsolnay, [1924]. Translated as: Verdi; a Novel of the Opera. New York, Simon & Schuster, 1926.

—— Verdi; the Man in His Letters. New York, L. B. Fischer, [1942]. Edited by Franz Werfel and Paul Stefan, translated by Edward Downes.

Werneck-Brueggemann, Fritz. Ueber E. T. A. Hoffmanns Oper Aurora: anlässlich der 3. Funk-Aufführung. Rudolstadt, Edda-Verlag, 1936.

Werner, Arno. "Briefe von J. W. Franck, die Hamburger Oper betreffend," SIMG VII (1905–1906) 125–28.

Werner, Arno (*Cont.*). "Sachsen-Thüringen in der Musikgeschichte," AfMw IV (1922) 322–35.

—— Städtische und fürstliche Musikpflege in Weissenfels bis zum Ende des 18. Jahrhunderts. Leipzig, B&H, 1911.

Werner, Theodor Wilhelm. "Agostino Steffanis Operntheater in Hannover," AfMf III (1938) 65–79.

—— "Zum Neudruck von G. Ph. Telemanns *Pimpinone* in den Reichsdenkmalen," AfMf I (1936) 361–65.

Wessely, Carl. Antike Reste griechischer Musik. [Vienna, 1891.]

Westerman, Gerhart von. Giovanni Porta als Opernkomponist. Munich Dissertation, 1921.

Westphal, Kurt. Die moderne Musik. Leipzig and Berlin, B. G. Teubner, 1928.

—— "Das musikdramatische Prinzip bei Richard Strauss," *Die Musik* (September, 1927) pp. 859–64.

Westrup, Jack Allan. "Monteverdi and the Orchestra," M&L XXI (1940) 230–45.

—— "Monteverdi's *Lamento d'Arianna*," *Music Review* I (1940) 144–54.

—— "The Originality of Monteverde," PMA LX (1933–34) 1–25.

—— Purcell. London, J. M. Dent; New York, E. P. Dutton, [1937].

White, Richard Grant. "Opera in New York," *Century Magazine* I (1881) 686–703, 865–82; II (1882) 31–43, 193–210.

White, Terence. "The Last Scene of Götterdämmerung; a New Production," M&L XVII (1936) 62–64.

Wiel, Taddeo. I codici musicali contariniani del secolo XVII nella R. Biblioteca di S. Marco in Venezia. Venezia, F. Ongania, 1888.

—— "Francesco Cavalli," MA IV (1912–13) 1–19.

—— I teatri musicali di Venezia nel settecento. Venezia, Visentini, 1897.

Wieland, Christoph Martin. Sämmtliche Werke, 26. Band: Singspiele und Abhandlungen. Leipzig, G. J. Göschen, 1796. Contains: "Versuch über das Deutsche Singspiel" (pp. 229–67, 323–42); "Ueber einige ältere Deutsche Singspiele, die den Nahmen Alceste führen" (pp. 269–320).

Wiese, Berthold. Geschichte der italienischen Litteratur. Leipzig and Wien, Bibliographisches Institut, [1898–]1899. Fourth to fifteenth centuries by Wiese; sixteenth century to present by E. Pèrcopo.

Wiesengrund-Adorno, Theodor. "Transatlantic," MMus VII, No. 4 (June–July, 1930) 38–41.

Willms, Franz. Führer zur Oper *Cardillac* von Paul Hindemith. Mainz, B. Schott, [1926].

—— "Paul Hindemith; ein Versuch," *Von neuer Musik* I (1925) 78–123.

Wimmersdorf, W. Oper oder Drama? Die Notwendigkeit des Niederganges der Oper. Rostock i. M., C. J. E. Volckmann, 1905.

Winckelmann, Johann Joachim. Sämtliche Werke. Donauöschingen, Im Verlage deutscher Classiker, 1825–29. 12 vols. Contains "Gedanken über die Nachahmung der griechischen Werke in der Malerei und Bildhauerkunst," I, 1–58; "Geschichte der Kunst des Alterthums," III–VI.

727-6650

Searches America Antiques

2620 Washington Avenue
Oceanside N.Y. 11572
Mikedealer@aol.com

Dear Customer,

Thank you for your winning bid. I hope you are pleased with our service and our item. If you are pleased, we would appreciate your positive feedback on eBay under the name mikedealer@aol.com. We look forward to having you visit our web site at http://searchesam.simplenet.com and see what we have coming soon to eBay. We have a lot more items coming in the near future and look forward to your continuing bidding. If there are any problems with the item you have received, feel free to contact me. Thank You.

Sincerely,
Mike Crawford
Searcies America Antiques

Winesanker, Michael. The Record of English Musical Drama, 1750–1800. Cornell Dissertation, 1944.

Winkelmann, Johann. Josef Myslivecek als Opernkomponist. Vienna Dissertation, 1905.

Winter, Marian Hannah. "American Theatrical Dancing from 1750–1800," MQ XXIV (1938) 58–73.

Winterfeld, Carl von. Alceste, 1674, 1726, 1769, 1776, von Lulli, Händel und Gluck. Berlin, Bote & Bock, 1851.

—— Johannes Gabrieli und sein Zeitalter. Berlin, Schlesinger, 1834. 3 vols.

Winternitz, Giorgio F. "I cimeli belliniani della R. Academia Filarmonica di Bologna," RMI XL (1936) 104–18.

Wirth, Helmut. Joseph Haydn als Dramatiker. Kiel Dissertation, 1937.

Witherspoon, Herbert. "Grand Opera and Its Immediate Problems," MTNA XXVII (1932) 148–49.

Wörner, Karl. "Beiträge zur Geschichte des Leitmotivs in der Oper [Teil I]," ZfMw XIV (1931–32) 151–72.

—— Beiträge zur Geschichte des Leitmotivs in der Oper (Teil 2, 3). Bayreuth, Ellwanger, 1932.

—— "Die Pflege Glucks an der Berliner Oper von 1795–1841," ZfMw XIII (1930–31) 206–16.

Wolff, Hellmuth Christian. Agrippina; eine italienische Jugendoper von Georg Friedrich Händel. Wolfenbüttel, Kallmeyer, 1943.

—— Die venezianische Oper in der zweiten Hälfte des 17. Jahrhunderts. Berlin, Elsner, 1937.

[Wolf-Ferrari, Ermanno.] See special number of Zeitschrift für Musik CVIII, No. 1 (January, 1941).

Wolzogen, Alfred von. Ueber die scenische Darstellung von Mozart's Don Giovanni. Breslau, Leuckart, 1860.

—— Ueber Theater und Musik; historisch-kritische Studien. Breslau, Trewendt, 1860.

Wolzogen, Hans von. Lebensbilder. Regensburg, Bosse, [1923].

—— "Wagners Siegfried," in Waldersee, Sammlung musikalischer Vorträge (Leipzig, B&H, 1879–98) I, 59–80.

Wortsmann, Stephan. Die deutsche Gluckliteratur. Nürnberg, Karl Koch, 1914.

Wotquenne, Alfred. Alphabetisches Verzeichnis der Stücke in Versen aus den dramatischen Werken von Zeno, Metastasio und Goldoni. Leipzig, B&H, 1905.

—— "Baldassare Galuppi (1706–1785); étude bibliographique sur ses œuvres dramatiques," RMI VI (1899) 561–79.

—— Catalogue thématique des œuvres de Chr. W. v. Gluck. Leipzig, B&H, 1904. Ergänzung und Nachträge . . . Leipzig, Reinecke, 1911, ed. by Josef Liebeskind. "Ergänzungen und Berichtigungen," Die Musik XIII (1913–14), Qt. 1, pp. 288–89, by Max Arend.

—— Etude bibliographique sur le compositeur napolitain Luigi Rossi. Bruxelles, Coosemans, 1909.

Wright, Edward. Some Observations Made in Travelling through France, Italy &c in the Years 1720, 1721, and 1722. London, T. Ward and E. Wicksteed, 1730. 2 vols.

Würz, Anton. Franz Lachner als dramatischer Komponist. München, Knorr & Hirth, 1928.

Wyndham, Henry Saxe. The Annals of Covent Garden Theatre from 1732–1897. London, Chatto & Windus, 1906. 2 vols.

Wyzewa, Teodor de. W. A. Mozart: sa vie musicale et son œuvre de l'enfance à la pleine maturité. Paris, Desclée, [1937]. G. de Saint-Foix is joint author of Vols. I and II and sole author of Vol. III.

Young, Karl. The Drama of the Medieval Church. Oxford, Clarendon Press, 1933. 2 vols.

Zademack, Franz. Die Meistersinger von Nürnberg; Richard Wagners Dichtung und ihre Quellen. Berlin, Dom-Verlag, 1921.

Zadig (pseud.?). "Ludovic Halévy," Revue politique et littéraire (1899) No. 2, p. 705.

Zambiasi, G. "Le date (a proposito de G. Verdi); bibliografia," RMI VIII (1901) 408–12.

Zarlino, Gioseffo. Le istituzioni harmoniche. Venetia, [Pietro da Fino?], 1558.

Zavadini, Guido. Gaetano Donizetti. Bergamo, Istituto italiano d'arti grafiche, 1941.

Zawilowski, Konrad. Stanislaus Moniuszko. Vienna Dissertation, 1902.

Zelle, Friedrich. Johann Philipp Förtsch. Berlin, R. Gaertner, 1893.

—— Johann Theile und Nikolaus Adam Strungk. Berlin, R. Gaertner, 1891.

—— Johann Wolfgang Franck. Berlin, R. Gaertner, 1889.

Zeller, Bernhard. Das recitativo accompagnato in den Opern Johann Adolf Hasses. Halle a. S., Hohmann, 1911.

Zelter, Carl Friedrich. "Ein Aufsatz . . . über Georg Benda und seine Oper Romeo und Julie," AMZ XIV (1879) 645–49.

Zenger, Max. Geschichte der Münchner Oper. München, Verlag für praktische Kunstwissenschaft, Dr. F. X. Weizinger & Co., 1923.

Zeno, Apostolo. Lettere. Venezia, F. Sansoni, 1785. 6 vols.

—— Poesie drammatiche. Orleans, Couret de Villeneuve, 1785–86. 11 vols.

Zichy, Géza. Aus meinem Leben. Stuttgart, Deutsche Verlags-Anstalt, 1911–13. 2 vols.

[Zille, Moritz Alexander.] Die Zauberflöte; Text-Erläuterung für alle Verehrer Mozarts. Leipzig, T. Lissner, 1866.

Zingel, Hans Joachim. "Studien zur Geschichte des Harfenspiels in klassischer und romantischer Zeit," AfMf II (1937) 455–65.

Zoref, Fritz. Wesen und Entwicklung des musikalischen Erinnerungsgedankens in der deutschen romantischen Oper. Vienna Dissertation, 1919.

Zucker, Paul. Die Theaterdekoration des Barok. Berlin, R. Kaemmerer, 1925.

Zuckerkandel, Viktor. Prinzipien und Methoden der Instrumentation in Mozarts dramatischen Werken. Vienna Dissertation, 1927.

Zur Nedden, Otto. Die Opern und Oratorien Felix Draesekes. Marburg Dissertation, 1926.

Zurita, Marciano. Historia del género chico. Madrid, Prensa popular, 1920.

Sources of Examples

1–5. Coussemaker, *Drames liturgiques du moyen âge*.
6. Coussemaker, ed. *Œuvres complètes du trouvère Adam de la Halle*.
7. *Ballet comique de la reine* (1582) p. 31.
8. Schneider, *Die Anfänge des Basso Continuo*, pp. 147–48.
9. Solerti, *Gli albori del melodramma*.
10. Eitner, *Publikationen* XXVI, 25.
11. *Ibid.*, p. 22.
12. *I classici della musica italiana* IV, Quaderno 10, p. 20. Realization of bass omitted, signature of one flat added.
13. Caccini, *L'Euridice* (1600).
14. Kretzschmar, *Geschichte der Oper*, p. 38. Realization omitted.
15. Torchi, *Arte musicale* VI, 117–18. Realization omitted.
16–17. Caccini, *L'Euridice* (1600).
18. Eitner, *Publikationen* X, 81–82. Realization omitted; chorus condensed from four staves, reduction omitted.
19. Monteverdi, C.E. XI, 31. Note values halved, score compressed.
20. *Ibid.*, p. 49. Note values halved, bar lines twice as frequent.
21. Monteverdi, *Orfeo*, facsimile of first ed. Figures in brackets correspond to Malipiero's realization, C.E. XI, 59.
22. Monteverdi, *Orfeo*, facsimile of first ed. Last two accidentals under bass notes correspond to Malipiero's realization, C.E. XI, 61.
23. Goldschmidt, *Studien* I, 159–60, bass only. Figures and brackets added.
24. *Ibid.*, p. 230.
25. *Ibid.*, p. 230. Time signature changed, brackets above line added.
26. *Ibid.*, p. 202. Condensed from five staves, names of instruments omitted.
27. *Ibid.*, p. 203. Condensed from five staves.
28. *Ibid.*, pp. 291–93. Condensed from five staves.
29. *Ibid.*, p. 305.
30. *Ibid.*, pp. 299–300. Slurring altered; sharp omitted below bass in measure 12 and before bass note C in measure 14.
31. *Ibid.*, p. 312.
32. Monteverdi, C.E. XIII, 80–81. Realization omitted.
33. *Ibid.*, p. 136. Signature changed from one flat; flat omitted under bass C in measures 1, 4, 8.
34. *Ibid.*, pp. 85–86. Realization omitted.
35. Eitner, *Publikationen* XII, 3, 4. Highest part only of five.
36. *Ibid.*, pp. 19–20. Reduced from four staves; flat added in last measure of bass.
37. *Ibid.*, pp. 79–80. Reduced from four staves; realization omitted.

38. Eitner, *Publikationen* XI, 147. Reduced from four staves; realization omitted.
39. DTOe III², 108. Continuo omitted.
40. Eitner, *Publikationen* XII, 154. Reduced from three staves, realization omitted, E-flat added in signature.
41. DTOe III², 9. Condensed, text omitted.
42. H. Hess, *Die Opern Alessandro Stradellas,* pp. 88–89. Introduction omitted (six measures of two parts over continuo).
43. DdT LV, 102. Bass and realization omitted.
44. *Ibid.,* p. 74. Realization and German text (translation) omitted.
45. DTB XXIII, 119–20. Condensed from five staves; realization omitted.
46. *Ibid.,* p. 159. Accompaniment (three-part strings) omitted.
47. *Ibid.,* pp. 163–64. Condensed from five staves; realization omitted.
48. SB 232. Accompaniment omitted.
49. Lully, *Phaëton* (1683) p. 36.
50. Lully, *Amadis.* Prunières ed. *Opéras* III, 95–96. Condensed from five staves; flat added before last bass note of measure 8.
51. Eitner, *Publikationen* XIV, 87–88. Reduced from six staves, E-flat added in signature.
52. Lully, *Phaëton* (1683).
53. Rameau, C. E. X, *Appendice,* p. 26.
54. *Old English Edition* XXV, 110. Slurs omitted.
55. *Ibid.,* p. 21. Reduced from three staves; realization omitted.
56. *Ibid.,* pp. 130–31. Realization omitted.
57. Purcell, C.E. XXVI, 41.
58. Purcell, C.E. IX, 17–18. Reduced from four staves, realization omitted.
59. Purcell, C.E. XIX, 49. Reduced from two staves; realization omitted.
60. MfMg XIII (1881).
61. DTB XXXVIII, 104. Realization omitted; all but one of inserted bar-lines omitted.
62. *Ibid.,* p. 147. Realization omitted.
63. *Das Erbe deutscher Musik, Landschaftsdenkmale Schleswig-Holstein* III, 18. Realization omitted.
64. Händel, C.E. Supplement VI, 104. Reduced from four staves; names of instruments changed from "violino e flauto dolce"; "(Bassi)" changed to "[Continuo]."
65. *Ibid.,* p. 26.
66. DdT XXVII/XXVIII, 38. Reduced from five staves; realization omitted; stage direction translated.
67. *Ibid.,* p. 202. Reduced from five staves.
68. Händel, C.E. LVII, 72. Accompaniment omitted.
69. Händel, C.E. LXVIII, 82–83. Recitative reduced from five staves, aria from six staves.
70. Händel, C.E. XCII. Three string parts omitted; ornamented version of melody by Dr. Putnam Aldrich.

71. Haas, *Aufführungspraxis,* p. 186. Signature changed from two flats.
72. Rolland, *Histoire de l'opéra en Europe,* Supplément musical, p. 9. Reduced from four staves.
73. Eitner, *Publikationen* XIV, 163–64. Reduced from three staves; realization omitted.
74. *Ibid.,* p. 166. Time signature altered from $C\frac{3}{4}$.
75. *Ibid.,* pp. 166–67. Realization omitted in first 2¼ measures; string parts condensed from three staves.
76. Dent, *Alessandro Scarlatti,* p. 110. Realization omitted; figure and accidentals in brackets correspond to Dent's realization.
77. Gerber, *Der Operntypus Hasses,* pp. 77–78. Slurs added, other slight changes in notation.
78. DdT XV, 166. Accompaniment reduced from four staves.
79. DTB XXV, 146–47. Accompaniment (first and second violins, viola, continuo) omitted; realization and reduction omitted.
80. DTB XXVI, 144. Accompaniment (four string parts) omitted.
81. DTOe LX, 46–47. Reduced from nine staves.
82. *I classici della musica italiana* XXIII, Quaderno 89–90, p. 11.
83. *I classici della musica italiana* XX, Quaderno 80, pp. 6–7. Reduced from three staves.
84. *Le Théâtre de la foire,* Vol. I.
85. Monsigny, *Le Déserteur,* piano-vocal score, Paris, Alphonse Leduc, no. A.L. 5204, pp. 10–11.
86. Grétry, *C. E.* I, 43–44. Orchestra parts condensed from seven staves.
87. *The Beggar's Opera,* 2d ed. (1728), p. [45.]. Repeat marks after first double bar omitted to conform with text.
88. Hiller, *Die Jagd* (Leipzig, 1772).
89. Dittersdorf, *Das rote Käppchen.* Ms. Vienna Nationalbibliothek.
90. Subirá, *La tonadilla escénica* III, [16–17].
91. Cherubini. *Les Deux Journées,* piano-vocal score, Universal Ed. 3157, p. 14; text underlaid from another ed., Braunschweig, Meyer, [before 1862].
92. Spontini, *Fernand Cortez.* Leipzig, Hofmeister, plate no. 1135, p. 282. Condensed from three staves.
93. Auber, *La Muette de Portici.* Novello piano-vocal score, p. 137.
94. Meyerbeer, *L'Africaine.* Edition Peters No. 2773, piano-vocal score, p. 127. Reduced from three staves; indication of instruments omitted.
95. Berlioz, *Les Troyens.* Piano-vocal score, Choudens, p. 420. Names of instruments translated; flat added before bass D in measure 11; first eighth rest added in measure 15.
99. Herold, *Le Pré aux clercs.* Piano score, Paris, Léon Grus, plate no. 1746, pp. 72–73.
100. Rossini, *Tancredi.* Piano-vocal score, Paris, Launer, plate no. 3237, pp. 50–51.
101. Bellini, *La sonnambula.* Novello octavo piano-vocal score.

102. Verdi, *Ernani*. Novello piano-vocal score, plate no. 8063, pp. 174–75. Condensed from six staves.

103. Verdi, *La traviata*. G. Schirmer piano-vocal score, p. 108.

104. Verdi, *Otello*. Ricordi piano-vocal score, plate no. 52105, p. 361.

105. Wagner, *Das Liebesverbot*. B&H piano-vocal score, plate no. E.B. 4520, p. 396.

106. Wagner, *Tannhäuser*. Eulenburg small score, plate no. E.E. 4850, pp. 648–49. Reduced from six staves.

107. Wagner, *Lohengrin*. B&H score, plate no. 25700, p. 140.

110. D'Indy, *L'Etranger*. Durand piano-vocal score (1902), pp. 149–50. Some notes enharmonically altered.

111. Debussy, *Pelléas et Mélisande*. Durand piano-vocal score (1907), p. 236.

112. Dukas, *Ariane et Barbe-Bleue*. Durand piano-vocal score (1906), pp. 72–74. Reduced from three or five staves to show only essential harmonic outline; recitatives (two soloists) omitted.

113. Puccini, *Madama Butterfly*. Ricordi piano score, plate no. 110001, p. 123.

114. Giordano, *Andrea Chénier*. Sonzogno piano-vocal score (1896), plate no. 929, pp. 88–89.

115. Montemezzi, *L'amore dei tre re*. Ricordi piano-vocal score, plate no. 114651, pp. 126–27. Reduced from four staves; first two measures notated with signature of three flats instead of three sharps.

116. Kienzl, *Der Evangelimann*. Bote & Bock piano-vocal score (1894), plate no. 14035, pp. 66–67. Upper staff of accompaniment omitted.

117. Pfitzner, *Palestrina*. Piano-vocal score cop. 1916 by Adolph Fürstner (A. 7403, 7415, 7418F), p. 5.

118. Glinka, *A Life for the Czar*. Piano-vocal score, Moscow, n.d., p. 212. Alto voice and accompaniment omitted.

119. Dargomyzhsky, *The Stone Guest*. Bessel & Cie. piano-vocal score, plate no. 5623, p. 132.

120. Mussorgsky, C. E. II, piano-vocal score, Universal Ed. 9313, pp. 324–25. Reduced from seven staves; original Russian transliterated and translated by Dr. Edward Micek.

122. Pedrell, *Los Pirineos*. J. B. Pujol piano-vocal score, plate no. P.25C., pp. 239–40. Time signature, tempo mark, and first "pp" inserted from previous directions.

123. Alfano, *Madonna imperia*. Universal Ed. 8796, p. 93. Reduced in some places from four staves, one stage direction omitted.

124. Ibert, *Angélique*. Heugel piano-vocal score, plate no. H29458, pp. 14–15. Reduced from three or four staves.

125. Honegger, *Antigone*. Senart piano-vocal score, plate no. EMS7297, pp. 51–52.

126. Milhaud, *Médée*. Heugel piano-vocal score, plate no. H31062, p. 84.

127. Berg, *Lulu*. Piano-vocal score, Universal Ed. 10745, p. 231. Accompaniment omitted.

Index

Index

Numbers in boldface type under titles or names
of person represent entries of special importance

Index

Index